Literacy Assessment

Helping Teachers Plan Instruction

Literacy Assessment
Helping Teachers Plan Instruction

J. David Cooper

Ball State University

Nancy D. Kiger

University of Central Florida

Houghton Mifflin Company   Boston   New York

Senior Sponsoring Editor: Loretta Wolozin
Development Editor: Lisa Mafrici
Project Editor: Amy Johnson
Senior Production/Design Coordinator: Sarah Ambrose
Senior Manufacturing Coordinator: Marie Barnes
Marketing Manager: Jay Hu

Cover design: Catherine Hawkes, Cat and Mouse
Cover art: Tiger, whale, and elephant by Milena Desenne
          Giraffe by Emily Gabriela

Acknowledgments

Chapter 3: pp. 92–93: List of developmental spelling stages and p. 94: Table 3.2.
Adapted by permission of J. Richard Gentry and Jean Wallace Gillet: *Teaching Kids to Spell* (Heinemann, A division of Reed Elsevier Inc., Portsmouth, NH, 1993).

All other acknowledgments appear on page 585, which constitutes an extension
of the copyright page.

Printed in the U.S.A.

Library of Congress Catalog Number: 00-133855

ISBN: 0-395-88816-6

4 5 6 7 8 9-CRS-04 03 02

To Isabelle, Melissa, and Michael, the three most important people in my life.

J. David Cooper

This work is dedicated to my daughters, Laura and Katherine, and to the memory of my son, Michael . . . they taught me most of what I know about literacy.

Nancy D. Kiger

Contents

Gathering Information II: Specific Tools and Techniques for Literacy Assessment

Instructional Strategies for a Balanced Literacy Program: An Overview 102

The Beginning Reading and Writing Stage 259

The Almost Fluent Reading and Writing Stage   312

The Fluent Reading and Writing Stage   361

Part Three   Using Special Tools for Reading and Writing Assessment

Informal and Qualitative Measures for Reading

Part Four   Beyond the Classroom   487

Preface

Success in literacy development is achievable for virtually every student with appropriate instruction. Appropriate instruction flows from knowledge about each student's stage of literacy development. Teachers acquire this knowledge through on-going assessment. *Literacy Assessment: Helping Teachers Plan Instruction* was written to help all teachers be effective literacy teachers.

Background

We have taught thousands of undergraduate and graduate students and worked with thousands of classroom teachers. An alarming number have told us they feel they don't know how to assess the literacy of their class. They feel overwhelmed by too many choices, too many mandated tests and instruments, too little time, too little organization, and too little relationship between what they have been told to do in assessment and what they need to know to plan appropriate day-to-day instruction for every child.

Literacy Assessment: Helping Teachers Plan Instruction grew out of the need to simplify the task of literacy assessment and instruction *for the classroom teacher*. We wanted to show teachers how to look at each child's literacy development in such a way that assessing and planning instruction both fit naturally into every-day classroom activities.

Our Framework

Our framework views literacy *as a developmental process*. We show how to look at children and infer where they are in that process. We do not presuppose that each stage of literacy development is tied to or limited to a certain age. We do not presuppose that you can understand a child's literacy by taking it apart and looking at pieces. Using Benchmarks, we show you how to assess literacy while "in the act of teaching." As a practical matter, we provide sample indicators you can apply to what you learn about children in your daily classroom activities. We ask you to accept the knowledge that you are never finished assessing, just as a person is never finished growing in literacy.

We believe that all teachers are capable of becoming skillful assessors with perseverance and practice. We also believe that collaboration with families and colleagues is important. Further, we believe that no teacher is ever finished learning about teaching, any more than one is finished growing in literacy. Our role is to give you the springboard you need.

This book takes a balanced literacy approach and is applicable regardless of your philosophy (or your school's) about literacy instruction. We share simple, practical ways to get to know about each child's literacy and then provide appropriate instruction. *Literacy Assessment: Helping Teachers Plan Instruction* was written as a text for preservice and inservice teachers.

Organization and Scope of the Text

The twelve chapters of the text are organized into four parts, each with a different focus. This is followed by the Resource File on the tabbed pages at the end of the book.

Part I: Getting Started   Chapters 1 through 4

Chapter 1: *A Framework for Assessment-based Literacy Instruction.* Here you learn the framework for literacy assessment that supports this text. We present an introduction to five stages of literacy development.

Chapter 2: *Gathering Information I: Generic Tools and Techniques.* We present a number of ways a teacher can gather information about students in any area. These include: observation, interest inventories, attitude or self-concept checks, checklists, work samples, conferences, self-reflections, and performance assessments.

Chapter 3: *Gathering Information II: Specific Tools and Techniques for Literacy Assessment.* We present ways to assess three areas of literacy: oral language, reading, and writing. We also suggest ways to organize information.

Chapter 4: *Instructional Strategies for a Balanced Literacy Program: An Overview.* We define and give models for a Balanced Beginning Literacy Program and a Balanced Literacy Program for Grades 3 to 8. We present eleven basic instructional strategies for use in assessment-based, balanced literacy programs. We also tell you how to select instructional strategies to meet diverse needs, including second-language learners and those who need intervention of some kind.

Part II: Assessing Literacy Learning for Instruction—Chapters 5 through 9

These five chapters cover the five stages of literacy development. We present benchmarks and sample behaviors or indicators for each stage. We show you how to use the benchmark behaviors in oral language, reading, and writing to determine if a child is at each stage. For each benchmark and behavior, we suggest instructional strategies. We also present ideas for planning instruction based on the assessed stage of literacy development. In each chapter we present a typical schedule for a classroom of students who are mostly at that literacy development stage and explain how a balanced literacy program works for that stage.

Each chapter contains a section that connects it to other chapters in the book. The following descriptions give an idea of content unique to each chapter.

Chapter 5: *The Early Emergent Literacy Stage.* We show you how to build a print-rich and language-rich environment and plan a balanced day for preschool-kindergarten students. We show you how to use instructional strategies and routines to foster development at this stage. We address students requiring special attention.

Chapter 6: *The Emergent Literacy Stage.* We show you how to plan a balanced literacy day for kindergarten or first grade. We show you how to meet the needs of all students in a diverse classroom. We discuss strategies and techniques for meeting the needs of a range of stages. We also show you two classrooms at work.

Chapter 7: *The Beginning Reading and Writing Stage.* We show you how to answer the questions about what to teach, how to teach it, and how to organize and manage a classroom with a range of stages. We then present a sample second-grade classroom and provide a detailed look at the literacy block of that schedule.

Chapter 8: *The Almost Fluent Reading and Writing Stage.* We show you how to assess and plan instruction for students who are moving beyond the beginning stage. We show you how to meet the needs of second-language learners, and describe a sample fourth-grade classroom at work.

Chapter 9: *The Fluent Reading and Writing Stage.* We show you what students at this stage are like in terms of oral language, reading, and writing. We tell you how to continue to support the literacy growth of students who have few word recognition challenges but instead are broadening their reading and writing and using both in every aspect of their lives. We show you a sample sixth-grade classroom at work.

Part III: Using Special Tools For Reading And Writing Assessment

Chapter 10: *Informal and Qualitative Measures for Reading.* Here we present the factors affecting the difficulty of materials and some information about measuring readability. We tell about how to administer informal reading inventories as well as other, more specialized published tests, and we discuss assessing special populations. We present the concepts of reading levels, interest levels, and using the cloze procedure to match students to materials.

Chapter 11: *Formal and Standardized Assessments.* In this chapter we include basic information about formal and standardized measurements in general and specifically those that are designed to assess literacy.

Part IV: Beyond the Classroom

Chapter 12: *Collaborating with Families, Peers, and Other Professionals.* We suggest ways to keep family and community members involved in literacy assessment and instruction. We show you ways to grow professionally through working with peers and colleagues and by affiliating with local and national professional organizations.

Text Pedagogy and Features

The following features are provided:

- A *graphic organizer* for each chapter includes page numbers.
- An *Eyewitness* feature takes the reader into a classroom and sets the stage for each chapter.
- *Focus questions* precede each Eyewitness and the body of each chapter, helping the reader prepare for reading as well as review.

- *Benchmarks* are provided for each stage of literacy development. These are presented and discussed in Part II and are listed as a single document in the Resource File.

- Issues related to assessing and instructing *second-language learners and other diverse students* are threaded throughout the text.

- *Figures* and *tables* make it easy to keep the organization of each chapter clear while reading.

- *Photographs* show children and teachers working together.

- A *summary* at the end of each chapter recaps the key ideas.

- *For Additional Reading and For Exploration*: Electronic Resources follow each chapter providing books, articles, and Web sites that relate to the chapter.

- *Classroom Applications* suggest brief projects to connect the concepts in the text to actual classrooms.

- A *bibliography* of all cited references is provided at the end of the text.

- A *glossary* provides definitions of key terms.

- The *Resource File* at the end of the text contains reproductions of various forms, checklists, figures, or tables that can be reproduced.

Instructor's Resource Manual

The Instructor's Resource Manual that accompanies this text contains many ideas for using the book both for preservice courses and for inservice training. For each chapter there are organizing tools, projects, suggestions for activities and discussion prior to the reading, alternative ways to have chapters read and presented, ideas for reviewing key ideas and terms, and transparency masters to aid in previewing and reviewing material.

Literacy Web Site

A new web site which offers literacy teaching and learning resources can be found at Teacher Education Station (*www.hmco.com/college*, and click on 'education'). At the core of this site will be an extensive self-testing program to help students check their knowledge of commonly assessed literacy topics.

Acknowledgments

This text reflects our lifelong dedication to helping teachers effectively help all children become literate. Many people have inspired us along the way and provided invaluable support:

- Thousands of teachers and children with whom we have interacted have taught us what we know about teaching and learning.

- Michael D. Robinson, Title I Building Coordinator, Center Elementary School, Marion, Indiana, gave invaluable suggestions throughout the text.

- David and Yvonne Freeman, Fresno Pacific College, Fresno, California, read the complete manuscript and gave suggestions for supporting second-language learners.

- Gary and Katrina Daytner, Ball State University, researched useful web site resources that are listed at the end of each chapter.

- Kathy Au, University of Hawaii, gave many suggestions during the early stages of the development of this text.

- Ali Sullo, Editor in Chief for Reading, Language Arts and Bilingual Products, Houghton Mifflin, provided many helpful ideas throughout the development of the manuscript.

- Irene Boschken, Janet McWilliams, and Lynne Pistochini read and responded to every chapter with many helpful suggestions.

- Doug Gordon, our developmental editor, did an outstanding job of supporting us in making the entire manuscript clear and user friendly.

- Brenda Stone Anderson keyed every chapter several times and helped design tables, figures, and diagrams to make the text appealing and clear.

- Our six outside reviewers gave many suggestions which helped us shape the manuscript: Darcy H. Bradley, Western Washington University; Ruth D. Farrar, Bridgewater State College; Fannye E. Love, University of Mississippi; Michael F. Opitz, University of Southern Colorado; Ray Ostrander, Andrews University; and Kenneth Weiss, Nazareth College of Rochester. Of these reviewers, we would especially like to acknowledge Dr. Farrar for her detailed reviews which challenged us to make this text as clear and as perfect as possible.

- Loretta Wolozin, Senior Sponsoring Editor, Houghton Mifflin, has given this project unbelievably strong support from the first time she heard about it.

- Lisa Mafrici, Senior Associate Editor, Houghton Mifflin, continuously monitored the project and made sure everything stayed on schedule.

- Amy Johnson, Project Editor, Houghton Mifflin, for her work in seeing our manuscript through the production process.

To all of these individuals, we say THANK YOU. And for all the preservice and inservice teachers who will use this text, we thank you for helping your students achieve success in literacy!

J. D. C.
N. D. K.

Getting Started

Part

1

A Framework for Assessment-Based Literacy Instruction

FOCUS   As you read the Eyewitness section, ask yourself the following questions:

1. Why is Dolores Alvarez doing these activities with her class?
2. Which of the specific activities Ms. Alvarez uses might be called "instructional" and which might be part of "assessment"? What do you notice about the two types of activities?

Eyewitness

It is early in the school year. Dolores Alvarez is listening to Sara, one of her third graders, read aloud a portion of the book The Three Little Javelinas *(Lowell, 1992). As Sara reads, Ms. Alvarez takes a running record (you will learn more about this later). After the reading, Ms. Alvarez asks Sara to retell what she has read. Ms. Alvarez notes that Sara read 100 percent of the words correctly, but she could retell only part of what she read.*

Later Ms. Alvarez will make notes on a 3" x 8" note card devoted to Sara's reading. She will write:

> Sara Brown
> Reading
>
> - Excellent fluency - 100%
> - Has developed many of the skills of a fluent reader
> - Needs instruction at the beginning stage of fluent reading with heavy emphasis on comprehension; was unable to retell story events

At the beginning of the year, Ms. Alvarez listens to all of her students read aloud as part of determining their stage of literacy development. By the end of the first few weeks of school, she will have heard all the students read.

While Ms. Alvarez has been listening to Sara, the other twenty-seven students in the classroom have been writing. Ms. Alvarez asked them to write at least two paragraphs about themselves, encouraging them to include some of the items she has listed on the chalkboard:

- *Favorite subject and why it's your favorite*
- *Best thing about school last year*
- *Activity you like to do best*
- *Types of books you like to read*
- *Most important thing about you*
- *Anything else you want to tell about yourself*

Such writing forms another part of Ms. Alvarez's method for determining each student's stage of literacy development. Besides looking at the writing fluency, she pays attention to the students' interests, self-concepts, and attitudes. For each student, she records her notes on a group of 5" x 8" cards.

The Eyewitness narrative portrays a teacher who is operating an **assessment-based literacy classroom**. Ms. Alvarez has started the year by looking at each student's reading, writing, and other language skills to make a tentative determination of each one's stage of literacy development. She is gathering the information she needs to plan the types of teaching activities and literacy experiences she will provide to help her students continue to progress in their literacy development. Finding out students' interests is an important part of this process.

In this chapter, you will learn more about the attributes of an assessment-based literacy classroom. To begin, notice these key features of Ms. Alvarez's method:

FOCUS As you read this
chapter, ask yourself
the following questions:
1. What is assessment-based literacy instruction?
2. For which students should you use assessment-based literacy instruction?
3. What are the stages of literacy development?
4. How will knowledge of these stages help you and your school foster literacy development?
5. What is the decision-making process for assessment-based literacy instruction?
6. What are the guiding principles for assessment-based literacy instruction?

- She uses **authentic assessment** activities, activities that involve real reading and real writing. For example, she has students read books and write about themselves.
- In a well-designed, well-managed, assessment-based classroom, you cannot tell instructional activities from assessment activities. In fact, Ms. Alvarez's assessment activities look just like good instructional activities.

This text is written for both preservice and inservice teachers. We assume you have some background in literacy development and instruction. Perhaps you have taken a course in literacy, reading, or language arts. Perhaps you have done some independent reading in the area or have experience in teaching literacy. If none of these is the case, we recommend that you supplement this book by reading some of the resources listed in the For Additional Reading section at the conclusion of this chapter. Another useful resource is the Glossary at the back of this book, which defines the terms that appear in **boldface**.

In this chapter, we develop the concept of an assessment-based literacy classroom, focusing on what it is and, broadly, how it operates. Further, we look at a framework for thinking about literacy learning as a series of stages.

Assessment-Based Literacy Instruction

Assessment is the process of gathering information about what students can and cannot do. **Evaluation** is using what you have gathered to make judgments about students' literacy development. For example, when Ms. Alvarez had Sara read from *The Three Little Javalinas,* she was assessing Sara's reading. When she wrote comments on Sara's information card, she was evaluating Sara's fluency and comprehension.

In assessment-based literacy instruction, you continuously gather information and use it to make instructional decisions about students' literacy growth.

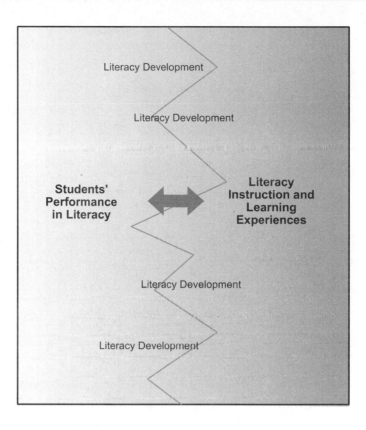

Figure 1.1
A Model for Assessment-Based Literacy Instruction

You gather the information through authentic assessment activities like the ones we saw in Ms. Alvarez's classroom, and you then look at each student's performance in relation to the stages of literacy development. In this way, you can determine the types of instruction students need to continue to gain power and strength in literacy—that is, in oral language (speaking and listening), in reading, in writing, and in viewing various media.

Figure 1.1 shows a diagram representing our model of assessment-based literacy instruction. As you examine this model, notice that students' performance and literacy instruction and experiences blend into each other, merging into a seamless whole. The double-headed arrow indicates that each continually influences the other: the instructional activities and experiences improve students' literacy and yield information about their performance; simultaneously, information about students' literacy performance leads to literacy instruction and experiences. As some educators like to say, "assessment informs instruction and instruction informs assessment."

As a teacher who uses assessment-based literacy instruction, you know and use many different tools and techniques for assessment. (We will survey these in Chapters 2 and 3.) The assessment process involves much more than just testing. It uses all teaching and learning experiences, as well as tests, in determining where students are and what they need to support their growth in literacy. You also use a variety of instructional tools and techniques (described in Chapter 4) to provide the instruction needed to help each student gain power in literacy.

Who Uses Assessment-Based Literacy Instruction?

The process of assessment-based literacy instruction must be sufficiently manageable to make it possible for all teachers to use it. Even though the process of literacy development is quite complex (Flood, Jensen, Lapp, & Squire, 1991), this text is about making the assessment-based process teacher-friendly and usable by any classroom teacher.

Some teachers have classes of twenty-five to thirty-five students or more, while others work with small groups or individuals. The assessment-based literacy process is one that can and should be used in all these settings. Similarly, it can be used not only by classroom teachers but also by all others responsible for literacy development: Title I teachers, resource room teachers, special education teachers, teachers of students acquiring English, and any others who take part in this process. For example, teachers of students acquiring English will select the procedures most appropriate for their students, keeping in mind what they know about the students' first-language literacy and second-language acquisition.

Assessment-based literacy instruction will help you create a **balanced literacy program,** one that combines the essential elements for effective literacy learning. This is the most effective type of program to use in helping all students achieve success in literacy development (Snow, Burns, & Griffin, 1998). This concept will be fully developed in Chapter 4.

The key to making the assessment-based literacy model work in a school is accepting the idea that each teacher works with colleagues as a team for each student's good. Regardless of where instructional programs are located—in the regular classroom, in a resource room, or elsewhere—*every teacher* should work from the same concept of literacy development. Students must not go from one classroom or program to another and find a totally different literacy focus. Learning to use the assessment-based literacy model helps you achieve consistency in all literacy programs within your school. This consistency leads to better learning for students (Allington & Walmsley, 1995).

Assessment-Based Literacy Instruction in Diverse Classrooms

The term *diverse classrooms* refers to the typically wide variety of individuals who make up a class. Think about classrooms with which you are familiar. Even if you have seen only a few, you probably realize that most classrooms today have students from many cultures and many language backgrounds. Some students speak languages other than English. Some come from cultural backgrounds quite different from the community in which the school operates. Some students are dealing with conditions that make learning especially challenging. Teachers need to recognize and accommodate diverse students, whatever the nature of that diversity.

Recently we were working with a group of teachers in the southeastern part of the United States who had children who spoke Chinese, Spanish, and English. Some classrooms have students representing as many as thirty or more languages and cultures. Projections indicate that by the year 2005, 50 percent of all public school students will be "minority" students, most of whom will be **second-language learners**—acquiring English as a second language (Jones, 1997). Another term you will frequently hear to describe these students is **English-language learners,** or *ELL students.*

A basic premise of this text is that assessment-based literacy instruction is for *all* students, not a select few. A diverse classroom is a strong classroom. The greater the diversity, the greater the opportunity to help all students develop literacy in a real-world environment.

We believe there are some constants in working with second-language learners:

- You will most likely have children whose first language is something other than standard English.

- Depending on their age and their stage of literacy, these children may or may not already be literate in another language, and this will influence how you help them become literate in English.

- Despite such potential differences, most of the assessment questions you ask will remain the same for all students. That is, you will need to find out the same things about second-language learners that you need to learn about any other children: Where are they now in terms of oral language, reading, and writing in English? What can they do now, and what are they ready to do next? How do they feel about themselves? How can you arrange instruction, materials, and the environment to help them?

Generalizations are risky for any group of children. For ELL students, lack of ability in English may be their only commonality. They may vary as to whether they are ready to speak in English or are still in the silent period that precedes attempts to speak a new language. Some may already be writing in the new language, some not. Further, ELL students may vary in terms of the educational background and literacy of their parents, whether English is being learned in the home, whether the family wants to maintain its language of origin, and more. The areas in which these children differ from one another may be more important than the single area that unites them: lack of proficiency in English (Krashen, 1982).

Another type of diversity in today's classrooms involves students who are "exceptional" in some way. As a result of **inclusion** programs, most students with disabilities are now placed in regular classrooms whenever possible. Typical classes may include, for example, students with **learning disabilities, attention-deficit disorder (ADD),** or **attention-deficit-hyperactivity disorder (ADHD)** (Lerner, 2000). Still other students may be exceptional by being classified as **gifted and talented**. Again, this wide range of variation need not change your basic approach to literacy. Assessment-based literacy instruction will serve you well for all these students.

As you develop an understanding of the process, you will learn how to assess your students regardless of their differences. As you study the Eyewitnesses, the classroom scenarios, and the instructional suggestions in this book, pay close attention to the ways of meeting the needs of *every* student in your classroom.

A Framework for Looking at Literacy Development

Literacy development, formally defined, is the process of learning to read, write, speak, and listen, with thinking being an integral part of each (Holdaway, 1979). Literacy may also include viewing, the process of looking at media such as television, films, and videos and using these sources in a critical, evaluative way. While some authorities do not discuss viewing as a part of literacy, we believe it is a vital component given our increasingly technological world. However, we do not deal with viewing separately, because it involves the same kinds of thinking skills that students learn for listening and reading.

In the process of learning or developing literacy, students go through what can be described as a series of stages (Juel, 1991; NAEP, 1987). This series is best viewed as a continuum, with the stages blending into one another. Progression from one stage to the next does not occur as smoothly as you might think it does (Adams, 1990). In any given classroom, there are likely to be students at several different stages. In fact, any given child may be doing some work that is typical of one stage while also doing some things that are typical of another stage.

We view literacy development in five basic stages that overlap and flow into one another. Figure 1.2 depicts the flow of these stages. A student might still be developing the characteristics, strategies, and skills of one stage while moving into and beginning development in another stage.

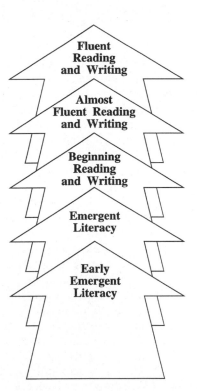

**Figure 1.2
The Stages of Literacy
Development**

Key Terminology

As you begin to think about stages of literacy development, two terms will come up frequently:

- **Standard** is a term that is receiving a great deal of attention in education. A standard is a degree or level of performance that is expected for students at a certain time. A widely circulated document, *Standards for the English Language Arts* (NCTE/IRA, 1996), defines what students should know about language and be able to do with language. This particular document sets out broad, general standards and leaves it up to each school or district to determine more specific standards.

- **Benchmarks,** as we use the term in this book, are behaviors exhibited by students that serve as evidence of a certain stage of literacy development. In education, the term *benchmark* has come to mean a reference point in relation to an individual's development, and our usage draws on that general meaning.

For example, in what we call the Early Emergent Literacy stage, one benchmark is that the child knows and repeats several nursery rhymes. This is a behavior one would expect to observe in a child at that stage of development. For each stage, this book describes a variety of benchmarks. By looking at the particular benchmarks a child demonstrates, it is possible to infer the stage of his or her development.

The terms *standard* and *benchmark* are often used interchangeably. In more precise usage, however, standards tend to be broad and general, whereas benchmarks indicate specific tasks that students might perform to show they have met a standard or one part of a standard.

With that terminology in mind, let's look more closely at the five stages of literacy development.

Stages of Literacy Development

The five stages of literacy presented in this text were developed by examining research sources spanning more than thirty years (Adams, 1990; Anderson, Hiebert, Scott, & Wilkinson, 1985; Chall, 1967; Hiebert, Pearson, Taylor, Richardson, & Paris, 1998; Juel, 1988, 1991; Learning First Alliance, 1998; Snow, Burns, & Griffin, 1998). In addition, we examined purported research-based curriculum guides from state and county departments of education and local school districts too numerous to list. We then identified benchmarks, common characteristics, and components for each stage. When we had no research to guide us, we used our combined wisdom and the wisdom of other colleagues in the field to guide our decisions.

Each stage and its benchmarks are discussed in more detail in Chapters 5 through 9. A complete list of the benchmarks for all stages can be found in the Resource File at the end of the book.

These, in brief, are the five stages:

1 **Early Emergent Literacy:** This is the stage during which children develop the foundations of literacy. It usually occurs before the student enters kindergarten, and it includes such aspects of literacy as developing oral language and being curious about print. Second-language learners usually have reached or surpassed this stage in their first language.

2 **Emergent Literacy:** During this stage, the child becomes more interested in literacy. He or she exhibits such behaviors as using more standard oral language patterns and forming and naming letters. Concepts about print, such as recognizing a word, also develop during this stage. Most children complete the majority of this stage by the end of kindergarten or at the beginning of grade 1.

3 **Beginning Reading and Writing:** In this stage, oral language expands and the student begins to actually read and write in conventional ways. Word analysis skills develop, and students begin to develop fluency in reading. Understanding of the meanings of many words increases. This stage continues through first grade for some students and into second or third grade for some.

4 **Almost Fluent Reading and Writing:** During this stage, the child is growing more sophisticated in all aspects of literacy. He or she reads silently more than in the previous stage, does more writing, and has an oral language that shows increasing vocabulary. For most students, this stage may begin toward the end of second grade and continue into the beginning of fourth or fifth grade.

5 **Fluent Reading and Writing:** By this stage, the student is using reading, writing, and oral language for a variety of purposes. She or he has attained most of the skills of reading and writing. This stage may begin in fourth grade for some students, and it continues through the upper elementary grades and into middle school and high school. In fact, fluent reading and writing development continues throughout one's life.

As you can tell from Figure 1.2 and from the description of the stages, there is much overlap among them. No student ever completely finishes one stage before moving into another. Moreover, some students reach a plateau and remain at a particular stage for a period of time. The stages of literacy development thus can be described as a "jerky continuum."

A Rationale for This Book's Approach

For many years, educators tended to be rigid in associating levels of achievement with specific grade levels; they did not allow for variation in individual development. Furthermore, literacy development was viewed as having a period of "readiness," during which time children mastered a discrete set of "prerequisite" skills. At the magical moment when they acquired these skills, children were supposedly ready to learn to read. However, research evidence indicates that this view is misleading (Durkin, 1966). Students do not learn one part or piece of literacy at a time (Teale & Sulzby, 1986). Rather, they gradually develop literacy as a whole, and they grow into literacy with the appropriate support and instruction.

Research over the past several decades has shown a strong relationship among all of the language arts: speaking, listening, reading, writing, viewing, and thinking. Essentially, what happens to a student's development in one area affects the other areas (Shanahan, 1990). That is why our descriptions of literacy development take into account a wide range of indicators rather than focusing solely on reading.

Research also supports the division of literacy development into stages. For example:

- Stages of development are clearly evident in beginning readers as they develop decoding and word identification skills (Juel, 1991).
- Studies of students' reading comprehension in the elementary grades show that students go through identifiable stages or phases as they develop their reading abilities (Rupley, Wilson, & Nichols, 1998). As they develop comprehension, students use a consistent set of strategies repeatedly, gradually becoming more sophisticated in their use (Cooper, 2000, Chapter 8).

You may wonder how our concept of stages relates to the traditional practice of measuring "reading levels." Considering a student's reading levels is important (Betts, 1946/1957), and we discuss the topic in detail in Chapter 10. However, students do not exhibit one absolute reading level or set of reading levels (Lipson & Wixson, 1997). Rather, an individual's reading levels can vary according to the particular text that he or she is reading.

For example, the informational book *Pelicans* (Patent, 1992) and the story *Barrio Boy* (Galarza, 1971) may be considered to be close to the same reading difficulty, and they may be rated at the same grade level. Therefore, it may be assumed that a student who is reading at that grade level can read and understand both. Yet a particular child who can read *Barrio Boy* independently may need instructional help to comprehend *Pelicans*. In part, this variation may occur because the student has more prior knowledge related to one text than to the other.

By describing literacy development in terms of stages, we can avoid some of the problems associated with the concept of reading levels. Overall, our model of five stages fits the knowledge accumulated about the various aspects of children's literacy and how it develops.

The Role of Skills in Literacy Development

What is the role of skills in literacy development? For many years, reading and language instruction were approached from a skills-based perspective (Smith, 1965). Researchers, however, challenged this perspective and came to realize that literacy is much more than a set of discrete skills that an individual must master to become literate (Rosenshine, 1980).

Unfortunately, the challenge to a skills-based perspective led many teachers to believe that skills were unimportant in literacy development and were not to be taught at all. *This simply is not true.* All literate individuals possess and use many different skills. Readers and writers develop literacy and learn to use skills by having many successful reading and writing experiences and by being given instruction with strategies and skills that will help them move forward in their literacy development.

The process is much like learning to play the piano. You learn your first little piece. You play it over and over, and in the process you develop "fluency." You are then taught a new chord, key signature, or rhythmic pattern (one that you lack or are unable to use). Once you learn the new "skill," you can learn new pieces.

Similarly, as students move through the various stages of literacy, they learn various skills and strategies. As we describe each stage in later chapters, we will have a good deal to say about these matters.

Making Decisions in Your Assessment-Based Literacy Classroom

The decision-making process in your assessment-based literacy classroom involves three steps, which are circular in nature (see Figure 1.3):

1 Take samples of each student's literacy (listening, speaking, reading, or writing).

2 Compare each student's performance to the stages of literacy development. By continuously doing this, you will be able to evaluate how each student is progressing and determine what is needed to help him or her further develop literacy skills.

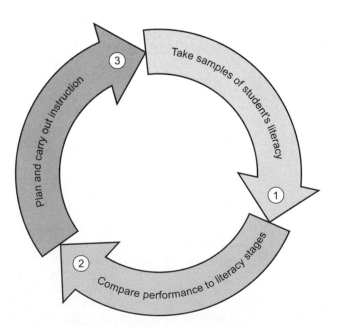

Figure 1.3
Steps for Making Decisions in the Assessment-Based Literacy Classroom

3 On the basis of what you learn from these first two steps, plan instruction and carry it out.

As you apply this decision-making process in your own teaching, you will find that it helps you plan instruction and determine each student's progress in literacy development. Further, this process will assist you in comparing each student's performance to local, state, and national standards.

We assume that when you provide instructional support, it will be **scaffolded;** that is, you will offer a great deal of support in the beginning and then gradually withdraw as the student becomes more proficient. In most cases, you will move gradually from teacher **modeling** (demonstrating) to guided practice and then to the achievement of student independence through practice and application (Pearson, 1985).

Preparing to Meet the Range of Needs in Your Classroom

Students bring to the classroom many characteristics and circumstances that can influence learning. These include home conditions, health and diet issues, language background, existence of disabilities or special gifts, and so on. While these various elements influence learning, they rarely are the direct or absolute cause of learning problems. As Lipson and Wixson note, "The majority of difficulties in reading and writing are more likely to result from a complex interaction between the learner and the reading and writing situation" (1997, p. 20) than from any underlying problems.

We will illustrate throughout this text how a teacher should consider these factors in planning instruction. It is our belief, however, that good instruction that is appropriate for the students will keep them progressing in their literacy development regardless of outside factors.

What students must accomplish to become literate is the same regardless of any special needs they may have. Therefore, all students should be viewed in relation to the same stages of literacy development. It is important to know how to provide quality instruction appropriate to the students' level of literacy development.

Within schools, there are many types of instruction that can support the needs of students. These can include, for example,

- The regular classroom instruction provided by a single teacher
- Inclusionary instruction, in which special-needs students stay in the regular classroom with the aid of support personnel such as special teachers or teaching assistants
- **Pullout programs,** in which individual students or small groups leave the classroom for a period of time for special instruction
- **Extended-day programs,** in which special instruction is provided before or after school

The value of all of these programs depends on how consistent or congruent they are with the classroom program (Walp & Walmsley, 1989). Pullout programs in particular have long been criticized as counterproductive (Allington & Walmsley, 1995). But whatever the arrangement in your school, we believe that using the decision-making process for the assessment-based literacy classroom will help you meet the needs of *all* students. The remainder of this text will illustrate how you can do this.

Guiding Principles for Assessment-Based Literacy Instruction

Three important principles should guide you as you develop an assessment-based literacy classroom. These principles have been inherent throughout this chapter, but we would like to make them as explicit as possible:

1 *Every teacher responsible for literacy in the school uses the same stages of literacy development as the core for planning each student's literacy instruction.* By focusing on the stages of literacy development, teachers will work with a common framework. This will help bring about consistency in literacy development for all students.

2 *Assessment of literacy development focuses on students' strengths in relation to the stages of literacy development.* Evidence from a variety of sources shows that students learn most effectively by focusing first on what they *can* do (Swartz & Klein, 1997). Then you provide new teaching activities and learning experiences to help students progress to the next stage of literacy development.

3 *Assessment should be an ongoing process based primarily on the results of instructional activities used to promote literacy development.* Your assessment may sometimes be supported by other formal and informal assessment procedures such as tests, but your daily instructional activities with students yield the most useful information. In the assessment-based literacy classroom, all of your teaching activities and experiences provide an opportunity to assess and evaluate students in relation to the stages of literacy development.

Using This Text

Literacy Assessment: Helping Teachers Plan Instruction is designed to be both a textbook and a handbook for preservice and inservice teachers. It offers many guidelines about how to look at students at the various stages of literacy and plan the types of instruction each student needs. After you have read the book, it will remain handy as a reference.

Special Features

Several features in each chapter will assist you as you read the book or use it as a reference tool:

- *Graphic Organizer:* Each chapter begins with a graphic organizer showing the main sections and subsections of the chapter with page numbers. Use these to preview the chapter or to locate specific sections.
- *Focus Questions:* Before each Eyewitness and before the body of the chapter, you will find a set of focus questions that will help you think about your purpose for reading. They may also be used to help you summarize what you have read or to guide your notetaking.
- *Summary:* Following the text of each chapter, a summary presents key points from the chapter. Use this feature to check your own knowledge of what you have learned.
- *For Additional Reading* and *For Exploration: Electronic Resources:* After the chapter summary you will find lists of relevant books, articles, and web sites that expand or extend chapter topics. Use these to learn more about an area of need.
- *Classroom Applications:* At the end of each chapter, we suggest brief in-school projects to help you apply concepts and knowledge presented in the chapter.

Organization

The text is divided into four parts, followed by a Resource File. Each part has a different focus.

Part One: Getting Started.   This section contains Chapters 1 through 4, which help you develop a framework for assessment-based literacy instruction and learn the tools, techniques, and instructional procedures that you can draw on in your classroom.

Part Two: Assessing Literacy Learning for Instruction.   Chapters 5 through 9 present each of the five stages of literacy development. The benchmarks for each stage are discussed in detail, and guidelines and suggestions are provided to help you plan instruction and apply the assessment-based literacy concept in whatever instructional role you play. Each of these chapters has an opening section that makes useful connections to other chapters.

Part Three: Using Special Tools for Reading and Writing Assessment. Chapters 10 and 11 provide in-depth information about informal and qualitative diagnostic procedures. They also develop the concepts you will need to understand and use standardized tests effectively.

Part Four: Beyond the Classroom.   Chapter 12 offers guidance in working with families, with your teaching peers, and with other professionals on the staff, as well as suggestions for maintaining and extending your own professional growth.

Resource File.   Following the text, the Resource File provides a complete list of the benchmarks as well as forms, checklists, and a variety of other resources to help you carry out assessment-based literacy instruction.

Summary

In assessment-based literacy instruction, the teacher continuously gathers information and makes instructional decisions about students' literacy growth by looking at their performance in relation to the stages of literacy development. The teacher's assessment is based on authentic activities—activities involving real reading and real writing. Assessment helps the teacher determine the kinds of instruction needed, and the instructional activities in turn provide more assessment information.

Using assessment-based literacy instruction, the teacher can create a balanced literacy program, one that involves all the essential elements for effective literacy development. At the core of this process are the five stages of literacy development: Early Emergent Literacy, Emergent Literacy, Beginning Reading and Writing, Almost Fluent Reading and Writing, and Fluent Reading and Writing. For each stage there are specific benchmarks, behaviors that provide evidence that the student has reached that stage.

This model and framework for instruction can and should be used to guide the literacy development of *all* students. It is relevant for English-language learners as well as students whose first language is English. Similarly, it is applicable to students with and without disabilities. To ensure consistency of instruction, we believe this approach should be used by all the teachers within a school who are responsible for literacy development, whether they teach in a regular classroom, a pullout program, an extended-day program, or any other setting.

FOR ADDITIONAL READING

Au, K. H., Mason, J. M., & Scheu, J. A. (1995). *Literacy instruction for today.* New York: HarperCollins.

Cooper, J. D. (2000). *Literacy: Helping children construct meaning* (4th ed.). Boston: Houghton Mifflin.

Freeman, D. E., & Freeman, Y. S. (1994). *Between worlds: Access to second language acquisition.* Portsmouth, NH: Heinemann.

Krashen, S. (1993). *The power of reading.* Englewood, CO: Libraries Unlimited.

Reutzel, D. R., & Cooter, R. B., Jr. (1992). *Teaching children to read: From basals to books.* New York: Merrill/Macmillan.

Spangenberg-Urbschat, K., & Pritchard, R. (1994). *Kids come in all languages: Reading instruction for ESL students.* Newark, DE: International Reading Association.

FOR EXPLORATION: ELECTRONIC RESOURCES

America Reads. **http://www.ed.gov/inits/americareads/** The America Reads Challenge is a national campaign that urges Americans to help all children learn to read. As part of this campaign, a web site has been developed to provide educators, parents, and students with some important general information on the topic of reading.

Language Arts. **http://instech.tusd.k12.az.us/LA/languagearts.htm** This web site provides balanced literacy booklets for use with elementary, middle, and high school students.

ProTeacher. **http://www.proteacher/com/** By following the links to "Reading & Language" and "Primary Reading," you can locate ideas for lessons and activities as well as resources for several topic areas, including emergent literacy.

Reading Online. **http://www.readingonline.org/** This site includes an online journal developed and maintained by the International Reading Association. The journal contains practical and research articles related to literacy education.

Standards for the English Language Arts. **http://www.ncte.org/standards/** This web site provides a list of the twelve standards for English language arts developed by the National Council of Teachers of English (NCTE) and the International Reading Association (IRA). The site, created by the NCTE, also includes information about obtaining supplemental materials designed to assist teachers in applying the standards to their classrooms.

TESL Lessons. **http://www.aitech.ac.jp/~iteslj/links/TESL/Lessons/** Providing a variety of links to articles from the *Internet TESL Journal* and other sources, this site also offers activities and lesson plans relevant to teaching English as a second language (TESL).

Understanding Authentic Classroom-Based Literacy Assessment. **http://www.eduplace.com/rdg/res/litass/** This web site, authored by Sheila Valencia from the University of Washington, highlights a number of topics related to authentic assessment of literacy and provides a case example in a fourth-grade classroom.

CLASSROOM APPLICATIONS

1. Select a classroom to visit or spend some time observing your own classroom. On the basis of this chapter's brief introduction to the stages of literacy development, try to identify the stages you see.

2. Interview one or two teachers. Ask them to tell you how they use assessment in their literacy program. Make notes about what they say. Get together with a partner and compare notes. Decide whether the teachers you have observed are operating an assessment-based literacy program.

Gathering Information I: Generic Tools and Techniques

As you read the Eyewitness section, ask yourself the following questions:

1. What aspects of literacy is Mrs. Logan assessing during the day?
2. Which activities seem to be specific assessments and which seem to be assessments "in the act of teaching"?

Eyewitness   *Polly Logan's third-grade classroom hums with activity. Some children are reading with a partner. Some are talking with a buddy about a piece of writing. Some are reading independently. As the children work, Mrs. Logan circulates with her clipboard and gummed address label sheets. From time to time she stops to talk with a child. Then she writes the child's name, the date, and a brief note on a label. She moves on. The child continues working. Afterward, Mrs. Logan will put the notes she has made into her notebook.*

Later in the day, Mrs. Logan sits at a table and has a brief conference with a child. It is one of several conferences she has scheduled for today. By the end of the week, she will have spent some time alone with each child in her class. During this particular conference, she asks the child to share a reading log and talk about his reading. Then she gives him an unfamiliar book to read aloud while she keeps track of his accuracy on a yellow pad. Later she inspects her records of the child's oral reading to help her decide whether he and a couple of others need a minilesson about a particular strategy. During conferences with other children, she may follow various other procedures.

On the same day, during their Writing Block, the children work from their writing folders. These contain prewriting clusters, rough drafts, and revisions. Not all children are at the same point in the writing process. Mrs. Logan refers to the folders when she plans instruction.

Today is Monday, so the children compile their individual spelling lists for the week. Some words they choose themselves—words they want to learn how to spell. Two children are working with the learning disability teacher to develop lists that combine student and teacher choice. Some words are drawn, with Mrs. Logan's help, from consistent misspellings in daily writing. Many children are confused about doubling the final consonant before adding inflected endings. Therefore, Mrs. Logan puts on the list several words that follow this pattern. She plans a whole-class minilesson on this useful generalization.

Today the children are also completing a unit on endangered animals. Each child has chosen one animal to study and has used several sources to complete a **K-W-L** *chart (Ogle, 1989). The* **K** *section shows what the child already* knows. *The* **W** *section lists the child's questions—"What I* want *to learn." The* **L** *section, which the children complete today, explains "What I* learned." *Each child now shares what he or she has learned. Mrs. Logan notes which children are unable to synthesize and summarize. She plans a series of minilessons on these skills before they embark on the next unit.*

Also, as the oral reports are given, Mrs. Logan pays close attention to the speaking and listening abilities of her students. Noting that Kathy is still painfully uncomfortable standing in front of the class, she decides to help her in two ways: (1) with techniques to overcome her shyness and (2) with alternative ways to share information. Mrs. Logan also notes that Sara is quite attentive and that she asks a question. Sara's facility with English is growing rapidly; a month ago, she would not have volunteered to speak aloud in class.

Finally, some children seem to have forgotten about how an audience should behave. It's time for a review of the listening guidelines that the class drew up at the beginning of the year. The students need to rededicate themselves to these guidelines or draw up new ones.

From the Eyewitness narrative, you can see that Mrs. Logan assesses her children's literacy daily in many ways. Every time she interacts with or observes the children in her classroom, she learns something that helps her to meet their needs. She knows that no one's memory is perfect, so she keeps very careful notes and organizes her information in such a way that she can refer to it when she plans individual, group, and whole-class instruction. She also uses the information during family conferences.

Teachers ask themselves many questions about each child: Who is this child? What is he doing during the day? During reading? During listening? What does this child think about himself? What is he interested in? How does he approach tasks? Where does he fit into the broad stages of literacy development? How do I gather, organize, and use data about all these things? In this chapter, you will begin learning about tools and techniques for answering such questions.

The Need for a Variety of Tools and Techniques

FOCUS **As you read this chapter, ask yourself the following questions:**

1. In which curricular areas might you use these various assessment tools and techniques?

2. Which tools and techniques might you use almost daily?

3. How can each tool or technique be adjusted or adapted to meet the diverse needs of students in any classroom?

4. Which tool or technique will be most difficult to find time for? Why?

5. Which do you think will be most useful to you? Why?

In describing the decision-making process in an assessment-based literacy classroom, Chapter 1 mentioned a number of reasons for using assessments. These include determining a student's literacy stage and progress, planning instruction, and comparing a student's performance against local, state, or national standards.

This and the next chapter present generic and specific assessment tools and techniques to help you begin the decision-making process. The generic instruments discussed in this chapter are useful in almost every curricular area. The specific literacy tools and techniques presented in Chapter 3 are for listening, speaking, reading, and writing. (*Thinking*, as you will recall from Chapter 1, is involved in all of these areas. *Viewing* involves applying the same thinking to nonverbal visual material.) Chapter 3 also addresses some ways to organize assessment information.

Together this and the next chapter form an introduction to basic tools and techniques. In each "stage" chapter, Chapters 5 through 9, we will refer to these tools again and again. Often we will elaborate and expand on procedures. We may give you more background on the development of a tool. We may suggest how to modify a tool or technique to suit a particular developmental stage or meet a particular need. You can always return to these introductory descriptions to refresh your memory about basic information.

Every teacher needs an assortment of tools and techniques that allow literacy assessment to be ongoing, nonintrusive, productive, and nonthreatening. As you read, it may seem there are far too many tools and techniques for any teacher to need or have time for. Just remember that we are giving you many so that you can make choices. In Chapters 5 through 9, we will guide you in choosing tools on the basis of your students, your setting, your materials, and your purpose for assessing.

Literacy can't be measured like a piece of string or weighed like a chicken. You can't use a ruler or a scale. Language goes on inside a child's head, where you can't see it. Your job is to find ways to look at what a child does and says and make inferences about what goes on in the child's head. These inferences help you plan a learning environment and instruction in which further literacy growth will flourish.

You need to look at children as they are actually engaged in listening, speaking, reading, and writing. Each of these language modes has many variations. The child reading a Goosebumps book such as *Piano Lessons Can Be Murder* (R. L. Stine, 1993) may use different strategies than when reading a book about sperm whales. The child who writes fluently when making up stories about ghosts and goblins may bog down when trying to write a report about President Lincoln.

We reaffirm that *you* are the decision maker. We can give you information about tools and techniques and how to use them. We can also help you determine how to think about decisions you need to make. But we cannot make the decisions for you.

Making Decisions for Diverse Learners

No classroom is made up of students who are all alike. In any class, you will find as many ways children differ from one another as ways they are alike. We believe these differences enrich your life as well as the lives of all the students in your classroom.

In terms of literacy development, you are apt to have students at more than one stage in any one classroom. Even those who seem to be at the same stage will exhibit many differences in such traits as personality, interests, attitudes, and work habits. We make suggestions throughout this book about adjusting assessment to fit the apparent literacy stage and other attributes of each individual student.

As we pointed out in Chapter 1, wherever you teach you will probably have learners for whom English is a second (or even a third) language, students whose culture or family background differs significantly from that of the rest of the community, and students whose learning is affected in some way by a learning disability or a physical, mental, or emotional condition. Whatever the variations in your classroom, the tools and techniques we introduce in this chapter can be used with all of your students.

We believe the same generalization holds true for assessment as holds for instruction: make the assessment fit the student. Therefore, you may need to make some adjustments or adaptations in using a given tool or technique. Sometimes you may need to seek assistance from specialists or community members. For example:

- If you have students who are not yet fluent in English, you may need to find someone to translate.
- If you have students whose hearing is impaired, you may need an interpreter or a microphone adaptation of some kind.

- If you have students who have difficulty holding a writing implement, you may need to ask a specialist for a device to assist the student to communicate.
- If you have students with low self-esteem, you will need to offer plenty of emotional support.

No matter what the need, your job will be to find a way to fit the assessment to the student, just as you will fit your instruction to the student.

Generic Assessment Tools and Techniques: An Overview

The following sections describe eight tools or techniques: observing, interest inventories, attitude/self-concept checks, checklists, work samples, conferences, self-reflections, and performance assessments. You will not use all of these assessment tools at one time. However, you do need to know about each one so that you can decide which to use to achieve your purposes for assessment.

For ease of organization, each section follows a consistent format. First, the section defines the particular tool or technique and states its purposes; then a series of subsections offer a description, a discussion of procedures, samples of how those procedures are used, and comments. Among the subsections you will find one called Diverse Learners, in which we present adjustments or adaptations you might make or ideas to keep in mind for students with diverse needs. These are not prescriptions; you may or may not choose or need to use them. We hope the ideas we give here will stimulate you to think of your own ways to make assessment work for each student in your classroom.

Observing

Observing involves close watching of a student's behavior while he or she is engaged in a particular activity or task. It serves a number of purposes:

- To look at students as they perform normal, authentic literacy tasks
- To look at the products or results of those tasks
- To plan instruction
- Sometimes to determine students' progress

Description

Observing, sometimes called kidwatching (Goodman, 1986), is perhaps the teacher's most powerful tool, but only if it stems from a thorough knowledge of the stages of literacy development. With such knowledge, you will know which responses and behaviors indicate typical growth and which indicate a need for special help, a change in support or materials, or a more detailed assessment. Bear in mind that no judgment about a child's literacy (or anything else) should ever be based on only one observation.

Later in this chapter you will find a discussion of checklists, which rely on observation: you observe whether or not a behavior is present and indicate this on the checklist. However, in this section we are dealing with observation that is not tied to a checklist. Rather than checking certain behaviors, you write a note about what you see—an **anecdote.** It is as though you are telling a very brief story about a moment in a child's day.

Procedures and Samples

Since nearly every classroom activity yields useful observations, most teachers have a favorite way to record and organize observational notes. No matter how you decide to do this, one thing is true for everyone: if you don't write it down, you *will* forget it.

Your observation notes need to be specific or they will be of no use to you later. Mostly you will write what a child does or says, not what he or she doesn't say or do, unless this child typically exhibits a particular behavior and today the absence of this behavior is important. For example, a note that says, "Tuesday: Johnny didn't ask for any help today" is not useful. You don't know which Tuesday or even perhaps which Johnny. Furthermore, you don't know what activity Johnny was engaged in that did not require help. You also don't know what inferences are possible. Should you rejoice because he didn't ask for help, seeing it as a sign that he is using strategies independently? Or should you be concerned because he doesn't seem to be aware of when he needs help, is still reluctant to ask, or may not be actually working at all but only sitting there daydreaming?

A more useful note might read:

10/7 Johnny M.
During paired reading, helped partner use context on unfamiliar word. Johnny seems to be using what was taught in yesterday's lesson.

You may decide to take observation notes (anecdotal records) on five or six children every day of the week so that you have at least one note per child per week. However, if a certain child is puzzling you, you may want to record several observations of that one child during a week, maybe even several each day. As you examine your notes over time, a picture may emerge that will help you make wise decisions.

There are many ways to record observation notes:

- *Sticky notes:* These can be identified with the child's name and the date and a brief statement (see Figure 2.1 for examples). The notes are transferred to a notebook or file folder where you are accumulating assessment information.
- *Gummed address labels:* As demonstrated by Mrs. Logan in the Eyewitness, gummed address labels can be used in the same way as sticky notes. After writing on them, the teacher peels them from the sheet and transfers them to the permanent file.

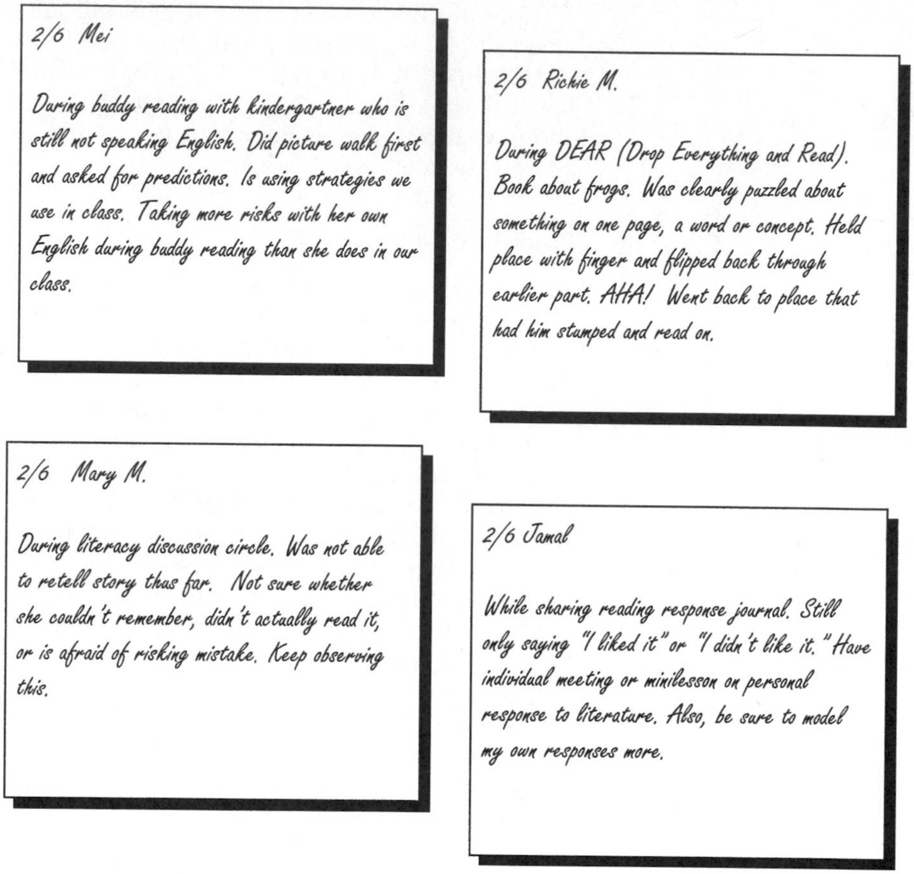

2/6 *Mei*

During buddy reading with kindergartner who is still not speaking English. Did picture walk first and asked for predictions. Is using strategies we use in class. Taking more risks with her own English during buddy reading than she does in our class.

2/6 *Richie M.*

During DEAR (Drop Everything and Read). Book about frogs. Was clearly puzzled about something on one page, a word or concept. Held place with finger and flipped back through earlier part. AHA! Went back to place that had him stumped and read on.

2/6 *Mary M.*

During literacy discussion circle. Was not able to retell story thus far. Not sure whether she couldn't remember, didn't actually read it, or is afraid of risking mistake. Keep observing this.

2/6 *Jamal*

While sharing reading response journal. Still only saying "I liked it" or "I didn't like it." Have individual meeting or minilesson on personal response to literature. Also, be sure to model my own responses more.

Figure 2.1
Observation Notes from
Mrs. Lacy's Second Grade

- *Index cards:* Cards, either 4" x 6" or 5" x 8" (3" x 5" are probably too small), can be taped to a clipboard, one for each child (see Figure 2.2). You can record several observations for each child before the card is full and must be filed and replaced.

- *Your own method:* Many teachers have devised their own methods that work well for them, and you may do the same. You need a method that is fast and easy to use; otherwise, you may be tempted to neglect this valuable tool. Whatever method you choose, record the date, the child's name, and a specific description of what you observed, along with a tentative conclusion based on the observation. Then add your note to a file that holds a growing picture of the child's literacy development over the course of the year.

Diverse Learners

You may want to ask a student's special teacher to observe the child in your classroom. For example, a child with a learning disability may behave quite differently

**Figure 2.2
Observation from Mr.
Montooth's Fourth Grade**

in your classroom than when with the exceptional education teacher. It would be helpful for that teacher to share observations with you. The same would be true of the second-language learner who may be quite at ease in the bilingual or ESL class but timid in the regular classroom. Everyone who teaches the child should share in both the assessment and the evaluation.

Comments

No one makes good observations right from the beginning. As you gain knowledge about the developmental stages of literacy, your ability to make good observations will grow. The best way to learn is simply to begin. Observe a child, write a note, and draw a conclusion. Put the note away and look at it a week later. Is it still helpful? Then make notes on several children, and keep doing it.

As you begin to use this tool, you may want an experienced observer to help you. Compare the specificity of what you have noted with that of the "expert." Compare your conclusions.

It takes time to get a feel for what to look for and how to record it so that it will be meaningful when you read it later. Don't abandon this tool just because you feel it is cumbersome and unhelpful at first. It is probably the most powerful tool a teacher has, but is of no use unless it leads to improved understanding of the individual child and thus to his or her literacy growth.

Interest Inventories

Interest inventories, as the term suggests, are instruments designed to reveal a student's interests, not only in school subjects but also in outside activities. These inventories have two major purposes:

- To determine each child's interests related to reading and writing
- To plan instruction

Clearly, when children are reading and writing about things that interest them, they are more highly motivated and better able to access their existing prior knowledge.

Description

Several types of interest inventories have been published over the years. Often these are meant also to assess attitudes (see the next section). For emergent readers and writers, the teacher may read items aloud and have the children mark pictures that indicate a scale from "I love it" to "I hate it." More competent readers and writers can read the items themselves and respond on a scale or in writing. You should also feel free to devise your own interest inventories. (See Figures 2.3 and 2.4 for partial examples.) Using what you learn from interest inventories, you can begin to build your classroom library and also help steer children to appropriate sections in the media center or on the Internet.

With very young children, responses on published interest inventories may not reflect their true interests. Little children like to please adults and may say what they think their teacher wants to hear. Other techniques, such as collages or all-about-me books (described in the next subsection), may be more helpful.

Procedures and Samples

If children are to respond on paper by marking pictures or symbols after you read to them, first describe the purpose and procedure briefly. Explain that the activity

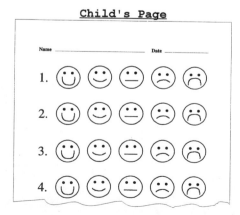

Teacher-Read Items

1. On the weekend I like to read comics.
2. My favorite books are about animals.
3. I like true stories best.
4. I like scary stories best.
5. . . . .
6. . . . .

**Figure 2.3
Partial Sample of Interest Inventory for Younger Children**

Name _____ Mark L. _____ Date _____ 9-11 _____

1. My favorite book is __don't have one.__

2. At the library I look for __nothing__ .

3. My favorite magazine is __don't know.__

**Figure 2.4
Partial Sample of Interest
Inventory for Older Children**

will help you find out what each child is interested in. Tell students that their interests may be things they already know about or things they have always wanted to learn about. Ask them to be completely honest; there are no right or wrong answers. Explain that you will read each item to them twice and give them time to decide on a response.

If children are to respond to open-ended items in writing, reassure them that they should feel free to use any word that is in their heads, spelling it as best they can. The variety of responses you receive can help you make significant discoveries about your students, even when the responses show an obvious reluctance. Look, for example, at the partial responses of an older child shown in Figure 2.4. It seems clear that this student is unwilling to share his interests (though he might be more forthcoming in an interview or a group discussion). He may feel that his interests would not be acceptable to you. He may be revealing a negative attitude or self-concept. In such cases, you need to do some serious observation for signs of interest in something. Take note of what he chooses during independent reading time. If you detect a spark of interest, gather books to share that you think he might like. Note his response when you read aloud from a variety of books about a variety of topics. He may want to read for himself the book you have just read, especially if his negative responses are masking his feelings of inadequacy.

What about children who are too young for a written interest inventory? Following are three procedures that are useful for such children:

1. **Interview:** Spend a few minutes alone with each child chatting about his or her interests. Leafing through picture books or magazines may be helpful. Questions about how the child spends free time are also helpful. Be sure to take notes.

2. **Collage:** First show the children a collage you have made about yourself, perhaps using pictures cut from old magazines. The pictures should reflect your interests. Let the children look at your collage closely and draw conclusions. They will probably be right on target. Then allow them to make their own collages. These may be mounted on construction paper or in file folders, and they are helpful to show during a family conference.

3   **All-about-me books:** These are books the children construct, with pictures or any other appropriate items, to help others know who they are and what they are interested in. Discuss the purpose of the books with the children, and brainstorm ideas for each page. Besides a page for personal information (appearance, age, and so on) and family items ("Who lives at your house?"), you may have pages such as the following: my favorite thing to do by myself after school, what I'd like to read about, where I'd like to go most in the world, my favorite game, my favorite sports star, my favorite books.

You may decide to have the children create some pages early in the school year and add to the book later. This technique is very open-ended. There is no wrong way to do it.

Diverse Learners

Students who are not yet fluent in English may be unable to reveal the extent of their interests through the inventories suggested here unless you can find someone who speaks their language to interpret for them. This might be a bilingual child in your school who is already fluent in English. It might also be a family or community member who is fluent in English and willing to spend some time in your classroom.

Pictures can also help you learn about a child's interests. For example, gather a group of pictures of different sports. Sit with the child. Pick up one picture and indicate through facial expression whether or not you like the sport. Then do another picture, then another. Finally, move the pictures toward the child and, with raised eyebrows, invite the student to choose his or her own favorites. The same simple strategy can be used to learn about such things as favorite foods, games, and leisure activities.

Comments

Our suggested techniques and instruments will give you a "ballpark" picture of the range of interests in your class and a little knowledge about individual interests. As time passes, you must be alert to additional hints from children about their interests.

Don't generalize about children's interests. Not all girls like Barbie dolls, and not all boys like basketball. Children need to see you model a wide range of interests that are not gender specific. There is no topic under the sun that is not valid. Whatever a child's interest, there are always things to read and write about it.

Part of your responsibility as a teacher is to help children become interested in new things. You will do this by sharing your own interests, reading aloud about a wide range of topics, and inviting children with unique interests to share. You must, however, avoid telling children that they "should" be interested in something. Let's celebrate diversity, not conformity.

Attitude/Self-Concept Checks

The instruments known as **attitude/self-concept checks** are used for three principal purposes:

- To learn about a child's attitude toward himself or herself (the self-concept)
- To learn a child's attitudes toward school, learning in general, and literacy in particular
- To plan instruction

Description

Attitude/self-concept checks include those that you administer as well as students' self-evaluations. Several instruments can help you gather such information. Obviously, close observation, discussed earlier, is invaluable. In addition, checklists, response scales, open-ended interviews, self-reporting, personal journals, and many other instruments can help you gather such information.

You can also devise ways to help children assess themselves in terms of attitude toward a given task and self-concept related to that task. Sometimes these are worksheets with specific items to be completed. Sometimes this is best done in an open-ended manner, such as in a journal.

Procedures and Samples

Caution is advised when using a scale, checklist, or other instrument on which either you or your students will be responding with writing or some other kind of mark. First, be sure children understand the purpose of the assessment. They must know there are no right or wrong answers; you are simply trying to find out how they feel about things.

Sometimes, as you read items aloud, children will either mark a picture (perhaps from a series of happy to sad faces) or check the response closest to the way they feel (see Figure 2.5). With such a procedure, be sure there are clear ways for children to keep their places, perhaps with a marker. Remember, some children

Teacher-Read Items

1. I am a good writer.
2. I make up good stories.
3. I am good at helping others read.
4. . . . .
5. . . . .

**Figure 2.5
Partially Completed
Attitude Survey for
Children Who Cannot Read
Items for Themselves**

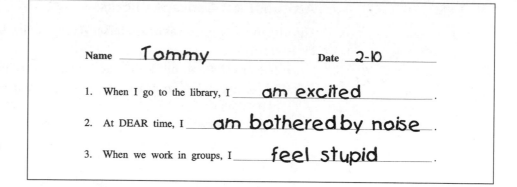

**Figure 2.6
Partially Completed
Attitude Survey on Which
Child Reads Stems and
Writes Answers**

may not read well, and they may need arrows or key symbols so they don't lose their place on the page.

Tell children not to mark until you have read each item twice. Then state how they are to respond. For example, "If this is exactly how you feel, put an X on the happiest face. If you never feel this way, put an X on the saddest face. If you feel somewhere in between, decide which one is closest to the way you feel most of the time."

Read each item without inflection, expression, or any verbal or facial clue as to which response might please you. Children will want to please you and are very skillful at judging such nonverbal clues.

Children who can read the items themselves may respond by marking a scale of some kind or by writing an open-ended response (see Figure 2.6). In either case, be sure they understand the directions and that there are no right or wrong answers. Allow them to ask for help decoding words, constructing meaning, and framing responses. Spelling is not important here.

In an interview or journal situation or in a self-evaluation, similar principles apply. It is vital that children feel free to respond honestly about their feelings. When students are self-evaluating, you must be sure they understand what they are to evaluate and how to think about it. They must understand that the only self-evaluation worth anything is the honest one. Perhaps most important, they must understand the purpose of such self-evaluation. It may be helpful for you to model how you evaluate yourself in terms of your attitude toward a task.

Figures 2.5 and 2.6 offer two partial samples of instruments you may find helpful. You will find complete forms of these types in the Resource File. Other forms appear in some of the references in the For Additional Reading section at the end of the chapter.

Diverse Learners

Even students who are fluent in English may respond in unexpected ways to attempts to determine self-concept or attitudes. Cultures vary widely in the ways they define acceptable behavior, and some children may have been taught that modesty and humility are more important traits than overt self-confidence. Some children may be extremely uncomfortable when asked to talk about what they are "good at." If you see a discrepancy between responses on a form such as we've shown and a child's actual performance, you may decide to probe further during a one-on-one conference. Pay attention to body language as children respond to your gentle probing.

Remember that each and every culture represented in your classroom has worth, no matter how divergent from yours or from the prevailing culture in the community. Your job is to try to understand the cultures from which the students come and help all students begin to feel at home in the culture in which they find themselves.

Comments

As with all assessments, attitude/self-concept checks are only samples of how the child felt on a particular day. You need to continue to add anecdotal records—your reports of incidents during the school day. You will probably need to use some assessments only at the beginning of the year or with a new student. You will quickly gain a "ballpark" idea of the attitudes of your children.

Be careful not to deny children their feelings. Teachers sometimes tend to respond to a child's negative comment, such as "I hate reading," by denying it: "Of course you don't hate reading, Susie. Reading is wonderful." Instead, find a way to accept the feeling honestly: "I'm sorry you feel that way. Perhaps you'll change your mind." Allowing children to save face is an important boost for their self-concept.

Checklists

A **checklist** is exactly what it seems to be—a list of items with a place to check whether or not each behavior is present and perhaps to what degree. In literacy assessment, checklists serve these purposes:

- To help you organize your observations or other information you collect about students' performance on given characteristics or items
- To plan instruction
- To compare evidence of behavior over time and thus help you determine student progress

Description

Checklists generally use symbols of one type or another (for instance, ✔, +, and 0) to note whether a behavior is present or absent. Sometimes the symbols indicate whether or not a trait is present consistently, occasionally, or not at all. At other times the symbols may indicate degree, such as "very effective," "somewhat effective," "not effective," and "not observed."

A checklist may focus on a single area, such as "using the writing process" or even "editing." It may list grade-level-appropriate decoding skills, such as these:

Reads unfamiliar words syllable by syllable

Reads on to use context

Refers to earlier part of book where word first appeared

Uses pictures

Substitutes a syntactically and semantically acceptable word for one he can't decode

Many published reading/language arts programs provide numerous check-lists to help teachers track student performance. Some schools develop checklists based on school-wide, district-wide, or state-wide benchmarks. Some teachers prefer to make up their own checklists so that they exactly match what they want to observe. You will find some sources for checklists in For Additional Reading. Benchmark checklists for each of the literacy stages are in Chapters 5 through 9.

Obviously you cannot use hundreds of checklists yourself. Your choice of which to use must be based on curricular decisions. You might ask yourself:

- What needs to be observed systematically?

- How can it be broken down into items that I can check as the children work independently or in groups?

- How can I word such a checklist so that it provides me with useful informa-tion for any one of a variety of purposes: for planning instruction, for shar-ing with the child, for sharing with families, for grade cards, for comparing my class and each child against my school's (school system's, county's, state's, or nation's) standards?

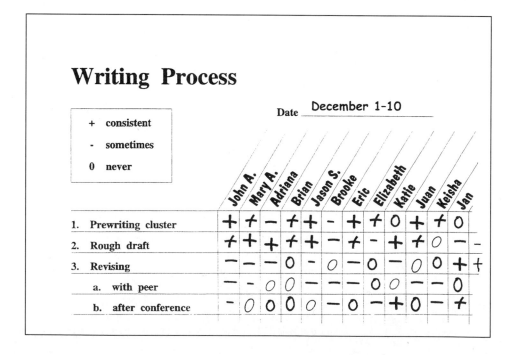

**Figure 2.7
Whole-Class Checklist
of Items Related to
Writing Process**

Procedures and Samples

Once you decide which checklist(s) to use, whether published or self-made, be sure to tell children that from time to time you may be marking things on a list and reassure them this will help you do a better job as their teacher.

Keep the list(s) handy, perhaps on a clipboard, during the time you plan to make observations. Have a place to file such lists when complete so that you can use them for whatever purpose they were meant to serve. Too often such checklists are completed but then get lost in a welter of paper on a teacher's desk.

Some checklists list items down the side and children's names across the top, allowing you to check the whole class on a single page (see Figure 2.7). The advantage of this format is that you can see at a glance which areas need attention for the whole class, for a group of children, or for individuals.

Some checklists, in contrast, are intended to be used for one child and to track performance on the same task over a period of time, such as a semester or school year (see Figure 2.8). This format allows you to see growth (or lack of growth). This kind of checklist is wonderful to share with families, especially those concerned about their child's progress.

Checklists can be used unobtrusively in the course of daily routines. They are not a test; they are a check of whether or not a certain behavior, skill, or ability is present on that day at that time.

As an example of what you might learn from a checklist, look again at Figure 2.7. Revising is clearly a weak area for most of the children listed here. A whole-class lesson should be planned. The checklist in Figure 2.8, devised to be used at

Constructing Meaning: Story

Name **Donald**

		Dates				
		9/9	**10/12**	**11/16**	**1/13**	**2/3**
1.	Topic	+	+	+	+	+
2.	Setting					
	Place	–	O	–	+	+
	Time	O	O	–	-	+
3.	Characters					
	Major	+	+	+	+	+
	Minor	O	–	–	+	+

Figure 2.8
Individual Checklist of Items Related to Constructing Meaning

intervals during an entire school year, is similarly enlightening. It shows that Donald was unable to retell a story successfully at the beginning of the year beyond the topic and main character's name. By February, however, he was recalling and retelling most of the significant elements in the story.

Diverse Learners

If you use a class checklist, you may want to code it in some way to remind yourself about behaviors that may relate to the diversity of the students. For example, if you use a class checklist to note participation in a discussion group, be sure to remind yourself of which children may not be participating because they are not yet confident enough in their own oral use of English. In such a case, failure to participate may have little to do with the child's understanding of the subject under discussion. You may want to have a private conversation about the topic with the child to allow him or her to speak without the whole class listening.

Similar reminders can be useful whenever the diverse backgrounds or characteristics of your students may significantly influence the behaviors on your checklist.

Comments

While checklists are useful tools, they can also be cumbersome. Be careful not to attempt so many checklists that you lose sight of their purpose or are unable to use the information to promote literacy growth in your children.

It may be wise for a beginning teacher to use checklists that are already prepared and have been found useful by colleagues. With experience, you may devise your own checklists to meet your own specific purposes. However, you may never be entirely satisfied and continue revising your checklists each year to better meet your needs.

As with other tools, the items must be specific to be useful. "Retells stories successfully" is too broad a behavior for a checklist. If any items in the student's retelling are missing or weak, you need to be able to indicate this, so it is probably best to break down the story elements on your list: for instance, Topic or Problem (conflict), Character(s), Setting(s), Significant Events, and Resolution. On many checklists, you will want to leave room for comments.

Work Samples

Work samples, which provide evidence of a child's actual work in the classroom, serve three important purposes:

- To look at students' work that results from learning
- To help in planning instruction as an ongoing activity
- To compare the level or quality of work over time and thus help you determine students' progress

Description

Samples of actual, authentic work done by a student yield direct evidence of performance. These may include everything from spelling tests to projects to published writing. Such samples are particularly good to share with families.

Samples of work collected over a period of time can show a child's growth. You, the child, and the family can all see clear proof of the child's progress from the beginning of the year.

Work samples may form part of a child's portfolio (a topic to be discussed in Chapter 3). Even if you do not have a portfolio as such, you should have a file folder for each child into which you put periodic samples of work.

Procedures and Samples

Decide what kinds of samples you will collect. This decision will depend on your purpose. For example, if you want to show the child's growth in reading, you might collect a cumulative list of all books the child has read, along with written responses to some of them. Figure 2.9 presents such a sample of a student's responses to independent reading. Each of Sam's responses is dated. The growth both in the child's ability to respond to literature and in his interest in reading are clear.

Name	Sam		Date	April 20

Book	Date	Comments
1. All About Snakes	9/3	I liked it.
2. Alligators All Around	10/15	It was good.
3. Who Lives in the Forest?	11/29	I learned new stuff.
20. Joe Goes to Work: He Sits Down to Draw	3/6	It was interesting to learn about a cartoonist. I think I'd be good at this, too.

**Figure 2.9
Samples of a Child's
Written Responses to His
Independent Reading**

Many teachers collect work samples for each child during the week and send them all home in a large envelope on Friday, along with a letter explaining what's been going on during the week. Sometimes the letter also outlines what will occur in the near future. The letter addresses all caregivers and has a place for you to jot a personal note for each family. A checklist of some kind is often included, perhaps tallying how many times homework was completed, how often books were returned on time, or any other information you wish to convey.

If you send a packet home weekly, ensure that the envelope is returned by having a place for responses and questions. This, then, becomes a means of communication between home and school—the beginning of a dialogue.

Figure 2.10 presents a sample cover page for a work packet to be sent home. This cover page could be inserted in a large envelope, along with samples of the child's work and a letter outlining the week's activities, future activities, and information about school events.

You may want to decide with each child which work samples to collect. You can tell children you want them to help you decide what work to save to show their families how much they are growing in literacy.

Diverse Learners

It does little good to send home a packet of work with a cover letter in English if the child's family cannot read English. Find out whether anyone in the family

**Figure 2.10
Cover Page for a First-Grade Packet Containing
Work Samples**

Name ___Susie_____   Date __10–18___

1. Homework returned: Ⓜ Ⓣ W Th Ⓕⓡ

2. Books returned: ⟨On time⟩   Late

3. Next week: ___Neighborhoods_____

4. Papers in packet:

   a. ___Spelling_____
   b. ___Math_____
   c. ___Social Studies Test_____

Teacher Comments: _Susie had a good week.___

Parent Comments: _____

knows English or whether there is a friend who can translate. If no one in the family knows English, try to find a community member or other professional who can translate the communications that go home from your class.

Such an effort will go a long way toward making a child feel part of your community. The fact that a family does not speak English or that you do not know the child's language does not relieve you of the necessity to communicate with the family.

Comments

We believe children should have some say about which samples of work are saved as "evidence." Everyone has an off day now and then, and not all samples are typical of a child's usual work. In our classrooms, we have often selected three types of work samples:

- *Yours:* This sample was selected by the student.
- *Mine:* This was a sample we (the teachers) wanted to include.
- *Ours:* This was a sample we and the student agreed together to include.

Selecting samples to save in this way helps students feel more involved in the process.

When sharing work samples with families, be careful to remind them that these are products—something produced after the child has gone through a process or a particular instructional phase. All work samples should be dated when collected. This is very helpful when trying to show progress. If the products show no improvement over time, perhaps you can reassure the family (and show evidence) that the child is becoming more comfortable with the process and therefore you expect to see improved products soon.

Look for ways to emphasize progress. For example, a child's spelling scores may still be low, but the nature of the misspellings may show growth. Perhaps Jill's wrong spellings at first reflected random letters, whereas now (though she still makes mistakes) there is clear evidence of her growing ability to connect phonemic segments with letters representing those segments.

Conferences

The term **conference** in this context refers to a meeting between the teacher and an individual student to discuss some aspect of the student's work. For the teacher, a conference of this type has several purposes:

- To provide a time to have direct interaction with one student
- To zero in on specific items or points
- To clarify some particular point
- To help plan instruction
- To determine students' progress

Description

In a general sense, a conference is a purposeful conversation between two or more people. When used with a clear purpose in mind, conferences are an essential part of a literacy environment (Calkins, 1986; Graves, 1983, 1991).

Many conferences for purposes other than assessment will take place during the day. Of course, any conference yields insights that will help you help children and therefore is a kind of assessment. This section deals with conferences designed specifically for assessment purposes.

The literacy assessment conference is short, about 5 to 10 minutes, and focused on gathering information about the child's literacy status. It may focus on construction of meaning, oral fluency, mechanical skills in writing, attitudes, or any other aspect of literacy. A conference often has several purposes. For example, while assessing oral fluency during a conference, you may also want to assess the child's attitude toward **risk taking,** or willingness to attempt to read even when not sure of accuracy.

As with all forms of assessment, it is vital that you organize your schedule, have a means of recording the data you gather, and have in place a way to use what you have learned to help the child take whatever next literacy step she or he is ready for.

Figure 2.11
Chart Showing Activities Children May Do While the Teacher Is Having a Conference with an Individual

---

TEACHER HAVING CONFERENCES? HERE'S WHAT YOU CAN DO

1. Read to yourself.

2. Read with a partner.

3. Write.

4. Use the computer (check schedule).

5. Go to the library (check schedule).

6. Work on research project.

7. Do any other quiet activity.

DO NOT INTERRUPT EXCEPT FOR EMERGENCIES!

YOU KNOW WHAT THEY ARE! ☺

Procedures and Samples

The following steps apply to all kinds of conferences, not just those you have targeted for assessment.

1 *Explain the purpose and procedure to students.* Role-play to establish behavior during the conference for those who are conferring and for the rest of the class. A chart can remind children what to do while the teacher is having a conference. Figure 2.11 shows one such chart.

2 *Use a timer.* Conferences should be short—no more than 5 to 10 minutes. Don't have a conference unless you have a valid purpose. The child's (and your) time could be better spent engaged in reading and writing.

3 *Have a chart of reminders for students.* To help children remember what to bring to a conference, post a chart with reminders like this:

HAVING A CONFERENCE TODAY?

Bring the following:
—Your book
—Your reading journal
—Your writing folder

4 *Post a schedule each day.* To help students keep track of who has a conference at what time and where, you can post a schedule:

LITERACY CONFERENCES TODAY:

WHO	WHEN	WHERE
Jamal	11:15	Round table
Chandra	11:40	Round table
Pete	1:30	Writing corner

At the same time, keep a master chart for yourself so you don't overlook anyone.

5 *Have a record sheet for each child.* Include a place for the date; the child's name, age, and grade; and notes. You may want to record notes about different areas, such as reading and writing. You may also want to record conclusions about the child's needs. (See Figure 2.12.) A half-sheet may be sufficient for your purpose.

6 *Monitor yourself as you begin assessment conferences.* You are trying, through your questions, to get a notion of what is going on in the child's head. Don't plant ideas, nudge, or give hints to try to get an answer you hope for. The child must feel free to respond honestly and openly.

7 *End each conference on a positive note.* Ask the child to tell you what he or she feels good about. If you use outright praise, focus on the work, not the child. Say, "This story was exciting to read" rather than "You are a good writer."

INDIVIDUAL CONFERENCE RECORD SHEET

Name _____ Date _____

Age _____ Grade _____

Purpose of today's conference:

Observations:

Conclusions/Instructional needs:

Goals for future:

Figure 2.12
Sample of a Form for Use in Conference

You will undoubtedly think of other ways to facilitate conferences. You can find other forms in some of the books listed in For Additional Reading. As with many areas of assessment and instruction, there is more than one way to do things.

Diverse Learners

We believe it is important to include all children in individual conferences, even a child who does not yet speak English. Until the child is comfortable beginning to speak some English, you might spend the time teaching each other the words for objects in the room or in pictures. Talk informally and naturally, accepting that only a little of what you say may be understood. Second-language learners will respond to the attention and your obvious caring attitude.

Students may exhibit cultural differences that puzzle you. For example, you may assume that children should look at adults when they speak, but in some cultures looking an adult in the eye is disrespectful, whereas looking down is a sign of respect. You may be used to patting a child's shoulder, but some children do not accept the touch of others. Some children may not understand when you are laughing *with* them and think you are laughing *at* them. Some children may never want to remove their coats because they have lived in an environment where personal belongings may be stolen if one lets go of them.

You'll need to try to accept and understand whatever cultural differences a child brings to your class. You and your students need to earn each other's trust.

Comments

Staying focused may be a problem for those just beginning to use conferences. Children are skilled at drawing teachers off task. Tell the child who does so that you'd love to hear about the new puppy (or whatever the child's enthusiasm may be) at another time, or suggest that the student write about it in his or her journal. Then get back on task.

During assessment conferences, remember that you are trying to learn about the child. Resist the effort to coach the child to the "right answer." Instead, suggest that the child pretend to be alone and talk out loud about what is going on inside his or her head. For some children, you may need to model thinking out loud several times.

Remember that what you learn during a conference is only a sample of literacy behavior—on that day, at that time. Many personal things may impinge on a child's behavior at any given moment. A single assessment conference is only a tiny piece of the whole picture.

Self-Reflections

Self-reflection means thinking about oneself. Here the term refers to the process as practiced by students. In literacy assessment, self-reflection serves these purposes:

- To help you find out how students perceive their own work and how they have performed
- To give you insight into why a particular student feels he or she is having difficulty in a certain area
- To help plan instruction

Description

As applied to literacy assessment, self-reflection includes thinking about broad ideas such as "What have I learned?" and "How do I feel about myself as a reader and writer?" For our purposes, self-reflection includes both self-assessment and self-evaluation:

- *Self-assessment* asks questions about process and product, such as:

    "What is giving me trouble?"

    "Did I do my part in a group project?"

    "What is my biggest problem in writing a report?"

- *Self-evaluation* seems to put a value on things, asking questions like these:

    "How did I do?"

    "Am I getting better?"

    "What am I good at?"

    "What still needs work?"

Later in this section, we show some sample forms you might give students for self-reflection. Many others are possible, of course.

You may want children to bring written self-reflections with them to conferences from time to time, though it is certainly not always necessary. The greatest value of reflection comes during the act itself as students think about their work. Sharing this reflection later may also be helpful.

Self-reflections serve two purposes. For children, such thinking should lead them to set their own goals and become more self-directed and independent learners. For the teacher, a child's self-reflection will deepen understanding of the child and help the teacher provide appropriate support.

Procedures and Samples

The following steps will help you get started with the process of having children reflect honestly about their own literacy.

1 *Model the process.* For example, you might share your own strategies when studying for a test and how you have evaluated yourself in terms of using those strategies. Imagine, for instance, that you are currently taking a science course to bolster your teaching in that area. You might compare your self-evaluation from an earlier study session with a recent one. You could explain what you learned about yourself from the process and how it will direct your literacy in the future.

Figure 2.13 presents an example of a teacher's own study checklist, along with a **think-aloud** commentary used to model self-reflection for fifth graders. You can adapt this process as necessary to allow you to use your personal self-reflections as a model for your students.

2 *Begin with just one simple form* (see Figures 2.14 and 2.15). For example, ask children to rate themselves in two or three areas and respond in writing to some questions. When you think children are comfortable with this process, you may want to introduce a more complicated form or additional forms for other areas (see Figure 2.16). Obviously, with very young children the process will be much less complicated. You are building a habit of self-reflection, something that does not come easily to many people.

MY PERSONAL CHECKLIST FOR STUDYING FOR A TEST

✚ = Done   ✓ = Close, but not quite   0 = Not done

Study Steps	Teacher Think-Aloud
✓ 1. Read chapter when first assigned.	*I used to wait to read the chapter until after the teacher had discussed it. I couldn't participate in the class discussion and I was always behind. This time I began reading on time but didn't finish.*
✓ 2. Make a K-W-L chart.	*For the last chapter I just began reading. This time, I tried to use a K-W-L chart to give me a purpose for reading. It helped, but I didn't think up "What I Want to Know" questions that fit the chapter. I need to get better at this or use a different strategy.*
✓ 3. Use sticky notes to mark major ideas.	*I can't mark in the book, so I used to try to remember the important parts or write them all down as I went along. Now I use sticky notes. Sometimes I find that an idea I put a note beside as I read is better stated later in the chapter and I can simply remove the note. I don't get so bogged down this way. I still need to work on using too many notes. Sometimes I can't tell an important idea that might be tested from one I just find interesting.*
✚ 4. Write vocabulary/ concepts on cards.	*Last time I tried to study by flipping back and forth from the page to the glossary. Putting important terms on cards with definitions on the back made it easier to review them for the test.*
✚ 5. Summarize sections in my head as I read.	*Last time I thought that if I understood each section as I read, that would be enough to do well on the test. That was not bad for multiple-choice questions, but not good enough for essay questions.*
✓ 6. Summarize in writing.	*I never used to write as I studied. This time I tried to take the time to write my summarizations when I reread. Writing forced me to organize my thoughts and use the vocabulary. I didn't start this soon enough, though, and didn't get all the way through the chapter.*
✓ 7. Feel prepared for test.	*On the day of the last test I felt worried even though I had studied. At least I had read the chapter and understood it. This time I was much more confident.*
✓ 8. Get a B or higher on test.	*I got a C last time! This time I got a B+!*
	I have improved in my ability to prepare for a test. And it feels good not to be scared on the day of the test. I found out I liked the subject more than before. I guess when you really work to understand something, you like it more. Next time I'll try to have a plus on every item in my list, and maybe I can get an A. Also, I need to revise my checklist. I forget to read the end-of-chapter summary first, and I forgot to use subheadings to help me predict.

Figure 2.13
Modeling of One Teacher's Self-Reflection Process for a Fifth Grade

Self-Reflection — Literature Circle

Name _____   Date _____

Title of Book _____

Author _____

Illustrator _____

Use the scale for each of the following:

(Scale: 5 = Wonderful, 4 = Pretty good, 3 = Okay, 2 = Not so good, 1 = Ooops)

How I felt about the book   _____

How well I read the book   _____

My part in discussion circles   _____

My journal response during the reading of the book   _____

Write about your literature discussion circle. What is the best part? What is the worst? How would you change it? How would you change the way you participate?

_____

_____

_____

Figure 2.14
Form for Children to Use After Reading a Book and Participating in a Literature Discussion Circle

3 *Encourage oral self-reflection as part of literature discussions and conferences.* As always, model such thinking yourself. For example, you might comment during a discussion that Linda gave you a whole new way of thinking about a story you thought you knew very well. You have learned from this that there is always more to learn.

4 *Ask children to file self-evaluations in their folders and bring them to conferences.* At the conferences, discuss these self-evaluations with the students, asking questions to help them think more about their own literacy.

Self-Reflection — Independent Reading

Name _____ Date _____

Title and Author _____

Mark the scales:

1. How I felt about the book:

             Loved it   Okay   Didn't like it

    Explain your marking _____

    _____

    _____

2. I understood the ideas:

             Mostly   Some   Not much

    Explain your marking _____

    _____

    _____

What else would you like to say about reading this book?

_____

_____

Figure 2.15
Form for Children to Use
After Independent Reading

The form shown in Figure 2.16 can be adapted in many ways. For example, for nonfiction, you might want to specify prereading behaviors related to whatever you have been teaching, such as examining graphics, making a K-W-L chart, or using a strategy such as **SQ3R,** which includes **s**urveying, **q**uestioning, **r**eading, **r**eciting, and **r**eviewing. Among the strategies to use during reading, you might want to specify summarizing at the end of each subsection, jotting down unfamiliar terms. Strategies for use after reading could include returning to the K-W-L chart.

Complete versions of the forms shown in Figures 2.14 to 2.16 are in the Resource File.

THINKING ABOUT MY READING

Name _____   Date _____

Title and Author of Book _____

_____

	All the time	Sometimes	Hardly ever
Before reading, did I * Preview the book			
* Predict			
During reading, did I * Stop and think			
* Change predictions			
After reading, did I * Retell to myself			
* Respond			

What do I need to do better? _____

_____

**Figure 2.16
Student Self-Monitoring
Checklist**

Diverse Learners

As we mentioned earlier, students from some cultures (but certainly not all) may find it difficult to admit they perceive themselves as good at anything. Try to find ways to allow them to express honest self-evaluations. For example, very young children might choose to wear a badge of some kind that shows how they feel about themselves that day.

Encourage appraisal that focuses on the work. Begin with simple statements, for example, "I wrote a good sentence today" or "I finished ten math problems." Help students begin to feel comfortable telling at least one positive thing about their school experience each day.

Also, help students begin to focus on one or more things they can do to help themselves and therefore raise the quality of their work. Help them learn to be specific. For example, instead of "I need to do a better project," a student should write, "My topic was too big. I couldn't cover it all. Next time, I'll choose better."

One other point should be made here, and it applies to all writing situations, not just to written self-reflections: if a second-language learner is not yet comfortable writing in English, encourage the student to write in whatever language she or he chooses. Gradually English words will appear.

Comments

Self-evaluation involves **metacognition**—knowledge and control of one's own thinking and learning—and is not easy for any of us, especially for young children. However, this is an important part of the learning process, and especially the process of learning to read, write, and become literate (Brown, 1980).

Be careful not to overuse self-reflection forms, or children will begin to see them as a chore rather than a means of growth. Know why you are asking for self-reflection, and be sure children understand the purpose as well. While your goal is to promote this kind of reflection independent of assigning it, overuse can have exactly the opposite effect.

Above all, remember that children may not feel free to be honest unless you have established an environment based on trust and risk taking. Once they feel comfortable with the thinking process and with responding openly both orally and in writing, consider involving them in devising appropriate self-reflection forms. For example, at the beginning of a collaborative project, children can work with you to decide how to evaluate the project, the group, and themselves as members of the group.

Continue to model your own self-reflections. Never underestimate the power of simply beginning to write as a way into reflection. Some children, if given a chance, may reflect daily about their learning, either by hand in a journal or by using a computer.

Performance Assessments

A **performance assessment,** an assessment based on a particular task performed by the student, serves three basic purposes:

- To see how well students apply what they are learning in real-world situations
- To help determine students' progress
- To help plan instruction

Description

Performance assessments involve authentic, real-world tasks that demonstrate a student's literacy knowledge and skill. Often they are part of ongoing instructional activities. Examples include posters, plays, oral or written reports, construction projects, graphic support of scientific experiments, and so forth. Such assessments affect both teaching and learning.

Procedures and Samples

Each performance assessment will be different and will depend on the specific things to be assessed. There are, however, some general criteria to follow in using any performance assessment.

1 *Identify the strategies, skills, and knowledge the task will demand.* Some of these may have been previously taught and presumed to be mastered. Others may be items you plan to teach prior to students' actually performing the task.

2 *Devise a task that requires the use of the strategies, skills, and knowledge.* You may devise the task yourself, or you may work in collaboration with your students.

3 *Develop a rubric to evaluate the performance task.* **Rubrics** are sets of guidelines or scoring guides and criteria for determining that a student has learned or accomplished something. Rubrics often include examples of acceptable responses or give several sample responses that show the degree to which an individual has attained something. For example, rubrics for writing often present three or four sample papers to show the varying degrees to which an individual has learned to do some type of writing. These sample papers are called **anchor papers,** because they give a point of reference to "anchor" the decision about the student's degree of success.

You may elicit the help of your students in developing your rubric. Each objective identified should be judged as having been met or not met and, perhaps, to what degree.

4 *Share the rubric with all students as the task begins.* Be sure students understand each part of the rubric. Encourage them to refer to it as they complete the task. Examples of writing rubrics appear in Chapter 8.

5 *Invite students to use the rubric to evaluate themselves independently.* Compare their results with your own. Collaboratively, decide which unachieved items were the result of a need for further instruction or reteaching (something for you to do). Alternatively, help students decide which items might have been achieved with more effort, better organization, and willingness to ask for help when needed (something for them to do).

The partial rubric shown in Figure 2.17 was used for assessing Ms. Leonard's culminating activity for a fourth-grade social studies unit. The unit grew from the state social studies curriculum framework. The overarching concept was that prejudice affects behavior and has far-reaching consequences.

To begin, Ms. Leonard identified some of the literacy strategies the children needed to pursue their study and prepare a culminating presentation. These included research in the media center, using the Internet, posing questions and framing tentative answers, synthesizing information, identifying significant information, distinguishing fact from opinion, presenting data in logical form both in writing and orally, and using visual aids. Of course, many other strategies could be involved. Other curricular areas, such as math and music, were also included in this unit. Each area might have items on the rubric.

Ms. Leonard had taught lessons on the appropriate skills and strategies before launching this unit, and she continued the lessons as the unit progressed over three weeks. The children were allowed to choose among several projects as possible culminating performances. Together with the children, Ms. Leonard

PROJECT RUBRIC — SOCIAL STUDIES UNIT

Name _____ Date _____

Unit _____ Project _____

Other Members of the Group _____

_____

Scale: O = Outstanding, P = Pretty Good, B = Beginning, N = Not Yet

Task	Achievement	
1. Gather information	O	Several print sources, Internet; synthesized, analyzed
	P	Several sources, information not synthesized, no conclusions
	B	Only one or two sources
	N	Only one source

Figure 2.17
Partial Rubric for a Fourth-Grade Culminating Activity

developed a rubric for assessing each type of project, describing each level of performance achievement. The children had copies of the rubric available as they prepared their projects so they could assess themselves as they worked. Ms. Leonard also encouraged them to log their actions as they worked.

Diverse Learners

You may find it nearly impossible to impose the same rubrics on the work of every student. We suggest that you develop choices of work to be assessed. Group projects are useful in this respect because they allow you to mix students of varying abilities and competence. For example, students who are not yet fluent in English might contribute graphics or music to a report. The students can work on a common goal, each individual doing whatever he or she is able to do. Each student might then be assessed twice. One assessment, of the product, would be the same for every student in the group. A second assessment might be based on your (and the student's) perception of individual participation. This second assessment would allow for the diversity in the group.

Comments

Performance assessments can be **summative;** that is, they can be used to derive a grade for a project. For example, each level of skill used to complete a project may be associated with a letter grade: the most competent performance might earn an A, a slightly lesser performance a B, and so on to the lowest possible grade.

Performance assessments can also be **formative,** yielding information you can use to meet the needs both of individual students and of your class as a whole. If you find that students score low on certain items on your rubric, it may be because you need to reteach, or teach differently, some of the strategies and skills.

Not every project needs to be assessed with the specificity of a rubric. There is no need to overassess your students. Sometimes you may want to allow your students to prepare and present a project with a simple pass/fail standard: if they do it, they pass. You don't want students working hard on projects only because of the payoff. You want them to discover the pleasure of working on something for the pure joy of pursuing an interest and sharing it with others.

Summary

A variety of generic tools and techniques can be used as part of literacy assessment.

In the technique known simply as observing, you watch students closely while they are engaged in a particular task and you record anecdotal notes—as specific as possible—about what you see.

Interest inventories help you identify materials and plan instructional activities that keep students involved and motivated. These inventories range from published pencil-and-paper measures to collages and all-about-me books.

Attitude/self-concept checks are similarly varied. Sometimes they take the form of a student's own reflections in a journal. Often, however, they involve a form on which the student marks a choice or writes responses. Whatever the format, these checks can help you determine a child's attitudes toward school, toward learning, and toward himself or herself.

Checklists are lists of items that allow you to mark whether a behavior is present or absent and (often) to what degree. With such a device, you can make a quick record of what you observe during a particular activity. Checklists may be designed for use with an entire class or with a single student.

Work samples are collections of a particular student's work. You can use them to gauge the child's progress over time and as a basis for discussion with the student and his or her family. Often you will want to involve students in the process of deciding which work samples to save.

Conferences, as discussed in this chapter, are short conversations between a teacher and an individual student. Though they last only 5 to 10 minutes, they provide invaluable information about a child's literacy status.

Self-reflections consist of a student's own thoughts about his or her progress. They may involve either self-assessment (thoughts about process and product, such as "What is giving me trouble?") or self-evaluation (value judgments, such as "Am I getting better?"). Even with young children, you can encourage the process of self-reflection by beginning with simple questions and modeling the process yourself.

Finally, performance assessments involve authentic tasks that demonstrate a student's literacy knowledge and skill. These assessments can be summative (used to derive a final grade) or formative (used to judge progress and guide your further teaching). To assess each type of performance, you use a specific rubric designed for that purpose. You may want to have your students collaborate in creating the rubric.

These tools and techniques will be helpful in assessing all students, no matter how diverse. Each technique is likely to be part of your literacy assessment at one time or another. Every teacher needs to command a variety of assessment options.

Chapters 5 through 9 will help you decide which tools to use and when. You will also learn how to use assessment to plan and carry out instruction. We can give you tools and techniques, but you must make informed choices.

FOR ADDITIONAL READING

Afflerbach, P. (1993). STAIR: A system for recording and using what we observe and know about our students. *The Reading Teacher, 47,* 260–263.

Gambrell, L. B., Palmer, B. M., Codling, R. M., & Mazzoni, S. A. (1996). Assessing motivation to read. *The Reading Teacher, 49*(7), 518–533.

Goodman, Y. (1978). Kidwatching: An alternative to testing. *Journal of National Elementary Principals, 57*(4), 441–445.

Harp, B. (1996). *Handbook of literacy assessment and evaluation.* Norwood, MA: Christopher-Gordon Publishers.

Hill, B. C., & Ruptic, C. (1994). *Practical aspects of authentic assessment: Putting the pieces together.* Norwood, MA: Christopher-Gordon Publishers.

McKenna, M. C., & Kear, D. J. (1990). Measuring attitude toward reading: A new tool for teachers. *The Reading Teacher, 43,* 626–639.

Rhodes, L. K. (1993). *Literacy assessment: A handbook of instruments.* Portsmouth, NH: Heinemann.

Rhodes, L. K., & Nathenson-Mejia, S. (1992). Anecdotal records: A powerful tool for ongoing literacy assessment. *The Reading Teacher, 45*(7), 502–509.

Worthy, J. (1996). A matter of interest: Literature that hooks reluctant readers and keeps them reading. *The Reading Teacher, 50*(3), 204–212.

FOR EXPLORATION: ELECTRONIC RESOURCES

Ideas and Rubrics.
http://intranet.cps.k12.il.us/Assessments/Ideas_and_Rubrics/ideas_and_ru brics.html   This web site provides general information about performance assessments and rubrics. Along with samples, it includes step-by-step guidelines for developing a rubric.

KidBibs Interest Inventory.
http://www.kidbibs.com/learningtips/inventory.htm   This site offers a model of an interest inventory for teachers to use with their students.

K-W-L Chart.
http://teams.lacoe.edu/documentation/classrooms/patti/k-1/activities/kwl.html   This web site provides a brief description of K-W-L charts, the materials needed, and the procedures for use.

Scholastic-Assessment.
http://teacher.scholastic.com/professional/assessment/index.htm   Sponsored by Scholastic, this web page devoted to assessment has links to a variety of articles by both researchers and practitioners. Some of the articles relate specifically to language arts assessment, others to more general aspects.

CLASSROOM APPLICATIONS

1. Take anecdotal records on one child (or several children) for several days and compare them with the records of someone else who has observed the same child (or children).

2. Try some of the other tools or techniques described in this chapter, using our forms or ones you make up.

3. Interview several teachers about one or more of the tools and techniques discussed in this chapter. Compile your results and draw conclusions.

Gathering Information II: Specific Tools and Techniques for Literacy Assessment

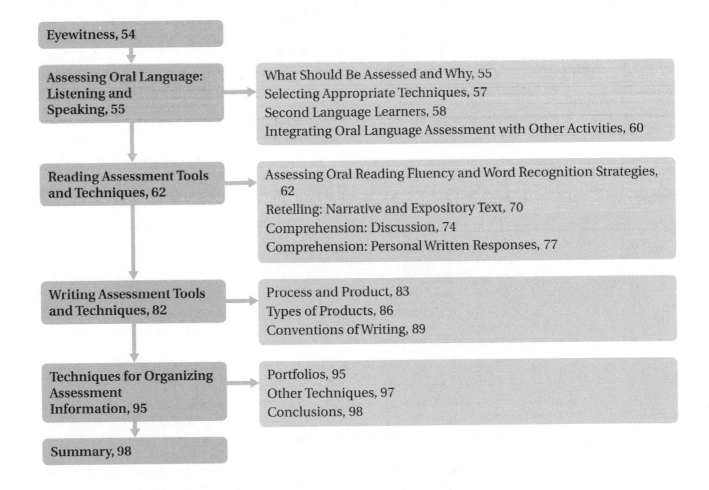

FOCUS

As you read the Eyewitness section, ask yourself the following questions:

1. How many examples can you find of assessment taking place during instruction?
2. How many different aspects of literacy could you assess during Alison's oral report?

Eyewitness   *It is first thing in the morning, and Jim Edwards's fourth graders are just arriving. The desks are arranged in groups of six. As the children settle into their places, they take out their journals. A suggested journal topic is on the board, but many children have chosen to write on their own topic.*

As the children finish journaling, they put their journals into a milk crate near Mr. Edwards's desk. Then they take out their writing folders, which are kept in containers on each group of desks. While the children begin work on their writing, Mr. Edwards responds to a few journals. We see that his written comments are almost a dialogue with each child. He responds only to content, not the mechanics.

(If we followed Mr. Edwards over the course of a week, we would see him respond in writing to every child's journal at least once. Usually, he reads two or three journal entries as students move into the next activity. Some he reads outside of school hours.)

Soon Mr. Edwards moves on to circulate among his students as they work on the writing in their individual folders. A bilingual volunteer has arrived; he confers with Mr. Edwards and then pulls up a chair beside one student. The children are at various stages of the writing process. Some are doing prewriting activities such as making semantic webs about their topics or brainstorming a list of ideas for topics. Some are writing first drafts. Some are conferencing with a peer, who suggests revisions to make the writing clearer and initials the draft when the conference is over. Some students are writing a revision. Some are doing final editing, checking spelling with hand-held spell checkers, looking at capitalization and punctuation. A couple are at the computers to input final drafts from their final edited revisions. The child who is being assisted by the bilingual volunteer is doing his first draft in Spanish; then, together, they will rewrite in English at the computer.

When writing time is over, the children break into literature circles. One group is reading Number the Stars *(Lowry, 1989). Mr. Edwards sits in on this discussion. Several times during the discussion, he marks a checklist on a clipboard. He participates in the discussion occasionally, but only as another reader, not as the leader.*

In the afternoon, Alison gives an oral report on penguins. She has used a variety of research sources, including a CD-ROM and a video. She speaks from notes and uses a chart on an easel. (She is also working on a HyperStudio presentation, she tells us, but it isn't finished yet. She and Mr. Edwards are both learning how to do this.) The rest of the class listens attentively and asks questions when she is finished. The questions are relevant, and Alison is able to answer some, but not all, of them. Those she can't answer she makes a note about. She tells the questioner she will try to find the answer later and suggests they search the Internet together.

Mr. Edwards is assessing his students all day long. During the Eyewitness account, we did not see any formal assessment, but we saw many opportunities for informal assessment tied directly to instructional activities. If we were to discuss the day with Mr. Edwards, he would be able to tell us what he learned about his class and about individual children and how this knowledge added to his literacy profile of each child. He would also be able to tell us how what he learned today will affect his instructional plans for the future.

In Chapter 2, you learned about some tools and techniques that are useful in assessing literacy as well as other curricular areas and affective factors. In this chapter, we introduce you to assessment tools and techniques specific to literacy: listening, speaking, reading, and writing. We also discuss some ways to organize information you gather, whether for instructional decision making or for building the literacy profile of an individual child. You will use these tools as you learn about the stages of literacy development in Chapters 5 through 9, where we link assessment to instruction.

Assessing Oral Language: Listening and Speaking

FOCUS **As you read this chapter, ask yourself the following questions:**

1. What areas of assessment are specific to literacy?
2. How will knowledge of the levels of language production help you in your diverse classroom?
3. What are the purposes for each type of reading assessment?
4. How is writing best assessed?
5. How can literacy assessment be integrated with the curriculum?

We believe that you, the classroom teacher, should closely observe each child's natural, everyday use of listening and speaking. In Part Two of this book, as you read the benchmarks for the stages of literacy development, it will be clear that listening and speaking play a critical role. These areas develop long before children come to school and continue to develop throughout their lives. As with all assessment, your first job is to decide what you need to know and why. Then you must devise ways to assess each child in terms of what you need to know.

You may use school-developed standards and sample indicators. Often schools have checklists tied to these standards. If so, what you learn in this chapter will help you use and interpret the instruments you are given. If your school does not have adequate indicators and checklists, you can use what you read here and in the "stage" chapters of Part Two to make up your own assessment instruments.

Note that we do not discuss hearing or articulation problems per se. If you have a child with a hearing impairment or speech articulation problem in your classroom, you must document the difficulty and refer the child for possible special help. As for listening comprehension, we discuss that subject in Chapter 10 in connection with informal reading inventories.

What Should Be Assessed and Why

For purposes of discussion, we look at listening and speaking separately, though they are closely interrelated. You will often assess both of them as you assess reading and writing.

Listening

There are three main kinds of listening. **Aesthetic listening** means listening for pleasure. This is what we do when we listen to a story, a play, or a sitcom on television. Aesthetic listening can be divided into various subcategories: for example, listening to relate to a personal experience, to retell, to predict, to enjoy the sounds of language, to detect nuance, or to recognize literary style. It is important to recognize that each facet related to listening also applies to reading. Children who cannot do these things while listening will undoubtedly have difficulty when trying to do them while reading—or writing.

A second kind of listening is **efferent listening,** which means listening for the purpose of learning. This too can be broken into subcategories: ability to note sequence, to compare and contrast, and to summarize material one has listened to. These, too, are ways of thinking that apply equally to reading and to writing.

A third variety is listening to make judgments, often called **critical listening**. Some subcategories are detecting bias, recognizing persuasive techniques of various kinds, synthesizing with prior knowledge, and recognizing validity of the source. These are also components of reading and writing.

Listening is not the same as "paying attention." A child can listen well without looking at you. Conversely, a child can look at you with seemingly rapt attention and be daydreaming rather than listening. A child may listen to you explain something to the class and immediately ask you to repeat it just for him or her. Usually this is not because the child didn't listen, or even because the child didn't understand; more likely, it is due to a lack of self-confidence. If you feel a child just isn't listening to you, don't label the behavior as a listening problem. Chances are that something else is going on: a need for attention, a negative attitude, or distractions on the child's desk, in the classroom, or outside.

On the other hand, a child may pay close attention but not understand what is being said to him. Such a child might have auditory memory problems. Or perhaps the child starts out paying close attention but gets distracted in his head as you talk. For example, in the first chapter of *Anastasia Krupnik* (Lowry, 1979), when Anastasia's teacher begins to explain an assignment on poetry, Anastasia stops listening to the teacher and begins listening to the words in her own head about a poem she wants to write. The main thing here is to be very careful about drawing hasty conclusions based on flimsy evidence.

Speaking

Speaking includes all the kinds of talk in which children may engage. Most of them you know from familiar labels: conversations, show-and-tell, oral reports, debates, discussions, storytelling, questioning, interviews, role playing, readers' theater, and video.

Another way to look at speaking is in terms of how successfully a child uses the language. You may know these as the seven **functions of language** (Halliday, 1975), and they apply to written language as well as oral:

1   *Instrumental:* conversations, satisfying a need
2   *Regulatory:* directions, rules, gestures
3   *Interactional:* conversations, discussions, sharing
4   *Personal:* show-and-tell, debates, discussions

5 *Imaginative:* dramatic play, storytelling

6 *Heuristic:* interviews, seeking information

7 *Informative:* reporting, telling, discussing, conveying information

Children begin learning all of these functions very early in life. The functions are not a prescription for what should be taught; rather, they are descriptive—how children (and adults) use language. Some children use all of them comfortably. Some do not. If you have children who seem to struggle with one or more of the functions of language, you may provide activities to help them become more comfortable.

Selecting Appropriate Techniques

Since listening and speaking are so pervasive in any classroom and both are part of everyone's daily life, it is important to assess them in a way that is useful to you, helpful for the child, and informative for the child's family. You don't usually need a test on a particular area of speaking and listening. Rather, you want to learn how the child is doing in oral language overall and whether there are particular areas that are troublesome.

Almost everything you do in the normal course of a day in the classroom affords opportunity for assessment of oral language. A number of the tools and techniques mentioned in Chapter 2 are especially useful, and the following sections offer a few suggestions for applying them.

Checklists

Checklists can be made for almost anything you want to assess. List what you expect to see, and check whether it is present when you observe. For example, if you have read a book aloud to your class, you can use a checklist to assess whether students were able to listen aesthetically. You discover this information by asking questions and leading or monitoring a discussion.

During a story retelling or a book talk, you might use a checklist to be sure the child followed the agreed-on format: giving an introduction, naming the book and author, telling the story elements, using story language, using gestures, and so forth. The items to be checked depend on your purpose.

Observation

Watch and listen to your children. Certainly you will want to note growth, but also observe any problems in usage, nonstandard English, failure to express ideas, and inability to follow directions.

Anecdotal Records

Write notes about what you observe. There is no need to keep anecdotal records about oral language separate from those about reading and writing, but be sure your records include what you observe about each child's speaking and listening.

Conferences

Whatever the primary purpose of a conference, this is a perfect time to note listening and speaking behaviors. You and the child are talking one on one. The child should feel free to express whatever feelings are present, while you listen and reflect.

Discussions

Use a checklist during a discussion to assess whether children are listening to one another (you know they are if they respond to the content of one another's comments), sharing, taking turns, being courteous to each other, and exhibiting other aspects of talking and listening appropriate to a discussion group.

Second-Language Learners

We live in an increasingly diverse society. One reflection of this diversity is the increasing number of children who come to school not yet speaking English or not yet fluent in English. These children as a group include a wide range of possible histories, of which the following are only a few:

1　The child may have been born in the United States but into a household where no English is spoken.

2　The child may have been born in another country. The family may have come to this country for a variety of reasons: refuge from war or other extreme hardship, a desire to pursue a better life, or a desire to live here temporarily with the goal of returning home within a few years. Each child has a different story, one that you must try to learn if you are to help the child learn.

3　The child may already be a reader and writer in another language or in several other languages.

4　The child may not yet be a reader or writer in any language.

5　The child may live in a family that wants to promote bilingualism at home, or the child may need to switch from learning in English at school to speaking his or her native language at home.

Many acronyms have been used over the years in an effort to name such children without using a label that acquires a pejorative connotation over time. For a time, these students were designated LEP, which stood for "limited English proficiency." Labels for programs designed to teach them have included ESL ("English as a Second Language") and ESOL ("English for Speakers of Other Languages"). Sometimes the children are simply called "ESOL kids." A more positive label would be "students acquiring English" or, as we mentioned in Chapter 1, "English-language learners" (ELLs). None of these labels roll trippingly off the tongue, however. Furthermore, any time we give a name to a group of kids, we are in danger of failing to see them as individuals. Despite some commonalities about students who are acquiring English, each is as unique as any native English speaker.

We will give you a little basic information about assessing these children. You should also read periodicals and consult specialists in your school. The issue of how best to meet the needs of these students is far from settled.

Levels of Language Production

The following are widely accepted stages of language production that students go through as they acquire English (Krashen & Terrell, 1983). *Production* in this sense refers to speaking, whereas *reception* means listening.

1 *Preproduction:* As students are just beginning to acquire English, they may not speak much. This level is often referred to as the *silent period.* You may elicit a response by asking such students to point to a picture, draw a picture, or hold up a yes/no card. The point is to recognize that this is a natural stage and that the child's lack of spoken response is not laziness or stubbornness but quite normal. In a supportive environment, the child will eventually begin to speak. First, perhaps, the child may respond orally to yes/no questions. From the beginning, children should be encouraged to use one another's names when responding.

2 *Early production:* When the child begins to respond orally, it is often with one- or two-word answers. The child's receptive (listening) ability is usually ahead of his or her productive (speaking) ability in English, just as in any child's natural language development. First responses may include only the key words, omitting articles, verb endings, inflections, adjectives, and adverbs. The wise teacher accepts these efforts with pleasure, perhaps elaborating what the child has said. Either/or questions can be helpful because they give the child the words necessary to answer appropriately and demonstrate comprehension.

3 *Speech emergence:* At this level, the child uses phrases or short sentences, though these are still incomplete and often nonstandard. As with any child, we don't know what is happening inside the child's head. Some talk may sound quite natural, as though the child is thinking in English. At other times, the child may still be thinking in his or her first language and attempting to translate into English. If you have ever learned a second language yourself, you'll recognize these attempts.

4 *Intermediate fluency:* After some time (a few months or a year), a student may be close in functioning to others of the same age or grade, though still building receptive vocabulary. True fluency may take several years (Cummins, 1996). Actually, we all continue to build receptive vocabularies throughout our lives. That is, we hear (or read) words we have never heard or read before—or at least we aren't aware that we have. As we continue to hear the word or meet it in reading, it acquires meaning for us. Eventually we feel secure enough in our understanding of the word to try using it in conversation and in writing. If those who hear us or read what we have written understand us and don't tell us we have used the word incorrectly, we continue to use it. The word has become a part of our vocabulary.

Using a Checklist to Measure Levels of Language Production

You may find that your school system has checklists designed to use in measuring a child's stage in language production. When a child is first registered for school, staff members often determine whether English is spoken in the home as a first language and, if not, what language is spoken. On the basis of that information, a specialist does an assessment to determine what level of help the child might need and how the school might best provide it. The child may be placed with special teachers for some or even most of the day but be in your classroom for the opening of the day, for special classes, for lunch, and for recess.

You may want to devise your own checklist for the levels of language production. You may also devise a checklist to use informally during discussions, allowing you to sample the child's language use at regular intervals over time. You, the child, and the family will be able to see how the child is growing in English usage. A sample checklist appears in the Resource File at the end of the book.

Most reading programs published within the last few years address the needs of students acquiring English. Whatever program you are using will provide many specific ways to include these children in your classroom language and reading activities.

Integrating Oral Language Assessment with Other Activities

The listening and speaking that children do in the classroom (aside from social use) should always be about something related to curriculum; that is, you should not devise special listening and speaking tasks simply for the sake of assessment. Children will use both listening and speaking all day long as they engage in activities related to their regular subjects. This will be true in the classroom in which subjects are dealt with separately as well in classrooms that integrate curriculum.

Many teachers like to discuss listening and speaking with children early in the year and cooperatively draw up guidelines to help children grow in these areas. Such guidelines can be posted in the classroom and revised as the year goes on. Here is one such set of guidelines suggested by third graders:

How to Have a Good Discussion

- Don't interrupt.
- Stick to the topic.
- Talk loud enough.
- Call people by name.
- Listen to other ideas.
- Don't argue.
- Don't hurt anyone's feelings.
- If one person hasn't said anything, ask what he or she thinks.

Most of the time, you will find you can assess many different things in the course of classroom instructional activities. For example, in Mr. Edwards's class described in the Eyewitness section at the beginning of the chapter, Alison was giving an oral report on penguins. The following areas of literacy could be assessed on the basis of this activity; undoubtedly there are more.

Listening

- Efferent listening by Alison (in preparing her report, she has listened to the audio portion of a CD-ROM and a video)
- Efferent listening to the report by the class

Speaking

- Alison's use of the informative function of speech
- Her presentation skills
- Her ability to synthesize
- Her ability to engage her audience
- The class's questioning after the presentation

Reading

- Allison's efferent reading (she read many sources to learn information)
- Her ability to synthesize those sources
- Her ability to read information on web sites

Writing

- Allison's prewriting: generating ideas, selecting topic
- Her notetaking (from the many sources)
- Her outlining of the presentation

We recommend that you subscribe to at least one professional journal such as *Language Arts,* as well as a professional magazine such as *Teaching K–8.* These will help you grow in your knowledge of theory as well as provide practical ideas for assessing oral language.

Although formal assessment of oral language probably is beyond the role of the classroom teacher, we believe that you, the classroom teacher, should closely observe each child's natural, everyday use of listening and speaking. When either seems significantly different from that of the typical child in your classroom and you suspect a language disorder of some kind, the first step is to confirm whether or not that is so, and refer the child to a specialist.

We will suggest some specific oral language assessments in the chapters about each stage of literacy development. You will often be able to use these assessments concurrently with reading or writing assessments.

Reading Assessment Tools and Techniques

In this section, we discuss reading assessment directly tied to making instructional decisions and yielding information that can be shared with the child and his or her family. Other kinds of assessment, such as those tied to published reading programs or to local or state standards, are discussed in Chapters 10 and 11.

We will address four areas of reading assessment: oral reading fluency and word recognition strategies, retellings of narrative and expository texts, comprehension as shown by discussion, and comprehension evidenced in personal written responses. For each tool or technique, as in Chapter 2, we state its purposes and then present subsections devoted to description, procedures and samples, ideas for diverse learners, and comments. Further information about each technique is threaded through Chapters 5 through 9.

Assessing Oral Reading Fluency and Word Recognition Strategies

Fluency in oral reading means the ability to read aloud words of connected text smoothly and accurately. Often fluency is described as rate of reading and accuracy. Along with fluency itself, a useful assessment considers the strategies the child is using to recognize words. Overall, the techniques described in this section serve multiple purposes:

- To infer the child's fluency when he or she is reading either unfamiliar or familiar text
- To infer the child's use of strategies to figure out unfamiliar words
- To assess quality of oral reading (for instance, good inflection versus word-by-word reading)
- To judge whether a child reads fluently in **grade-level** materials (for instance, whether a second-grade child reads a second-grade book)
- To judge whether a child reads with similar fluency regardless of genre
- To note the child's attitude, self-concept, and risk-taking behaviors
- To use individual results to plan instruction
- To determine student progress and share this information with the child and family

As we will explain later in this chapter, reading involves constructing meaning from text. To do this, the reader must recognize many (or most) words automatically and quickly. The reader must also know and use several strategies when a word is not recognized automatically—and must be confident about his or her ability to do so.

Description

The first step in assessing a child's oral reading fluency and use of strategies involves having the child read a book or selection to you. As the student reads, you

- **Substitution:** Write what the child said instead of the correct word; if what is said is not a real word, write the best phonetic representation you can.

penny ←(what child said)

~~*pony*~~ ← (word in text)

- **Omission:** Write the word and circle it.

(daylight)

- **Self-correction:** Put **SC** next to the substitution or omission.

SC ←(indicates child corrected self)

penny ←(what child said)

~~*pony*~~ ← (word in text)

- **Teacher-pronounced:** Write the word and put **T** above it.

*happiness*ᵀ

**Figure 3.1
One Possible Coding
System for Oral Reading**

keep a record on a piece of paper indicating both the words read correctly and the **miscues** (mismatches or errors).

There are several systems for coding oral reading fluency. Each is somewhat different, though all provide a way to know exactly what the child said while reading. Figure 3.1 shows one useful coding system; see Goodman and Watson (1987) for another.

Later you can examine your record of the child's miscues to determine their acceptability in both **semantic** (meaning) and **syntactic** (word order) respects. You can also look at how similar a miscue is to the text in terms of letters or sounds. This helps you infer which strategies a child is or is not using.

Clay (1985) calls this kind of fluency assessment a **running record.** As a part of the Reading Recovery Program, begun in New Zealand and now widely used in the United States, running records may be taken for a book that was introduced on the previous day, so it is somewhat familiar, or with new material. Reading Recovery requires special training. However, the concept of "taking a record" of oral reading may be applied in many other situations with different kinds of text and different purposes.

Some teachers regularly take a fluency record of whatever book a child is currently reading independently. They use the results from these running records to plan minilessons for individuals, small groups, or the whole class. Other teachers take running records from whatever book the class (or group) is currently reading to judge whether the difficulty level seems appropriate for each child.

Some teachers use passages from unfamiliar books or from published informal reading inventories. They assess each child with the passage designated at his or her grade level (the grade in which the child is currently enrolled) and judge whether the child is below, on, or above grade level—a practice that implies an acceptance of the concept of a text's "readability." Some teachers use an assessment that bases the running records on a collection of small books of various difficulty levels. One such assessment, the *Developmental Reading Assessment* (Beaver, 1997), which acknowledges the prior work of Clay, has been widely field tested. We discuss these concepts and instruments further in Chapter 10.

Some teachers like to take two running records: one on material with which the child is familiar and another on unfamiliar material. Another choice also involves two running records: one on **narrative** material (a story) and one on **expository text** (information). The procedures for actually taking the running record are much the same regardless of your purpose or choice of material.

Procedures and Samples

The procedure that follows incorporate ideas from many sources. There is no one right way to code oral reading. You can use the coding suggested here or a code you already know.

Although it takes considerable practice to become comfortable with the process, anybody can learn to do it, including aides and volunteers. However, conclusions and inferences should be left to the teacher.

Other things besides actual reading fluency may be noted while taking a running record, such as attitude, self-concept, style of reading (good inflection or word by word and labored), and much more. If you are going to have others take running records, train them also to note behaviors and attitudes. In this case, a tape recording of the child's reading may also be helpful.

A Suggested Procedure.   Here is the procedure we suggest for assessing oral reading fluency and word recognition strategies:

1   Choose a book or selection (or have the child choose). The sample should have about one hundred words.

2   Sit where you will not be disturbed for a few minutes. You will need a piece of paper. A form such as the one shown in Figure 3.2 helps, but any lined paper will do. Record the child's name, the date, and the selection title and pages. Sit beside the child so you can see the text as she or he reads, or make a copy of the text for yourself.

3   Until children are accustomed to the procedure, reassure them about the purpose. You want a sample of how the child reads when there is no one to coach him, so resist your natural inclination to teach as you take a running record. If the child simply balks at an unknown word and refuses to go on, tell him or her the word and mark it *T.*

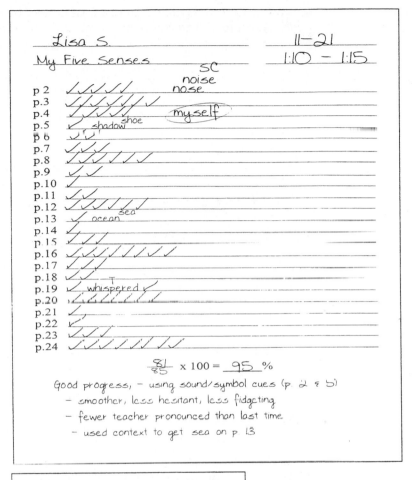

**Figure 3.2
Partial Marked Form of a
Running Record**

- Each ✓ indicates a word correctly said.
- SC indicates child self-corrected miscue.
- Word written on line is in text; word above is what child said.
- Circled word was omitted.
- T indicates word pronounced by teacher.

4 As the child reads, keep track of accuracy line by line, writing a check mark for each word read correctly. Record the starting and stopping times for the reading.

5 At the same time, if a child miscues (makes an error) or leaves out a word, record the type of error using the coding system presented in Figure 3.1 or whatever other system you are comfortable with. Figure 3.2 shows an example of a coded record sheet.

6 Calculate the percentage of words correct by dividing the total number of words read correctly by the number of words in the sample and multiplying by 100:

$$\frac{\text{Total Words Read Correctly}}{\text{Number of Words in Sample}} \times 100 \ = \ \rule{1.5cm}{0.4pt} \ \% \text{ Accuracy}$$

For example, the record sheet in Figure 3.2 shows 81 correct words out of a possible 85, which works out to 95 percent:

$$\frac{81}{85} \times 100 \ = \ 95\% \text{ Accuracy}$$

Note that in this system, a **self-correction**—a child's spontaneous recognition and correcting of a miscue—is counted as correct.

Anything above 90 percent is usually considered acceptable. A score below 90 percent indicates that the material is probably too difficult for the child. If the child scores above 94 percent, you probably won't have learned much about the child's use of strategies and may want to choose a more challenging passage.

7 Look at the amount of time it took the child to read the text. This is important in determining the rate aspect of fluency. If the child read smoothly and quickly, he or she shows fluency with the text. If the child read very slowly, he or she may be calling words accurately but not be reading fluently.

Divide the number of words the child read correctly by the number of minutes it took him or her to read the text. This will give you the words-correct-per-minute score. For example, if Mark, a second grader, read 93 words correctly in 2½ minutes, his rate of reading would be approximately 37 words correct per minute. Some educators recommend norms for evaluating students' oral reading fluency (Hasbrouck & Tindal, 1992).

8 Examine the miscues for insight about the child's use of strategies. (See the discussion following these steps.)

9 Another analysis that may be useful involves judging whether the meaning of a sentence was maintained even when miscues occurred. Look at each sentence in the context of the whole passage and ask: Is the meaning essentially the same? Does it still sound the way language should sound? For example, assume the text sentence reads, "The bicycle is painted red." The following are some judgments you might make:

Acceptable	"The bike is painted red."	Maintains meaning and sounds like language.
Possibly acceptable, depending on context	"The bike was painted red."	Past tense may or may not change meaning significantly.
Unacceptable	"The bark is painted red."	Meaning is lost.
Unacceptable	"The bicycle painted red."	Bicycles do not paint; omission of the word *is* changes both

language and meaning. However, if the omission results from a dialectic or second-language usage difference, you might judge it acceptable and plan instruction based on verb forms.

Possibly acceptable or unacceptable	"The bicycle is painted blue."	Acceptability depends on how critical the color is to the passage.

When you have judged each sentence in terms of acceptability, you can calculate a percentage score for this aspect of the child's reading:

$$\frac{\text{Total Sentences Read Correctly}}{\text{Number of Sentences in Sample}} \times 100 = \underline{\hspace{1cm}} \% \text{ Acceptability}$$

For example, if the reading sample had 20 sentences total and you judged that 18 of them were read acceptably, the student's score would be

$$\frac{18}{20} \times 100 = 90\% \text{ Acceptability}$$

Analyzing Miscues. Analysis of the miscues from running records allows you to make some inferences about the strategies, skills, and information a child is using. Let's look at Lisa's miscues as recorded in Figure 3.2. In practice, we would never draw dramatic conclusions from single examples, but this exercise will help you understand the possible inferences you might make.

First, does the child base her choice of a word on what would make sense in the story (semantics)? Lisa said "sea" for "ocean" on page 13, for example. Lisa clearly thought about meaning as she read this. She hardly needed to note the letters on the page; she said the word that made sense. This is a strength.

Second, does she base her choice on what kind of word belongs in a certain slot in the sentence (syntax)? If so, when she substitutes a word for one she doesn't recognize, the substitution will yield a sentence that sounds like English even if it doesn't make any sense. For example, Lisa said "shoe" for "shadow." Both are (or can be) nouns, though with this substitution the meaning is lost. If this kind of miscue occurs frequently, Lisa needs to be taught to monitor her own reading, asking, "Does this make sense?"

A third possibility is saying a word that matches what she sees, whether or not it results in a sentence that sounds like language and makes sense. A child who does this might say "horse" instead of "house." Visually, these two words are quite similar. They are similar phonetically at the beginning and end. The child who pays attention primarily to such **graphophonic cues** (symbol and sound—the letter on the page and the sound that it stands for) may read right on, undisturbed by the lack of semantic or syntactic fit. Lisa's substitution of "noise" for "nose" may fit this explanation. An abundance of this kind of miscue may indicate an overreliance on **phonics,** using sound/symbol knowledge to figure out the probable pronunciations of words. Lisa needs to balance her phonics strength with self-awareness and learn that what she reads must sound like language and make sense.

Another significant piece of information is related to how a child treats her miscues. Self-correction indicates competence. If a child has substituted "home" for "house," she will probably feel no need to self-correct, since meaning was not interrupted. The competent reader, however, will self-correct if she says "horse" rather than "house." Such a child often giggles at herself, recognizing that she made a "silly mistake." Lisa self-corrected the miscue "noise" on page 2 in Figure 3.2.

Some children will not attempt any word they think they do not recognize. They are not risk takers. Somewhere along the line, they have learned to feel that they cannot make an attempt unless they are absolutely sure they are correct. This kind of child may need support for risk taking as a part of reading instruction.

As you can tell, a great deal can be learned from taking a record of a child's fluency. In order to open a little window into the child's thought processes, the child must be reading material that challenges but does not overwhelm her. If it is too easy, she will not miscue often enough for you to tell what is going on. If it is too hard, she will stumble so often and get so discouraged that she will miscue on words that normally give her no trouble. Table 3.1 presents some possible miscues and examples of what they might indicate for instruction.

Table 3.1
Examples of Miscue Patterns and What They Might Mean for Instruction

Miscue Pattern	Instructional Meaning	Comments
1. High ratio of self-correction of miscues that changed meaning	A strength. Child knows if meaning is lost and looks again and corrects. If child is reading fast, you might suggest more attention to visual cues.	Self-correction (which, of course, requires repeating a word or more) used to be ignored as a strength. In fact, repetition was considered a serious failure. Now we welcome self-correction as a sign of attention to meaning.
2. Miscues show a high percentage of graphophonic similarity (that is, miscues have many of the same sounds and letters as the target words) with few self-corrections	Child needs to be taught more strategies to use when meeting an unfamiliar word. Focus should be on meaning of text first, then confirming with letters on the page.	If the child's miscues are similar to the target words but result in nonsense, either nonwords or words that clearly make no sense, *and* if the child reads right on, this may indicate an overreliance on phonics to the exclusion of other strategies. Obviously, phonics is an important part of decoding, but it is not successful unless combined with attention to meaning.

(continued)

Table 3.1
Examples of Miscue Patterns and What They Might Mean for Instruction (cont.)

Miscue Pattern	Instructional Meaning	Comments
3. High number of teacher-pronounced words	Not enough information to make an instructional decision. Try to figure out why the child will not try to say the words independently: Fear of failure? Lack of knowledge of other strategies? Knows other strategies but does not use them unless prompted? Past experience with expectations of absolute accuracy? More observation in other settings is necessary.	There is a danger in drawing too many conclusions from too few data. Patterns of miscues occurring only during running records aren't enough. Sometimes the best instructional decision is to gather more information. For example, you might take another fluency record with different material.
4. Substitutions such as "he be going" for "he is going"	The child is, in effect, translating written text into his or her own language patterns—a pretty sophisticated thing to do and one that works only if the child does, in fact, understand the words on the page. You might make plans to deal with the need for school language (that of teachers and books) as well as everyday language.	When children restate text in their own dialect, it is not a reading problem. One of your goals will be to help them be comfortable with book language, but do not mistake this for a reading difficulty.
5. Large number of miscues that show little or no graphophonic similarity to target word, do not retain meaning, and do not make syntactic sense.	More information is needed. Child appears not to use any strategies and not to be bothered by lack of sense. Text may simply be too difficult. It is also possible that something else is going on in the child's life that keeps him or her from focusing on text. You need to explore further.	If the child makes this kind of miscue frequently and the total percentage of words correct is less than 90%, you need to try an easier passage. But if the percentage correct is above 90% and all miscues are of this kind, it appears that the child can deal only with words already "memorized" and has no idea how to approach an unfamiliar word.

Diverse Learners

Inability to use word recognition strategies is only one way to account for less than fluent oral reading. Sometimes oral reading of written text deviates in ways that simply reflect the student's oral language. An example is shown in the fourth pattern in Table 3.1. Such deviations are not necessarily indicative of reading difficulty. In fact, they may indicate a high degree of comprehension in that the student has read the material, understood it, and rephrased it in his or her own vernacular.

Other conditions may also inhibit a student's performance on this task. Second-language learners may still be shy about their pronunciation of words in English even though they may read fluently to themselves. Further, students may have low self-esteem, speech articulation difficulty, distractibility, lack of interest in the subject matter, lack of background for the subject matter, vision problems, hunger, family concerns—the list is almost endless.

Comments

A running record or fluency record, whatever you call it, is simply a sample of a child's reading on a given day with a given piece of text. Conclusions should always be tentative, not set in stone. You are looking for clues to help you help the child. You are not judging, evaluating, or looking for a place to put blame. Whatever you may think you know about the child's life is of little consequence here. Take the running record for what it is worth—an authentic piece of evidence about the child's reading that day. Use it to plan ways to help the child grow.

You want your children to participate in this assessment willingly and confidently. Therefore, keep the experience focused, businesslike, and pleasant. Greet each child warmly; thank him or her when you are finished. At first, children may feel intimidated, fearful, or shy. They will not be quite sure what is expected of them in terms of performance. Reassure them. In time, the procedure will be routine for both you and the children.

Continue to read about running records, take advantage of workshops, consult colleagues, and practice. Each time you take a running record, you will improve. See the sources listed in For Additional Reading at the end of the chapter for more elaborate descriptions and additional samples of forms to use.

Retelling: Narrative and Expository Text

Retelling involves having a student read material silently or orally and then orally tell about it using his or her own words. Sometimes the term **summarizing** is used for this process. Retelling has several key purposes:

- To assess comprehension of narrative and expository material
- To assess the ability to tell specific story elements of narrative material

- To assess the ability to tell important ideas and significant details of expository text, as well as factors related to text structure such as sequence, comparison and contrast of ideas, and fact and opinion
- To make instructional decisions and plans

Description

Retelling of narrative material often involves presenting all the elements of the story—characters, setting, problem, events, and resolution—in basically the same sequence in which they occurred in the story. Children may use story language as they retell, sometimes repeating whole phrases verbatim, though they use mostly their own words. Here is a partial retelling of *The Little Red Hen:*

> *A little red hen found some grains of wheat. She asked, "Who will help me sow the wheat?" The duck said no. The pig said no. Everybody said no. So she did it herself. Then she asked who would help her. . . .*

A student may also retell in more summary form by stating the main problem and resolution or the theme:

> *This story is about a hen who finds some wheat. She keeps trying to get other animals to help her plant it and cut it and make bread from it. No one will help. She does it all herself. . . .*

Retelling of expository material (nonfiction or informational material) differs somewhat from retelling of narrative material. Such retelling should not include every detail but should make clear that the reader understood the topic, the main idea(s), and the significant details. Expository retelling should also indicate that the reader grasped how the ideas were organized and how they related to one another.

Procedures and Samples

The following procedures have evolved from Morrow's (1989) guidelines for the use of retelling diagnostically as well as from our own experiences with students and teachers.

1 Either you or the student may select the text to be read. If you are using retelling at intervals to show growth, the texts should be conceptually comparable.

2 Before the retelling begins, read the text yourself. (It is possible to listen to a retelling of a story you don't know and assess whether or not all the elements are present in the retelling, but this is not usually recommended.)

3 If you have chosen the text to be read, identify the story elements or ideas that you expect the reader to include to demonstrate understanding. You might use a retelling form such as those shown in Figures 3.3 and 3.4. (Blank versions are in the Resource File.)

4   Have the student read silently and immediately retell. Give only generic prompts such as "Keep going; you're doing fine." Check off items if you are using a form. Make notes if you are not using a form.

5   If anything important was omitted, probe a bit to determine whether the student can tell about what was omitted. Indicate on your record which parts of the retelling emerged only with prompting.

6   Make notes regarding other aspects of the retelling, such as whether the student adopted story language, recalled story-specific words, injected personal comments, was precise in recalling details, and attempted total recall or verbatim retelling.

In the narrative retelling form shown in Figure 3.3, Jamal's strengths are apparent from the checks in the "Unaided" column. Since this form is only for the

---

RETELLING: NARRATIVE

Name   Jamal   **Date**   10-9

Title of Story and Source   The Doorbell Rang (reader)

✓ = indicates whether student told about element unaided or after prompting by teacher
— = indicates student could not tell even with prompting

Elements Included	Unaided	Prompted
1. Setting (time, place, weather)	✓	
2. Character		
Major(s)	✓	
Others		✓ (some)
3. Problem	✓	
4. Story Events		
Includes all major events		NO ✓
Tells mostly in sequence		—
5. Solution		
Tells how the problem was solved	✓	
Tells how the story ended		—

Comments/Analysis: Needed much prompting. Reluctant to speak unless he was sure he was right.

Future support needed: Model and encourage risk taking. Minilesson sequence (small group). Reinforce "how authors and stories" during discussions and analyze and compare.

Figure 3.3
Marked Retelling Record:
Narrative Text

RETELLING: EXPOSITORY TEXT

Student Name   Brenda   Date   2/6

Selection/Author   Scaly Babies. G. Johnston & J. Cutchins
                    Ch. I Baby Snakes — intro pp. 4–5

Parts Included	Unaided	Prompted
Topic	✓	
Main idea(s)		✓
Supporting details	✓ (3) but could not elaborate	
Explanation/relating ideas/conclusion	—	—

Comments/Analysis: After prompting elicited the main idea,
asked Brenda why she thought the author wrote the book.
She couldn't think of any reason. Prompting failed to elicit
any details about how the information was presented or ideas
about why an author might have chosen to organize it that way.

Future support needed: Plan minilessons on text structure. Be
sure to explore how authors might decide about organization.
      Plan lessons on identifying main idea(s) — first when
stated literally, then when implied — whenever it occurs in
a paragraph — then in a longer selection

Figure 3.4
Marked Retelling Record:
Expository Text

teacher's use, the comments have to do with Jamal's needs and ideas for instructional support. If you referred to this form during a family conference, you would naturally comment first about Jamal's strengths.

Figure 3.4 shows a form you might use to assess a child's ability to retell, or summarize, expository text. Depending on the text read (and perhaps only with older students), some teachers also ask readers about the author's purpose: to entertain the reader, inform the reader, or persuade the reader to think or behave in a certain way. Brenda, the student whose retelling is recorded in Figure 3.4, shows strength in her ability to tell the topic and some details. She needed prompting, however, to tell the main idea. She was unable, even with prompting, to discuss any of the ideas further, show how the ideas related to one another, or draw any conclusions. The form allows the teacher to comment on Brenda's performance and note future instructional needs.

Diverse Learners

Students whose oral language is inhibited by some factor such as lack of fluency in English may find retelling particularly difficult. Although such students may be able to demonstrate understanding of what they have read when asked direct questions, generating the language necessary for retelling may present challenges they cannot meet. We suggest that at first you give students options, such as drawing pictures of parts of a story or responding to either/or questions. Then you can ease these students into retelling through prompting.

For example, you might say, "Tell me who this story was about . . . the main characters. Who else was it about? Tell me about the setting. . . . Where did it happen? When? Tell me about the problem [the main character] had. Now let's talk about the events in the story. . . . What happened first?" Continue in this vein, guiding, prompting, and leading through the retelling. As you do so, you are putting the language of retelling as well as the language of the story into the students' heads.

Gradually diminish your prompts as students' confidence in English grows. Don't confuse inability to generate the words during retelling with inability to comprehend.

Comments

Retelling, by and large, is tied directly to the passage read and does not call on prior knowledge or require critical thinking, though both are aspects of literacy. Be cautious, however, about judging a student to be inadequate at retelling narrative or expository text. You need to determine if retelling of both kinds of text has in fact been taught.

One problem is that young children tend to retell everything—all the details—when asked to recount an experience such as a trip to the zoo. Retelling of narrative or expository text, in contrast, is selective. Your students may need to be taught how to identify and retell just the key parts. On the other hand, if they tend to leave out key elements, they may need to be taught why those elements are important.

Retelling of expository material in particular may be neglected in the elementary grades, yet it is an essential tool in higher grades. We urge you to make retelling of expository text just as much a part of your daily activities as retelling of stories.

Comprehension: Discussion

In the current view of reading comprehension, the meaning a reader finds in a text arises not merely from the printed page but also from the reader's process of interacting with the text to create or "construct" meaning (Cooper, 2000). Classroom discussions of literature can be particularly useful in this process, and they give you a golden opportunity to assess individual students' ability to construct meaning.

As children discuss literature they have read, you can also assess their use of appropriate discussion behaviors such as how well they listen to one another and share ideas. The information you gain about construction of meaning and discussion skills will have a direct influence on your instructional plans.

These, then, are the main purposes for literacy assessments based on discussion:

- To assess construction of meaning or any of several related aspects of reading, such as retelling, summarizing, locating text to support a point, fluency in oral rereading, understanding of idiomatic and other figurative language, and appreciation of authors' craft

- To assess use of appropriate discussion behaviors such as participation, listening to others, and accepting ideas without censure

- To make instructional decisions

Description

While there may be a structure or set of guidelines that children follow during a discussion, the actual event is unpredictable and may veer off in unplanned directions. Whatever happens, you can glean valuable insights.

While you can certainly focus on one child during a discussion, it is also possible to track all the children in a discussion circle. A number of indicators can be listed on a grid vertically, with children's names across the top, as shown in Figure 3.5. (A blank version of the form is in the Resource File.)

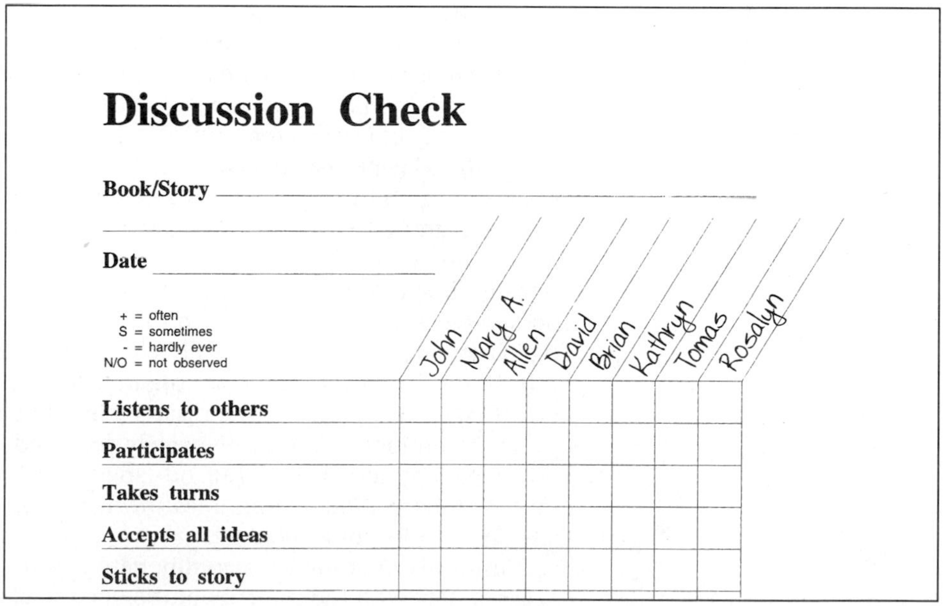

Figure 3.5 Discussion Observation Grid

Discussion Check

Book/Story _____

Date _____

```
+   = often
S   = sometimes
-   = hardly ever
N/O = not observed
```

Names (written diagonally): John, Mary A., Allen, David, Brian, Kathryn, Tomas, Rosalyn

	John	Mary A.	Allen	David	Brian	Kathryn	Tomas	Rosalyn
Listens to others								
Participates								
Takes turns								
Accepts all ideas								
Sticks to story								

We believe the best discussion assessment is devised by each individual teacher to meet individual needs. You might, for instance, want to observe behaviors related to participation, listening to others, accepting ideas without ridiculing, and so forth. In addition, you might want to observe the ability to retell certain portions, the ability to predict, knowledge of idiomatic language, fluency in oral rereading, and so forth. You make up the list on the basis of what you want to know. It can vary as time goes by and as your purposes change.

Procedures and Samples

Using a grid like the one in Figure 3.5, devise a code for marking behaviors. A simple one would be as follows:

> *+ = often*
> *S = sometimes*
> *— = hardly ever*
> *N/O = not observed today*

Inform the children that you will be observing during their discussion and making notes. Sit where you can observe without interrupting the flow of a natural discussion. Some teachers are even able to record observations as they participate. In such cases, it is almost impossible to separate assessment from instruction, nor is there any reason to do so. *Assessment should be a natural part of instruction.*

Review your data after the observation. Use what you have learned to plan instruction. After instruction, use the same form to assess both your success in instructing and the children's growth as a result of the instruction.

Diverse Learners

Children who are not yet fluent in English may feel quite at sea in a group discussion. Imagine how you might feel sitting in a crowd of people throwing ideas back and forth in a language you are only just beginning to learn. If you are assessing a student's ability to take part in a discussion, you'll want to keep in mind how the lack of fluency in English may inhibit full participation.

Trying to keep up with ideas coming from several sources at once is especially difficult for a child not yet fluent in the language. You might want to keep the discussion group very small at first so the second-language speaker can follow the conversation more easily.

English-speaking class members probably will use informal language, idioms, and sentence fragments. These too make it hard to follow a conversation. The English-language learner may still be translating into his or her own language to understand. The reverse may be true in responding: thinking of the words in his or her first language and then translating into English. Oral rereading may be halting, and pronunciation may be heavily accented. The discussion group needs to be very patient and give the second-language learner a chance to feel part of the group. For more about communicating in a second language, see Johnson (1995), listed in For Additional Reading.

Help all your students accommodate and include the not-yet-fluent English speakers. Talk with the class about the need to clarify idioms for all listeners, not just second-language speakers. Model how a good listener in a discussion may paraphrase the speaker's words to ensure that the meaning was understood before responding. Model using mispronounced words correctly in a discussion but not "correcting" mispronunciation. Everyone should follow the same good rules: each person should be allowed whatever time is needed to gather his or her thoughts and formulate a comment.

Comments

It takes time for children (and adults) to learn to have good discussions. At the beginning of the school year, you may want to assess your students' ability to conduct a discussion and to show construction of meaning as they do so. This, then, will provide baseline data on which to build instructional plans. These plans will involve teaching, modeling, developing guidelines, devising ways for children to assess their own discussion behavior, and much more.

The indicators you choose to use will arise from what you feel you need to assess. You could, for example, choose to assess only discussion behaviors at first, believing that children first need to learn how to treat one another and how to participate in a successful discussion. When these behaviors are fairly well established, you might then move on to assessing evidence of construction of meaning during discussions.

Assessment of one discussion gives you information only for that day, based on that piece of literature. Many factors may affect a single day's participation: prior knowledge, interest, hunger, the sniffles, what happened at home last night, the weather, and so on. This is only a piece of a large, multifaceted picture.

Comprehension: Personal Written Responses

Teachers have always asked children to write in response to what they have read. For the teacher, these personal written responses serve several purposes:

- To assess cognitive aspects of literacy such as prior knowledge, construction of meaning, and understanding of story elements and text structure
- To assess knowledge of subject matters and concepts
- To assess affective aspects of literacy such as interests, self-concept, and attitudes

Description

In past years, written responses to reading have ranged from answering questions to doing a book report. Responses to expository text, such as a social studies chapter, might have involved simply answering a series of questions. Teachers often thought they learned about a child's comprehension from such assignments. In reality, they were often "prove to me you really read it" assignments that the student could complete with little or no construction of meaning. Furthermore, they yielded little useful instructional information.

These days, teachers use a wide variety of written responses that can yield useful information about a child's literacy. Among these are **story maps** (graphic representations that visually show the story elements), journals, individual K-W-L or other charts, **learning logs** (students' own daily records of their learning activities and the concepts they have learned), and variations of these devices.

Certainly such responses can be used for summative assessment—to help you assign a grade on a project, mark grade cards, or in some other way judge the quality of a student's work. However, these responses can also be used to help you learn about a child's interests, self-concept, attitudes, prior knowledge, ability to construct meaning in general, and knowledge about literary elements and text structure.

The use of written responses for assessment purposes is perhaps the most open-ended of all. There are no set guidelines, specific checklists, or forms to fill out. *In fact, every time you read something a child has written about a piece he or she has read, you will learn valuable information about that child.*

Procedures and Samples

As you get started, you may decide to structure the children's written responses, at least part of the time. Until you are comfortable with the notion of using everything that happens in the classroom as assessment, structure will help to keep you on track.

Here is one idea. Establish a set of items to which you want children to respond in writing after they read a story independently. These can be posted on a chart or put on a worksheet and photocopied. The items will depend on what you want to know. They might include such things as these:

Write about your favorite character.

Write about something that puzzled you.

Tell why you would (or would not) like to read another story by the same author.

In two sentences, say something about the story to make others want to read it.

After the children have read an informational book, your items will differ somewhat. They might include questions such as these:

What was the most important new thing you learned?

What else do you want to know about the subject?

Tell why you would (or would not) recommend this book to a friend.

Obviously the items will vary widely depending on the age of the children, but children of any age can respond in writing on some level.

In a typical *response journal,* in which students write about what they are reading, there are no specific questions and no right or wrong things to say. Let's say you and your students all keep such reading response journals and share

Chicken Little got hit with a nut. She thought the sky was falling. She told all the others. They all went to tell the king. They all believed her. It shows how silly people are. They beleive anything.

Figure 3.6
Lee's Retelling of
Chicken Little

The chicken wanted to see the King. The turkey and the goose went with her. The book kept saying all the names.

Figure 3.7
Sheryl's Retelling of
Chicken Little

them frequently. As you read children's journals, note which students have little to say, responding with only one or two words. You'll want to help them learn to respond more fully or find books that engage them more.

Written retelling of a story, in a journal or elsewhere, can reveal both the strengths and weaknesses in a student's comprehension. Figures 3.6 and Figure 3.7 are two sample written retellings of *Chicken Little*. Note that Lee has included all the essential elements in his retelling, whereas Sheryl has omitted key elements. You would investigate further to decide what kind of instructional help Sheryl needed.

In a *dialogue journal,* the teacher provides ongoing responses in writing to the student's own comments. Figure 3.8 shows such an exchange. Jamal is retelling almost the whole story. The teacher models retelling only important parts and giving a personal response. The teacher also tries to motivate Jamal to explore some other kinds of books.

9-10 (Jamal)
   First he went in the house. Then he got scared by a noise. Then a cat ran out. Then he went home. Then he came back.

9-11 (Teacher)
   You really remembered everything, didn't you? I just read a mystery about horses that were being given drugs to make them run faster. It was very bad for them. In the end, of course, they caught the bad guys. I'm glad, because I love horses.
   See me if you'd like a mystery to read next.

Figure 3.8
Dialogue Journal with
Teacher as Child Is Reading
a Book from a "Horror"
Series

> September 9
> Blubber by J.
> Blume
> Predictions
>
> Jill will be nice to
> Linda because Jill
> is telling the story.
>
> A teacher's job is
> to make them stop
> being mean.
>
> What happened
>
> Jill laughed at Linda with
> everyone else. I think they are
> mean.
>
> The teacher didn't find out why
> they were laughing.

Figure 3.9
Liz's Double-Entry Journal
Entry, Written While She
Was Reading Judy Blume's
***Blubber* (1974)**

Figure 3.9 shows another variation, a double-entry journal with separate columns for the student's predictions and later responses. Liz's entries show that she reacted strongly to this book, *Blubber* (Blume, 1974). She may be more sensitive to her own weight problem than anyone realized. Her prediction that the children who were so mean would be punished reflects an idealized view. Her teacher might consider having a class discussion about why life isn't always fair or perhaps one about group mentality.

Figure 3.10 shows a reading log with Erika's personal response to the book *Song and Dance Man* (Ackerman, 1988). She didn't seem to see any point to the story. You would want to be sure Erika took part in a literature discussion circle with children who dug a little deeper. You would sit in on the circle.

> october 12
>
> Song and Dance Man
> by Karen Ackerman
> This was a dumb book.
> Who wants to
> read about an old man?
> I didn't like the pictures.

Figure 3.10
Erika's Reading Log
Response to *Song and*
Dance Man

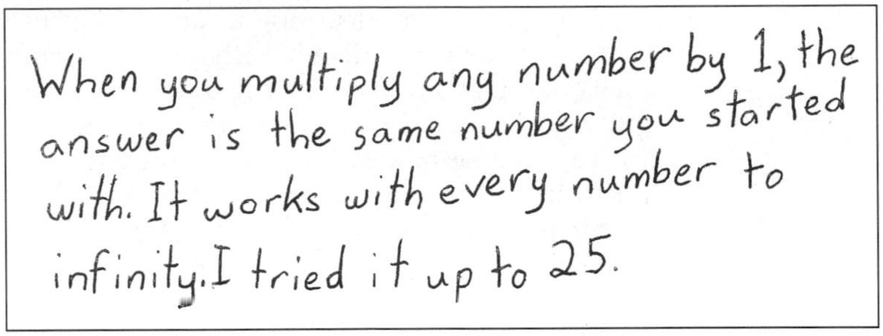

When you multiply any number by 1, the answer is the same number you started with. It works with every number to infinity. I tried it up to 25.

Figure 3.11
Paul's Learning Log:
Multiplying by 1

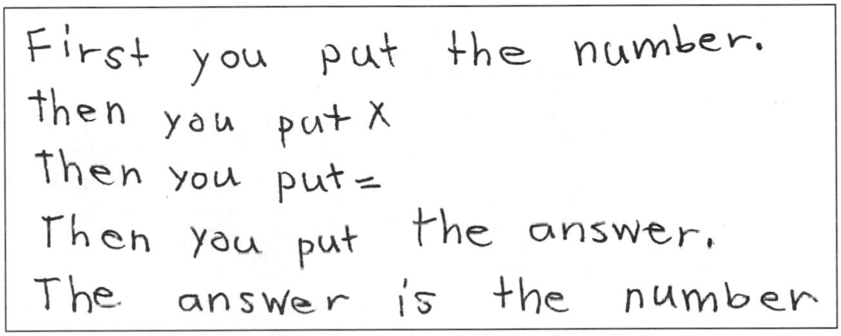

First you put the number.
then you put X
Then you put =
Then you put the answer.
The answer is the number

Figure 3.12
Sammy's Learning Log:
Multiplying by 1

Learning logs can be similarly revealing. Your children may keep learning logs for math or science, for instance. After the children record what they have learned, you can read the entries and discover which children understood the concepts and which need more work. Figure 3.11 is a sample learning log written by third grader Paul after an introductory lesson on the concept of multiplying by 1. Figure 3.12 was written by Sammy after the same lesson. Which boy clearly grasps the concept and which needs further teaching?

Diverse Learners

Written responses to reading can be marvelously helpful to you, providing insights into students' comprehension of reading material, interests and attitudes, and grasp of concepts—but only if they can write with enough skill to truly reflect these things about themselves in writing. Some students will find it difficult, if not impossible, to demonstrate anything about their reading ability through writing.

For example, a second-language learner may not yet be fluent enough to write in English. If students are comfortable writing in their first language, encourage such writing even if you cannot read it; the idea is to build the habit of responding in writing. If a student is just beginning to write in English, you may need to adapt the activity to whatever degree of written ability he or she currently exhibits. While open-ended writing may be appropriate for most of your students, the nonfluent student might respond better to a series of written questions or perhaps written questions with a choice of answers. Such a student might also dictate to an English-speaking buddy or volunteer who acts as scribe. Another possibility is oral responses, perhaps using a cassette recorder.

A student with a learning disability that makes written expression difficult may read widely and deeply with admirable comprehension but be able to produce only scratches when trying to express a response on paper. One of our own children was such a reader and writer. He read and understood content far beyond his years, but his handwriting was labored and his spelling such that it was virtually impossible to know what he intended to write. To judge his reading ability by his written responses would have been a huge mistake.

Some students may feel free to write more fully if they can write on a word processor and store their responses on a disk. Others may best be assessed through oral means. Not every assessment method works equally well with every student.

Comments

There is virtually no limit to the kinds of written responses you can use as part of your collection of tools. Anything a child writes will allow you to make inferences about his or her thinking. This is not to say that you need to analyze everything in great detail. It does mean that, although some written responses may be used to assign a grade, a more useful purpose is to help you plan instruction. As you grow more comfortable using written responses as a measure of construction of meaning, you can add variety to the types of writing you assess.

In your zeal to accumulate information, be wary of turning all writing into assessment. We don't want to kill children's joy in writing. There is a danger that the response journal could become as deadly as the old-fashioned book reports many of us remember.

A final note: as you analyze a child's written response to reading, keep your purpose in mind. If your purpose is assessment of the child's ability to construct meaning, only content is relevant. The conventions of writing—mechanics such as spelling, usage, and punctuation—are not part of assessing construction of meaning. While you may note these, do not let poor mechanics cloud your judgment. In the next section, we discuss writing assessment.

Writing Assessment Tools and Techniques

We have discussed using written responses to text as a way to learn about a child's reading. In this section, we discuss using writing of many kinds, including response to text, as a way to assess writing. Throughout the Part Two chapters devoted to the stages of literacy development, you will find references to what is discussed here, with elaborations and modifications appropriate to each stage.

This section is divided into three main parts: (1) process and product: assessing a student's use of the writing process as well as the final product; (2) types of products: reports and other kinds of writing suitable for assessment evidence; and (3) conventions: grammar/usage, mechanics, and spelling.

Process and Product

Children do a great deal of writing in today's classrooms. Some of it involves what is called the *writing process:* prewriting, drafting, revising, editing, and publishing. This process is appropriate when children write stories, reports, essays, and other kinds of writing that lead to a final, finished product. We will discuss other kinds of writing, such as journals, in the next section. Here we limit our discussion to those that involve process as well as product.

Process

Children should have individual writing folders in which they store their works-in-progress. Each piece of work should have the child's name and be dated. The folder should contain "evidence" of all stages of the process, beginning with whatever prewriting techniques the child used to generate ideas and organizational plans. These include, but are not limited to, drawings, lists, semantic webs (a variation of semantic maps, illustrated in Chapter 4), and free-writing.

The various drafts should also be stored in the folder, labeled "First Draft," "Second Draft," and so forth. When a child has a conference, whether with you or with a peer, the person who conferred should initial the draft and date it. After revisions have been made, the last draft should show editing and proofreading marks to be followed when creating the final version for publication.

As you check children's folders, you will be able to note which children are having trouble with which steps of the process. You can make a checklist to help yourself determine how you might group children for further instruction. As with so many other assessments, you'll need to determine what might cause a problem. If a child is missing evidence of prewriting, for example, is it because she or he didn't do any prewriting, doesn't know how, knows how and thinks it's a waste of time, or lost it? Your instructional decisions depend on answers to these kinds of questions.

Perhaps the most common explanation for a child's failure to make good use of the writing process is the simplest: he or she was never taught how to use it or given adequate guided practice. Ask yourself if you have actually taught—that is, modeled, presented, collaborated, practiced, and so forth—each step of the process. No matter what grade you teach, no matter whether you believe this process was thoroughly taught in a lower grade, you need to reteach and reteach and reteach. Good, clear writing is seldom "mastered."

Every writer knows that revision is perhaps the most important part of writing. Hardly ever is a first draft polished enough to be a final draft. Still, we see classrooms where children go directly from first draft to editing. We want children to understand and accept that writing well involves a process. So we recommend that you regularly assess evidence of children's use of the process.

When you assign writing that does not allow for revision, such as an essay question, we urge you not to require best thinking, best handwriting, correct spelling and mechanics, and correct usage, all on what may essentially be considered a first draft. You probably have experienced how difficult it is to think clearly and at the same time pay attention to careful handwriting, let alone remember your own personal spelling/usage demons, such as whether one "elicits" or "illicits" critical thinking. (It's *elicits.*)

If your children are writing directly with a word processing program, you will need to adapt your assessment procedures. Most writers revise continuously as they write on a computer. It is almost impossible, therefore, to see a clear succession of revisions. Until you are sure a child is indeed revising, you may ask that each draft be printed before revisions are made. Even so, this will not allow you to know when a writer changes a phrase almost as soon as it is written. You will need to find ways to monitor children's writing on the computer. All children need to feel comfortable writing in this way, and you need to feel comfortable letting them, even though you may not have pieces of paper showing each step in the process.

Product

Sometimes you will want to assess a final product to help you make instructional decisions and in order to share results with a child's family. Yet a single mark on a piece of writing, whether a number or a letter grade, is of little use to you, to the child, or to the family if the basis for the mark isn't clear. What does 87 mean? Or C+? Very little. In fact, when you give (or receive) such a grade, you want to know the criteria. What counted? Spelling? Grammar? Content?

One assessment technique being used widely is known as holistic scoring. **Holistic scoring** of writing involves assigning a single score to a piece of writing based on the overall quality of both content and mechanics. The key to effective holistic scoring is to spell out the criteria clearly. Often rubrics are prepared or drawn from previously written papers. The rubrics may be accompanied by sample responses—sometimes called *anchor papers,* as we mentioned in Chapter 2— for each of the possible number scores. Numbers usually run from a high of 6 to a low of 1, but other ranges, such as 4 to 1, are possible. Student papers are compared to the anchor papers, and a paper receives the number score of the closest match.

If you are going to assess your students' writing holistically for a state-, district-, or schoolwide program, you will be given directions and rubrics. You probably will not score the papers yourself. For these kinds of assessments, special readers are trained in applying the rubrics to ensure a high degree of **inter-rater reliability;** that is, a given paper will be assigned the same score no matter who reads it. However, you should understand how the rubrics are used and apply them to the writing your children do in preparation for the assessment. Otherwise, you will not be successful in coaching them to do their best.

Holistic scoring may be applied to writing in response to a prompt, to so-called creative writing, or to expository writing. When such assessment is carried out on a schoolwide basis, it assesses how well we are teaching writing every bit as much as it assesses each child's writing.

If you examine the reasons for your children's scores, holistic scoring may be useful in illuminating areas that need more instruction. First, score your class's papers. Then analyze them. Perhaps you may find that many students lack the ability to organize their thoughts logically. Don't fall into the trap of blaming the students. Instead, analyze how you have been teaching writing. Have you ever really taught your students how to organize their thoughts as they write? Maybe you just assumed they should be able to do it. Maybe you assumed that those who didn't were lazy, learning disabled, or rebellious. *The simplest, and perhaps likeliest, explanation of why a child is unable to do something is that no one has taught it sufficiently.*

To apply holistic scoring to classroom assignments, decide first how many levels you want. (An even number will force you not to score everyone in the middle.) Next, prepare descriptors for each level. These can be stated both as something present in the paper or as something missing. There should be clear differences between levels. The descriptors may include elements related to the following: content, conceptual level, thoroughness, organization, use of the language, conventions (spelling, punctuation, grammar), interest, freshness, and any other items you have established. For example, for a report you may stipulate that there should be at least four chapters and that each chapter should have at least two illustrations.

In many cases, you and your students together can establish what makes a paper a 6 or a 5, an A or a B. Then the students can apply such rubrics to their own writing by rereading their work and checking the descriptor statements that apply. They can assign themselves a score based on which level had the most checks. Figure 3.13 presents a partial generic rubric. As you can see, each step down from a 6 would retain some of the same standards, but to a lesser degree.

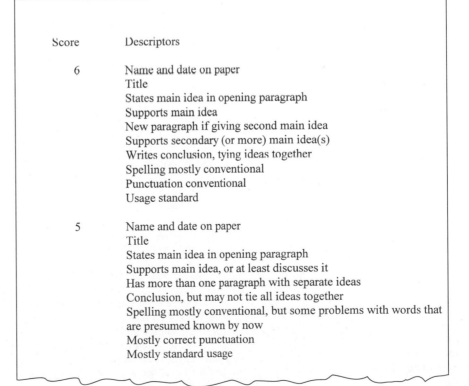

Score	Descriptors
6	Name and date on paper Title States main idea in opening paragraph Supports main idea New paragraph if giving second main idea Supports secondary (or more) main idea(s) Writes conclusion, tying ideas together Spelling mostly conventional Punctuation conventional Usage standard
5	Name and date on paper Title States main idea in opening paragraph Supports main idea, or at least discusses it Has more than one paragraph with separate ideas Conclusion, but may not tie all ideas together Spelling mostly conventional, but some problems with words that are presumed known by now Mostly correct punctuation Mostly standard usage

Figure 3.13
Partial Generic Rubric for a Writing Assignment

The rubric presented in Figure 3.14 is part of one developed for a specific culminating project in grade 4 following a unit of study on state history. The students worked with the teacher to develop the rubric and used it to guide them as they wrote their final reports. Then each student evaluated his or her own report. The teacher also evaluated each report. Both scores were recorded and shared with the students' families.

Students should understand not only the descriptors used for making judgments but also why these are considered elements of a good paper. Too often we see teachers simply mandating certain things, for example, that children should have three supporting ideas with examples to go with their main idea. The children are so involved in trying to follow what they perceive as a rule that they lose sight of why they are doing it.

Types of Products

Many types of writing yield useful information about children's growth in writing. We already talked about using pieces of work produced through the writing process to learn about the child's understanding and application of that process. In this section, we discuss some of the other types of writing you can use to assess writing progress.

Reports

Written reports are usually the culminating product of some process or activity. They can take many forms: research reports, book reports, science experiment reports, interview reports, and others. If a report is to be assessed, students need to know in advance what is expected of them. This can be done by developing a

**Figure 3.14
Partial Rubric for "Our State" Report, Fourth Grade**

Score	Descriptors
6	Name and date
	Title
	Gives at least three sources
	Synthesizes ideas from sources
	Introductory paragraph
	Subheadings
	Main idea for each subheading
	Supporting ideas for each subheading
	At least two visuals to support ideas
	Facts are accurate
	Conclusion pulls together ideas
	Correct spelling
	Correct punctuation
	Correct language use

rubric for the report. As we mentioned earlier, students may even help draw up the rubric and guidelines to follow. Then they can follow these guidelines as they complete their reports.

Another way to proceed is to use a checklist on which you itemize each component of the project that will be assessed. Children can check each item, and you can check the same items. The child's checklist can be submitted along with the report.

Figure 3.15 shows a sample of a checklist for a research project. As you can see, the components are simply to be checked as absent or present. You could also assign a number of points to each component, allowing yourself to make a judgment regarding the quality of each in addition to its presence or absence.

Of course, you and the students will have discussed exactly what each item on the list means. For example, the first item in Figure 3.15, "Topic appropriate,"

RESEARCH REPORT CHECKLIST

Name _____   Date _____

Title of Report _____

	You	Teacher
1. Topic appropriate		
2. Cluster or other graphic organizer		
3. Three or more references		
4. Information synthesized		
5. Appropriate paragraphing		
6. Rough draft(s) showing revision		
7. Editing (with editor identified)		
8. Cover page		
9. Bibliography		
10. Work submitted on time		
11. Final copy reflecting all of the above		

Figure 3.15
Checklist Used for Research Project in a Fourth Grade

might mean that the topic was narrow enough to research thoroughly, that it fit the overall theme, and that it was introduced in the first paragraph.

You might have an additional checklist to provide a picture of your entire class. From this, particular instructional needs might become clear. For example, one item might have called for using a cluster or other organizer prior to writing a rough draft. If many children did not do this, or seemed unable to do it in a way that truly aided their writing, you would know you needed to teach more about this step in the writing process.

A checklist such as the one in Figure 3.15 is very effective in helping children learn what to think about as they gather information and formulate a report. However, children can satisfy each of the listed items and still need further instruction in many areas. For example, a child may have the required number of references but have chosen them unwisely. You might decide, then, that you need to provide many additional lessons on locating and evaluating references for authenticity and suitability.

We have seen arbitrary requirements such as "Must have three revisions." We don't believe this kind of stipulation leads to thoughtful writing. Instead, we urge you to help children to accept that all writing needs revision; no writer gets it exactly right the first time. Help your students learn how to judge when they have revised sufficiently. If you keep your goals and objectives in mind, you will establish guidelines that truly lead to better writing.

Other Types of Written Products

Some other kinds of writing you may want to assess include journals, learning logs, and letters. For example, you may urge your children to write in personal journals every morning. You may suggest topics or allow children to choose their own. Of course, you will read these journals and respond to the ideas expressed. That is one of the joys of journaling with children.

You might also, however, keep anecdotal records of a child's growth in fluency as evidenced in his or her journal. Duane might have only drawn a picture at the beginning of the year, whereas now he is adding a sentence about his picture. Lois might have written only stilted sentences a couple of months ago ("I did this. . ."; "We had fun. . ."), whereas now she is writing such things as "The coolest thing I did this weekend was teach my little brother how to tie his shoes. What a great feeling! He was so proud of himself, and I was proud of him and of myself. It feels good to teach someone something."

Along with fluency, you can note increased complexity of language use. For example, note when a child has begun using dependent clauses at the beginning of sentences, when an awareness of audience begins to emerge, when figurative language and fresh metaphors turn up. You could also note growth in areas such as conventional spelling and punctuation, even though these are not emphasized in journals. This is, of course, the true test of acquiring skill in these areas: competence even when it doesn't "count."

We suggest that you ask children to note such growth about themselves. This isn't a formal or complicated process. Just say to a child, "You have grown so much in your writing this year. Let's talk about what you are doing now that you didn't do at the beginning of the year." This kind of discussion is particularly valuable with a child who is feeling discouraged about writing.

Finally, remember that each of the written responses to reading discussed earlier in this chapter could be assessed in terms of writing as well. Whatever goals and objectives you have for writing can be monitored through every piece of writing children do. It is not necessary to assign a special piece of writing solely for the purpose of assessing writing, unless your school mandates this.

Conventions of Writing

No one would argue with the need to teach students to write clearly, use language correctly, and spell and punctuate accurately. Conventions of writing are agreed-on standards: ways of doing things that are judged to be "correct." For example, all of us agree that proper names should begin with a capital letter. We agree that a complete sentence needs both a subject and a predicate. We agree that there is (generally) one correct way to spell a word. We agree that noun and verb should agree in number; that is, we shift from "he goes" (singular) to "they go" (plural). The number of such conventions is almost endless. For the most part, they are not open to debate, nor are they subjective.

Some conventions apply to both oral and written language. Some, however, such as spelling and punctuation, apply only to written language. Conventions for written language are important because they allow others to read what we write. In many computer programs, aids in applying such conventions are called writing "tools," and these are found on a Tools menu or an Edit menu.

Although the use of these conventions may emerge only when children begin to attend school, many children have begun writing long before that point. The urge to express oneself in writing is strong. Little children don't let their lack of knowledge of conventions inhibit them. They make marks that look sort of like what they see others do and call it writing. And it *is* writing because they know it "says" something.

The difficulty with conventions arises from differences of opinion about how and when children learn to do these things. Should we encourage them to write whatever they want to say, even before they know how to spell all the words or use punctuation? Or should we teach conventions early on? This is not a debate we can resolve here, but we do want to give you some idea of how to assess children's use of writing conventions.

As with other types of assessment, you gain the best information by using authentic tasks. For example, you may assess spelling through weekly spelling tests, but spelling in authentic writing, in our view, is the only way to assess where a child is developmentally. You may also give tests of one kind or another that purport to assess usage and punctuation; for instance, some teachers use a daily language exercise that involves correcting the grammar, mechanics, and spelling of an incorrect sentence written on the chalkboard. While this and other group editing tasks may be helpful, true assessment should be of real pieces of children's writing. When assessment matches curriculum, teachers can be sure they are measuring what is taught (Salvia & Ysseldyke, 1998). You will find stage-specific assessment ideas in Chapters 5 through 9.

Diverse Learners

Some children may be inhibited from acquiring the conventions of writing as soon as others do. These may include children with various learning disabilities and those with delayed language. If you suspect that some of your children have these conditions, you need to document with anecdotal records and checklists exactly what the children are doing. Try direct and explicit teaching of the absent skills, using more than one strategy if necessary. If your attempts fail, you will probably want to consult with special education teachers to discuss further assessment.

Children for whom English is a second language may also lag in their use of the conventions of writing. Not all languages construct sentences with words in the same order as in English. In some languages, the adjective follows the noun rather than preceding it. In some languages, each noun is designated masculine or feminine and requires a different article, unlike English. In some languages, verb endings are derived differently than in English. As students from such language backgrounds acquire English, they may not display conventional usage at first.

Spelling may be particularly difficult for some English-language learners who already spell in their first language. If a student's first language has a strict one-to-one correspondence between a sound and the letter that represents that sound, the multiple ways to spell sounds in English (difficult for most people!) will undoubtedly be confusing.

One of your important jobs is to help all children move toward comfortable use of conventional English, which includes oral and written language that follows grammatical standards as well as correct punctuation and spelling in written language. You do this in the same way for all children. Pay attention to what they are doing now. Then plan instruction to help them learn what comes next. Remember that children do not progress in lockstep but according to their individual characteristics.

Grammar/Usage

The category of conventions grouped under grammar/usage includes noun-verb agreement, run-on sentences, sentence fragments, misplaced modifiers, and much more. A checklist drawn from your local list of objectives probably is the best way to track your children's acquisition of these skills. You need to keep assessment of development separate in your thinking from evaluation for the purpose of assigning a grade.

Mechanics

The area of mechanics includes capitalization and punctuation (periods, exclamation points, question marks, commas, semicolons, dashes, apostrophes, and so on). Again, a simple checklist may be the best way to keep track of your children's skills in this area. You may want to use individual checklists to show when children acquire each ability. Or you may have a class checklist to point to overall instructional needs.

Spelling

In our college classes over the years, the teaching of spelling has sparked more heated discussion than almost any other aspect of literacy. Those preservice teachers who are "good" spellers are convinced that whatever method was used to teach them made them that way. Those who consider themselves poor spellers are convinced that if only their elementary teachers had used a different method, they wouldn't have trouble spelling.

Most published reading programs have a language program with a spelling component woven in. Some schools use this as their sole language/spelling program. Some schools use a separate language program that includes spelling. Some use a separate language program and yet another, separate spelling program. Some teach spelling directly, some indirectly. Some prefer programs based on high-frequency words, some on word families, and some on high-utility words.

Probably you will have little to say about how you teach spelling: the school system in which you teach will likely mandate a certain methodology. Yet it will be up to you to become informed and remain open to emerging research. If you feel strongly about the best method, perhaps you will be a change agent in your school.

Here we will not discuss the issue of spelling instruction and tests. Rather, we will address the developmental nature of spelling acquisition, which often begins before children enter school and extends over many years, throughout the literacy stages. Many view spelling ability as essentially developmental (Gentry & Gillet, 1993; Henderson, 1990; Templeton & Bear, 1992); that is, even without formal instruction, children who write every day will grow in their ability to spell conventionally. Some children seem able to spell virtually any word they can say from kindergarten on. Others seem perpetually unable to spell conventionally, even into adulthood, despite their best efforts (see Gentry [1987] in For Additional Reading).

Stages of Spelling Acquisition. While the terminology used differs among researchers, the stages of spelling acquisition are remarkably similar for nearly all children. Before producing anything that looks remotely like a letter, children begin making scribble marks. The marks may be made from right to left, left to right, or top to bottom. As children see others writing and watch readers move their hands from left to right, they begin producing scribble lines in left-to-right order. Then they begin making marks that look rather like letters. Soon after, children begin to use actual letters, though these seem to be random because they don't yet consistently represent sounds. However, this use of letters marks the beginning of spelling development; children have come to understand that all writers must use the same set of marks to enable others to read what is written.

From then on, children progress through several more stages as they move toward spelling words conventionally—that is, correctly. Each child moves through the acquisition of spelling competence idiosyncratically in terms of speed, but almost all go through these stages in sequence. As with all learning, most children are partly in one stage and partly in another, or at one point on one day and another on another day. Learning is not tidy.

The following list of labels and descriptions of the developmental spelling stages is drawn from Gentry and Gillet (1993), a source listed in For Additional

Reading. As you read through the stages, think how your knowledge of spelling acquisition might affect instructional decisions about teaching spelling. It has been said that not until a child has reached the conventional stage will he or she benefit from formal instruction. You may decide, however, that there is appropriate instruction for every stage as long as one does not try to teach something to a child who is not developmentally ready to learn it.

1 Precommunicative Stage

The writing represents a message, though only the writer can read it and only immediately after writing it.

Children do not yet know the **alphabetic principle:** that letters represent sounds.

Children use letters and marks that resemble real letters.

Letters may or may not seem to follow a left-to-right organization.

Children mix upper- and lower-case letters and may prefer upper case.

Letters are in random order.

Children may include numerals with letters.

Children may use a few letters or many.

2 Semiphonetic Stage

Children begin to acquire the alphabetic principle, the sense that letters represent sounds. This is a stunning discovery.

Letters represent words, but there is not a complete representation of each sound in a word. Words may often begin with a consonant. In fact, a whole word or syllable may be represented by the initial consonant.

The sounds of words are often represented by the sound of a letter's name rather than the sound the letter stands for. For example, the word *elephant* may begin with the letter *L,* and the word *are* may be spelled *R.*

There is increasing evidence of left-to-right arrangement of letters.

Character formations look more like actual letters.

There may or may not be spaces between words.

3 Phonetic Stage

The next major step in a child's acquisition of spelling ability is the realization that certain letters stand for certain sounds and that all words can be represented with symbols for the sounds. This understanding grows by leaps and bounds as children learn to read.

Particular sounds may always be spelled the same way.

Words are spelled on the basis of sound alone.

As children write, they say words to themselves, listening for the sounds. We say they have developed **phonemic awareness** when they can segment a word into individual sounds. When they write, they use letters for each sound.

Children at this stage may use visual memory for some words because of exposure or drill, but mostly they spell words the way they sound. This is what is meant by *invented spelling:* spelling a word the way it sounds. Of course, this spelling may not be correct, but it usually is close enough that others can read it. Once children realize they can write this way, they usually increase their writing fluency and the amount they write. If the word is in their heads (they can say it and know what it means), they feel free to write it, matching sound segments with written letters.

4 Transitional Stage

Writers begin to pay attention to what words look like as well as to the sounds, though they may not yet recognize when a word is spelled incorrectly.

Vowel sounds are represented in every syllable.

Writers begin to know alternative spellings for various sounds.

Writers begin to rely on their knowledge of **morphology,** that is, the meaningful parts of words such as verb endings, prefixes and suffixes, and root words.

Writers begin to discover the more mysterious aspects of spelling: for instance, doubling final consonants or dropping them; spelling the past tense *-ed* even when it doesn't sound that way, except when the verb has an irregular past tense.

Common patterns appear. Sight words are spelled correctly, and those patterns are applied to the spelling of other words.

Writers begin to understand what to do with syllables and how spelling sometimes needs to be changed when a syllable (representing a meaning change) is added. Some examples are *glad* and *gladdest; happy* and *happier; live* and *living.*

5 Conventional Stage

Most words are spelled correctly.

Writers are catching on to the fact that if they know how to spell a word such as *compete,* they need not struggle with what letter to use for the second vowel sound in *competition.* The words are related both in meaning and in spelling, so even though the sound is a long *e* in *compete* and a schwa in *competition,* the spelling remains *e.*

Writers at this stage have developed a "spelling conscience" (Hillerich, 1977), a positive attitude toward spelling and a desire to spell conventionally.

Writers also have developed a sense of when a word just doesn't look right and can vary the spelling as they search for the conventional spelling.

Writers show increased understanding of the spellings of affixes, contractions, compounds, and homonyms (words that sound alike but are spelled differently).

Writers benefit from systematic spelling instruction.

Assessing Spelling Development. In addition to outlining the stages of spelling acquisition, Gentry and Gillet (1993) have suggested a developmental spelling test that allows you to use just ten words to determine an individual child's stage. Table 3.2 presents the ten words along with possible responses indicative of each spelling stage. If you decide to use this assessment, we suggest that you consult the source cited. Chapter 8 presents other ways to look at spelling assessment.

You may decide to analyze each child's spelling at the beginning of the school year. If so, you can use a recent piece of spontaneous (that is, unedited) writing. Make a list of misspelled words and match them to the characteristics of each stage.

Comments

Remember that acquisition of all writing conventions is uneven and varied. In any one classroom, you may find children not only at various stages of spelling development but also using the other conventions inconsistently. That is, a child might be at the transitional stage in spelling but apparently ignoring punctuation altogether and still expressing himself or herself with immature or nonstandard language.

The following three children might be in the same class:

Child A   Spelling: phonetic
               Grammar/usage: standard
               Mechanics: not yet paragraphing; no commas or semicolons
Child B   Spelling: conventional
               Grammar/usage: conventional
               Mechanics: conventional
Child C   Spelling: semiphonetic
               Grammar/usage: nonstandard
               Mechanics: none secure yet

A few lucky children seem to have acquired all conventions by age 6 or 7. Others are still struggling as they finish middle school and even into adulthood. Some children can acquire conventions through diligence, good teaching, and support. Others try but seem unable to reach the conventional stage even with all the support you can give them.

As the teacher of a probably widely diverse group, you will want to know which children are already doing what conventionally. You'll want to know where a

Table 3.2
Student Spelling Responses Indicating Stage of Development

Word	Precommunicative	Semiphonetic	Phonetic	Transitional	Conventional
1. monster	random letters	MTR	MOSTR	MONSTUR	monster
2. united	random letters	U	UNITD	YOUNIGHTED	united
3. dress	random letters	JRS	JRAS	DRES	dress
4. bottom	random letters	BT	BODM	BOTTUM	bottom
5. hiked	random letters	H	HIKT	HICKED	hiked
6. human	random letters	UM	HUMN	HUMUM	human
7. eagle	random letters	EL	EGL	EGUL	eagle
8. closed	random letters	KD	KLOSD	CLOSSED	closed
9. bumped	random letters	B	BOPT	BUMPPED	bumped
10. type	random letters	TP	TIP	TIPE	type

Source: Gentry, J. R., & Gillet, J. W. (1993). *Teaching kids to spell.* Portsmouth, NH: Heinemann.

child is developmentally in spelling to provide developmentally appropriate instruction and practice. The same is true for the other conventions of writing. Assess your children's writing to learn what they are now doing. Then plan instruction based on helping them move forward.

As you read what children have written, you need to separate the content from the spelling, grammar, and mechanics. The content reflects emotions, analytical ability, life experiences, thinking process, self-awareness, and much more. The spelling, grammar, and mechanics simply represent developmental stages in narrow aspects of writing. We believe children should be free to write whatever they have to say regardless of their ability to follow writing conventions, just as they are encouraged to express ideas orally regardless of articulation problems, mispronunciations, or occasional wrong words.

It is difficult for some teachers to see past the spelling and mechanics to the ideas. Read first without a red pencil. Respond to the child's ideas. Then make notes about development in writing conventions and any instruction you think may be needed.

Techniques for Organizing Assessment Information

The point of gathering information—assessing—is to help you meet the needs of your children. Therefore, you must find a way to organize data that works for you. We will suggest a few ways, but there is no one right way. You are the only one who can judge if a method of organization is working for you. You will know it is working because you will be able to put your hands on the information you need when you need it. If asked, you will be able to justify any lesson you plan by pointing to evidence of the need for such a lesson, whether for the whole class, a small group, or a single child.

We acknowledge that this isn't easy. You will probably try many ways of organizing information over the years, always searching for the one perfect way. You may never find it. After all, you are dealing with a roomful of individual children, each with his or her own needs and abilities. Further, children change from day to day: some move away while new ones move in; and children who seemed unable to do something one day can magically do it the next, while children who have been able to do something one day suddenly seem unable to do it at all. So your data are continually changing—and thus your plans have to change.

Still, as a teacher, you have to find a way to keep it all organized, up to date, and available for use as you plan instruction. The following sections offer a few ideas. Also, ask your colleagues to share what they do. Read articles. Make up your own method. Just don't give up. You'll find a way.

Portfolios

A **portfolio** is a collection of a student's work gathered over time. It shows both progress and achievement. Further, it includes self-assessment and reflection. It can be kept in any kind of folder or container, such as a box or plastic pocket. It includes items the student has chosen, with reflections about why those choices were made. It includes both formative (showing progress) and summative (showing achievement) items.

The portfolio content represents a collaboration between a student and the teacher and should be accessible to both at all times, but to no one else. Portfolios are particularly useful during student-teacher conferences, teacher-family conferences, and three-way conferences (student-teacher-family).

Following is a brief description of one way to get started using portfolios. Refer to For Additional Reading for sources that discuss portfolios further. The school system in which you teach may have policies, procedures, and guidelines in place for the use of portfolios. If not, these steps should help you get started.

1   *Introduce the concept and perhaps show a portfolio from a previous year or one you keep for yourself.* Elicit ideas from children about a portfolio's purpose. Talk about how you and they will work to build the portfolio.

2   *Identify the categories of information to be included.* Use students' ideas as well as your own. For young children, you may want only two or three categories to start with, such as, work samples, records of independent reading, and some checklists you have used. Later you may decide to add student self-evaluations, your anecdotal notes, tests, and other records related to assessment of reading and writing.

3   *Establish a procedure.* Pick a place to store the portfolios that is easily accessible. Decide the following and make a chart:

   a. How to select materials

   b. How to place them in the portfolio

   c. How to use entry and reflection slips for each student-selected item (see Figure 3.16 for a sample)

   d. How and when to use the portfolio; when to file and retrieve items

   e. How to use the portfolio in conferences

   f. When to review, weed, and reevaluate the contents

4   *Be sure to inform the child's family* about the purpose, the process, and the procedures of portfolios.

5   *Plan regular times* with each child to review the portfolio.

Be careful not to let the portfolio become a case of the tail wagging the dog. You don't want children to spend time on portfolios that might better be spent on reading and writing.

Children must see the value in the portfolio; otherwise, it will become a chore—an end in itself—rather than a support. Children should be able to peruse their portfolio contents and feel proud of what they have accomplished and how much they have grown.

Simplicity is best at the beginning. Just start. Keep asking yourself whether or not your objectives are being met by what you are doing. Make adjustments. Keep reading and refining. Eventually you will have a system that works well for you and for your children. You may find the process overwhelming at first, or you may not see the value. We urge you to stick with it and make it your own. It *is* worth your while.

PORTFOLIO ENTRY SLIP

Name _____ Date _____

Work placed in portfolio _____

I included this in my portfolio because _____

_____

_____

It shows that I am good at _____

_____

_____

It shows that I need to work on _____

_____

_____

**Figure 3.16
Sample Entry and
Reflection Slip for Placing
Items in a Portfolio**

Other Techniques

You can use many other techniques to organize assessment information. We will discuss several of them here.

File Folders

You may choose to keep carefully identified file folders of information. One set might contain a folder for each child. Another set might contain class results of tests, checklists, or other kinds of records. Still another set might be grouped by skill, each with a cover sheet on which you identify which children are using the skill and which still need to acquire it.

File folders have been in use for many years. Each person finds his or her own way to use them. The biggest danger is giving a folder too broad a name, such as "Literary elements"; you may need a separate folder for each story element.

Notebooks

A thick notebook can have dividers to form a section for each child. Three-hole-punched pocket folders make it easy to file things. Various record sheets for each child can be duplicated. Even if your children use portfolios, you may want to duplicate reading logs and put them into a notebook. As with all recordkeeping devices, each page should include the child's name and the date(s). Anecdotal records that were written on self-stick labels or sticky notes can be peeled off and put into the notebook.

Cards

Some teachers like to keep records on note cards, usually 5"x 8", with a card for each child. The cards may be taped in alphabetical (or any other logical) order, overlapping, onto a clipboard so that the entire set can be carried around easily. (Look back at Figure 2.2 on page 25.) When a child's card is filled, it is removed, filed in a box, and replaced with a new card.

Computer Programs

More and more computer programs are becoming available to help teachers keep records and organize information. Your school probably will have several to choose from.

These programs pose a possible danger, however. Some reduce everything to numbers and averages, a method inconsistent with the kind of assessment that may be most useful in making instructional decisions. But the cliché is true: the program is only as good as the person using it. So acquaint yourself with the program and discover its strengths and weaknesses.

Once you decide a program will be useful, enter data in a timely manner, double-check accuracy, and be sure you are using the information in a way that helps the children, not just producing statistics.

Conclusions

Organizing information and recordkeeping may seem like a far cry from what drew you into teaching in the first place. However, you must do it or you will fall short of what you want for your children. Accept that it will take more time than you think. Accept that you will forget things unless you write them down. Establish habits of attention to detail. Make a checklist to remind yourself of the steps you must take to organize information.

Summary

In this chapter, we have described tools and techniques specifically aimed at helping you assess children's literacy: oral language, reading, and writing.

To assess a child's oral language development, you pay attention to both listening and speaking. You may use any of a variety of techniques, such as observing, checklists, and conferences. For second-language learners, you should be aware of the stages of language production that people typically pass through as they learn a new language.

Reading assessment focuses on several different areas. To assess oral reading fluency and word recognition strategies, you have the child read aloud a selection to you. You take what is often called a running record, noting the words read correctly and the miscues. Later you analyze not only the child's overall score but also the particular types of miscues he or she is prone to make. With this information, you then plan the instruction the child needs.

Retelling, another type of reading assessment, involves having a student read material and then tell you about it. Again you record the results and analyze them to determine the child's needs.

Classroom discussions allow you to assess reading comprehension, abilities such as retelling and summarizing, and appropriate behaviors for participating in a discussion. To learn how to conduct a good discussion, children frequently need teacher modeling and guidelines.

Children's written responses to what they have read can help you assess their construction of meaning, their self-concepts, their attitudes, and more. You can have them write in journals, learning logs, or a variety of other formats.

In assessing writing, you will sometimes want to focus on children's use of the writing process: prewriting, drafting, revising, editing, and publishing. During a project that involves the writing process, each student should store every stage in a writing folder. For assessing final products, holistic scoring is often used. This provides a single score for a piece of writing based on the overall quality of both content and mechanics. The key is to develop clear rubrics and anchor papers to which students can refer as they work.

The types of writing you assess will be extremely varied. For reports, you will again want to develop a rubric or checklist by which students can judge their own progress. You'll also want to look at journals, learning logs, letters—virtually everything your students write.

There is much controversy about assessment and instruction for the conventions of writing: spelling, grammar/usage, and mechanics. Many researchers see spelling ability as largely developmental, pointing out that nearly all children go through the same stages of learning to spell no matter how they are taught. Understanding these stages can help you determine when instruction is needed and what precisely you should teach.

For all of these types of literacy assessment, you will need an efficient means of organizing the information you gather. Portfolios—collections of an individual student's work over time, with reflections and self-assessments by the student—are a vital resource. Many other organizational methods, such as file folders, notebooks, cards, and computer programs, may also prove useful.

The tools and techniques from this chapter, as well as those from Chapter 2, will be used as you learn about assessing the stages of literacy development in Chapters 5 through 9. We will show you how to use them to assess benchmark behaviors and plan instruction.

FOR ADDITIONAL READING

General Sources

Cambourne, B., & Turbill, J. (Eds.). (1994). *Responsive evaluation*. Portsmouth, NH: Heinemann.

Glazer, S. M., & Brown, C. S. (1993). *Portfolios and beyond: Collaborative assessment in reading and writing*. Norwood, MA: Christopher-Gordon.

Goodman, K. S., Goodman, Y. M., & Hood, W. J. (Eds.). (1989). *The whole language evaluation book*. Portsmouth, NH: Heinemann.

Harp, B. (Ed.) (1994). *Assessment and evaluation for student centered learning*. Norwood, MA: Christopher-Gordon.

Hill, B. C., & Ruptic, C. (1994). *Practical aspects of authentic assessment: Putting the pieces together*. Norwood, MA: Christopher-Gordon.

Johnson, K. (1995). *Understanding communication in second language classrooms*. New York: Cambridge University Press.

Sources for Reading Assessment Tools and Techniques

Clay, M. (1985). *The early detection of reading difficulties* (3rd ed.). Auckland, New Zealand: Heinemann.

Clay, M. M. (1993). *An observation survey of early literacy achievement*. Portsmouth, NH: Heinemann.

Fountas, I. C., & Pinnell, G. S. (1996). Using running records. In *Guided reading: Good first teaching for all children* (Chapter 7). Portsmouth, NH: Heinemann.

Johnston, P. H. (1992). *Constructive evaluation of literate activity*. White Plains, NY: Longman.

Rhodes, L. K. (1993). *Literacy assessment: A handbook of instruments*. Portsmouth, NH: Heinemann.

Scott, J., & McCleary, S. (1993). *Diagnostic reading inventory for primary and intermediate grades*. Akron, OH: Scott & McCleary Publishing Company.

Sources for Writing Assessment Tools and Techniques

Gentry, J. R. (1987). *Spel . . . is a four-letter word*. Portsmouth, NH: Heinemann.

Gentry, J. R., & Gillet, J. W. (1993). *Teaching kids to spell*. Portsmouth, NH: Heinemann.

O'Neill, J. (1994). Making assessment meaningful: "Rubrics" clarify expectations, yield better feedback. *ASCD Update, 36*(1), 4–5.

Sources for Techniques for Organizing Assessment Information

Bergeron, B. S., Wermuth, S., & Hammar, R. C. (1997). Initiating portfolios through shared learning: Three perspectives. *The Reading Teacher, 50*(7), 552–562.

Farr, R., & Tone, B. (1994). *Portfolio and performance assessment*. Fort Worth, TX: Harcourt Brace.

Salvia, J., & Ysseldyke, J. (1998). Performance and portfolio assessment. In *Assessment* (Chapter 13). Boston: Houghton Mifflin.

FOR EXPLORATION: ELECTRONIC RESOURCES

Dialogue Journals: Interactive Writing to Develop Language and Literacy.
http://www.cal.org/NCLE/Digests/DIALOGUE_JOURNALS.HTML   An article from the National Clearinghouse on Literacy Education, written by Joy Kreeft Peyton, describes the use and benefits of dialogue journals.

ELA Best Practices–Grades K–4.
http://www.bcdinteractive.com/philadelphia/gridmenu/ela/bestk403.htm
("Story Retelling");
http://www.bcdinteractive.com/philadelphia/gridmenu/ela/bestk406.htm
("Reflections About My Story Retelling");
http://www.bcdinteractive.com/philadelphia/gridmenu/ela/bestk408.htm
("Student Story Retelling Assessment") These three related web pages provide
valuable information regarding story retelling: a five-point rubric, a handout
to facilitate student reflection, and a chart for use in assessment. For other
language arts "best practices" from the Philadelphia school district, go to
http://www.bcdinteractive.com/philadelphia/gridmenu/ela/ and click on any
of the links provided.

CLASSROOM APPLICATIONS

1. Practice taking a running record on several children, and draw conclusions.

2. Try some other tools or techniques described in this chapter, using our forms or ones you make up.

3. Find out which of these tools and techniques are already in use in your school. What are the teachers' opinions of them? Synthesize the information and share it.

4. Interview several special teachers—such as teachers for ELLs, students with learning disabilities, or students with hearing impairment—about one or more of the tools and techniques from this chapter. Compile your results and draw conclusions.

Instructional Strategies for a Balanced Literacy Program: An Overview

CONTINUED ON NEXT PAGE

FOCUS

As you read the Eyewitness section, ask yourself the following questions:

1. How is Mr. Aroyo meeting the different needs of students in his classroom?
2. What evidence do you see that Mr. Aroyo is assessing the use of specific skills and strategies?

Eyewitness   *Mr. Aroyo's fifth-grade class consists of thirty-one students: eighteen girls and thirteen boys. Nine students are Hispanic; their families are from Mexico, Central America, and Puerto Rico. All of these Spanish-speaking students have achieved the level of intermediate fluency in English (as described in Chapter 3) and have made the transition from reading Spanish to reading English. They participate in all class activities, even though twice a week they still go to ESL tutoring for work on academic English.*

Today the class has divided into three groups; each group is reading a different book related to the theme the class has been studying: catastrophes. Mr. Aroyo begins by meeting with the group reading Predicting Earthquakes *(Vogt, 1989). He introduces the semantic map shown in Figure 4.1, and he models for students how to use it to organize the information they will gain from reading the text.*

Next, Mr. Aroyo moves on to another group reading Emergency *(Gibbons, 1994). He guides and talks students through the first six pages of the book to prepare them for better comprehension of the text. The students then read silently. This group is reading considerably below grade level, and Mr. Aroyo is trying to accelerate their reading development by using highly structured lessons. He follows a method known as* reciprocal teaching, *an interactive process in which teacher and students take turns modeling reading strategies. (See Chapter 8 for a detailed discussion of this method.)*

Mr. Aroyo moves on to the third group, where he participates and observes as students discuss their book using written prompts that he has previously given them. As students complete their discussion, Mr. Aroyo makes notes on his clipboard about each student's response. At the conclusion of their discussion, he tells the group, "You identified almost all of the main points!"

This brief glimpse into Mr. Aroyo's classroom shows how he operated a **balanced literacy program** in a classroom of students from several different cultures. On this day, he was having his students read **developmentally appropriate books**. These are books that are at the students' instructional reading levels, that is, books they can read capably with good guidance and instruction. If we observed on other days, we would see that Mr. Aroyo sometimes had the entire class reading the same book, in which case he used different types of activities to meet the individual needs of students.

We saw Mr. Aroyo use several different instructional strategies. When he used the semantic map shown in Figure 4.1, he was employing a type of **graphic organizer,** a visual representation of the way a text is organized. (The story maps mentioned in Chapter 3 are another type of graphic organizer.) When Mr. Aroyo talked students through the first six pages of *Emergency* before they began reading, he was using a technique known as a **text walk**. Finally, the third group of students, who discussed their book using his prompts, were an example of a **discussion circle** (also known as a **discussion group**). As he participated in and observed the discussion circle, Mr. Aroyo was assessing how students were using previously taught skills.

Mr. Aroyo's students were functioning at several different stages of literacy development. Although most were at the Almost Fluent Reading and Writing Stage, we noticed some variation in their literacy stages, as well as in their fluency in English. Yet Mr. Aroyo accommodated all of the children's needs comfortably in the same classroom.

This chapter provides an overview of a balanced literacy program and reviews eleven key instructional strategies that you can use with students at all stages of literacy development. This chapter is *not* intended as a comprehensive presentation of instructional strategies; rather, it is a brief survey of strategies we will refer to frequently in Chapters 5 through 9 as we consider each stage of literacy development in detail. If you have questions about a particular instructional strategy and want to read more about it, you can refer to the sources listed in For Additional Reading at the end of this chapter.

**Figure 4.1
Partial Semantic Map
Used by Mr. Aroyo to
Model a Graphic Means
of Organizing Information
from a Text**

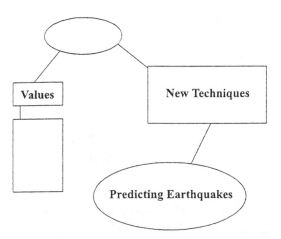

Values

New Techniques

Predicting Earthquakes

Balanced Literacy Instruction

FOCUS **As you read this chapter, ask yourself the following questions:**

1. What are the components of a balanced literacy program?
2. What are the eleven basic instructional strategies discussed in this chapter? Meet with a partner to discuss how each strategy would help you develop a balanced literacy program.
3. What types of text are needed for a balanced literacy program?
4. What is "intervention"? When and why should you use it in your program?

Balanced literacy instruction is a widely supported concept (Au, Carroll, & Scheu, 1997; Freppon & Dahl, 1998; Pressley, 1998; Snow, Burns, & Griffin, 1998; Strickland, 1994). Of course, various educators have slightly different points of view as to what balanced literacy is. Yet as we examine these points of view, we find that all point to the idea that a balanced literacy program is one that places emphasis on the right combination of elements each student needs to achieve success in literacy. These elements include both direct instruction in skills and strategies for those who need it (Delpit, 1986) and indirect instruction through a variety of meaningful literacy experiences.

As Au and her colleagues note, we must balance skills-and-strategies instruction with meaningful literacy experiences to help students achieve success (Au, Carroll, & Scheu, 1997). In fact, a well-designed balanced literacy program meets the needs of *all* students, whatever their cultural or language background (Moll, 1988; Strickland, 1994).

Models for a Balanced Literacy Program

Figures 4.2 and 4.3 present an effective way to think of a balanced literacy program. These figures should help you as you organize your assessment-based literacy classroom on a daily basis.

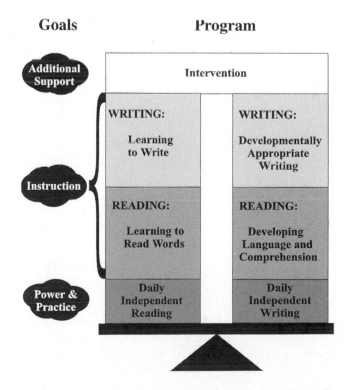

**Figure 4.2
Balanced Beginning
Literacy Program,
Generally Appropriate
for Grades K–2**

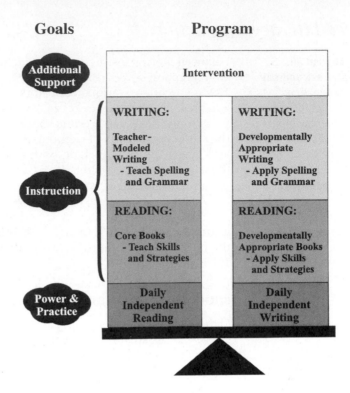

Figure 4.3
Balanced Literacy Program
for Grades 3–8

The figures present two models: a Balanced Beginning Literacy Program, generally appropriate for kindergarten through second grade, and a Balanced Literacy Program 3–8, generally suitable for third through eighth grades. As students progress through the stages of literacy development, their needs change, and therefore the program must change. As you study both models, note that there are similarities and differences.

Both models share these characteristics:

- They focus on the same goals.
- They are developed in blocks.
- They have **independent reading** and **independent writing** on a daily basis.
- They have two reading blocks devoted to instruction.
- They have two writing blocks devoted to instruction.
- They have a block of intervention.

The most significant differences between the two models are that the K–2 model has a reading block that focuses on learning to read words and one that emphasizes developing language and comprehension. In the model for grades 3 through 8, the reading blocks change to focusing on core books and developmentally appropriate books.

At the beginning literacy stages, learners need to focus more on learning to read words (decoding), expanding their language base, and developing oral comprehension. When students achieve independence in decoding words, they can apply their strategies and skills to many different texts at a variety of levels. They begin to focus much more heavily on comprehension. Therefore, the texts they read need not be as carefully sequenced as at the beginning stages of learning (Clay, 1991).

Even though we have designated the two models as pertaining to grades K through 2 and grades 3 through 8, the shift from one to the other is not smooth and precise. It is much like the stages of literacy development: a "jerky continuum." For most students, the shift from one model to the other usually occurs around the end of second grade, the time when most students achieve independence in decoding. However, this is not an absolute. Some students achieve this independence earlier, and some achieve it much later. Therefore, whatever grade you teach, it is important that you understand both models.

Some older English-language learners may not have developed literacy in their first language. Therefore, they may need the elements of the Balanced Beginning Literacy Program even though they are in the upper grades. However, if they have developed basic oral English, they will need the Balanced Literacy Program 3–8.

The following sections discuss the components of each model. As you read, keep two points in mind. First, within a given classroom, you may be using elements from both programs, depending on your students' needs. Second, even though our program models stop at grade 8, literacy development continues throughout life.

A Balanced Beginning Literacy Program

As you can see in Figure 4.2, the three primary goals of our Balanced Beginning Literacy Program are power and practice, instruction, and additional support. For *power and practice*, students do independent reading and writing on a daily basis. *Instruction* focuses on learning to read words, developing language and comprehension, learning to write, and developmentally appropriate writing. Both power and practice and instruction are needed for all students. *Additional support* is provided for students who are experiencing difficulty in learning to read or write and for those who have special learning needs. (For a more extended discussion of this Balanced Beginning Literacy Program, see Cooper [2000], listed in For Additional Reading at the end of the chapter.)

Within this balanced program, there are six blocks (shaded in Figure 4.2) that all students receive. These six blocks require a minimum of 3 hours per day in kindergarten and approximately $3\frac{1}{2}$ hours per day in grades 1 and 2. *Any intervention instruction is in addition to these times.* Now let's take a closer look at each block.

Independent Reading and Writing Blocks

Daily Independent Reading and *Daily Independent Writing* comprise the first two blocks of the Balanced Beginning Literacy Program. These blocks provide stu-

During daily independent
writing, students choose
their own topics.
M. K. Denny/PhotoEdit

dents with the practice they need to become effective, fluent readers and writers. *Daily Independent Reading and Writing are the only two blocks that must be provided in all classrooms on a daily basis.* An average of 10 to 15 minutes per day should be allotted for *each* block, with adjustments for the grade level you teach.

During the Independent Reading Block, students read self-selected books, magazines, and newspapers. At the beginning literacy stages, children may begin by looking at pictures. You may read to model independent reading part of the time, but you should also monitor students' reading and hold conferences with individuals.

Similarly, during the Independent Writing Block, students choose what to write. You also monitor and confer with students during this block, even though you may write some of the time to model for students that you value writing, too.

Reading Instruction Blocks

Reading: Learning to Read Words, one of the two blocks for reading instruction, is the block in which you systematically and explicitly teach students the strategies and skills they need to become independent decoders. During this block, students are given texts in which they can read and apply the strategies and skills you have taught.

   Reading: Developing Language and Comprehension is the block in which you build and expand oral language and teach students comprehension strategies they need to develop their ability to construct meaning. The instruction in this block involves the use of big books, read-alouds, shared reading, and guided reading. You will find more about these teaching methods later in this chapter.

Writing Instruction Blocks

In the *Writing: Learning to Write* block, you teach children how to write. This includes teaching them to form letters and write words and sentences. Writing plays an important role in developing students' knowledge and use of concepts of print, phonemic awareness, and letter-sound associations. During this block you also model different types of writing, such as stories and informational pieces. Spelling and grammar are taught as a part of writing. This block may be provided to small groups or to the whole class.

   Writing: Developmentally Appropriate Writing is the block in which students write their own pieces. By **developmentally appropriate writing,** we mean students do the type of writing that was modeled in the Learning to Write block, but they *always select their own topics.* In the beginning, students may write only sentences or captions for their pictures. Gradually they begin to write stories and even informational pieces. This block provides time for practice and application of spelling and grammar.

Intervention

Intervention is the additional support block that is provided only for students who are experiencing difficulty in learning to read or who have special learning needs. This block is designed to stop or prevent failure for students. Students receiving intervention also take part in the six other blocks. Later in this chapter, we will discuss intervention in more depth.

   Now let's see how this Balanced Beginning Literacy Program compares with the Balanced Literacy Program 3–8.

A Balanced Literacy Program for Grades 3 to 8

Look back at Figure 4.3. Notice that the principal change in the Balanced Literacy Program 3–8 is that the two reading blocks now focus on reading core books and developmentally appropriate books. There are still six blocks for all students, plus an extra intervention block for students who need additional support.

Rather than the 3 to 3½ hours per day in the beginning program, the amount of time required for the six basic blocks is approximately 1½ to 2 hours per day in grades 3 through 8.

Independent Reading and Writing Blocks

Daily Independent Reading and *Daily Independent Writing* continue. Their goal is the same: power and practice. The main change in this block is the amount of time, which increases to 15 to 20 minutes per day for each block. Students can and should be reading and writing more.

Reading Instruction Blocks

Core Books and *Developmentally Appropriate Books* comprise the next two blocks of the Balanced Literacy Program 3–8. These two blocks now replace the Learning to Read Words and Developing Language and Comprehension blocks.

In the beginning of kindergarten and first grade, the two reading instruction blocks usually take place daily. As students progress through the grades and stages and read longer texts, it becomes appropriate to alternate between the two blocks— Core Books on one day, Developmentally Appropriate Books on the next day.

By **core books,** we simply mean books experienced by all students in the class. Using the same book for all students during this block serves three main purposes:

1   It helps all students see that they can learn from a common book, even though everyone may not do the same kinds of activities with the book. This helps to elevate self-esteem.

2   The core book provides a basis for developing a common body of prior knowledge, vocabulary, and background.

3   Through the use of minilessons (described later in this chapter), key strategies and skills are taught within the meaningful context of the literature using direct, explicit instruction.

For the majority of the class, the book used for the core book should be *slightly* more difficult than the students' reading levels (Snow, Burns, & Griffin, 1998). For a few students, the core book will be less challenging. For others (for instance, some English-language learners who lack English proficiency), the book may be more challenging. Through the use of small groups, you meet the needs of these students by providing different types of instruction. This process is further illustrated in Chapters 7, 8, and 9.

In the Developmentally Appropriate Books block, students read books appropriate to their reading levels and receive instruction from the teacher. Think back to our Eyewitness: Mr. Aroyo was having the Developmentally Appropriate Books block on the day we visited his classroom. In this block, students work in small groups that change as students grow in their ability to read. *Groups are never static or constant.* The purpose of this block is to give students opportunities to apply the strategies and skills learned while reading the core book and to develop the skills they need to further their reading growth. Minilessons are provided to teach skills needed to read the developmentally appropriate books.

The two reading instruction blocks, Core Books and Developmentally Appropriate Books, help you combat the pitfalls of static ability grouping and build on the best that we know about effective reading instruction (Cunningham, Hall, & Defee, 1998).

Writing Instruction Blocks

Teacher-Modeled Writing and *Developmentally Appropriate Writing* are basically the same as the two writing blocks in the Balanced Beginning Literacy Program. By **teacher-modeled writing,** we mean that you demonstrate a particular type of writing, such as a story, and share your thinking about the process. In the Developmentally Appropriate Writing block, you give students the opportunity to practice writing in line with their levels of ability; although you specify the type of writing to be done, you allow students to select their own topics. You also teach grammar and spelling in ways connected to students' writing. The phonic and word structure patterns that you are teaching for reading should also be reflected in spelling instruction.

Intervention

Intervention, the seventh block, is again designed only for students who need more than regular instruction to help them continue to grow in their ability to read. As with the Balanced Beginning Literacy Program, the primary focus of the intervention block is to stop failure for students who have fallen behind and help them accelerate their reading so they can read at an age-appropriate level.

English-Language Learners and Balanced Literacy Instruction

The concept of a balanced literacy program and the instructional strategies presented in this chapter are all appropriate for English-language learners (ELL students). Of course, adjustments in the use of these strategies and concepts should be made to accommodate the students' language proficiency.

When planning an instructional program for ELL students, we believe you should give serious consideration to the recommendations of the Committee on the Prevention of Reading Difficulties in Young Children (Snow, Burns, & Griffin, 1998, p. 325):

- *If language-minority children arrive at school with no proficiency in English but speaking a language for which there are instructional guides, learning materials, and locally available proficient teachers, then these children should be taught how to read in their native language while acquiring oral proficiency in English and subsequently taught to extend their skills to reading in English.*
- *If language-minority children arrive at school with no proficiency in English but speak a language for which the above conditions cannot be*

met and for which there are insufficient numbers of children to justify the development of the local capacity to meet such conditions, the initial instructional priority should be developing the children's oral proficiency in English. Although print materials may be used to support the development of English phonology, vocabulary, and syntax, the postponement of formal reading instruction is appropriate until an adequate level of oral proficiency in English has been achieved.

In addition to the second point, keep in mind that delaying reading instruction too long only puts English-language learners further and further behind. The most widely accepted line of thinking is to do lots of reading to and with students, having them write from the beginning to develop academic English as well as conversational English (Krashen, 1993). Recall, too, the many adaptations for assessment procedures to meet the needs of diverse learners that we outlined in Chapters 2 and 3.

Assessment: Maintaining a Balanced Literacy Program in Diverse Classrooms

A balanced literacy program is an assessment-based literacy program. In other words, as you work with your students, you will continuously think about their performance in relation to the stages of literacy development and use a variety of tools and techniques to determine students' strengths, needs, and progress. Without such continuous assessment, you cannot maintain a balanced program.

In our classrooms, we always looked at our students' performance and made changes in our instructional programs on the basis of what we observed. At some times we grouped, at other times we taught the whole class, and at still other times we worked with individuals. Our balanced literacy classroom was constantly changing as students grew and changed. You will find this happening in your own classroom as you develop your teaching skills. The next section looks at a variety of instructional strategies that you will use as you adapt your program to meet the needs of your diverse learners.

Basic Instructional Strategies for Use in Assessment-Based Balanced Literacy Programs

In Chapters 2 and 3, we presented a variety of tools and techniques for assessment and stressed how you would become selective in deciding which ones to use. As you make decisions about students' instruction, you will similarly need a variety of instructional strategies and techniques.

These strategies will help you provide the much-needed ingredient in a successful classroom, **explicit teaching** (Hancock, 1999), the process of clearly modeling for students what they are to learn. Some of these strategies fall into the category of an **instructional routine,** a pattern of instruction that you will use repeatedly.

This section summarizes eleven key instructional strategies: the literacy lesson, minilessons, the explicit phonics/structural elements routine, the explicit comprehension routine, the decodable words routine, the phonetically unpredictable words routine, modes of reading, response activities, discussion circles or groups, modes of writing, and the daily blocked plan. You are likely to use all of these strategies at all stages of literacy development, though not all every day. We will further discuss each of these strategies and show you when to use them in Chapters 5 through 9. Here we define and describe each strategy, list the procedures, and offer some additional comments. For each strategy, you can find more resources in the For Additional Reading section at the end of the chapter.

Instructional Strategy 1: The Literacy Lesson

The *literacy lesson* provides a framework for planning instruction using a piece of text for reading and writing instruction. It has three parts (Cooper, 2000): Introducing, Reading and Responding, and Extending. Table 4.1 identifies these parts, outlines their basic procedures, and explains their rationale.

You can use the literacy lesson in the instructional portion of your balanced literacy program, whenever you have students read any type of book for instructional purposes. As you can see from Table 4.1, the lesson also involves writing. At times you will model how to write the particular type of text students are reading. For example, if students are reading a story, you will model for them how to write a story (in the Learning to Write or Teacher-Modeled Writing block) and then have them write their own story (in the Developmentally Appropriate Writing block). You will not need to model a new type of writing every time you do a literacy lesson because the writing is likely to extend over several days.

Procedures

You will find that the literacy lesson framework is appropriate at many times throughout your literacy program. While maintaining the basic structure, you can adjust the lesson to your students' needs and to the types of text they are reading. The following procedures can help you plan your lessons:

1. Look at your students' strengths and needs; consider where they are in the stages of literacy development. Decide what strategies and skills will help them move on to the next stage.

2. Select the type of text your students need at this point. You will probably use a published program that has an anthology as well as a variety of other types of text. Selectively use these texts to teach your students the lessons they need to move forward in their literacy development.

3. Read the text and the suggestions given in the manual that accompanies it. If the text is narrative, outline on paper or in your mind the story map (the setting, characters, problem, actions, and outcome). If the text is expository, outline the main ideas and supporting details. This information helps you identify the key background concepts that need to be developed and helps you see what big ideas should be brought out in the reading.

Table 4.1
The Literacy Lesson: An Instructional Framework

Lesson Part	Procedures	Rationale
Introducing	• Activate and develop prior knowledge and background for the text. • Help students set purpose for reading.	Utilizes the research-based findings that prior knowledge/background and a purpose for reading are essential to effective comprehension.
Reading and Responding	Students: • read text using one or more of the modes of reading (described later in this chapter). • respond to the text through discussion and/or writing. • apply decoding and comprehension strategies and skills. • discuss which strategies and/or skills helped them read the text successfully. • summarize orally and/or in writing what they read.	Builds on these research-supported ideas: • Readers must receive scaffolded support, moving toward independence as they learn to read. • Talking about strategies and skills used helps students apply what they are learning and make the strategies and skills their own. • Responding and summarizing lead to improved comprehension.
Extending	• Students use the knowledge and information gained in a follow-up activity. • Writing is taught on the basis of the type of text being read.	Using knowledge gained from reading helps students see the value in learning to write. Writing and reading are best taught together.

Also, look at the text to identify places that give students the opportunities to **practice** (use in reading under teacher guidance) and **apply** (use in reading independently) what they need to help them move to the next stage of literacy.

4   Outline each part of your lesson. Table 4.2 presents a set of questions that can guide you as you develop lessons. In the beginning, you may write out the lessons. As you gain more experience, you will outline your lessons mentally.

Comments

The literacy lesson framework is similar to the Directed Reading-Thinking Activity (DRTA) (Stauffer, 1969) and the Experience-Text-Relationship (E-T-R) method (Au, 1979). The major difference is that the literacy lesson brings reading and writing together more consistently. For further information on the literacy lesson, the DRTA, or the E-T-R, see For Additional Reading.

Table 4.2
Questions to Guide Development of a Literacy Lesson

Introducing	a. What key prior knowledge and background concepts need to be brought out or developed? (Look at your story map or main ideas and supporting details.)
	b. How will you develop this prior knowledge in an *interactive* way in a short amount of time (10–15 minutes or less)?
Reading and Responding	a. What key strategies and skills do you want your students to practice and/or apply in this text? How will you bring these out after reading?
	b. How do you want students to read this text? (See Instructional Strategy 7: Modes of Reading.)
	c. What types of response prompts and/or activities will you use?
Extending	a. What type of follow-up activities would give students a chance to use what they have learned in this text? (Follow-up activities are not always necessary; they depend on the text.)
	b. What type of writing will you teach using this text as the basis for your modeling?

Instructional Strategy 2: Minilessons

Minilessons (Calkins, 1994; Cooper, 2000) are short, focused lessons (5 to 15 minutes) that may be taught to a small group or the whole class. They are used to teach a specific skill, strategy, concept, or process based on students' needs.

Minilessons can be used in any of the four instructional blocks of reading and writing in a balanced literacy program. They may precede or follow a literacy lesson.

Procedures

You can use the following steps to teach minilessons:

1 *Introduction:*   Tell students what they are going to learn.

2 *Teacher modeling:*   Model the skill or strategy. To demonstrate, use text from literature students have read or from students' own writing. The following is an example of a teacher model for explicitly teaching students how to select a topic for writing:

When I start to select a topic for writing, I think about things I know the most about or like the most. I make a list of them. [Write a list for students to see such as the one below.] Then I look over my list and circle the one I want to write about now. [Circle one topic.] I put the others in my writing folder and save them for later.

−pets

⟨−collecting rocks⟩

−bicycles ·

−my friends

3　*Student modeling and guided practice:*　Have students model the same procedure you modeled.

4　*Summarizing and reflecting:*　Guide students to summarize in their own words what they have learned and tell when they would use the process, skill, or strategy.

5　*Follow-up:*　Provide repeated opportunities for independent practice and application of what was taught. Application should take place within the actual process of reading, writing, speaking, or listening as opposed to isolated worksheet activities. Draw students' attention to their successful application of what was taught.

When you are planning minilessons for your students, you will find the following procedures useful:

1　Identify what students need to be taught. Do this by referring to your ongoing assessment data in relation to the stages of literacy development.

2　Use the questions in Table 4.3 to guide your planning of the specific parts of the minilessons. (Students' performance during the minilesson is part of your ongoing assessment.)

Table 4.3
Questions to Guide Minilesson Development

Introduction	What are you going to teach? (Tell or show students directly what you will teach.)
Teacher Modeling	Does this skill, strategy, or concept lend itself to modeling? How will you model the process? What "think-alouds" will you use?
Student Modeling and Guided Practice	Where will students be able to find other examples of what has been taught? What questions do you need to ask to guide students in modeling what they have learned?
Summarizing and Reflecting	What questions will you ask to guide students in summarizing and reflecting on what has been taught?
Follow-up	What authentic reading and writing tasks will be used for repeated practice and application of skills and strategies?

3 Reflect on each lesson after you teach. What worked well? What would you change?

Comments

Minilessons are useful tools throughout your literacy program whenever you need to teach a particular skill or strategy. Some educators object to the term *minilesson*, claiming it implies too casual an attitude or too short a time to teach thoroughly. We obviously disagree.

The primary purpose of the minilesson is to keep the instruction focused and succinct. Whether you use the term *minilesson* or just *lesson*, remember that these lessons are always based on students' needs. See For Additional Reading for more information on minilessons.

Instructional Strategy 3: Explicit Phonics/Structural Elements Routine

The five-step routine we call the *explicit phonics/structural elements routine* builds on the best research we have to date on explicitly teaching sound elements (Adams, 1990; Eldredge, 1995; Moustafa, 1997). It incorporates five steps: (1) awareness, (2) segmentation, (3) association, (4) reading, and (5) spelling.

This routine provides a pattern that you can use repeatedly for explicitly teaching phonic and structural skills. You can use it in the Learning to Read Words block of the Balanced Beginning Literacy Program or in the Core Books or Developmentally Appropriate Books blocks of the Balanced Literacy Program 3–8. Teachers often teach a phonics/structural routine for certain sound elements before reading text that contains examples of those elements. Other teachers use the routine following the reading of the text. Research does not offer a definitive answer as to which way is best.

Procedures

We recommend the procedures outlined in Table 4.4 to explicitly teach phonics and structural skills. Each of the five steps should be incorporated within every lesson. Depending on students' needs, however, each step can be given more or less emphasis.

The following guidelines will help you plan explicit phonics/structural element instruction:

1 Using your ongoing assessment data, identify students who need instruction in a particular phonics or structural element or elements.

2 Use the explicit phonics/structural elements routine as outlined in the example in Table 4.4.

3 Follow the instruction with practice by having students read and reread books containing the element numerous times.

Table 4.4
Routine for Explicitly Teaching Phonics: Sample Lesson for Initial Sound /b/

Step	Procedures
1. *Awareness*	a. "Today you will learn to use the sound for the letter *b* at the beginnings of words to help you read and spell."
	b. "Listen to this word (pronounce *boat* slowly, each sound slightly exaggerated) /b/–/ō/–/t/." (Say it again slowly.) "How many sounds do you hear in this word?" (Students respond: "Three.") "What is the first sound you hear?" (Repeat using the words *big, boy, box.*)
	c. If students respond correctly, move on to the next step. If students do not respond correctly, do further work in phonemic awareness.
2. *Segmentation*	a. "The first sound in *box* is /b/. What is the first sound in *barn*?" (Students respond: "/b/.") Repeat using the words *bet, bang, bake.*
	b. If students respond correctly, move on to the next step. If they do not, provide more teaching and practice in segmentation.
3. *Association*	a. Write the words *box, boy,* and *bear* on the chalkboard. Underline the *b.* Say, "Each of these words begins with the same letter and the same sound. The letter is *b*; the sound is /b/." Say each word slowly, emphasizing the /b/ sound. Have children repeat with you.
	b. Show a picture card with a bear. Say, "This bear's name is Boris—Boris Bear. He will help us remember the sound for b: /b/."
	c. Write groups of words on the chalkboard. Have students read the words with you and decide which ones begin with the same letter and sound as Boris Bear:
	band, car, bell
	hat, beg, big
	top, Bob, cap

Bb

Boris Bear

(continued)

Table 4.4
Routine for Explicitly Teaching Phonics: Sample Lesson for Initial Sound /b/ (cont.)

Step	Procedures
4. *Reading*	a. Write a few words on the chalkboard that students are likely to know: *funny, say, pig.*
	b. For the first word, say, "This word is *funny*. If we change the beginning letter to *b*, what sound will be at the beginning of this word?"
	b ̸funny
	(Students respond: "/b/.") "What is the new word?" (Students respond: "Bunny.")
	c. Repeat using the other words.
	d. Write a silly sentence on the chalkboard:
	Big bear went to box the baby boy.
	Ask students to read it, emphasizing the sound for *b*.
5. *Spelling*	a. Using small chalkboards, magic slates, or sheets of paper, ask students to write the following:
	• the letter that stands for the sound you hear at the beginning of *bake*
	• the letter that stands for the sound /b/
	b. Dictate several words, mixing in words that begin with other sounds that students know *(bank, best, cup, zoo, box).* Have students write the words. Look for accuracy in using the *b* and any other sounds that have previously been taught.

The texts used for step 3 (see page 117) are often called **decodable texts** because they contain mainly words with phonic elements students have been taught. Sometimes these texts are created to focus on certain sound elements, and at other times they are trade book literature. See Trachtenburg (1990), listed in For Additional Reading, for a list of trade books useful for applying phonic elements. Gradually you'll want to move students to more natural-language texts, encouraging them to apply what they have been learning and practicing in decodable texts.

Comments

> The use of routines for explicit teaching of phonics is not new (Cooper, Warncke, Shipman, & Ramstad, 1979). Many teachers have found them effective for years. Placing the use of such routines within the framework of a balanced literacy program helps to make them more effective. We believe that when they are taught within this kind of framework, explicit phonics routines are important for all students, including those with special learning needs (Chard & Osborne, 1999). For English-language learners, however, these routines will not be useful until the students develop adequate understanding of the English sound system. For more information on phonics routines, see For Additional Reading at the conclusion of this chapter.

Instructional Strategy 4: Explicit Comprehension Routine

In the *explicit comprehension routine,* the teacher models a comprehension strategy at each of three levels: concept, listening, and reading. This routine is appropriate for the Core Books and Developmentally Appropriate Books blocks.

Procedures

You can use the procedures outlined in Table 4.5 to teach comprehension strategies. The guidelines that follow will help you plan comprehension strategy lessons.

1   Identify students who need explicit instruction in a comprehension strategy. (You will learn how to do this in Chapters 5 through 9.)

2   Use the minilesson framework to teach the strategy. Incorporate the routine outlined in Table 4.5.

3   Provide repeated practice and application through reading until students are comfortable using the strategy.

Comments

> Routines for teaching comprehension have been recommended for many years and have been refined as our knowledge about comprehension has increased. The five most significant strategies are *inferencing, identifying important information, monitoring, summarizing,* and *generating questions* (Pearson, Roehler, Dole, & Duffy, 1992; Pressley, 1999). For more information on teaching comprehension routines, see Cooper (2000), listed in For Additional Reading.

Table 4.5
Explicit Comprehension Routine: An Example Based on the Strategy of Inferencing in Narrative Text

Step		Procedures
1. *Concept*	a.	Begin by developing the concept of inferencing. Use concrete materials and examples:
		Say, "Look outside. Is the sun shining? Is it cloudy?" and so on. (Students respond.) "What do these things indicate the weather is likely to be in a few hours?" (Students respond, depending on the conditions.)
	b.	Discuss with students how they arrived at their answer (important information they gained by looking outside, prior knowledge they had, logic). Tell students that this process is called *inferencing*.
2. *Listening*	a.	Read aloud a short paragraph that requires students to infer. Say, "Listen to this paragraph and tell what happened about Mr. Lind's appointment":
		Mr. Lind only had fifteen minutes to make his appointment. He hurried from his office and pushed the elevator button, but the elevator didn't come. Finally, after some nervous moments of waiting, it arrived. Down the forty-two floors and out into the parking garage he ran. As he got into his car, he noticed it was leaning to the right. He got out and went to the other side to find a flat tire. Mr. Lind looked at his watch and saw that he had five minutes and eight miles to go. (Cooper, 1986, p. 208)
	b.	Recall the purpose for listening to this passage: "What happened about Mr. Lind's appointment?" Note that because of all his problems, he was likely to be late. Discuss students' responses. If they have difficulty with this process, provide more models using a think-aloud and repeat the process using several additional examples.
3. *Reading*	a.	Select a piece of text students have read that requires inferencing. (Note: All texts require inferencing; some, however, have more opportunities than others for students to use this strategy.)
	b.	Model the use of inferencing with a think-aloud.

Instructional Strategy 5: Decodable Words Routine

The *decodable words routine* is used to teach high-frequency words or any other words that are completely decodable (such as *at, it, prefer, dissatisfied*) as soon as students have learned the decoding elements involved in the word.

Before students read a text for instructional purposes, it is often necessary to teach some key-concept or high-frequency words that may cause them difficulty in reading. Thus, the decodable words routine becomes a part of the literacy lesson discussed earlier. This routine can be used in both the Learning to Read Words block and the Developing Language and Comprehension block of the Balanced Beginning Literacy Program and in the two corresponding reading instruction blocks of the Balanced Literacy Program 3–8.

Procedures

As an example of the decodable words routine, assume you are teaching the word *fan.* You will follow these procedures:

1   *Review the sounds.*

Show the key pictures for sounds needed to decode the word:

Ask students to give the sounds /f/, /ă/, and /n/. If they are unable to do so, use the phonetically unpredictable words routine (described in the next section) and reteach the sounds later.

Say, "We are going to use these three sounds to read a new word."

2   *Sound and blend.*

Print the new word on the board:

fan

(Do not say the word.)

Point to each letter. Ask students to give the sound. Model or coach as needed.

Say, "Now, let's blend the sounds to read the word" (or "Let's read the word"). Sweep your hand under the word as children blend. Model or coach as needed.

3   *Read the word.*

Print the word in a sentence:

The fan is red.

(All words in the sentence except *fan* are known words or are decodable.)

Ask children to read the sentence.

Comments

Following the reading of the word in the sentence, you can give each child a 3" x 5" card. Tell the child to copy the word on one side and the sentence on the other side. Then each child should place the word in alphabetical order in his or her *word bank,* a personal file of words the child has learned or is interested in learning:

Two or three times each week, have children play games with words in their banks. For instance, they can draw words from another person's bank and read it, or they can play a game like FISH.

Instructional Strategy 6: Phonetically Unpredictable Words Routine

Students will often encounter words that are phonetically unpredictable or words for which they do not yet have the necessary decoding knowledge. The *phonetically unpredictable words routine* can be used as part of the literacy lesson to teach vocabulary needed before reading a selection. This routine is appropriate for the Learning to Read Words block or the Developing Language and Comprehension block of the Balanced Beginning Literacy Program and for the Core Books or Developmentally Appropriate Books blocks of the Balanced Literacy Program 3–8.

Procedures

You can use the following procedures for the phonetically unpredictable words routine. Imagine you are teaching children the word *the.*

1 *Read the word.*

Write a sentence on the board with the word:

> The car is red.

Read the sentence aloud to the group. Ask the children to read the sentence with you.

2 | *Match the word.*

Distribute several 3" x 5" cards containing the word. Ask each child to find the word, match it by holding the card under it, and read the sentence aloud. Have the other children clap their hands softly if the child is correct.

3 | *Write the word.*

Hold up a word card containing the word, or point to the word in the sentence. Say, "This word is *the, t-h-e.*"

Say, "Now you say and spell it."

Ask children to write the word on their papers or slate boards, saying and spelling the word as they write.

Comments

You should follow your instruction with many opportunities for children to read text containing the words you have taught. You will want to provide repeated practice like that described for the decodable words routine.

Instructional Strategy 7: Modes of Reading

The ***modes of reading*** concept helps you provide appropriate scaffolding of instruction as students read texts. Each mode provides a different level of instructional support. By varying the way students read a text, you vary the amount of instruction given.

The five modes of reading are teacher read-aloud, shared reading, guided reading (observational and interactive), cooperative/collaborative reading, and independent reading. Figure 4.4 shows how these modes of reading provide decreasing instructional support and increasing independence. This concept is based on what Pearson (1985) calls the "gradual release of responsibility."

The various modes of reading can be used during the Core Books and Developmentally Appropriate Books blocks. Within your literacy lessons, you will use different modes of reading to meet students' needs. Even after students read independently, you will return to other modes as needed to deal with more challenging ideas and texts.

Procedures

Table 4.6 presents a summary of the basic procedures and the purpose for each mode of reading. If the modes concept is new to you or if you need more information on one or more modes, see For Additional Reading at the end of this chapter. Here we will discuss key points about the use of each mode.

Teacher Read-Aloud. Reading a text aloud for instructional purposes is an important strategy to use when concepts or ideas might challenge students. However, be cautious; don't use texts that are so difficult that you always feel you need to read the texts aloud. Unfortunately, many teachers have done this as they began

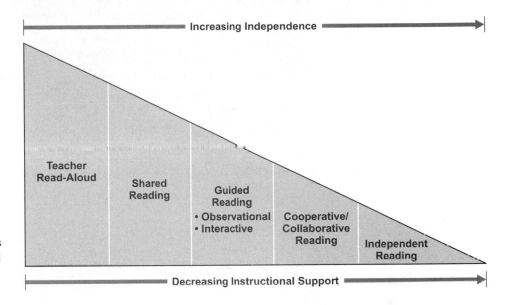

Increasing Independence

Teacher
Read-Aloud

Shared
Reading

Guided
Reading
• Observational
• Interactive

Cooperative/
Collaborative
Reading

Independent
Reading

Decreasing Instructional Support

**Figure 4.4
The Relationship of Modes
of Reading to Instructional
Support and Students'
Independence**

using literature-based instruction. Teacher read-alouds for instructional purposes should not be confused with read-alouds for enjoyment, which take place at a variety of times during the classroom day.

Shared Reading.　The concept of *shared reading* was introduced by Holdaway (1979) as a way to start beginning readers, but it can be equally effective with older students and second-language learners. Basically, the teacher reads a text aloud as students look at the text and follow along. Students are encouraged to join in or chime in when they can. Chapter 5 describes the process in more detail.

Guided Reading.　The practice of **guided reading** has been used to teach reading for many years (Betts, 1946/1957). As the name implies, the teacher guides students' reading. Many variations of the concept exist. We present two basic types: observational (Fountas & Pinnell, 1996) and interactive (Cooper, 2000).

During *observational guided reading*, students read a text with a minimum of new skills or concepts. They construct meaning while using strategies to decode words and solve other problems. A complete text is usually read. The teacher observes and coaches.

During *interactive guided reading*, students read text that has been divided into meaningful chunks. Under the teacher's guidance, students make predictions or pose questions that become their purpose for reading. After they have read each chunk, the teacher guides discussion, helps students look at any difficult words, and supports students as they make predictions about the next chunk to be read.

Cooperative/Collaborative Reading.　In *cooperative/collaborative reading*, students read with a partner. Though some teachers set up cooperative reading

Table 4.6
Procedures for Using Different Modes of Reading

Modes of Reading	Type of Text and General Procedures	Time to Use
Teacher Read-Aloud *Purpose:* Develop concepts, vocabulary, sense of story, text structure, and comprehension	⌐ Use with any type of text. • Teacher reads text aloud; students do not have a copy of text. • Teacher and/or students set a purpose before reading. • Discussion follows to check purpose and summarize what was read.	• When text is beyond students' independent or instructional levels (see Chapter 10 for a discussion of these levels). • When the greatest amount of teacher modeling and support are needed.
Shared Reading *Purpose:* Model reading; develop concepts of print, decoding skills, and comprehension skills	⌐ Often used with big books; may be done with any book. • Text is usually predictable or patterned. • Teacher reads aloud from book, tracking lines of print with hand or pointer. • Children are encouraged to join in as they can. • Texts are reread many times to build fluency and comprehension. • Skills are taught using examples from the text.	• When students need heavy teacher support and modeling. • As a way to introduce reading when students are at the Early Emergent Literacy, Emergent Literacy, and Beginning Reading and Writing stages. May be used with older students who are having difficulty with a particular type of text.
Guided Reading • *Observational Guided Reading* *Purpose:* Have students apply strategies and let teacher observe students' use of strategies	⌐ Texts are at students' instructional level with just a few new words and/or concepts. • Teacher introduces text by building background. • Students make some predictions. • As students read, teacher observes to see how they are using various skills and strategies. • Follow-up discussion is held to check predictions and talk about text. • One or two new skills or concepts may be taught. (continued)	• When teaching literacy lessons. • When students are in the beginning stages of reading. Students may read the text aloud softly as a group, each reading at his or her own pace.

Table 4.6
Procedures for Using Different Modes of Reading (cont.)

Modes of Reading	Type of Text and General Procedures	Time to Use
• *Interactive Guided Reading* *Purpose:* Help students read a challenging text successfully	Any texts. • Teacher divides text into meaningful chunks. • Teacher introduces text. Together students and teacher make predictions or pose questions. • Students read first chunk silently. • Discussion is held to check predictions or answer questions. • New predictions or questions are posed. • Silent reading continues.	• At all stages of literacy development. • When teacher support and scaffolding are needed.
Cooperative/ Collaborative Reading *Purpose:* Practice reading with limited partner support	Any texts. • Teacher introduces text. • Students read meaningful chunks with a partner; reading may be done orally or silently, followed by discussion. • *Note:* Mix student pairs. Don't always put better reader with less able reader.	• When students are approaching independence at their current level of development but still need some support. • When motivation is low for students. Working with another student can be encouraging.
Independent Reading *Purpose:* Practice reading by oneself	Any texts. • Teacher introduces text. • Students and/or teacher make predictions or pose questions. • Students read silently. • Follow-up discussion is held.	• When students are independent at their current level of development. • When students need to try using strategies on their own. • At all stages of literacy development.

groups of three, this often results in an "odd person out." Therefore, we believe it is best to use partners for this type of reading. Cooperative reading is generally used as a follow-up to shared or guided reading. During cooperative/collaborative reading, the teacher moves among partners and coaches as needed.

Independent Reading.   In this mode, students read alone. They have reached a point in their development at which they are able to independently apply decoding and comprehension strategies when given text appropriate for them. All students at every stage of literacy development need experience with independent reading.

Independent reading for instructional purposes is different from and in addition to the Daily Independent Reading block in a balanced literacy program. In the Daily Independent Reading block, students select reading materials *they* want to read. In contrast, instructional independent reading sometimes is not self-selected.

Comments

> Learning to think about reading in the modes concept helps you see how the various types of reading function together in the instructional process. All modes of reading should be used for all students at numerous times throughout their stages of literacy development. By observing your students, you will be able to determine when a particular mode is needed to help them continue to gain power in reading. You will learn to vary the mode on the basis of student needs, developmental stage, and materials being read.

Instructional Strategy 8: Response Activities

Response activities help students develop comprehension and learn to construct meaning. After reading a text, students react to it orally or in writing or do some other type of activity using the information from the text. The types of activities students do should be things that one naturally does after reading a text. For example, it is normal to follow up the reading of a good book by talking about it with others. However, children who are developing literacy also enjoy some activities that would not be usual for adults, such as drawing or acting out some parts.

Response activities fit into any of the reading blocks in a balanced program. Many suggestions for response activities can be found in the teacher's manuals of published programs.

Procedures

The following procedures will help you plan and use response activities:

1   Have students read the text using the literacy lesson framework.

2   Give students at least two suggestions of response activities they might do, and let them choose. Students should always be free to devise or choose their own way to respond. Table 4.7 provides examples of several response activi-

Table 4.7
Sample Response Activities

Activity	Comment
Journals	Students write responses in a journal.
Art	Students use drawing, painting, or other creative forms of expression to respond to what they have read. Initially, give prompts such as: <ul><li>Draw your favorite part. Be ready to tell why it's your favorite.</li><li>Paint a picture that shows how this book makes you feel.</li></ul>
Readers Theater	Students write a script of the story and read it aloud as a play.
Debate	Students form teams and debate an issue raised in an informational piece or story.
Posters	Students create a poster about a favorite character or part.
Mobile	Students create a mobile of the story events or the important ideas.
Retelling	Students retell to a partner what they have read.
Discussion groups	Students discuss their reactions in a small group. (See Instructional Strategy 9.)

ties. The For Additional Reading section lists texts that offer many additional suggestions.

3 Share and discuss responses in small groups or with the whole class .

Comments

Students' responses to their reading are a critical part of developing comprehension. You should always have some type of response activity following any instructional reading, but you don't want to overdo responses. Keep in mind that it is not the number of activities the students do that will help them learn to read; it is the amount of reading they do.

Remember too that English-language learners often need to respond in visual or graphic ways because their level of language production may not allow them to successfully respond orally. In some cases, ELLs might work in small groups, organized by primary languages, to discuss the reading in their first language and then report back to the whole class in English.

Instructional Strategy 9: Discussion Circles or Groups

Discussion circles (also known as *discussion groups*) provide time for students to talk about what they have read. We saw one in Mr. Aroyo's class in the Eyewitness at the beginning of this chapter. Discussion circles are small groups of students (usually three to five) who meet together to talk about what they have read. Initially these discussions are prompted by the teacher, who participates and observes as students discuss. As students become more proficient in discussion, they decide for themselves what to discuss, and the teacher's prompts are not needed.

In both balanced literacy programs, discussion circles can be used in all of the reading blocks, including Independent Reading. A discussion circle may focus on a core book that all students have read or experienced, or it may be used following small—group reading of developmentally appropriate books. Discussion during the Independent Reading block includes telling others about each book; it may also involve comparing such things as characters, events, and authors' techniques.

As part of the Learning to Read Words/Core Books and Developing Language and Comprehension/Developmentally Appropriate Books blocks, students should always have some time for discussion of what they have read. This is an important part of developing students' ability to comprehend.

Procedures

After students have completed their reading, the following steps will help you organize and manage discussion circles:

1 Introduce the concept of discussion circles or groups. Role-play the procedures. Develop with students a list of guidelines for class behavior during this time, and post the guidelines where everyone can see them. For instance:

Class Guidelines for Discussion Time

(1) Move quickly to your groups.

(2) Listen while others share.

(3) Think about what each person says. Add your comments.

(4) Stick to your task. Watch your time.

2 Form groups of three to five students; do this by random assignment, your assignment, or student choice. Vary the way in which groups are formed.

3 In the beginning, give two or three written discussion prompts. For *A River Dream* (Say, 1988), the prompts might look like these:

Today's Discussion
Talk about . . .

(1) how Mark and Uncle Scott differed in their feelings about fishing.

(2) what Mark learned about fishing.

(3) anything you feel is important about this story.

4 As students discuss, circulate among the groups, observing and/or participating.

5 As you become more comfortable with the procedure, use it as a form of assessment. Use a simple checklist like the one in Figure 4.5 to observe students as they discuss.

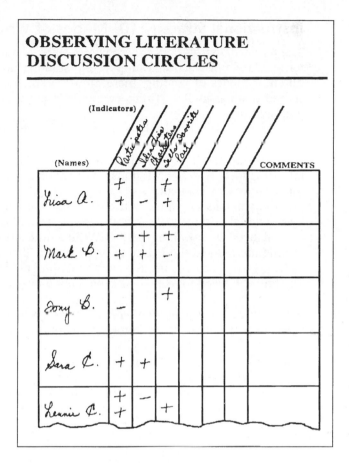

**Figure 4.5
Sample Observation
Checklist for a
Discussion Circle**

6 Provide a time limit for discussion groups to help keep students focused. Usually 3 to 5 minutes is enough in preschool, kindergarten, and first grade. In grades 3 through 8, 5 to 10 minutes is generally sufficient. You will need to use your judgment about the amount of time your students need for discussion. In some instances, it may be more or less than we recommend.

7 Have students share and discuss as a whole class.

Comments

Discussion circles are useful in all aspects of literacy development and throughout the curriculum. They are an important part of teaching students how to comprehend. Through discussions, students demonstrate their use of strategies and have many opportunities to use their thinking processes.

Instructional Strategy 10: Modes of Writing

The *modes of writing* concept is a way to think about different types of writing in terms of their instructional support and student independence. Just as there are different modes of reading, there are different modes of writing: write-aloud, shared writing, guided writing, cooperative/collaborative writing, and independent writing.

Figure 4.6 shows how these modes of writing move from heavy teacher support to student independence, with write-aloud having the greatest amount of teacher support and modeling. Again, this concept is based on Pearson's (1985) idea of gradual release of responsibility. Writing is taught by moving through the modes of writing concept.

You will find that you can use the modes of writing concept throughout the instructional writing blocks in both the Balanced Beginning Literacy Program and the Balanced Literacy Program 3–8. Write-aloud, shared, guided, and cooperative writing are used in the Learning to Write and Teacher-Modeled Writing blocks. Independent writing is used in the Developmentally Appropriate Writing block. The following sections explain the main features of each mode.

Write-Aloud.   In the *write-aloud* mode, the teacher writes something and thinks aloud for students to model thinking that occurs during the writing process. You may do this with students at all stages of literacy development to show them how to use a particular type of writing.

Shared Writing.   *Shared writing* is a process in which students and teacher write a common piece. The teacher does some of the actual writing, and the students

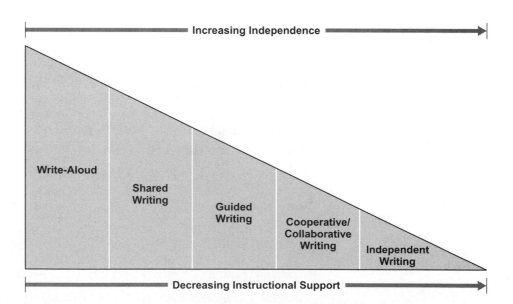

**Figure 4.6
Relationship of Modes of
Writing to Instructional
Support and Students'
Independence**

do some of it. When students actually write the words on the chart or transparency, it becomes **interactive writing.**

The key to shared writing is that both teacher and students have input into the piece. The teacher serves as a model for how to write in a particular domain of writing, such as persuasion or simple description. Shared writing is an effective way to model and teach writing for any age level and is appropriate whenever a difficult concept or task is introduced. The child who writes a report independently in grade 3 may need shared writing again in grade 4 while learning to write more complex reports.

Guided Writing. *Guided writing* takes place when students work on their individual pieces of writing and the teacher models, coaches, and prompts the students, serving as editor as well.

Cooperative/Collaborative Writing. *Cooperative/collaborative writing* occurs when two students work as partners on developing a single product. They take turns writing things down and contributing to the overall piece of writing. The teacher continues to model, coach, and support the students as they need it. Cooperative/collaborative writing is especially motivating for students who dislike writing.

Independent Writing. *Independent writing* is used when students are ready to write on their own, using all the processes, strategies, and skills they have learned. The product from independent writing is usually evaluated.

In this context, *independent writing* refers to a way of scaffolding teacher instruction. This form of independent writing, used in the Developmentally

Students work in pairs to read and respond to each other's writing. Sometimes they discuss possible revisions. Sometimes they act as editor.
© Elizabeth Crews

Appropriate Writing block, should not be confused with what occurs in the Daily Independent Writing block, when students are writing for power and practice on topics and products of their own choosing.

Procedures

The following guidelines will help you use the modes of writing concept:

1   Determine students' writing strengths and needs on the basis of your ongoing assessment and your knowledge of the stages of literacy development.

2   Select the type of writing students need to learn.

3   Begin with write-aloud and proceed through the modes of writing until you achieve student independence with the type of writing you are teaching. This process will take from several days to several weeks depending on the age and grade level you are teaching.

4   Remember that progression from one mode of writing to the next will not necessarily be smooth and continuous. You will often find that you do shared writing and move on to guided writing, only to discover that students need more modeling through shared writing. This process once again illustrates that literacy development is a "jerky continuum." The nature of the writing process and tasks also dictates moving back and forth among the modes.

Comments

The modes of writing concept gives you a clear way to see how to actually teach writing. By moving students through the various modes of writing, you will be able to provide the direct instructional support they need to progress through the stages of literacy development. The modes of writing concept also provides the framework you need to meet individual needs of diverse learners. For more reading on the various modes of writing, see Au et al., Calkins, Cooper, and Graves in For Additional Reading at the conclusion of this chapter.

Instructional Strategy 11: Daily Blocked Plan

The *daily blocked plan* is a pattern for organizing a balanced literacy program on a daily basis. Consisting of blocks and subblocks, it can help you fit in all the components of a balanced literacy program. Table 4.8 presents a sample plan using the blocks of our balanced programs. As you can see from the table, the total amount of time for the daily blocked plan ranges from 90 to 210 minutes per day.

Procedures

You can begin using the daily blocked plan by considering the following guidelines:

1   Think about the grade level you are teaching and the stage of development of your students. Following are *minimum* suggested times for a daily literacy block by grade level:

Table 4.8
Outline of a Sample Daily Blocked Plan for a Balanced Literacy Program

Block	Time Range in Minutes
Daily Independent Reading	10–20
Daily Independent Writing	10–20
Reading	
Learning to Read Words/Core Books	
• Literacy lesson	15–40
• Explicit phonics/structural elements routine *or* explicit comprehension routine	15–20
Developing Language and Comprehension/ Developmentally Appropriate Books	
• Guided reading *or* other modes of reading	15–40
Writing	
• Learning to Write/Teacher-Modeled Writing *or* Developmentally Appropriate Writing	15–40
• Minilessons for writing procedures	5–15
• Minilessons for grammar and spelling	5–15
Total minutes	90–210

Kindergarten	3 hours
Grades 1–2	$2\frac{1}{2}$–$3\frac{1}{2}$ hours
Grades 3–5	$1\frac{1}{2}$–2 hours
Grades 6–8	$1\frac{1}{2}$ hours

2 Study the outline presented in Table 4.8. Develop a schedule appropriate for your class situation. The blocks of the plan may be moved around and taken in different orders.

3 Post the schedule in your classroom. Discuss it with students.

4 Try out the plan and revise it as needed.

Comments

No one schedule or plan works for all teachers. The daily blocked plan provides a flexible framework that allows you to organize and manage a balanced literacy program. Examples of using this plan flexibly are presented in each of the chapters in Part Two. For further reading, see Cooper (2000), listed in For Additional Reading.

Selecting Instructional Strategies To Meet Diverse Needs

You will use the eleven key instructional strategies we have presented throughout your assessment-based balanced literacy program. As you develop your teaching skills, you will learn other strategies to help meet the needs of your students. But how will you select among so many possible strategies?

Think back to Mr. Aroyo's classroom, which we visited at the beginning of this chapter. How did he know what to teach his students? How did he decide which instructional strategies to use? He had to make some important decisions about what to teach and how to teach it.

Mr. Aroyo selected his instructional strategies by considering several factors:

- *The strengths and needs of his students.*   He was continuously assessing what his students could do well in literacy and where they needed to grow and improve their literacy development.

- *Each student's stage of literacy development.*   Prior to our visit, as Mr. Aroyo identified students' strengths and needs, he was always thinking about the stage of development each student had achieved and what was coming next.

- *Students' levels of English proficiency.*   Mr. Aroyo had a number of students who were second-language learners, and he adapted his instruction to their lower level of academic English proficiency. If we had visited his classroom daily for a week or two, we would have seen him provide extra help for ELL students in reading academic content-area texts. Similarly, we would have noticed them responding to the readings in a variety of ways, including labeled pictures, graphics, and short writing assignments.

- *Difficulty of texts in relation to students' achievement levels.*   Mr. Aroyo knew his students' reading abilities, and he was able to match students to texts that were appropriate for them. See Chapter 10 for a full discussion of this topic.

- *How students had learned with previously used instructional strategies.* Each time Mr. Aroyo used an instructional strategy, he was aware of how well it worked with his students. This information helped him make the decisions he needed to make next.

- *Students' interests.*   Mr. Aroyo knew his students' likes and dislikes in terms of reading. He used this information to help him select the books to use with the instructional strategies. Sometimes students themselves selected the book they read or the group with which they worked.

All of these factors guided Mr. Aroyo's selection of instructional strategies to use with his class. Sometimes he was pleased with his decisions, sometimes he wasn't. He made adjustments daily. He built his knowledge and experience through trial and error. This is the same process you will use in selecting instructional strategies for your classroom. It all takes place through ongoing assessment.

Throughout the next five chapters (Chapters 5 through 9), we will illustrate how you can use assessment to help you make decisions in planning instruction and selecting instructional strategies for students at each stage of literacy development.

Materials for Balanced Literacy Instruction

A variety of materials is needed to operate a balanced literacy program, and part of your decision-making process will involve choosing materials appropriate for your students, as Mr. Aroyo did in the Eyewitness section. We will explore this topic more fully in Chapter 10; here we introduce some general ideas about the types of text you will use, how you will level them (that is, decide their degree of difficulty), and how you can organize your materials.

Types of Text

Different texts are used for different purposes. Texts can be divided broadly into two types, authentic literature and decodable texts:

- *Authentic literature* (or text) refers to any piece of text that is in the original form as written by the author. This includes narrative text (stories), expository text (informational), and procedural text (directions). Authentic literature can be used for any aspect of reading instruction.

- *Decodable texts,* as already mentioned, are those specifically written to use only certain decoding elements and high-frequency words that students have been taught. These are often called *controlled vocabulary texts* or *created texts.* They are short, and they are used for immediate practice and application of decoding skills, whether related to phonics or to structural analysis.

All children can learn to read using authentic literature. However, in the beginning stages children may benefit from texts that let them "try their wings of reading" by immediately using the skills they are learning. Decodable texts are used for this purpose because it is often very difficult to find authentic literature that covers only the phonics and decoding skills taught to beginning readers.

As soon as children develop independence in decoding (most by the end of grade 1), decodable texts become less important. Many teachers, however, will continue to use decodable texts through third grade to provide students with practice in fluency. These texts are used along with authentic literature as the core for literacy instruction.

You will hear many other terms related to types of text, including the following:

- *Anthology:* a collection of texts bound in one volume. Some collections may not include all the illustrations of the original work.

- *Literature sets:* books that you have in multiple copies. These are often called *class sets* or *small-group sets.*

- *Library books (trade books):* authentic literature books available in single copies. Usually they are the books students select for independent reading. Literature sets may be multiple copies of such books.

Knowing these terms will help you as you read and listen to what is being said about literacy instruction.

Leveling Texts

Leveling texts—that is, placing them in order of their difficulty—is important in beginning reading instruction because students need to ease gradually into the process of reading until they become independent in decoding (Clay, 1991). Clay calls this creating a "gradient of difficulty" for books.

There is no one right or absolute way to level or sequence texts. We do not believe, however, that the use of the traditional readability formula is the best way to level texts in light of what we know about literacy learning (Weaver & Kintsch, 1991). (See Chapter 10 for a full discussion of readability.) Table 4.9 presents one set of criteria for leveling and sequencing texts at the beginning stages of reading (Peterson, 1991). These criteria can be used through about second grade. These leveling guidelines simply give you a way to order texts from simple to complex. The level numbers do *not* equate to grade levels.

Even beyond the beginning stages of literacy development, it is often helpful to level texts, especially for students who are experiencing difficulty in learning to read. Table 4.10 presents a set of leveling criteria that were developed for use in grades 3 to 6 (Cooper, Boschken, McWilliams, & Pistochini, 1999). Again, the category numbers do not equate with grade levels; they just provide a framework for putting more complex texts in order of difficulty.

Organizing Materials

Having instructional materials organized for easy access and use within a school is especially important when selecting books that are developmentally appropriate for students. We recommend that criteria similar to those presented in Tables 4.9 and 4.10 be used to organize all of the sets of books within a central location in a school. If your school isn't doing this, you might want to try it within your own class and then encourage other staff members to consider the idea for the entire school. This will help facilitate the creation of a school-wide balanced literacy program that is assessment based.

Intervention Models

Recall that there are three goals for the balanced literacy program: power and practice, instruction, and additional support (refer back to Figures 4.2 and 4.3). The third goal, providing additional support, is for those students who are experiencing difficulty in learning to read or who have special learning needs. The extra instruction they receive, called *intervention,* is provided *in addition to* the regular classroom instruction. Let's examine the concept of intervention.

Intervention Defined

Intervention, according to *The American Heritage Dictionary,* is the act of coming into or between to hinder or alter an action. A **reading intervention program** provides students with additional instruction in reading that is designed to accelerate

Table 4.9
Criteria for Leveling Texts for Beginning Readers

LEVELS 1–4
- Consistent placement of print
- Repetition of 1–2 sentence patterns (1–2 word changes)
- Oral language structures
- Familiar objects and actions
- Illustrations provide high support

LEVELS 5–8
- Repetition of 2–3 sentence patterns (phrases may change)
- Opening, closing sentences vary
- Or, varied simple sentence patterns
- Predominantly oral language structures
- Many familiar objects and actions
- Illustrations provide moderate–high support

LEVELS 9–12
- Repetitions of 3 or more sentence patterns
- Or, varied sentence patterns (repeated phrases or refrains)
- Blend of oral and written language structures
- Or, fantastic happenings in framework of familiar experiences
- Illustrations provide moderate support

LEVELS 13–15
- Varied sentence patterns (may have repeated phrases or refrains)
- Or, repeated patterns in cumulative form
- Written language structures
- Oral structures appear in dialogue
- Conventional story, literary language
- Specialized vocabulary for some topics
- Illustrations provide low–moderate support

LEVELS 16–20
- Elaborated episodes and events
- Extended descriptions
- Links to familiar stories
- Literary language
- Unusual, challenging vocabulary
- Illustrations provide low support

Source: © Peterson, B. (1991). Selecting books for beginning readers. In D. E. DeFord, C. A. Lyons, & G. S. Pinnell (Eds.), *Bridges to literacy* (pp. 119–147). Portsmouth, NH: Heinemann.

Table 4.10
Criteria for Leveling Texts for Grades 3 to 6

Category I

- Small amount of print per page. (The majority of pages have one to three sentences.)
- Pictures/illustrations are clear and uncluttered, and they directly support the text.
- Text for both fiction and nonfiction is narrative, with a clear, easy-to-follow storyline.

Category II

- Still a small amount of print per page, but text can increase to one or two paragraphs on the majority of pages. Short lines of dialogue may increase the amount of text per page.
- Pictures/illustrations still give direct text support; two or three spot vignettes on a page are appropriate.
- Expository nonfiction on highly focused topics with simply stated main ideas and few supporting details. (Often a picture or photograph illustrates each main idea.)
- Short captions (a word, a phrase, or one sentence) may accompany pictures. Simple diagrams with clear labels are appropriate.
- Narrative storylines remain simple.

Category III

- Increasing print with several paragraphs per page. Books themselves become longer.
- Pictures/illustrations are less supportive of text. Captions may increase in length.
- Narrative texts have a clear storyline, but now multiple characters are appropriate.
- In expository texts the topics may broaden; main ideas increase in complexity with more supporting details.
- Text may contain a secondary element, such as sidebars or speech balloons.
- More inferencing is required by the nature of the text.

Category IV

- Text increases to fill the page.
- Narrative storylines become more complex: there may be subplots, mysteries, or multiple problems that require critical thinking.
- In expository texts the topics expand to include subtopics, which may be organized by chapter; main ideas increase in complexity and contain more details, requiring readers to organize and analyze information.

(continued)

Table 4.10
Criteria for Leveling Texts for Grades 3 to 6 (cont.)

- Picture support is less direct; pages may be designed more for visual effect than to help readers with the text. Chapter books may contain spot art or **none at all.**

Category V

- Number of chapters increases.

- Size of print decreases as amount of text per page increases.

- Picture support is minimal or nonexistent. Book length may increase to 80–100+ pages.

- In narrative texts, greater inferencing skills are required to follow complex story lines containing multiple characters. Problems, which are multiple, are more sophisticated.

- In expository texts, an increasing amount of new information is presented with more complex text organization. Readers may be required to sift through information and make decisions about how relevant each detail is to the topic at hand.

Source: Cooper, J. D., Boschken, I., McWilliams, J., & Pistochini, L. (1999). *A study of the effectiveness of an intervention program designed to accelerate reading for struggling readers in the upper grades—Final report.* Boston: Houghton Mifflin Company.

their reading to an age-appropriate level. The primary goal of reading intervention is to prevent or stop reading failure. Students who receive intervention instruction are given the program *only for as long as they need it.*

Reading intervention is very different from remedial reading, which has been the model used for years to plan instruction for students who are having difficulty learning to read (Harris & Sipay, 1985). Remediation has been based on the assumption that teachers should wait until children have a problem and then try to correct it; most of the time it was too late for the students, and the overall remediation never worked (Allington & Walmsley, 1995). The concept of reading intervention is replacing the concept of remediation because intervention is more effective in preventing or stopping failure in reading (Hiebert & Taylor, 1994).

You cannot think about reading intervention, however, without considering the entire balanced literacy program we have discussed throughout this book and specifically in this chapter. The primary goal of the balanced literacy program is to prevent failure in literacy learning. According to existing research, *all* children need the highest-quality literacy instruction to learn how to read and write; however, *some* children need all of this instruction *plus* intervention to achieve success in literacy, especially reading (Snow, Burns, & Griffin, 1998).

Reading intervention can be provided in three ways:

- *Within the classroom:* This can be done by the classroom teacher with a small group at some time during the day, or a specialist may come into the room to teach the small group. All existing evidence suggests that intervention should be provided by certified teachers (Snow, Burns, & Griffin, 1998). If an aide or assistant is available, the teacher should provide the intervention while the aide monitors the remainder of the class.

- *Pullout program:*   With this model, students leave your classroom for a period of instruction. Many problems exist with this model (Allington & Walmsley, 1995), the major one being indicated by the question: *When* do students leave the classroom? The only acceptable answer to this question is: *any time other than when literacy instruction is being provided.*

- *Extended-day program:*   In this model, students come to school early or stay later for additional instruction. A certified teacher provides the instruction.

Regardless of the model used to provide intervention, it is critical that the intervention support be consistent with the overall classroom literacy program.

Most intervention programs developed to date focus on the beginning reading levels because evidence supports the idea that the earlier the intervention is provided, the better it is for students (Snow, Burns, & Griffin, 1998). Although this is true, some students beyond the beginning reading levels are still reading considerably below their age-appropriate level (Mullis, Campbell, & Farstrup, 1993; NAEP [National Assessment of Education Progress], 1995). Therefore, models for intervention are needed for upper-grade students as well.

In the rest of this section, we will present brief descriptions of four types of reading intervention programs that have solid research evidence supporting their effectiveness: total school reorganization programs, individual tutorial programs, small-group models for beginning readers, and a small-group model for intermediate-level students. Refer to For Additional Reading and the references cited in the chapter to find further information on the programs of interest to you.

Total School Reorganization Programs

Success for All (Slavin et al., 1996) is an example of a reading intervention program that requires total school reorganization in grades 1 through 3. Students are regrouped homogeneously across the three grades and given 90 minutes of direct instruction daily. Individual tutoring sessions are provided for students who show signs of falling behind. This model has been implemented in many inner-city school districts throughout the United States.

Individual Tutorial Programs

Another type of intervention program focuses on tutoring of individual students. *Reading Recovery,* for example, is an individual tutorial program for first-grade children developed in New Zealand (Clay, 1985) and transferred to the United States (Pinnell, Fried, & Estice, 1990). Each student receives 30 minutes of instruction per day for a set number of days in addition to balanced classroom instruction. The goal of the program is to get students up to level; if the program doesn't work, a different alternative is sought after the set number of days.

A great deal of research has been conducted with Reading Recovery (Swartz & Klein, 1997). While the program usually seems effective in its initial stages, issues have been raised about its lasting gains and transfer effects for students (Snow, Burns, & Griffin, 1998). Schools considering Reading Recovery should look carefully at the cost effectiveness of the program in comparison to other alternatives available.

Small-Group Models for Beginning Readers

There are many small-group models for reading intervention (Hiebert & Taylor, 1994). Three that have received much attention are *Early Intervention in Reading (EIR)* (Taylor, Frye, Short, & Shearer, 1992), *Right Start* (Hiebert, Colt, Catto, & Gury, 1992), and *Facilitating Reading for Optimum Growth (FROG)* (Hall, Prevatte, & Cunningham, 1992). All three of these small-group models are designed for first- and second-grade students. A comparison of these and other models (Pikulski, 1994) revealed that they have many common characteristics:

- Small-group instruction (three to five students)
- Intervention instruction provided in addition to quality classroom instruction
- Simple texts with natural language, leveled and sequenced in difficulty
- Structured, fast-paced lessons
- Repeated reading of texts
- Instruction on word parts
- Writing
- Ongoing assessment
- Home-school connections
- Strong teacher preparation

Small-Group Model for Intermediate Students

Project SUCCESS (Cooper, Boschken, McWilliams, & Pistochini, 1999) is a small-group (five to seven students) intervention model designed specifically for students in grades 3 through 8. While it builds on what has been learned from early intervention programs, it has special features that accommodate the needs of below-level readers in the upper grades.

Project SUCCESS has a system for leveling and sequencing literature that is used in structured lessons incorporating the research-proven strategies of reciprocal teaching (Palincsar & Brown, 1986) and graphic organizers (Pehrsson & Robinson, 1985). Table 4.11 presents an outline of the lesson structure for Project SUCCESS, which is taught by a certified teacher 40 minutes per day in addition to the balanced classroom program the students receive.

Research with Project SUCCESS using fourth graders in a national study showed that statistically significant gains were made after an average of 76 days of instruction (Cooper, Boschken, McWilliams, & Pistochini, 1999). Project SUCCESS has been used as the basis for a published program, *Soar to Success* (Cooper, Boschken, McWilliams, & Pistochini, 1998), which has also been very effective for English-language learners.

Table 4.11
The Project SUCCESS Instructional Model

Key Features

- Forty minutes per day in addition to regular classroom instruction
- Fast-paced lessons using reciprocal teaching and graphic organizers
- Taught by certified teachers
- Uses trade books

Component	Description	Rationale
Revisiting (5 minutes)	• Students reread, alone or with a partner, previously read SUCCESS books. • Teacher takes a running record of a retelling or coaches individuals. *or* • A group conference about independently read books is held.	• Builds fluency. • Develops comprehension. • Builds connection between learning to read and independent reading.
Reviewing (5 minutes)	• Students summarize previous day's reading using graphic organizers. • Students and teacher discuss strategies used and share examples of use beyond SUCCESS.	• Develops comprehension. • Keeps students focused on the same four strategies. (See the Reading section later in this table.)
Rehearsing (10 minutes)	• A quick text talk, guided preview, cooperative preview, or independent preview is done for new text to be read. • Students may predict, question, or start a K-W-L chart.	• Builds background, specifically for the text to be read. • Sets purpose for reading.

Reading (15 minutes)	• Students silently read a predetermined meaningful chunk of text to verify predictions or answer questions.
	 • Following reading, reciprocal teaching is employed, with students and teacher taking turns assuming the role of teacher modeling for these four strategies:
	
	    Summarize *Clarify*
	    Question *Predict*
		• Applies strategies and develops comprehension.
		 • Develops students' ability to construct meaning.

(continued)

Table 4.11
The Project SUCCESS Instructional Model (cont.)

Component	Description	Rationale
Responding/ Reflecting (5 minutes)	• Students do one or more of the following: 　Make a written response 　Complete graphic organizers 　Reflect on strategies 　Discuss and share	• Develops comprehension. • Develops use of strategies.
Home Connection	• The completed book is sent home with a letter to be signed and returned with the book.	• Shares student success with home. • Builds self-esteem.

Using Intervention Models with Title I and Special Education Programs

All the models of intervention described in this section are appropriate for use with special education students. The same is true for children in Title I programs (federally funded programs for students in high-poverty schools and other at-risk children). The intervention models provide the type of structured, fast-paced, focused instruction that will help students with special needs achieve success.

When considering the use of an intervention model for Title I or special education, remember that intervention is *in addition to* the basic core program. Look back at Figures 4.2 and 4.3. Note that the bar of intervention is supported by the six blocks in the classroom. For example, if your school has a pullout concept for special education, sending students to a resource room for part of the day, those students should *never* miss their reading or language arts instruction in the regular classroom. This is also true for English-language learners. Students who are having difficulty learning to read need good instruction in the classroom *plus* good intervention instruction (Snow, Burns, & Griffin, 1998).

Summary

This chapter has presented two models for a balanced literacy program: a Balanced Beginning Literacy Program for grades K through 2 and a Balanced Literacy Program 3–8. Each model contains components to meet the needs of diverse learners. Each provides blocks of time for students to build power through independent reading and independent writing. Each provides blocks for whole-group, small-group, or individual instruction and practice in oral language, reading, and writing. An intervention block provides additional support for students who are experiencing difficulty in learning. Both models are assessment-based programs; that is, the teacher continuously thinks about students' performance in relation to the stages of literacy development and uses assessment information to plan further instruction.

We have described eleven basic instructional strategies that are important in such a program: the literacy lesson, minilessons, the explicit phonics/structural elements routine, the explicit comprehension routine, the decodable words routine, the phonetically unpredictable words routine, modes of reading, response activities, discussion circles or groups, modes of writing, and the daily blocked plan. These strategies can be used repeatedly with students at various stages of literacy development. At any given point in your instruction, you can select among the strategies on the basis of your students' strengths, needs, and interests.

A balanced literacy program requires a variety of materials. There are uses for both decodable texts and authentic literature of various types. It is important to level all of these books in terms of difficulty according to an appropriate set of criteria.

For students who need additional support, a reading intervention program helps to prevent reading failure. Intervention programs may involve total school reorganization, individual tutorial programs, or small-group models. Whatever the type of intervention, it should be given in addition to, not in place of, the regular literacy instruction.

This chapter concludes Part One, which has provided the theoretical basis, background information, and framework necessary for understanding assessment-based instruction in a balanced literacy program. Part Two focuses on specific stages of literacy development.

FOR ADDITIONAL READING

Au, K. H., Carroll, J. H., & Scheu, J. A. (1997). *Balanced literacy instruction: A teacher's resource book.* Norword, MA: Christopher-Gordon Publishers. See especially the sections on these topics: Experience-Text-Relationship (E-T-R) lessons (pages 113–119), minilessons (pages 88–91, 223–225), responses to literature (pages 127–135), and discussion groups (pages 148–152).

Blair-Larson, S. M., & Williams, K. A. (Eds.). (1999). *The balanced reading program.* Newark, DE: International Reading Association. Good chapters on all aspects of a balanced program at various grade levels.

Calkins, L. M. (1994). *The art of teaching writing* (Rev. ed.). Portsmouth, NH: Heinemann.

Cooper, J. D. (2000). *Literacy: Helping children construct meaning* (4th ed.). Boston: Houghton Mifflin. See especially the sections on these topics: literacy lessons (pages 55–58 and sample lessons at the conclusions of Chapters 2, 3, 4, and 5), minilessons (pages 59–60), modes of reading (pages 34–43), modes of writing (pages 43–47), responses (Chapter 6), discussion circles (pages 321–325), comprehension strategies (Chapter 8), and daily blocked plans (Chapter 10).

Eldredge, J. L. (1995). *Teaching decoding in holistic classrooms.* Englewood Cliffs, NJ: Merrill/Prentice Hall. Chapter 10 is especially strong in routines for teaching phonics. The entire text is a good reference on teaching all aspects of decoding.

Fountas, I. C., & Pinnell, G. S. (1996). *Guided reading: Good first teaching for all children.* Portsmouth, NH: Heinemann. This text focuses on observational guided reading; good information for K–3 teachers.

Gambrell, L. B., & Almasi, J. R. (1996). *Lively discussions! Fostering engaged reading*. Newark, DE: International Reading Association. The entire text is helpful in understanding the use of discussion.

Graves, D. H. (1983). *Writing: Teachers and children at work*. Exeter, NH: Heinemann Educational Books.

Graves, D. H. (1994). *A fresh look at writing*. Portsmouth, NH: Heinemann.

Hiebert, E., & Taylor, B. (Eds.). (1994). *Getting reading right from the start: Effective early literacy interventions*. Needham Heights, MA: Allyn & Bacon. A good discussion of early literacy intervention.

Moustafa, M. (1997). *Beyond traditional phonics: Research discoveries and reading instruction*. Portsmouth, NH: Heinemann.

Peregoy, S. F., & Boyle, O. W. (1997). *Reading, writing and learning in ESL* (2nd ed.). New York: Longman. See especially the sections on these topics: English-language learners in school (pages 1–24), second-language acquisition (pages 27–56), and classroom practices for English-language learners (pages 59–97).

Pikulski, J. J. (1994). Preventing reading failure: A review of five effective programs. *The Reading Teacher, 48*(1), 30–39.

Roser, N. L., & Martinez, M. G. (1995). *Book talk and beyond*. Newark, DE: International Reading Association. This entire text is useful for discussions and response activities.

Strickland, D. S. (1998). *Teaching phonics today: A primer for educators*. Newark, DE: International Reading Association.

Tierney, R. J., Readence, J. E., & Dishner, E. K. (1990). *Reading strategies and practices: A compendium* (3rd ed.). Boston: Allyn & Bacon. See especially the section on Directed Reading-Thinking Activity (pages 12–20).

Trachtenburg, P. (1990). Using children's literature to enhance phonics instruction. *The Reading Teacher, 43*, pp. 648–654.

FOR EXPLORATION: ELECTRONIC RESOURCES

A to Z Teacher Stuff: LessonPlanZ.com–The Lesson Plans Search Engine. **http://LessonPlanz.com/Language_Arts_Lesson_Plans/** This web site features links to language arts lesson plans for use with students of all ages, from preschool through high school, along with links to a wide variety of other resources. The main web site, **http://www.atozteacherstuff.com/**, contains links to other subject areas as well.

Best Practices Portfolio: Language and Literacy. **http://www.osr.state.ga.us/bestprac/language/ll_toc.htm** Created by the Georgia Office of School Readiness, this site offers teachers and parents information about expressive (oral and written) and receptive (listening and reading) language literacy skills important for children entering kindergarten. The site provides links to activities and instructional strategies that teachers can use to develop early literacy skills.

Literacy Components. **http://www.beth.k12.pa.us/schools/spring_garden/Bethmann/mainmen .html** For each of a variety of instructional strategies—including strategies that this chapter has described as modes of reading and modes of writing—the site discusses implementation in the classroom and summarizes the relationship between the strategy and current research about the brain.

Literature Circles.
http://toread.com/strategies.html   Besides information about setting up literature circles, this site discusses the various roles played by teacher and students and lists useful assessment techniques.

Preventing Reading Difficulties in Young Children.
http://books.nap.edu/html/prdyc/   This web site provides full access to the report from the Committee on the Prevention of Reading Difficulties in Young Children, established by the National Academy of Sciences. The report, *Preventing Reading Difficulties in Young Children* (Snow, Burns, & Griffin, 1998), is one of the most current and comprehensive investigations of reading problems and reading instruction.

Reading Recovery.
http://connwww.iu5.org./cvelem/ReadingRecovery.html   This site provides a detailed outline of a Reading Recovery lesson, along with information about some of the reading strategies children use as they progress through the program.

Soar to Success: The Intermediate Intervention Program.
http://www.eduplace.com/rdg/soar/   The web site for the Soar to Success reading intervention program offers information about the intensive training model, research articles regarding the intervention's success, comments from classroom teachers, and a discussion forum.

Winston-Salem Project.
http://www.ncrel.org/sdrs/areas/issues/students/atrisk/at7lk23.htm   This site describes the Winston-Salem literacy instruction project, designed by Patricia Cunningham of Wake Forest University in collaboration with teachers Dorothy Hall and Connie Prevatte, as well as the project's support program, Facilitating Reading for Optimum Growth (FROG), which provided daily instruction in small, heterogeneous groups.

CLASSROOM APPLICATIONS

1. Locate a school or classroom that claims to have a balanced literacy program. Observe several classes; note how English-language learners and other special-needs students receive instruction. Compare the program to the balanced literacy models presented in this chapter.

2. Obtain access to a small group of students. Select one or more of the instructional strategies presented in this chapter and use it with the group. Write a reflection about how it worked for you.

3. Visit a school that has a Title I reading program. Observe a group and interview the teacher. Compare what you see to what you learned about intervention in this chapter. Would you say the school has a remedial program or an intervention program?

Assessing Literacy Learning for Instruction

The Early Emergent Literacy Stage

FOCUS

As you read the Eyewitness section, ask yourself the following questions:
1. What has the teacher done to encourage literacy growth?
2. Which activities are related to literacy development?

Eyewitness *We are looking through the doorway into a bustling prekindergarten class. At first, we don't even see the teacher. Children are busy everywhere.*

In one center, a little girl is putting her dolly to bed. She tucks the covers around her "baby's" shoulders and kisses it on the forehead. Then she takes a book and settles down in a rocking chair nearby to read a bedtime story. She turns pages as she tells the story, holding the book for her baby to see the pictures.

In another center, children are shopping for groceries, consulting a list, choosing cans and boxes, paying, and putting things in bags. Another group is listening to a story read aloud by an adult who stops from time to time for children to predict what they think will happen next. Two children are in a writing center. They have drawn pictures and are writing captions with markers and signing their names. One child is using the computer in the far corner. She knows how to turn it on and find a game she likes to play. Then she goes back to the screen she started from so the computer is ready for the next child.

Finally, we spot the teacher, Mr. Gomez. He is holding a clipboard and making notes as he observes the children. After a while, he calls all the children to a rug in front of the rocking chair. Together they recite nursery rhymes while Mr. Gomez points to the words in a big-book version.

Jeff Gomez is the bilingual head teacher in this very busy, diverse, assessment-based preschool. He notes what each child is doing throughout the day. He keeps a folder on each child, recording anecdotal evidence of growth in language and literacy as well as in other areas of development.

In this classroom, children explore using all of their abilities, including language. The tools of literacy are everywhere, within easy reach. There are books, paper, pencils, crayons, markers, a computer, an old typewriter, magnetic letters, word cards, movable cardboard letters, and alphabet blocks. Wherever the children look, they see print, both in the classroom and in their greater environment. Often this print is in more than one language.

These children already sense that print plays an important part in life, even though they may not yet be able to articulate this understanding. They are learning which life situations call for the use of print. Children who are steeped in such a rich literacy environment will learn to read and write more easily because they know how the process is supposed to work. They *expect* print to be an important part of their lives.

For all teachers, this is one of the most thrilling stages of literacy development to witness. It is also the most critical stage of literacy development. A thorough review of the research on preventing reading difficulties in young children verifies that what happens in this early stage influences all aspects of the child's future literacy development (Snow, Burns, & Griffin, 1998).

In this chapter, we focus on the period of development just before the one most commonly called "emergent literacy." We call this stage **Early Emergent Literacy,** yet much of what we discuss here could be considered part of the

Emergent Literacy stage. The lines between stages are blurry rather than clear-cut. Actually, children are emerging into literacy from the day they are born.

You observe a child at this stage and say, "He's getting there. It won't be long now. He's so curious about all of this literacy stuff." If the emergent reader and writer is like a butterfly emerging from a cocoon, the Early Emergent Literacy stage perhaps is the cocoon stage: hidden, but growing and developing until it can't help but emerge.

BENCHMARKS ▶ for the Early Emergent Literacy Stage

The following outline shows benchmarks for the Early Emergent Literacy stage. Read over these benchmarks before you read the chapter. You will want to refer to them as you study the remainder of the chapter. The sample indicators or behaviors given for each benchmark are just that: samples. Many other behaviors could also indicate the presence or achievement of a benchmark. Be aware, too, that the indicators for oral language, reading, and writing often relate closely to one another; none of these behaviors happens in isolation.

These behaviors are typical of children 3 to 5, preschool through kindergarten. In some rare cases, a child will display some or all of these behaviors as early as age 2. In other rare cases, these behaviors may still reflect the extent of the literacy development of an older child.

Oral Language

The child shows through both receptive (listening) and productive (speaking) behaviors that language development is occurring.

BENCHMARK ▶ **The child shows pleasure in stories, poems, and informational texts.**

✔ Attends to read-alouds

✔ Attends to programs on television and will predict future events during commercials

✔ Can retell stories in sequence or tell what a story or an expository text is "about"

✔ Uses book language when retelling a story (example: "Once upon a time . . . ") and an informational text

✔ Likes to make up stories

✔ Tells a story or gives information to go with a picture

BENCHMARK ▶ **The child shows growing facility with the functions (uses) of language.**

✔ Retains oral directions to do more than one thing; usually can tell the directions back

✔ Makes verbal requests or gives verbal orders that others understand

✔ Asks questions for information and for permission

✔ Converses with peers and adults

✔ Reports orally on events in his or her life

BENCHMARK ➤ **The child enjoys word play.**

✔ Likes to play word games

✔ Pretends or role-plays using appropriate language

✔ Repeats and uses (sometimes inappropriately) new words

BENCHMARK ➤ **The child shows increasing knowledge of grammar and other language conventions.**

✔ Tells you a sentence doesn't make sense or sound right if incorrect syntax or incorrect facts are presented

✔ Is generalizing about such language oddities as irregular plurals and verb forms

✔ May be able to identify what is or is not a complete sentence, though cannot tell why

Reading and Book Knowledge

BENCHMARK ➤ **The child has acquired many concepts about print.**

✔ Has concepts about books and print

✔ Knows that labels name products or tell about something

✔ Asks questions about print and about own writing, scribbling, or drawing

✔ Knows the purpose of some print

✔ Likes playing with movable and/or magnetic letters, arranging them into "words" and "reading" them or asking an adult, "What word did I make?"

BENCHMARK ➤ **The child is familiar with various genres.**

✔ Knows several/many nursery rhymes

✔ Knows several/many traditional stories such as fairy tales

BENCHMARK ➤ **The child begins to construct meaning.**

✔ Predicts what will happen next or what word or phrase comes next during read-aloud

✔ Makes up stories to go with pictures

✔ Can retell a story he or she has heard

✔ Can play games such as "What if . . . "

BENCHMARK ➡ **The child enjoys literature and language.**

> ✔ Enjoys listening to stories read aloud
> ✔ Wants favorite stories read over and over
> ✔ Looks at books independently
> ✔ Pretends to read
> ✔ Enjoys playing with sounds and words

Writing and Uses of Writing

BENCHMARK ➡ **The child knows the purpose of writing.**

> ✔ Understands that the marks on a paper mean something
> ✔ Wants to write messages, letters, greeting cards, and shopping lists

BENCHMARK ➡ **The child tries to communicate in writing.**

> ✔ Uses paper and pencil (marker, crayon, chalk, typewriter, computer) to attempt to write
> ✔ Arranges movable letters, writes string of letter-like shapes, or hits random string of letters on a keyboard, then asks, "What did I say?"

BENCHMARK ➡ **The child connects reading and writing.**

> ✔ Wants to label own pictures
> ✔ Understands that stories are made up by a person who thought of the story and then wrote it down, and that he or she can do this also
> ✔ Can spin out a story to go with attempts at writing and with drawings

Connecting To Other Chapters

In each of the five "stage" chapters, Chapters 5 through 9, we present assessment information and instructional ideas based on the child's stage of literacy development. Bear in mind that while most children who are at a particular stage are also at a similar age, not all children are at the same stage at the same time.

If the assessments for a given stage are not appropriate for a particular child in your class, you may need to use some of the assessments suggested for an earlier or a later stage. For example, if you teach preschool children, you would use the suggestions in this chapter to assess the benchmark behaviors for the Early Emergent Literacy stage. However, if you have a child in your class who already knows some letters and words or is already reading, you would not administer the assessment about concepts of books and print given in this chapter. Instead, you would use assessments from the Emergent Literacy stage described in Chapter 6.

Keep in mind, too, the foundations laid in earlier chapters: the framework for assessment-based literacy instruction presented in Chapter 1, the assessment

techniques described in Chapters 2 and 3, and the instructional strategies outlined in Chapter 4. All of these are relevant as you begin reading about the five
stages of literacy development.

Using the Benchmarks to Assess the Child and Determine the Stage of Instruction

FOCUS As you read this chapter, ask yourself the following questions:

1. How will you assess oral language, reading and book knowledge, and writing in young children?

2. How can you use what you learn to make instructional plans for each child?

3. How will your understanding of English-language learners lead to assessment and instructional decisions?

4. How will you plan a balanced day for children at this stage?

Three areas of Early Emergent Literacy can be assessed informally: oral language,
reading and book knowledge, and writing and the uses of writing. In this chapter,
we show you how to assess benchmarks in each of these areas. We also suggest
some ways to promote achievement of each benchmark in those children who are
not there yet.

Your job as the teacher of a group of children is to use the appropriate assessments for each child's literacy development, whatever his or her age. At the same
time, we recognize that teachers are often required to assess children using prescribed benchmarks for certain ages or grades. After you comply with the school
requirements, we suggest that you consider whether you have found out what you
need to know to teach each child appropriately. If not, you may need to go beyond
the school-required assessment.

Figure 5.1 will help you visualize the areas to be assessed and their component parts. Think of the figure as a menu. As we discuss each area, we will show
details of each part.

As we present informal assessments and suggest instructional activities, we
will occasionally add commentary about how a behavior, assessment, or instruction might vary for English-language learners (ELL students). Benchmark behaviors for these children may not occur in the same way or in the same sequence as
for those for whom English is the first language. Such children face a temporary
hurdle as they learn English, but they should not be treated as having a learning
disability (unless that condition coexists with their status as ELL students). Most
important, we caution you not to think that what we say here is all you need to
know about such learners; rather, we just want to alert you to differences that may

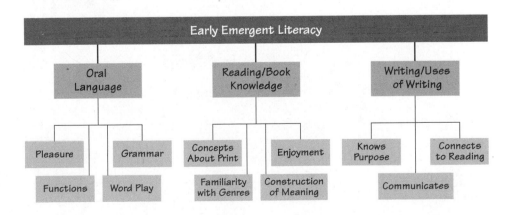

**Figure 5.1
Menus for Assessing
the Early Emergent
Literacy Stage**

have more to do with the child's status of learning English than with his or her literacy development.

Oral Language

Most oral language can be assessed in the routine course of your day with the children. You do not need a special activity or a special instrument. Observation is your best tool.

For this stage, there are four key areas of oral language: pleasure in stories, poems, and information (Figure 5.2); functions of language (Figure 5.3); word play (Figure 5.4); and grammar and other conventions (Figure 5.5). We show you how to assess each behavior and give some instructional strategies to use if a behavior is not yet present. At the end of the section, you will find a sample class checklist that includes all areas of oral language (Figure 5.6). A sample individual checklist is in the Resource File.

BENCHMARK

The child shows pleasure in stories, poems, and informational texts (Figure 5.2).

✔ Attends to read-alouds
✔ Attends to programs on television and will predict future events during commercials

Read-alouds, as you know from Chapter 4, are sessions in which you or someone else reads aloud to the children. As you read aloud to a group or as the children watch television, note their behavior. Which children are attending? Do some pay attention for some reading or some programs and not for others?

Do some children offer predictions as they watch a particular show or commercial? Are the predictions logical? That is, are they supported by the picture(s), the title, previous story or program events, typical story or program structure, and background experience?

Instructional Strategies. Unless you are delivering curriculum-dictated content, it may not be necessary for every child to attend to everything you read aloud or everything watched on television. It is unreasonable to expect all chil-

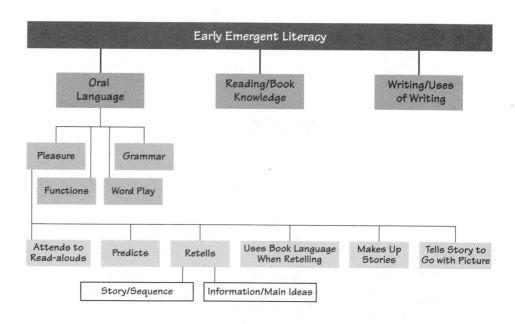

Figure 5.2
Oral Language: Pleasure

This teacher is sharing good literature with children.
© Elizabeth Crews

dren to like everything. Try a variety of books and poems; try to match children's interests. Work to improve your oral reading ability through practice.

Try to motivate attentive listening by engaging children in predicting; showing a picture, film, or object related to the story; changing seating arrangements; or monitoring the duration of your reading. When appropriate, model good listening.

When children cannot make logical predictions, you need to model the process. When illogical predictions are offered, gently examine why they probably are not acceptable. Often children at this stage simply need more experience in being asked to predict and then to pay attention to whether their predictions come true.

✔ Can retell stories in sequence or tell what a story or an expository text is "about"

✔ Uses book language when retelling a story (example: "Once upon a time . . . ") and an informational text

When you ask children to retell the story, or when you overhear a child retelling a story to a doll, a stuffed animal, or a friend, is the retelling basically complete and accurate? Did the child use book language, that is, begin with a phrase such as "Once upon a time . . . "?

Instructional Strategies. If retelling is not consistently present, model it. Talk about what is included and what is omitted. Try modeling retelling, first using your own everyday language and then using book language: "Listen to these two ways to begin retelling a story: 'A little girl went for a walk.' 'Once upon a time, a young girl went into the woods to walk.'"

✔ Likes to make up stories

Give each child a chance to make up a story based on an event, an object, or pure fantasy. Invite children to come to you individually when they are ready to tell you a story they have made up. As they tell their stories, listen to see if story elements are present.

Instructional Strategies.   Most children will learn to make up stories if given a chance. At this stage, a chance is usually all they need. If children continue to omit certain story elements, reinforce these in group discussions based on stories you read aloud. Also, guide the children with questions such as "How about giving Susie a problem to solve?"

> ✔ Tells a story or gives information to go with a picture

As you circulate observing children's artwork, ask for a story to go with the picture. Not all pictures, of course, will produce a story. Some will simply be representations of things, nature, or feelings. In this case, the child may offer descriptive comments rather than a story. But try to elicit a story from each child based on a picture he or she has drawn or one that you provide.

Instructional Strategies.   If a child is unable to make up a story to go with a picture, you'll need to demonstrate what you see when you look at a picture. Comment on big ideas as well as details. Then demonstrate thinking: "What if the people who live inside this house had never heard music? One day, some music comes in through the window and frightens them. What would they do? How would it all turn out?"

> **BENCHMARK**
>
> The child shows growing facility with the functions (uses) of language (Figure 5.3).
>
> ✔ Retains oral directions to do more than one thing; usually can tell the directions back

Directions from a parent or teacher often involve more than one thing. For instance, a parent might say to a child, "First wash your hands and dry them. Then go upstairs and get my glasses, please, and bring them to me." You will give similar oral directions in the classroom, often related to completing one activity and preparing for the next. When you do so, note which children follow such directions. You could give each child a set of two or more things to do to assess ability to follow directions, but we think this is better assessed in the normal course of activities. Note which children can restate directions given orally.

Instructional Strategies.   If a child did not follow directions, ask yourself how this behavior might be explained. Was it because the child was so involved that he or she literally did not hear you? Have a signal that means "Stop—Look—Listen." The signal can be a hand clap, a rap, a bell, a light, or a chord on an instrument. Before children can follow directions, you must get their attention.

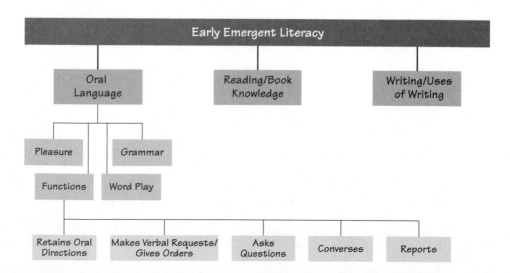

Figure 5.3
Oral Language: Functions

If the child hears and wants to comply but doesn't understand, demonstrate what is required, model it, explain the rationale, and guide practice. Failure to follow directions for completing a project or worksheet is often due to lack of understanding, lack of coordination, or disinterest.

If a child hears and understands but doesn't obey, this is a problem with compliance. Lack of compliance is not a listening problem, though you will want to explore the behavior with the child.

✔ Makes verbal requests or gives verbal orders that others understand

✔ Asks questions for information and for permission

✔ Converses with peers and adults

Observe whether or not the child can make himself understood when asking about something and when telling someone to do something.

Instructional Strategies.   Paraphrase to help children express themselves more clearly. Role-play with them, pretending you are trying to follow a child's orders but failing to understand what she means; this will encourage the children to be more precise.

Listen to the children as they talk with each other and with adults. Are they able to make themselves understood? Do they initiate conversations? Are they actually exchanging ideas with others, or are they simply engaged in **parallel talking,** that is, taking turns without really having a conversation?

Instructional Strategies.   Parallel talking is typical for this age. While you accept it as typical, you certainly can model what conversations should be: an exchange of ideas, taking turns, responding to what the other person says, and so forth.

If a child cannot make himself or herself understood by others, you must try to figure out a possible explanation so you can attempt to help. If the problem is articulation—that is, the child cannot form sounds clearly—start keeping a list of specific sounds. Unless you are a speech specialist, you probably cannot determine whether or not a true speech delay or problem exists. If the articulation difficulty is with certain particular sounds, such as /l/ or /r/, chances are this is merely immaturity, but monitor it closely. Share what you have noted with a speech specialist. The child may need help beyond what you can give in the classroom.

If the child is an English-language learner, lack of conversation is likely related to levels of comfort and competence with the new language. Model conversing with the child even though he may not understand much.

If a child never initiates conversations, she may be shy. You can help by gently encouraging conversation but not insisting. Some children remain shy. Forcing them to talk may do more harm than good. Patience is the key here.

✔ Reports orally on events in his or her life

Is the child able to report on daily activities or events that occurred at home in such a way that others understand?

Instructional Strategies.   Give children many opportunities to report on events to others. If a child cannot make other children understand, listen carefully to determine the nature of the problem; then model, paraphrase, and demonstrate. Adequate reporting involves good listening as well.

BENCHMARK

The child enjoys word play (Figure 5.4).

✔ Likes to play word games

As you engage in various kinds of word play, note what children do in response and whether or not they participate. For example, play a game such as "I'm going to Grandma's house and I'm taking a . . . book." Each child repeats everything that has been said before and adds one more thing. Most children this age find this fun and enjoy trying to remember the string of items and adding a new one.

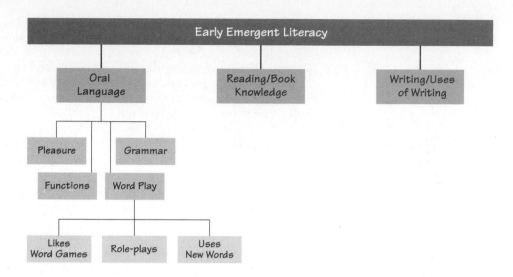

**Figure 5.4
Oral Language: Word Play**

Instructional Strategies.   If a child doesn't participate in word games, you'll want to encourage and support such participation. Some children may simply be embarrassed or afraid of looking foolish. You may need to act silly yourself to help them relax. Some children may feel they are failing if they cannot remember how to play a game. They need reassurance.

✔ Pretends or role-plays using appropriate language

Often you will see children role playing on their own, and you can observe whether they use language appropriate to the roles. For instance, you may notice that a child in a housekeeping center is playing at being a parent and using that person's tone and language.

After you have read a story to children, you can encourage them to act it out. Note which children use appropriate language for the character they are playing.

Instructional Strategies.   Modeling is the best instructional strategy for role playing. Take a part yourself to model the process. Also, before asking children to role-play, talk about character traits, feelings, and events, and how a character might react to events in the story.

✔ Repeats and uses (sometimes inappropriately) new words

When you use "big" words, which children try them out in their own oral language? When you introduce new vocabulary related to concepts in science, music, art, math, and so forth, do children begin using these words with growing confidence? This is a global judgment on your part. You should not try to "test" vocabulary but simply observe whether each child continues to add to his or her vocabulary.

Instructional Strategies.   Make a game of "use a new word today." Announce the word early in the day. Make it a useful word, perhaps a concept related to weather (such as *frigid*) or ethical behavior (such as *trustworthy*). Use the word often, and ring a little bell or otherwise note every time a child uses it that day. As you complete a group presentation or discussion, make vocabulary part of your review of what was learned. After reading a story, ask children to think of words they heard that were new to them. Then locate the words and talk about their meaning.

Elaborate basic sentences. If a child says, "See my truck," respond, "Yes, indeed, I do see your truck. What a beautiful shade of green it is painted. I notice it has special windows in the back and a place to carry things." When a child points and says, "Pretty flower," you say, "The flower is a geranium. It *is* pretty. In fact, I think it is gorgeous! Look at the blossoms and the fuzzy leaves." Informally, note whether children are producing more elaborate sentences as a result of your modeling.

Which children are using conventional sentence construction? Can they fix a sentence with incorrect word order (**syntax**) such as "That is a cow big"? Will they tell you if a sentence presents wrong facts—for instance, if someone says, "That is a cow" when in fact the animal is a dog?

Instructional Strategies.   Most children have a clear grasp of word order in the English language almost from the time they begin speaking—if English is their first language. If it is not their first language, you will need to provide many models of syntax, gently restating and paraphrasing what a child says until he or she can switch to English syntax when speaking English, even while retaining the first language's syntax when speaking that language.

Do your students use irregular plurals such as *feet* and *women,* or are they still overgeneralizing their growing understanding of plurals to *foots* and *womans*? Do they affix *-ed* to all verbs, as in *goed,* or are they using the irregular past *went*?

Instructional Strategies.   There is no need to correct immature construction. Rather, repeat the child's idea using the correct form. Model, model, model.

If the child uses **nonstandard English,** model correct usage. There is little to be gained by interrupting a child who is trying to communicate to "correct" the child's grammar. That tactic is unlikely to result in more standard usage. What will more likely result is a decreased willingness to speak to you at all.

As you talk with children individually or in small groups, ask them to listen and tell you if what you say is a complete sentence. Make up several examples of each.

BENCHMARK

The child shows increasing knowledge of grammar and other language conventions (Figure 5.5).

✔ Tells you a sentence doesn't make sense or sound right if incorrect syntax or incorrect facts are presented

✔ Is generalizing about such language oddities as irregular plurals and verb forms

✔ May be able to identify what is or is not a complete sentence, though cannot tell why

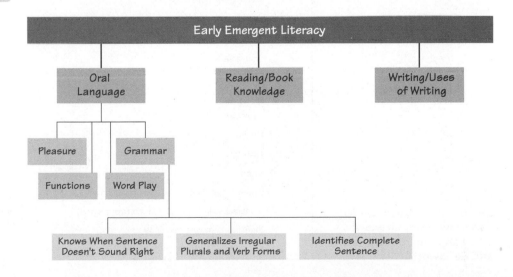

**Figure 5.5
Oral Language: Grammar and Other Language Conventions**

If a child recognizes the difference, the behavior is present. You cannot expect these children to give grammatical explanations, but their ears tell them what "complete" is.

Instructional Strategies.   Continue to attune children to complete sentences by modeling and "catching yourself," using incomplete sentences and fixing them aloud.

ORAL LANGUAGE CHECKLIST:
EARLY EMERGENT LITERACY STAGE

Date _____   Class/age group_____

Key: Y = behavior present consistently   **Student Names**
         S = behavior sometimes present
         N = behavior not yet present

Benchmark

Pleasure in Stories, Poems, Information

Attends to read-alouds

Predicts

Retells:

    story/sequence

    information/main ideas

Uses book language when retelling

Makes up stories

Tells story to go with picture

Functions of Language

Retains oral directions

Makes verbal requests/gives orders

Asks questions

Converses

Reports

Word Play

Likes word games

Role-plays

Uses new words

Grammar

Knows when sentence doesn't sound right

Generalizes irregular plurals and verb forms

Identifies complete sentence

Figure 5.6
Sample Class Checklist for Early Emergent Literacy: Oral Language Benchmarks and Behaviors

Comments

> Both children's **receptive language** (listening) and their **productive language** (speaking) are, to a great extent, the result of the language spoken in the home. While you cannot change, nor should you denigrate, the language used in the home, you can model appropriate language when the children are with you and support their efforts to use school language.
>
> Figure 5.6 sums up the benchmarks and behavioral indicators for oral language in the form of a sample checklist that you might use in class. A checklist for individual students appears in the Resource File.

Reading and Book Knowledge

Assessment of reading and book knowledge consists of four related areas: concepts about print (Figure 5.7), familiarity with genres (Figure 5.10), construction of meaning (Figure 5.12), and enjoyment of literature and language (Figure 5.13). We show you how to assess each area and give some instructional strategies to aid development of each.

Assess each child at the beginning of the school year or whenever a child enters your care. Record which behaviors are present. Continue to assess children for behaviors that are absent during your initial assessment. Record when the behavior appears consistently. A sample checklist is provided in Figure 5.14.

This area deals with knowledge about books and print. Children at this stage may have acquired some of the important basic concepts. They will often realize, for instance, that the marks on a printed page stand for something. When handling a book, they may know where it begins and when it is right side up. You can actually assess many related concepts, as the checklist in Figure 5.8 shows. You assess these concepts directly, one on one with each child. The rare child who has acquired all the concepts is at the next stage, Emergent Literacy, discussed in Chapter 6.

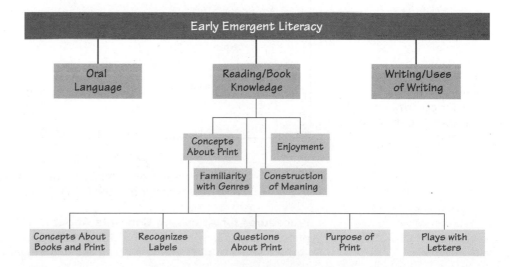

**Figure 5.7
Reading and Book
Knowledge: Concepts
About Print**

CHECKLIST FOR CONCEPTS ABOUT BOOKS AND PRINT:
EARLY EMERGENT LITERACY STAGE

Name_____   Year_____

Key: Y = has concept
      N = does not have concept
      B = beginning signs of concept

Concept	Date							Comments
Books								
• Front of book								
• Print carries message								
• Directionality								
• Voice-to-print match								
• First and last								
• Inverted picture/print								
• Left before right								
• Word order								
Print								
1. Punctuation								
a. period								
b. question mark								
c. exclamation mark								
d. other								
2. Upper-case match								
3. Lower-case match								
4. Upper- to lower-case match								
5. Frame one letter								
6. Frame two letters								
7. Frame one word								
8. Frame two words								
9. Found and named letters								
10. Found and named words								

Comments:

Figure 5.8
Sample Checklist for
Early Emergent Literacy:
Concepts About Books
and Print

In the following discussion, which explains how to assess the concepts listed in Figure 5.8, we have drawn on Clay's (1985) "Concepts About Print" assessment.

Procedures for Assessing Concepts About Books and Print.   Use any simple picture book. Sit where you and the child will not be disturbed. Tell the child you are going to read and talk about the book together. Explain that you will be making notes as you talk so you won't forget anything. Keep your manner friendly but business–like. Discontinue this assessment if the child becomes frustrated or clearly doesn't understand.

Assessing Concepts About Books. Use the following steps to assess the child's concepts about books:

1 *Front of the book.* Dangle a picture book by the spine and ask the child to take it and show you the front, or where it begins.

2 *Print carries the message.* Tell the child you are going to read the story. Ask the child to point to where you should begin in the book. The child should point to the print, not the picture.

3 *Directionality.* The concept of **directionality** involves the understanding that print goes from left to right and top to bottom on the page. Ask the child to point to where you should start on a page (should point to the first word), then in which direction to go (left to right), then what to do at the end of the line (move to the left side of the next line down).

4 *Voice-to-print match.* Ask the child to point to the words as you read somewhat slowly but with normal inflection. The **voice-to-print match** tells you whether the child seems to understand that the marks on the page are related to the sounds coming from your mouth. Though an exact match may not occur, the child's finger should move along as you read.

5 *First and last.* Ask the child to show you the first and last parts of the story.

6 *Inverted picture and print.* Present the child with a "page" you have made up on which a picture is inverted (Figure 5.9A). Do not use the term *upside-down.* Ask the child to show you the bottom of the picture. If the child has the concept, she or he will either turn the page or point to the appropriate place. Then show a "page" with inverted print (Figure 5.9B) and ask where to begin reading. Again, if the child has the concept, he or she will either turn the book or point to the correct place even though the print is upside-down.

Figure 5.9
(A) Page with Inverted Picture. (B) Page with Inverted Print

(A)

(B)

7 *Left page before right.* Return to the picture book. Showing a double spread of pages, ask which page to read first.

8 *Word order.* Read a sentence with the words out of order and ask what's wrong (we talked about this with oral language). The child should say it doesn't sound right.

Assessing Concepts About Print. Continue to use the picture book. As the child responds to the following items, you may sense many more questions you want to ask. That's perfectly all right. While you don't want to put words in the child's mouth, you do want to find out what the child knows. Sometimes you have to probe gently.

1 Point to random punctuation marks and ask what they are for. Accept any words that indicate the child understands the concept. That is, a child may not name the exclamation point, but he or she may tell you it means to say the words louder or with excitement. Or the child may demonstrate by saying something in that manner.

2 Point to random upper-case letters and, for each one, ask the child to find another one like it.

3 Do the same with lower-case letters.

4 Point to an upper-case letter and ask the child to find a lower-case one like it. If the child doesn't seem to understand, demonstrate first. You can assess a few letters this way, using the book you have in hand. If the child seems to know many letters, you may want to move on to a more elaborate assessment of every letter, upper and lower case. We will discuss this further in the next chapter, on the Emergent Literacy stage.

5 Ask the child to show you one letter by framing it with an index finger on each side. Do this a few more times.

6 Ask the child to frame two letters.

7 Ask the child to frame one word.

8 Ask the child to frame two words.

9 Ask the child to find and name any letters he or she knows.

10 Ask the child to find and say any words in the book he or she knows.

Instructional Strategies. If children have not yet acquired some of the concepts just described, teach them. Acquisition of the concepts results from direct instruction and exposure to books. Many children get this at home, but others find it only in school.

Demonstrate, show, and discuss all of these concepts in the normal course of your day with children. All you need to do is address each concept frequently as you read and write with the children.

✔ Knows that labels name products or tell about something

Observe which children recognize some products or objects in the room by the labels. While they may not yet recognize the words on the labels in other contexts, recognition that the words tell about the product or object is an important indicator.

Instructional Strategies.   Label objects in the room, including doors, windows, blinds, directions, paper supplies, crayons, and so forth. As you use products with brand names, reinforce with commentary: "There are many kinds of fruit juice in the grocery store. I choose the one I want by reading the label on the can." Children will associate pictures, logos, containers, and print.

✔ Asks questions about print and about own writing, scribbling, or drawing

Observe which children demonstrate interest in print by asking what letters and words are when they see them. Which children question their own writing? After scribbling, which children ask what they have "said"?

Instructional Strategies.   Children will develop an interest in print when an adult or other literate person makes print a significant part of the day. Write while children watch you, thinking aloud, saying what you are writing, helping them make the connection between your spoken words and these same words in print. Reassure them that they too will learn to do this.

✔ Knows the purpose of some print

Watch behavior and listen to conversations to make inferences about each child's awareness of the purposes of print and books. The following list suggests some everyday events and responses on which you can base inferences about this indicator:

- If you ask, "Shall we have a story?" the child asks for a familiar story or goes to the bookshelf to get a book.
- If you wonder what to watch on television, the child gets the TV guide.
- If you are making a shopping list, the child says, "Write *peanut butter*, please."
- If a grown-up is writing a letter, the child says, "Tell Gramma I love her."
- If you wonder aloud about whether a certain animal has more than one baby at a time, the child prods you to "Look it up."
- The child pretends to read and write, mimicking adult behavior. (We witnessed one three-year-old "reading" to her baby brother, stopping from time to time to take a sip of "coffee" just as her mother did.)
- The child urges an adult to use, or pretends to use himself or herself, such things as telephone books, dictionaries, greeting cards, and cookbooks.

Instructional Strategies.   You don't need to wait for the dawning of such awareness to happen naturally. You can encourage it by modeling the use of many kinds of print, commenting on what you are doing, explaining how the print is helping you. Some examples follow:

- Show children a cookbook or a recipe from a newspaper or magazine, and tell them that someone wrote this recipe to help us know how to make some good cookies. Ask them to think what would have to be in a recipe to enable someone else to cook something, and hypothesize about what would go wrong if ingredients were missing, directions were wrong, or the cookies were baked at the wrong temperature.
- As you read aloud, tell children that a person wrote this funny story so you could have a good laugh when you read it.
- Send letters, by either regular mail or e-mail. Talk about the many reasons for writing letters.

- When children ask questions about concepts they are studying, ask, "Where can we look it up?"

Comments

> Lucky children grow up in families where reading and writing are an important part of daily life. Their understanding of the purpose of books and writing is as natural to them as their knowledge of the purpose of a bed or a spoon. Not all children are so lucky. You need to immerse such children in literacy. Surround them with books, and model the use of books. Keep talking about what you are doing and why, giving them the language they need to talk about books and writing.

✔ **Likes playing with movable and/or magnetic letters**

Simple observation will show you which children are interested in playing with various kinds of letters you have in your classroom, moving them around to make words and matching them to words on charts and in books.

Instructional Strategies.   Children who do not show an interest in playing with letters this way may simply have not yet had an opportunity. Make sure many ways of making words are available, such as alphabet blocks, magnetic letters, cardboard letters, and foam letters. Encourage play.

BENCHMARK

The child is familiar with various genres (Figure 5.10).

We suggest that you keep anecdotal records as evidence accumulates about each child's familiarity with various genres of literature. Note both global and specific information related to this aspect of book knowledge. Figure 5.11 shows some sample observation notes.

✔ **Knows several/many nursery rhymes**

Note which children chime in as you recite traditional nursery rhymes. Children whose first language is not English may know nursery rhymes in another language. Some native English speakers may know rhymes specific to a particular culture rather than the rhymes you consider traditional.

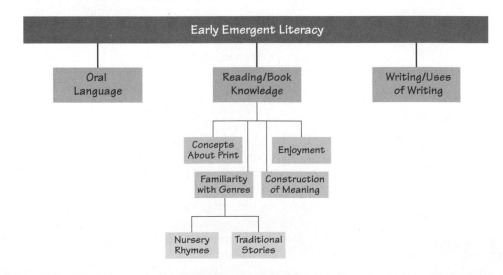

**Figure 5.10
Reading and Book Knowledge: Familiarity with Genres**

8-28 Gina — knows the movie version of "Beauty and the Beast" but apparently hasn't heard the original version.

8-28 John — did not join in when we did "Jack and Jill." Note whether or not he participates in future nursery rhymes.

8-28 Jamal — told me he had "about a million" books at home and his grandma read to him every night.

8-28 Amy — had all the stuffed animals lined up in front of her and was retelling "Pinocchio" to them. We have not read this in class yet, but she knows it well. Could be she saw the old movie. Ask her.

8-30 Douglas — brought a watered-down version of Pooh story to be read. I substituted the original and read it aloud instead. He had never heard it before, but volunteered the opinion that it was better than his version. Next time, talk with him about what he thinks is "better."

Figure 5.11 Sample Teacher Observation Notes for Children's Familiarity with Genres

Instructional Strategies. Children who already know nursery rhymes will delight in hearing and saying them over and over as others learn them for the first time. Nursery rhymes and other poems develop a sense of rhyme, rhythm, alliteration, onomatopoeia, plays on words, and many more twists and turns of language. Hearing and saying rhymes also develops an ear for the sounds in words.

✔ Knows several/many traditional stories such as fairy tales

Which children are already familiar with some traditional stories such as fairy tales and legends (in any language)? Some may know these stories only through a contemporary, rewritten, or cartoon version.

Instructional Strategies. The classc fairy tales, as well as modern classics, bear rereading over and over, as parents will attest. When children ask for the same story many times, it isn't because they have forgotten what happened. They know exactly what happened. It is the very familiarity that they crave—that and the story language. We sometimes talk about "anchoring the sounds of language in the child's ear." Children who know these favorites and have heard them many times are acquiring a sense of book language.

Read aloud (and suggest that parents do likewise) the rich, authentic versions of stories. When you read a watered-down version of any classic fairy tale such as "Beauty and the Beast," you deprive children of the richness of the language.

When you read to children, it doesn't matter that they don't yet understand every word. When they begin to read for themselves, they know what book language should sound like. Encourage children to talk about their favorite stories and why they like them. As you expose children to new stories, encourage comparison with their favorites. Talk about your favorite stories and why they are favorites.

Comments

> Teachers need to expose children to many nursery rhymes, poems, and fairy and folk tales, as well as good contemporary classics such as *Where the Wild Things Are* (Sendak, 1963). All of these anchor language in the ears. They help children appreciate the sounds of language as well as such delights as puns, similes, and metaphors. Children at this age don't need to identify or label these literary techniques; in fact, you don't need to discuss them at all if you don't want to. The point is to put these things into the ears and heads of children long before they are reading and writing for themselves.

BENCHMARK

The child begins to construct meaning (Figure 5.12).

✔ Predicts what will happen next or what word or phrase comes next during read-aloud

Much of the evidence for this benchmark parallels the oral language benchmarks of predicting, retelling, making up stories, and playing with language. Assessment at this stage is observational. Keep anecdotal records to support your judgment.

As you read, stop at certain points to ask what might happen next. Can the child predict a reasonable event? Can the child tell you why he or she is making a certain prediction? The child who consistently makes reasonable predictions—based on story events or characters, knowledge of story structure, awareness of human nature, or personal experience—has achieved this benchmark. For example:

- When hearing a folk tale about a child who goes off into the woods, many children will predict that something bad will happen to the child. They

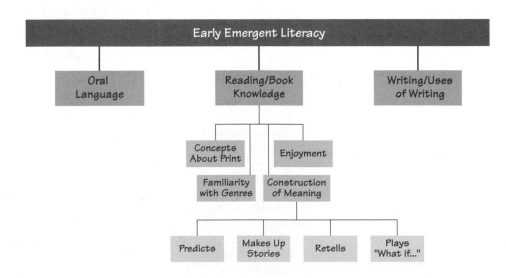

**Figure 5.12
Reading and Book
Knowledge: Construction
of Meaning**

explain their prediction by telling you that woods are dangerous or that that's what happens in stories like this.

- If a character does something naughty, children can predict that the child will be sorry and may get punished because that's what happens to them when they do something naughty.
- If a character is walking down the street and the picture shows a banana peel on the sidewalk, they predict that the character might slip and fall because they've seen that happen in a movie.

If ELL students are still at the silent stage of English production, ask them to give predictions in their first language, even though you may not understand the words.

Instructional Strategies. Model predicting by thinking aloud as you read to children or watch videos with them. Explain what leads you to think as you do: "I bet he's going to surprise her with a ring, and then she'll have to tell him she . . . " or "He's never going to get her that ring she wants, because . . . " Give children many opportunities to predict and talk about why a prediction is logical on the basis of story events and personal response.

Also talk about the author's task of deciding what to have happen in a story. How might such decisions be made? An adult concept of a good story is one in which events surprise us yet seem inevitable. Even little children can think about and talk about such things: Why did the author have the character do that? Could the author have made a different decision? How would that have changed the story? Why couldn't the character behave in a certain way? When you give little children a chance to explore these ideas as you share stories with them, their ability to think about story grows enormously.

✔ **Makes up stories to go with pictures**

Assessment of this behavior is quite informal. Ask children to make up a story based on a picture they have seen or drawn. Note whether story elements are present: character, setting, problem, events, and solution.

Instructional Strategies. Reinforce children's growing awareness of story by tying stories they hear to stories they make up. Model making up stories. Omit an element, such as setting, and ask children to tell you what is missing. Probe to get children to expand stories by asking "Why?" as they tell you what a character does.

Children may also enjoy describing a picture or giving information about what is portrayed. For example, children can be encouraged to describe and tell about pictures of animals, food, or space shuttles.

✔ **Can retell a story he or she has heard**

After a story is read aloud and the book is closed, ask what the story was about. Children on the brink of Emergent Literacy can remember the main characters, what the problem was, some of the events, how the problem was solved, and how the story ended. Even if they leave out some of these elements, they usually can recall them with a little prompting.

Read aloud an informational book or watch a video; then ask, "What did you learn?" Does the child say something such as "It was about penguins. It told where the penguins live, and what they eat, and how the daddy holds the eggs on his feet"? Like most of us, children are apt to talk most about the part they found most interesting, but with prodding they usually can remember other information.

Instructional Strategies.   Make retelling of stories and information a regular part of your day after read-alouds and viewings. Applaud all efforts, even when they include every single little detail. Improve retelling through stronger prereading activities. Help children focus as they listen. After listening, probe for recall of additional information.

Some children may not be able to retell at all. Your job is to help them acquire this critical ability. You are the scaffold, providing whatever support they need for as long as they need it. You model, collaborate, prod, guide, support—and then do it all over again, as often as needed for as long as needed. You know that children will acquire these abilities in a supportive environment.

✔ Can play games such as "What if . . ."

Use a story children know, and ask "What if . . . " questions. For example: "What if Goldilocks stayed to live with the three bears? Where would she sleep?" Can the child hypothesize an alternative story that is reasonable?

Instructional Strategies.   Play this kind of game frequently. Model by making up alternatives for children. Accept all suggestions while helping children see which could work and which could not, and why. An activity such as this helps children learn about story, a vital element in literacy.

BENCHMARK
The child enjoys literature and language (Figure 5.13).

The components for this benchmark are very similar to those described for oral language. There we focused on the ability to express verbally. Here we are assessing what the behaviors tell us about the child's appreciation of books and language. Assessment is through observation. Keep anecdotal records.

✔ Enjoys listening to stories read aloud

Note each child's response to read-aloud time. Does the child show interest? Come willingly? Sit attentively? Participate in discussion?

Instructional Strategies.   Motivate children by showing enthusiasm, giving a hint of delights to come, and making them feel wanted in the group. Accept that not every child will be interested in every story, but teach all to sit quietly to accommodate the interests of others. If a child continues to be reluctant to join the group, look for a social reason, such as the child's being bothered by others. Avoid embarrassing the shy children; invite, don't demand.

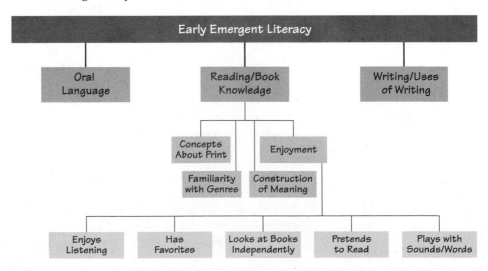

Figure 5.13
Reading and Book Knowledge: Enjoyment

You can encourage attentiveness by engaging children in predicting and allowing ample time for looking at and talking about pictures. Second-language learners will maintain attentiveness better if you not only show pictures but also make generous use of gestures, vocal inflections, and facial expressions to support the words as you read.

✔ **Wants favorite stories read over and over**

Note whether the child asks for favorite stories and asks to hear them read aloud or to listen to audiotapes.

Instructional Strategies. Help children become familiar enough with stories to begin to have favorites. Then allow them to hear their favorites as often as requested. Learning is happening as children listen to favorite stories: learning about story structure, character, beautiful language, and human nature.

✔ **Looks at books independently**
✔ **Pretends to read**

Does the child look at books during free time? Does the child pretend to read, retelling stories and turning pages?

Instructional Strategies. No instruction is required for these components. However, time and freedom to engage in looking at books independently are needed. Be sure to allow for this activity each day. After reading a book aloud, leave it on a shelf where children can choose it. Model choosing a book as a free-time activity. Provide books in children's first language, if possible.

✔ **Enjoys playing with sounds and words**

Does the child show enjoyment of the rhymes, alliteration, and onomatopoeia in poems and stories? Can the child substitute sounds? That is, when you ask for rhymes for *cat*, will the child give you such words as *fat, mat, rat*?

Instructional Strategies. Games with sounds and words support developing phonemic awareness as well as increasing delight with the sounds of language. Play such games with children daily; for instance: "*A:* My name is Alice, my husband's name is Al, we live in Alabama, and we sell apples." Use rhythm instruments, clapping, marching, and other means to reinforce the rhythm of language. Talk about onomatopoetic words you find in stories and poems, and show your own pleasure in such words as *buzz, hiss, whoosh, squish,* and *thump.*

Comments

You will sometimes find preschool-age children who already read fairly fluently. Such children will not necessarily announce that they can read, but you certainly want to know if they can. The easiest way to find out is simply to ask if anyone can already read. Invite whoever says yes to choose a book and read it to you privately. Some can indeed read unfamiliar text with accuracy, fluency, and understanding. Such children are beyond this Early Emergent Literacy stage. Use the assessment procedures designed for one of the next stages.

Other children may say yes and run to bring a book to you, but in fact they are not yet reading independently. It is wonderful that these children see themselves as readers, but you should use the assessments suggested in this chapter.

Figure 5.14 presents a class checklist for summarizing reading and book knowledge. An individual checklist appears in the Resource File.

READING AND BOOK KNOWLEDGE CHECKLIST:
EARLY EMERGENT LITERACY STAGE

Date _____   Class/age group _____

Key: P = behavior present   **Student Names**
      S = some knowledge
      L = little knowledge
      N = behavior not present

Benchmark

Concepts About Print

     Has concepts about books and print*

     Recognizes labels

     Questions about print

     Purpose of print

     Plays with letters

Familiarity with Genres

     Nursery rhymes

     Traditional stories

Construction of Meaning

     Predicts

     Makes up stories

     Retells

     Plays "What if . . ."

Enjoyment

     Enjoys listening

     Has favorite stories

     Looks at books independently

     Pretends to read

     Plays with sounds/words

* See also separate checklist in Figure 5.8

Figure 5.14
Sample Class Checklist for Early Emergent Literacy: Reading and Book Knowledge Benchmarks and Behaviors

Writing and Uses of Writing

In this section, we show you how to assess what the child is doing in an effort to write. We want to note whether the child understands some of the purposes of writing (Figure 5.15), whether and in what way the child is attempting to communicate in writing (Figure 5.16), and whether the child is beginning to connect reading and writing (Figure 5.17). There is, of course, a great deal of overlap between the reading and writing assessments. You may find that you have enough data from reading assessments to judge this area without separate observations.

Even though children at this stage are not producing what you would call writing, *they* generally know they are writing. If asked to talk about a picture drawn, the child may not tell you it is a picture of something; rather, he or she may tell you what it "says." Often children attempt to write before they attempt to read. We want to encourage all efforts; therefore, we celebrate each child's attempt and recognize it as an important step forward.

Some children at this stage simply grasp a crayon in a fist, bear down on the paper, and beam at you, saying, "See what I wrote?" It is sometimes tough to know how to respond. They know they are writing, not drawing. They had in mind something they wanted to say, though you cannot read it. Usually the best thing to do is ask them to tell you about it. Your anecdotal record will note which children are beginning to use writing to communicate, though not yet making letter-like marks.

In terms of spelling, this is the precommunicative stage, as described in Chapter 3. Writing is made up of scribbles, letterlike forms full of vertical, horizontal, and diagonal lines and occasional curves, numbers, and some actual letters, usually upper case. As yet there is no connection between letters and the precise sounds they represent, nor is there a match between the number of letters and the number of sounds in a word. These children have not grasped the alphabetic principle that letters represent sounds. They do not yet have phonemic awareness, that is, an awareness of the separate sounds in speech, or at least have not used such awareness to guide them as they attempt to write. There is often no space between the "letters" to indicate word boundaries. Some children at this point seem to write left to right and top to bottom, while others do not. All of these variations are normal and developmental.

Little direct instruction in writing is warranted at this stage. Rather, your role is to model writing: reading to children what you have written and talking about what you are doing and why you are doing it. Ask questions. Guide. For example, when you see a child showing another child something, say, "How could you share that if you couldn't show it? . . . Yes, you could write it down for her." Collect samples of children's efforts frequently, identifying them with the child's name and the date. As these are reviewed later, it is easy to see how the child is growing in writing.

> **BENCHMARK**
>
> The child knows the purpose of writing (Figure 5.15).
>
> ✔ Understands that the marks on a paper mean something

With regard to this benchmark, see also the section on understanding the purpose of print in the reading section earlier in this chapter.

Assessment is observational. You will already know something about this understanding from your assessment of concepts about books and print. If you need further evidence, informal conversation with the child will reveal whether she or he knows that the print—that is, the "marks"—carries the meaning.

Instructional Strategies.   Continue to point to text as you read aloud from big books, and point to labels and print in the classroom as you say the words. Reinforce with children why a sign, picture, or product needs to have print to let others know exactly what it is. No direct teaching is required.

> ✔ Wants to write messages, letters, greeting cards, and shopping lists

Again, assessment is observational. Note if the child attempts to write messages. Does the child draw a greeting card such as a valentine and "write" on it? Does the child make a list of presents wanted for a special occasion? Does the child make a grocery list while playing in the housekeeping corner of the classroom?

Instructional Strategies.   Continue to model the uses of writing in your own life and in the life of your classroom. Make lists that the children help you compose.

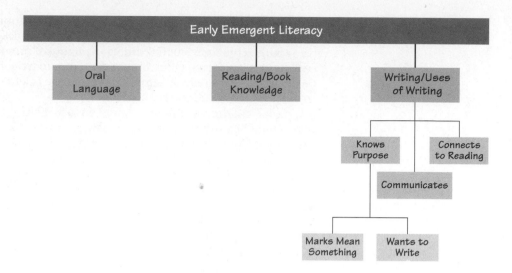

Figure 5.15   Writing: Purpose

Write thank-you letters to visitors, talk about the purpose of the thank-you letter, and let the children help you compose it. Take every opportunity to let the children see you engage in purposeful writing and to contribute to that writing. Encourage families to do likewise.

Observe which children are using various writing tools available in the classroom. These include paper and pencil, markers, crayons, chalk, typewriter, and computer. Note whether the child asks, "What did I write?" or tells you what the writing "says," or at least knows that the writing should say something.

Instructional Strategies.   If a child does not seem at ease with any writing tools, introduce them one at a time, with brief instructions and demonstrations. For example, demonstrate using crayons on paper. Talk about where not to use the crayons. Show the child how to put them away. Then get out of the way and let the

> **BENCHMARK**
>
> The child tries to communicate in writing (Figure 5.16).
>
> ✔ Uses paper and pencil (marker, crayon, chalk, typewriter, computer) to attempt to write

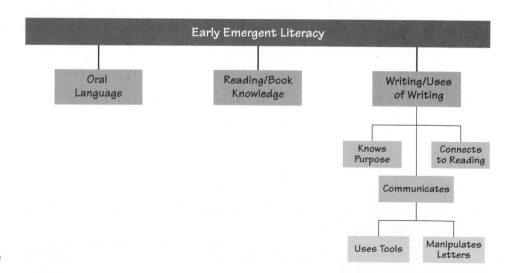

Figure 5.16   Writing: Attempts to Communicate

child experiment, but watch to be sure he or she uses the tool safely as well as to ensure that property is not destroyed.

Children will use whatever tools are available to them. Some children have not grown up with access to and freedom to use pencils, crayons, markers, and so on. It is important to provide a wide variety of tools for children at this stage to experiment with. Don't worry about whether they are using the tools correctly (except, of course, to avoid damage or injury). Simply make the tools available, along with something to write on, such as paper or chalkboard. We see no reason to withhold any tools from little children as long as there is reasonable supervision.

> ✔ Arranges movable letters, writes string of letterlike shapes, or hits random string of letters on a keyboard, then asks, "What did I say?"

Combine this assessment with the use of tools discussed above. If a child arranges movable letters or hits a random string of letters on a keyboard *and* wants to know what the result "says," this indicates understanding that print can help one communicate. See also the assessment of concepts about print in the earlier section on reading.

Instructional Strategies.   Support children's seemingly random production of print, whether by hand or on a keyboard. If children ask what the letters "say," you might respond, "You tell me," and also comment gently that before long they will learn to make marks that others can read and be able to read for themselves. Informal comments about the nature of print will help children grasp that print is stable: the same string of letters always says the same thing.

> **BENCHMARK**
> The child connects reading and writing (Figure 5.17).
>
> ✔ Wants to label own pictures

Assess through observation. A child's desire to label his or her own pictures is simply a sign that the child is beginning to understand the connection between print and objects, concepts, and events.

Instructional Strategies.   If a child is not yet showing the desire to label his own pictures, demonstrate, doing it for him until he begins to request it for himself.

> ✔ Understands that stories are made up by a person who thought of the story and then wrote it down, and that he or she can do this also

When you read a story, does the child ask who wrote it? Through group conversation, note which children know that a person (the author) makes up a story and writes it down for others to read. Which children are beginning to see them-

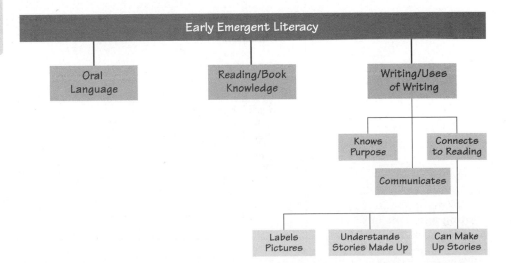

Figure 5.17   Writing: Connection to Reading

selves as authors—people who can make up stories and write them down or have someone else write them down?

Instructional Strategies.   Whenever you read aloud or talk about a book, tell children the name of the person who wrote it. Help children see the author as a real person—one who was once a child as they are. Share information about the lives of authors. As children make up stories, perhaps ones that you record for them, include a short biography so readers will know something about the author.

✔ Can spin out a story to go with attempts at writing and with drawings

Which children are able to spin out a story to go with their attempts at writing and with drawings? Those who can are showing they understand that the print

---

Writing and Uses of Writing Checklist:
Early Emergent Literacy Stage

Date _____   Class/age group _____

Key: P = behavior present
     S = some knowledge
     L = little knowledge
     N = behavior not present

Student Names

Benchmark								
Purpose								
Marks mean something								
Wants to write								
Communicates								
Uses tools								
Manipulates letters								
Connects to Reading								
Wants to label own pictures								
Understands stories are made up and he or she can do this also								
Can make up stories								

Figure 5.18
Sample Class Checklist for Early Emergent Literacy: Writing and Uses of Writing Benchmarks and Behaviors

carries the words of the story and that the picture usually is not enough to tell the whole story.

Instructional Strategies. Help children by asking them to make up a story and writing it for them. Let them talk a story onto a tape, and then type it out for them. If you have older children, reading buddies, who come to your class, this is a good activity for them to share.

Comments

Figure 5.18 presents a sample class checklist for writing. An individual checklist is in the Resource File.

Keep in mind that all children are on a continuum in terms of growth toward literacy. Children do not reach literacy through a series of steps that are separate and discrete. Other, more apt analogies might be a pool, surrounded on all sides with literacy experiences; a carousel, on which children grab more and more of the brass rings of literacy each time around; a garden, with a plethora of possible experiences to pick from and freedom to choose which path to take and when.

Happily, many—perhaps most—children have numerous literacy experiences before coming to school. For these children, you assess and go on. For those who have missed such experiences, you make up for it by providing a rich environment in the classroom.

Planning Instruction Based on Assessed Stage of Development

You have just learned how to assess individual children at the Early Emergent Literacy stage to learn where they are developmentally in oral language, reading and book knowledge, and writing. Finding out which children have reached which benchmarks takes time. However, *do not delay instruction* in order to complete assessment.

As your time with children goes on, you will gradually tailor instructional experiences to particular children based on your assessment. At the outset, however, you begin gathering information while at the same time establishing an environment that supports literacy growth and lends itself to adjustments for individual children.

Three conditions are necessary for appropriate instruction: (1) a print-rich, language-rich environment, (2) a balanced literacy day, and (3) a way to meet the needs of students who require special attention. You were introduced to the concept of a balanced literacy program in Chapter 4. Here we show you what such a program looks like in a prekindergarten setting, adapting and adjusting the balanced model to meet the needs of individual students at this level. In addition, we will describe a typical day in the kind of classroom we recommend.

Creating a Print-Rich, Language-Rich Environment

The terms **print-rich** and **language-rich environment** have been used for a long time to describe the kind of environment in which children's growth in literacy will flourish. Many parents have provided such an environment quite naturally in their homes. They have read to their children from birth and have surrounded them with books, magazines, newspapers, and other print. They have talked to their children, sung to them, told them nursery rhymes, written notes to them, and shared conversations. They are readers and writers themselves, so their children see reading and writing as a natural part of life.

Your job is to provide for children at school the same rich environment you wish all children had at home. At this stage, you will provide more "play" opportunities than you might for older children. You will have many kinds of materials for children to experiment with, such as sand tables, water, plants, blocks, and so forth. Here we are discussing prekindergarten, but most kindergartens and primary grades need the same environment, even though some materials will change or be eliminated (for example, sand and water tables are seldom found beyond kindergarten).

The materials and physical arrangement described in the following sections are directly related to literacy and should be part of every classroom from prekindergarten through primary grades, though their use will change for older children.

Materials, Tools, and Furniture

Children use many materials and tools independently for part of the day, with teacher supervision but little direct instruction. For reading, here are a few of the items they use:

- Big books
- Picture books
- Wordless picture books
- Books to be read aloud
- Board books
- Manipulative books
- Magazines
- Poetry books
- ABC books
- Counting books
- Comfortable chairs, couches, mats, pillows, or beanbags
- Low bookshelves
- Means for displaying books with the covers facing out, such as racks or plastic pockets

For writing, the tools, materials, and furniture include these:

- Tables and chairs
- Chalkboards
- Paper
- Magnetic boards and letters
- Typewriters
- Computers
- Pencils, crayons, markers, and chalk
- Clay or another substance for shaping letters

Physical Arrangement

Children at this stage are mostly in prekindergarten settings. Though the room probably has tables and chairs, it seldom has desks. The setting is informal but structured to the extent that activities are planned to encourage development in all types of learning, including literacy. In its physical arrangement, the classroom has various areas, including the following.

Learning Centers.   **Learning centers** provide one kind of comfortable environment for children at the Early Emergent Literacy stage. Even before educators used the term *learning centers,* good preschool environments included such areas as these: housekeeping, doctor's office, grocery store, sand and water tables, tools, painting, pets, clay, reading, and writing.

These children are choosing fresh vegetables in the grocery store center. In the background, environmental print names several products.
© David Young-Wolff/PhotoEdit

We encourage you to use books and writing implements in every center. If children find books about animals in the pet center, they will look at them. If they find paper and pencil in the housekeeping center, they will make grocery lists. In this way, you can demonstrate on a daily basis how reading and writing are part of everyday life.

Read-Aloud Area.   One area, preferably with a rug and a rocking chair, can be a designated read-aloud area. This is where your entire class can gather comfortably while you read aloud to them and do shared writing.

Listening/Viewing Area.   In a listening/viewing area, children can listen with headphones to favorite stories while following the story in a book. In this area, they can also listen to music or view videos of books.

Cubbies.   Labeled cubbies allow children to store their personal belongings. Also, you may want to have individual mailboxes for messages that are to go home.

The Teacher's Part in the Environment

Perhaps the most important thing the teacher can do, besides reading aloud, is talk to children. On occasion the talk may be somewhat formal, as in a presentation or demonstration of some concept to the entire group. More often, however, it is informal; the teacher circulates as children work on various tasks and talks with them about what they are doing.

Such talk gives children the words for the concepts they are learning, expanding their oral language. The growth of oral language in young children is amazing. (See Norton [1997], who cites several studies.) By three to four years of age, children have vocabularies of about 1,500 words and use most language patterns—an astounding feat that they have accomplished without any formal instruction. By ages four to five, the number of words is up to 2,500. By five to six years of age, children understand approximately 6,000 words. They acquire this vocabulary and facility with language through interactions with adults and other children. It is a good example of the principle of the zone of proximal development: learning something most easily when there is someone handy who already knows it (Vygotsky, 1978). It is also an example of scaffolding, providing temporary support as needed while someone learns something.

To create a language-rich environment, many teachers of children at this stage and the next collaborate with the children to label virtually every object in the classroom. They don't formally teach children to read the words; they certainly don't make a flash card drill of it, but there are labels everywhere the child looks. No matter what the object, the child hears and sees the word for it. This kind of rich environment promotes an easy transition to the next stages of development.

Despite differences among classrooms, effective learning environments have some things in common. They are comfortable and inviting. They make it easy for children to use the tools of literacy. They are staffed by adults who delight in children and in literacy.

Planning a Balanced Literacy Day for Preschool or Kindergarten

Though we recommend a great deal of free time for children to explore the tools of reading and writing on their own at this stage of development, several instructional techniques and strategies are appropriate beginning at this stage. Some are so natural that adults often do them without realizing they are teaching. We presented many such instructional strategies during our assessment discussion. In this section, we focus on several that are particularly important in creating the kind of balanced literacy program described in Chapter 4.

Read-Alouds

Reading aloud to children may be the single most important activity you do to promote literacy growth. The value of reading aloud to children has been well documented (Strickland & Taylor, 1989). Reading aloud to children is recommended for all stages, though one reads aloud differently to 3-year-olds than to 10-year-olds. We know that children who learn to read on their own usually have been read to repeatedly (Durkin, 1966).

With children at the Early Emergent Literacy stage, reading aloud several times a day is appropriate. Not all children will like the same kinds of books. The books in your classroom should reflect all cultures and include all genres, classics and old favorites as well as newly published books, books by award-winning authors and books by lesser-known authors. You will also want to share information about authors' lives with your children. You may want books in other languages. It's hard to imagine a child who will not want to read when he or she is read to by an adult who loves books.

Reading aloud seems so simple it hardly bears discussing. Still, there is so-so reading and then there is wonderful reading. You want to do the latter, so we offer some simple steps to follow:

Before Reading

1. Read the story to yourself first so you know it well, can pronounce all the words, know what is important to emphasize, are familiar enough to make frequent eye contact, and know logical places to stop for talk and predictions.

2. Call the children to sit on the floor for a story while you sit in a rocking chair, positioned so that everyone can see you.

3. Show the cover. Tell the title, author, and illustrator, showing the children where the information is found. You may discuss the publisher, copyright, and any other concepts about books, such as naming the spine, the front and back, and the top and bottom.

4. You may want to do what is often called a **picture walk** before reading. This involves looking at each picture with the children, talking about it, and hypothesizing about the story that goes with the picture. You can do this with a regular-size trade book or with an oversize big book. Of course, you won't show pictures that might give away a surprise ending.

During Reading

1. Read the book, pausing to show the pictures to the entire group. Be careful not to sweep the book in front of the group; it's hard to look at a moving picture. Rather, hold the book still for one side of the group to see, then for the center of the group, then for the other side. Allow plenty of time. As you read the story, stop whenever it seems appropriate to discuss what has happened so far and what might happen next.

2. If you are reading a big book, it will probably be on an easel. This makes it easy for all the children to see both the print and the pictures. It is then logical to sweep a pointer or your hand under the words as you read. As you do this, children acquire a solid sense of the connection between your voice and the print. This procedure is an integral part of shared reading, which we describe later in this section.

After Reading

1. Talk about the story: what the children liked, what they didn't like, how it made them feel, and anything else they want to say about the story or book.

2. Have the children retell the story, recalling favorite parts, characters, problems, and so forth. If the book was not a story, have them tell what they remember. Though the children are not yet reading, you are teaching thinking skills that they willl use in reading.

It is not necessary to perform all these steps every time you read a story, except that you should always first read the book to yourself. Sometimes you will just read a book straight through for sheer pleasure and let it go. If you put the books you have read aloud on a bookshelf that children can reach, you'll see them "reading" the books to themselves and each other frequently. They already know the story, so it's easy for them to retell it to themselves.

Activities for Oral Language Development

We have talked about the language-rich, print-rich environment children need and the importance of talk as children work in this environment. In every center, there is opportunity for talk. There are many other specific activities that a teacher can provide to further encourage oral language growth. A discussion of a few follows.

Dramatic Play.   Children in learning centers often will play roles appropriate to the center. In the store center, for example, children adopt roles as storekeeper, shopper, or stock person. Often teachers keep large supplies of costumes so children can act out all sorts of roles, from princess to firefighter to knight.

Stories offer perfect opportunities for dramatic play. After hearing *The Three Billy Goats Gruff,* children will become the billy goats or the troll, changing their tone of voice and their actions. If you keep props handy, children can act out stories even without adult supervision. This is not "putting on a play." It is spontaneous dramatic play, and it is an important way for oral language to develop.

Puppets.   Children develop oral language by using and responding to puppets. These may range from full-size, realistic puppets to tongue depressors, Styrofoam boxes, and old socks.

Music.   Singing songs expands oral language, especially when children have learned the songs by heart and then make up their own words to fit their lives. For example, after learning "Row, row, row your boat," children may add "Zip, zip, zip your coat." After learning "The wheels on the bus . . . , " they may innovate "The siren on the truck goes . . . "

Art.   Encourage children to talk as they paint, draw, or use clay. Let them watch you and talk about what you are doing.

Poems, Rhymes, Chants, and Finger Plays.   No need for explanation here. Combining movement with language enhances both. Such activities never grow old, either for adults or for children. We've never met a teacher who didn't take continued pleasure in "Itsy, bitsy spider" even after doing it thousands of times over many years.

Comments

> To become competent language users, children need to hear and use language. Adults need to talk to them, listen to them, and provide materials and activities that encourage them to use all their senses as well as their imaginations. Children find virtually everything in the world interesting. We can give them the language to talk about what they are learning. Once they have the language in their ears and in their heads, they are on the road to becoming literate. When they meet those same words in print, they will be familiar with them. They will have expectations about how language in print will "sound" because they have had such rich experiences in the sounds of oral language.

Shared Reading

Chapter 4 introduced you to shared reading as a part of the modes of reading concept. The word *share* is a good one for this instructional strategy. As you read aloud to children, you invite them to share the reading task with you whenever it feels comfortable. You continue to "revisit" the story as many times as you and the children are interested in order to learn about print and about story.

While there are many ways to do shared reading, the following steps will provide guidelines as you conduct a shared-reading experience with children at the Early Emergent Literacy stage.

Introducing the Book

1   Bring the children together so they can all see the book. (Many times this is a big book; however, it is not always necessary to use a big book.)

2   Discuss the cover, title, author, illustrator, and other book elements.

3   Look at and talk about pictures, unless doing so gives away the ending.

4   Encourage predicting. If children are reluctant to predict or are predicting wildly, model the process. Make a prediction and explain what you saw in a picture or thought about the words in the title that makes your prediction appropriate. You may record the predictions that you and the children make and read them aloud when you discuss the story later.

Reading and Responding to the Book

1   Read the story aloud. Be sure the children can see each page. Run a pointer under the words as you read them, being careful not to block the print. Allow children to chime in if they want to. This is especially likely in stories that have a repetitive refrain.

2   Stop at key points for reactions, but don't linger. Get the story read.

3   Encourage the children to talk about the story. The discussion may be unprompted, or you may ask specific questions such as:

Were your predictions right?
What was your favorite part?
Describe how the story made you feel.
Which character did you like, and why?

Rereading and Responding Further to the Book

1   Reread the book, inviting children to join you in some manner. For example, during a second reading of *The Gingerbread Man,* children quite naturally will chime in for the repeated refrain, "Run, run, as fast as you can. You can't catch me. I'm the gingerbread man." Repeat the rereading process as many times as children want. Each time, they will participate more and more because they have the story almost memorized. As you point to the words, the children will connect the oral words to the print.

2   Encourage other responses to the book besides discussion. Examples:

Draw a picture.
Tell the story to a friend.
Make up a new ending and tell a friend.
Dramatize the story.

As you reread and reread books during shared reading, you will find many opportunities to emphasize certain things about language and sounds, such as beginning consonants in poems that use alliteration or ending sounds in rhymes.

Shared Writing

Like shared reading, shared writing was introduced in Chapter 4. Shared writing experiences are just as powerful with children at this stage of literacy development as shared reading. Shared writing will continue to be part of the instructional environment well beyond this stage. However, remember that by modeling the purposes and pleasures of reading and writing at this stage, you help children see where they are going in their development. Here we describe two shared-writing activities: morning messages and collaborative stories and reports.

**Figure 5.19
Sample of a Teacher-
Written Morning Message**

Today is Tuesday, October 14, 2001.
We are going to visit a farm today.
Kristen is 4 years old today. It is her birthday.
We will make decorations for our room this afternoon.

Morning Message.   A **morning message** is just what the term implies: a written activity with which to start the day. There are almost as many ways to do morning message as there are teachers. We will describe two here; others will be described in Chapter 6.

Teacher-Written Morning Message.   The teacher writes a message on the chalkboard before the children arrive (see Figure 5.19). He or she names the day and date, tells what will happen that day, and gives other information the children will find interesting. When the children are all settled, the teacher reads the message aloud to the group, sweeping a pointer under the words. Sometimes she or he reads the message more than once. The teacher usually spends some time asking children what they notice about the message. Table 5.1 shows a sample of dia-

**Table 5.1
Sample of Dialogue After Morning Message**

(The teacher has read aloud the morning message shown in Figure 5.19 and then reread it with the children.)

Teacher: Tell me something you notice about the message.

Child 1: Some dots.

Teacher: Point to them. (Child does so.) These are periods. We put them at the end of each sentence. It shows that the sentence has ended.

Child 2: Big letters.

Teacher: Yes, capital letters. Point to each one. (Child does so.) We need capitals at the beginning of each sentence. Where else do you see capitals?

Child 3: (Points to *Tuesday, October,* and *Kristen.*)

Teacher: Right! Sometimes the names of things begin with capital letters. (Points.) This is the name of the day, Tuesday. This is the name of the month, October. This is the name of a person, Kristen.

(Dialogue can continue as long as children are interested.)

logue related to the message in Figure 5.19. Though we call this shared writing, it is almost impossible to separate reading and writing—nor should you try.

Though a conversation such as the one in Table 5.1 is quite informal, it is instruction. It can continue as long as it seems interesting to the children. The things you call attention to or ask children to locate will depend on your assessment and on what the children have been learning. If your children have no knowledge yet of the kinds of writing conventions mentioned in Table 5.1, you may be more didactic. Your conversation might begin differently. Pointing while talking, you might say:

> *When we write, certain words need capital letters at the beginning. Sometimes we call these "big letters," but their name is "capital letters" or "upper case." Watch where I point. We use a capital letter for the first word of every sentence [pointing to each]. We also use a capital letter for the names of the day, the month, and a person [pointing to each]. Now who can tell me one place where we need a capital letter?*

This is not a formal lesson, but it is certainly teaching.

Child-Dictated Morning Message.   You may write the morning message with your children. Begin by asking the children to discuss what they should include in their message. After several ideas are put forth, ask a child to dictate a sentence. Use this opportunity to reinforce a sense of what makes a complete sentence. For example, if a child dictates, "Tuesday, October 14," prompt, "Let's make that a complete sentence." If the child doesn't understand, prompt further by cuing with the beginning, "Today is . . . " You are not giving a grammar lesson; after all, these children are very young. However, you are modeling and reinforcing. Children acquire a sense of what is or is not a complete sentence long before they can tell you anything about subjects or predicates. You continue to encourage dictated sentences, prodding, prompting, and nudging as the message takes shape.

Use the message to instruct about writing features children do not yet know and to reinforce those they do. Focus on a few conventions at a time. Keep up a running commentary as you record the children's dictated sentences. For example, say such things as:

> *I'm beginning this word with a capital because it is the name of a month. . . . I need an apostrophe here to form the contraction* isn't. *. . . I start the word* tomorrow *with the same letter that starts Tim's name. . . . That's a question, so I use a question mark to let whoever reads this know it is a question.*

There is no prescribed set of steps. You simply comment about what you are doing and why. If it seems appropriate, you ask the children to tell you what to do and why. If they know, fine. If not, tell them. It is an informal, comfortable, risk-free—and very powerful—way to teach.

Eventually you can use the children's own message to develop phonemic awareness and a sense of how phonics will help them figure out words. For example, let's say the children had dictated, "We are going to visit the farm today." You might have the following discussion with them about the words in the sentence:

Let's look and listen as we read this sentence: "We are going to visit a farm today." [Teacher and students read it together several times, the teacher pointing to the words.]

[Pointing to we*] I hear two sounds, and the first one almost isn't a sound—it's a way I make my mouth when a word begins with the letter* w. *[Teacher exaggerates slightly and confirms the two sounds.]*

When we write, every sound in a word we say has at least one letter to stand for that sound. When we say the word we, *we hear two sounds. The letter* w *stands for the first sound, and the letter* e *stands for the second. In this word, there are two sounds and two letters.*

There is no specific lesson being prescribed here, nor should there be. Children at this stage are developing their phonemic awareness and getting ready to use phonics to help them decode words when they read as well as figure out what letters to use when they write. We do not advocate a particular sequence for introducing the sounds of letters at this point. Virtually every sound in the English language will turn up within a few days in any dictated message or story. Use these words from the children's mouths to call attention to the separate sounds in words and the letters that can stand for those sounds. See the sources in For Additional Reading at the end of the chapter for more background and instructional ideas.

Collaborative Stories and Reports.   Almost any event that takes place during the day is reason for shared writing. Let's say a storm has blown up with thunder, lightning, and hail, causing the lights to go out and canceling outside playtime. What more perfect time to write a story?

- Ask the children to describe what the weather was like and how it made them feel. Put your own ideas in, too; collaboration means everyone has input.
- After you have talked about the storm for awhile, suggest writing a story.
- Take ideas from several children.
- Talk with the children about each idea before you write it to be sure you are writing just what you and they want to say.
- If you write on the chalkboard or a transparency, you can revise.
- As the children observe you write, talk about what you are doing and why. Think aloud about what a writer needs to consider. The most important thing to talk about is content: what are we trying to say, and are we saying it the best way we know how? Will our words make the reader know how the storm frightened us? Talk about choosing certain words to express certain ideas.
- Also talk about some of the mechanics of writing: the capitals, the punctuation, the choice of letters for certain sounds, and the need to form the letters carefully so others can read them.

Throughout the day, lead children to grasp the many purposes and uses of writing. For example, if you are planning a field trip, ask children, "How can we make sure we remember everything we have to do?" You want the children to suggest making a list. Then have them dictate what should go on the list and help you put the tasks in logical sequence. Or say, "How can I let each of your families know about our party?" The children should suggest a letter to go home and then help you compose it.

Language Experience

Language experience is a beginning reading approach closely related to the shared writing just discussed (Allen, 1976; Stauffer, 1969). There is a critical difference, however, between language experience and shared writing. In the language experience approach, the teacher serves only as the scribe, not as a collaborator; that is, the teacher writes down a story exactly as the child tells it and then uses it as reading material for the child. This is a useful instructional technique with children at the Early Emergent Literacy stage and the next two stages, as well as with bilingual students (Wilson & Cleland, 1989), struggling middle-school students (Sharp, 1990), and adult nonreaders (Mulligan, 1974).

The language experience approach is based on the theory that one learns to read most easily if what one reads sounds like the same language one speaks and is about something one knows. When a child dictates a story about his or her experience and the teacher writes down what the child says, the child has a better chance of reading the resulting story successfully than if the language and topic are unfamiliar.

Language Experience Procedures: Individual.   The purest use of language experience is with individual stories, since no two children share exactly the same experience or have exactly the same oral language. Table 5.2 shows the basic steps.

Table 5.2
Basic Steps for Language Experience Story with One Child

1. The teacher and child have a brief discussion and decide on a topic.
2. The teacher and child sit side by side with the teacher on the right so the child can see the teacher as she or he writes (unless the teacher is left-handed).
3. The child dictates and the teacher records exactly what the child says, saying the words aloud as they are written and commenting on conventions of print.
4. The teacher reads the completed story aloud, pointing to the words, as the child follows along.
5. The teacher rereads the story, inviting the child to join in.
6. The child is invited to read the story alone, or more rereadings together take place. This process will vary from child to child.
7. The story can be the basis for lessons about print.
8. A copy is made available to the child for multiple rereadings and for illustrating.

There are many ways to continue to get mileage from language experience stories. Some are rather formal and not appropriate for this stage, for instance, rereading a copy each day for a certain number of days, underlining the words retained, and then putting those words into a word bank. We believe that at this stage, language experience can be a valuable technique if it is not belabored. Do it from time to time. Enjoy the stories the children dictate. Help those who can to read their own stories. Compile the stories into a book—a sort of anthology. Send them home to families. But *don't* turn this into a formal ritual.

Language Experience Procedures: Group Dictation.   If several children contribute to a dictated story, it may take the form of what you may recall as an "experience chart." Unlike the individual story, in which you record the child's exact language, you can avoid nonstandard usage when taking group dictation. Keep such corrections low key: for example, simply comment after a dictated *ain't* that when writing we use *isn't*. You may want to indicate which child contributed which idea by writing such things as "David said: Today we will take a trip to the petting zoo."

As with the individual dictated story, many kinds of instruction can flow from the dictation, depending on what the children are ready for and interested in. Copies can be made so that each child who contributed has a personal collection of stories to reread as well as to illustrate.

While we do not recommend milking each dictated story to the extent that the children get bored with it, remember that reading a familiar story, written with one's own words and about one's own experience, almost guarantees a high degree of success. The more times children reread a story, the better they know it and the more likely they are to begin to recognize words from their own stories when seen in other places.

Helping Children Develop Phonemic Awareness

Phonemic awareness, as we noted in Chapter 3, refers to the child's understanding that speech is made up of individual sounds, which are the basis for forming words and syllables. This awareness, and the eventual ability to segment words into sounds, is a necessary part of learning to read and write.

To refresh your memory, **phonemes** are the speech sounds of language. They have no meaning in themselves. A single phoneme may be represented in print by one or more letters. For example, the word *cat* is made up of three phonemes, or sounds. In this case, each phoneme is spelled with one letter. The word *that* is also made up of three phonemes, but the first one is spelled with two letters: *th*. When we talk about knowing which letters are associated with which sounds, we are talking about phonics, a topic we will discuss further in later chapters.

How Phonemic Awareness Develops.   Many children acquire phonemic awareness and concepts about print quite naturally, independently of instruction. Chances are that such children have been read to a great deal and have seen both reading and writing modeled in their homes. They recognize and make rhymes. They play with sounds in words. They probably have been "writing" for some time. When you listen to such children talk to themselves as they write, you will hear them segmenting speech sounds: for example, /c/ – /a/ – /t/. They will write a letter (or a letter-like shape) for each sound. They will slow down when they want to write and deal with one word at a time, often repeating what they have said before going on.

All successful readers and writers have acquired phonemic awareness and concepts about print. The acquisition is not like learning to tie one's shoes, however. Learning to tie shoes involves a huge leap in manual dexterity. After fumbling and total failure, suddenly one day you can do it, and you can continue to do it forever. With phonemic awareness, acquisition is gradual.

For example, little children who know fairy tales may tell you that the first word is *onceuponatime*. They hear that group of words as a continuous sound— and, in fact, it *is* continuous sound when we speak. (Try it!) We do not pause between words in this phrase or in most groups of words. The group of words also has semantic unity for children: it tells them all kinds of things about the type of story that will follow. Therefore, children may write these four words as one when they write stories. We applaud all such efforts to express oral language in writing. Yet we may call attention to the conventional writing of *"once upon a time"* the next time we read a story with the children. After a while, the children's writing will reflect awareness of the separate words. Eventually their writing will reflect awareness of individual sounds in each word.

What to Do in the Classroom.   Direct instruction in phonemic awareness is seldom needed at the Early Emergent Literacy stage. (Older children who have not yet acquired phonemic awareness may need such instruction.) Generally, at this stage informal, indirect teaching is most appropriate. (For further discussion and references, see the position paper issued by the International Reading Association and the National Association for the Education of Young Children listed in For Additional Reading.)

Following are some ideas for reinforcing phonemic awareness throughout the day's activities.

Rhymes.   A regular part of every day should include reciting many familiar rhymes, emphasizing the rhyming words (in a poem) and then adding other words that also rhyme. This helps children develop an ear for rhyme.

You may also call attention to print. For example, take the words *bed* and *head* from a nursery rhyme and begin a **word wall** of rhyming words. As you build an ear for rhyme, you also build awareness for segmentation of sounds, separating *b-e-d* and *h-ea-d* as you write them. At the same time, you may note the two spellings for the same sound in the middle of the two words.

Finger Plays.   Finger plays help children build phonemic awareness because of the rhythmic nature of the recitation. If you do "Five little monkeys jumping on the bed . . . " with gestures, each word, and sometimes each syllable, gets attention.

Singing.   Songs reinforce concepts about words, since each word is often on a separate note. Sometimes each syllable is a separate note. It is a short leap from this awareness to awareness of individual sounds.

Clapping. Clap as you recite rhythmic poems. Then say the words and have children clap the syllables, stamp their feet, snap their fingers, or shrug their shoulders.

Playing Games with Words. You will think of many ways to turn learning activities into games throughout the day. For example, "I'm thinking of a word that begins like *baby* and is what I take to get clean," or "I'm thinking of a word that rhymes with *hot* and is something to cook in."

We suggest weaving instruction that will develop phonemic awareness into everything you do all day long. As Yopp (1995) says, "Phonemic awareness should not be addressed as an abstract isolated skill to be acquired through drill type activities." Later we will discuss more formal instruction for children who do not seem to be acquiring the skills naturally.

Scheduling the Balanced Literacy Day

The balanced literacy models presented in Chapter 4 cover preschool through grade 8. At the preschool level, the model is adjusted to meet the developmental needs of the students. Schedules will vary widely depending on a number of factors: how long the children are in a school setting (whether a half-day, full day, or extended day), the nature of the physical facility (whether part of a public school or a separate preschool), the philosophy of the school, the availability of aides and volunteers, the materials on hand, and much more.

While this text focuses on developing literacy, other equally important types of development are taking place with children at this time. Children are having experiences with numbers and shapes, with animals and plants, with art, and with music. They are learning to get along with others, to follow rules, to pay attention, to work and play with new materials, to visit new places, to relate to new adults, and perhaps to relate to children who are culturally quite different from them. Each teacher must find a way to schedule time so that all aspects of a child's development are supported, including but not limited to literacy.

The school day for children at this stage should not look like it would in a traditional primary-grade classroom. Children are not sitting at desks doing seatwork. They are participating in a wide variety of activities all over the classroom. Some of these involve interacting with books and writing materials, but not all. However, literacy activities may very well glue the day together. For example, each day may begin with children looking at books quietly (or drawing or writing) for a short period of time. This may be followed by the morning message and a read-aloud. More read-alouds take place throughout the day, along with other writing. Later in this chapter, we will look at a sample schedule.

Students Requiring Special Attention

You may find that some of your students at the Early Emergent Literacy stage need special attention. In this section, we offer some ideas concerning two types of such students: those with exceptionalities and those who are learning English as a second language.

Exceptionalities

Even at the early stage (and young age) we address in this chapter, development varies widely. Some variations are attributable to the natural differences in the population and some to specific difficulties in language, intellectual, behavioral, or physical development.

As you assess children at this stage, you will find some who do not yet exhibit all of the behaviors listed as benchmarks. Perhaps this is simply a lag in development that does not require special attention; for most children, all the behaviors will emerge naturally with time. Some children, however, are almost totally lacking in these behaviors, though they are the same age as most children at this stage. If this is the case, you may need to initiate steps to get special help for the child. Follow the suggested procedures for your school. You will usually begin by keeping careful anecdotal records, checklists, and other documentation. After you have gathered the requisite information, you will probably refer the child for further assessment by a specialist.

When a child is referred for special assessment and possible special placement, he or she will likely remain with you for at least part of the day as part of a mainstreaming or inclusion policy. Educators are a long way from settling issues regarding the identification of special learning problems (including giftedness) and how best to help children who exhibit some kind of exceptionality. For the purposes of this book, we take a simple and uncomplicated view. We understand there is justification for identifying and labeling certain groups of children to get appropriate help for them. We are concerned, however, with how *you* help these children *while they are with you.*

- You are responsible for doing for each child whatever that child needs to the best of your ability.

- You must not assume that others will take care of children who fall outside the parameters of "normal" on either end. In any given classroom, you are the teacher for the entire range of developmental stages found in the age group you teach. If you are a prekindergarten teacher, most children will be at the Early Emergent Literacy stage, but some may have little oral language at all and some may already be reading and writing independently.

- If some of your children are pulled out for special attention, you must find out what is being done for them and reinforce it while the children are with you.

- You must continue to read books and articles that teach you more about the kinds of problems your children face.

- You must get to know the families of your children in order to encourage and support them.

You may need to adapt some procedures or materials for certain children in your class. You will want to accommodate differences without isolating those who need special attention. You may have to accommodate a wheelchair, for instance. You may need large-print books for visually impaired children or microphones for those with hearing impairments. You may need special computer programs. But whatever special attention a child needs, you are not alone; you will be able to provide what is needed with help and support from your colleagues, special teachers, the child's family, and professional organizations.

We believe that good teaching is good teaching, regardless of the recipient. This means that a classroom environment should support and foster language development for all children, regardless of their literacy stage. So if some of your children have not yet developed much oral language or begun to show the other behaviors described in this chapter, your job is to assess them carefully, refer them to specialists if appropriate, but keep on teaching them every single day, giving them the language they need.

Second-Language Learners

To be certain that second-language learners are receiving the special attention they may need, you should focus both on what the school does for such students and on what you as an individual teacher can do.

What the School Does. Your school system may have a series of questions that are asked about each child at enrollment. Examples are:

- What is the primary language spoken in the home?
- Does the child speak English or the first language at home?
- Does the child speak English outside the home?
- What degree of oral English fluency does the child demonstrate?
- Are the parents bilingual?
- Is the child already literate in any language?

Depending on the answers to such questions, the child may be assigned to a class for English as a Second Language children or to a bilingual classroom in which the child is taught in his or her native language while concurrently being taught English.

What You Do. Even when a child in your class is assigned to a special program, you will want to do your own assessment using the levels of language production discussed in Chapter 3. Listen and observe carefully as the child interacts with other children and with adults. Many factors impinge on a child's oral language usage, not the least of which is fear of a new situation. The child who refused to speak at all during enrollment may show a more advanced level of production when relaxed in the safe environment you provide in the classroom.

A simple technique to encourage speech is to expand what a child has said. For example, the non-English speaker points to the water fountain and grunts or says, "*Agua.*" You reply, "Water. You want a drink of water." You elaborate and rephrase, though you keep it simple. The other children will mimic you, of course, so you will soon hear them all doing the same kind of elaborating and rephrasing. As the non-English speaker reaches for paper and crayons, another child says, "Do you want some paper? Here is a piece of paper. You may use my crayons, too. What color do you want? The yellow one?"

The first thing the child needs is the words for necessities in the environment: bathroom, lunch, drink, home, bus, coat, book, paper, hurt, cold, hot, sick, tired, teacher, and so forth. The other children in the class are probably the best teachers. At the same time, you will continue to label orally (and in print) objects in the room, and the labels may be in more than one language. In addition, you will find opportunities to embed labels in elaborated sentences: "This is the window. Look out the window. See the bird? The bird is in the tree. We can look out the window and see a bird in a tree." This technique will benefit all the children and will be especially helpful for second-language learners.

Be sure to have audiotapes of stories. They are tireless, retelling stories over and over, and building language in the process.

We know this is probably not necessary to say, but we have observed classrooms in which the second-language speaker is isolated from virtually all normal activity, put in a corner with paper and crayons, and ignored. On the contrary, we also have seen classrooms that welcome the child with open arms, the teacher bubbling with speech. It doesn't matter that the child doesn't understand all the words. What matters is that the child feels a part of the class.

We believe that what these learners need is no different from what all learners need: instructional support that is developmentally appropriate—in other words, pleasure in where they are now and scaffolding or support in helping them grow. For these learners, steeping in the English language is a huge need. Therefore, all the usual activities are appropriate: reading aloud, rereading, finger plays, songs, nursery rhymes, acting out stories, drawing, building, splashing, and stirring—all accompanied by language.

A Diverse Classroom at Work

Let's return to Jeff Gomez's prekindergarten classroom, described in the Eyewitness section at the beginning of this chapter. Table 5.3 shows his daily schedule for his 4-hour preschool program. Look at the schedule and then read the descriptions that follow.

8:00–8:20: Arrival; check-in; independent activity.   As children enter the room, they turn over their tags on the big attendance chart so Mr. Gomez can tell at a glance who is here. The tags have the children's photos as well as their names. The children put their wraps in individual cubbies and check their mailboxes.

Next, the children engage in quiet literacy activities. There are no desks or assigned seats. Children settle wherever they are comfortable. There are pillows, bean bag chairs, writing tables, an old sofa, and, of course, the floor. Some children look at books independently. Some talk quietly in pairs as they share a book. Some are writing. Some are drawing and writing captions. While there is a hum in the air, the atmosphere is quiet and focused.

During this time, and at other times when children are working quietly, classical music is played softly.

8:20–8:40: Calendar; world and local news; personal news.   Mr. Gomez first talks about the calendar—the month, the day, special events—then the weather, and finally news. He reports these in English and in Spanish, which is the first

Table 5.3
Daily Schedule for Mr. Gomez's Class: a Four-Hour Preschool Program

Time	Activity
8:00–8:20	Arrival; check-in; independent activity
8:20–8:40	Calendar; world and local news; personal news
8:40–9:00	Child-dictated morning message
9:00–9:15	Independent reading and writing
9:15–9:30	Rug time; story
9:30–10:00	Centers
10:00–10:15	Snack and rest
10:15–11:00	Centers
11:00–11:15	Rug time; informational book
11:15–11:40	Science/math experiment or manipulatives
11:40–12:00	Clean-up; story/song/poem/finger play

language of several children. All the children are invited to share something they heard on the news or something their parents read to them from a newspaper. Some days they share personal news, such as the birth of a baby sister or brother. Children are encouraged to use their first language if they are not fluent in English.

8:40–9:00: Child-dictated morning message. Teacher and children compose the morning message together. Mr. Gomez writes on chart paper using a felt marker. Once a week, a bilingual aide composes a morning message with the Spanish-speaking children. All morning messages are read and discussed.

9:00–9:15: Independent reading and writing. The children continue independent activities while Mr. Gomez completes daily "housekeeping" chores. This time may also be used for individual assessment of one or two children.

9:15–9:30: Rug time; story. The children come to sit on the rug in front of the teacher's rocking chair. This is a time for shared reading of some kind. Mr. Gomez has some Spanish books as well as some that show both English and Spanish.

9:30–10:00: Centers. Children work at assigned learning centers. Each child has a clothespin with his or her name written on it. The centers are listed by name and with a picture on a large chart. Mr. Gomez clips each child's clothespin to the center where the child should go. Every child is assigned to each center at least twice a week. Some of the centers are art, housekeeping, water and sand, store, listening, blocks, book nook, dramatic play, pets, and computer. Some of the activity at centers is "free," while at other times a specific task may await the children.

Some days, Mr. Gomez leads the children in whole-class music during this time. Many instruments are available, though not always in free reach of the children. There is a piano in the room, and a guitar. Even when nothing particular is planned, Mr. Gomez uses odd moments for songs and dancing.

10:00–10:15: Snack and rest.   Family members take turns providing healthful snacks each day. Children distribute the snacks. Following snacks, all close their eyes and rest for a few minutes.

10:15–11:00: Centers.   Mr. Gomez circulates as the children work at centers, using this time to make notes and occasionally pulling a child aside for individual assessment.

On some days, this long period of centers is scheduled tightly. On other days, it is broken into a defined period of assigned centers and a longer period of free time. The children spend a great deal of time at the beginning of the year learning procedures for conducting themselves during this kind of activity.

Books are everywhere, including many books in Spanish. The children are free to take out and read any book in the classroom. It is clear from the way they handle the books that they have been taught to respect them. Some books are in plastic tubs, grouped by topic and labeled. For example, the tub that holds books about snakes and reptiles has a picture of a snake on the front, and the ABC book tub has letters on the front. There are also shelves with picture books, both with print and wordless. Books with audiotapes are in the listening center.

Writing tools and paper are available in several places. Each child knows where things are and knows the procedures for getting and returning materials. Each child also has a take-home envelope for special things to share at home. By next year, Mr. Gomez hopes to have at least two computers available for the children to use for games and information on CD-ROMs.

11:00–11:15: Rug time; informational book.   Mr. Gomez is very interested in science and math. He takes time every day to read aloud an informational book about a topic in one of these curricular areas, and he follows the reading with an activity related to the book content.

11:15–11:40: Science/math experiment or manipulatives.   This time is directly related to the book Mr. Gomez has just read. He may demonstrate a physics principle or present children with a problem and lead them to hypothesize. Often these activities stretch over several days. They may be related to matter, plants, the elements, weather, motion, animals, or any other area of science. They may also be related to counting, shapes, quantities, estimating, or anything else related to mathematics. This period ends with shared writing of some kind.

Sometimes the activities from 11:00 to 11:40 are reversed. Mr. Gomez may begin with an experiment, demonstration, or problem and end the period with a book. The time is flexible, but it always includes an activity, a book, and writing.

11:40–12:00: Clean-up; story/song/poem/finger play.   After everything is cleaned up and put away, Mr. Gomez takes a few minutes to review the day. The children talk about what they did that day and what they learned. This is, of course, exactly what families will ask when the children get home: "What did you learn in school today?" The children also talk a bit about what they will be reading, writing, and doing the next day.

Finally, there is a story, a poem, a song, or a finger play, one that Mr. Gomez has planned in advance. The Spanish-speaking children have taught the others many songs, stories, and poems in Spanish, and these are included frequently. By the end of their year with Mr. Gomez, these children will know hundreds of stories, songs, poems, and finger plays.

Accommodating Variations

Despite the schedule just described, the day in Jeff Gomez's classroom seems to flow from one thing to the next, and many deviations from the posted routine occur. All kinds of things disrupt the regular schedule: a thunderstorm, a butterfly, a new sprout in a garden, baby guinea pigs—all are good reasons to vary the usual agenda.

The exact activities in any class vary widely, of course, but some things are common to all language-rich classrooms. Children talk a lot—to the adults, to one another, and to themselves. They spend a lot of time with print: books, magazines, maps, signs, packaged and canned goods, and so on. They write a lot. Perhaps most in common is the frequent request they direct to any adult: "Will you read us a story?"

Summary

In this chapter, we have examined the benchmarks and behaviors that indicate a child is at the Early Emergent Literacy stage. You have seen how to assess oral language, reading and book knowledge, and writing using informal assessment, and you have learned some appropriate instructional strategies for use in your classroom.

At this stage of children's literacy development, it is especially important to create a language- and print-rich environment with appropriate materials, tools, and furniture. The physical arrangements in your classroom—for instance, learning centers and a listening/viewing area—can help support literacy development. You can also foster literacy development by reading aloud, talking constantly to the children to expand their oral language, labeling objects in the classroom, and making the environment comfortable and inviting.

At this stage of development, several instructional strategies are especially important for a balanced literacy program: read-alouds; oral language activities, including dramatic plays, puppets, poems, and so forth; shared reading; shared writing, including morning messages as well as collaborative stories and reports; language experience activities, in which children read something they themselves have written; and phonemic awareness activities. Although schedules may vary a great deal, these literacy activities should take place frequently throughout the day.

Some students may require special attention. For example, children with various exceptionalities may need adaptations in procedures and materials. Children who are learning English as a second language need to have their production of English encouraged on an everyday basis. Overall, though, the instruction for such students differs little from what you have already learned about teaching reading and language arts. That's because we believe that good teaching is good teaching; meeting the needs of each child is mostly a matter of matching appropriate instruction to the child's developmental stage. We are all in the process of reaching a new stage of literacy—it is a lifelong process.

FOR ADDITIONAL READING

Adams, M. J. (1990). *Beginning to read: Thinking and learning about print. A summary.* Urbana, IL: Center for the Study of Reading, University of Illinois at Urbana-Champaign.

Campbell, R. (Ed.). (1998). *Facilitating preschool literacy.* Newark, DE: International Reading Association.

Glazer, S., & Burke, E. M. (1994). *An integrated approach to early literacy.* Needham Heights, MA: Allyn and Bacon.

International Reading Association/National Association for the Education of Young Children. (1998). Learning to read and write: Developmentally appropriate practices for young children. A joint position statement of the International Reading Association (IRA) and the National Association for the Education of Young Children (NAEYC). *Young Children, 53,* pp. 30–46.

Salinger, T. (1996). *Literacy for young children.* Englewood Cliffs, NJ: Prentice-Hall.

Strickland, D. S., & Morrow, L. M. (Eds.). (1989). *Emerging literacy: Young children learn to read and write.* Newark, DE: International Reading Association.

FOR EXPLORATION: ELECTRONIC RESOURCES

Center for the Improvement of Early Reading Achievement.
http://www.ciera.org/   This web site offers much research-based information on the early stages of literacy development, as well as links to other sites.

PALS: Activities.
http://curry.edschool.virginia.edu/curry/centers/pals/pals-activities.html PALS stands for Phonological Awareness and Literacy Screening, and this site offers dozens of activities related to rhyming, letter sounds, alphabet recognition, and the like, as well as links to teaching resources.

The Perpetual Preschool: Language and Literacy Area.
http://www.perpetualpreschool.com/languageideas.html   This web site contains a variety of language activities used by teachers in their classrooms.

Read*Write*Now! Activities for Reading and Writing Fun.
http://www.ed.gov/Family/RWN/Activ97/   This online booklet, developed as part of the national America Reads Challenge, offers literacy games and other activities for children at various stages, including preschoolers.

Rebus Rhymes: Mother Goose and Others.
http://www.enchantedlearning.com/Rhymes.html   This web site contains dozens of nursery rhymes that teachers can use in their preschool and kinder-garten classrooms, plus visual cues to help children learn the words they are seeing and hearing.

CLASSROOM APPLICATIONS

1. Observe a class of children ages 3 to 5. Using the benchmarks in this chapter, try to determine if most children fall within this stage of literacy development. How did you tell? Are any not exhibiting these behaviors yet? Do any seem well beyond this stage? How did you document this?

2. Assess one child's book knowledge using the guidelines provided in this chapter. Then describe the kind of instructional support that would most benefit this child, and explain your rationale.

3. Combine the results for the child you assessed with similar assessments for several other children. Assume all of these children will be in your class. Plan a classroom literacy environment that would meet the needs of all of them.

4. Assess the environment of two prekindergarten classrooms in terms of centers, materials, schedule, arrangement of activities, and so forth. Devise a checklist to help you remember what to look for. Discuss what you found as well as what changes you would recommend and why.

5. Plan a balanced literacy preschool day for a group of children who attend a full-day program.

The Emergent Literacy Stage

FOCUS

As you read the Eyewitness section, ask yourself the following questions:

1. On the basis of what she observes, what notes might Mrs. Bullock be making to be transferred to individual records later?
2. What do you know about the children's ability to construct meaning when you learn their response to *Amelia Bedelia*?

Eyewitness

We are looking into Mrs. Bullock's kindergarten class. The twenty children in this class are engaged in independent literacy activities of various kinds. Over in the reading corner, two boys sit side by side on floor cushions, sharing a book. As we watch, one boy turns the pages and seems to be pointing to and talking about the pictures. The other child adds comments and points to other things, then continues turning pages. The two boys go through the entire book this way, talking about the pictures. Then they turn back to the beginning, and one boy appears to be reading the story. He points to words as he reads. From where we are, we cannot tell whether he has memorized the story or actually recognizes the words, but he seems to be matching his words with the print on the page.

We glance around the room to see what else these children can do. Two are sorting alphabet cards to match upper- and lower-case letters. Another is paging through a child-made personal dictionary with both words and pictures, naming the pictures and pointing to the word on each page. Another bends low over a piece of paper, the tip of his tongue moving back and forth between his lips, fiercely concentrating on what he is writing. A little girl is telling two friends about a book she just heard on an audiotape.

During these independent activities, Mrs. Bullock moves about the room, observing and making notes. She also uses this time to hold individual conferences with five children. A chart tells, both with words and pictures, which children are to have conferences today and what to bring to the conference. Today each child is to bring his or her writing folder to the conference.

Later in the day, the children come to the rug at the front of the room, where Mrs. Bullock sits in a rocking chair and reads aloud Amelia Bedelia *(Parish, 1963/1981). The children chuckle with delight as Amelia Bedelia makes such silly mistakes as "changing the towels" by cutting holes in them.*

In Mrs. Bullock's classroom, we have witnessed children in the process of growing toward literacy: the **Emergent Literacy** stage. They already see themselves as readers and writers. All make reading and writing an important part of their daily lives. They make good use of the reading and writing materials that surround them and are available to them throughout the day. They *are*, in fact, readers and writers.

Some teachers believe this is the most exciting stage of literacy to share with children. In classrooms with children at this stage, the students joyfully embrace their growing literacy. Most of the children are experiencing success. As teachers provide solid instruction for these children, they also try to identify those who are struggling and provide the extra scaffolding they need not to falter.

BENCHMARKS for the Emergent Literacy Stage

No matter where you teach, your school system is likely to have its own set of benchmarks or standards beginning with kindergarten, or with what we are calling the Emergent Literacy stage. Each such set probably has been written through the considerable efforts of a committee whose members have read about and studied children of this age. Often these sets of standards are at the same time too broad and too limiting to be truly helpful. Still, they represent what each child (and his or her teacher) is held to in terms of achievement each year.

The United States does not (yet) have national standards. So states, local school districts, and sometimes individual schools often devise their own sets of standards, stating what competencies, behaviors, and attitudes are expected at each grade level. This is a tough job. The very simple final product, which is often a checklist, doesn't begin to reflect the enormous struggle for consensus that went on during the drawing up of these standards.

We do not have a quarrel with any of these sets of standards. We do, however, remind you that for us, the definition, purpose, and use may be somewhat different. We present behaviors that will indicate to you that a child is indeed *at* a particular stage of literacy development, thus helping you plan appropriate instruction for that child.

No two sets of benchmarks (along with sample behaviors) will match exactly; however, most agree on the big ideas. Children develop through the stages mostly in the same sequence, though not always at the same rate. Think of the process as crossing a creek on stepping stones—one stone for each stage. We slip occasionally. We may have one foot on one stone and one on the next. As we reach for the next stone, we may fear slipping and retreat to a previous, more secure stone. But having had a glimpse of things to come, we try again, and this time we are more confident because we know where we are going.

The following benchmarks and behaviors are typical of children ages 5 to 7, kindergarten through first grade. Some children are already beyond this stage when they begin kindergarten. Others may still be at this stage beyond first grade. Remember as you read that the behaviors are samples: they are neither limiting nor inclusive.

Oral Language

BENCHMARK → **The student exhibits behaviors of the Early Emergent Literacy stage to a greater degree.**

BENCHMARK → **The student uses standard sentence construction and grammar.**

✔ Is recognizing use of nonstandard language in self and others

✔ Is developing a sense that school/book language is perhaps different from home or neighborhood language

BENCHMARK → **The student's facility with oral language is growing.**

✔ Makes self understood by peers and adults

✔ Follows "rules" for conversation and discussion

✔ Retains oral directions

✔ Can ask questions for clarification

✔ Can paraphrase what others have said

✔ Participates in sharing

BENCHMARK ➧ **The student's oral language reflects literature to which he or she is exposed.**

✔ Uses new words from stories

✔ Uses "book language" when appropriate; that is, storytelling narrative is clearly different from conversation or simply relating an event

✔ Enjoys "making a play" of a favorite story

BENCHMARK ➧ **The student shows pleasure in language.**

✔ Enjoys jokes related to words, such as puns

✔ Enjoys tongue twisters

✔ Enjoys hearing humorous books related to idioms

✔ Is proud of learning new words

✔ Tries out new words and asks what words mean

Reading

BENCHMARK ➧ **The student exhibits behaviors of the Early Emergent Literacy stage to a greater degree.**

BENCHMARK ➧ **The student has acquired most or all of the concepts about print.**

✔ Handles book in correct position; knows where to begin reading and in what direction to read

✔ Can point to a word, two words, a letter, two letters

✔ Knows that print should match the voice of the reader

✔ Knows about such book parts as title, author, and so forth

BENCHMARK ➧ **The student is using print in everyday life.**

✔ Can locate a specific book, record, tape, and so forth

✔ Recognizes some environmental print such as brand names and fast-food restaurant signs

BENCHMARK ➧ **The student is acquiring word recognition skills.**

✔ Recognizes and can name most letters

✔ Can match many upper- and lower-case letters

✔ Recognizes and can name some words

✔ Recognizes own name in print and perhaps other names

✔ Shows evidence of phonemic awareness

✔ Has a sense that letters "make sounds"

✔ Is beginning to use phonics; knows many letter-sound associations, including both consonants and vowels

✔ Is beginning to use other decoding strategies such as sight words, context, graphics, and word structure

BENCHMARK ➧ **The student is constructing meaning.**

✔ Can retell a story page by page

✔ Can summarize

✔ Participates in small-group and whole-class discussions about books and stories

✔ Talks about books with others

✔ Responds to books in writing

✔ Begins to see self as a reader

Writing

BENCHMARK ➧ **The student exhibits continued growth in many of the Early Emergent Literacy behaviors.**

BENCHMARK ➧ **The student is using spelling and other writing conventions.**

✔ Can write own name (perhaps first name only), with all or most of the letters present, though not necessarily formed correctly

✔ Can name most letters in random presentation

✔ Forms letterlike shapes and some correct letters

✔ Uses some punctuation

✔ Shows phonemic awareness and beginning association of letters and sounds in attempts to spell

✔ Can give a letter sound or say a word that begins with the letter sound

BENCHMARK ➧ **The student is using writing for own purposes.**

✔ Can keep a journal that may combine drawing and writing

✔ Attempts to read others' writing

✔ Shares writing with others

✔ Shows interest in practicing writing, often through copying favorite stories from books

BENCHMARK ➧ **The student is becoming familiar with the writing process.**

✔ Uses the steps of the process appropriately with guidance

✔ Understands that the author of what is read has also gone through a process of some kind

BENCHMARK ➤ **The student is constructing meaning in writing.**

✔ Responds to reading

✔ Composes both narrative and expository pieces

✔ Expresses and reports on personal events and feelings

Connecting to Other Chapters

FOCUS

As you read about the Emergent Literacy stage, ask yourself the following questions:

1. How does this stage differ from the previous one in terms of assessment and planning instruction?
2. What are some ways you can adjust for the range of stages in your classroom?
3. How does a blocked literacy schedule work in kindergarten and in first grade?

It is impossible to isolate literacy behaviors and address them in only one stage. As we have emphasized throughout this book, literacy development occurs along a continuum; therefore, behaviors don't occur at one precise point. They give hints that they are coming before they appear consistently. They also sometimes disappear briefly long after we have thought they were secure. Your assessment-based instruction must reflect this understanding.

The Emergent Literacy stage usually occurs when children are in kindergarten or first grade. However, some children in these grades will be at the previous literacy stage, while others will be at a subsequent stage. Children who display few emergent literacy behaviors need the assessment and instructional ideas presented for the Early Emergent Literacy stage in Chapter 5. Children who already exhibit all of the emergent literacy behaviors and more need the assessments and instructional strategies discussed for the Beginning Reading and Writing stage in Chapter 7, or beyond.

As you read this chapter, remember that we are talking about children who are at the Emergent Literacy stage, regardless of their grade or age, and that your assessment and instruction must be adjusted to fit each child. Keep in mind the assessment techniques and instructional strategies presented in Part One of this text.

Using the Benchmarks to Assess the Child and Determine the Stage of Instruction

In this section, we show you how to assess informally the three major areas of literacy—oral language, reading, and writing—building on the Early Emergent Literacy stage and adding the new benchmarks for the Emergent Literacy stage. Along with the assessments, we suggest strategies to help children who do not yet exhibit the sample behaviors consistently.

If your school system requires you to use its benchmarks, you may want to supplement that assessment with some or all of the assessments presented here. In fact, many of these tools may be used to assess local benchmarks.

Keep in mind that you should begin both instruction and assessment on the very first day of school using the kinds of materials, methods, and strategies that you know promote literacy development in all children. As the days pass, you begin to gather information about each child in each of the areas. In other words,

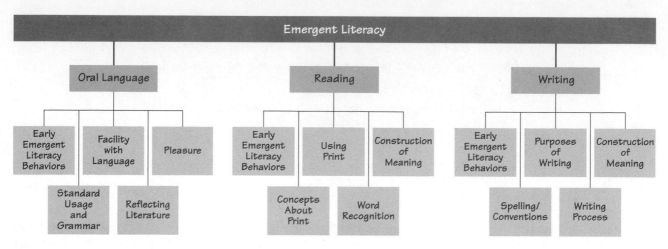

Figure 6.1
Menus for Assessing the Emergent Literacy Stage

assessment takes place as you teach. For English-language learners, assess literacy behaviors in students' first languages, if possible. If assessment is in English, expect to see some delay for second-language students, but continue to provide these students with comprehensible input in English.

Figure 6.1 presents the three areas to be assessed, with menus showing the major components of each area. As we discuss each area, additional figures will show the discrete items of each component. Sample class checklists are presented at the end of our discussion of each of the three areas. Sample individual checklists are in the Resource File. From time to time, we will also note how cultural and language differences affect both assessment and instruction.

Oral Language

Children's oral language continues to grow rapidly as they move from the Early Emergent Literacy stage into the Emergent Literacy stage. Much of the development is refinement of language begun earlier. With the influence of school, some new behaviors also begin to emerge. Your assessment of these areas will be largely based on observation during whole-class, small-group, and individual activities. We do not suggest using a specific assessment instrument; rather, you make inferences based on what you observe so that you can continue to support further development.

The major areas we address are continued development of behaviors from the Early Emergent Literacy stage; standard usage and grammar (Figure 6.2); facility with oral language (Figure 6.3); reflecting literature (Figure 6.4); and pleasure in language (Figure 6.5). A class checklist for oral language (Figure 6.6) appears near the end of the section. An individual checklist is in the Resource File.

BENCHMARK

The student exhibits behaviors of the Early Emergent Literacy stage to a greater degree.

Recall the oral language benchmarks in the Early Emergent Literacy stage from Chapter 5. Most of these behaviors will be present with increasing consistency and maturity as children move into the Emergent Literacy stage. This growth is not a leap. Nor is it a sudden "aha" experience such as a child might have

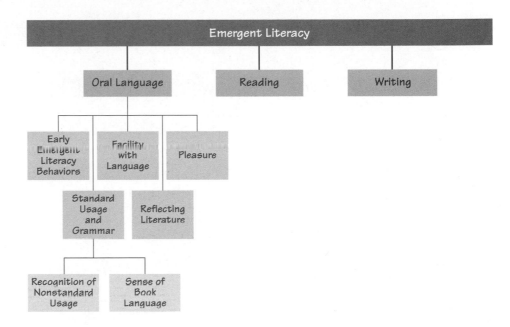

**Figure 6.2
Oral Language: Standard
Usage and Grammar**

in math when suddenly grasping the principle of multiplying by zero. This growth is gradual and mostly steady, given continued good support.

Listen to children who have come to school using nonstandard English, whatever its root. Note which are beginning to "catch themselves" in such usage and change their wording to standard usage. When you ask direct questions, perhaps during a collaborative writing activity, which children can suggest a way to word ideas using standard language? Note which children are beginning to switch language from playground usage, which reflects home or neighborhood, to classroom usage, which reflects school and book language.

Instructional Strategies.   This may be one of the most ticklish and divisive areas of teaching. You must walk a path between two somewhat conflicting notions. On one hand, you know it is important for all children to eventually be able to use standard English comfortably. On the other hand, you value whatever language a child brings to school as reflecting the child's culture and family.

Interrupting a child's speech to correct his or her usage may not result in more standard usage and may make the child reluctant to speak at all. Instead, continue to model standard usage. When revising and editing written work that requires standard English, focus on the work, not the child, so that changes make the work stronger rather than appearing to denigrate the child's language. Praise specific instances of self-correction. Keep in mind that some students are adjusting to regional or cultural differences or dialects of English, while second-language learners face the dual task of learning a new language and distinguishing between informal, conversational language and book language.

Though some of the following behaviors were discussed in Chapter 5, we elaborate here because children at this level are almost certainly in a school setting. Facility in oral language includes the cultural aspects of communicating, such as

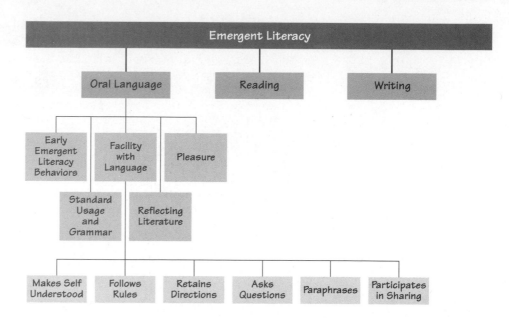

**Figure 6.3
Oral Language: Facility
with Language**

knowing acceptable ways to address elders or when to remain silent and when to speak. Second-language learners may acquire basic vocabulary and structures of English long before they are comfortable with the cultural differences.

✔ **Makes self understood
by peers and adults**

Note which children are able to communicate with classmates and adults. Most probably will have no difficulty. If some do, ask yourself the following: Is it a matter of inability to articulate the sounds of language clearly? If so, should I consider referral to a language or speech specialist? Is it lack of vocabulary? Is it social—that is, do the other children not want to listen to this child for some reason? Is the child's behavior making others not want to understand?

Instructional Strategies.   If you have children who struggle to make others understand, and the problem is not rooted in difficulties with articulation (which call for a speech specialist), you may need to build more opportunities for children to communicate directly with each other. For example, if a child relates something to a group, other children should be free to ask questions if they don't understand. Such talk should not be filtered through you but instead should be directly child to child.

✔ **Follows "rules" for
conversation and
discussion**

Note which children are abiding by guidelines established for discussions in the classroom as well as which are comfortable in informal conversation.

Instructional Strategies.   Keep emphasizing why guidelines are necessary for effective verbal interaction with others to work. Lead children to express the reasons for guidelines; praise their efforts to monitor themselves.

✔ **Retains oral directions**
✔ **Can ask questions for
clarification**

Observe which children are able to remember a series of oral directions such as "First finish your rough draft. Put the rough draft in your writing folder. Then you may work on your math or read with a buddy. Check the schedule to see when you are to work on the computer." Note which children seem aware of when they do not understand something and ask questions to help themselves.

Instructional Strategies.   If children cannot remember oral directions, consider writing the directions on the chalkboard so everyone can refer to them. As children begin to write with more ease, introduce the habit of taking notes about what to do.

We want children to be aware of when they don't understand something and to ask questions as needed. Be sure children feel free to ask questions. Don't assume that the child who has questions wasn't listening.

Some children are not aware they do not understand. When you ask, "Are there any questions?" no hands go up, but as a child begins to work, she or he is full of questions. Children cannot always anticipate what will be difficult to understand in advance of beginning the task. One way to help children monitor their own understanding of directions is to ask them to retell what to do.

Some children, in contrast, ask more questions than needed, seemingly because they need the special attention from the teacher. You find that when the child asks for clarification, he or she understands perfectly and can tell you exactly what to do, but needs reassurance. In this case, give whatever support is needed while gradually working to build the child's confidence.

✔ **Can paraphrase what others have said**

The ability to paraphrase relates to the child's understanding of what was heard as well as the child's own language for putting something "into his or her own words." Note which children are able to do this consistently.

Instructional Strategies.   Model paraphrasing when you talk with children. Demonstrate the difference between repeating exact words and putting ideas into one's own words. Help children see how paraphrasing helps others know we have understood them.

Paraphrasing may be difficult for some second-language learners. At first, accept virtual repetition of what was heard and ask questions to be sure of understanding. Continue to model paraphrasing until these students are able to do it independently.

✔ **Participates in sharing**

Note which children are willing to participate in sharing time.

Instructional Strategies.   If a child never wants to share, try to determine the reason privately. Is it shyness? Would sharing in a small group be easier? Is it because the child has tried to share but the other children didn't listen? Do you need to reaffirm polite behavior during sharing?

Is the child unsure of what to say? Perhaps you need to provide some structure for sharing time. For example, if you have "show-and-tell," teach this procedure: Show your item. Name it. Tell what it's for. Tell why you wanted to share it. Ask for questions.

BENCHMARK

The student's oral language reflects literature to which he or she is exposed (Figure 6.4).

✔ **Uses new words from stories**

Note whether children incorporate words from stories they hear into their everyday language. There is no specific number of new words to count, of course. Just observe which children experiment with new words and which do not.

Instructional Strategies.   Discuss words as you engage in read-alouds and in shared reading. Encourage children to use story words both during discussions of the story and at other times during the day. Acknowledge those who do so with specific praise: "That word was in the story we read this morning." Share your own experience of learning new words and beginning to "try out" new words first orally and then in writing.

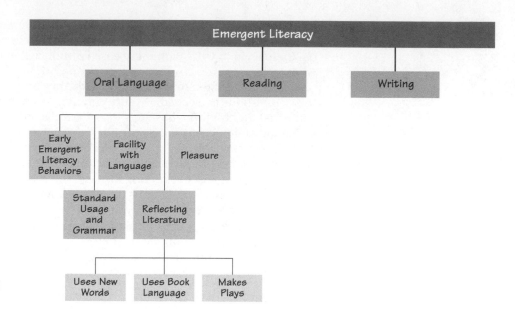

Figure 6.4
Oral Language: Reflecting Literature

✔ Uses "book language" when appropriate; that is, storytelling narrative is clearly different from conversation or simply relating an event

✔ Enjoys "making a play" of a favorite story

BENCHMARK
The student shows pleasure in language (Figure 6.5).

✔ Enjoys jokes related to words, such as puns
✔ Enjoys tongue twisters
✔ Enjoys hearing humorous books related to idioms

Note which children use the story language as they retell a story.

Instructional Strategies. Model retelling that uses book language. Demonstrate the difference between retelling in your own language and using that of the book. Both are important, of course, but you want to encourage a sensitivity to book language. Help children see the difference between "Pooh wasn't very smart and he was always wanting to eat honey" and "Pooh was a bear of very little brain. When he was hungry, he always said it was 'time for a little something.'" If such story language was a part of your family language, share that with children.

Note which children participate in making stories into plays. Which are comfortable using the story and character language? The ability to assume the role of a character in a story shows both a grasp of the story's meaning and oral language facility.

Instructional Strategies. Allow children time and space to role-play stories, both under your supervision and independently. Consider taking a part yourself to model using the language of a story character.

Note which children are enjoying language-related jokes such as puns. Which are beginning to enjoy tongue twisters and books whose humor depends on understanding idiomatic language? You saw an example of this behavior in the Eyewitness at the beginning of the chapter. Mrs. Bullock's children "caught on" to the humor that relies on understanding that Amelia Bedelia was interpreting directions such as "change the towels" literally; she changed the towels by cutting holes in them. Children at this stage understand that she should have changed them by replacing them with fresh towels.

Some humorous books are particularly based on knowledge of homonyms. Fred Gwynne has written several, including *The King Who Rained* (1970). This book and others are listed in For Additional Reading at the end of the chapter.

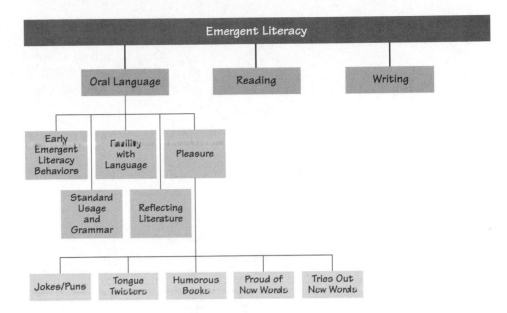

**Figure 6.5
Oral Language: Pleasure**

For second-language learners, absence of the behaviors discussed in this section should not be construed as indicative that a child is at an earlier literacy stage. Jokes are among the most difficult things to understand in another language, because they usually involve language play. Perhaps you have tried to explain to a friend "why" something is funny.

Note which children are pleased to use new words, trying them out and freely asking what unfamiliar words mean. Such pleasure indicates an active interest in language that contributes to growth in all aspects of literacy. The child meets a new word through listening or reading and begins to get an idea of its meaning. Next, the child begins trying out the word orally. If that seems successful—that is, people understand—the child may begin using the word in writing.

Instructional Strategies. No direct instruction is necessary beyond your usual vocabulary-building instruction. Vocabulary develops best through wide reading (and listening), along with risk-free opportunities to try out new words. Everyone misuses a word now and then, and no one should be made to feel embarrassed.

✔ Is proud of learning new words
✔ Tries out new words and asks what words mean

Comments

The checklist in Figure 6.6 includes all the behaviors we suggest as typical of this stage. Remember that these are neither comprehensive nor limiting. You may choose to add other behaviors or group some items differently. You should make such checklists meet your personal needs in terms of local standards and the particular children in your classroom.

Reading

You can easily do much of your reading assessment informally as you teach and as you observe children during their regular daily activities. Some assessments re-

Oral Language Checklist: Emergent Literacy Stage

Teacher_____ Date_____ Grade_____

Student Names

+ = behavior present
- = behavior absent
✓ = somewhat present

Benchmark

Early Emergent Literacy Behaviors												
Standard Usage and Grammar												
Recognition of nonstandard usage												
Sense of school/book language												
Facility with Oral Language												
Makes self understood by peers and adults												
Follows "rules" for conversation and discussion												
Retains oral directions												
Can ask questions for clarification												
Can paraphrase what others have said												
Participates in sharing												
Reflecting Literature												
Uses new words from stories												
Uses "book language" when appropriate												
Enjoys "making a play" of a favorite story												
Pleasure in Language												
Enjoys jokes related to words												
Enjoys tongue twisters												
Enjoys hearing humorous books												
Is proud of learning new words												
Tries out new words												

Figure 6.6
Sample Class Checklist for Emergent Literacy: Oral Language Benchmarks and Behaviors

quire one-on-one time with each child and are best accomplished during conference time. These are usually sprinkled throughout the day and week, giving you time alone with perhaps five children each day.

The five areas of reading are: continued development of the Early Emergent Literacy behaviors, concepts about print (Figure 6.7), using print (Figure 6.8), word recognition (Figure 6.9), and construction of meaning (Figure 6.10). A sample class checklist for reading benchmarks appears in Figure 6.11, and a similar checklist for individual students is in the Resource File.

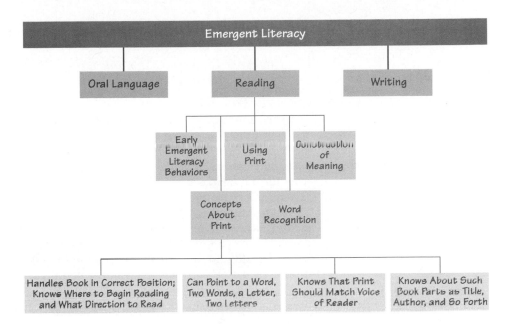

Figure 6.7
Reading: Concepts About Print

Recall the benchmarks for reading and book knowledge in the Early Emergent Literacy stage, described in Chapter 5. Whereas at that stage a child is just beginning to demonstrate the behaviors, at the Emergent Literacy stage the behaviors are exhibited consistently. All of the suggested instructional strategies in Chapter 5 are equally appropriate for children at this stage and beyond.

Note that children are handling books in right-side-up position, starting at the beginning of the story and turning the pages appropriately. If they are pretend-reading and pointing to print, note that they are moving their fingers left to right and top to bottom.

Instructional Strategies. If children do not exhibit these behaviors consistently, demonstrate frequently, verbalizing as you do so:

Watch how I hold the book so the pictures and print are right side up. I begin here, the front of the book. I turn the pages this way. When I read the words, I start at the top and move my eyes from left to right like this. (Move your finger to demonstrate.) When I come to the end of the line, I move down to the beginning of the next line and go from left to right again.

By verbalizing as you demonstrate, you give children important concepts such as *up, down, left, right,* and *front* as you model them. As children become comfortable with these concepts, you can have them take turns coming up as you read a big book together and showing these things to the other children.

This behavior can be assessed individually in just a few minutes with a child. A child who can do this shows an important understanding about the boundaries in printed language that are not so apparent in oral language.

Instructional Strategies. Children who cannot yet isolate letters and words in print may simply need to be shown. Don't wait for children to "catch on." Use any text, such as a big book or the morning message. Point to one letter and then frame it with your two index fingers, saying:

This is one letter (you can name it if you like, but it isn't necessary). This is two letters (move your fingers). This is one . . . this is two . . . one . . . two. Now you do it.

The same activity can be done with one word and two words.

✔ **Knows that print should match the voice of the reader**

You can best determine if a child has this concept through chatting as you sit with the child and a book. Ask the child to point to the words as you read. Note whether the child seems to understand the connection between the words you say and the marks on the page.

Instructional Strategies.   If a child doesn't yet seem to have made this connection firmly, he or she will benefit from many experiences of shared reading during which you move a pointer, finger, or marker under the words as you read aloud. In addition, the child will be aided in grasping this concept through one-on-one read-alouds with you, an aide, a volunteer, or a reading buddy.

Research shows that a child's eventual ability to finger-point to words being read depends on prior letter knowledge and phonemic awareness (Ehri & Sweet, 1991). Demonstrating that there is such a connection between voice and print is worthwhile, however, even before the child can point to the words independently.

✔ **Knows about such book parts as title, author, and so forth**

Determine each child's knowledge during group activities such as shared reading as well as during individual book conferences. It is not expected that the child can read the titles or the authors' and illustrators' names at this point. Instead, look for an understanding of the parts of the book: "This tells the name of the book. This tells who wrote it . . . who drew the pictures . . . who published it . . . when it was published . . . this is the front, the back, the spine . . . that tells you what some of the words mean (if there is a glossary)," and so on.

Instructional Strategies.   Children who don't have this knowledge of book parts probably haven't been taught about them yet. The knowledge is easily taught (and learned) through your continual reference to book parts as you conduct activities such as read-alouds and shared reading.

BENCHMARK

The student is using print in everyday life (Figure 6.8).

✔ **Can locate a specific book, record, tape, and so forth**

✔ **Recognizes some environmental print such as brand names and fast-food restaurant signs**

Children at this stage of development begin to show in various ways that they understand some of the many ways print is used in daily life. Assessment is informal and observational.

Note which children are able to go to the book shelf or tape and video storage and select a particular item. Even before a child is able to read the words on the cover of the book or in other places, she or he can often tell one book from another, one tape from another, and so on. The child knows that the print tells which book or tape it is.

Note also which children recognize environmental print in newspapers, television commercials, products, and so forth in the classroom. A child may first think *Crest* says "toothpaste." While that is not the right word, this behavior shows that the child knows the print tells what the product is.

Instructional Strategies.   Demonstrate frequently your own use of print to inform you about items in the environment. For example, read to children from newspapers and magazines, look up the time of a television program, locate a

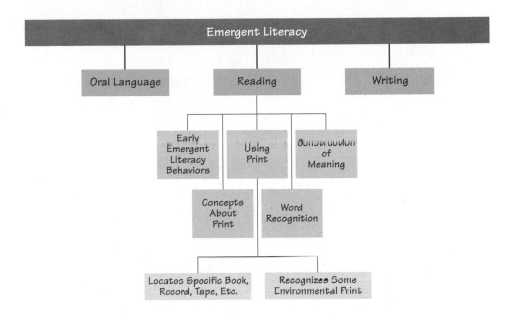

Figure 6.8
Reading: Using Print

word in a dictionary to verify pronunciation, check the daily menu to see what's for lunch, and note the manufacturers of items such as sneakers, book bags, and other personal items.

Scaffold instruction. For example, when a child points to the word *Crest* and says "toothpaste," use this to build understanding: "Yes, the name is Crest. Let's say the letters together. What do you hear at the beginning?"

BENCHMARK

The student is acquiring word recognition skills (Figure 6.9).

Decoding, a process referred to in earlier chapters, is what the reader does to determine what a printed word is. Some words are recognized instantly (at sight); they have been memorized. Words that are not recognized instantly require the use of one or more strategies for decoding. These include the use of background knowledge and vocabulary, phonics, the structural nature of words (such as prefixes, suffixes, and roots), surrounding text (what you may think of as "context clues"), and graphics (such as illustrations) on the page. Keep in mind that phonemic awareness, phonics, and knowledge of the structure of words also play a large part in attempts to spell.

Readers must be able to decode unfamiliar words. The child who has to struggle to figure out each and every word has little chance of constructing meaning at the same time. And without meaning, the child is just saying words. Therefore, fluent decoding is necessary, but not sufficient, for acquiring literacy.

Most of the words that emergent readers will meet in print are already in their oral vocabulary. They understand the word when they hear it and may use it when they speak; they just don't yet recognize it in print. However, if the child is reading meaningful text of some kind rather than isolated words, the pronunciation arrived at through the application of word recognition skills, even if not exactly correct, probably will trigger the correct word in the child's mind. Children will benefit from applying their burgeoning skills to decoding isolated words, but this activity must be balanced with significant blocks of time spent with meaningful text.

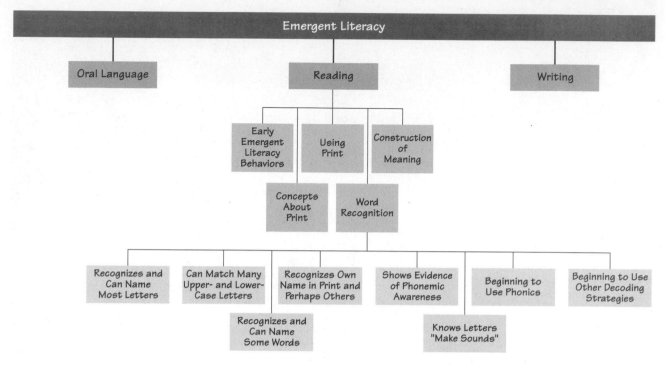

Figure 6.9
Reading: Word Recognition

✔ Recognizes and can name most letters

✔ Can match many upper- and lower-case letters

You need to know which print letters each child can name and find. Following is a set of individual assessments. Begin with task 1, which shows the most knowledge. Each time, if the child seems unable to do the task, go to the next assessment. You can quickly tell if you need to discontinue a task and move to the next. Do so casually: "Let's do something else now. How about . . . "

1 Use a set of alphabet cards, both upper and lower case and in mixed-up order. Go through the stack (or train an aide to do so), asking the child to name each letter. Sort into two piles: known and unknown. If most are unknown, use the next task.

2 Use the same set of cards. Ask the child to find and name as many letters as he or she can and put them in a pile.

3 Use the same set of cards. Display a few at a time, and ask the child to point to the letters you name.

4 Use the same set of cards, but separated by upper case and lower case. Ask the child to match upper- and lower-case cards.

5 Use two sets of upper-case cards and then two sets of lower-case cards. Display in groups of eight or so letters at a time. One at a time, hold up a letter card and ask the child to find one on the table just like the one you are holding.

A child matches upper- and lower-case letters.
© David Grossman/Monkmeyer

6 Display cards randomly (in small batches), and ask the child to find and name any he or she knows.

Group assessment of letter knowledge may seem quicker, but the information obtained is not as precise. A paper-and-pencil assessment presents rows of randomly ordered letters. You ask the children to circle or put a mark on the letter you name. This gives you a broad notion of your entire class, but not enough to be truly helpful, in our opinion. Most such paper-and-pencil assessments do not assess every letter, both upper and lower case. Furthermore, they test only whether a child can find a letter when you name it, not whether the child can name the letter.

Instructional Strategies.   The same tasks you used for assessment can be used for children to play games of matching letters. Besides the lessons you may routinely use to teach the alphabet, many daily activities offer opportunities to teach and reinforce letter knowledge. Here are just a few:

- Name aloud the letters you use to write on the chalkboard, chart paper, or computer.
- Call attention to "new" letters as you revisit stories you have read during shared reading.

- Hold up a letter and ask a child to come to the big book or morning message, name the letter, and find where else it appears.
- Have available and share ABC books.
- Provide tactile experiences as needed: sand, salt, pudding, bumpy rubber manipulative letters, sandpaper or flocked letters.

Comments

The relationship between letter knowledge and ease in learning to read is strong (Durkin, 1966; Snow, Burns, & Griffin, 1998). Though it is possible for a child to begin reading before knowing the names of all the letters, letter knowledge is required for grasping the alphabetic principle—the notion that letters systematically represent phonemes. However, do not hold up instruction because some children do not yet know the names of *all* the letters. Proceed with teaching letter recognition, letter names, and the sounds associated with letters, along with other aspects of word recognition.

✔ Recognizes and can name some words

✔ Recognizes own name in print and perhaps other names

At this stage, there is no set of words that all children "should" know. Many children, of course, can read some words, their own names, and perhaps the names of some classmates. You will learn this informally within a couple of days as children find their cubbies or collect their drawings from a pile.

You want to find out if children can recognize and read other words besides their names and, if so, which words. We see little value in the group paper-and-pencil assessments that ask children to mark a word you say aloud. What you need to know is whether the child can recognize and say the word when he or she sees it. How you assess this depends on your first observation of each child's interaction with books. If item 1 in the following list isn't true of a child, proceed to item 2 or 3.

1 *If a child is reading books independently from the first day:* Arrange an individual conference and have the child read to you. If the reading is fluent, find a book with which the child is unfamiliar. If the child is fluent with this book as well, take a running record of fluency.

2 *If a child frequently looks at books and appears to recognize some of the words there and in the environment:* Have a conference. Ask the child to bring a book and either read to you or find words that are familiar and say them. If the child knows quite a few, you might assess his or her knowledge of what are called *basic sight words* using word cards. (A list of basic sight words appears in the Resource File.)

3 *If a child spends little time with books or pages through quickly, looking only at the pictures:* Spot-check any words recognized as you do daily activities such as calendar, time, morning message, shared reading, and shared writing.

Instructional Strategies.   Reinforce the connection between print and the spoken word in your everyday activities. You may or may not choose to teach a group of words before reading a story. Published reading programs may have vocabulary lessons (which are also word recognition lessons) built into each selection's instruction.

Also, provide many opportunities for children to become familiar with frequently used words through shared reading and rereading, choral reading, and the use of prerecorded books on tape. Encourage children to read with a friend; each will help the other learn to recognize words. A buddy program that brings older readers into your class is also a fine way for children to build recognition of words through repeated reading of familiar books.

✔ Shows evidence of phonemic awareness

This indicator and the next two emerge in order, though with some overlap: first comes an ear for the separate sounds, then the alphabetic principle (the idea that letters represent phonemes, or individual sounds), and then the actual association of certain sounds with certain letters (Stahl, Duffy-Hester, & Stahl, 1998). Each indicator applies both to reading and to writing; that is, a child who uses phonics to decode an unfamiliar word will likely also use phonics to aid in spelling a word not yet learned.

One test for assessing phonemic awareness in young children is the Yopp-Singer Test of Phoneme Segmentation, which appears in the Resource File. The article supporting this test is listed in For Additional Reading at the end of this chapter. You may also quite informally assess each child by saying some individual words and demonstrating isolation of the sounds: "Listen to me say a word: *cat.* Now listen as I say each sound separately: /c/–/a/–/t/." After giving some examples and doing several with the child, say a word and then ask the child to segment the sounds alone. There is no need to assess every sound, of course. You just want to find out whether the child has the concept—the awareness of the separate sounds in words.

Instructional Strategies.   Continue the activities suggested in Chapter 5 for the Early Emergent Literacy stage: rhymes, finger plays, singing, and other games with words. Children can learn to manipulate sounds through games, rhyming patterns, and analogies. For example, the child who can say *book* and can segment sounds into the onset *b* and the rime *-ook* can figure out the new word *took.* (The **onset** is the consonant sound that precedes the vowel in a syllable; the **rime** includes the vowel and any consonant sounds that follow.)

Comments

Phonemic awareness assessment and instruction may not work in the same way for students for whom English is a second language. Until they know English phonology, or sounds, efforts to impose typical phonemic awareness activities (as well as subsequent phonics activities) may not only be inappropriate but actually impede learning. (See a discussion of this issue in Freeman & Freeman [1999], listed in For Additional Reading.) Keep this idea in mind as you read about associating sounds and letters in the next section. Also, remember that associating sounds with letters may not result in understanding of a word, even if the child pronounces the word correctly. As with all readers, if the word is not in the child's oral language, it will simply be a meaningless sound, no different from a nonsense word.

✔ Has a sense that let-
ters "make sounds"

This indicator overlaps a good deal with indicators for writing development; the sense of letters making sounds is also used as students learn to spell.

Kindergarten programs often provide activities that combine phonemic awareness with the introduction to letter names and to the sounds associated with letters. Children will begin to use their growing sense of how print works as they decode (read) and perhaps even more as they encode (write). In fact, some children may be segmenting sounds and making a separate mark for each sound before learning all the letters of the alphabet and which letters represent which sounds.

To assess whether a child seems to have a sense that letters represent individual sounds—the alphabetic principle—you must observe two kinds of activities:

1 As the child tries to read unfamiliar words, note the application of known sounds, such as the beginning sound in the child's name. Similarly, during group activities, note which children are able to substitute sounds in rhyming words: "This word is *cat*. If we take off the beginning sound, /c/, and substitute the sound we hear at the beginning of Mary's name, what word will we have? [*mat*]." Children may be able to do this without yet knowing the names of all the letters and which sounds go with which letters.

2 As a child is writing and attempting to spell an unknown word, does he or she segment sounds, writing a letter or letterlike form for individual sounds? (See more about this aspect of phonemic awareness in the section on writing benchmarks later in this chapter.)

Instructional Strategies.   Continue activities that support the development of phonemic awareness through games, songs, and rhymes. Help children break syllables into onset and rime. At a later stage, they will use analogies independently to figure out how to read and write new words with the same rime. At the same time, show children how letters are associated with sounds. This may occur during instruction in letter formation (handwriting), during reading, and during writing.

✔ Is beginning to use
phonics; knows many
letter-sound associa-
tions, including both
consonants and vowels

Phonics helps children figure out the probable pronunciation of an unknown word by associating letters with sounds. How you assess children's ability to use phonics will depend largely on which approach to phonics (and reading instruction) you are using. Your assessment may be largely observational as children read and write, or you may use the assessments that accompany a published program.

Most published basal reading programs incorporate a phonics strand and provide systematic and periodic assessment to check whether children are learning the skills that have been taught. Stand-alone phonics programs also have periodic tests. Keep in mind that performance on a phonics test is not necessarily an indication of a child's ability to use phonics while actually reading.

Instructional Strategies.   We recommend that you apply the explicit phonics/ structural elements routine suggested in Chapter 4 when children show a need for it. Whatever program your school uses, such explicit routines will help your children see clearly how phonics can become a tool for them to figure out the pronunciation of unfamiliar words in reading and writing. It is a valuable decoding strategy, though not the only decoding strategy readers need.

Comments

While this is not the place for a detailed discussion of phonics, we will remind you of some basic ideas to keep in mind as you help children:

- Reading requires constructing meaning; pronunciation of words is not enough.
- It is sometimes possible to determine meaning without pronunciation.
- English is not completely phonetically regular: the same letter can represent different sounds in different words (*cat, city*); the same sound can be spelled with different letters in different words (*do, due*).
- Readers use phonics even when they don't realize it. Most readers can make a stab at the pronunciation of a word they have never seen. Phonics, the ability to associate sounds with letters, makes this possible.
- You can't treat children like automobiles on an assembly line, stamping the same instruction on all of them. If there were indeed one perfect way to teach every child to decode every word, educators would simply do it and end the debate about a "best" way. What we do know is that some ways seem to work for some children and some for others. Bear in mind that most children learn to read with comparative ease—any approach would likely work for such children.

That being said, Snow, Burns, and Griffin (1998) summarize how three basic teaching approaches develop phonics skills, but caution that these vary a great deal from teacher to teacher:

1. *Whole language.* The teacher teaches phonics as opportunities arise during authentic reading and writing. The emphasis is on **connected text,** groups of words that convey meaning. Learning regarding the alphabet is assumed to take place implicitly.

2. *Embedded phonics.* Phonics instruction is sequenced according to a list of word families. Children substitute sounds at the beginnings of words and generalize the patterns as they figure out new words. Teachers use trade books that contain the target patterns. They also use the patterns in writing and spelling. This approach appeared to be more effective with disadvantaged students than whole language (Hiebert, Colt, Catto, & Gury, 1992).

3. *Direct code instruction.* Once children understand how print works (concepts of print), letter-sound correspondences and spelling conventions are explicitly taught and practiced. Children read books designed to review the words and phonics lessons they have experienced up to that point. The strategy emphasized is: if you don't recognize a word, sound it out. Then children use anthologies and trade books to develop reading and writing. According to the report by Snow, Burns, and Griffin (1998), children taught via this approach improved in word reading at a faster rate and had higher word recognition skills than those taught by the other methods.

Given the wide variation among classrooms with similar stated philosophies, some classrooms may use a published explicit phonics program as part of each day's activities regardless of the system philosophy or the adopted basal reading program. Some teachers may tie lessons in a separate phonics program to their other reading activities, while others teach the phonics lessons apart from any application to the material children are reading. Stahl, Duffy-Hester, and Stahl (1998) discuss several phonics instruction approaches in detail; these include analytic and synthetic methods such as those used in the 1960s and 1970s and contemporary approaches such as spelling-based, analogy-based, and embedded. Most experts agree that further research is needed and that while we are learning a great deal about effective ways to teach phonics, we do not yet have all the answers.

Your school system will have embraced an approach to teaching reading that probably includes a position on phonics. You will need to reconcile your beliefs about phonics instruction with your school's stated philosophy. Keep in mind that *all* teachers share a common goal, regardless of philosophy: to help children learn to read and write successfully.

Phonics is not the only strategy readers use when encountering an unfamiliar word. Use of each of these other strategies can be assessed informally during regular reading instruction:

✔ Is beginning to use other decoding strategies such as sight words, context, graphics, and word structure

- *Sight words.* Words recognized at sight, without the need to apply any other decoding strategy, are known as **sight words**. As readers become more competent, each builds a body of words that are recognized instantly. The term *sight words* or *basic sight words,* as mentioned earlier, also refers to a given group of high-frequency words. (See the list in the Resource File.)

- *Context.* When a child uses the words surrounding an unfamiliar word to hypothesize about the target word, he or she is making use of **context**. The surrounding text may be a phrase, a sentence, a paragraph, or the entire work. Readers who are constructing meaning as they read have expectations about what words will appear in certain contexts. For example, if the story is about a zoo, the reader expects to find animal names. Thus, even if an unfamiliar animal name appears, context helps the reader at least infer that the word names an animal of some kind. A hypothesis about an unfamiliar word can then often be confirmed or rejected by applying phonics.

- *Graphics.* Any **graphics** available on the page or in the text can help a reader decode the text. Very young children often use pictures to make "guesses" about an unfamiliar word; this is a good strategy up to a point. Readers also use captions under illustrations, tables and charts, maps and other insets, and typographical aids such as boldface and underlining. All of these help to create an expectation of what kind of word might appear in the text.

- *Word structure.* Understanding of **word structure**, especially the fact that certain parts of words carry meaning, is an important decoding tool. The meaningful parts of words include prefixes and suffixes; children learn, for instance, that *un-* before a word often means *not.* Word structure also includes inflected endings such as those that denote the tenses of verbs or those that denote plurals, possessives, gender, or comparisons. The child who has learned that *-ed* at the end of a word often means the past tense of an action word can apply that knowledge in figuring out an unfamiliar word.

Instructional Strategies.   If children are not using these decoding strategies when appropriate or are using them inefficiently, provide direct and explicit instruction. If the children show a need, you may isolate a skill to teach it, but keep in mind that these strategies are best learned and practiced during meaningful reading experiences.

Comments

Skilled readers use each of these strategies to varying degrees. Emergent readers benefit from having them taught and reinforced as they engage in the appropriate reading and writing activities in any balanced literacy day. Being taught how to approach unfamiliar words helps children build fluency and confidence in their ability to become independent readers and writers.

We believe that meaning must always be central in children's minds as they read; therefore, the first thought about an unfamiliar word probably should be "What would make sense here?" Then children should think about the familiar parts of the word such as endings, prefixes, and so forth; apply phonics if needed; and confirm that the word fits in the context.

BENCHMARK
The student is constructing meaning (Figure 6.10),

The most authentic way to assess a child's construction of meaning is during actual reading experiences rather than with a test of some kind. As you conduct

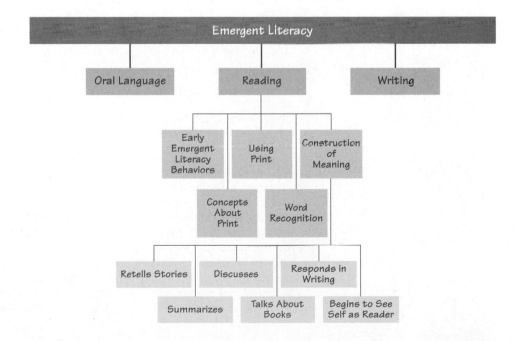

Figure 6.10
Reading: Construction of Meaning

literacy lessons and minilessons, you will learn which children are struggling to construct meaning. What you learn then changes how you plan your next literacy lesson or minilesson.

Some techniques described in Chapter 3 are particularly useful for assessing construction of meaning: retelling or summarizing, discussion, and personal written responses. You may want to refresh your memory by reviewing those sections of Chapter 3 before you read on.

Instructional Strategies.   You help children learn to construct meaning as they read by providing good basic instruction. The following strategies, all of which you read about in Chapter 4, are important:

- Provide the blocks of time necessary for complete literacy learning.
- Use the various modes of reading: teacher read-aloud, shared reading, guided reading, cooperative/collaborative reading, and independent reading.
- Plan and carry out literacy lessons.
- When needed, plan and carry out minilessons.
- Use the explicit comprehension routine when appropriate.
- Provide for response to reading through discussion and writing.

As you use these basic instructional strategies, note whether your children are struggling to construct meaning. If so, ask yourself questions such as the following:

1   Did I motivate the children before reading?
2   Do these children lack background experience?
3   Should I have introduced new concepts before reading?
4   Was vocabulary not sufficiently defined in context?
5   Did we read too much in one chunk?
6   Was the text structure confusing to the children?
7   What do I need to do next?

The following discussions of individual indicators for this benchmark should help you focus your assessment and instruction.

✔ Can retell a story page by page
✔ Can summarize

Ask children individually to retell (or summarize) a story or other text as they page through a book. Use a book they have heard read aloud. Children at this stage can look at the pictures, and perhaps part of the print, and tell you what went on during each part of the story. They remember the characters, setting, and events. They can tell you how the story ended. If the text was expository, they can tell you the important ideas and some of the details. This retelling response gives you an idea of children's understanding of story structure or expository structure and usually of whether they can relate the content to their own lives.

Instructional Strategies.   Continue to make retelling part of your daily instructional strategies. As you talk with children during shared reading and during and after read-alouds, engage them in recalling and retelling story elements and information from informational text. Encourage personal responses, tying story events to the children's experiences. Encourage broader and deeper thinking through modeling and prompting.

✔ Participates in small-group and whole-class discussions about books and stories
✔ Talks about books with others

Observe which children talk about the books and stories they have been listening to and reading. For example, note the child who recommends a book to another child or snags another child to listen to a retelling.

At the same time, note how children are participating in group and class discussions. Which children participate willingly, staying focused but sharing personal responses to the story or topic? Which children never participate? Are they shy? Have others ridiculed their ideas in the past? Do they lack background experience for the concepts in the story? Were they not participating during the read-aloud or shared reading? In other words, lack of participation in a discussion may not have a single explanation. Keep looking.

Instructional Strategies. If children are not talking about books and stories with each other and in discussion groups, search for a reason. It may have nothing to do with reading but rather with the social dynamics of your class. Establish a climate in which all ideas are valued, while at the same time modeling staying focused on the book under discussion and related experiences. Second-language learners will benefit from very small discussion groups.

Even though your children may not yet be able to read, you may want to post some discussion guidelines on which you all agree, such as these:

Discussion Guidelines

1 Take turns.
2 Don't talk while someone else is talking.
3 It's okay to disagree, but not to argue.
4 Speak loudly enough for everyone to hear.
5 When you say something about someone else's ideas, talk to that person—not to the teacher.
6 Never say anything bad about anyone else's ideas.

When necessary, you can refer to the chart and read the pertinent item aloud.

✔ Responds to books in writing
✔ Begins to see self as a reader

Note which children respond to books in writing. Children who are responding to stories in personal ways will have something to say. At first, their responses may include or be limited to drawing a picture. Responses may also take the form of a log of books read, a response journal in which children record feelings about books they are listening to or reading, writing a play, or writing an innovation—a new version using the same pattern. Note, too, whether children tell you "I can read."

Instructional Strategies. Continue to show by word and deed that response to a story is personal and important. Share your own written responses to your own reading. Provide time for children to respond in writing to what they are reading. When you respond to children's written responses, comment on content, not mechanics. If the child writes, "Ths wuz a gd bok," don't correct the spelling.

Just say something like "I'm so glad you loved that book. It was a favorite of mine when I was a child." Second-language learners should be encouraged to write in any language or in a mixture of English and their first language. Help all children see themselves as readers even though they may not yet know every word.

Comments

> You may be used to thinking of constructing meaning as "comprehension," a term that traditionally comprises a collection of discrete skills: knowing the main idea, significant details, supporting details, sequence, and cause and effect; drawing conclusions; distinguishing fact and opinion; and so forth. If you use a published reading program, you may find lessons devoted to these separate skills. If you teach such lessons, be sure children integrate such learning into the whole act of constructing meaning. Isolated performance of skills is not enough.

Figure 6.11 presents a group checklist for all the Emergent Literacy reading benchmarks. An individual checklist is in the Resource File.

Writing

As with reading, you will determine if children are at this stage in writing by examining their work and by observing and listening to them as they work. Some information can be gleaned as you observe and work with children in groups or as a whole class. Some is best gathered in individual conferences.

The areas we address in this section are: continued development of the Early Emergent Literacy behaviors, spelling and other conventions (Figure 6.12), purposes of writing (Figure 6.13), the writing process (Figure 6.14), and construction of meaning (Figure 6.15). A class checklist (Figure 6.16) appears near the end of the section, and an individual checklist is in the Resource File.

All of the assessment and instructional strategies presented in Chapter 5 continue to be appropriate for children at this stage and beyond.

On the first day of school you can ask children to write their names if they already know how. Tell those who say they cannot that you will help them. Often teachers have pre-made name cards ready for children to use as a model to copy their names, but first ascertain which children can write their names without copying.

Instructional Strategies.   Names are important. Children should learn to write their own names as soon as possible. Provide models for the children to copy. Regardless of the sequence in which you intend to teach letter formation, help each child learn to write the letters in his or her own name. Gently help children to reform incorrectly formed letters. Remember that children at this stage frequently write letters backwards or stroke in a different direction from what you will teach. For most children, this will straighten out in good time; intervention is seldom necessary.

An assessment with alphabet cards, as described earlier in the reading section (page 218), will quickly tell you whether students can name letters.

BENCHMARK

The student exhibits continued growth in many of the Early Emergent Literacy behaviors.

BENCHMARK

The student is using spelling and other writing conventions (Figure 6.12).

✔ Can write own name (perhaps first name only), with all or most of the letters present, though not necessarily formed correctly

✔ Can name most letters in random presentation

Reading Checklist:
Emergent Literacy Stage

Teacher_____   Date_____   Grade_____

Student Names

+ = consistently present
- = not present
✓ = somewhat present; recheck

Benchmark

Early Emergent Literacy Behaviors

Concepts About Print
Handles book correctly
Points: word, two words; letter, two letters
Knows print matches voice
Knows book parts

Using Print in Everyday Life
Locates specific book
Recognizes some environmental print

Word Recognition Skills
Names most letters
Matches upper- and lower-case letters
Recognizes some words
Recognizes own name
Phonemic awareness
Alphabetic principle
Phonics
Other strategies:
    sight words
    context
    graphics
    word structure

Constructs Meaning
Retells stories
Summarizes
Discusses
Talks about books
Responds in writing
Begins to see self as reader

Figure 6.11
Sample Class Checklist for Emergent Literacy: Reading Benchmarks and Behaviors

✔ Forms letter-like shapes and some correct letters
✔ Uses some punctuation

Examine children's writing wherever it occurs–on drawings, in journals, in assigned papers. Which children are writing some correct letters and shapes that look like letters? Note, too, which children are putting down some kind of mark to indicate the boundaries of their thoughts. Many children will be using periods at this stage. Some may become especially fond of exclamation points once they discover them.

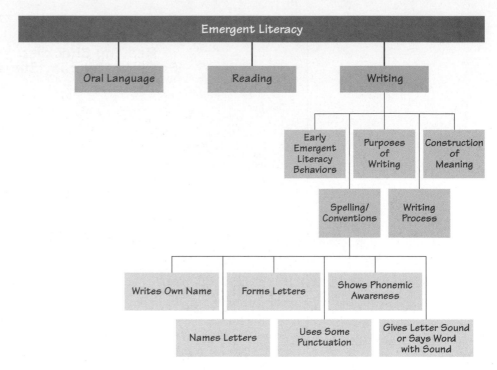

**Figure 6.12
Writing: Spelling and Other
Conventions**

Instructional Strategies.   For the formation of letters, the same kinds of activities and games described earlier for reading will help the child in writing. Teaching of punctuation will take place informally every time you write in front of the children, when you discuss morning messages and other collaborative writing, and when you revisit big books. At this stage, we do not believe isolated explicit lessons on punctuation are needed, but we do urge frequent, repetitive commentary, first from you and then from the children themselves.

Earlier in the chapter, we discussed phonemic awareness and letter-sound connections as decoding skills for reading. Evidence of the use of phonemic awareness to aid in writing is available from two sources: a child's self-talk as he or she writes and the product that results from writing.

> ✔ Shows phonemic awareness and beginning association of letters and sounds in attempts to spell
> ✔ Can give a letter sound or say a word that begins with the letter sound

1   *Self-talk.* Sit with children individually as they write. Listen to what they say to themselves. You may hear them segment sounds and see them write a letter or a shape to represent each sound as they say the word. This ability will increase as children's literacy grows. Gradually, as they learn both the names of letters and the sounds associated with letters, they will put their ability to segment the sounds in a word together with letter-sound knowledge and move toward conventional spelling.

2   *Product.* As you read what a child has written, segment the sounds in your mind to see if a letter (or letterlike form) has been used to represent each sound. Review the stages of spelling development described in Chapter 3,

beginning on page 91. You will note whether phonemic awareness is demonstrated at all, once or twice, or most of the time. Remember that awareness of separate sounds and acquisition of the alphabetic principle that letters represent sounds may precede knowledge of exactly which letters represent which sounds. Here you need to note whether a child is "getting the hang" of how the system works.

Instructional Strategies. Good basic teaching of the sort described in Chapter 5, along with your regular curriculum related to introducing letter names, sounds, and the association between the two, will be sufficient for most of your children. Children who are not acquiring phonemic awareness as expected will need additional and specific instruction. As you write on transparencies or the chalkboard, encourage children to help you segment sounds, decide which letter(s) to associate with the sounds, and then write those letters. As you circulate while children write, guide them to use their growing knowledge of the alphabetic principle to segment words into sounds and write letters for sounds.

As we mentioned in Chapter 3, the term *invented spelling* refers to this very process. It is not guessing. On the contrary, it is the thoughtful invention of an unknown word's probable spelling, using one's ability to segment words into separate sounds and one's knowledge of which letters are associated with which sounds. All writers "invent" spelling whenever they write words they are not sure of how to spell; some may look up and verify spelling as they write, though many save this process for the editing step. To use a dictionary for spelling, of course, one must first have been able to invent a likely spelling.

Comments

Some children for whom English is a second language may have already begun attempting to spell in their first language. It is likely that spelling knowledge in another language may not develop in the same way it does for native English speakers (Freeman & Freeman, 1997).

BENCHMARK

The student is using writing for own purposes (Figure 6.13).

✔ Can keep a journal that may combine drawing and writing

In addition to other kinds of writing, you undoubtedly will ask your children to do personal writing every day in some kind of journal. In kindergarten and first grade, you will probably tell them at first that they may draw as well as write. Gradually you will encourage more and more writing. Note which children willingly comply with this request and show increased interest in expressing personal thoughts and events in writing.

Instructional Strategies. Encourage personal writing by modeling it daily; share your own journal writing with your children. Support their efforts by reading and responding to their journals frequently. If you read and respond to five or so journals each day, you will get through your entire class in a week without spending an inordinate amount of time daily. Share the many kinds of things children can write about: events at home, vacations, pets, holidays, movies, story ideas, and feelings.

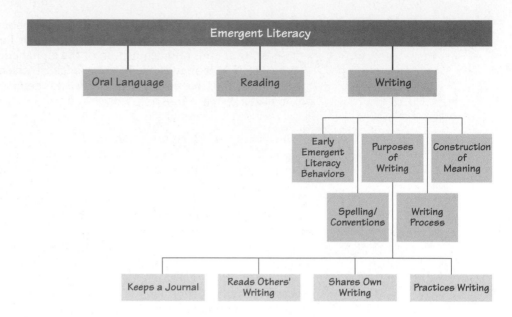

Figure 6.13
Writing: Using Writing for Own Purposes

✔ Attempts to read others' writing

Note which children are attempting to read what others have written, whether published authors or classmates. Such attempts indicate that the child has grasped that just as he or she can record ideas, so can others.

Instructional Strategies. Point out to children that the same words they are using as they write are in the writing of others. If they can read their own words, they can learn to read the words others write.

✔ Shares writing with others

Note which children are willing to share their writing. If you have a time when children are invited to read aloud either their stories or their journals (but never *require* a child to do either), which children volunteer? If some children are not willing to share with the entire class, note which ones will share with a friend or with you.

Instructional Strategies. Sharing writing is risky, as many successful authors will testify. When you share what you have written, you expose yourself to others. No child should be required to share personal writing, but you should encourage sharing of nonpersonal writing such as reports or stories. Many teachers have a special chair labeled **Author's Chair**. Children who are ready to share something they have written are invited to sit in the special chair as they read aloud and then receive comments and questions from their audience.

✔ Shows interest in practicing writing, often through copying favorite stories from books

Note which children enjoy writing, the act of putting pencil to paper. Which children make copies of poems or favorite passages from stories?

Instructional Strategies. Many children enjoy practicing the physical act of writing as they gain control over their eye-hand coordination and shaping letters. Allow time for such practice. Children need to practice letter formation; they might as well practice while copying a favorite story or poem. At the same time, children learn something about the art of composition through copying good literature. Just as the sound of wonderful language can become anchored through listening, the flow of words can become anchored through copying wonderful language.

As you do shared and collaborative writing with children, note which ones are beginning to be comfortable with the process used for creative writing: generating ideas, making a rough draft, revising, editing, and publishing. Children at this stage may not yet do much independent revising and editing, but they are beginning to understand the process that leads to a finished piece of writing.

Instructional Strategies. Continue to model, demonstrate, guide, and teach the processes used to produce a publishable piece of writing (as opposed to journal writing, logs, lists, and so forth). Use the minilesson format to teach and reteach each part of the process. For example, you may devote several lessons to generating ideas or brainstorming. When children are becoming comfortable with generating ideas, you can begin to present minilessons on producing a rough draft, then revision, then editing, and finally producing a "publishable" piece of writing.

No particular assessment is needed here, nor are any instructional strategies. Rather, you must build this awareness for children to accept that writing is hard work that hardly anyone gets perfect on the first try—and that it is worth the hard work. Try to find information about how authors write, and read it aloud to children or paraphrase if it is difficult to understand. For Additional Reading at the end of this chapter gives several sources; others are available on the Internet.

Readers construct meaning by assigning meaning to a text, using information in the text and in their own background experiences; they must monitor their thinking, pay attention to their purposes, and understand the text structure. Similarly, writers construct meaning to tell a story or present information in an organized fashion or to express a personal response to something internal or ex-

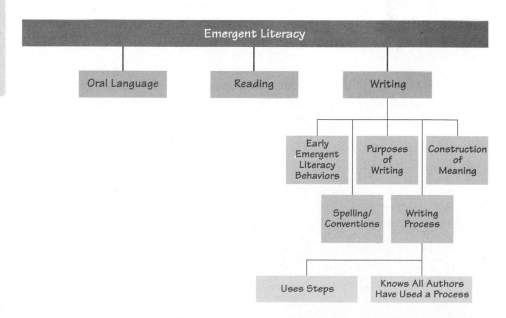

Figure 6.14
Writing: Familiarity with the Writing Process

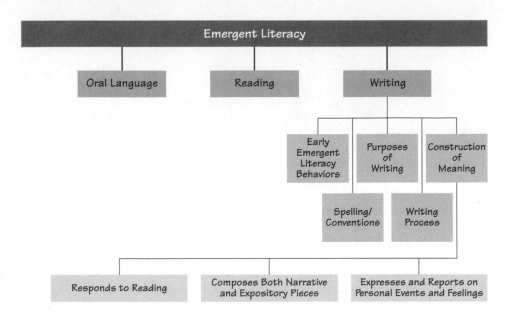

**Figure 6.15
Writing: Construction of
Meaning**

ternal. Writers also are aware of audience. In other words, much the same kinds of thinking are needed both for reading and writing.

As children engage in writing tasks, those of their own choosing as well as those you have assigned, you assess their success in constructing meaning as they write by talking with them, examining their efforts, helping them revise, and evaluating their final products.

Instructional Strategies.   As with reading, children learn to write by doing it frequently, accompanied by good basic guidance and instruction. Examining their writing, including their written responses to reading, should help you determine what instruction they need to grow in their ability to construct meaning as they write.

For example, if a child's story is disorganized, with no clear sequence of events, you need to help the child evaluate his or her own work and then teach how to plan and write something in which the sequence of events is clear to the reader. If several children show the same need, you can teach a minilesson to a small group.

With English-language learners, apparently unorganized writing may reflect a cultural writing pattern differing from that of English. If several different cultures are represented in your classroom, you probably won't be able to familiarize yourself with the writing patterns of each, but do be aware that difference exist. Provide support as you help students move toward the patterns and forms needed to communicate in English.

As we've said before, many problems may be the result of inadequate teaching. When you find problems with children's assigned writing, again ask yourself some questions:

1 Was the assignment or task clear?

2 Was the assignment or task reasonable for these children?

3 Did I model what I wanted the children to do?

4 Did I provide enough guided practice?

5 What are the particular problem areas (for example, no clear purpose, lacks sense of audience, does not stick to topic, omitted one or more story elements, did not support ideas, no conclusion)?

6 What do I need to do next?

There is more to teaching writing than what we have discussed here, of course. Beyond these broad aspects of writing are many other important considerations, such as sentence construction, choice of words, misuse or overuse of adjectives and adverbs, tone, mood, color, research, and much more. Several fine books to help you teach writing are listed in For Additional Reading.

Comments

As you look at a child's written work to judge construction of meaning, you may also note instructional needs in the area of mechanics, conventions, and usage. Do not, however, equate ability in those areas with construction of meaning. A child may have advanced ability in those areas but write in a disorganized fashion. On the other hand, a child may write a beautifully cohesive piece that has many problems with conventions. Some children, of course, are skillful at both and some at neither.

Figure 6.16 presents a group checklist for all the writing benchmarks. The Resource File provides an individual checklist.

Planning Instruction Based on Assessed Stage of Development

This section is arranged around two major concerns: planning the day and meeting individual and group needs in your Balanced Beginning Literacy Program.

You must provide a balanced literacy day for all your children. Within that day you will provide a classroom environment in which literacy can flourish and a time for literacy instruction, practice, and application. Throughout the day, you will continue to assess children, often while in the act of teaching. On the basis of that continuous assessment, you will be able to select appropriate strategies, techniques, and materials to meet the needs of both individuals and groups, including children with special needs.

Planning a Balanced Literacy Day for Kindergarten or First Grade

We address three areas related to planning the balanced literacy day for kindergarten and first grade: the balanced classroom, the blocked schedule, and continuous assessment.

Writing Checklist:
Emergent Literacy Stage

Teacher_____ Date_____ Grade_____

Student Names

+ = consistently present
- = not present
✓ = sometimes present/needs instruction

Benchmark

Early Emergent Literacy Behaviors

Spelling and Other Conventions
Writes own name
Names most letters
Forms letterlike shapes/letters
Uses some punctuation
Shows phonemic awareness
Gives letter-sound or says word with sound

Purposes of Writing
Keeps a journal
Attempts to read others' writing
Shares writing with others
Practices writing

Writing Process
Uses steps
Knows all authors have used a process

Construction of Meaning
Responds to reading
Composes narrative and exposition
Expresses/reports personal events and feelings

Figure 6.16
Sample Class Checklist for Emergent Literacy: Writing Benchmarks and Behaviors

The Balanced Classroom

Children at the Emergent Literacy stage need the same print-rich, language-rich environment as those at the previous stage. The materials, tools, furniture, and the overall physical arrangement of your classroom are all important.

Materials, Tools, and Furniture.   Materials, tools, and furniture at this stage of literacy development look very much like those described for the previous stage, with just a few differences. You may not have sand or water tables in your kindergarten, and almost certainly will not have them in a first grade. All of the same reading and writing materials need to be available, however, and you may want to add ruled paper as children become ready to use it in writing.

By first grade, children may have individual desks or at least tables and chairs. We know of one first-grade teacher who accommodated her children's preferences by lowering one or two large tables so that some children could sit or kneel on the floor as they worked on the table surface. Tables were left at regular height for those children who preferred sitting on chairs.

Physical Arrangement.   The physical arrangement of the room will depend on many factors, such as available cubbies, shelves, display tables, chalkboards, sinks, and so forth. What you have in your classroom matters less than what you do with what you have.

Children need a classroom that is inviting and comfortable. They need places where they can work independently without being disturbed, as well as places where groups can collaborate. If the children have individual desks and you cannot group these for some reason, you need at least one table at which a group can meet. There should also be a place where the whole class can gather to listen to a story or discuss a news item. You'll want to have a place for animals, plants, and science experiments. You need listening posts, computer stations, and centers to meet your curriculum needs. You need a place to display work—walls are not enough; hang things from the ceiling or clip them to miniblinds if you need to.

Your classroom will be unique, a combination of what is available for you to work with, the size and arrangement of the room, your own ideas of what will work, and your children's wishes. You will probably change things as time goes by. However your room is arranged, it should work for the children. They should know where everything is and, after guidelines are established, be able to function with increasing independence.

The Blocked Schedule

Recall from Chapter 4 that the Balanced Beginning Literacy Program is based on blocks of time allocated to three major areas: power and practice, instruction, and additional support as needed. The amount of time allocated to each block and the nature of the activities will vary as children move along the continuum of literacy development. We will discuss the blocks as they look at kindergarten and first grade for children who are at the Emergent Literacy stage. Remember that you may need to make alternative arrangements for kindergartners or first graders who are not yet at this stage or are at a subsequent stage.

How much time you devote to your literacy program may depend in part on your school system's requirements. We suggest a minimum amount of time for each block, but scheduling is flexible. Some days you may devote more time to one block and less to another. However, remember that literacy development occurs best in an environment that balances instruction with opportunities for independent reading and writing and provides for these every single day.

Later in this chapter you will read more about strategies, techniques, and materials appropriate for this stage. The section "Two Classrooms at Work," beginning on page 249, suggests both a kindergarten schedule and a first-grade schedule, and presents possible activities for each segment of the day.

Power and Practice.   During the two power-and-practice blocks—Daily Independent Reading and Daily Independent Writing—your children read and write independently. This vital part of the program allows for the extended practice necessary to build fluency in both reading and writing.

Daily Independent Reading.   During this time, children choose books that interest them. Group books by topic to help children make selections. Quiet time for independent reading for children at the Emergent Literacy stage may not be entirely quiet. These children often talk to themselves as they look at books. Some teachers allow partners to look at books together during this time in kindergarten. You could also schedule individual children to listening stations during this period.

Teachers who read to themselves during this time are providing a powerful message about the pleasure of reading. However, you may also want to use part of this block to hold individual conferences with children. The Independent Reading block will require at least 10 minutes each day.

Daily Independent Writing.   A second block of time is allocated for writing the children choose to do. Again, you may spend some of this block doing your own writing. You may also want to use part of it to hold individual conferences with children. The Independent Writing block should be at least 10 minutes each day.

Comments

It takes some time to establish independent reading and writing behavior with children in kindergarten and first grade. Don't expect the process to work perfectly at the beginning of the year. You may begin with very short blocks, perhaps only 5 minutes in kindergarten. Gradually expand the blocks as children become able to sustain independent work for a longer period of time.

Talk with the children about what they will be doing during each block. Collaborate to draw up guidelines. Rehearse and role-play such things as the following:

- Responding to a signal that independent reading (or writing) time is beginning, such as playing a tape or CD of Bach or Mozart.

- Behavior during the block: do not bother anyone else, don't talk out loud, don't walk around.

- What to do if . . . (for instance, I need to use the bathroom, I finished my book). Bathroom routines will vary. If a pass is required, work out a system that does not require speaking. If a book is completed, the child should not get up to get another but should reread the book or enter it in a reading log. This point may require further discussion later about being sure to have enough reading material on hand.

- How to behave if coming to a conference: lift chair to push in, tip-toe, don't touch anyone on the way.

> • What to do when signaled that the block has ended: put materials away; stand, stretch, and wiggle; get ready for the next activity.

Figure 6.17 presents a sample chart you might post to help children remember guidelines for the Daily Independent Reading and Writing blocks.

Instruction.   Four blocks comprise this part of the Balanced Beginning Literacy day. (1) Reading: Learning to Read Words, (2) Reading: Developing Language and

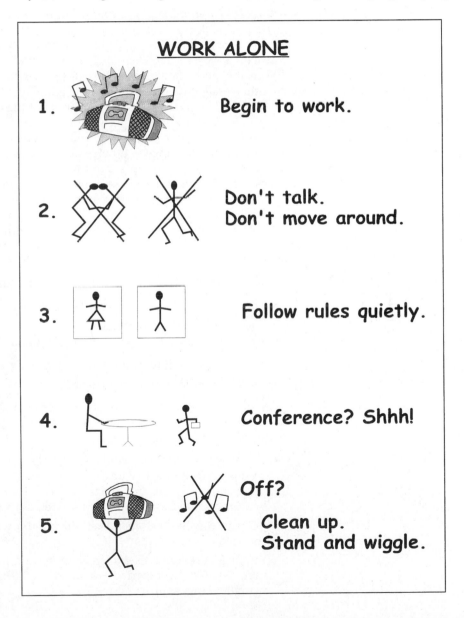

**Figure 6.17
Independent Reading or
Writing Chart**

Comprehension, (3) Writing: Learning to Write, and (4) Writing: Developmentally Appropriate Writing.

Reading: Learning to Read Words.   During this block, you teach explicit lessons on strategies and skills you have determined are needed through your informal assessment. At this stage, the main skills the children need are related to word recognition, and children will read from books specially designed to foster particular word recognition skills. These skills, which will help them become independent decoders, should also be reinforced during other blocks.

Reading: Developing Language and Comprehension.   In this block, instruction is carried out with big books (and multiple small-book copies of the same book), read-alouds, shared reading, and guided reading. Students develop their ability to construct meaning through listening and then moving on to reading.

Even though some children may not yet be at the Emergent Literacy stage while others may be at the Beginning Reading and Writing stage or beyond, the same book can be used for instruction some of the time. Together you enjoy the story, predict, explore ideas, discuss literary elements, compare the story with other stories, talk about vocabulary, and examine various components of words. To accommodate the range of literacy development you may have in your group, you can use multilevel prompts, varying the kinds of questions and expected responses according to children's level of development. For example, after reading the big book *If You Give a Mouse a Cookie* (Numeroff, 1985, 1989), you might begin by asking children to look at the first page and tell something they notice. Comments will vary depending on the children. Some comments about the words or print on page 1 ("If you give a mouse a cookie,") might include:

- The first word has a capital.
- The sentence isn't over because there's just a comma.
- That word (pointing to *mouse*) rhymes with *house*.
- The word *a* is there two times.
- The "oo" in that word (*cookie*) is like the word *book*.
- The "ou" in *you* sounds different from in *mouse*.
- I can hear three sounds in the word *give*.

Children need practice in generating these kinds of observations. Begin by modeling and then invite comments. Make it part of your routine.

You can also direct observations for particular children:

- You might turn to page 6 and ask Miguel to come up. "Point to all the words on this page that begin with the same first letter as your name," you tell him (the words being *mirror, make, milk,* and *mustache*). "Now use your two first fingers and frame that letter and tell us its name."
- On page 8, you might ask Susie to "Find a word that rhymes with *deep*" (*sweep*).
- You might ask Jonah to explain what the author means on page 9 when she says, "He might get carried away and . . . " (this requires understanding of figurative language).

- Melissa might be asked to explain how the picture of a refrigerator on page 23 helps a reader predict that the word on the next page probably has something to do with eating or drinking something.
- You might ask Greg to respond to the question "How do we know how the mouse liked the story? Read the page that tells us" (page 15).

No matter where each child is on the literacy continuum, every one of them can participate in this book experience. During this block, you may occasionally form groups of children with like needs. Such groups are changed frequently as needs change. This block is 15 minutes or more.

Writing: Learning to Write.   You may alternate between this block and Developmentally Appropriate Writing, teaching a lesson one day and then allowing several days for children to work on the type of writing you taught. You teach several related aspects of literacy concurrently:

- You demonstrate a particular type of writing. As you do so, you help children understand aspects of genre, audience, text structure, and story elements, as well as style and tone. You may simply model writing or combine modeling with collaborating. For example, you may demonstrate writing a circular story such as the one you just read. As you progress, children may contribute so that the task becomes collaborative.
- You teach the grammar and spelling needed for the writing. While you may teach separate grammar and spelling lessons during another part of the day, they may be isolated from authentic use. Here children discover how these lessons are applied. For example, as you first model and then guide collaborative story writing, you verbalize that you begin each sentence with an upper-case letter and end each sentence with a period.
- You reinforce the phonic and structural patterns the children are learning in reading. Such learning has equal use in both reading and writing. As you write, verbalize about choices you make about letters to use to represent certain sounds and how many sounds a word has. For example: "Our story is about a cat. How many sounds can we hear in the word *cat*? What letter can I use for each sound?"
- At this stage, you are also teaching children about letter formation: handwriting. During this block, you can reinforce the importance of careful letter formation in communication: "Watch how I write the letter *t*; I start here, just above this line, and move the chalk down to the base line. Then I cross the *t* here. Notice that the letter is not slanted and that I left just a tiny bit of space after the *a*—not as much as between words."
- The teaching of handwriting may combine lessons related to phonemic awareness and sound-letter associations: "I need to write the word *kite*. How many sounds do you hear? What's the first sound? What letter can stand for that sound?"

Be careful not to overdo verbalization as you do collaborative writing with children. Be selective, calling attention most often to skills that have most recently been taught or that you have learned need reinforcement.

Writing: Developmentally Appropriate Writing.   During this block, you assign the type of writing that has recently been taught, though students may choose their own topics. For example, you might assign children to write a friendly letter following a lesson on that form, but you would not assign whom the letter goes to or what the content should be. The extent of the writing task is adjusted to individual abilities. This may mean that one child is directed to write "one good sentence," while another is directed to "draw a picture and tell me what you want to say about it; I'll write it for you," and still another is asked, "How many pages do you think your letter will be?"

Comments

If we expect children to write competently and with pleasure, we must begin in the early grades. The two instructional writing blocks in the Balanced Beginning Literacy Program ensure that ample time is given to writing. Children come to see writing as a normal part of every day.

Though these two blocks are designated as instructional periods, children will write during other times of the day as well, such as during the Daily Independent Writing block. They may also write in journals first thing in the morning, collaborate on writing morning messages, write reports for science or social studies, write letters to pen pals, and so forth.

Additional Support: Intervention.   As we emphasized in Chapter 4, intervention is in addition to (not instead of) the daily literacy blocks just described. These programs may be pullout, in-class, or extended day. They may be delivered by you or by another qualified teacher. See the description of intervention programs and the sources for additional reading in Chapter 4.

Continuous Assessment

Throughout this book, we have stressed the concept of continuous assessment. By that we mean that assessment is not something you do once with each child at the beginning of the year, and then only when required to give tests for grade cards. Continuous assessment means you use every moment of the day as an opportunity to learn about your children.

Here, in conjunction with the way you plan a balanced literacy day for students at the Emergent Literacy stage, we want to stress this point once again. Continuous assessment means adjusting the way you listen to and view children as you interact with them during daily activities. The children are changing from day to day, and you need to be continuously aware of their development so that you can change your instruction accordingly.

Meeting Individual and Group Needs in Diverse Classrooms

You need to think about four areas when planning to meet the needs of individual children as well as your whole class: the range of stages in your classroom, the strategies and techniques appropriate for the children at each stage, materials to use during appropriate instruction, and accommodating children with special needs. We dealt with each of these areas earlier in this book, often in several ways. Here we review the kinds of thinking necessary to incorporate these needs into your everyday classroom.

Range of Stages

You must accept that you *will* have a range in your classroom. As children grow in years, the range in any given classroom is apt to widen. Though we identify children by stage, based on assessment, each child is unique—even within a stage. There are differences among children from the day they are born. These differences may be related to intellectual capacity (such as that measured on an intelligence test), to life experiences, to health, to home and neighborhood milieu, to interests, and more. Whatever the cause of the differences, you must acknowledge that they exist.

At one time, educators put more stress on causation of reading difficulties. Formulas were devised to figure out a child's **reading expectation level** based on IQ, chronological age, and years in school. While such notions were tempting, they usually were not helpful in planning instruction for most children. Educators working with children who have special needs may still take such a clinical view of literacy differences, but we do not do so here.

While you cannot be a private tutor to each child, you must do your best to meet individual needs. How you do that depends on allocating time for different modes of reading and writing and on building into your day time for one-on-one instruction for children who need it.

Strategies and Techniques

All of the strategies and techniques emphasized in Chapter 5 are appropriate at this stage as well:

1. Teacher read-alouds
2. Activities for oral language development
3. Shared reading
4. Shared writing
5. Language experience
6. Developing phonemic awareness

Additional strategies and techniques from Chapter 4 are used at the Emergent Literacy stage, including these:

1. The literacy lesson
2. Minilessons
3. Explicit phonics/structural elements routines
4. Explicit comprehension routines
5. Modes of reading
6. Response activities
7. Discussion circles
8. Modes of writing

The teacher has involved the children in composing the morning message and incorporating counting.
© Ellen Senisi/The Image Works

We already discussed some of these strategies as we described the literacy blocks. Now we will elaborate on several to illustrate typical ways of incorporating reading and writing into every day at this stage.

Modes of Reading and Modes of Writing.   Most of your time with children at this stage will involve providing heavy support through teacher read-alouds, teacher write-alouds, and shared reading and writing.

Shared Writing: Morning Message.   We described two kinds of morning message in Chapter 5: teacher-written and child-dictated (collaborative). Here are two more:

Formula.   Provide a pattern, or formula, for children to follow as they begin to compose morning messages themselves. For example, you may post the names of two children each day whose first task of the day is to compose the morning message. They may write on chart paper; perhaps each uses a different color of felt-tip marker. They follow a pattern that you have provided, such as the following:

- Month, day, and year in upper right-hand corner
- Begin with "Today is . . . "
- Write about the weather.
- Write about something you heard on a news program.
- Write about whatever special class is today.
- Add something personal if you want.

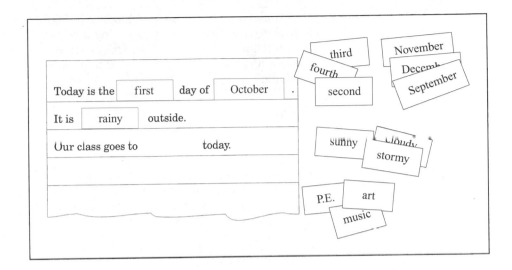

Figure 6.18
Frame in Pocket Chart for Children to Complete Morning Message

Frame.   If children cannot yet deal independently with a formula or pattern, provide a frame for them to complete. You can photocopy frames, use a transparency, or use a pocket chart. An example is shown in Figure 6.18.

Explicit Phonics and Comprehension Routines and Minilessons.   As you do literacy lessons and writing with children, you will teach explicit routines designed to build decoding strategies and enhance the children's ability to construct meaning. Some of these lessons will be for the entire class; others may be with small groups. Most are minilessons in that they are tightly structured, focused, and quick.

Response Activities.   Sometimes you will encourage children to use response activities after a read-aloud, a shared reading, independent reading, or developmentally appropriate reading. We know that responding to literature aids in construction of meaning as well as contributing to a child's pleasure. The following discussion elaborates on ways to carry out some of these activities with children at this stage.

Art.   Many children at this stage naturally enjoy drawing pictures to express their interests and ideas. In response to a story, they might draw their favorite part and talk about it or dictate a summary statement about it. They might also draw a character, an alternative ending, an illustration for an event that does not have a picture in the book, or something to express mood. Such visual imagery aids understanding.

Art responses might also involve clay, collage, posters, mobiles, and felt- or magnetic-backed characters and settings. The idea is to encourage children to have a personal response to a story and show it in some way. Art responses are especially appropriate for English-language learners whose comprehension exceeds their language production.

Retelling.   Retelling is part of your everyday activities related to story. The form of retelling used with expository text—summarizing—is also part of everyday instructional practice. As an individual response activity, children can retell or summarize to a partner or to you during a conference. If children have a problem with retelling, review your instructional strategies to be sure you are incorporating retelling regularly. You may need to provide a series of minilessons devoted to retelling.

Journals.   Even children at the Emergent Literacy stage can keep a reading response journal. At the very least, they can record the name of the book, the author, the illustrator, and the date; these can be copied from the book and the calendar. They can also write or draw a comment. You could begin by suggesting happy-, indifferent-, or sad-face drawings, but be sure to allow any other drawing that expresses a personal response. The children may also contribute to and refer to a word wall of possible response words and phrases from which to copy. For example, the wall might list:

> Wonderful!
> Made me laugh!
> You should read it!
> Made me sad.
> Good story!
> Good pictures.

Always tell children they may choose their own drawings or words to put in the journals if they like.

Discussion Circles or Groups.   This stage is not too early to introduce the pleasure of talking about books with a small group of friends. Whole-class discussion is not sufficient because it limits comments to only a few children, whereas a small group gives everyone an opportunity to talk. Discussion groups can fit in any of the reading blocks of the literacy program.

You will need to describe, role-play, and participate in such discussion groups until children learn to take over for themselves. By participating, we mean you will model sticking to the topic, listening to others, accepting and responding to the ideas of others, and general small-group behavior. Later you may continue to sit in from time to time, sometimes participating and guiding and sometimes observing and assessing.

Role-Plays and Puppets.   Before children are capable of actually writing a script and reading it (Readers Theater), role playing or puppets can serve as a way to respond to a story. Children assign parts and act out major events of a story. This is an informal activity, entirely carried out by the children for their own pleasure, though they may choose to show it to classmates who have not read the story. Limit the time spent on this response. Remember that children's growth in literacy is the direct result of time spent actually reading and writing.

Debate.   Most debate is highly structured and follows specific guidelines. With children at the Emergent Literacy stage, this is neither possible nor desirable. Instead, introduce children to the notion of dealing with different views about an informational piece or a story. You might begin with an issue that has two clear sides to it, for example, school uniforms. Survey children and count how many are on each side. Work with each side to develop and record points to support the children's views.

Selecting Materials

At the Emergent Literacy stage, you will need abundant examples of both authentic literature and decodable text.

Authentic Literature. *Authentic literature,* as you learned in Chapter 4, refers to any text that appears in its original form, whether narrative, expository, or procedural. It may be used in any literacy reading block.

For children at this stage, authentic literature that is appropriate in content is most likely found in picture books; children can enjoy these even without reading the text, or you can read them aloud. However, you may also have children who are at one of the next stages, so you need to provide books for these children to read as well.

Authentic literature will be available in your classroom in big books, literature sets (class sets), trade books, and anthologies that are part of a published program (sometimes referred to as a *basal*). Note that not all published programs include authentic literature. Some contain rewritten or edited versions of authentic text, and others are actually decodable text.

Decodable Text. Decodable text, written specifically to follow a sequence of decoding elements and high-frequency words, is particularly useful with emergent and beginning readers and writers, since it provides practice and helps children build fluency. Decodable text is available in these forms:

- *Literature sets, either for classes or for small groups.* Several publishers offer short books, some only 8 or 16 pages long, with limited words per page and colorful illustrations. Some limit the words to those of high frequency. Some focus on a particular phonic element, such as /-ar/; such a story might be about a *farm* with a *barn,* and so on. These books allow children to develop independence in decoding unfamiliar words in stories that contain many words with the same phonic element.

- *Anthologies.* Some publishers offer a series of anthologies of stories with controlled vocabulary and other decoding control.

- *Trade books.* Some trade books (that is, books not published especially for schools) also stress controlled vocabulary or limited phonic elements.

Comments

As you gather material for use in your classroom, you may find some decisions have already been made for you. Your school system may dictate not only the philosophy you are expected to espouse but also the materials you are expected to use. Even so, you can supplement any program with both authentic literature and decodable text for children at the Emergent Literacy stage.

Make books accessible; this means putting them where children can reach them and return them easily. Some teachers keep plastic tubs of books on each group of desks or in the centers of large tables. These tubs usually contain books children may choose to use during independent reading, though they may also contain developmentally appropriate books such as decodable texts.

You may borrow books from the school media center or the public library to keep available in your classroom during a certain unit. For example, you may gather books about reptiles, stars, the ocean, or different cultures. These become part of your library temporarily.

Your media specialist can help you build your library of authentic literature. At the same time, you need to keep reading new books at your library as well as reviews of new children's literature in journals and newspapers. You should also check web sites such as Amazon.com (http://www.amazon.com/). For children at the Emergent Literacy stage, you'll want wonderful illustrations and content that interests your children even though they cannot yet read the words. These books can be read aloud by you, by aides or volunteers, or by older reading buddies.

Be sure there are books available that represent all the diverse ethnic and cultural backgrounds of your students. Readers want books that reflect their own experiences. At the same time, such books can help your students begin to learn about one another and about cultures different from their own.

Students Requiring Special Attention

In your kindergarten or first-grade class, you may have some children who need special attention. Here we look at three broad categories of such children: those with exceptional gifts, those with special physical, emotional, or intellectual needs, and those who are second-language learners.

Gifted Children.   Schools may give less attention to children reading beyond the expected stage than to those who seem at risk for falling behind. Yet the child in your kindergarten or first-grade classroom who already reads fluently also deserves appropriate instruction. Such children should still participate in the Daily Independent Reading and Writing blocks and may be very happy as part of group instruction with grade-level materials. After all, even though they read fluently, they are still only five or six years old. During the Developmentally Appropriate blocks, they may be content to be a "group of one." Sometimes such children spend part of each day in another teacher's classroom with readers who are at the same literacy development stage. This is a fine solution only if everyone concerned, including the child, agrees.

Children with Special Physical, Emotional, or Intellectual Needs.   You will need to consult specialists in your school system for ways to adjust your classroom literacy program to accommodate special physical, emotional, or intellectual needs. The accommodations may include such items as large-print books for children with visual impairments, special microphones for those with hearing disabilities, tables that allow for wheelchairs, and communication devices for children who cannot control the usual writing tools or whose speech is unintelligible. While such children may receive help outside your classroom for some of the day, they remain a part of your class.

At the Emergent Literacy stage, you may find you can deal with most children who seem to be "not catching on" through rigorous attention to informal assessment followed by instruction that targets the need. In other words, now is the time to deal with children who are struggling. Do not wait for a serious lag to develop and then rely on special classes or teachers to try to compensate.

Whatever your assessment has revealed as behavior not yet present or not consistently present, that's where you need to focus your attention. This is often best done in the normal course of delivering a balanced literacy program, for the whole class or a small group, during the literacy lesson or during minilessons. What you emphasize in your class must make sense in terms of the particular children you teach. For example, you may need to spend more time on oral language development in one school than in another or provide more explicit instruction in helping children hear sounds and connect letters with those sounds.

Be a thoughtful user of school-dictated programs and materials. No program is an exact fit for every child. You must adjust instruction and materials to fit the particular needs of the children in your class. Your most important job is not "covering" a set of materials or a set of skills; rather, it is getting to know each child and adjusting materials and instruction to fit his or her needs.

Second-Language Learners.   Many of the activities that support the acquisition of English are also appropriate for all children who are acquiring literacy. With children at the Emergent Literacy stage who are in kindergarten or first grade, much daily activity for all children is oral, building vocabulary and developing phonemic awareness. Keep in mind, though, the wide variety of profiles that second-language learners may present when they come to your class: from absolutely no English yet to fairly adequate conversational English. Some may already exhibit many benchmark behaviors of the Emergent Literacy stage; some may not. Some may have begun to acquire English vocabulary while their oral speech still reflects the sounds of their first language, making the attainment of phonemic awareness of English more difficult for them. In fact, some may have sounds in their first language that don't even exist in English. They also face greater cognitive demands when asked to develop literacy skills at the same time they are wrestling with acquiring oral language.

Though many views exist about the best way to teach these children, it is dangerous to generalize about them. No single approach can meet the needs of this diverse group. Chamot and O'Malley (1994) found, after examining the research of many others, that most instructional suggestions for ELLs are the same as for any group of learners, though you may need more variety and adaptation. It will help–as it does with all children–if you can relate the materials you use to each child's cultural background and experiences. We believe you must not wait for English proficiency to develop. Just begin including the children in all activities. Your native English-speaking children will help you.

Two Classrooms at Work

To illustrate many of the suggestions made in this chapter, we will give brief descriptions of the schedule and the daily activities in two classrooms: first, Mrs.

Bullock's kindergarten, featured in the Eyewitness at the beginning of the chapter, and then a first-grade classroom.

Kindergarten

The kindergarten schedule varies from school to school but always contains literacy blocks similar to those in the preschool schedule presented in Chapter 5. Table 6.1 shows Mrs. Bullock's daily schedule for her half-day kindergarten. This is only one possible way to arrange a day.

In the following descriptions, you will see that many of the activities are similar to those in the preschool classroom presented in Chapter 5. Remember, too, that literacy learning takes place during the entire school day, even when the schedule shows another subject such as science or math.

7:45–8:00: Arrival; check-in; personal journals.   Mrs. Bullock encourages her children to write in personal journals each morning as soon as they have checked in. When they swarm about her trying to tell her something, she simply puts a finger to her lips and says, "Tell me in your journal." Children often begin by rereading previous entries in their journals. They also read the comments Mrs. Bullock has written. They are free to talk softly to a partner as they work to decode Mrs. Bullock's words.

8:00–8:30: Reading: Developing Language and Comprehension.   The children gather on the rug for a literacy lesson using a big book. Say this is their second day of reading with *If You Give a Mouse a Cookie* (Numeroff, 1985, 1989). The children begin by retelling the story. Then they reread it, with many chiming in confidently at various points as others still silently follow Mrs. Bullock's pointer. They discuss how the story made them feel and talk about the techniques the author used to make them feel that way. Mrs. Bullock then begins a literacy lesson with a new book. Children make predictions based on the cover and title.

Table 6.1
Daily Schedule for Mrs. Bullock's Kindergarten: a Half-Day Program with Literacy Blocks

7:45–8:00	Arrival; check-in; personal journals
8:00–8:30	Reading: Developing Language and Comprehension
8:30–8:45	Daily Independent Writing
8:45–9:15	Special classes (art, music, PE)
9:15–9:30	Bathroom/snack/morning message
9:30–9:45	Daily Independent Reading
9:45–10:30	Math/science/social studies/centers
10:30–11:00	Writing: Learning to Write/Developmentally Appropriate Writing
11:00–11:30	Reading: Learning to Read Words
11:30–12:00	Clean-up; story, song, finger play; dismiss

Mrs. Bullock does a picture walk. These activities with the new book will continue the next day.

8:30–8:45: *Daily Independent Writing.* The children know that independent writing comes next. As they return to their seats, they take individual folders from the plastic tub on each table. Each child works on a writing task of his or her choosing. Mrs. Bullock always begins the period by taking out her own writing folder to model the importance of daily writing.

After all the children are working, she holds two 5-minute individual conferences. In these conferences, she may discuss writing folders or reading logs, or may do a brief individual assessment.

8:45–9:15: *Special classes (art, music, PE).* When a timer goes off, the children know they should put their writing folders away and get ready to go to whichever special class takes place that day.

9:15–9:30: *Bathroom/snack/morning message.* Children gather on the rug at the front of the room to go over the morning message, which has been written on chart paper.

Early in the year, Mrs. Bullock treats the morning message as a big book, moving her pointer under the words as she reads them. She guides the children to note features of written text such as upper and lower case letters, the date, and punctuation. She reinforces identification of letters and associated sounds and leads the children to segment sounds.

Mrs. Bullock writes the message herself at the beginning of the year. As she finds some children who are moving out of the Emergent Literacy stage and into Beginning Reading and Writing, she encourages them to take over this task. If children are doing the morning message, they use the first block of time in the morning as other children write in personal journals.

9:30–9:45: *Daily Independent Reading.* To signal that the Daily Independent Reading block is beginning, Mrs. Bullock starts a tape playing some Bach *Two-Part Inventions*. The children settle down to read. At the beginning of the school year, the children did not yet know what was expected of them during this block, so Mrs. Bullock spent several days discussing, modeling, and guiding. She developed behavior guidelines with the children and created a poster that uses words and pictures to show the children what to do.

For the first couple of weeks, Mrs. Bullock chose and distributed a book to each child. She set the timer for 5 minutes. The children were to look at (read) their books until the timer rang. Then she collected the books.

When the children were comfortable with that routine, Mrs. Bullock began putting tubs of books on each table. The children selected a book when they arrived in the morning and put a marker in it with their name. They were thus able to begin reading promptly when the Bach music began. Eventually, the children were taught to choose a book from any shelf, put a marker in it, and put it at their places for Independent Reading time. Some children began to choose two books.

Gradually Mrs. Bullock extended the time until, by the end of the year, the children read independently for 15 minutes. Mrs. Bullock allows children to talk softly with a friend during this time because she values the importance of sharing books with friends. Even when her children are able to manage their independent reading consistently, Mrs. Bullock continues to model by reading her own book during this time. Sometimes she uses part of the time for individual conferences.

9:45–10:30: Math/science/social studies/centers.   Mrs. Bullock often reads aloud from a trade book as part of whatever math, science, or social studies unit she is currently doing. Children may refer to other books and also write about related topics. Sometimes this period is devoted to whole-class demonstrations, sometimes small-group activities, and sometimes centers. Sometimes there is a mix of activities. It is a very flexible time in this kindergarten.

10:30–11:00: Writing: Learning to Write/Developmentally Appropriate Writing. Mrs. Bullock likes to have this literacy block immediately after content areas. Often the writing she teaches or models is related to the content just learned. She alternates days between teacher-modeled writing and developmentally appropriate writing. However, every day she presents a minilesson on the mechanics of writing, such as letter formation and punctuation. Fourth-grade writing buddies come to Mrs. Bullock's class twice a week. Each kindergartner has a buddy; the buddy may take dictation, help compose or revise a story, collaborate on a report, or share any other appropriate task.

11:00–11:30: Reading: Learning to Read Words.   To teach word recognition skills, Mrs. Bullock may use a familiar book, such as *If You Give a Mouse a Cookie.* For example, to teach a minilesson on phonemic awareness, she turns to a page in the book and points to the word *might* as she says it aloud slowly. Starting with that word, she helps children segment the sounds into onset and rime and then replace the beginning sound with another sound such as /t/ to make the word *tight.* She does this with several words. Some children can perform the task with ease. Others struggle. Still, they all participate. Mrs. Bullock notes which children may need additional small-group lessons and which now seem to segment sounds with little or no difficulty.

Mrs. Bullock also works with small groups of three to five children during this period, meeting each group two to three times a week. The groups are flexible, changing as needs change.

11:30–12:00: Clean-up; story, song, finger play; dismiss.   Just before cleaning up, each child tells one thing he or she learned that day. During clean-up, the children often sing a familiar song or recite nursery rhymes. Then Mrs. Bullock may teach them a new song or finger play. Finally, because Mrs. Bullock wants the children to leave with wonderful language in their ears, the children settle down for a read-aloud story before going home.

Comments

There is no "right" way to schedule a kindergarten day. We have suggested only one of many arrangements. In fact, Mrs. Bullock may change this schedule when she feels it isn't working. The important thing to remember is that for literacy to develop, time must be built into the everyday schedule for children to read and write, both independently and with the guidance of a teacher. Only rarely does literacy develop without a teacher. Simply exposing children to good literature is not enough. Children need to be taught.

First Grade

The first-grade schedule shown in Table 6.2 is a sample; again, schedules vary widely. Whole school days may be only about 2 hours longer than half days and include time for lunch and perhaps additional breaks.

As you can see from the table, all literacy blocks are present, but more of the additional time is allocated to daily math, spelling, and handwriting lessons. Teachers use such schedules flexibly, extending some periods and cutting short others to accommodate the interests of the children, special events or holiday celebrations, special units of study in science or social studies, or sometimes just because everyone feels like a change.

We will comment briefly about some of the periods that differ from those in kindergarten.

9:30–10:15: Spelling; explicit minilessons for groups; centers. Part of this time is spent with the mandated basal spelling program. The teacher relates the elements in the prescribed lessons to phonemic segments, letter-sound associations, and elements of word structure that the children are learning during other parts of the day.

After spelling, small groups of children who have shown a need are given minilessons of explicit instruction in phonics or comprehension. The other

Table 6.2
Sample Daily Schedule for a First-Grade Class with Literacy Blocks

8:15–8:30	Arrival; check-in; personal journals
8:30–8:45	Daily Independent Writing
8:45–9:30	Reading: Learning to Read Words
9:30–10:15	Spelling; explicit minilessons for groups; centers
10:15–10:30	Break; snack; morning message
10:30–10:45	Read-aloud
10:45–11:30	Reading: Developing Language and Comprehension; minilessons
11:30–12:00	Lunch
12:00–12:15	Handwriting
12:15–12:30	Daily Independent Reading
12:30–1:05	Special classes (alternating music, art, PE)
1:05–1:30	Math
1:30–1:45	Recess and/or read-aloud
1:45–2:15	Science/social studies (units alternate)
2:15–2:40	Writing: Learning to Write/Developmentally Appropriate Writing
2:40–3:00	Clean-up; story, song, finger play; dismiss

children work at centers that may be tied to reading, writing, or other content areas. The children rotate through the centers according to a schedule.

10:30—10:45: Read-aloud.   The book read aloud during this time may relate to a content-area unit.

10:45—11:30: Reading: Developing Language and Comprehension; minilessons. The teacher does guided reading with one group as others use a different mode such as reading with a partner or alone. Groups are flexible. The children struggling the most may meet with the teacher every day, while others may meet with the teacher three times a week.

1:05—1:30: Math.   The words for math concepts are learned as sight words, though the teacher reinforces those that fit phonic elements the children have learned. Some time is spent practicing recognition of number words, arithmetic operation words, and direction words necessary for independent practice of math skills.

1:45—2:15: Science/social studies (units alternate).   As with math, some important concept words are taught as sight words. Others are used to reinforce children's growing decoding ability.

Science and social studies units are of varying length. They are planned by grade-level teams, and materials for teaching each unit rotate among the classrooms on a prearranged schedule. The "packaged" materials include reading material with big books and trade books, though each teacher often uses his or her own favorite materials as supplements. These materials are also the basis for lessons about text structure as well as such comprehension skills as compare and contrast, fact versus opinion, and main idea and supporting details. During this time, the teacher may also incorporate lessons on searching the Internet for related information as well as using the computer for projects related to the unit. (See the two books by Grabe and Grabe in For Additional Reading.)

Comments

Though we show separate blocks for math, science and social studies, and literacy, in some first grades the entire day is integrated, making such divisions misleading. For example, a class doing a unit on endangered species may address almost every part of the day to the overarching themes related to that unit, tying reading, writing, math, and even spelling to the topic of study.

Summary

The Emergent Literacy stage, an exciting stage of literacy to share with children, follows the Early Emergent stage. Children usually reach this stage during kindergarten or first grade, though some reach it earlier and some later. Assessment of the benchmark behaviors continues to be mostly informal, and it takes place continuously; that is, teachers focus their observation on certain behaviors while carrying on routine classroom activities. When a child has not yet reached a benchmark, instructional strategies are planned to foster continued literacy growth.

In kindergarten and first grade, the classroom needs a wide variety of materials for reading and writing, including many examples of both authentic literature and decodable text. The physical arrangement should allow comfortable spaces for individual work, small groups, and whole-class activities.

The schedule for each day should reflect the seven blocks of the Balanced Beginning Literacy Program described in Chapter 4: two blocks for power and practice (Daily Independent Reading and Daily Independent Writing), four blocks for instruction (Reading: Learning to Read Words; Reading: Developing Language and Comprehension; Writing: Learning to Write; and Writing: Developmentally Appropriate Writing), and one block for additional support (intervention) for those children who need it. The blocks are used flexibly within each classroom, however, and the amount of time devoted to each depends partly on the continuous assessment the teacher does. Schedules also vary widely from school to school. While some schools allot separate times for separate subjects, many integrate the curriculum so that virtually all activities relate to a particular topic or unit of study.

Teachers of kindergarten or first grade typically must meet the needs of a range of literacy stages. In addition to the instructional strategies used at the Early Emergent stage, several other strategies and techniques become especially useful, including the literacy lesson, minilessons, explicit phonics/structural elements routines, explicit comprehension routines, modes of reading, response activities, discussion circles, and modes of writing. Teachers should also be prepared to adapt their instruction to meet the needs of children who are gifted, those who have special physical, emotional, or intellectual conditions, and those for whom English is a second language. Such children may benefit from adaptive equipment or additional professional support from special teachers or classrooms; however, we believe that all children can be well served by the assessment-based teaching you will do in the regular classroom.

FOR ADDITIONAL READING

Books About Children's Authors

1. Meet the Author series published by Richard C. Owen Publishers, Katonah, New York. One example is *A Letter from Phoenix Farm* (1992) by Jane Yolen.

2. Two books of interviews with authors of books for children by Lee Bennett Hopkins: *Books Are by People* (1969) and *More Books by More People* (1974) (New York: Citation Press).

3. Books about writing for children such as *Worlds of Childhood: The Art and Craft of Writing for Children* (1998), edited by Maurice Sendak and William Zinsser (Boston: Houghton Mifflin). When you learn more about writing for children, you are better able to help children write and understand the process.

4. Annotated editions of books that help children understand that authors have revised and revised. One such book is *The Annotated Charlotte's Web* (1994), with an introduction and notes by Peter F. Neumeyer (New York: HarperCollins). This book contains the entire text of *Charlotte's Web* by E. B. White and the drawings by Garth Williams, along with copious notes about the process through which the author went as he developed the book. Also included are some facsimile pages showing White's many revisions.

Books About Teaching Writing

Calkins, L. M. (1991). *Living between the lines.* Portsmouth, NH: Heinemann.

Graves, D. H. (1994). *A fresh look at writing.* Portsmouth, NH: Heinemann.

Tompkins, G. E. (1994). *Teaching writing: Balancing process and product* (2nd ed.). New York: Merrill/Macmillan.

Language arts texts are also excellent sources for help in teaching writing. For example:

Norton, D. E. (1997). *The effective teaching of language arts.* Upper Saddle River, NJ: Merrill/Prentice Hall.

Templeton, S. (1991). *Teaching the integrated language arts.* Boston: Houghton Mifflin.

Children's Books with Word Play

Gwynne, F. (1970). *The king who rained.* New York: Windmill Books.

———— (1976). *A chocolate moose for dinner.* New York: Windmill Books.

———— (1988). *A little pigeon toad.* New York: Simon & Schuster.

Parish, P. (1963/1981). *Amelia Bedelia.* New York: Harper & Row/Avon Camelot. (Also other volumes in the Amelia Bedelia series by the same author.)

Terban, M. (1983). *Eight ate: A feast of homonym riddles.* New York: Clarion Books.

Other Additional Reading

Cole, A. D. (1998). Beginner-oriented texts in literature-based classrooms: The segue for a few struggling readers. *Reading Teacher, 51,* 488–501.

Freeman, D., & Freeman, Y. (1999). The California reading initiative: A formula for failure for bilingual students? *Language Arts, 76*(3), 241–248.

Grabe, M., & Grabe, C. (1998). *Integrating technology for meaningful learning* (2nd ed.). Boston: Houghton Mifflin.

———— (2000). *Integrating the Internet for meaningful learning.* Boston: Houghton Mifflin.

Johnston, F. R. (1998). The reader, the text, and the task: Learning words in first grade. *Reading Teacher, 51,* 666–675.

Martens, P. (1996). *i already know how to read: a child's view of literacy.* Portsmouth, NH: Heinemann.

Morrow, L. M., & Tracey, D. H. (1977). Strategies used for phonics instruction in early childhood classrooms. *Reading Teacher, 50,* 644–651.

Opitz, M. (1998). Children's books to develop phonemic awareness—for you and parents, too! *Reading Teacher, 51,* 526–528.

Ramirez, G., & Ramirez, J. L. (1994). *Multiethnic children's literature.* Albany, NY: Delmar.

Spangenberg-Urbschat, K., & Pritchard, R. (1994). *Kids come in all languages: Reading instruction for ESL students.* Newark, DE: International Reading Association.

Stahl, S. A., Duffy-Hester, A. M., & Stahl, K. A. D. (1998). Everything you wanted to know about phonics (but were afraid to ask). *Reading Research Quarterly, 33*(3), 338–355.

Wagstaff, J. M. (1997/1998). Building practical knowledge of letter-sound correspondences: A beginner's word wall and beyond. *Reading Teacher, 51,* 298–304.

Yopp, H. K. (1995). A test for assessing phonemic awareness in young children. *The Reading Teacher, 49,* 20–29.

Zarillo, J. (1994). *Multicultural literature, multicultural teaching.* Fort Worth, TX. Harcourt Brace.

FOR EXPLORATION: ELECTRONIC RESOURCES

Carol Hurst's Children's Literature Site: Children's Books.
http://www.carolhurst.com/titles/allreviewed.html   Useful reviews of children's books by the site's author. Each review contains a brief summary of the story along with a critique.

Effective Decoding Instruction for Diverse Learners.
http://www.cs.oswego.edu/~borgert/OCM/rdagenda-1.html   Designed for use in a workshop, this web page provides links to various types of information about decoding instruction, including a five-step lesson plan.

Predictable Books. http://monroe.lib.in.us/childrens/predict.html   This web site, developed by the Monroe County Public Library in Indiana, provides a list of predictable books—books that encourage children to predict what will come next—in eight different categories.

Ready to Read: Building Skills Through Early Care and Education.
http://www.ed.gov/pubs/startearly/ch_2.html   This chapter from the U.S. Department of Education's publication *Start Early, Finish Strong: How to Help Every Child Become a Reader* provides valuable information about supporting literacy development during the early years. The chapter describes a number of useful activities and highlights several exemplary programs from around the country.

Use the Web to Enhance the K–2 Reading Curriculum.
http://www.education-world.com/a_curr/curr150.shtml   This curriculum article on the *Education World* site discusses using the Web to enhance reading curricula in kindergarten through second grade. The article contains links to a number of sites that teachers can use to augment their reading instruction.

CLASSROOM APPLICATIONS

1. Locate one of the word-play books suggested in For Additional Reading. Read it with a group of children and talk about it with them. Immediately after, write what you have learned about the children in terms of their reaction to the book, and describe the instructional decisions you might make on the basis of this information.

2. After reading a story aloud to a group of children, suggest several response activities. Monitor the children as they carry out these activities, and then assess what you have learned about each child's ability to construct meaning.

3. With a small group, use words from a familiar story or nursery rhyme to informally assess each child's ability to segment sounds. Using what you learn, plan an explicit lesson on phonemic awareness and phonics using the model presented in Chapter 4.

4. Interview a bilingual teacher or one who teaches English as a second language. Prepare interview questions in advance to learn about how children are selected for the program, how the program works, the philosophy on which the approach is based, and any other information you would like to know. Observe a class, if possible.

The Beginning Reading
and Writing Stage

FOCUS
As you read the Eyewitness section, ask yourself the following questions:

1. What things are Mr. Pulaski and Ms. Farrieas doing that will help them be assessment-based literacy teachers?
2. Most children in these two classrooms are at the Beginning Reading and Writing stage. Keeping this in mind, ask yourself:
   • How do these children compare to children you saw in the Eyewitnesses in Chapters 5 and 6?
   • What evidence do you see in these classrooms that there are children at several different stages of literacy development?
   • How are these teachers accommodating the needs of second-language learners?

Eyewitness *Today we are visiting two assessment-based literacy teachers in the Livingston School: Mr. Pulaski, who teaches first grade, and Ms. Farrieas, who teaches second grade. Each teacher has twenty-one students. Mr. Pulaski has three second-language learners: two Spanish-speaking students and one student who speaks Hmong. Ms. Farrieas has four Spanish-speaking students.*

In Mr. Pulaski's room, we see him teaching the consonants m *and* t *and the short vowel* a *to a group of ten students, including the second-language learners. He is using an explicit phonics routine (see Chapter 4). At the conclusion of his lesson, he distributes copies of a little book that contains text requiring the use of the phonics skills he has just taught. He tells the children to use what they have learned in today's lesson and the other skills they know to read the text silently to find out what problem the children in the story are having.*

As the children read silently, Mr. Pulaski moves from child to child, asking each one to softly read aloud two pages from the text. He listens to the second-language learners first to be sure they are gaining the ability to do sequential beginning decoding in English. He makes notes about each student's performance in decoding the words in the text. With the second-language learners, he is aware that their pronunciation may still not match standard English; what he checks is that they are developing basic decoding skills.

While Mr. Pulaski teaches this group, the remaining eleven students are working at learning stations or centers, completing a written task related to sorting words by a spelling pattern; they must also do an activity requiring them to complete a chart about two characters from a trade book they have read.

Next door in Ms. Farrieas's class, we see similar types of activities. One group is silently reading the book Eek! There's a Mouse in the House *(Yee, 1992). As the children finish, they write responses in their journals. Another group, including the four Spanish-speaking students, is working with a bilingual teaching assistant who is following up on the lesson Ms. Farrieas taught yesterday. The assistant is guiding the students in locating words in a big book that consist of two or three sounds. As they find the words, the assistant says them slowly and the children repeat them. Then they write the words under columns headed "Two Sounds" and "Three Sounds." The final group is doing guided reading (see Chapter 4) with Ms. Farrieas. Ms. Farrieas is noting their reading behaviors on a checklist.*

As you looked at these classrooms, did you notice how the children are becoming readers and writers? For example, Mr. Pulaski teaches some phonics skills that students immediately apply in a book that they read silently. At the same time, the other children are working at learning centers and completing a task related to a trade book they have read. Although we did not see it today, Mr. Pulaski's second-language learners receive daily English-Language development lessons, which include literacy-based activities in which the students listen to others read books in person or on tape. Notice that he was quick to check that the second-language learners had sufficient oral language skills to handle the assigned reading task.

The excitement of the **Beginning Reading and Writing** stage is also apparent in Ms. Farrieas's room. Some children are responding to what they have read, while others are applying strategies and skills they are learning through guided reading. It is also evident that some children in Ms. Farrieas's room are still close to the Emergent Literacy stage. These are the students who are working on phonemic awareness with the teaching assistant.

BENCHMARKS for the Beginning Reading and Writing Stage

The benchmarks for the beginning reading and writing stage are typical of children ages six to eight in first and second grades. Read through the following benchmarks for this stage before proceeding with the remainder of the chapter.

Oral Language

BENCHMARK The student exhibits behaviors from the Emergent Literacy stage to a greater degree.

BENCHMARK The student's use of standard English continues to develop.

- ✔ If speaker of nonstandard English, is learning to switch between two languages
- ✔ Self-corrects while speaking

BENCHMARK The student's facility with language is growing.

- ✔ Listens to classmates and can paraphrase what others have said
- ✔ Oral language reflects increasing vocabulary
- ✔ Will ask for meanings of unknown words used in class
- ✔ Is interested in collaborative work with classmates
- ✔ Can participate in a discussion
- ✔ Can plan and ask oral questions
- ✔ Will plan and present an oral report

BENCHMARK The student continues to show pleasure in words.

- ✔ Makes jokes related to plays on words
- ✔ Shows interest in the history of words
- ✔ Enjoys nonsense and silly poems such as those by Shel Silverstein and Jack Prelutsky
- ✔ Enjoys making own dictionary

Reading

BENCHMARK ➤ **The student continues to show growth in many of the behaviors from the Emergent Literacy stage.**

BENCHMARK ➤ **The student is acquiring additional word recognition skills and strategies.**

✔ Recognizes and can name all letters in random order

✔ Recognizes and can name many words at sight

✔ Uses phonics and structural elements to determine the pronunciations of words

✔ Chooses appropriate strategies and skills to sound out words

✔ Uses context to determine word meaning

BENCHMARK ➤ **The student constructs meaning from print.**

✔ Can read and retell familiar stories

✔ Reads own writing

✔ Is beginning to use critical strategies such as predicting, identifying important information, self-questioning, monitoring, summarizing, and evaluating

✔ Attempts to read and retell unfamiliar texts (narrative and expository)

✔ Self-corrects when reading

✔ Is confident and willing to take risks

✔ Chooses to read during free time

✔ Sees self as a reader

✔ Likes to read to others

✔ Begins to explore using research tools and skills such as glossary, table of contents, dictionary or picture dictionary, beginning encyclopedias, and reference sources on CD-ROM and in library

Writing

BENCHMARK ➤ **The student exhibits continued growth in many of the Emergent Literacy behaviors.**

BENCHMARK ➤ **The student exhibits a variety of general writing behaviors.**

✔ Enjoys writing

✔ Is confident about own writing

✔ Communicates with others spontaneously

✔ Attempts to read others' writing

✔ Shows interest in writing

✔ Writes in a variety of formats for different purposes, such as journals, learning logs, notes, lists, stories, poems, reports, and labels

BENCHMARK ➤ **The student is growing in the use of mechanics and conventions of writing.**

✔ Forms letters conventionally for the most part

✔ Shows increased phonemic awareness along with increased visual memory and spelling sense

✔ Invents spelling when conventional spelling is not yet known and edits/proofreads later if writing is to be published

✔ Is beginning to learn spelling patterns that reflect phonics knowledge

✔ Recognizes nonstandard usage and grammar in own writing and edits/proofreads

✔ Uses word processing

BENCHMARK ➤ **The student uses the writing process.**

✔ Participates in and understands the purpose of all steps of the writing process

✔ Uses the writing process collaboratively and independently

✔ Listens to or reads the writing of others and makes appropriate positive comments related to story parts or text structure

Connecting to Other Chapters

FOCUS

As you read about the Beginning Reading and Writing stage ask yourself the following questions:

1. What are the major differences between this stage of literacy and the preceding one?

2. How does assessment at this stage differ from assessment at earlier stages?

3. What are some critical elements in organizing and managing a classroom containing a range of stages of development?

For most children, the Beginning Reading and Writing stage usually occurs during first and second grade. The higher the grade, however, the greater the range of stages you are likely to encounter in your classroom. The first- and second-grade classroom is likely to have children at two or three different stages of development, and perhaps more. Think about each stage discussed so far, and compare your thoughts to the following points:

- *Early Emergent Literacy stage.* By first or second grade, nearly all children who have been given appropriate instruction should be beyond the Early Emergent stage of literacy development. If you discover children who are still functioning at this stage, you need to use the ideas presented in Chapter 5. Further, you should consult with your school learning specialists to determine whether these children need special support in addition to the classroom program.

- *Emergent Literacy stage.* Some children in first grade are still likely to be functioning at the Emergent Literacy stage. These children need the type of instructional support suggested in Chapter 6 plus the support discussed in this chapter. By grade 2, most children will be well beyond this stage; if some are not, besides referring to the ideas presented in Chapter 6, you should consult with school learning specialists to determine whether the children need additional support beyond the regular classroom program.

- *Beginning Reading and Writing stage.* This is the stage, discussed in this chapter, at which most children in first and second grade are likely to be functioning. Some first graders and many second graders are likely to be well into this stage of development as the school year begins.

- *Almost Fluent Reading and Writing stage.* For most children, this stage begins toward the end of second grade or at the beginning of third grade and is likely to continue through grade 4 or beyond. It is possible, however, to have some children in first and second grade who are functioning at this stage. For these children, you should refer to the ideas presented in Chapter 8. A first or second grader who has reached this stage also needs many opportunities to participate in reading and writing activities with peers who are functioning at other stages of development.

- *Fluent Reading and Writing stage.* This stage typically begins around grade 4 or 5. However, you may have a first or second grader who is at the fluent stage. The ideas suggested in Chapter 9 would be appropriate in this case.

Meeting the needs of an increasingly wider range of stages requires that you use a variety of small-group and individual activities throughout your program. This chapter frequently refers back to the instructional strategies presented in Chapter 4, which will help you create the appropriate mix of activities. You may want to review the relevant sections of Chapter 4 as you read on.

Using the Benchmarks to Assess the Child and Determine the Stage of Instruction

In this section, we show you how to assess students' oral language, reading, and writing at the Beginning Reading and Writing stage. This assessment takes place primarily through instructional activities, although some specific informal and formal procedures are suggested. Figure 7.1 presents the benchmarks and their major components for this stage. As an assessment-based literacy teacher, you will continuously adjust instruction on the basis of what you determine about each student's performance in relationship to the benchmarks.

Oral Language

At the Beginning Reading and Writing stage, children's oral language continues to expand. As before, it serves as the foundation for reading and writing (Menyuk, 1988). We present four major areas in this stage: continued development of Emergent Literacy behaviors, use of standard English (Figure 7.2), growing language facility (Figure 7.3), and pleasure in words (Figure 7.5). A class checklist for all of these behaviors appears in Figure 7.6 and an individual checklist in the Resource File. Assessment of all these oral language benchmarks is based simply on observation and the use of checklists.

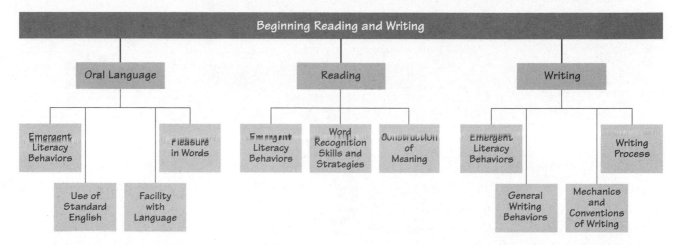

Figure 7.1
Menus for Assessing the Beginning Reading and Writing Stage

BENCHMARK

The student exhibits behaviors from the Emergent Literacy stage to a greater degree.

BENCHMARK

The student's use of standard English continues to develop (Figure 7.2).

✔ If speaker of nonstandard English, is learning to switch between two languages

✔ Self-corrects while speaking

Think back to the Emergent Literacy stage. What behaviors were identified for the oral language benchmarks? Refer to Chapter 6 to refresh your memory. Most children will continue to show these behaviors, but to a greater degree. For example, children will keep developing their abilities to retain oral directions and use new words they learn from stories.

As you listen to students talk, note that some are using standard English while others are using nonstandard English. Second-language learners are likely to be using their native language and making attempts to use English. As children are learning standard English, they often continue to use nonstandard English as well. Note which students are learning how to switch between standard and non-standard forms according to the situation. Mastery of standard English is not a prerequisite to proficient reading; however, it is important for all students to acquire standard English because it is the language of formal writing and of the books they will read.

At this stage, you will often note that a child's oral language directly influences his or her use of phonics. For example, a child who drops endings in speaking will often drop endings in reading. This is not a reading problem; it is a language difference. For second-language learners, this influence is even more significant. Until students develop good use of oral English, their progress in learning phonics and other decoding skills is likely to move more slowly (Freeman & Freeman, 1999).

As children develop more facility with standard English, they will often correct themselves while speaking. Support efforts to switch to "school language." Don't allow nonstandard usage to become an embarrassment.

Instructional Strategies. The best way to help children's use of standard English grow is to provide many good models and opportunities to interact with these models. Offer many opportunities for children to listen, discuss, and re-

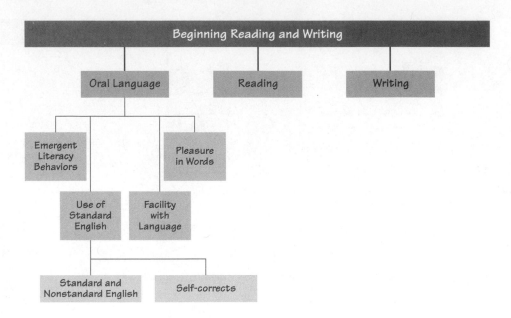

Figure 7.2
Oral Language: Use of Standard English

spond: read-aloud, daily sharing time, role playing with other students or using puppets, class visitors who use standard English, and so forth.

As other students are talking or reading aloud, note which students pay attention and can respond by stating what they have heard in their own words.

Instructional Strategies.   Provide many opportunities for students to give oral reports or do oral reading for the purpose of sharing books, not just orally reading around a group. Ask other students to tell in their own words what they have learned from the presentation. From time to time, model this process yourself, especially if students are having difficulty.

During discussions, model paraphrasing the previous speaker's statements before adding your own comments. Reduce the number of times you restate students' ideas; rather, encourage students to speak directly to each other and to listen to (and paraphrase) each other's ideas.

Note that students' vocabulary increases over time. Be aware of which students ask for word meanings, thus showing an interest in words. Some primary teachers take a sample of a child's oral language by having the child describe a picture or photograph on tape. Several months later, the process is repeated using the same picture, and growth in the child's vocabulary is usually obvious. This is also a good way to show parents evidence that their child's vocabulary is increasing.

Instructional Strategies.   Increasing oral vocabulary does not require direct instruction. Rather, it requires many opportunities for students to listen, respond, talk, and interact with others. Use activities such as the following to expand oral language:

BENCHMARK

The student's facility with language is growing (Figure 7.3).

✔ Listens to classmates and can paraphrase what others have said

✔ Oral language reflects increasing vocabulary
✔ Will ask for meanings of unknown words used in class

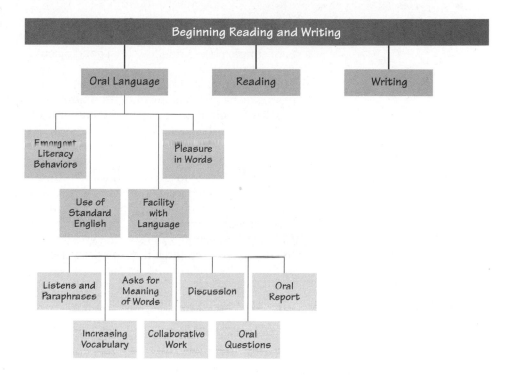

Figure 7.3
Oral Language: Facility with Language

- Have a daily sharing time during which students, you, and other adults talk about something of interest.
- Keep and discuss a bulletin board with labeled pictures.
- Have a "Word of the Day" displayed on the chalkboard or bulletin board. The word is discussed and used in a variety of sentences and can be provided by you or your students. Focus on general vocabulary as well as technical vocabulary related to particular topics or areas of study.
- Read aloud and discuss books that contain rich vocabulary.

✔ Is interested in collaborative work with classmates

✔ Can participate in a discussion

Children naturally like to talk. During this stage, they start to actually collaborate with their peers on projects and begin to participate in discussions about what they have read and many other areas of work and play. Note the students who do this well and those who need extra encouragement or guidance.

When working with second-language learners, keep in mind that they can participate in group discussions (Martinez-Roldan & Lopez-Robertson, 1999/2000), though they may not take part as readily until they feel more confident in their use of oral English. Often second-language learners will respond more favorably when they work with just one other student until they are comfortable working with a larger group.

Instructional Strategies. Set up many opportunities for collaborative work and discussions. Follow the guidelines for discussion groups presented in

Chapter 4. As students are starting to learn to participate in discussions, model the process. Discuss and evaluate how things are going. Generate with students a set of simple class guidelines for a good discussion as well as for good behavior during a discussion.

Second-language learners who have not developed the ability to discuss in English may be grouped together from time to time to discuss in their native language. The student with the best command of English could then report the group's ideas to the class. This procedure works best when there is also an adult who speaks the students' native language.

✔ **Can plan and ask oral questions**

Note who is able to ask good questions during lessons, following read-alouds and talks by special guests or other students, and so forth. Are the questions logical, and do they focus on things pertinent to the situation?

Instructional Strategies.   Discuss and model the process of asking good questions. Guide children to see that good questions focus on important aspects of the topic. Teach children how to ask a variety of types of questions focusing on *who, what, when, where,* and *why.*

✔ **Will plan and present an oral report**

As students make oral presentations, look for such signs as the following:

- Has a logical order
- Sticks to the topic
- Uses complete thoughts or ideas
- Has a beginning, middle, and end to the report

Instructional Strategies.   Model the process of good oral reporting. Stress the importance of the role of the presenter and the role of the audience. Use guidelines such as those behaviors just suggested to show students how to plan and give an oral report. Plan an oral report as a class, and have different students give parts of it. After the report, discuss ways to improve it. Develop a chart of guidelines, generated by the students themselves, about how to give a good oral report (Figure 7.4).

BENCHMARK

The student continues to show pleasure in words (Figure 7.5).

✔ Makes jokes related to plays on words
✔ Shows interest in the history of words
✔ Enjoys nonsense and silly poems such as those by Shel Silverstein and Jack Prelutsky
✔ Enjoys making own dictionary

This part of the Beginning Reading and Writing stage is really fun for teachers and children. Note children who show an interest in words through behaviors like the ones listed under the benchmark. Add any other such behaviors that are appropriate for your classroom. Keep in mind, though, that second-language learners often lack the language and cultural background to understand certain jokes, word plays, or figurative language. When you notice that second-language learners start to get jokes, it is a sure sign of English acquisition.

Instructional Strategies.   Do as many things as possible to interest children in words. Some of the following strategies should be very helpful:

- Have children keep personal Joke Books.
- Share your own "word of the day." Make a big deal out of it. Reward those who can use the word during the day.

Our Guidelines For A

GOOD

Oral Report

- Have a clear topic.

- Stick to your topic.

- Have a beginning, middle, and end.

- Speak clearly.

- Be natural.

**Figure 7.4
Sample Student-Generated
Guidelines for Oral Reports**

- Use a bulletin board to display information about word histories and origins. For ideas, refer to Bear, Invernizzi, Templeton, and Johnston (2000), listed in For Additional Reading.
- Share lots of nonsense poems. Encourage children to recite them. Use such poets as Jack Prelutsky, Judith Viorst, and Shel Silverstein.
- Have children make individual word banks or dictionaries to collect their own special words.

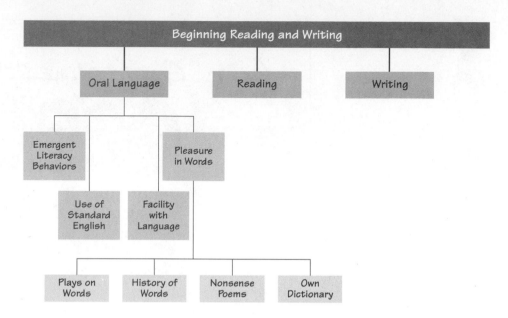

Figure 7.5
Oral Language: Pleasure in Words

Figure 7.6 presents a class checklist for all the oral language benchmarks. An individual checklist is in the Resource File.

Reading

You can easily do much of your reading assessment informally during instruction. From time to time, you will do more formal things to assess students' application of a variety of reading strategies and skills.

There are three main areas of Beginning Reading behaviors: the continued development of behaviors from the Emergent Literacy stage, *word recognition* skills (Figure 7.7), and construction of meaning (Figure 7.11). A sample class checklist for reading benchmarks appears in Figure 7.14 and an individual checklist in the Resource File.

Students will continue to show growth in many of the behaviors from the two previous stages, especially the Emergent Literacy Stage. It is not necessary—or defensible—to wait until a student shows development in *all* aspects of earlier stages to begin instruction that will foster growth of the behaviors in the Beginning Reading and Writing stage.

Children at this stage should be able to name all the letters of the alphabet, both upper and lower case. You can assess this knowledge informally:

- As various class writing activities are done, note which children use the letter names to refer to letters as they write.
- When children line up to leave the room and you have a few extra minutes, ask different children to name various letters in the room as you point to them.

BENCHMARK

The student continues to show growth in many of the behaviors from the Emergent Literacy stage.

BENCHMARK

The student is acquiring additional word recognition skills and strategies (Figure 7.7).

✔ Recognizes and can name all letters in random order

Oral Language Checklist:
Beginning Reading and Writing Stage

Teacher_____   Date_____   Grade_____

Student Names

+ = behavior present
- = behavior absent
✓ = somewhat present

Benchmark

Emergent Literacy Behaviors

Use of Standard English
Switches between standard and
    nonstandard English
Self-corrects

Facility with Language
Listens and paraphrases
Increasing vocabulary
Asks for meanings of words
Works collaboratively
Participates in discussion
Plans and asks oral questions
Plans and presents oral report

Pleasure in Words
Makes jokes related to plays on words
Shows interest in word history
Enjoys nonsense and silly poems
Makes own dictionary

Figure 7.6
Sample Class Checklist for Beginning Reading and Writing: Oral Language Benchmarks and Behaviors

However, by this stage of literacy development, you may want to assess letter-name knowledge more directly. A quick, efficient way to do this is to have a set of 3" × 5" index cards printed with upper- and lower-case letters. Mix up the cards, and ask each child to name the letters at random. Record your results on a sheet like the one in Figure 7.8; a blank copy of this form is in the Resource File.

Instructional Strategies.   If children do not know the letter names, use the following strategies to help them gain this knowledge:

1   After determining the letters children do not know, provide direct instruction on several of the unknown letters at one time.

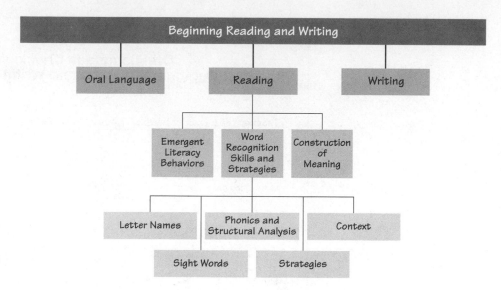

Figure 7.7
Reading: Word Recognition Skills and Strategies

a. Show the letter on a card. Include the name and picture of an object to help children remember the letter name:

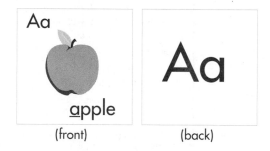

(front)   (back)

b. Say the letter and name the object.
c. Have children repeat the name.
d. Follow this procedure with several other letters.
e. Shuffle the cards with only the letters showing. Have children name the letter. If they have difficulty, turn the letter to the picture side to help children link the name of the picture with the letter name. Repeat as often as needed.

2 Play games that require children to match upper- and lower-case letters and name them.

3 Read aloud many alphabet books. Share the illustrations and discuss the letter names. Have children join in reading aloud the books.

4 During write-aloud and shared writing, have children name letters of the alphabet as they write. Do the same as they observe you write.

5 If you are using a published reading, spelling, or handwriting program, use the index of the teacher's manual to locate activities that teach the letter names.

Letter-Name Knowledge

Name _Jean R._   **Date** _10-10_

Upper Case   **Match**   **Lower Case**

___ A		___ a
___ B		___ b
___ C		___ c
___ D		___ d
___ E		___ e
___ F		___ f
___ G		___ g
___ H		___ h
___ I		___ i
___ J		___ j
___ K		___ k
___ L		___ l
___ M		___ m
___ N		___ n
___ O		___ o
___ P		___ p
___ Q		___ q
___ R		___ r
___ S		___ s
___ T		___ t
___ U		___ u
___ V		___ v
___ W		___ w
___ X		___ x
___ Y		___ y
___ Z		___ z

Observations

___ Says all upper- and lower-case letters by name

___ Matches all upper- and lower-case letters

___ Needs help with:

Q and X (upper-case). p and q (lower-case)

matching upper and lower q

**Figure 7.8
Sample Letter-Name Sheet**

Children who are having serious problems learning the names of letters may need several months to develop as you continue with other reading skills and strategies. If this is the case, use strategies suggested in Chapters 5 and 6, and continue to provide short periods of instruction and practice with the alphabet each day until children's knowledge of it is automatic. Lack of alphabet knowledge, however, should not stop you from teaching other skills and strategies of Beginning Reading.

Children at the beginning reading and writing stage are starting to build an extensive sight vocabulary. This vocabulary will consist of high-frequency words as well as other words they are able to decode independently and automatically

✔ Recognizes and can name many words at sight

(including the Dolch words, which we will discuss in Chapter 10). In addition to assessing a child's sight-vocabulary knowledge, you are assessing fluency.

The best way to assess a child's sight vocabulary and fluency is to periodically sample oral reading of the connected text being used for instruction. In Chapter 3, you learned to take an oral reading sample or running record. Use this procedure to assess students' increasing knowledge of sight vocabulary.

At the Beginning Reading stage, it is important that you assess students' sight-vocabulary knowledge on a regular basis until you are confident they have attained a large stock of sight words. Do this by taking an oral reading sample or a running record for each child at least once every two or three weeks. Save the sheets you used for coding the children's oral reading and compare them over time to note the number of words children read instantly by sight. The same oral reading samples will also provide information on children's other skills and strategies, such as the phonics skills discussed in the next section.

Instructional Strategies.   To help children attain an increasing sight vocabulary, you should do four primary things:

1   Systematically teach decoding skills so that children become independent in figuring out words they do not know when they are reading. This ultimately leads to an increase in sight vocabulary.

2   Introduce high-frequency words or any other words you think students may be unable to decode before they read a text.

3   Provide daily opportunities for students to read and reread, both orally and silently, books in which they know all the words. Occasionally, time students' reading. Have students keep a graph or other type of record of their reading times. (See the section "Assessing Oral Reading Fluency and Word Recognition Strategies" in Chapter 3.)

4   Provide daily reading practice with books at students' instructional reading level—that is, books they can read capably with guidance and instruction—or with slightly more difficult books. This will give them the opportunity to use the skills and strategies they are learning (Snow, Burns, & Griffin, 1998). This activity can form a part of the Reading: Learning to Read Words block or the Reading: Developing Language and Comprehension block of the Balanced Beginning Literacy Program.

For the introduction of high-frequency vocabulary or words students are unable to decode before reading a selection, use the decodable words routine and phonetically unpredictable words routine suggested in Chapter 4. In the next section, we will discuss systematic decoding.

Daily practice reading in books appropriate to the student's reading level, or slightly harder, can be provided in several ways. Use books that have been leveled as described in Chapter 4. If your school is using a published program, that program probably has sets of leveled little books to use for guided reading. If your school does not use a published program, you can obtain sets of leveled books from such publishers as Houghton Mifflin Company, Rigby Educational Publications, the Wright Group, or Richard C. Owen Company.

To provide additional practice, place sets of books in tubs or baskets in your room. Each tub or basket can be color coded to correspond to the level of the book, and you can also place a colored dot on the back of each book to signify its level:

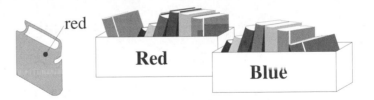

Post a chart in the reading center or reading area to help children determine the order of moving from one color-coded set of books to another. Children can also have individual lists of book titles to check off as they read. Most often, students should read the books silently. From time to time, students may read cooperatively to add interest and fun to fluency practice.

Another good way to reinforce learning of sight vocabulary is through the **word wall,** an idea we introduced in Chapter 5. As high-frequency words and other words are introduced, place them on the wall under the letter with which they begin, as shown in Figure 7.9. Students should be encouraged to use the word wall to identify words needed for writing. Each day words on the wall should be reviewed with a short activity such as "Who can read the words listed under *D*?" Words should remain on the wall until most students have mastered them. Mastered words are removed to make room for new words. For a detailed discus-

Two children review a word wall. All words in each column contain the same vowel with varying sounds.
© Ellen Senisi/The Image Works

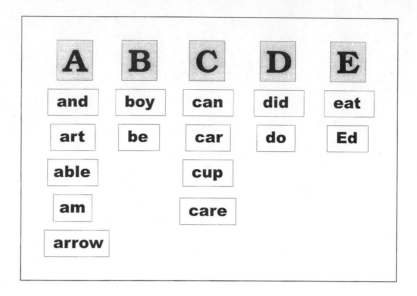

Figure 7.9
Sample Word Wall

sion of word walls, see Cooper (2000) and Cunningham (1995), listed in For Additional Reading at the end of the chapter.

✔ Uses phonics and structural elements to determine the pronunciations of words

✔ Chooses appropriate strategies and skills to sound out words

We have chosen to discuss these two behaviors together because to be of real value to students, they must be taught together. Within the categories of phonics and structural analysis, there are many subskills that students must learn. For a detailed discussion, see the Handbook Resource section titled "Word Skills: Phonics and Structural Analysis for Teachers" in Cooper (2000), listed in For Additional Reading.

As with sight vocabulary and fluency, the best way to assess the use of phonics, structural analysis, and the ability to use strategies to sound out words is to listen to a child's oral reading. As you listen, take a running record and then examine the miscue patterns. This will allow you to determine which phonic and structural skills the student uses and how he or she uses strategies to figure out unfamiliar words. The running record is a natural part of routine activities, which keeps assessment where it belongs—as a part of instruction.

Sometimes you may note in a running record that a student has difficulty using certain phonics skills or structural elements. In such cases, you might turn to specific skill tests for these items. (See Chapter 10 for a discussion of such tests.) If you are using a published program, it will include specific skill tests. However, you should not rely on these tests too heavily because they often assess the skills in isolation rather than in the context of real reading or writing. We believe it is much better to use samples of students' oral reading.

Looking at students' writing is another good way to determine their knowledge of phonics and structural skills. By analyzing how students spell words in their writing, you can tell which skills they are using. Again, use caution in drawing absolute conclusions. Writing is an **encoding** process in which students go from sounds to letters. Reading, as we have mentioned before, is a **decoding** process in which students go from letters to sounds. It is possible for students to use certain skills in one process and be unable to use them in the other. When making a determination about a student's use of certain skills, it is best to look at both a reading and a writing sample. By comparing the two, you can determine where to place emphasis in instruction. For example, if you see that a student uses digraphs and inflectional endings in decoding words but does not use them in spelling words as she or he writes, you know that in teaching the structural elements you need to emphasize the connection between reading and spelling.

Instructional Strategies.   Three of the instructional strategies we outlined in Chapter 4 will be most useful in helping students develop the use of phonics and structural skills: the literacy lesson, minilessons, and the explicit phonics/structural elements routine.

If you are using a published program, it will include a **scope and sequence** of strategies and skills that your students are expected to learn. Or your district may have a curriculum guide listing skills students need to achieve the standards or benchmarks for beginning readers. You should use that sequence of skills to help you determine what to teach, and you should make adjustments based on your own determination of your students' needs. As you teach the needed phonic and structural skills, provide decodable books for practice and application, and use the guided reading strategy described in Chapter 4. Periodically take a running record using these books to determine how students are applying the skills and strategies they have been taught.

For students who need help in learning to use strategies for sounding out words, teach them a plan like the one shown in the poster in Figure 7.10. This strategy helps students sound out words by looking first for word parts they know (structural elements). If that doesn't lead them to the word, they then try looking at the letter-sound associations (phonics). Following each step, they read or reread, checking whether the word they have sounded out makes sense. Finally, if these steps don't work, students can ask someone for help or use a dictionary. Even students at the Beginning Reading and Writing stage use simple dictionaries. The goal of all decoding instruction is to help students independently apply phonics and structural analysis along with other skills to figure out unknown words.

✔ Uses context to determine word meaning

The middle box in Figure 7.10 indicates the role of context as part of the strategy for sounding out words. Context is even more important, however, as a skill in determining word meaning. Students use context to verify the word they have sounded out by determining whether it fits into the sense or meaning of the sentence or paragraph. If the word is in the child's oral vocabulary and he or she has pronounced the word orally or silently, the context helps to verify the meaning. If the word is not in the child's oral vocabulary, the context may help the child predict the type of word that the unknown word must be (thing, descriptive word, and so forth) or predict the word's general meaning (fruit, form of transportation, and so on).

You can assess students' use of context to determine the meanings of words through oral reading and follow-up discussion, and also by taking a running record. Here are some examples:

- A student who miscalls a word in oral reading but corrects it after reading to the end of a sentence shows use of context. In the following example, the

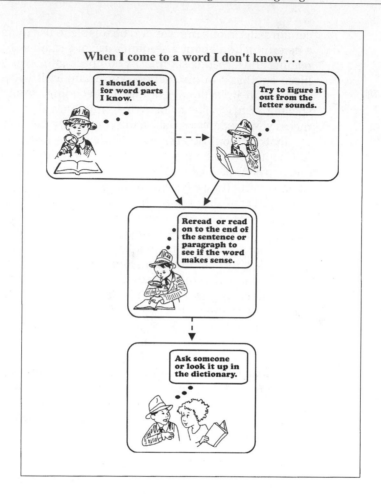

Figure 7.10
Poster for Decoding
Strategies

student originally read *apple* as *ape,* but then self-corrected the miscue after realizing that *ape* did not have the appropriate meaning for the context:

The big red ~~apple~~ ^ape sc^ was delicious.

- A student who substitutes a word that means the same or nearly the same thing as a given word shows the use of context. In fact, if a student does this often, it may indicate an overdependence on context, which can lead to inaccurate reading. In the following example, the student has used the context to determine the meaning for *mountain*:

The boy climbed to the top of the ~~mountain.~~ ^hill^

- In a follow-up discussion, you can ask the child to explain how he or she figured out the meaning of a particular word, and the answer will often reveal the use of context. For example, after reading silently or aloud,

The big red apple was delicious. *It was very sweet and juicy.*

you might ask the child how he or she could figure out the meaning of *delicious*. The child might say, "I could tell it was a word that meant the apple tasted good by the words *sweet* and *juicy*."

Instructional Strategies. A good way to teach the use of context to determine word meaning is to use the cloze procedure (discussed in Chapter 10 for assessment purposes) with big books or chart stories written by the teacher. Choose a text that children can decode, and place a self-adhesive note over key words that are easily determined by using the context. Have the text read aloud, asking children to supply the covered words. List all possibilities given by the students; then discuss which ones make sense in the text. The goal is not to get the exact word but to get one whose meaning fits the text. Finally, uncover each word and talk about how the letter-sound associations would be used to determine the exact word and the context would help to verify the meaning.

Another good way to develop students' abilities to use context is through read-alouds. After reading aloud, go back and discuss the meanings of selected words and how the context would help to determine the meaning. Model your thinking by explaining to students how you would figure out word meaning using the context.

Context is especially important for second-language students who are still developing standard English. Since phonics may be difficult for these students, they should be particularly encouraged to use context cues as well as their own background knowledge to comprehend texts.

BENCHMARK

The student constructs meaning from print (Figure 7.11).

✔ Can read and retell familiar stories
✔ Reads own writing

Many children come into the Beginning Reading and Writing stage having been read to a great deal. They have heard many wonderful stories such as *The Three Bears* (Galdone, 1972), *The Three Little Pigs* (Marshall, 1989), and *Brown Bear, Brown Bear* (Martin, 1967), to name just a few. A sign of children's beginning ability to construct meaning is that they often begin to read these stories and

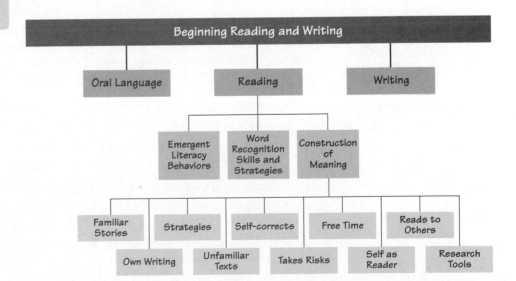

Figure 7.11
Reading: Construction of Meaning

retell them on their own. Because some of these stories are **predictable texts,** with repeated patterns that children can recognize, children often memorize them. This is a natural part of the beginning reading process and helps children see themselves as readers.

Many children at this stage will read these familiar stories aloud, but some will move toward silent reading. Children often think that silent reading is softer oral reading; they may mumble to themselves or subvocalize. This is quite natural at this stage.

The assessment for this behavior is primarily observational. You will observe children sitting with favorite storybooks, often reading to a stuffed animal or a real friend. You can often hear children retelling the story after they have read it. You can check for decoding and construction of meaning by using the retelling and running-record procedures described in Chapter 3. Keep in mind, however, that when children are reading favorite stories that have been read aloud to them, they may not be able to decode every word correctly because they are relying partly on what they have memorized or on picture clues.

Children also begin to read their own writing at this stage. You will observe children reading something they have written to a friend, to a stuffed animal, or to the group. As children progress through this stage, they will share more and more of what they have written. Even when the children "read" an elaborate story, however, you may see very few scribbles, letters, or words on their papers.

Instructional Strategies.   If children are unable to read and retell favorite stories, this may indicate they have not been read to outside of school. These children need a strong oral language program, with lots of time for stories to be read aloud, retold, and discussed. Second-language learners will also need a strong oral language program.

For children who seem to lack interest in reading their own writing to others, you should use the write-aloud and shared-writing techniques presented in Chapter 4. The read-alouds plus write-aloud and shared writing will give children who need this background a strong foundation.

✔ **Is beginning to use critical strategies such as predicting, identifying important information, self-questioning, monitoring, summarizing, and evaluating**

Research shows that the six strategies included in this behavior are critical for readers across all stages to become effective constructors of meaning. At the Beginning Reading and Writing stage, children are beginning to use all of these strategies. (For a detailed discussion of strategies, see Chapter 8 of Cooper [2000], listed in For Additional Reading.)

The best form of assessment for these strategies is observation of students' reading during reading lessons. Look for such behaviors as these:

- Makes logical predictions based on text information and own knowledge
- Begins to see that predictions change as more information is acquired
- Begins to ask questions based on logic and own knowledge
- Can answer own questions and those of others after reading
- Begins to know when something read does not make sense (monitoring)
- Rereads, looks at illustrations, or asks for help when something does not make sense (monitoring)

- Can summarize stories with key elements: setting, characters, problem, events related to problem, and outcome related to problem
- Can summarize informational texts by giving the main idea with a few details
- Begins to evaluate by noting likes and dislikes for text

Instructional Strategies. To help students develop their abilities to use the critical strategies, you will need to model frequently and provide many opportunities to use the strategies with increasingly difficult text. The literary lesson, minilesson, and explicit comprehension routine are the instructional strategies most pertinent here.

✔ Attempts to read and retell unfamiliar texts (narrative and expository)

At the Beginning Reading and Writing stage, students typically begin with texts that are heavily decodable and then move into trade book literature as they become independent decoders. To assess students' increasing ability to read unfamiliar text, use the retelling procedure presented in Chapter 3. You may do this retelling informally as a part of everyday instruction, or you may designate specific times or points in your instructional program when you take a retelling for each student. Actually, it is best to use both procedures. We suggest that every two or three weeks, you combine retelling and the running record using the same text. First, have the child read the text silently and retell it to you. Then have the child read the same text orally. By having the two samples of behavior with the same text, you are able to determine if the child is having problems with comprehension, decoding, or both. This helps you decide how to focus your instruction.

When you perform these assessments, always note the approximate level designation for the text. Save the record sheets (often known as *protocols*) for each assessment, and compare them over time to determine the child's progress.

Instructional Strategies. Ongoing assessment of students' ability to read increasingly difficult texts is critical. As you look at each sample of a student's behavior, you must determine what instruction will help that student continue to grow. Study the information for two students in Figures 7.12 and 7.13. How would you make decisions about these students? Here is the analysis we would suggest:

- Becky Smith (Figure 7.12) is having difficulty with the primer-level text; it is too difficult for her, so an easier text is needed. It also looks like she needs direct instruction with vowel patterns. Therefore, we would use the explicit phonics/structural elements routine and provide a lot of reading with decodable texts using the vowel patterns taught. We would also continue work with story elements through listening activities until we were sure she was overcoming any decoding problems.
- Roger Bickel (Figure 7.13) is decoding and comprehending accurately at the primer level. We would continue instruction with new skills and strategies and gradually increase the difficulty of his text. Since Roger is exhibiting no problems with decoding, he may be approaching independence and be ready to move into more trade book literature.

As you can see from these two examples, the instructional strategies you select must be based on the students' strengths and needs. Only through ongoing assessment can you make this determination.

Figure 7.12
Retelling and Running Record Data for Becky Smith

Name: Becky Smith

Date: 10-1

Text Level: Preprimer

Type of Text: narrative

Retelling: 75%
(Gave setting, problem, some events, part of outcome)

Running Record: 95%
(Good self-corrections, missed two hf words— saw & was; no other patterns)

Date: 10-18

Text Level: Primer

Type of Text: narrative

Retelling: 40%
(Only able to give characters & setting)

Running Record: 70%
(Had problems with words using long vowel patterns oa, ai, ea)

✔ **Self-corrects when reading**

Self-correcting means that, during oral reading, students correct miscues they have made because the meaning of the text does not make sense. This behavior is a part of the monitoring strategy discussed earlier. Self-corrections clearly indicate that a student is constructing meaning while reading. You assess this behavior using oral reading or a running record. We assume that when children self-correct in oral reading, they also self-correct in silent reading.

Instructional Strategies. Self-correction is best taught through teacher modeling and discussion. Talk to students about the importance of rereading and self-correcting, and periodically model the process yourself:

Figure 7.13
Retelling and Running Record Data for Roger Bickel

Name: Roger Bickel

Date: 10-1

Text Level: Preprimer

Type of Text: narrative

Retelling: 100%
(good complete retelling)

Running Record: 98%
(no pattern of miscues)

Date: 10-19

Text Level: Primer

Type of Text: expository

Retelling: 100%
(good use of strategies— summarizing & monitoring)

Running Record: 100%
(no problems)

Today as I was reading the story to myself, I read a sentence that said Harry was a house. *That didn't make sense to me because houses don't usually have names. I reread the sentence to myself and looked more carefully at the last word. It had* orse *on the end. It had to be* horse—Harry was a horse. *Now it made sense.*

Sometimes students don't self-correct because they lack the necessary understanding of language or background knowledge about the text topic. In these cases, it is necessary to teach the needed skills or concepts. Sometimes students are so focused on decoding that they forget about meaning. This is apt to occur if the child is trying to read text with too many decoding challenges. Second-language learners are especially likely to focus on decoding at the expense of meaning; therefore, you should encourage them to use background knowledge and context cues to check comprehension. It is our responsibility as teachers to guide and encourage students to use a variety of strategies to construct meaning effectively.

Observation of children in a variety of reading situations will give you many opportunities to determine which students exhibit these behaviors. Some teachers like to make up their own checklists to guide their observations. Here are some signs that we suggest you look for:

> ✔ Is confident and willing to take risks
> ✔ Chooses to read during free time
> ✔ Sees self as a reader
> ✔ Likes to read to others

Risk Taking

- Tries harder texts
- Attempts to sound out a word even when unsure
- Volunteers to read aloud
- Not afraid of reading

Free-Time Reading

- Picks up books or magazines as soon as other work is completed
- Wants longer independent reading times; often groans when it is time to stop
- When given time to play, often reads

Seeing Self as Reader

- Attempts to read familiar stories that have been read aloud
- Says "I can read"

Reading to Others

- Volunteers to read aloud to class or group during instruction
- Often seen reading aloud a book to a friend

Instructional Strategies. The development of these behaviors in students comes through the general classroom atmosphere and the overall approach to your balanced literacy program. You must create an exciting, print-rich environment that supports and promotes reading and writing. At the same time, you must express an attitude that encourages children to take risks, to see reading as important, to read during free time, and to read to others.

✔ Begins to explore using research tools and skills such as glossary, table of contents, dictionary or picture dictionary, beginning encyclopedias, and reference sources on CD-ROM and in library

Students at the Beginning Reading and Writing stage will have had minimal introduction to the use of research tools. They may have limited knowledge of such tools as the table of contents, glossary, and library sources. Some students may be familiar with CD-ROMs and Internet sources. The best way to assess students' knowledge of these tools is through observation of tasks requiring their use in the classroom.

Reading Checklist:
Beginning Reading and Writing Stage

Teacher_____   Date_____   Grade_____

Student Names

+ = consistently present
- = not present
✓ = somewhat present; recheck

Benchmark

Emergent Literacy Behaviors

Word Recognition Skills/Strategies
Names letters in random order
Recognizes many sight words
Uses phonics and structural analysis
Chooses strategies for sounding words
Uses context to determine meaning

Construction of Meaning
Reads and retells familiar stories
Reads own writing
Begins to use:
 - predicting
 - identifying important information
 - self-questioning
 - monitoring
 - summarizing
 - evaluating
Reads and retells unfamiliar texts
(narrative/expository)
Self-corrects
Takes risks
Reads in free time
Sees self as reader
Reads to others
Begins to use research tools and skills (list:)

Figure 7.14
Sample Class Checklist for Beginning Reading and Writing: Reading Benchmarks and Behaviors

Instructional Strategies. To introduce research tools and skills to students, we suggest you use minilessons. If more time is needed for the initial instruction, expand the amount of time devoted to the lesson.

The most effective way to teach research tools and skills also involves using short projects related to selections students are reading; themes or topics of study; or science, social studies, or other subject areas. Systematically identify the specific tools and skills you want to teach, and develop projects around them.

Figure 7.14 presents a sample class checklist for all of the reading benchmarks at the Beginning Reading and Writing stage. An individual checklist appears in the Resource File.

Writing

Most of your assessment in writing is done informally through observation of instructional activities and through group and individual conferences with students. There are four main areas of writing in this stage: continued development of Emergent Literacy behaviors, general writing behaviors (Figure 7.15), mechanics and conventions of writing (Figure 7.17), and use of the writing process (Figure 7.18). These aspects of writing grow together, not sequentially, as students develop literacy. A sample class checklist for the writing benchmarks appears in Figure 7.19 and an individual checklist in the Resource File.

In their writing, just as in their oral language and reading, children should show continued development in the benchmarks from the preceding stage. You should watch for further growth in the writing behaviors described in Chapter 6:

> **BENCHMARK**
>
> The student exhibits continued growth in many of the Emergent Literacy behaviors.

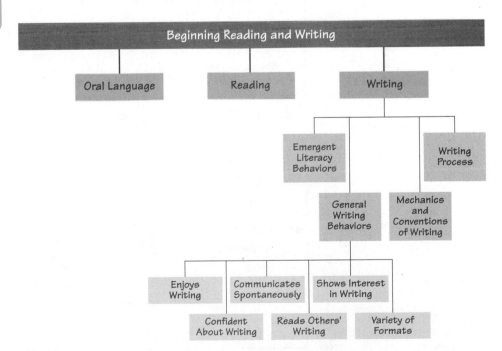

Figure 7.15
Writing: General Writing Behaviors

for instance, use of a journal, sharing of writing with others, and ability to report in writing on personal events and feelings.

These behaviors are assessed through observation of children as they write independently and during writing instruction. Some teachers use a checklist like the one in Figure 7.16 to keep track of these observations. Others simply make notes about students in a notebook or on cards and transfer them later to individual records.

BENCHMARK

The student exhibits a variety of general writing behaviors (Figure 7.15).

✔ Enjoys writing

✔ Is confident about own writing

✔ Communicates with others spontaneously

✔ Attempts to read others' writing

✔ Shows interest in writing

General Writing Behaviors Checklist: Beginning Reading and Writing Stage

Teacher_____   Date_____   Grade_____

Student Names

Y = yes
N = no
S = somewhat

Behaviors

Enjoys writing

Is confident about own writing

Communicates with others spontaneously

Reads others' writing

Shows interest in writing

Formats:

– Journals

– Logs

– Notes

– Lists

– Stories

– Poems

– Reports

– Labels

– Other (_____)

**Figure 7.16
General Writing Behaviors
Checklist**

Instructional Strategies. To achieve these behaviors, children must be taught how to write and they must have time to write. The classroom should have a writing center or area. Using an Author's Chair is one way children enjoy sharing what they have written. Use the modes of writing strategy described in Chapter 4 to model many kinds of writing.

Assessment of this behavior is mostly observational. However, for the various formats and purposes for which students write, you should use rubrics for evaluating the quality of the writing. If you are using a published reading—language arts program, rubrics and anchor papers are probably provided. Collect samples of students' writing over time as a basis for measuring progress.

Instructional Strategies. To support children's growth in this behavior, model the various types of writing using the modes of writing strategy. Move your modeling across all the modes, beginning with write-aloud and shared writing, until children are using each type.

Assessment of all of these behaviors comes primarily through analysis and evaluation of students' writing. When students begin formal spelling instruction (about two or three months into grade 1 in most schools), spelling tests serve as an additional assessment.

By this stage of development, phonemic awareness is more firmly connected to writing and spelling. Therefore, looking at students' use of spelling patterns provides additional information about their phonemic awareness.

The use of word processing should be a standard part of all students' learning. Many very young children will come to school knowing how to use the com-

---

✔ Writes in a variety of formats for different purposes, such as journals, learning logs, notes, lists, stories, poems, reports, and labels

---

BENCHMARK

The student is growing in the use of mechanics and conventions of writing (Figure 7.17).

✔ Forms letters conventionally for the most part

✔ Shows increased phonemic awareness along with increased visual memory and spelling sense

✔ Invents spelling when conventional spelling is not yet known and edits/proofreads later if writing is to be published

✔ Is beginning to learn spelling patterns that reflect phonics knowledge

✔ Recognizes nonstandard usage and grammar in own writing and edits/proofreads

✔ Uses word processing

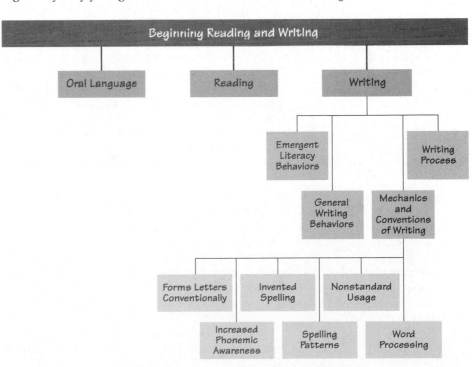

Figure 7.17
Writing: Mechanics and Conventions of Writing

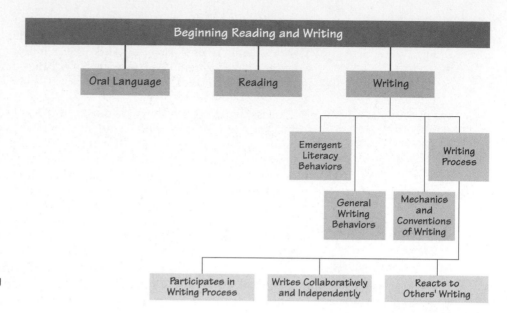

Figure 7.18
Writing: Use of the Writing Process

puter for games and for a variety of Internet resources. Therefore, word processing is a natural extension of what many students already know about computer technology.

Instructional Strategies.   Appropriate instruction comes primarily through the modeling of writing as discussed earlier. The explicit phonics/structural elements routine incorporates phonemic awareness development, reading instruction, and spelling instruction in relation to each letter-sound association pattern. Continue to help children make letter-sound associations in both reading and spelling. For a detailed discussion of the teaching of phonemic awareness, spelling, and grammar, see Cooper (2000) in For Additional Reading.

At this stage, students become more adept at using all steps of the writing process alone and in collaboration with others. Students are able to read and give suggestions for improving the writing of peers. Assessment of these behaviors occurs through observation as students write, have peer conferences, and share their writing with others.

Instructional Strategies.   The Balanced Beginning Literacy Program has two blocks of writing instruction, Learning to Write and Developmentally Appropriate Writing. Consistently providing these blocks throughout the daily instructional program using the modes of writing instructional strategy affords you many opportunities to model the steps of the writing process: selecting the topic, drafting, revising, proofreading, and publishing. (For in-depth reading on the writing process, see For Additional Reading.)

Figure 7.19 presents a class checklist for the writing benchmarks at the Beginning Reading and Writing stage. An individual checklist is in the Resource File.

BENCHMARK

The student uses the writing process (Figure 7.18).

✔ Participates in and understands the purpose of all steps of the writing process

✔ Uses the writing process collaboratively and independently

✔ Listens to or reads the writing of others and makes appropriate positive comments related to story parts or text structure

**Writing Checklist:
Beginning Reading and Writing Stage**

Teacher_____ Date_____ Grade_____

+ = consistently present
- = not present
✓ = sometimes present/needs instruction

Student Names

Benchmark									
Emergent Literacy Behaviors									
General Writing Behaviors									
Enjoys writing									
Is confident about writing									
Communicates spontaneously									
Reads others' writing									
Shows interest in writing									
Writes in a variety of formats									
Mechanics and Conventions of Writing									
Forms letters conventionally									
Shows increased phonemic awareness									
Uses invented spelling and edits									
Learning spelling patterns									
Recognizes nonstandard usage and edits own writing									
Uses word processing									
Writing Process									
Participates in writing process									
Writes collaboratively and independently									
Reacts to others' writing									

**Figure 7.19
Sample Class Checklist
for Beginning Reading
and Writing: Writing
Benchmarks and Behaviors**

Planning Instruction Based on Assessed Stage of Development

Now that we have looked at the benchmarks for the Beginning Reading and Writing stage, we need to think about how to plan instruction based on each student's stage of development. This section is organized around three important questions:

What do I teach or emphasize for students?

How do I teach what needs to be taught?

How do I organize and manage my class when I have a range of stages and needs?

What Do I Teach?

Through systematic, ongoing assessment using the benchmarks as guidelines, you are able to tell where students are in their development and determine what needs to be taught and emphasized within their instructional program. Most students in a typical first- or second-grade classroom will be functioning at the Beginning Reading and Writing stage. However, within this classroom you will have a range of stages.

Meeting the Needs of Diverse Learners

Remember that as you go up the grades, the range of stages within each grade increases. Meeting the needs of students entails the use of whole-class, small-group, and independent activities.

English-language learners (ELL students) at the Beginning Reading and Writing stage follow the same basic patterns and stages of development as other learners (Gibbons, 1993). However, as a part of your assessment of these children's needs, you must ask two questions:

- Do my ELL students know how to read in their native language?

- Are my ELL students proficient in English? (See Chapter 3 for a discussion of levels of oral language production.)

These two questions will guide you toward the type of instruction that is best for these students (Snow, Burns, & Griffin, 1998).

Ideally, as we pointed out in Chapter 4, if beginning ELL readers and writers are speaking only their native language, they should be taught to read in that language and then make the transition to English. However, this may not be possible for all languages. The next best step is to start ELL students with a strong oral English program before they are taught to read (Snow, Burns, & Griffin, 1998). Then their oral language will continue to develop as they learn to read in English. Oral language development should include many experiences with book language through read-alouds and taped readings. In the regular classroom, ELL students should take part in the oral language lessons, read-alouds, and shared reading during the Reading: Developing Language and Comprehension block. They will, however, still have a separate time to begin learning to read in English.

Starting ELL students with oral English first means they may not reach the benchmarks of the Beginning Reading and Writing stage at the same rate as other students. However, having the oral language activities take place at the same time as learning to read in English minimizes the delay these students will face in learning to read. Once they start to read in English, their rate of growth will increase. For many excellent suggestions for ELL students at the Beginning Reading and Writing stage, see Gibbons (1993) and Freeman & Freeman (1994), listed in For Additional Reading.

Making Decisions Using Ongoing Assessment

As you start each school year, use the tools and procedures suggested in the first portion of this chapter and in other places throughout this book to determine each student's stage of development and needs. Begin this process each year by looking at records from previous teachers, keeping in mind that this is only an indication of where the student was functioning at the end of the previous school year. This does not account for any growth the student might have made over the summer.

Some teachers don't like to look at previous records because they don't want to bias their judgment before they get to know a child. Biases can indeed occur; however, valuable time is often wasted in trying to find out about a particular student's development. Therefore, we recommend that you keep all these points in mind and use the previous records to help you determine how much initial assessment you will need. You can summarize the information you gain using *some* of the checklists and forms presented in this text. If all teachers in your school operate using the same basic stages of literacy development, this task will not be an overwhelming one.

As you provide instruction and literacy learning opportunities, keep your assessment ongoing. Constantly refer to the benchmarks for each stage as guidelines to help you determine how each child is progressing. This procedure will help you answer the question "What do I teach?" and plan your instruction accordingly.

How Do I Teach What Needs to Be Taught?

Once you have made your initial decisions about each student's stage of development and what needs to be taught, you must decide how you will teach and support your students. This process involves thinking about three principal matters: selecting materials for instruction appropriate for each child, continuing the Balanced Beginning Literacy Program, and choosing instructional strategies appropriate for each child. This section focuses on each of these points in turn.

Selecting Materials for Instruction

Most likely you will be teaching in a school that uses a published reading—language arts series. You should familiarize yourself with *all* of the materials in the series and make sure you understand the purpose of each type of text. For example, look at the anthologies, the teacher's manual, and so forth. Make certain you have appropriate decodable texts and trade book literature. If you don't, you should talk with your principal or supervisor about what you need and why you need it.

Recall that beginning reading has two big jobs, decoding and comprehension. At this stage of development, the bigger of these two jobs is still decoding. Therefore, children must have many opportunities to read texts in which they can apply the strategies and skills they are learning. You will need decodable texts that focus on the phonic and structural elements you are teaching.

As we mentioned in Chapter 4, decodable texts may be created (written by someone using a list of given words or letter-sound patterns) or may be authentic trade books selected because they offer many opportunities to use certain skills. In either case, decodable texts are usually single-story books. However, some publishers issue them in anthologies or as big books. The form they come in is unimportant. The main point is that you will need lots of these texts; children read them very quickly because their ability to decode is growing so rapidly. For a list of trade books grouped by the phonic elements used, see Trachtenburg (1990), listed in For Additional Reading.

You will also need plenty of authentic trade book literature, narrative and expository texts that offer richer language because they have not been selected to contain a limited number of decoding elements. Trade book literature may come in single-title form, big books, or anthologies. You'll use these books to provide reading practice and rich language development beyond the decodable texts.

Your trade books should be sequenced from simple to complex. If you are using a published reading series, most of this literature is likely to be in an anthology. A good way to organize all the books needed for instruction beyond the anthologies is to create a room in the school where the books are organized by level. See Chapter 4 for criteria for doing this.

In addition to the decodable texts and trade book literature, you'll need a classroom library for independent, self-selected reading. We recommend that you have a rotating collection that stays in your room for 6 to 8 weeks and is then replaced by another one. These collections can come from the school's central library or a local public library, or they can be rotated among several classrooms. By having rotating classroom collections rather than static ones, you always have fresh, new titles at the children's disposal. These collections should include magazines and newspapers that show environmental print appropriate for the beginning reader and writer.

You also need many titles for reading aloud to the class. These books are also trade books, but they can be even richer and more challenging to help students expand their oral vocabularies and overall general listening abilities. They are chosen for the children's interest as well as for being conceptually appropriate, even though they may be beyond the students' decoding abilities.

Continuing the Balanced Beginning Literacy Program

In Chapter 4, we described a Balanced Beginning Literacy Program for grades K through 2 and a slightly different balanced program for grades 3 through 8. In a first- or second-grade classroom, you will still be using the first of these two programs, though your students will be close to making the transition into the second program.

But what does the Balanced Beginning Literacy Program actually look like in a first- or second-grade classroom in which most students are at the Beginning Reading and Writing stage and some are at other stages? Remember that six blocks should occur every day for all students: Daily Independent Reading, Daily Independent Writing, Reading: Learning to Read Words, Reading: Developing Language and Comprehension, Writing: Learning to Write, and Writing: Developmentally Appropriate Writing. For those students needing additional support, an Intervention block is also provided. Let's examine these blocks one by one.

Daily Independent Reading.   By the time students reach the Beginning Reading and Writing stage, the habit of independent reading should be somewhat established. You should allot five to fifteen minutes per day for this activity. At the be-

Independent Reading and Writing Log Sheet

Name	Reading	Writing
Mark A.	10–10 Enjoying book on frogs. 10–19 Book too difficult. Suggested he select a different one.	
Lisa C.		
Andy D.		10–1 Drew picture in log. Did not write about it but could tell about it. Encouraged him to write one or two words about his drawing.

Figure 7.20
Independent Reading and Writing Log Sheet

ginning of grade 1 and even grade 2, you will still need to build up independent reading time by starting with five minutes and gradually increasing the time until you reach fifteen minutes.

You should read during part of this time to model reading. However, you should also move through the class coaching and monitoring students' reading. From time to time, have short conferences; for example, listen to individuals read orally to check their decoding and the appropriateness of the text. Ask children to retell what they have read. You might use a log sheet like the one shown in Figure 7.20 to keep track of observations as part of your ongoing assessment. A blank copy of this form is in the Resource File.

Daily Independent Writing.   This block requires 10 to 15 minutes per day of actual writing time, not counting the time spent getting out materials and so forth. The goal is to give children practice with their writing and help them establish the habit of writing for their own purposes. At the Beginning Reading and Writing stage, some children will be drawing and labeling while others may be writing full sentences.

Children at all stages of development often need help with ideas for their independent writing. A good way to help students make selections is to have a class chart for independent writing ideas (see Figure 7.21). The chart does not list specific topics; rather, it suggests types of writing that students might try. You can keep adding ideas as the year progresses.

For children who need help with selecting topics, you can offer two ideas to pick from. For example, suggest that a child write about a pet or a family member. Gradually increase the number of suggestions to three or more until children are selecting their own topics. You want them to choose their own topics as soon as possible because doing so leads to better writing (Graves, 1994).

As with independent reading, you should model the process yourself, in this case by writing some of the time. Share your writing with the children often. Use part of your time to coach, monitor, and conference with children as they write. A form like the one in Figure 7.20 can help you keep a record of your observations.

In addition to the suggestions just offered, many of the ideas given in Chapter 6 for independent reading and writing may be used for children at this stage of development.

Reading: Learning to Read Words.   During this block, you provide systematic, explicit instruction in decoding. Students read decodable texts that gradually in-

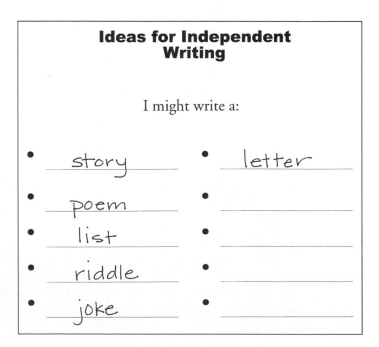

**Figure 7.21
Chart for Independent
Writing Ideas**

crease in difficulty as you teach more and more decoding skills. As soon as students become independent in decoding, the need for this block decreases in the literacy program, and the block is ultimately replaced by the Core Books block in the Balanced Literacy Program 3–8.

Exactly what you teach is determined by two factors: (1) students' needs from previous stages that you have identified through ongoing assessment and (2) strategies and skills that are reflected in the benchmarks for the Beginning Reading and Writing stage. If you are using a published series, the scope and sequence of skills will help guide you.

This block is not the only one in which students will learn decoding skills. During the next block described, Reading: Developing Language and Comprehension, students also develop some abilities to decode through listening to texts, shared reading, and guided reading.

Reading: Developing Language and Comprehension. In this block, students expand oral language and vocabulary and learn comprehension strategies. Because students at the Beginning Reading and Writing stage are still unable to read much text independently, you also provide richer text by reading aloud or doing shared reading. As students begin reading more, you move them into guided reading.

Writing: Learning to Write. In this block, you model how to write in various forms as well as how to use the process of writing. Further development of spelling and phonemic awareness takes place. Through many shared writing experiences, students learn to write, compose their own writings, spell, and use standard grammar.

Writing: Developmentally Appropriate Writing. As soon as students learn to do one type of writing in the Learning to Write block, they have the opportunity to perform the same type of writing on their own, but selecting their own topic. For example, if you model how to write a sentence about a picture or drawing in the Learning to Write block, children can draw their own pictures and write about them during the Developmentally Appropriate Writing block. Some children may still be labeling, while others are writing full sentences.

Intervention. For those students who appear to be having difficulty learning to read, you must add a component of intervention (not remediation; see the distinction in Chapter 4). You will be able to identify those students who need intervention quickly through your ongoing assessment. At the first- and second-grade levels, intervention usually can be handled in a small, flexible group within the classroom. This instruction should be delivered by a certified teacher, not a paraprofessional or volunteer.

Choosing Instructional Strategies

Many of the instructional suggestions given in Chapter 6 for students at the Emergent Literacy stage are also useful for students at the Beginning Reading and Writing stage.

By this stage, you will be making full use of all the instructional strategies presented in Chapter 4. The summary presented in Figure 7.22 shows where you

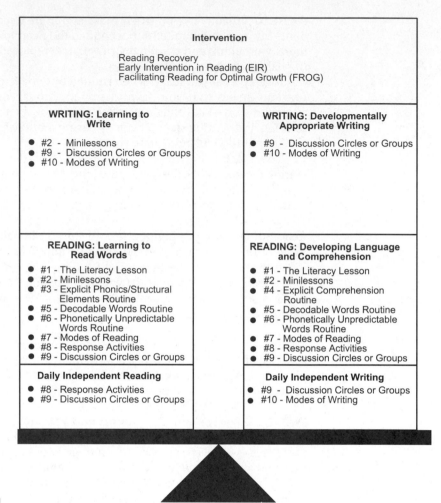

Figure 7.22
Use of Basic Instructional
Strategies in the Balanced
Beginning Literacy Program

would use these strategies in your program. Note that many of the strategies are used in several blocks. You select strategies that are appropriate to your instructional goals and the individual needs of your students.

You will want to adjust each strategy to serve your teaching purpose. For example, notice that Instructional Strategy 9, discussion circles or groups, is used in all six of the core program blocks, but it will serve different purposes:

- In Daily Independent Reading and Daily Independent Writing, discussion groups are used for students to share what they are reading independently or what they are writing on their own.

- In the Reading: Learning to Read Words block, discussions are used following the reading of a simple decodable text as a way to bring out the understandings students have developed.

- In the Reading: Developing Language and Comprehension block, discussions are used following listening, shared reading, or guided reading activities to focus on strategies or enjoyment of what was read.
- In the two instructional writing blocks, discussions allow students to talk about elements of the writing process as well as to share their writing, perhaps using the Author's Chair.

A later section of this chapter, "A Second-Grade Classroom at Work," gives some examples of how different strategies are used.

Now that we have examined what to teach and how to teach it, we turn to how to organize and manage a classroom with a range of stages and needs.

How Do I Organize and Manage a Classroom with a Range of Stages?

You may have noticed that Figure 7.22 does not include the last instructional strategy introduced in Chapter 4: number 11, the daily blocked plan. That is because it applies to all the blocks as a whole. The daily blocked plan is the basic structure we suggest you use for organizing your classroom.

Before you can develop a daily blocked plan, however, you especially need to consider four areas: your children's attention spans and interests; how to use whole-class, small-group, and independent activities; developing routines to manage a classroom using a variety of types of groups; and using learning centers.

Attention Spans and Interests

First and second graders at the Beginning Reading and Writing stage have attention spans of varying lengths. When planning instruction, you must keep this point in mind. As the year progresses, attention spans typically will increase.

During the first few days of school, you should try to identify students who have long attention spans and those whose attention spans are exceptionally short. Note and record who sticks to a task until completion, who stops before a task is done, and who requires lots of your attention to get tasks finished.

Directly related to attention span are students' interests. If students are doing tasks that interest them, their attention spans are likely to be longer. Knowing something about each child's interests becomes even more important in planning instruction.

This kind of information will help you organize groups and plan instructional activities. It will help you decide how long activities should last, the types of activities you need, and how many activities you need for a given amount of time. For example, students with short attention spans require shorter, more interactive activities to keep them focused.

Using Whole-Class, Small-Group, and Independent Activities

Three types of activities will help you meet the range of needs in your classroom: whole-class, small-group, and individual activities.

With w*hole-class activities,* as the name implies, everyone in the class does the same task. Sometimes these are independent; at other times they are teacher directed or coached. For example, a shared writing lesson focusing on how to write a letter or note might be done with the whole class.

Small group activities bring together two or more students who have the same needs to focus on a particular activity or to give them more individual attention. For example, you might conduct the shared reading of a big book with a group of six to nine students who need to expand their vocabulary and language; the small-group situation allows you to observe each student's progress more closely.

Individual activities are used when each student needs to work alone on a task or when only one student has the need for particular instruction. For example, you may have one student who needs more help with the comprehension strategy of predicting. You may decide to meet with this student and use the explicit comprehension routine to show him or her how to make predictions.

Using different types of groups with varied activities helps you meet the range of stages and needs in your class. You can also meet that range of needs by using what Cunningham and Allington (1994) call *multi-leveled activities* during whole-class instruction. In Chapter 6 we used an example based on the big book *If You Give a Mouse a Cookie* (Numeroff, 1989), describing how you might ask different students different questions about the book. That is an illustration of a multi-leveled activity, because the questions are based on each student's particular stage of development.

Developing Routines to Manage a Classroom Using a Variety of Types of Groups

Managing the first- and second-grade classroom (or any other classroom) requires that students learn some routines. Think of it as teaching a brief social studies unit on helping children learn to work together in the classroom. There are five important steps for developing student routines: (1) develop class guidelines, (2) appoint monitors, (3) identify independent activities, (4) role-play working in groups, and (5) evaluate with students. Let's look at how to carry these out.

Develop Class Guidelines   Having guidelines for students to use while working in the classroom is important, especially when you have several groups doing different things and you are meeting with one group. At the beginning of the school year, talk with your class about the need for everyone to know how to act while you are working with another student or a group. Ask students for their suggestions. Give one or two examples of what the guidelines might include. During the discussion, elicit or suggest such things as the following:

- Do your own work.
- If you need to talk with someone, use a soft voice.
- Go to a class monitor for help if the teacher is busy.
- When your work is done, do a special activity from the Activity Box.
- Try to solve your own problems first.

As children give suggestions and you add your own, write them on the board. Make sure you keep the ideas reasonable. Don't include such unreasonable abso-

Our Class Guidelines

1. Do your own work.

2. If the teacher is busy, go to a monitor.

3. Use soft voices.

4. Get an Activity Box pack when your work is done.

5. Solve your own problems.

**Figure 7.23
Sample Class Guidelines
Chart**

lutes as "Never interrupt the teacher working with a group"; after all, an emergency might arise that requires a student to interrupt the teacher. When you have the guidelines assembled, you can post them on a chart like the one in Figure 7.23.

Appoint Monitors.   Whenever you are working with a group, some other children may need help. Appoint monitors who can answer simple questions about an assignment, where to find materials, and so forth. You may have special monitors for different subjects, such as reading, spelling, or math, or you may have general monitors. One teacher we know gives the monitors special badges to wear so the other children will know who they are. Monitors may be changed daily or weekly so all children have an opportunity to be a monitor.

Identify Independent Activities.   You'll find that you need to establish activities for students to do after completing their assigned work. Such activities help keep children busy and prevent problems; they ensure that students never have idle waiting time. Independent or partner activities work best. Make available a limited set of activities, and change them frequently. These are a few possible types of activities:

- Self-checking folder games or activities
- Independent reading of books
- Assessment tasks for particular strategies or skills (you will check them later)
- Math practice, such as counting pictures and simple addition or subtraction
- Independent writing for the student's own purposes or for a special project
- Listening center activities
- Map activities
- Learning centers (see the next section)
- Computer activities

The important thing about all of these activities is that they be meaningful and constructive. They should always provide problem-solving experiences, practice or reinforcement, or extension of basic learning.

Children are working at the science center. They are recording their observations.
© David Young-Wolff/Photo Edit

Role-Play Working in Groups.   Once you have your class guidelines, monitors, and independent activities, you need to take a "dry run." Role-play the class doing an assignment while you are working with a group. First, talk the class through the way this would work. Next, walk through the procedures with no one actually doing work. Finally, actually carry out your plans. Keep times short and tasks simple.

Evaluate with Students.   After your first full trial of your routine, discuss with students how things went. Refer to the class guidelines: Did they work? Do some need to be added? Do some need to be deleted? During the first few weeks of school, evaluate regularly. Don't get discouraged. It takes first and second graders a few weeks to establish these routines. As children become comfortable with your pattern of working, the evaluation step can be done less frequently.

We have used these types of guidelines to develop management routines in our own classrooms. We have seen thousands of successful teachers use them. They work!

Using Learning Centers

As you saw in Chapter 5, **learning centers,** sometimes called *learning stations,* are places in a classroom where students perform tasks that have specified objectives. Effective learning centers have several common characteristics:

- *Manipulative activities.* Students often do matching and sorting types of activities involving hands-on manipulation. Sometimes writing is involved.
- *Specific focus.* Each learning center has a specific focus: for instance, to practice using vocabulary from a recently completed story.
- *Provision of all needed materials.* Everything students need to do the job is provided: pencils, paper, cards, crayons, tape recorders, and so forth.
- *Self-checking system.* Usually some system allows students to check their own work. This may be a simple answer key or some other type of coding system. Figure 7.24 shows an example of self-checking cards for a vocabulary activity. After pairing a word on one card with its definition on another, the student can check the match by looking to see if the images on the backs of the cards fit together to form a whole picture.

**Figure 7.24
Self-Checking Cards for a
Vocabulary Game**

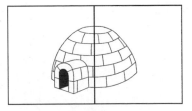

igloo | a house made of ice blocks

Front
(Match word and definition)

Back
(Check by seeing if picture pieces
go together. The picture does not
always have to relate to the word.)

- *Specified place to put completed work.* Students know exactly where to put their completed work. This may be a file box, a shoe box, or a storage tray on your desk.

- *Recordkeeping system.* A system is provided to help the student and you know whether all the activities of a particular center have been completed. This might be a simple card like the one in Figure 7.25. If it is laminated, students can mark on it with an erasable marker and use it over and over. These cards can be stored in the center area so you can easily see how each student is doing.

- Notice in Figure 7.25 that Larry Brown wrote the name for center 2, but he apparently didn't do the activity. Maybe he couldn't get to it because the

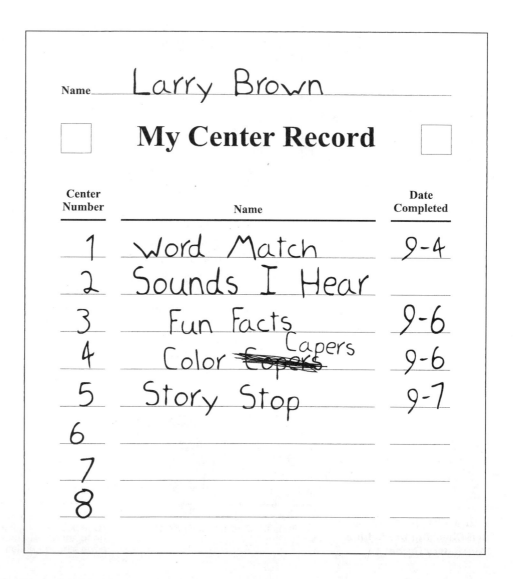

Figure 7.25
Learning Center Record Card for Students

center was occupied. Maybe the activity was too difficult or he didn't understand it. You would want to check on this. The record card plus any completed work sheets become a part of your ongoing assessment. (A blank copy of the record card is in the Resource File.)

If space is limited, you may have to be inventive. Figure 7.26 shows how you can create a set of four learning centers using a table placed near an electrical outlet. Some teachers just push together several extra desks to create learning centers. Still others construct learning centers in file folders. Students pick up the center and take it to their desk or work area.

Some first- and second-grade teachers use learning centers to carry out a major portion of their program. Students rotate through all the centers each day, meeting with the teacher daily in one of the centers. Centers are usually changed daily.

A Second-Grade Classroom at Work

Now let's look at how all of the concepts discussed in this chapter work in a second-grade classroom that contains native speakers, second-language learners,

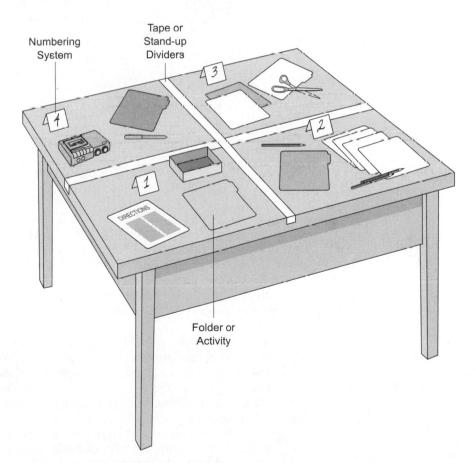

Figure 7.26
Table Divided into Four Learning Centers, with Materials Needed for Each Activity

Table 7.1
Daily Schedule for Mr. Russo's Second Grade

8:15	Arrival (children sign in each day)
8:25	Morning message
8:45	Literacy block
	• Reading
	• Writing/handwriting
	• Spelling
	• Oral language
	• Daily Independent Reading
	• Daily Independent Writing
12:00	Lunch and recess
12:30	Math
1:00	Special classes (art, music, PE) three days per week. On the two days with no special classes, second-language learners and children who need intervention go to the appropriate teachers; other students have project/activity time or teacher conferences.
1:40	Science/social studies/health (alternating units; some children go to intervention teachers during this time, and second-language students go to English Language Development)
2:20	Activity time
2:40	Read-aloud
2:50	Prepare to dismiss
2:55	Dismiss

and inclusion students. Mr. Russo's class has twenty-two children at various stages of literacy development, and he meets their needs with a Balanced Beginning Literacy Program. Table 7.1 presents his full-day schedule.

Four students in Mr. Russo's class who need reading intervention are pulled out at 1:00 on two days and at 1:40 on two additional days. This allows these students to get intervention without missing the classroom literacy block or the art, music, or PE classes; they miss some but not all periods of science, social studies, and health.

There are also four students who are second-language learners. They speak Spanish and can read some materials in their native language. They are at the Early Production level (see Chapter 3) in their oral language; this means they listen attentively, speak a few words of English, but most often use key words. They go to a language specialist for English Language Development lessons at the same times other students go to intervention.

In the following section, we take a detailed look at Mr. Russo's literacy block on one sample day. Study the plan carefully, read the discussion that follows it, and complete the questions at the end of the plan.

FOCUS As you read Mr. Russo's Plan:

1. Note how he incorporates the blocks of the Balanced Beginning Literacy Program.
2. Look for the variety of routines he uses.
3. Ask yourself whether he meets the needs of a range of stages by using different types of groupings or by using the same basic core activity and varying the way different students do it. Or does he use both approaches?
4. Note how he manages small groups by using independent reading and learning centers.
5. Look for evidence of ongoing assessment.
6. Note ways in which instruction differs from what you have seen at earlier stages.

Mr. Russo's Literacy Block Schedule (22 second graders)

Time

8:45 to noon daily (includes morning break)

Arrangements for independent work

Five learning centers: one for writing, one for vocabulary, one for spelling practice, and two for phonics practice

8:45 READING: Developing Language and Comprehension

Activities

• Reread the big book *The Lady with the Alligator Purse* (Westcott, 1988)
• Discussion

Routines

• Shared reading routine (Instructional Strategy 7: Modes of Reading)
• Discussion circles (Instructional Strategy 9)

Comments

This previously read book provides application of letter-sound associations and high-frequency words taught earlier. The activity also serves as a warm-up for the day. Since shared reading is a group-type choral reading, the four second-language learners can successfully participate. After the shared reading, the class divides into four small groups to discuss the book.

9:00 Daily Independent Reading

Activities

• Conferences with Jeff, Leisa, Elaina, and Martha

Comments

During this time, students are practicing reading. Conferences help Mr. Russo check for decoding and other skill applications to self-selected books. Elaina, one of the second-language learners, is reading a Spanish book. Mr. Russo discusses the book with her in Spanish.

9:10 READING: Learning to Read Words

Activities

• Teach digraphs *sh, ch, th*
• Practice and apply digraphs
• Read *Charlie's Shoes*

Routines

• Explicit phonics/structural elements routine (Instructional Strategy 3)
• Decodable words routine (Instructional Strategy 5)

- Observational guided reading routine (see Instructional Strategy 7: Modes of Reading)
- Phonetically unpredictable words routine (Instructional Strategy 6)

Comments

Mr. Russo is continuing to teach the decoding skills students need. Meeting with three small groups, he uses the phonetically unpredictable words routine as well as three other routines. While he meets with one group, the other children go to an assigned learning center. Because the four second-language learners are not yet ready for this skill, they go to one of the learning centers that has a taped story; they follow along in a picture book while listening to the story and then respond to it with a short writing (in English or in their first language) or with labeled pictures.

10:10 Daily Independent Writing

Activity

- Children add to their journals.

Comments

Mr. Russo moves from child to child to check how each is spelling using the letter-sound associations taught so far this year. He also notes how their overall writing is developing. He encourages the second-language learners to draw and write in both Spanish and English. The inclusion students also participate in this activity.

10:20 WRITING: Learning to Write

Activities

- Writing a group story
- Spelling words with *sh, ch, th*: *chair, show, think, much, shop*

Routine

- Shared writing routine (Instructional Strategy 10: Modes of Writing)

Comments

Mr. Russo is connecting the explicit phonics instruction with spelling. The children help him write a group story. He works the spelling words into the story. The second-language learners have a list of five other words that they have identified with Mr. Russo from their English Language Development class that they will use for spelling.

10:40 Morning Break

10:55 READING: Learning to Read Words

Activities

- Practice spelling words with digraphs *sh, ch, th*

- Add spelling words to word wall
- Review words on word wall

Routines

- Making words (a routine in which students build words using letter cards; see Cooper [2000])
- Word wall

Comments

Mr. Russo returns to this block to provide more individual and small-group practice and connections for students. All students participate in these activities.

11:15 WRITING: Developmentally Appropriate Writing

Activities

- Children write own stories
- Use of words from word wall is encouraged

Comments

This is a follow-up to the teacher modeling through shared writing done earlier in the day. Mr. Russo moves from student to student to provide coaching. He is looking for application of skills previously taught and evidence of students' writing progress.

11:30 READING: Developing Language and Comprehension

Activities

- Read aloud *The 500 Hats of Bartholomew Cubbins* (Seuss, 1938) to teach students about identifying important information using a story map
- Partner practice reading (each pair of students selects any book already read)

Routines

- Read-aloud (Instructional Strategy 7: Modes of Reading)
- Cooperative reading (Instructional Strategy 7: Modes of Reading)

Comments

Mr. Russo is teaching listening comprehension in preparation for teaching reading comprehension.

   Children select any books they have read today or on another day. They read with a partner. Mr. Russo moves from pair to pair to note fluency and application of skills.

11:50 Closing the Literacy Block

Activities

- Discuss what was learned today. Make a list on the board.

Comments

Mr. Russo concludes his literacy schedule for the day by having children talk about what they have learned. For example, children might say, "I learned a new word" or "I learned to read better." This helps to keep children focused and helps them see the value of their day.

12:00 End of Literacy Block/Lunch/Recess

A Discussion of Mr. Russo's Literacy Block Plan

Now that you have a picture of how Mr. Russo's day works, let's look at how instruction for children at the Beginning Reading and Writing stage differs from instruction for children at the earlier stages. We can do this by looking at each time block during the day.

8:45: Reading: Developing Language and Comprehension. Mr. Russo uses shared reading as might be done with children at an earlier stage. Children at the Beginning Reading and Writing stage, however, are likely to join in the reading sooner than children at an earlier stage might.

Although his class has children at several different stages, Mr. Russo can use shared reading in the same book to support all the children, including the second-language learners. He uses different questions and prompts and calls different students' attention to different skills or elements of the text.

9:00: Daily Independent Reading. Children at the Beginning Reading and Writing stage will begin to read increasingly difficult texts. However, some children at this stage like reading simpler texts until they feel more secure in reading.

9:10: Reading: Learning to Read Words. The instruction being provided in digraphs was selected on the basis of students' strengths and needs. This is a review for some children and a skill need for others. While Mr. Russo teaches one group, children who have other needs work at learning centers on tasks more appropriate for them. The second-language learners work at a learning center using some oral language tapes.

10:10: Daily Independent Writing. Children at the Beginning Reading and Writing stage are writing more than in earlier stages. Even though the class includes children at various stages, Mr. Russo can meet the needs of all the children by working with individuals as they write their own pieces.

10:20: Writing: Learning to Write. During this time, Mr. Russo models writing. He connects phonics, spelling, and writing by using shared writing. He is combining what children have been taught about phonics and showing them how to write using what they have learned.

10:40: Morning break. This is basically a restroom and stretch break.

10:55: Reading: Learning to Read Words. Since his class contains a range of stages, Mr. Russo provides more time for practice for those who have just received instruction in the skill of digraphs. This gives him time to work with other students with different needs.

11:15: Writing: Developmentally Appropriate Writing. The children at the Beginning Reading and Writing stage are ready to write their own stories based in part on the modeling Mr. Russo did earlier during shared writing. This time block gives him time to work with the children who are ready to write full stories as well as with those who need more teacher modeling.

11:50: Closing the literacy block. Mr. Russo and the children discuss what they have done for the day and what individuals think they have learned.

After Reading Mr. Russo's Plan

Answer the following questions and discuss with a peer:

1. How did Mr. Russo work all parts of his balanced program into the schedule?
2. Where did you see instances in which Mr. Russo was meeting the needs of a range of stages and students' abilities?
3. Where did you see indications that Mr. Russo was making use of the concept of ongoing assessment?
4. What questions do you have at this point?

Summary

At the Beginning Reading and Writing stage, students take on more and more of the characteristics of readers and writers. There are many different procedures for assessing the benchmarks for this stage, most of which are informal, carried out as a part of assessment-based literacy instruction.

Students at this stage expand their use of standard English and grow in their facility to use language. They continue to show pleasure in knowing more words and in word play.

In reading, students acquire additional word recognition skills and strategies. At the same time, they learn to construct meaning more readily by using key strategies such as predicting, identifying important information, self-questioning, monitoring, summarizing, and evaluating. They also begin to use and explore many research tools and skills.

Students at the Beginning Reading and Writing stage exhibit a variety of general writing behaviors, showing increased interest and enjoyment of writing, reading others' writing, and writing on their own using a variety of formats for a variety of purposes.

Benchmarks at this stage are usually achieved by most students in first or second grade. Within any classroom, there will be students at various stages of literacy development. Some of these will be second-language learners, and others may be students who have a variety of disabilities. Instruction in the classroom for all students should be adjusted to their needs, interests, and attention spans.

For students at this stage, the Balanced Beginning Literacy Program described in Chapter 4 is still appropriate, and all the instructional strategies detailed in that chapter come into play through a mixture of whole-class, small-group, and individual activities. To organize and manage your classroom, you will need to develop class guidelines, appoint monitors, identify independent activities, role-play working in groups, and evaluate your routines with your students. Effective use of learning centers also becomes particularly important at this stage. In Mr.

Russo's classroom, you saw an example of how a teacher pulls all these elements together to provide a balanced literacy block for a diverse group of students.

FOR ADDITIONAL READING

Bear, D. R., Invernizzi, M., Templeton, S., & Johnston, F. (2000). *Words their way* (2nd ed.). Columbus, OH: Merrill.

Calkins, L. M. (1994). *The art of teaching writing* (rev. ed.). Portsmouth, NH: Heinemann.

Cooper, J. D. (2000). *Literacy: Helping children construct meaning* (4th ed.). Boston: Houghton Mifflin. See especially Chapters 4, 7, and 8.

Cunningham, P. M. (1995). *Phonics they use* (2nd ed.). New York: HarperCollins.

Freeman, D. E., & Freeman, Y. S. (1994). *Between worlds: Access to second language acquisition.* Portsmouth, NH: Heinemann.

Freeman, Y. S., & Freeman, D. E. (1997). *Teaching reading and writing in Spanish in the bilingual classroom.* Portsmouth, NH: Heinemann.

Gibbons, P. E. (1993). *Learning to learn in a second language.* Portsmouth, NH: Heinemann.

Graves, D. H. (1983). *Writing: Teachers and children at work.* Exeter, NH: Heinemann Educational Books.

Trachtenburg, P. (1990). Using children's literature to enhance phonics instruction. *The Reading Teacher, 43,* 648—654.

FOR EXPLORATION: ELECTRONIC RESOURCES

Activities for Teaching Reading.
http://toread.com/activities.html   Specific guidelines for a number of useful reading instruction activities.

Activities for Teaching Writing.
http://www.sil.org/lingualinks/library/literacy/fre371/vao852/fre218/krz315/index.htm   Guidelines for using dialogue journals, guided writing, and other activities for writing instruction.

Center for the Improvement of Early Reading Achievement.
http://www.ciera.org/ciera/   Sponsored by the Center for the Improvement of Early Reading Achievement (CIERA), this site includes information on early literacy acquisition and effective strategies for teaching reading, as well as links to CIERA publications.

Read to Succeed: How Schools Can Help Every Child Become a Reader.
http://www.ed.gov/pubs/startearly/ch_3.html   This chapter from the U.S. Department of Education's publication *Start Early, Finish Strong: How to Help Every Child Become a Reader* discusses the components of effective literacy instruction, the role of teacher preparation, the importance of the school community, and a variety of other topics.

Teaching Word-Identification Skills and Strategies: A Balanced Approach.
http://www.eduplace.com/rdg/res/teach/   A comprehensive discussion by John J. Pikulski of a balanced approach to instruction for beginning readers.

CLASSROOM APPLICATIONS

1. Using one of the group checklists provided in this chapter as a guide, observe a first- or second-grade classroom alone or with a peer for a full language arts block. Make notes about children's behaviors in relation to the benchmarks for the Beginning Reading and Writing stage. What are you able to tell about the children in terms of their stage of development?

2. Observe a first- or second-grade classroom during the language arts block over several days. Using the guidelines discussed in this chapter for the Balanced Beginning Literacy Program, make notes about what you see. How are second-language learners accommodated? What provisions are made for students with disabilities? Does the classroom indeed have a balanced literacy program? What are the strengths in this classroom? What areas need to be improved?

3. Using the guidelines for developing and using learning centers presented in this chapter, create a learning center for a strategy, skill, or specific area of oral language, reading, or writing. Try it out in a first- or second-grade classroom. Evaluate its effectiveness.

4. Meet with a first- or second-grade teacher to discuss his or her management procedures and routines. How do the ideas compare to what we presented in this chapter? Meet with a peer to discuss your findings.

The Almost Fluent Reading and Writing Stage

FOCUS **As you read the Eyewitness section, ask yourself the following questions:**

1. In terms of their literacy behaviors, how do Mrs. Barnes's students compare with the children you have seen in the Eyewitness classrooms visited in Chapters 5, 6, and 7?

2. What evidence do you see that Mrs. Barnes is using on-going assessment to decide where her students are in their literacy development and what they need next?

Eyewitness   *Mrs. Barnes, a fourth-grade teacher at Center Elementary School, has invited us to visit her classroom today. She has twenty-seven students, thirteen boys and fourteen girls. One boy is Vietnamese and three girls are Puerto Rican. All of the second-language learners have made the transition from their native language and now do all of their reading, as well as their work in other subjects, in English.*

One group of students at a round table is discussing a selection they just finished reading in their anthology. One boy is directing the discussion by referring to four ideas Mrs. Barnes has listed on the board. As students take turns adding to the discussion, they all write in their journals.

In another part of the room, Mrs. Barnes is teaching a group of students a lesson on summarizing. She is modeling how she would write a summary. As she writes, she shares with the students why she wrote what she did in her summary. Afterward, Mrs. Barnes and the students develop a chart of guidelines for a good summary. She directs students to return to their desks to write a summary of the article on turtles they have just read, using the guidelines from the chart to help them.

Mrs. Barnes now moves to her desk, where she makes notes on several students. Then she calls for another group to meet at the table. She tells the students they are going to work on ways to decode unfamiliar long words and infer the words' meanings from the text.

In terms of their reading and writing, were you able to see a difference between the students in Mrs. Barnes's room and those you met in earlier Eyewitness classrooms? In this class, notice that students were taking a leadership role in the discussion, even though they were focusing on points the teacher had listed on the board. Notice too the range of student needs: to one group Mrs. Barnes was teaching the strategy of summarizing, while with other students she continued to give some instruction in decoding.

All of the behaviors we observed in Mrs. Barnes's classroom are typical of students in the Almost Fluent Reading and Writing stage. Even though Mrs. Barnes has students who are at other stages of development, most of them are at this Almost Fluent stage.

BENCHMARKS for the Almost Fluent Reading and Writing Stage

Benchmarks for the Almost Fluent Reading and Writing stage are typical of children ages seven to nine, from the end of second grade through fourth or fifth grade. In these higher grades, we usually find an increasing range of stages of literacy development. Even at fourth grade, a teacher may have a student who is still at the Beginning Reading and Writing stage and one who can read adult material with understanding. The challenge becomes greater as the range increases. Read through the following benchmarks for the Almost Fluent Reading and Writing stage before proceeding with the remainder of this chapter.

Oral Language

BENCHMARK ➧ **The student exhibits continued growth in many behaviors from the Beginning Reading and Writing stage.**

BENCHMARK ➧ **The student's use of standard English continues to develop.**

✔ Is aware of own problem areas

✔ Accepts diverse usage or varieties of English from others without criticism

BENCHMARK ➧ **The student's facility with language is growing.**

✔ Uses new vocabulary

✔ Collaborates with classmates in speaking and listening situations

✔ Participates in discussion without adult supervision

✔ Can listen to and then question or respond to (use an idea expressed by) a speaker

✔ Speaks in front of a group using written notes but no script

BENCHMARK ➧ **The student continues to take pleasure in the use of language.**

✔ Appreciates symbolic language such as metaphor

✔ Enjoys listening to and telling riddles and jokes

✔ Begins to appreciate shades of meaning, connotation, precise word choice, and the evocative power of certain words

✔ Recognizes and begins to use persuasive techniques

Reading

BENCHMARK ➧ **The student exhibits continued growth in behaviors from the Beginning Reading and Writing stage.**

BENCHMARK ➧ **The student regularly uses all word recognition strategies.**

✔ Uses structure, phonics, and syntax (language structure) to determine word pronunciation

✔ Uses context

✔ Selects appropriate skills and strategies to sound out unknown words

✔ Reads orally with 90 percent accuracy in grade-level materials

✔ Self-corrects

✔ Takes risks

✔ Uses a dictionary both for pronunciation and for meaning

BENCHMARK ➤ **The student's ability to construct meaning is growing.**

✔ Enjoys listening to selections that may be beyond his or her reading ability

✔ Reads independently

✔ Enjoys reading a variety of genres

✔ Reads outside of school even without reward

✔ Prefers to read silently

✔ Continues to grow in the use of strategies for constructing meaning: predicting, identifying important information, self-questioning, monitoring, summarizing, and evaluating

BENCHMARK ➤ **The student reads for a variety of purposes.**

✔ Appreciates levels of meaning in stories

✔ Has a growing interest in authors, illustrators, and genres

✔ Is aware of own purpose(s) for reading

✔ Is beginning to understand text structure in expository text

✔ Uses a variety of print sources for information

✔ Is learning to synthesize information from more than one source

BENCHMARK ➤ **The student is learning research skills.**

✔ Uses card catalog or the computer equivalent

✔ Operates the computer

✔ Is learning to narrow search for both print and Internet sources

✔ Is learning to read graphic materials such as graphs, charts, tables, timelines, and maps

✔ Uses dictionary, thesaurus, encyclopedia, and other references, either in book form or on CD-ROM

Writing

BENCHMARK ➤ **The student exhibits continued growth in behaviors from the Beginning Reading and Writing stage.**

BENCHMARK ➤ **The student writes for a variety of purposes.**

✔ Is aware of the power of the written word

✔ Can identify a topic and theme and develop a paper to fit a given rubric

✔ Can plan and put together a report

✔ Writes stories with all the literary elements present

BENCHMARK ➡ **The student shows growth in the mechanics and conventions of writing.**

✔ Uses spelling patterns to attempt to spell words

✔ Uses increasingly conventional spelling, demonstrating increased visual memory and spelling sense

✔ Uses increasingly appropriate grammar and punctuation in writing

✔ Uses word processing tools to check spelling, to format, to revise, and to edit

BENCHMARK ➡ **The student shows pleasure in writing.**

✔ Sees self as a writer

✔ Offers constructive comments to peers about their writing

✔ Seeks suggestions for revision during peer and teacher conferences

✔ Chooses to write in free time and at home

✔ Enjoys sharing writing with peers either by reading aloud or by publishing in print

✔ Enjoys and supports the writing of classmates

BENCHMARK ➡ **The student connects reading and writing.**

✔ Uses elements of narrative writing, such as form, theme, literary techniques, style, idioms, and colorful language, in own writing

✔ Uses elements of text structure in expository writing and attempts to use a variety of structures in informational writing

✔ Appreciates poetry forms and attempts to write them

Connecting to Other Chapters

As you read about the Almost Fluent Reading and Writing stage, you may want to refer to other chapters for ideas about assessment and instruction to meet varying needs. The range of stages you will find in your classroom continues to increase as you progress through the grades. Many students will begin the school year functioning at the Beginning Reading and Writing stage and look more and more like fluent readers and writers at the end of the year. Therefore, it becomes increasingly important to know the assessment procedures and instructional strategies used at all the stages of development.

Using the Benchmarks to Assess the Student and Determine the Stage of Instruction

FOCUS **As you read about the Almost Fluent Reading and Writing stage, ask yourself the following questions:**

1. How does the Almost Fluent Reading and Writing stage differ from the previous stage?
2. What are some procedures for assessment of students at the Almost Fluent Reading and Writing stage?
3. What are some key procedures for organizing and managing a classroom with students at a range of stages?

Assessment of each benchmark for the Almost Fluent Reading and Writing stage can be done informally during instruction as well as through more structured informal procedures and some formal procedures. In this section, we discuss ways to assess each benchmark and provide some suggestions for instruction.

Figure 8.1 presents the major components of the benchmarks for the Almost Fluent Reading and Writing stage. As we discuss each area, we will show some of the behaviors associated with each benchmark.

Oral Language

Oral language becomes increasingly important as students progress through the Almost Fluent Reading and Writing stage. Students have many more opportunities, as well as a greater need, to listen critically and speak distinctly. The four main areas of oral language behaviors for the Almost Fluent Reading and Writing stage are: continued growth in Beginning Reading and Writing behaviors, use of standard English (Figure 8.2), growing facility with language (Figure 8.4), and pleasure in using language (Figure 8.6). A sample class checklist appears in Figure 8.7, and an individual checklist is in the Resource File at the end of the book.

BENCHMARK

The student exhibits continued growth in many behaviors from the Beginning Reading and Writing stage.

Children in the Almost Fluent Reading and Writing stage will continue to develop in the behaviors characteristic of the Beginning Reading and Writing stage, described in Chapter 7. For example, they will ask about the meanings of words

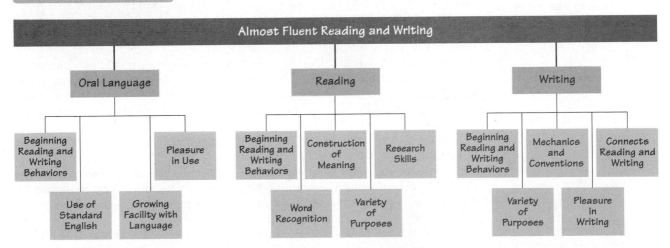

Figure 8.1
Menus for Assessing the Almost Fluent Reading and Writing Stage

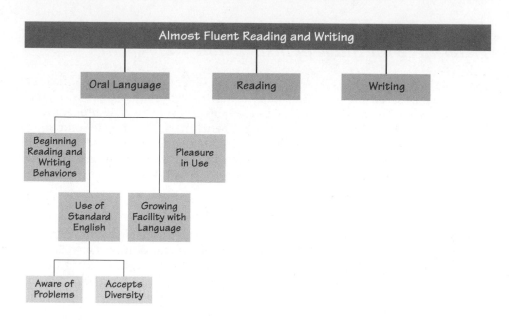

Figure 8.2
Oral Language: Use of
Standard English

they don't know, and they will show an increasing ability to paraphrase what others say.

Students must begin to assess their own speaking and listening abilities and become aware of any problem areas. This can be encouraged by providing students with a checklist for their own use of language, such as the one in Figure 8.3, that they can complete periodically. By comparing checklists completed by a student several times during the year, you can note changes in perceptions.

Instructional Strategies.   By talking about and modeling the process of self-evaluation in speaking and listening, you can help students develop this ability in themselves. You want them to see how important it is to be aware of one's own problem areas. A checklist like the one in Figure 8.3 offers a good basis for discussion with your students. Be sure they realize that most people have areas of language use that need improvement. For instance, we often speak one way in a more formal situation and another way in a less formal situation, and making the shift is not always easy.

When you are working with English-language learners (ELL students), keep in mind that they may have a more difficult time evaluating their use of English than native speakers do. For example, it takes a long time for ELL students to master the use of prepositions and noun-verb agreement. Therefore, a bit more teacher guidance may be required when asking ELL students to do self-evaluation.

You can observe whether students exhibit this behavior as you listen to and watch them interact with other students in the classroom. For example, when students are on the playground or in the lunchroom, listen to the language they use with peers. Do you hear students make fun of the way(s) someone speaks? Do you hear students correcting others in a demeaning manner?

BENCHMARK

The student's use of standard English continues to develop (Figure 8.2).

✔ Is aware of own problem areas

✔ Accepts diverse usage or varieties of English from others without criticism

ORAL LANGUAGE
SELF-EVALUATION

Name_____ Date _____

Think about your use of listening and speaking. Check the areas where you feel you have strength.

LISTENING

_____ I pay attention as others speak.

_____ I ask appropriate questions.

_____ I listen to responses to questions.

SPEAKING

_____ I speak clearly and distinctly.

_____ I use appropriate words.

_____ I choose language that fits the audience.

_____ My subjects and verbs agree when I speak.

_____ I use articles and prepositions appropriately.

Strengths	Areas Where I Need to Improve

(Use the back if needed)

**Figure 8.3
Student Self-evaluation
Checklist for Oral Language**

Instructional Strategies. The principal strategy here is to create an atmosphere in your classroom that promotes and accepts diversity. You do this mainly by example. You let your students see that you yourself are accepting of diversity in language.

In addition, during your language lessons, you can discuss how different people talk differently. Have students look for examples from television and other media of people talking with variations of the same language. Be sure everyone in the class realizes that although the second-language students are just learning English, they speak their native language very well. If problems arise among your

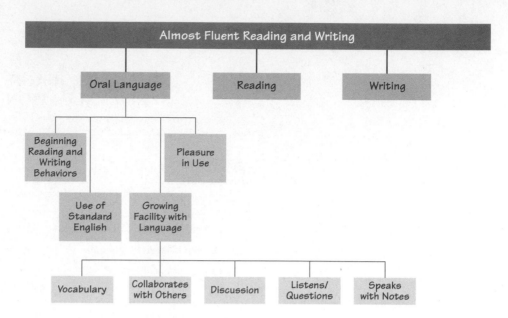

**Figure 8.4
Oral Language: Growing
Facility with Language**

students, have open and honest discussions about how people express themselves differently depending on their heritage. At the same time, all students should realize that there is a standard form of English that is considered most appropriate for school, and the goal for all is to use this form comfortably.

These five behaviors are best assessed by observing students in a variety of speaking and listening situations. As you observe, ask yourself the following questions and make notes about their behaviors:

1   Does the student use a variety of words in expressing himself or herself?

2   Does the student tend to use the same words over and over?

3   Does the student use new words orally that she or he encountered during reading?

4   Does the student pay attention when classmates are talking?

5   Does the student participate in discussions with other students in a polite and cooperative manner?

6   Does the student participate in discussions with other students in your absence?

7   While listening to classmates, does the student raise relevant questions?

8   Is the student able to give a talk in front of a group using just notes?

Figure 8.5 shows a form for recording your answers to these observational questions.

Instructional Strategies.   Many of the suggestions given in Chapter 7 for increasing facility with language (see pages 266–270) are also useful at this stage. Wide reading plays an increasingly important role in expanding students' oral

LANGUAGE FACILITY
RECORD SHEET

Name_____   Date_____

	Yes	No	Comments
1. Uses a variety of words.			
2. Uses same words over and over.			
3. Adds new words to usage.			
4. Pays attention while others talk.			
5. Participates in discussion politely and cooperatively.			
6. Participates in discussion without teacher present.			
7. Raises questions when listening to others.			
8. Gives talk in front of group using notes.			

**Figure 8.5
Form for Recording
Observations of a Student's
Facility in Use of Oral
Language**

language. Make sure you include the Daily Independent Reading block in your balanced literacy program.

Continue to make students aware of new words. For instance, have students listen for new words they hear others use, then post these words on a bulletin board and discuss them. Also, continue to teach lessons focusing on effective listening.

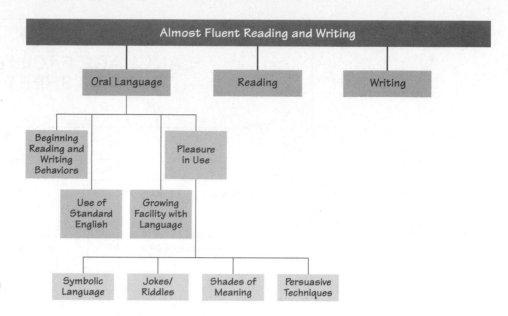

Figure 8.6
Oral Language: Pleasure in Use

To develop their ability to give a talk or report using notes alone, teach students how to create an outline and write key words on cards. Then provide many opportunities for them to practice giving talks.

Observation of students in a variety of listening and speaking situations is the best way to assess these behaviors. To see what persuasive techniques your students use, for example, note how they conduct themselves during discussions.

Instructional Strategies.   Students' pleasure in the use of language begins with the rich literature they are reading and listening to. From time to time, discuss the shades of meaning represented by certain words in a story or note a particular technique an author has used to sway the reader. Encourage students to use these elements in their own oral language. With the shared-writing method, you can also model the use of these elements in writing.

You may use the minilesson strategy to teach lessons on metaphor, similes, connotation, and various persuasive techniques. But, above all else, have fun with language yourself. Share jokes and riddles with your students, and encourage them to do the same with the class. Serve as a good language model by using and talking about exciting or interesting words and different ways to express oneself.

Figure 8.7 presents a class checklist for all the oral language benchmarks at the Almost Fluent Reading and Writing stage. A sample individual checklist appears in the Resource File.

BENCHMARK

The student continues to take pleasure in the use of language (Figure 8.6).

✔ Appreciates symbolic language such as metaphor

✔ Enjoys listening to and telling riddles and jokes

✔ Begins to appreciate shades of meaning, connotation, precise word choice, and the evocative power of certain words

✔ Recognizes and begins to use persuasive techniques

Reading

The five main areas of reading behaviors for the Almost Fluent Reading and Writing stage are continued growth in Beginning Reading and Writing behaviors,

Oral Language Checklist:
Almost Fluent Reading and Writing Stage

Teacher_____   Date_____   Grade_____

Student Names

+ = behavior present
- = behavior absent
✓ = somewhat present

Benchmark

Beginning Reading and Writing Behaviors

Use of Standard English
Is aware of own problems
Accepts diverse usage

Growing Facility with Language
Uses new vocabulary
Collaborates in speaking and listening
Participates in discussion without adult
Listens to and questions speakers
Speaks with notes

Pleasure in Use
Appreciates symbolic language
Listens to and tells jokes/riddles
Appreciates shades of meaning
Recognizes and uses persuasive techniques

Figure 8.7
Sample Class Checklist for Almost Fluent Reading and Writing Stage: Oral Language Benchmarks and Behaviors

word recognition (Figure 8.8), construction of meaning (Figure 8.10), variety of purposes (Figure 8.13), and research skills (Figure 8.15). A sample class checklist appears in Figure 8.17 and an individual checklist in the Resource File.

As with oral language, you should notice that your students at the Almost Fluent stage show continued development of various reading behaviors from the preceding stage: for instance, the ability to read and retell both familiar and unfamiliar texts, sense of self as a reader, and growth in the number of words recognized at sight.

BENCHMARK

The student exhibits continued growth in behaviors from the Beginning Reading and Writing stage.

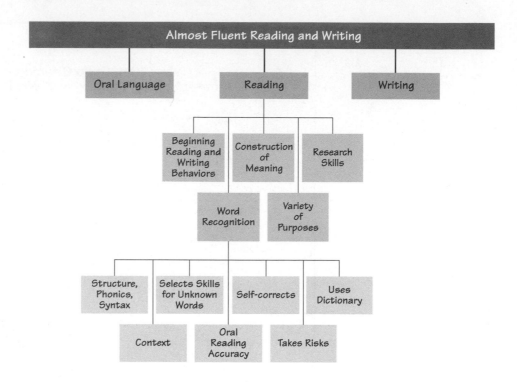

**Figure 8.8
Reading: Use of
Word/Recognition
Strategies**

The student regularly uses
all word recognition strategies (Figure 8.8).

✔ Uses structure, phonics,
  and syntax (language
  structure) to determine
  word pronunciation
✔ Uses context
✔ Selects appropriate
  skills and strategies to
  sound out unknown
  words
✔ Reads orally with 90
  percent accuracy in
  grade-level materials
✔ Self-corrects
✔ Takes risks

These behaviors are natural to assess together. Most students at this stage have a solid repertoire of skills and strategies for decoding.

Oral reading of connected text is the best way to assess these behaviors. You will be able to tell what skills students are using to pronounce words by studying their oral reading behaviors and analyzing their miscues. As we have noted before, you must look for a pattern of miscues (at least two or three examples) before you can draw conclusions about a student's reading. Table 8.1 presents examples of behaviors that would indicate a student has achieved the various benchmark components. All of these behaviors are observable during a student's oral reading.

When students get to the Almost Fluent Reading and Writing stage, they have many decoding skills. As beginning readers, they depended more heavily on let-ter-sound associations and sequential decoding. Now, as they become more flu-ent readers, they will use context to determine what type of word fits in a slot and then use structure and phonics to determine the actual pronunciation of un-known words.

Sometimes it is hard to pinpoint the exact problem students are having be-cause they are using so many different skills and strategies at once. If you en-counter this situation, you might check a student's decoding abilities by giving him or her a list of pseudo-words (made-up words) to read. For example, if you suspect a problem with vowel sounds, have students read aloud some pseudo-words containing common vowel patterns to see if they are pronouncing the words according to the generalizations they should be following:

Table 8.1
Oral Reading Behaviors Showing Benchmark Accomplishment for Word Recognition

Benchmark Behavior	Oral Reading Behaviors
Phonics and/or structural analysis	• Pronounces most words correctly • Miscues show student pronounces phonic/structural elements correctly; for example: ~~debate~~ *dehat* (knows beginning consonants or syllable *de*; does not know the v̄ce generalization; should self-correct) ~~unselfish~~ *unselish* (knows prefix *un* and suffix *ish*; does not focus on middles of words; should self-correct) • Slowly analyzes word in oral reading but blends together in reading: *pre-his-tor-ic;* finally says *prehistoric*
Syntax	*The snake moved across the grass in a sinewy, slithering motion.* (Can't pronounce *sinewy* but knows it must be a word that describes how the snake moves because of its position in the sentence)
Context	*The rhea displayed beautiful feathers.* (Is unable to pronounce *rhea,* but comments, "It's some kind of pretty bird")
Selects appropriate skills and strategies to sound out unknown word	• Breaks an unknown word into parts and finally blends it together in oral reading: Says: dĕv-ə-stāte Blends: *devastate* (Shows good use of chunking and application of vowel generalizations) • Skips an unknown word and reads to end of sentence to get a sense of the type of word that belongs in the slot. Then goes back and tries to analyze the word: *Larry and Ted were having a* <u>*heated*</u> *talk.* (Skipped *heated*; then sounded it out: hēat-əd — *heated.*)
Oral reading 90% accurate	• Reads orally 90% or more of the words correctly • Reads with fluency
Self-corrects	• Miscues in oral reading and then corrects: *galloping sc* The dinosaur was ~~gobbling~~ up everything in sight. This correction might result from re-examination of the letters, but more likely from meaning because *galloping* doesn't make sense
Takes risks	• Does not stop when oral reading and comes to an unknown word; tries to analyze the word even if not totally correct: for *lubricate,* says *lub rick at*

zeat (zēₐt)
rapple (răpp el)
lakint (lăk ĭnt or *lā kĭnt)*
darump (dar ŭmp or *dā rŭmp)*

There is disagreement among literacy specialists about using pseudo-words with students. We have found them useful in some situations. Be cautious about reading too much into the way students pronounce nonsense words because they may try to make them "real." Also, be aware that second-language learners are often confused by pseudo-words. However, this is one way to better pinpoint a student's specific decoding problems at the more advanced levels of reading.

Instructional Strategies.   If students are having problems with decoding at this stage, first try to identify their specific needs as suggested earlier. Then use the instructional strategies suggested in Chapter 4 to meet those needs.

Some students who are entering and moving through the Almost Fluent Reading and Writing stage know the various decoding elements but do not apply them when they encounter longer words. We suggest that you teach students the following steps to guide them as they attempt to decode a longer word:

- Look for chunks or parts of words you recognize. These chunks might include prefixes, suffixes, base words, or root words (*not* little words within big words). Try to orally say or silently think the word. Then use context to verify the word's meaning.

- If you are unable to recognize the word by using the chunks, look to the letter-sound associations. Again, say the word orally or silently in your head; then use context to check or verify meaning.

- If neither word chunks nor letter-sound associations lead to the pronunciation, ask someone or go to the dictionary.

Figure 7.10 (page 278) presented a poster to remind students about this decoding strategy. Its simple steps give the reader a system for thinking about an unknown word.

We strongly suggest that most decoding instruction for students who have reached the Almost Fluent stage be developed around this strategy. We recommend teaching and modeling it using longer, multisyllabic words, followed by many opportunities to practice and apply the strategy in reading experiences. Table 8.2 shows a sample lesson for teaching students to decode longer words. Use your ongoing assessment of students' reading to determine the amount of reteaching, practice, and application your students need.

Another approach to teaching students to decode longer words is the *Making Big Words* system developed by Cunningham and Hall (1994), listed in For Additional Reading at the conclusion of this chapter. This is an interactive system in which students manipulate chunks of words to build and decode longer words.

✔ Uses a dictionary both for pronunciation and for meaning.

This word recognition ability involves a variety of skills, including:

- Use of alphabetical order to the second and third letter
- Knowing the elements and symbols in a dictionary such as the entry word, the phonetic respelling of a word, the definition, the pronunciation guide, various symbols (n = noun, v = verb), and so forth

Table 8.2
Model for Lessons in Decoding Longer Words

Objective	Teach students a systematic strategy for decoding longer words and applying known phonics and structural elements.
Materials	• Transparency or poster showing the strategy (see Figure 7.10, page 278) • List of multisyllabic words in sentences
Procedures	
Teach	1. Tell students that the purpose of this lesson is to teach them how to approach a longer unknown word when they encounter it in reading.
	2. Display the poster. Ask students to read each step aloud. Discuss and explain the meaning of each step.
	3. Present a multisyllabic word underlined in the context of a sentence: The students in the science class were studying the <u>muscular</u> structure of the human body.
	4. Model how you would approach the word by saying: When I came to this word in my reading (point to *muscular*), I didn't know it. I started thinking about the steps of our strategy. I looked for chunks I knew. I knew *mus* (/mŭs/) and I knew *ar* (/ar/). I thought of three chunks: *mus•cul•ar*. I couldn't quite say the word. I looked at *cul* and thought about the letter-sound associations. I knew the /c/ and /l/ sounds. I also knew that the vowel in the middle of a chunk is usually short. I said /mŭs/•/cŭl/•/ăr/. I read the sentence aloud, and it didn't sound like any word I knew. Then I put the /l/ with the /ăr/. The vowel (*u*) at the end of a chunk is usually long. I said mŭs•cŭ•lar. I had heard *muscular*. I read the sentence and it made sense. I knew the students in this class were studying the muscles of the body.
	5. Repeat modeling with several examples as needed.
Practice	Provide students with several sentences containing multisyllabic words. Have pairs of students select any multisyllabic word and tell how they would use the strategy to approach the word.
Apply	Give students a piece of text (narrative or expository) you believe is *slightly* more difficult than their usual reading material. Direct them to read the text silently, looking for places where they could use the strategy for determining an unknown word. After reading, ask different students to name a word they have found and explain how they used the strategy.

DICTIONARY CHECKLIST

Name_____ Date_____

	Uses Appropriately	Needs Improvement	Comments
LOCATING WORDS			
Locates words by first, second, third, fourth letter			
Uses guide words			
Finds words whose exact spellings are unknown			
PRONUNCIATION (uses)			
Parts of dictionary entry			
Abbreviations in entry			
Pronunciation guide			
Phonetic respelling			
Diacritical marks			
Accent marks			
Alternate pronunciations			
WORD MEANING AND USAGE			
Understands abbreviations			
Recognizes different definitions given			
Selects appropriate definition			
Relates derived forms to base word			
Understands etymologies			

Figure 8.9
Checklist for Assessing Student's Use of the Dictionary

- Rapid location of entries
- Selecting the appropriate definition

There are two primary ways to assess students' ability to use the dictionary: (1) give specific tasks for students to do in relation to each skill mentioned above, and (2) observe their behaviors as they actually use the dictionary on their own during daily literacy activities or to complete tasks or answer questions that you give them. If you are using a published program for reading/language arts, use some of the suggestions given in the teacher's manual for this purpose. Also, see Pavlak (1985), listed in For Additional Reading, for further suggestions. The checklist presented in Figure 8.9 should help you keep track of students' progress in learning to use the dictionary.

Instructional Strategies. The dictionary can become a valuable tool in helping students pronounce unknown words and determine their meanings. Most students will come into this stage with some familiarity with the dictionary. As early as the Emergent Literacy or the Beginning Reading and Writing stage, students learn to use a picture dictionary or make their own simple dictionaries. By the Almost Fluent stage, students should receive more formal instruction in the use of the dictionary. They should be introduced to all elements of the dictionary and show increased use of the dictionary on their own.

Once students have been taught the basics of using the dictionary, the best way for them to master its use is through many authentic opportunities involving actual reading or writing. Avoid giving students long lists of words to look up; students usually write the first or shortest definition. They gain nothing from this kind of activity. Rather, encourage dictionary use for authentic reasons in reading or writing: looking up the meaning or pronunciation of an unknown word or verifying spelling.

Be cautious, however, about thoughtlessly telling students to use the dictionary to find the spelling of an unknown word. Unless they have some idea about how a word is spelled, the dictionary is of limited value for spelling. Therefore, you need to teach students to hypothesize probable spelling as a starting point.

Listening to stories and informational texts beyond their actual reading level continues to be a good way for students to expand their oral language and vocabulary, which in turn expand their foundation for constructing meaning. You assess this behavior through observation.

BENCHMARK

The student's ability to construct meaning is growing (Figure 8.10).

✔ Enjoys listening to selections that may be beyond his or her reading ability

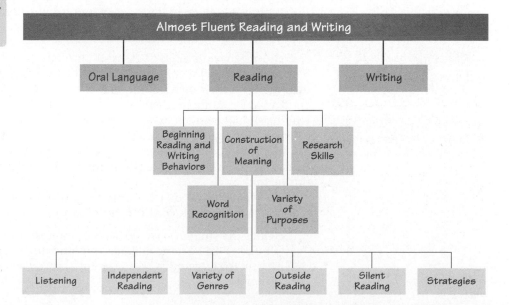

**Figure 8.10
Reading: Construction of Meaning**

Good contemporary literature captures a reader's interest.
© Elizabeth Crews

Instructional Strategies.   Continue to read aloud to students for enjoyment on a regular basis. Include a variety of types of texts in your reading, and provide opportunities for discussion and reaction to what you have read. Do not turn enjoyable listening experiences into tests or formal lessons by requiring students to write or do other activities following the listening experience.

Some students may find more pleasure in listening to tapes if they have a choice of what to listen to.

✔ Reads independently
✔ Enjoys reading a variety of genres
✔ Reads outside of school even without reward
✔ Prefers to read silently

These behaviors are best assessed through observation. By the time students reach the Almost Fluent Reading and Writing stage, they should be reading a great deal more on their own both in and out of school. The form in Figure 8.11 is a good way for students themselves to keep track of these behaviors. Students' reading should be silent except when they are reading aloud to share information, prove points, or entertain others.

Instructional Strategies.   These behaviors require no real instruction, but students must have ample opportunities to do independent, self-selected reading during the day.

Occasionally you may have students who don't seem to enjoy independent reading. In these cases, consider the following:

- Does the student have books that interest him or her? Independent reading can also be done in magazines and newspapers. You might need to use an interest inventory (see Chapter 2) to get a better picture of the student's interests.

Independent Reading Record

Name _____

		In-School		Out-of-School	
		Date	Minutes	Date	Minutes
Title _____					
Author _____					
Type of Book _____					
Started _____ Completed _____					
Comments: _____					
_____					
_____					
Title _____					
Author _____					
Type of Book _____					
Started _____ Completed _____					
Comments: _____					
_____					
_____					
Title _____					
Author _____					
Type of Book _____					
Started _____ Completed _____					
Comments: _____					
_____					
_____					

Figure 8.11
**Independent Reading Form
for Students to Use**

- Are the books the student is trying to read too difficult? You may need to talk with the student about selecting books that he or she can read. Show the whole class how to select a book by reading a page silently and looking for unknown words. If there are five or more unknown words on a page, the student may want to select a different book.
- Is the student interested only in one type of book or series of books? This is not really a problem; the important thing is that the student is reading.

However, you might want to make other books available on related topics. Also, be sure to introduce a variety of books when you read aloud to students.

If you have students at the Almost Fluent Reading and Writing stage who are still reading aloud to themselves, you should look at their overall reading behavior. Is there a problem with decoding or comprehension? Are the students having difficulty remembering what they read? If so, does the problem occur with all types of text or just with certain types? Are the texts too difficult? Examining all of these factors will help you determine ways to encourage students to read silently.

✔ Continues to grow in the use of strategies for constructing meaning: predicting, identifying important information, self-questioning, monitoring, summarizing, and evaluating

Assessing students' use of strategies for constructing meaning can take place in two ways: through an informal reading inventory (see Chapter 10) and through listening to daily text reading. In Chapter 7 (page 284), we discussed a variety of behaviors to look for as students read to note their use of strategies. Those same procedures should be used for students at this stage of development. You'll notice that students are becoming more sophisticated in their use of the strategies. For example, as students use the evaluation strategy, they will judge a greater range of things, such as an author's qualifications to write on the topic and how clearly ideas were presented and supported.

Instructional Strategies. Think back to Mrs. Barnes in our opening Eyewitness and how she modeled summarizing. This is the kind of procedure that should be used for students at this stage. The strategies remain the same as at earlier stages, but the materials the students read become more difficult. In addition, for students who have reached the Almost Fluent Reading and Writing stage, we suggest that you use the research-based strategy called *reciprocal teaching* (Palincsar & Brown, 1984, 1986; Rosenshine & Meister, 1994).

Reciprocal teaching is an interactive process; teacher and students take turns modeling four strategies after reading a meaningful chunk of text silently. The four strategies are *predict, question, clarify,* and *summarize.* This process was developed to help struggling readers in upper elementary and middle schools accelerate their reading growth and learn to construct meaning more effectively. It is one of the cornerstone strategies in the proven intervention program Project SUCCESS and its published program *Soar to Success* (Cooper, Boschken, McWilliams, & Pistochini, 1999). An additional benefit of reciprocal teaching is improved ability to decode words (Rosenshine & Meister, 1994). Reciprocal teaching is not difficult to use, but it does take practice on the part of both teacher and students. Table 8.3 presents the steps.

BENCHMARK

The student reads for a variety of purposes (Figure 8.13).

✔ Appreciates levels of meaning in stories
✔ Has a growing interest in authors, illustrators, and genres
✔ Is aware of own purpose(s) for reading

By the Almost Fluent Reading and Writing stage, students begin to realize that stories have multiple levels of meaning. For example, students should already know that any story has the basic elements of characters, setting, plots, and so forth. However, they also begin to know that stories have a theme, a lesson, or a moral. At the beginning of this stage, many students will recognize the basic elements but will need instructional support in becoming aware of additional levels of meaning. By observing students' responses as they write and talk about what they have read, you can easily tell whether they are able to get multiple levels of meaning from stories.

The best way to ascertain whether students are becoming aware of different authors, illustrators, and genres is to observe their independent, self-selected

Table 8.3
Model for Using Reciprocal Teaching

1. Make a poster for the four strategies like the one shown in Figure 8.12.

2. Introduce the four strategies to students using a *very easy, short* piece of text (not more than two pages). Present the poster and explain each strategy. Model one strategy at a time for students, having students model right after you model. Remember, your goal is just to introduce the strategies. After your introductory lesson (40–60 minutes total), use the process on a daily basis with students.

3. Select a narrative or expository text for your students to read.

4. Divide the text into meaningful sections or chunks. In the beginning, use fairly short sections or chunks (3–5 pages each).

5. Introduce the text by activating prior knowledge and building background.

6. Have students *predict* or pose *questions* for the first chunk of text.

7. Remind students to use the four strategies as they *silently* read the chunk of text.

8. After the silent reading, have students verify their predictions or answer the questions posed. As students answer, have them locate places in the text to support their answers and read them aloud.

9. Model a *summary* for the chunk of text read. Then call on different students to give a model. In the beginning, students' models will be very similar to yours.

10. Next, model either *clarify* or *question*. For example, to model use of the question strategy, you might say, "One question I had while reading this text was . . . " In the beginning stages of this process, model using a literal question. Over time, use inferential and critical questions. A student should then answer the question posed in your model. Always follow your models by having students themselves model.

11. Conclude the reading of the first chunk by having students talk about what they think they now know and *predict* what they think they will learn next or what will happen next.

12. Continue by reading the next chunk, or wait until the next day to read it. (If continued on a different day, spend some time reviewing the previous day's lesson.)

13. After students complete each day's reading, have them talk about the strategies they used and how the strategies helped them in their reading.

Points to Remember

- Continue to make your models more sophisticated over time.

- When students have difficulty with a strategy, provide another model and then have another student present a model.

- Gradually increase the difficulty of the books over time.

- Students should do more and more modeling as you withdraw support and become more of an observer and coach. Eventually, you provide modeling only when needed.

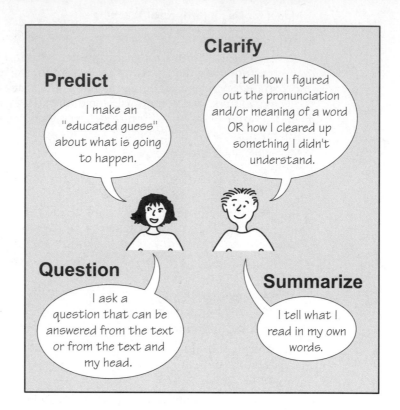

**Figure 8.12
Reciprocal Teaching
Strategy Poster**

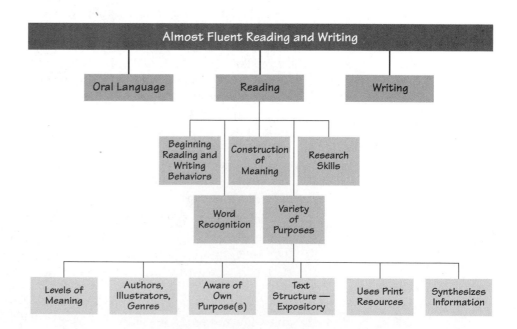

**Figure 8.13
Reading: Variety of
Purposes**

reading. The form presented earlier in this chapter (Figure 8.11) can be useful in making this assessment.

The third behavior in this group, awareness of one's purpose for reading, is important because knowing your purpose for reading influences the way you approach the reading task and the rate at which you read. The best way to assess this behavior is to ask students their purpose for reading. You might do this from time to time when students are reading for pleasure or reading science, social studies, and so forth. Note the differences in how they respond. You may find that sometimes even good readers are vague about their purpose for reading, but really do have one. For example, a student might say, "I thought this book about turtles had neat photographs, and I don't know much about turtles, so I decided to read it to find out more information."

Instructional Strategies. Strategies to help students develop these behaviors include the literacy lesson, response activities, and discussion circles or groups, all of which were described in Chapter 4.

When you read aloud to students, talk about different authors, illustrators, and genres. Share your favorites and talk about why you like them. Use classroom bulletin boards to promote various authors, illustrators, and genres.

When you read aloud to the class, talk about reading and listening for pleasure as opposed to other types of reading and listening that may require more care, such as listening to directions. Make the connection to reading. Before students begin reading, talk about their purpose. Help them formulate a purpose and write it down before they read. After reading, ask students to return to their purpose and evaluate whether it was accomplished. Help them to articulate how their reading varies according to their purpose; for example, when reading technical material such as a computer manual, one reads much more carefully.

> ✔ Is beginning to understand text structure in expository text
>
> ✔ Uses a variety of print sources for information
>
> ✔ Is learning to synthesize information from more than one source

Assessment of these behaviors takes place most often when students are working with expository texts in science, social studies, and other curricular areas. The following ideas should be helpful in your assessment:

- When students read a content text (science, health, and so forth), have them identify the main ideas and supporting details. This will let you know whether they understand text with expository structures.

- Assign a report on a topic related to a theme students are studying. Ask each student to create a bibliography, and note the sources they use. By this stage, students should be using a variety of sources such as books, magazines, newspaper articles, CD-ROMs, encyclopedias, and the Internet.

- As students write reports, note whether they can actually pull together ideas from various sources and synthesize those ideas. Do they create their own synthesis of the ideas they have encountered, or do they just copy from a particular book or present ideas from each source separately?

Instructional Strategies. You can use the following instructional strategies to develop students' understanding and use of expository text material:

- Use the reciprocal teaching strategy suggested earlier in this chapter. It will help students develop an understanding of expository text structures by focusing them on summarizing the main ideas and important details.

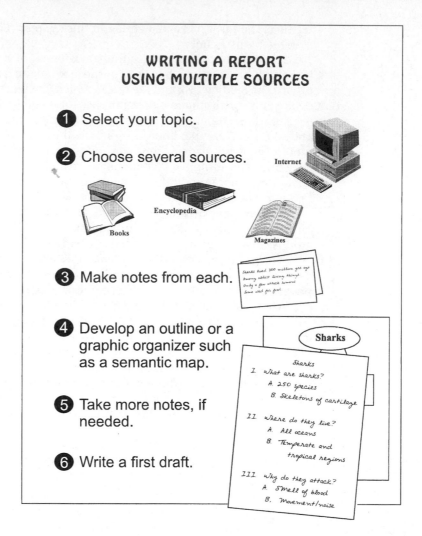

Figure 8.14
Poster Showing How to Write a Report Using Multiple Sources

- Combine the use of the minilesson and the explicit comprehension routine to teach students a lesson on main ideas and supporting details, showing how these are used in different types of texts such as science and social studies.

- Teach students to write a report using the shared-writing mode. As you work with them on a shared group report, use minilessons to teach students how to use encyclopedias, magazine articles, CD-ROM sources, and so forth. Make class posters recording the procedures and guidelines for using multiple sources and writing reports (see Figure 8.14 for an example of such a poster). This procedure will teach students to use multiple sources as well as synthesize information.

BENCHMARK
The student is learning research skills (Figure 8.15).

Students who have reached the Almost Fluent Reading and Writing stage are making a great deal of use of their ability to both read and write. Therefore, they become involved in projects and other types of activities that require them to do research.

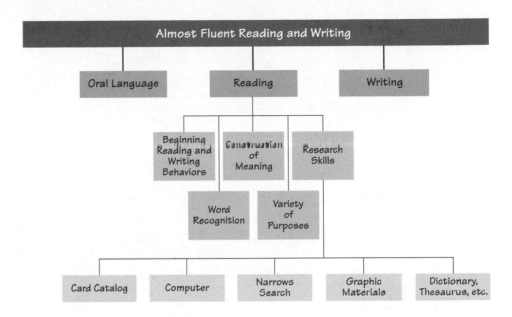

**Figure 8.15
Reading: Research Skills**

✔ Uses card catalog or the computer equivalent

The best way to assess students' acquisition of this behavior is through tasks requiring them to use the card catalog or its computerized equivalent. For example, give students a project related to an area of study such as developing a timeline about certain events in their state. This will require them to locate books, topics, and so forth in the catalog. Observe their behaviors as they perform this task.

Instructional Strategies. Use the minilesson strategy to teach students how to use the card catalog or whatever means your school uses for searching. Incorporate in your lessons the following topics:

- Cards (or entries) are arranged alphabetically by author, subject, or title
- All entries contain the same information
- How to read each type of entry
- How to narrow the subject
- How to evaluate whether a book is worth pursuing

As you teach the use of the catalog, provide many opportunities for students to use this skill in the library.

✔ Operates the computer

Actually having students use the computer is your best assessment of this behavior. Some of the skills you would look for include turning the computer on, accessing web sites, and using a CD-ROM to get information. For more information on assessment of this behavior and on related instruction, see Grabe and Grabe (1998), listed in For Additional Reading at the end of this chapter.

✔ Is learning to narrow search for both print and Internet sources

This behavior is related to a behavior we discussed earlier, using multiple sources. We suggest that you incorporate the assessment and instruction for this behavior in the process of teaching students to write a report. Narrowing the search on a topic means being able to come up with specific terms for a topic as opposed to more global ones. For example, a student writing a report on moun-

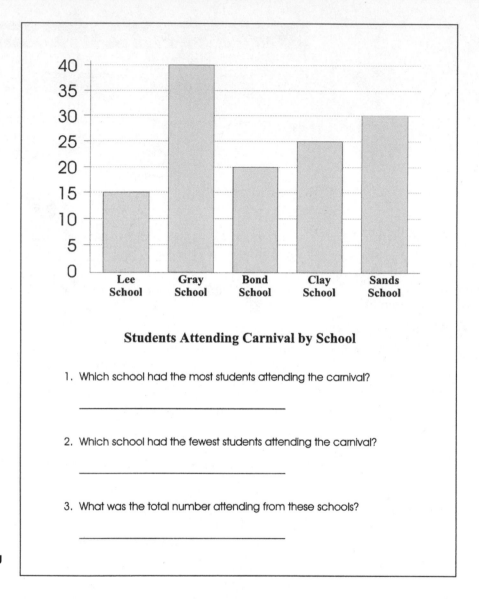

Students Attending Carnival by School

1. Which school had the most students attending the carnival?

   _____

2. Which school had the fewest students attending the carnival?

   _____

3. What was the total number attending from these schools?

   _____

**Figure 8.16
Sample Sheet for Assessing
Ability to Read a Graph**

tains and their influence on pioneers' travel might start with a search focusing on mountains and then narrow it to a specific area of the country.

✔ Is learning to read graphic materials such as graphs, charts, tables, timelines, and maps

Two processes are related to using graphic materials: reading them and making your own to depict information you want to share with others. These two processes should be taught together.

These behaviors are best assessed by giving students projects or activities that require them to use graphic materials. You can also give them samples of graphic material and ask questions that call for understanding of the material (see Figure 8.16 for a sample sheet that poses questions about a graph). Similarly, students can be given tasks to see if they can construct graphs.

Reading Checklist:
Almost Fluent Reading and Writing Stage

Teacher_____ **Date**_____ **Grade**_____

+ = consistently present
- = not present
✓ = somewhat present; recheck

Student Names

Benchmark

Beginning Reading and Writing Behaviors

Word Recognition Strategies
Uses structure
Uses phonics
Uses syntax
Uses context
Selects appropriate strategies
Reads orally at 90% accuracy
Self-corrects
Takes risks
Uses dictionary

Construction of Meaning
Enjoys listening
Reads independently
Enjoys reading a variety of genres
Reads outside of school
Reads silently
Continues to grow in use of:
  - predicting
  - identifying important information
  - self-questioning
  - monitoring
  - summarizing
  - evaluating

Variety of Purposes
Appreciates levels of meaning
Has growing interest in authors, illustrators, genres
Is aware of own purpose
Begins to understand expository text structure
Uses variety of sources
Synthesizes information

Research Skills
Uses card catalog/computer
Operates computer
Narrows search
Reads:
  - graphs
  - charts
  - tables
  - timelines
  - maps
Uses:
  - dictionary
  - thesaurus
  - encyclopedia
  - CD-ROMs
  - internet

Figure 8.17
Sample Class Checklist for Almost Fluent Reading and Writing: Reading Benchmarks and Behaviors

Instructional Strategies.   Use the minilesson strategy to teach students to read each type of graphic material. Connect this teaching to report writing, as discussed earlier. When you teach students to read graphic materials, also teach them to construct their own. Encourage students to use some of these graphics in their reports.

To assess these behaviors, provide an opportunity for students to use the actual materials and then note how they have done. See Pavlak (1985) and Miller (1995), listed in For Additional Reading, for many appropriate suggestions.

Instructional Strategies.   Use the minilesson strategy to teach lessons showing students how to use these resources. Again, remember to connect these lessons to your lessons on report writing.

Figure 8.17 presents a sample class checklist for all of the reading benchmarks at the Almost Fluent Reading and Writing stage. For an individual checklist, see the Resource File.

> ✔ Uses dictionary, the-saurus, encyclopedia, and other references, either in book form or on CD-ROM

Writing

The writing benchmarks for the Almost Fluent Reading and Writing stage are divided into five categories: continued growth in behaviors from the previous stage, variety of purposes (Figure 8.18), mechanics and conventions (Figure 8.21), pleasure in writing (Figure 8.24), and connection of reading and writing (Figure 8.25). A class checklist for the writing benchmarks for this stage is presented in Figure 8.26, and an individual checklist is in the Resource File.

> BENCHMARK
> The student exhibits continued growth in behaviors from the Beginning Reading and Writing stage.

Keep in mind that students just moving into the Almost Fluent Reading and Writing stage may still exhibit many behaviors from the previous stage. These behaviors should show continued improvement. Even if some students are having difficulty in one or two areas, it is not necessary to drop back totally to the earlier

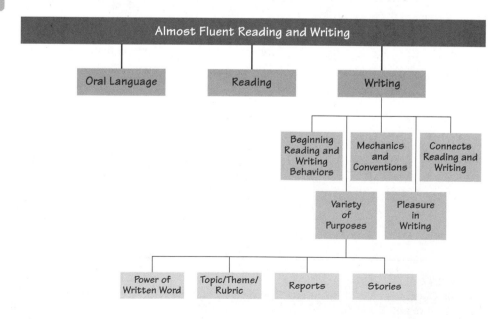

**Figure 8.18
Writing: Variety of Purposes**

**Figure 8.19
Criteria for Writing a
Personal Narrative and
Sample Scoring Rubric
(Houghton Mifflin
Company, *Invitations to
Literacy,* Grade 4, Theme 1.
Used by permission.)**

Criteria for Evaluating a Personal Narrative

- The story is about a personal experience and is told in the first person.
- The story has a beginning, a middle, and an end.
- The beginning gets the reader's attention.
- Details, including dialogue when appropriate, are used to help the story come to life.

Sample Scoring Rubric

1	2	3	4
The paper does not tell about a personal experience; or, if it does, there is no or little narrative structure.	The story is sketchy. There may be gaps in sequence that cause confusion. Details and dialogue are insufficient.	The story has a beginning, middle, and end. Details and dialogue are included but could be enhanced. Significant usage, mechanics, or spelling errors may keep the story from rating a 4.	The story has a strong narrative structure, including a good beginning, with realistic and well-distributed details and dialogue. It has a minimum of usage, mechanics, and spelling errors.

stage in your assessment or instruction. Rather, provide strong support for students' individual needs as they move toward fluency.

The first of these behaviors, awareness of the power of words, may be evident when you observe students using writing to move people to action or to change opinions. It is also evident as students share personal writing that affects classmates (or you) emotionally.

To assess the other three behaviors, have students write pieces and then evaluate them through the use of rubrics. Figures 8.19 and 8.20 present two appropriate rubrics, one for a personal narrative and the other for a research report.

BENCHMARK

The student writes for a variety of purposes (Figure 8.18).

✔ Is aware of the power of the written word

✔ Can identify a topic and theme and develop a paper to fit a given rubric

✔ Can plan and put together a report

✔ Writes stories with all the literary elements present

**Figure 8.20
Criteria for Writing a
Research Report and
Sample Scoring Rubric
(Houghton Mifflin
Company, *Invitations to
Literacy,* Grade 4, Theme 4.
Used by permission.)**

Criteria for Evaluating Research Reports

- The report presents factual information about a topic.
- The report includes topic sentences that present main ideas.
- Relevant details support the main ideas.
- An introduction presents the topic and leads into the report.
- A conclusion sums up and closes the report.

Sample Scoring Rubric

1	2	3	4
The paper is not a report, or it meets the criteria only minimally. The report lacks focus and structure.	The report topic is clear. The facts included support the topic, but they need to be better organized into paragraphs with clear topic sentences. The introduction and conclusion are missing or weak.	The report is focused and organized, with an introduction and a conclusion. Topic sentences are supported by relevant details. The report might rate a 4 except for significant usage, mechanics, or spelling errors.	The report meets all the criteria. It is well organized, well developed, and clear. The introduction and conclusion open and close the report appropriately. There are few errors.

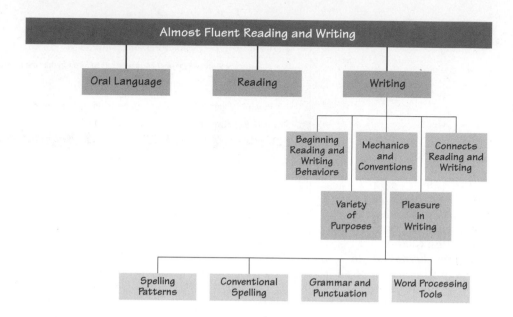

Figure 8.21
Writing: Mechanics and Conventions

Instructional Strategies.   Instruction provided for students at this stage of development should entail using all the modes of writing from write-aloud to independent writing. Using the modes of writing strategy, as outlined in Chapter 4, gives you the basic support you need to teach your students to become better writers. For other suggestions, see Cooper (2000), listed in For Additional Reading.

These behaviors are quite closely related, and you can best assess them through analysis of students' writing samples. In the last section, we suggested the use of rubrics to assess students' level of writing. Here we suggest you do a further analysis by looking at students' spelling patterns and use of grammar and punctuation.

For spelling analysis, you can make a list of student spelling errors from a piece of authentic writing. A form like the one shown in Figure 8.22 is helpful. List the correct spelling and then the student's spelling, and look for patterns of errors (three or more mistakes of the same type would constitute a pattern). You can cat-

Table 8.4
Categories for Analyzing Patterns of Spelling Errors

Beginnings	Middles	Ends
Consonants	Single vowels	Inflectional endings
Blends	Vowel patterns	
Digraphs	Double consonants	Plurals
Prefixes		Suffixes
Vowels	Digraphs	

SPELLING ANALYSIS GRID

Name _____ Grade _____ Date _____

Writing Sample _____

Correct Spellling	Student Spellling	Possible Problem

Patterns of Errors:

Figure 8.22
Spelling Analysis Grid

egorize the patterns of errors using the simple system presented in Table 8.4. The patterns will help you determine each student's instructional needs. For a more detailed discussion of spelling analysis, see Bear, Invernizzi, Templeton, and Johnston (2000), listed in For Additional Reading.

For grammar and punctuation, we suggest you use a checklist for each student similar to the one in Figure 8.23. From this analysis, you can determine where students need more instruction.

GRAMMAR, PUNCTUATION, AND USAGE ANALYSIS

Name_____ Grade_____ Date _____

	Uses Appropriately	Needs Instruction	Comments
CAPITALIZATION Beginning of sentence			
Proper nouns			
Titles of books, magazines, etc.			
PUNCTUATION End punctuation (period, question mark, exclamation point)			
Quotation marks			
Commas			
GRAMMAR/USAGE Run-on sentences			
Sentence fragments			
Noun/verb agreement			
Paragraphing			

Figure 8.23
Grammar and Punctuation
Analysis Checklist

Assessment of each student's use of word processing will depend on available technology.

Instructional Strategies.   Instructional strategies helpful at this stage include the modes of writing strategy and minilessons. You can use these to provide instruction that targets each particular need you have discovered.

BENCHMARK

The student shows pleasure in writing (Figure 8.24). Sees self as a writer

✔ Offers constructive comments to peers about their writing

✔ Seeks suggestions for revision during peer and teacher conferences

✔ Chooses to write in free time and at home

✔ Enjoys sharing writing with peers either by reading aloud or by publishing in print

✔ Enjoys and supports the writing of classmates

BENCHMARK

The student connects reading and writing (Figure 8.25).

✔ Uses elements of narrative writing, such as form, theme, literary techniques, style, idioms, and colorful language, in own writing

✔ Uses what is learned about text structure in expository writing and attempts to use a variety of structures in informational writing

Assessment of these behaviors takes place through observation. As students participate in various writing experiences and lessons, observe whether these behaviors are apparent. For example, do students talk with peers about their writing, and give and seek suggestions? Do students write during free time? Do they show that they are interested in writing and enjoy hearing and reading what others have written?

Instructional Strategies. The primary way to ensure that students achieve this benchmark is to provide a classroom atmosphere that promotes and supports writing. This includes having a balanced literacy program that provides time for daily independent writing, teacher-modeled writing, and developmentally appropriate writing. Share some of your own writing from time to time, and encourage students to do the same. Ask students for suggestions about ways you could improve your writing.

Daily independent writing is one of the most effective ways to promote students' pleasure in writing. Take some part of this time each day to have students share their writing with the class or with a partner. You can use the Author's Chair for this purpose.

Provide many suggestions for students to use in sharing and publishing their writing. These can include reading aloud, posting on a bulletin board, or producing a book.

Observation and analysis of students' writing is the best way to determine whether students are making a connection between their reading and writing. For example, do students use in their own writing structures used in materials they have read? Do they use language from authors they have read, thus making their own writing more colorful and exciting?

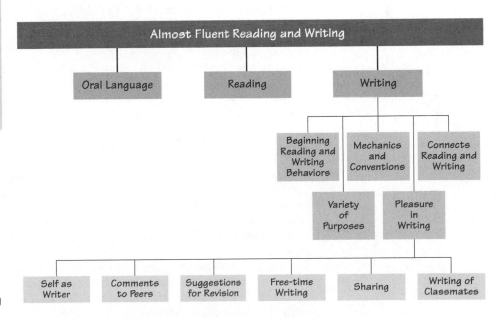

**Figure 8.24
Writing: Pleasure in Writing**

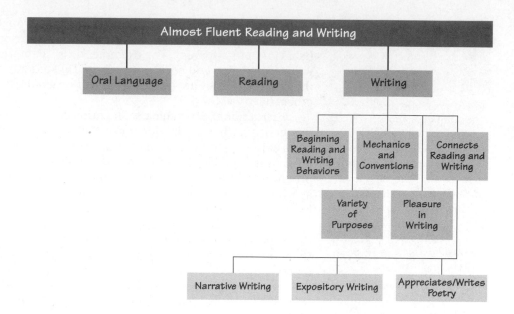

**Figure 8.25
Writing: Connection of
Reading and Writing**

Instructional Strategies.   One of the most effective ways to help students make connections between reading and writing is to directly connect them in your teaching. This means that instead of teaching reading and writing as separate subjects, you teach integrated language arts, systematically blending reading, writing, spelling, and grammar.

When students are reading a persuasive piece, for example, you teach them how to write using persuasion. You help students note the features in the piece that make it persuasive, and then you use the write-aloud and shared-writing modes to model how to write persuasively, drawing parallels from the reading. Finally, you move to developmentally appropriate writing in which students write persuasive pieces on topics of their own choice. For more discussion of teaching writing, see Cooper (2000), listed in For Additional Reading.

✔ Appreciates poetry forms and attempts to write them

Observation of students' daily independent writing is a good way to assess this behavior. Do students write poetry? Do they enjoy listening to poetry?

Instructional Strategies.   The first step in getting students to appreciate and enjoy poetry is to read it aloud to them on a regular basis. Begin with poetry that is fun and has lots of rhyme and rhythm. Read such authors as Shel Silverstein and Jack Prelutsky. Follow poetry read-alouds by writing poetry together as a group. Students should then be encouraged to write their own poetry and share it in many ways, such as read-aloud, booklets, and bulletin boards. In our classrooms, we always kept a class anthology of poetry to which students added from time to time. For a detailed discussion of teaching poetry, see Heard (1989), listed in For Additional Reading.

Figure 8.26 presents a sample class checklist for the writing benchmarks of the Almost Fluent Reading and Writing stage. An individual checklist appears in the Resource File. Now let's look at how we use all of the benchmarks presented in this chapter to plan instruction.

**Writing Checklist:
Almost Fluent Reading and Writing Stage**

Teacher_____   Date_____   Grade_____

Student Names

\+ = consistently present
\- = not present
✓ = sometimes present/needs instruction

Benchmark

**Beginning Reading and Writing
Behaviors**

Variety of Purposes for Writing
Is aware of power of writing
Writes paper to topic/theme/rubric
Writes reports
Writes stories

**Mechanics and Conventions
of Writing**
Uses spelling patterns
Uses increasingly conventional spelling
Uses increasingly appropriate grammar
Uses increasingly appropriate punctuation
Uses word processing tools

Pleasure in Writing
Sees self as writer
Offers constructive comments to peers
Seeks suggestions for revision
Writes in free time
Enjoys sharing
Supports classmates

Connects Reading and Writing
Uses/learning about narrative writing
Uses/learning about expository writing
Appreciates and writes poetry

**Figure 8.26
Sample Class Checklist for
Almost Fluent Reading and
Writing Stage: Writing
Benchmarks and Behaviors**

Planning Instruction Based on Assessed Stage of Development

Recall that in Chapter 7 we posed three questions you should consider in planning instruction based on each student's assessed stage of development. Those same questions should guide your decision making for students at the Almost Fluent Reading and Writing stage:

What do I teach or emphasize for students?

How do I teach what needs to be taught?

How do I organize and manage my class when I have a range of stages and needs?

In this section, we look at some possible answers to these questions in relation to the Almost Fluent Reading and Writing stage.

What Do I Teach?

By using some of the assessment techniques we have suggested, you can determine each student's strengths and needs and pinpoint what you need to teach. Even more than at younger ages, however, you will find that your students represent an increasing range of literacy stages. For that reason, it becomes especially important to use ongoing assessment based on the benchmarks from several stages. Beyond your initial assessment at the beginning of the school year, you must continuously assess students' growth by using some of the suggestions given in the benchmark discussions in this chapter as well as in Chapters 5, 6, and 7.

For most students, the Almost Fluent Reading and Writing stage occurs somewhere between third and fifth grade. For some, it may start as early as the end of second grade (or even earlier for a very few). Thus, in grades three through five, the majority of your students will be at the Almost Fluent Reading and Writing stage. Typically, though, students will range from the Beginning Reading and Writing stage through the Fluent Reading and Writing stage. Few students in these grades are still at the Early Emergent or Emergent Literacy stage, and those who are must be given very specialized attention in your classroom, supported by a learning specialist in your school.

Meeting the needs of this range of stages requires consistent use of flexible grouping along with many instructional activities that allow students at different stages to participate successfully. You will find many uses for the multi-leveled types of activities described in Chapters 6 and 7.

How Do I Teach What Needs to Be Taught?

In deciding how to teach what needs to be taught, you need to consider the same three basic areas discussed in Chapter 7: selecting materials for instruction appropriate for each student, maintaining a balanced literacy program, and choosing instructional strategies appropriate for each student. Let's look at how these these areas apply to the Almost Fluent Reading and Writing stage.

Selecting Materials for Instruction

Since your school is likely to be using a published reading—language arts series, much of your instructional material will come from this resource. The anthologies provide core trade book literature, and your series will probably include a range of paperback books as well. The materials in your reading—language arts series will already be organized by level of difficulty. However, in some cases, you may find you do not agree with the publisher's leveling. In such a case, use the criteria for leveling we discussed in Chapter 4 to guide your decisions about text difficulty (see Table 4.10, page 141; also see Chapter 10 for a discussion of readability formulas).

In addition to the published series, you will need sets of trade books. Because of the range of stages you will probably have in your classroom, your instructional materials should include a wide spectrum of trade books, organized by level of difficulty. Each set should consist of five to nine copies of each title. The most efficient and useful way to organize these trade books is for all the teachers in the upper grades to work together to establish a central materials resource center where the books are stored for easy access. Many schools have a reading specialist who works out of this center and helps teachers select materials and determine appropriate instructional strategies. In schools that do not have such a center, the upper-grade teachers work together to organize and manage one.

We cannot stress enough the importance of every school having some way to provide a range of trade book literature for teachers to use for instruction. Without this resource, the teacher's hands are virtually tied in trying to meet the reading and writing needs of students functioning at a range of stages.

To meet the needs of second-language learners and to expose native speakers to other languages, some books in other languages are needed. By this stage, second-language learners who have been in school several years have made or are making the transition to English. However, you may get older students from other countries who do not speak English and have not been in school until now. Books in their native language are critical. Where available, books on tape in English and in other languages are also helpful.

In addition to sets of trade book literature, you will need the resources of a library (either a school library or a nearby public library) to support independent reading and to help you find books for reading aloud to students. Finally, you will need some decodable texts for students functioning at earlier stages who are still developing independence in decoding. Usually these texts are needed for at least some students in grade three and perhaps beyond.

The Balanced Literacy Program

Up to this stage, we have focused primarily on the Balanced Beginning Literacy Program. By the time students reach the Almost Fluent Reading and Writing stage, however, this program will give way seamlessly to the Balanced Literacy Program 3–8. This means, as you will remember from Chapter 4, that some of the blocks become slightly different in focus. For a full discussion of the two programs, review Chapter 4 and see Cooper (2000), listed in For Additional Reading.

The Balanced Literacy Program 3–8 contains six blocks for all students: Daily Independent Reading, Daily Independent Writing, Reading: Core Books, Reading: Developmentally Appropriate Books, Writing: Teacher-Modeled Writing, and Writing: Developmentally Appropriate Writing. For those students needing additional support, there is a block of Intervention as well. Let's examine each of these blocks in relation to the Almost Fluent Reading and Writing stage.

Daily Independent Reading. Daily Independent Reading continues to be an important block in the balanced literacy program for students at the Almost

Fluent Reading and Writing stage. Research strongly supports the importance of this block as a part of a student's continued literacy growth (Snow, Burns, & Griffin, 1998). You should allow 15 to 20 minutes per day for this block.

Students at this stage should be doing much more independent reading in school as well as at home. Yet the following problems may arise even at this stage:

1 *Selecting books that are too difficult.* Some students always want to read books that are beyond their abilities. Usually this is brought on by peer pressure and the student's belief that it will please you, the teacher. One of the best ways to handle this situation is to share books you are reading. Select a book that would appear to be too easy for you. Talk about how you really enjoyed the book even though you thought it was too easy. Also, discuss with students how to select books. Focus on making an initial selection based on interests. Then show students how to test a book by reading the first paragraph or two to determine whether it will be hard to read. Model this process as often as needed to help students select their materials for independent reading more effectively.

2 *Changing books frequently during independent reading.* Teachers frequently ask us, "How do you deal with a student who wants to change books every two or three minutes?" Students should select their reading material (books, newspapers, magazines, and so forth) prior to the independent reading time. Encourage students to stick to what they have selected. However, if a student has selected a book or other material that is too hard or that he or she does not like, alternate choices should be at hand. You yourself don't continue books that you can't read or don't like.

3 *Not wanting to stop reading.* What a great problem to face! However, some students really do want only to read and don't want to stop when the time is up. Provide some extra time during the day for independent reading for these students, and be sure they are free to check books out to take home to read.

4 *Not wanting to read.* Some students at the Almost Fluent Reading and Writing stage may have a negative attitude about reading. They *can* read, but they don't *want* to. This is a tough situation to deal with, and there are no simple answers. One way to approach this problem is to be supportive and to talk about times when you yourself may not have liked to read. Reading aloud to students is another good way to motivate them to read. Try to capitalize on the students' interests. Provide books on tape. Encourage them to read comics, magazines, pages on the Internet, books on CD-ROM, and other types of materials. Provide some special materials for each such student. Try to find out why a particular student doesn't like to read. However, you must keep in mind that not everyone is an avid reader.

Daily Independent Writing.   Allow at least fifteen to twenty minutes per day for this block. It should involve whatever kind of writing students select; *it is not assigned writing.* The purpose of this block is to help students build power in writing and to practice their writing. During some of this time, you should write to serve as a model. However, you should devote much of your time to conferencing with students and monitoring what they are doing. Even though the writing students do during this time will not be evaluated, this is a good time for you to note how students are writing and applying the various techniques and skills you have been developing through instruction.

Problems and issues similar to those we described for Daily Independent Reading are also likely to occur during Daily Independent Writing. Some of these may include a student's not knowing what to write about, not wanting to write, and not wanting to stop writing. You can approach these issues in a manner similar to the ways we suggested for reading. Many of the suggestions for independent writing given in Chapter 7 can also be used with students at the Almost Fluent Reading and Writing stage.

Reading: Core Books.   During this block, all students work with the same text. This text may be a selection from the anthology of your published reading—language arts series, or it may be a trade book that you want everyone to experience.

Even though everyone works with the same book, not everyone does the same things with it. You use small groups to provide different types of instruction and activities designed to meet the assessed needs of individual students.

Reading: Developmentally Appropriate Books.   In this block, all students read books that are appropriate to their reading level and receive needed instruction with these books. This block provides an opportunity for students to apply strategies and skills taught in the Core Books block.

By the time students reach the Almost Fluent Reading and Writing stage, their books are too long to read in one day. Therefore, the Core Books block and the Developmentally Appropriate Books block do not take place on the same day. Most teachers spend two or three days with the Core Books block and the remaining days of the week with the Developmentally Appropriate Books block. Some teachers alternate, having one block each week.

Writing: Teacher-Modeled Writing.   Showing students how to write continues to be important at this stage. During the Teacher-Modeled Writing block, you model various types of writing for students, focusing more on voice and style than you would at earlier stages. Also, teach students the elements of spelling and grammar needed to help them continue to grow into more effective writers.

By this stage, students will be able to understand various types or domains of writing. The **domains of writing** are usually described as sensory/descriptive, imaginative/narrative, practical/informative, and analytical/expository. Select the domain to be modeled for the class on the basis of students' assessed needs.

Writing: Developmentally Appropriate Writing.   In this block, all students write, focusing on the domain of writing you have modeled. The topic of the writing is the student's choice. During this block, students apply what they have learned about the particular domain of writing and the strategies and skills of grammar and spelling. The writing done during this block can be evaluated (as opposed to the writing done in the Daily Independent Writing block).

These six blocks comprise the balanced literacy program for all students in grades three to eight. For students experiencing difficulty in learning to read, an

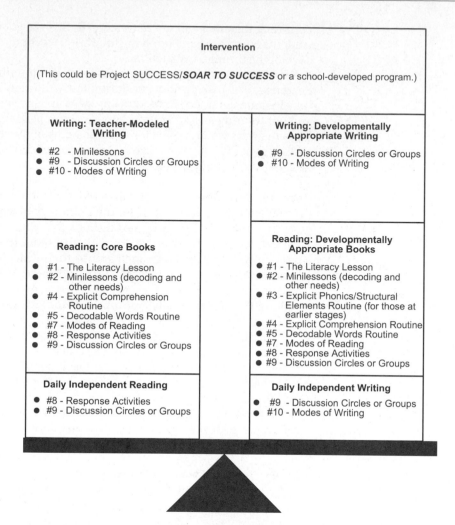

Figure 8.27
Use of Basic Instructional Strategies in the Balanced Literacy Program 3–8

additional block of Intervention is provided. See Chapter 4 for a detailed discussion of intervention methods.

Choosing Instructional Strategies

The basic instructional strategies presented in Chapter 4 continue to be used with students at this stage, with adjustments for the types of materials being used and the sophistication of the strategies and skills being taught. Figure 8.27 shows where these strategies are typically used in the Balanced Literacy Program 3–8. By comparing this figure to Figure 7.22 (page 296), you can see the subtle but significant changes that occur as the students reach a more advanced stage in their literacy development. Of course, your ongoing assessment will play a key role in helping you determine which strategies to use and how to use them.

We have addressed two of the important instructional questions, "What do I teach?" and "How do I teach what needs to be taught?" Now let's turn our attention to the final question.

How Do I Organize and Manage a Classroom with a Range of Stages?

Knowing how to organize and manage your classroom in grades three to five becomes increasingly important because you have students functioning at so many stages. In Chapter 7, we discussed the answer to this question in detail in relation to the Balanced Beginning Literacy Program. The same principles apply for organizing and managing your classroom when most students are at the Almost Fluent Reading and Writing stage. The following discussion builds on what we said in Chapter 7.

Know Your Students

Throughout this text, we have discussed the importance of getting to know your students and using ongoing assessment to keep track of where they are in developing their literacy skills. You must, however, go further than this: you need to determine which students have good independent work habits and which need continuous guidance and support. Use the first few days of school to note how students work. Make a list of the names of students who can work well independently and those who cannot. This information will help you manage your class more effectively.

Use Flexible Groups and Activities

There is no effective way to teach a class of twenty to thirty students in grades three, four, or five without using flexible groups and individual activities. Flexible groups usually range from five to nine students who are grouped together or who choose to work together for a particular need or task. They remain together until the need is met or the task is completed, and then the grouping is dropped.

There are many reasons to form flexible groups in grades three, four, and five, including the following:

- To teach a lesson to students who are at a stage of development different from most others in the class
- To discuss a core book or selection
- To teach a strategy or skill minilesson
- To have small groups reading the same developmentally appropriate book
- To conduct group conferences
- To allow several students to discuss the same type of book

At times, each student will be doing a different activity. The trick to successful classroom organization and management is to use the appropriate balance of small, flexible groups and individual activities to meet the range of needs in your class. Many teachers in grades three to five mistakenly try to teach everything to the whole class as one large group. Even when the entire class reads the same book, small groups are necessary to meet individual needs.

Develop Routines

In order for you to work with small, flexible groups and with individuals, your students need to know the classroom routines and follow them. In the upper grades, students work more independently. However, we have found that it is still important to take time at the beginning of the school year to develop the routines you want students to follow in your classroom.

In Chapter 7, we discussed five steps for developing routines. These same steps can also be applied in grades three, four, and five: (1) develop class guidelines, (2) appoint monitors, (3) identify independent activities, (4) role-play working in groups, and (5) evaluate with students. Developing a system of routines is critical to organizing and managing your classroom.

Meeting the Needs of Second-Language Learners

Classrooms throughout the United States represent a cross-section of our society. They include children who represent many cultures and many countries of origin. Some of these students come to school speaking English; others do not. Some start school at age five or six; others don't come to this country until they are much older, still speaking their native language. Although most students in grades three, four, and five are at the Almost Fluent Reading and Writing stage, some may be unable to speak English proficiently.

If your ELL students started school in kindergarten, they probably have made the transition to English by now or are very close. For students still acquiring English, the following procedures may help ease their acquisition of the language:

- *Buddies.* Provide a "learning buddy" for each ELL student to serve as a model in the use of English. If a buddy is bilingual, he or she can also provide short previews before reading in the ELL student's native language or in English. Even for ELL students who have made the transition to English, a learning buddy is a good way to expand their English.

- *Tapes, software, CD-ROMs, and videos.* These materials also provide good models of English and can help students expand their vocabularies. Most published reading—language arts series provide tapes of anthology selections as well as software technology that can support ELL students in improving their use of English.

- *Volunteers.* Invite volunteers from the cultures of the ELL students to bring both the language and the culture into the classroom. These types of experiences are excellent for helping to make your classroom truly multicultural as well as multilingual.

- *Minilessons.* Conduct minilessons as needed on figures of speech and phrases in English that have a meaning other than the literal one. This is very helpful to ELL students and any others who need support in improving their English. Teaching students the meanings of such idioms as "big as an ox," "turned green with envy," and "grew as big as a house" helps them develop a more authentic understanding of the English language. These lessons should be taught not in isolation but in relation to texts students are reading.

For other suggestions for teaching ELL students, see Freeman and Freeman (1994, 1998), listed in For Additional Reading.

A Fourth-Grade Classroom at Work

Now let's see how an upper elementary class, in which most students are at the Almost Fluent Reading and Writing stage, functions. We will focus on Ms. Boyd's fourth-grade class. Table 8.5 lists her full-day schedule. Notice that her literacy block is shorter than the one for the second-grade classroom you saw in Chapter 7. Ms. Boyd has two hours per day for literacy instruction, including time for independent reading and writing.

Ms. Boyd has twenty-four students, thirteen girls and eleven boys. Two students are functioning at the end of the Beginning Reading and Writing stage, nineteen at the Almost Fluent Reading and Writing stage, and three at the Fluent Reading and Writing stage. One student at the Beginning Reading and Writing stage is an English-language learner from Puerto Rico who is making the transition to English. Four other students at the Almost Fluent Reading and Writing stage are also from Puerto Rico but have made a complete transition to English.

In the following section, we present a detailed look at Ms. Boyd's literacy block. Study the plan carefully, read the discussion, and complete the questions at the end.

Table 8.5
Daily Schedule for Ms. Boyd's Fourth Grade

8:15	Arrival
8:25	Daily news
8:40	Literacy block
	• Reading
	• Writing (including spelling and grammar)
	• Daily Independent Reading
	• Daily Independent Writing
10:40	Morning break
10:50	Math
11:45	Lunch and recess
12:20	Science/health (alternating units; students who need intervention go at this time; second-language learners go to English Language Development)
1:00	Special classes (art, music, PE, computers) for four days each week; the fifth day is used as an activity period in the room.
1:45	Afternoon break
1:55	Social studies
2:50	Prepare to dismiss
3:00	Dismiss

FOCUS   As you read Ms.
Boyd's plan:
1. Notice how Ms. Boyd fits in all the blocks of a balanced literacy program.
2. Note how she uses flexible groups to meet individual needs.
3. Identify the instructional routines used.
4. Look for places where you think Ms. Boyd is conducting ongoing assessment.

Ms. Boyd's Literacy Block Schedule (24 fourth graders)

Time:

8:40—10:40 daily

Arrangements for independent work:

Four learning centers: two for comprehension, one for writing, one for decoding longer words

8:40 Daily Independent Reading

Activities

- Independent reading
- Small group (eight students, lesson on decoding longer words)

Routine

- Minilesson (Instructional Strategy 2)

Comments

While some students read independently, Ms. Boyd pulls out a small group who need instruction in decoding longer words. Students in this group will read independently at another time.

9:00 READING: Core Books/Developmentally Appropriate Books

Activities

- Introduce *Koya Delaney and the Good Girl Blues* (Greenfield, 1992).
- Read first chapter in *Koya Delaney* (twelve students read independently; six students read cooperatively; six students read with teacher).

Routines

- Literacy lesson (Instructional Strategy 1)
- Modes of reading (Instructional Strategy 7)
- Learning centers for those who finish early

Comments

- Everyone is introduced to the same book.
- Using different modes of reading helps to meet individual needs.

9:30 Activity

- Discussion of *Koya Delaney*

Routine

- Discussion circles or groups (Instructional Strategy 9)

Comments

The discussions focus on the portion of the book that has just been read.

9:40 WRITING: Teacher-Modeled Writing/Developmentally Appropriate Writing

Activities

- Students write story of own choosing.
- Teacher-student conferences are held during writing

Routine

- Modes of writing (Instructional Strategy 10)

Comments

- Students practice writing own story.
- Ms. Boyd assesses students' writing for strengths and needs.

10:10 Activity

- Spelling lesson (words with suffixes *-ness* and *-tion*)

Routine

- Minilesson (Instructional Strategy 2)

Comments

Ms. Boyd does direct teaching of spelling elements.

10:25 Daily Independent Writing

Activities

- Independent writing
- Grammar lesson (run-on sentences) for ten students

Routine

- Minilesson (Instructional Strategy 2)

Comments

Grammar is taught as an outgrowth of assessed writing needs and Ms. Boyd's knowledge of new skills that have not yet been taught.

10:40 Morning Break

A Discussion of Ms. Boyd's Literacy Block Plan

You now have a sense of Ms. Boyd's literacy block schedule. You probably have many questions as to why she did what she did. We will try to anticipate your questions by discussing each block.

8:40: Daily Independent Reading. Ms. Boyd starts off her literacy block with independent reading. This choice provides her with a management tool: she can pull out a small, flexible group to teach the skill of decoding longer words. The students who receive this instruction were identified over the past several days.

She varies the type of strategy or skill taught according to the students' needs. Ms. Boyd is very careful not to pull out the same students two days in a row.

Students who miss the scheduled independent reading get a chance to do it at other times during the day. No one is ever denied independent reading. This pattern of instruction allows Ms. Boyd to meet a wide range of needs and stages in her classroom. Remember too that this block makes it possible for *all* students to read developmentally appropriate books every day.

9:00: Reading: Core Books/Developmentally Appropriate Books.   Each day Ms. Boyd does one or the other of these two blocks. (Note: In the lower grades, especially kindergarten and grade 1, both of these blocks are usually done on the same day.) Typically Ms. Boyd works three to five days on a core book, depending on its length. First, she introduces the book and uses small groups to meet students' individual needs by having the first chapter read in different ways by different groups. This is what we see her doing with the book *Koya Delaney and the Good Girl Blues*. The following discussion allows all students to discuss and share this common book.

9:40: Writing: Teacher-Modeled Writing/Developmentally Appropriate Writing. Today Ms. Boyd is doing developmentally appropriate writing because for the past two days she has been doing teacher-modeled writing, using shared and guided writing of a story. Now students are writing their own story on a topic of their choice. She usually does not try to do both types of writing on the same day.

This block also provides time to directly teach spelling. On some days, Ms. Boyd teaches a grammar lesson if most students need it.

10:25: Daily Independent Writing.   During this block, Ms. Boyd may pull out a small group for a short period of time, as she does today in teaching a grammar lesson to a group of ten students. On many days, she does not teach a grammar lesson but uses the time to conference with individuals or small groups.

After Reading Ms. Boyd's Plan

Answer the following questions and discuss with a peer:

1 How did Ms. Boyd work in all the parts of her balanced literacy program?

2 How and when did Ms. Boyd use small, flexible groups?

3 Which instructional routines were used, and why were they chosen?

4 What ongoing assessment opportunities did you see?

5 How did Ms. Boyd's schedule compare to those of other classes you have seen in person or in this text?

Summary

Students at the Almost Fluent Reading and Writing stage continue to exhibit growth in literacy development. Their oral language becomes increasingly important as they expand their use of standard English and become more aware of their own areas of need. They note and accept diversity in the use of language in themselves and in others. They use more vocabulary and participate in discussions, responding with questions or comments as they listen to others. At this stage, students are developing a deeper appreciation for an ability to use all aspects of language.

In reading, students at this stage are using all the word/recognition strategies and selecting the ones appropriate for sounding out an unknown word. Their use of the dictionary for both pronunciation and meaning is growing. Students' ability to construct meaning is also improving. They read independently from a variety of genres, both in and out of school. Throughout this stage, they grow in their ability to use strategies such as predicting, identifying important information, self questioning, monitoring, summarizing, and evaluating. In addition, students are learning to understand different text structures and learning to conduct research using a variety of sources. This requires them to synthesize and organize information in many ways.

In their writing, students at this stage continue to develop their ability to write for a variety of purposes. They make connections between reading and writing, seeing how their own writing can incorporate techniques learned from what they have read. Their use of the mechanics and conventions of writing also continues to grow.

Assessment of students' individual behaviors continues to be primarily informal. The increasing range of stages within a classroom makes it even more important for teachers to plan an assessment-based, balanced literacy program, using small groups and multi-leveled activities to address the needs of all students.

Second-language learners who have reached this stage have generally made or are in the process of making the transition to English. However, there may be some ELL students who are new to this country and are performing at a much earlier stage of development. For these students, learning buddies, volunteers, mini-lessons, and a variety of tapes and other resources can help ease the transition.

Ms. Boyd's classroom showed how a fourth-grade teacher working predominantly with students at the Almost Fluent Reading and Writing stage can pull all of these ideas together to meet the needs of a range of stages within the classroom. Using flexible, small groups is a key ingredient.

FOR ADDITIONAL READING

Bear, D. R., Invernizzi, M., Templeton, S., & Johnston, F. (2000). *Words their way* (2nd ed.). Columbus, OH: Merrill.

Cooper, J. D. (2000). *Literacy: Helping children construct meaning* (4th ed.). Boston: Houghton Mifflin. (See Chapter 7 on writing and Chapter 10 on organization and management.)

Cunningham, P., & Hall, D. M. (1994). *Making big words.* Parsipanny, NJ: Good Apple.

Freeman, D. E., & Freeman, Y. S. (1994). *Between worlds: Access to second language acquisition.* Portsmouth, NH: Heinemann.

———— (1998). *ESL/EFL teaching: Principles for success.* Portsmouth, NH: Heinemann.

Grabe, M., & Grabe, C. (1998). *Integrating technology for meaningful learning* (2nd ed.). Boston: Houghton Mifflin.

Heard, G. (1989). *For the good of the earth and sun: Teaching poetry.* Portsmouth, NH: Heinemann Educational Books, Inc.

Miller, W. H. (1995). *Alternative assessment techniques for reading and writing.* West Nyack, NY: The Center for Applied Research in Education.

Pavlak, S. A. (1985). *Informal tests for diagnosing specific reading problems.* West Nyack, NY: Parker Publishing Company.

FOR EXPLORATION: ELECTRONIC RESOURCES

General-Purpose Learning Strategies: Reading Comprehension.
http://muskingum.edu/~cal/database/reading.html   From the Center for Advancement of Learning at Muskingum College, this site is a valuable resource for teachers interested in reading comprehension. It contains both general information and descriptions of many specific strategies for classroom use.

Issues in Literacy Development.
http://www.eduplace.com/rdg/res/literacy/   An extensive discussion of literacy development research and instructional practices, written by John J. Pikulski and J. David Cooper.

Reciprocal Teaching.
http://www.ncrel.org/sdrs/areas/issues/students/atrisk/at6lk38.htm
Maintained by the North Central Regional Educational Laboratory (NCREL), this site describes reciprocal teaching and outlines the common strategies used.

CLASSROOM APPLICATIONS

1. Using one of the group checklists provided in this chapter as a guide, observe a third-, fourth-, or fifth-grade classroom alone or with a peer for a full language arts block. Make notes about children's behaviors in relation to the benchmarks for the Almost Fluent Reading and Writing stage. Note the English-language learners who are present and what they are doing in this class. What can you tell about the various children in terms of their stage of development?

2. Observe a third-, fourth-, or fifth-grade classroom during the language arts block over a period of several days. Using the guidelines discussed in this chapter regarding a balanced literacy program, make notes about what you see. Does the classroom in fact have a balanced literacy program? What are the strengths in this classroom? What changes would you suggest, and why?

3. Locate a small group of students in a third-, fourth-, or fifth-grade classroom. Select two or three of the assessment procedures suggested for the Almost Fluent Reading and Writing stage. Use the procedures with the group, and write a summary of the students' strengths and needs.

4. Interview a third-, fourth-, or fifth-grade teacher about how he or she carries out ongoing assessment. Summarize your findings and discuss them with peers.

The Fluent Reading and Writing Stage

FOCUS

As you read the Eyewitness section, ask yourself the following questions:

1. What assessment opportunities do you notice in each classroom?

2. How might assessment in a departmentalized fifth grade differ from that in a self-contained classroom?

Eyewitness   *We will look in on Mrs. Collins's fifth-grade language arts class in just a moment. But first, a word about how this fifth grade is organized. At this school, the fifth grade is departmentalized to help students make the transition into middle school next year. The fifth-grade teachers work as a team of three. Students have a homeroom teacher with whom they do routine activities. The homeroom groups are heterogeneous: that is, each group has students at more than one literacy stage, as well as students representing several first languages and various exceptionalities.*

The homeroom groups rotate among the three teachers for major curriculum areas. Mr. Herbert teaches the social studies and science units. Ms. Street teaches the math units. Mrs. Collins teaches the language arts classes.

The three-teacher team plans units carefully for the entire year so as to integrate learning whenever possible. (Often the physical education, music, and art teachers also integrate their activities with the curriculum.) Each teacher is aware of what is occurring in the other classes and helps students make connections. For example, when students are preparing a final project for a science unit, Mrs. Collins collaborates with Mr. Herbert to plan lessons focused on research and report writing.

Today we begin by visiting Mrs. Collins during her morning literature block. She is reading aloud from The Lion, the Witch, and the Wardrobe *by C. S. Lewis (1950/1994). Most of her students could certainly read this independently (and, in fact, many already have), but it is a book rich with potential for discussion, so she plans to read a chapter a day and then have students discuss whatever they have found interesting—words, plot development, author's craft, character traits. Mrs. Collins has already shared some information about C. S. Lewis's life. Today, after the first chapter, Mrs. Collins asks the students to discuss the pictures they have made in their minds about the house, the attic, and the faun. Then they spend some time talking about why an author might choose to tell a story that was pure fantasy. Mrs. Collins seems to be leading the class to the notion of the theme of the novel. The students share other fantasy and science-fiction stories they have read and enjoyed.*

Students then take out their writing folders and begin to work independently on reports for science class. They are choosing topics to research further and write about. Some may use computer programs to create multimedia presentations. Some may choose expository writing. Some may choose design/art/graphic presentations with supporting text. Some may make oral presentations. Mrs. Collins moves among the students, helping each think through what to report on and possible ways to approach the task. The students will do the actual research for the report while they are with Mr. Herbert in science class.

Next, Mrs. Collins has the students examine a piece of writing displayed on a transparency. It is part of one student's science report from a prior year, and the name has been obliterated. The class reads the piece, and a general discus-

sion follows about how it might be revised to make a stronger statement and make the ideas clearer to the reader. Then pairs of students work on actually revising the piece. Following this, the students work on revising their own writing; then each person shares with his or her partner, who offers feedback. The students are clearly comfortable giving and accepting comments about revision.

Finally, the class breaks into literature discussion groups. Each group has been reading a different genre. One group has read biographies. Another has read poetry. Another has read novels by Katherine Paterson. Another has read nonfiction about the Titanic. *Each group functions well, sharing ideas, clearly following the posted guidelines for that group. Mrs. Collins sits in on two groups for a short while. She is not the leader of either group; rather, she is a participant. Her comments do, however, spur more divergent and deeper thinking than might have occurred without her.*

Next, we follow the students to Mr. Herbert's science class, where he will supervise their research for their reports. Each student has brought the science writing folder from Mrs. Collins's room. Mr. Herbert explains various methods of research available: Internet, encyclopedias in the classroom, other references in the classroom, the school library, and so forth. Then each student is asked to choose one of these sources to pursue first. Mr. Herbert lets students work in pairs so they can help each other.

After school, we sit in as the three fifth-grade teachers have a grade-level meeting. Mr. Herbert is generally pleased with the students' ability to choose a narrow enough topic to research and report on. He asks Mrs. Collins to work with him to develop some minilessons focused on evaluating the validity of sources, especially on the Internet. For the next few days, Mrs. Collins and Mr. Herbert will work together to develop lessons on planning a research report format, outlining, notetaking, attributing sources, rough drafts, revision, editing, and final product.

Ms. Street, who teaches mathematics, is beginning a unit on ratio, and she asks that both Mrs. Collins and Mr. Herbert stay alert to examples of ratio in literature and science. They agree that both the music and art teachers will be able to contribute many examples of the importance and role of ratio in those fields.

The fifth-grade students in the Eyewitness are mostly at the **Fluent Reading and Writing** stage. They are able to do many things independently, but they still need strong teaching and guidance to help them develop critical thinking skills and apply such thinking to various curriculum areas.

Attaining this stage does not mean students have finished growing in literacy. On the contrary, they are at a perfect age to grow in leaps and bounds with good teaching. They are capable decoders; they understand how fiction and nonfiction are organized; they understand the writing process and the many purposes for writing. They are reading wonderful literature independently. They are ready to examine authors' craft, read critically, weigh opinions, recognize persuasion, and write purposefully as well as for personal pleasure.

This chapter examines the benchmarks and behaviors of the Fluent Reading and Writing stage, as well as instructional strategies you can use to keep students progressing in their literacy development.

BENCHMARKS ➤ for the Fluent Reading and Writing Stage

The benchmarks for the Fluent Reading and Writing stage are typical of students in grades four or five and up, ages nine or ten and above. Yet even those who are not yet fluent at grade 5 may function fairly well in other academic areas and understand the concepts of various content areas.

Before reading the rest of the chapter, read the following benchmarks carefully. These are some of the indicators children will exhibit when they are at the Fluent Reading and Writing stage.

Oral Language

BENCHMARK ➤ **The student exhibits continued growth in behaviors from previous stages.**

BENCHMARK ➤ **The student's facility with language is growing.**

- ✔ Oral language reflects increasing vocabulary
- ✔ Shifts from formal to informal usage to suit occasion
- ✔ Listens to oral presentations with understanding

BENCHMARK ➤ **The student uses oral language for a variety of purposes.**

- ✔ Discusses literature with pleasure and understanding
- ✔ Enjoys role-playing and Readers Theater
- ✔ May enjoy debate or speech competition

BENCHMARK ➤ **The student continues to enjoy language.**

- ✔ Is sensitive to body language and tone of others and self
- ✔ Appreciates the importance of speech in interpreting the written word, for example, news reporters, actors, comedians

Reading

BENCHMARK ➤ **The student continues to display many of the behaviors from the Almost Fluent Reading and Writing stage.**

BENCHMARK ➤ **The student seldom seeks or needs assistance with word recognition.**

BENCHMARK ➤ **The student uses a wide variety of strategies to construct meaning.**

- ✔ Grasps differences among genres

✔ Perceives text structure

✔ Appreciates levels of meaning in a story

✔ Varies reading according to purpose for reading

✔ Effectively uses strategies to construct meaning: predicting, identifying important information, self-questioning, monitoring, summarizing, and evaluating

✔ Can verbalize process used to construct meaning; that is, is aware of own thinking (metacognition)

✔ Is learning study strategies such as taking notes

✔ Uses graphic material to construct meaning

`BENCHMARK` ➤ **The student enjoys reading.**

✔ Recommends books to others

✔ Is exploring young adult and adult fiction and nonfiction

✔ Sees self as a competent reader

✔ Sets goals and self-evaluates

✔ Is aware of own purposes for reading

`BENCHMARK` ➤ **The student is refining research skills begun at the previous stage.**

✔ Can plan a research project

✔ Knows how to locate information

✔ Takes notes in a variety of ways; attributes sources

✔ Synthesizes information into a final product

Writing

`BENCHMARK` ➤ **Prior writing behaviors strengthen and deepen.**

`BENCHMARK` ➤ **The student writes for a variety of purposes and reasons.**

✔ Is aware of how writing can contribute to self-awareness

✔ Uses writing to persuade

✔ Can write in response to a prompt to fit a given rubric

`BENCHMARK` ➤ **The student is growing in the mechanics of writing.**

✔ Edits own work

✔ Can edit the work of others

✔ Can independently verify spelling, grammar, and usage

`BENCHMARK` ➤ **The student is using the writing process.**

✔ Uses all steps of the writing process independently

✔ Varies prewriting techniques according to task

✔ Revises own work extensively

✔ Is developing a personal writing style, or voice

BENCHMARK ➧ **The student sees self as a competent writer.**

✔ Sets goals and evaluates own writing

BENCHMARK ➧ **The student connects reading and writing.**

✔ Recognizes author's craft and uses in own writing

✔ Is experimenting with writing in many forms and genres

Connecting to Other Chapters

As you read and think about the benchmarks in this chapter, you will see references to prior stages as well as ideas, concepts, tools, techniques, and strategies introduced in Chapters 1 through 4. Many students at the Fluent Reading and Writing stage continue to exhibit some of the behaviors from prior stages, while other literacy behaviors are firmly rooted, automatic, and no longer developing.

Some students in grade 4 or higher may not yet be fluent readers and writers. For such students, teachers should use the information and suggestions from previous chapters, both for assessment and for instruction.

Remember, even a child showing all the behaviors of the Fluent stage will need strong teaching to continue to grow. At this stage, every behavior is one that can be enhanced, extended, and carried further. No one is ever finished learning about being literate. Everyone continues to grow throughout his or her lifetime.

Using the Benchmarks to Assess the Student and Determine the Stage of Instruction

FOCUS As you read about the Fluent Reading and Writing stage, ask yourself the following questions:

1. How does this (our final) stage differ from the preceding stage?

2. Does a fluent reader need further instruction? If so, why and what kind?

3. Why is one never finished with the development of literacy?

In this section, we show you how to assess students' reading, writing, and oral language to determine whether they are at the Fluent stage. Most of this assessment will occur during regular instructional activities. Because your instruction is assessment based, you will make frequent instructional adjustments as you detect a need.

Figure 9.1 presents the benchmarks for the Fluent Reading and Writing stage. As we discuss each area, another "menu" figure will show some discrete indicators for that area. After discussing assessment of each indicator or group of indicators, we will describe instructional strategies that encourage and support continued growth.

Oral Language

Assessment of most oral language benchmarks will occur during normal classroom activities. You will rely almost entirely on observation and checklists.

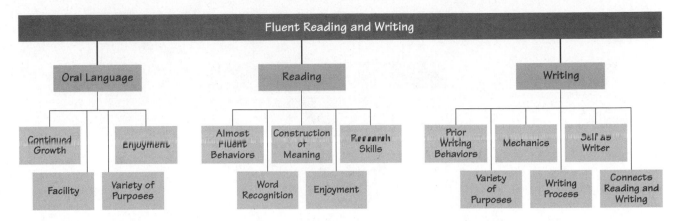

Figure 9.1
Menus for Assessing the Fluent Reading and Writing Stage

Particular projects that involve oral presentations may sometimes require rubrics and special checklists specific to those presentations only.

We discuss four major benchmarks for oral language: continued growth in prior behaviors, facility with language (Figure 9.2), use of language for a variety of purposes (Figure 9.3), and enjoyment of language (Figure 9.4). Near the end of this section you will find a sample class checklist (Figure 9.5) An individual checklist is in the Resource File.

By now you are comfortable with the developmental nature of literacy, which includes facility with oral language, that is, speaking and listening. At the Fluent stage, the oral language benchmarks from earlier stages, especially the Almost Fluent stage, do not disappear; rather, they continue to develop. For instance, fluent readers and writers are increasingly aware of their own problem areas. They can accept and enjoy diverse usage, and they use language with more ease and pleasure. In fact, many of the Almost Fluent behaviors are never mastered; rather, they continue to grow and develop over one's lifetime.

Observation will inform you which students continue to use new words in their oral language. Students will be encountering many new words as they read widely and listen to you read from more and more adult texts. These words will begin to find their way into students' everyday usage, and you will find you have an "ear" for the language students are using.

Instructional Strategies.   Make a point of discussing words during literature discussions, guided reading, and read-aloud sessions. Be sure to include derivation and word history as you discuss words, along with subtleties of denotation and connotation.

For example, share the origin of such words as *afghan,* which comes from the long-pile rugs that were once woven in Afghanistan, and *kindergarten,* the term Friedrich Froebel coined from the German words *kinder* (children) and *garten* (garden) to describe what he believed to be the kind of place children need before beginning school—a place to play and grow, a "garden of children." Also, share how some words have shifted in connotation over time. For example, the word

> **BENCHMARK**
> The student exhibits continued growth in behaviors from previous stages.

> **BENCHMARK**
> The student's facility with language is growing (Figure 9.2).
>
> ✔ Oral language reflects increasing vocabulary

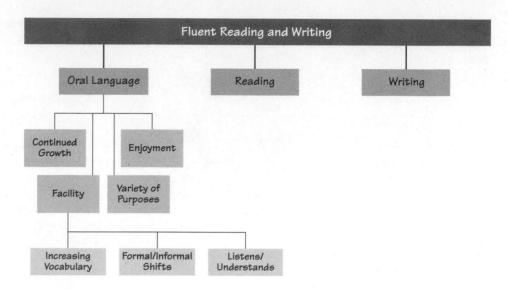

**Figure 9.2
Oral Language: Facility**

square once denoted something true, upright, and honest. More recently the connotation in some contexts has become pejorative, so that a square is someone who is not "cool."

Provide resources to support students' growing interest in word histories, the history of language, idioms, and foreign language words and phrases commonly used in our language. Students who are familiar with another language may particularly enjoy researching the history of words that have entered English from the other language.

Because students whose first language isn't English find figurative language, especially idiomatic language, particularly difficult, some books of idioms may be helpful: *There's a Frog in My Throat* (Leedy & Street, 2001), *In a Pickle and Other Funny Idioms* (Terban, 1983), *Put Your Foot in Your Mouth and Other Silly Sayings* (Cox, 1980), and *From the Horse's Mouth* (Nevin & Nevin, 1977). Be alert to idioms in reading materials as well as in oral language, and provide explanations or discuss the meanings. You may want to begin a class collection of idioms in a notebook or on a poster.

✔ Shifts from formal to informal usage to suit occasion

Observe that students are comfortable switching usage when situations change. By now they should have a good idea of the language appropriate to various situations. While language on the playground is apt to be informal and perhaps nonstandard, you should note students' increasing efforts to use standard English within the classroom.

If some students are not switching usage appropriately, direct intervention may be needed. Pay particular attention first to see whether the student *can* use standard English. If so, you need to determine why the student is not using it when appropriate; it could be lack of sensitivity to the situations, or it could be an act (however minor) of defiance.

Second-language learners may prefer to speak to each other in their first language, especially in informal situations. However, these students need to develop an awareness of when it is appropriate to use their first language and when it is not.

Instructional Strategies.   If you find that a student is unable to use standard English comfortably, you will need to do some direct instruction such as that discussed for earlier stages. If the student can use standard English comfortably but doesn't seem to realize when and where it is required, or why, open discussions and modeling are in order. You may want to have students role-play various situations. For example, they could role-play how they might tell a friend about a ball game if they were visiting at that friend's home or on the playground. Then role-play how they might talk if they were in the classroom, or at church, or in a group of adults.

A frank discussion about the language children hear around them and on television may be in order. The fact that they hear famous, respected people using nonstandard English in public does not give them license to do the same at school.

Remember that second-language students may retain some accent for many years, perhaps for a lifetime. This is especially true if they have begun speaking English at a relatively late age. With such students, you should focus on syntax and vocabulary rather than on pronunciation, which is difficult to change.

Students at this stage often give oral reports after completing a unit of study. Observe which students listen carefully to oral presentations, and check how well they have understood the main ideas. You may want to devise a series of items for students to discuss or write about after listening to oral presentations. At the least, you (or the presenter) will want to lead a discussion to be sure the ideas were understood. If they were not, your next step is to figure out why, with the help of your students. Failure to understand might be the result of inadequate listening, but it might also stem from a poorly prepared or poorly presented speech.

As with other oral language indicators, these are best observed during regular classroom activities. Note which students participate fully when discussing literature, as well as which participate willingly during role playing or Readers Theater.

The third indicator, debate or speech competition, may or may not be present. Some Fluent readers and writers may never be comfortable with the public nature of debate or speechmaking. Some teachers require all children to partici-

> ✔ Listens to oral presentations with understanding

> **BENCHMARK**
> The student uses oral language for a variety of purposes (Figure 9.3).
> ✔ Discusses literature with pleasure and understanding
> ✔ Enjoys role-playing and Readers Theater
> ✔ May enjoy debate or speech competition

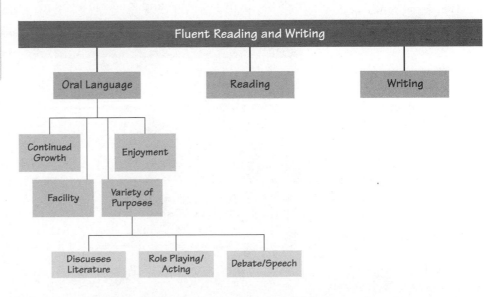

Figure 9.3
Oral Language: Variety of Purposes

pate in speech competitions; perhaps they believe this allows children to discover abilities or interests hitherto unknown. You will need to decide for each of your students how far to push him or her into speaking in front of an audience.

Instructional Strategies. Normal activities are probably sufficient to bring out each of these behaviors in your students. Perhaps most important are encouragement and opportunity. In other words, provide many activities that will allow students to express themselves orally. Encourage all children to do so, and accept such expression with pleasure.

When discussing literature, solicit comments from every participant. Be sure to model acceptance of all ideas. Students should feel free to express personal opinions in such discussion without fear of ridicule or argument. Your comments should support the understanding that discussion is an occasion for expanding thinking, not for finding right answers.

Readers Theater does require direct instruction and supervision until students are comfortable with it. If your students don't already know about this, teach them how to turn a story into drama. You may do this collaboratively until students are comfortable taking over the task entirely. See For Additional Reading at the end of this chapter for some sources on ways to teach Readers Theater.

Debate has formal rules of procedure that you may or may not decide to teach to your students, depending on their level of maturity. Even if you do not teach them format debating, you and they may develop guidelines for presenting both sides of an issue. If your school participates in speech competitions, the sponsoring organization undoubtedly has guidelines that must be followed. You can help your students prepare and rehearse their presentations.

> BENCHMARK
>
> The student continues to enjoy language (Figure 9.4).
>
> ✔ Is sensitive to body language and tone of others and self

At this stage, students will be acquiring an extra layer of awareness to add to their enjoyment of language. Observe them to judge their sensitivity to subtleties of oral language such as body language and tone. By fourth or fifth grade, children have been aware of some such elements for years; you have heard them say, "He looked at me funny!" "She's mad at me!" "Don't talk to me in that tone of voice!" Because body language and tone convey many things to one's audience, it is im-

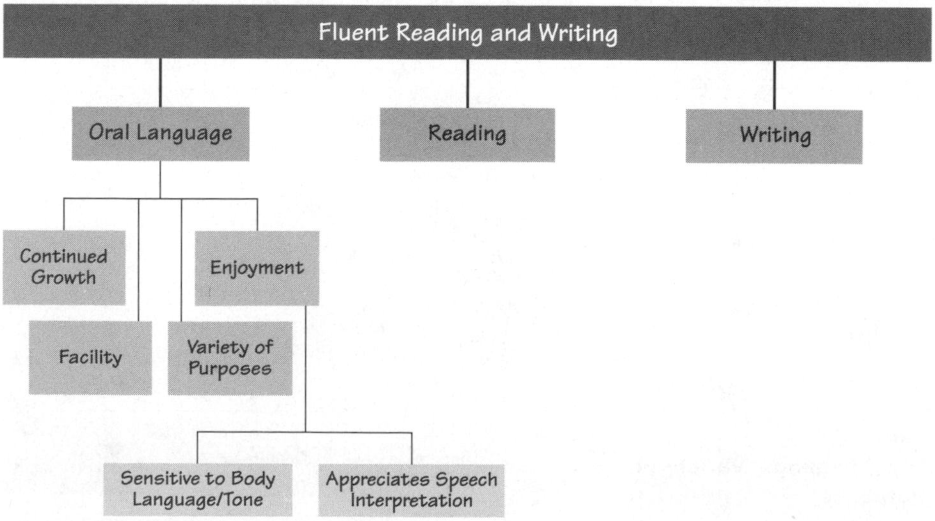

Figure 9.4
Oral Language: Enjoyment

portant that students become aware of their own body language and tone when they speak. They also need to be sensitive to others' use of the same indicators.

Instructional Strategies.   You can help your students become more aware of both body language and tone of voice. Along with them, you might watch some television or film with no sound and try to use the characters' body language and facial expressions to decide how they are feeling. Or you can have students role-play a situation wordlessly; the art of mime is built partly on the ability to convey feelings and ideas without words. Similarly, as you watch television or movies with your students, you can make them aware that acting requires the use not only of body language but of tone and inflection to convey meaning beyond the actual words.

Body language, facial expression, and vocal inflection may be culture specific. Students new to the United States may find the nonverbal communication they encounter quite different from what they grew up with. You can help them learn this kind of communication in U.S. culture. You can also encourage them to investigate similarities and differences between their first culture and the prevailing culture in which they now live. All students will benefit from raised awareness of cultural differences as long as you are careful not to suggest that one way is better than another.

✔ Appreciates the importance of speech in interpreting the written word, for example, news reporters, actors, comedians

Observe your students and enjoy with them the skill involved in using one's voice to enhance and lend additional meaning to the written word. Call attention to such oral interpretation when appropriate.

Instructional Strategies.   You can help students become sensitive to the way different interpretations elicit diverse reactions. For example, one of the authors used the children's book *Love You Forever* (Munsch, 1986) to illustrate how interpretation can influence response to text. The book was read to one group of undergraduates in a sweet and gentle tone of voice; the listeners were moved, some almost to tears. Then the same book was read to another group in a slightly sarcastic tone; that group laughed and hooted at almost every page. Of course, we then discussed what had occurred with both groups.

Figure 9.5 presents a class checklist for the entire set of oral language benchmarks and behaviors. An individual checklist is in the Resource File.

Reading

Five main areas of Fluent reading behaviors are continued growth from the previous stage, word recognition, construction of meaning (Figure 9.6), enjoyment (Figure 9.7), and research skills (Figure 9.8). A sample class checklist for Fluent reading benchmarks appears in Figure 9.9 and an individual checklist in the Resource File.

BENCHMARK
The student continues to display many of the behaviors from the Almost Fluent Reading and Writing stage.

Growth from the Almost Fluent stage to the Fluent stage may be fluid and seamless. Most behaviors from the previous stage have been refined. These students are now using reading abilities skillfully and automatically.

Students at the Fluent Reading and Writing stage deal with print independently most of the time, and we do not break out discrete skills or behavioral indicators in this category at this stage.

BENCHMARK
The student seldom seeks or needs assistance with word recognition.

You will have no trouble tracking which children display this benchmark. Actually, it is *lack* of the behavior you need to note. In other words, note which

Oral Language Checklist: Fluent Reading and Writing Stage

Teacher _____ Date _____ Grade _____

Student Names

+ = consistently present
- = not present
✓ = somewhat present; recheck;
      insufficient evidence

Benchmark

Continued Growth in Previous Behaviors

Facility
Shows increasing vocabulary
Shifts from formal to informal language
Listens to presentations with understanding

Variety of Purposes
Discusses literature
Enjoys role-playing/Readers Theater
Enjoys debate/speech competition

Enjoyment
Is sensitive to body language and tone
Appreciates speech interpretation

Instructional Plans:

_____
_____
_____

Figure 9.5
Sample Class Checklist for Fluent Reading and Writing: Oral Language Benchmarks and Behaviors

children are continuing to request help with word recognition. Then try to determine why they are asking for help. It might be that their word recognition skills are still at an earlier stage, even though their overall reading is strong.

Frequent requests for assistance might also indicate a lack of confidence; that is, if you nudged the student to apply decoding skills, he or she would be able to say the word.

You may also find that some students need assistance but do not recognize their own need. You will note this when students have read an assignment without requesting help, but further activities such as discussion, a report, or a quiz reveal that they have misread one or more significant words. This calls for individual consultation with each student to try to get at the root of the problem. Is it too hasty reading? Is it failure to keep in mind that what is read must make sense and, if it doesn't, a word may have been misread? Is it fear of asking for help? Is it lack of ability in using a word recognition skill you thought everyone in the class knew, such as suffixes, context, or a rare grapheme/phoneme relationship? Is it lack of background knowledge or concepts?

Asking yourself such questions can help you decide what to do. Do you need to reteach a skill? Do you need to boost self-confidence? Do you need to devise a way for the student to become more aware of misreading caused by haste or lack of focus?

Instructional Strategies. If your observation reveals that a student (or group of students) is not using a word recognition skill competently or appropriately, you need to plan minilessons to address that need. These lessons will likely involve reteaching; that is, the word element or the strategy will have been taught in an earlier grade and will probably seem familiar to the students. For example, students will have received lessons about using the structure of words to help figure out both the probable pronunciation and the probable meaning. Your task now is to reteach the skill and provide grade-appropriate practice opportunities. As students work independently and in small groups, you can coach them to use the skill.

For those students who seem to know the skill but don't use it, you may just have to build self-confidence, helping them see that they have all the skills they need to deal with unfamiliar words if they are not afraid to try.

The most difficult word recognition problem at this stage may involve students who don't seem to know when they have misread a word. Actually, this may or may not be a word recognition difficulty. Some students may have wonderful word recognition skills but remain oblivious to the need for text to make sense. These students can read right through an incorrect word without being bothered at all. The focus for them is not necessarily on slowing down and "reading more carefully." Rather, the emphasis is on helping them maintain focus on meaning as they read.

In this case, you would remind students to have a purpose in mind as they read, a question to answer, a fact to search for, a clue to detect. Remind them, too, that when a sentence doesn't seem to make sense, it might mean they have misread a word and should take another look. Discuss with them how lack of background knowledge can inhibit word recognition, and encourage them to ask for help when they feel ill prepared to read a particular passage. Share instances in your own reading when you have misread something and realized it only because what you were reading didn't make sense. With this focus on meaning, students will catch miscues and self-correct or at least look again; they will also learn when they need help because they are insufficiently prepared to deal with the conceptual load of a text.

> **BENCHMARK**
> The student uses a wide variety of strategies to construct meaning (Figure 9.6).

Students at this stage are able to read, learn from, and enjoy a wide variety of materials. They begin to employ their skills as adult readers. You will be able to observe which students have reached this benchmark during your normal everyday activities. At this stage, the student is not learning new reading strategies and skills so much as learning to apply them to a wide range of materials and for a variety of purposes. Everything previously learned is now strengthening and deepening.

Keep in mind that reading can never be "mastered." Any reader, no matter how fluent, will struggle if he or she has insufficient background information to

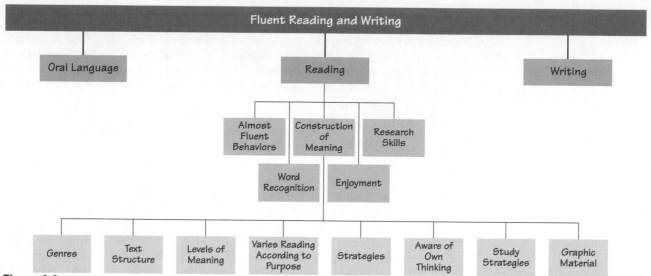

Figure 9.6
Reading: Construction of Meaning

understand the text or is trying to grasp new concepts and deal with unfamiliar vocabulary, symbolic language, allusion, and so forth. Still, the following behaviors will be evidence of attaining the Fluent Reading and Writing stage.

✔ Grasps differences among genres
✔ Perceives text structure
✔ Appreciates levels of meaning in a story
✔ Varies reading according to purpose for reading

Students at the Fluent Reading and Writing stage are beginning to have a firm grasp of various genres; that is, they recognize what makes a text contemporary fiction, historical fiction, nonfiction (including information and opinion), poetry, science fiction or fantasy, or a play. You will be able to note during class and small-group discussions which students can both talk about the distinguishing characteristics of various genres and recognize them while reading.

As your class reads and responds to nonfiction, note which students demonstrate awareness of text structure. You can detect this through discussion and by examining written responses. For example, after reading a book about reptiles that has one chapter about each of several reptiles, students may recognize this structure as only one way the author might have chosen to present the material. They also should be able to discuss some other ways the same information might have been organized: a chapter on each of several topics (habitat, feeding, appearance, reproduction), a chapter on each of several parts of the world and reptiles found there, a comparison of one kind of reptile to another, or a sequential presentation showing the evolution of reptiles since the beginning of recorded history. Students should also be able to discuss advantages and disadvantages of various kinds of text structure.

As students read and respond to a story, observe which individuals read beyond the plot and are able to deal with theme, character development, conflict, and subplot. Such readers won't just say that *Charlotte's Web* by E. B. White (1952) is a story about a pig and a spider who saves his life. They will recognize the underlying themes of friendship, life cycles, self-esteem, and death.

Also notice whether your students are approaching every reading experience in the same way. At this stage, they should vary their reading approach according to the purpose they have in mind. For example, a student who is beginning a novel may very well open to the first page and just begin, but even with novels there should be some variation in pace. The mini-thriller, for example, demands little thought and can be read quickly; a more substantial novel such as *Hatchet* (Paulsen, 1987), though equally thrilling, requires more careful and thoughtful reading.

With nonfiction, you should see an even more pronounced difference in approach. For example, when a student is beginning a book about deserts, note whether he or she surveys the book; looks at the table of contents; leafs through to examine charts, maps, and tables; and notices whether there is a glossary and an index. In other words, before beginning an informational book, the student should get acquainted with it, not just open to page one and begin.

Instructional Strategies. If some students seem unfamiliar with various genres, you may need to teach minilessons about the characteristics of each genre. Such lessons might be largely deductive, because by now all the children will have read almost every genre. You should be able to elicit from them the distinguishing characteristics. Then, as you continue to use a wide variety of texts in your class, make genre part of your introduction and your follow-up discussion. For example, as your students read *Roll of Thunder, Hear My Cry* (Taylor, 1976), review with them the characteristics of historical fiction, touching on historical accuracy, setting, appropriate language, characterization, plot and theme, and illustrations.

You may have students who are not yet familiar with various kinds of text structure or perhaps can pay lip service to the kinds but in fact do not recognize them as they read. Some of the most familiar organizational patterns used in information writing are description, collection, cause and effect, problem and solution, and comparison. See Table 9.1 for examples of each pattern.

If your students have had little instruction about text structure, you will need to plan a series of lessons devoted to each kind of structure and include many chances for students to examine informational writing to detect the structure. Follow the guidelines for any good teaching: explain, show examples, analyze familiar text, and analyze unfamiliar text. You may want to have students apply what they have learned in their own writing. For example, students may have read an article about the fires in Yellowstone Park organized in a cause-and-effect pattern. Then, when students are preparing to write a report of their own on some topic, you can help them recall this pattern and decide whether it is appropriate for what they are writing.

Your students, no matter how fluent, may typically read superficially; that is, they may read only for facts or for plot rather than digging for deeper meaning. It may be tempting, since they have few word recognition problems, just to leave them to read on their own and discuss their reading with their peers. This is probably a mistake. You are the more experienced reader. You are aware of the depth of meaning one can derive from literature. It is up to you to help make the deeper levels of meaning apparent to children by guiding discussions, asking open-ended questions, and probing. With your prompting, students can read beyond the story line of a book such as *Charlotte's Web* (the spider sees the worth of a pig and devotes herself to saving him from slaughter) to the bigger issues of life, death, balance of nature, and friendship, not to mention the impact and power of words. Students can compare pieces of literature on the same theme, different

Table 9.1
Examples of Expository Text Structures

Expository Structure	Example
Description	The tiger is the master of the Indian jungle. It stalks its prey in deadly silence. For half an hour or more, it carefully watches and then slowly, placing one foot softly in front of the other, closes in.
Collection	As master of the Indian jungle, the male tiger plays a number of roles. First, he is the hunter of prey who stalks in deadly silence. He is the beauty of the jungle, an expert at doing nothing in order to rest to be ready for his hunt. Finally, the lord of the jungle is the active seeker of mates, who begins his mating with a nuzzle but ends with a roar.
Causation, or cause and effect	We observed the tiger from our vehicle as it stalked the herd of deer. As a result of the slight noise from our running camera, the tiger turned and knew we were there. This didn't stop it from returning to its intended prey. Slowly and carefully it moved forward, not making a sound. The deer were initially unaware of its presence, but because of the shifting winds they caught the tiger's scent. This was enough to scare them away.
Response, problem-solution, question-answer, or remark-reply	One problem to be resolved in tiger watching is transportation. How is it possible for observers to get close enough to a tiger without scaring it away or being attacked? Nature has helped solve this problem by making the tiger and the elephant friends. It is possible for an elephant carrying several people to get very near a tiger without even being noticed. If it weren't for this natural friendship, tiger watching would be virtually impossible.
Comparison	The great tiger displays terrific power. With one steady lunge, it can destroy its prey, seemingly without any effort at all. Unlike other predators, the tiger basks in the sun after an attack in order to prepare for its next kill. The power and actions of the tiger resemble those of no other animal in the Indian jungle.

books from the same author, similar plot lines in different genres, different viewpoints, and much more.

Students can also be nudged to vary their reading according to their purposes for reading: "Why are you going to read the encyclopedia?" you might ask. "What are you looking for? If you are looking for only certain pieces of information, you might scan. If you are trying to decide if the entry will tell you what you want, you might skim to get a general idea." Give them the same kind of guidance with fiction and poetry: "If you are beginning a novel that will be the focus of a discussion, you'll want to read thoughtfully. If you are reading a mystery for pleasure, you can read as quickly as you like. If you are reading poetry, you might read it aloud to yourself to savor the language." Students who are unable to vary their reading even when prompted may need more direct instruction and modeling.

These strategies and abilities have been emphasized for students since they first began to read—or even earlier, as they listened to stories. The Fluent reader uses them all, though he or she may no longer be aware of it on a conscious level.

Whenever you guide prereading, reading, and postreading activities, you have an opportunity to check that students are using basic strategies that aid in constructing meaning. Before beginning a new book (or proceeding in an ongoing book), ask for predictions to check whether students are combining what they already know about the book with their own experience to make logical predictions. Then check to see whether they are adjusting predictions as they read on the basis of new evidence.

Particularly with informational reading, check that students are preparing for reading by asking questions focused on what they expect or hope to learn from their reading. As they read, some questions should be answered while others should arise.

Fluent readers monitor their own reading; that is, they keep asking themselves such questions as "Am I getting it?" "Do I understand what I'm reading?" "Is it making sense to me?" "Am I finding answers to my questions?" "Do I understand why that character did what he did?" Not only do Fluent readers monitor their reading, but they take action if the answer is *no.* They reread, ask for help, or choose another book.

Summarizing during reading, which involves identifying important information, helps the reader monitor his or her reading. Fluent readers can do so overtly if asked. From time to time, interrupt a student who is reading independently and ask him or her to summarize what has been read so far.

Fluent readers also evaluate what they read, whatever the genre. This means they don't simply take in the words and ideas; they connect their own experiences and prior reading to what they read and evaluate it in some way. Ask students to form opinions about what they read and to support those opinions with what they have read elsewhere or with personal experience.

Finally, Fluent readers are able to verbalize what they do and how they do it. One way to assess whether a reader is using the strategies we have discussed is to ask the reader to describe what he or she did while reading. Remember, though, that children can sometimes verbalize the acceptable behavior while not actually performing that behavior in real reading situations.

This area of assessment can be tricky, and what you think is evidence may be misleading. For example, if you call attention to a strategy by directly asking a child to demonstrate it to you, you haven't really learned what you want to know. Fluent readers use the strategies all the time, even when no one is asking them to do so.

Instructional Strategies. Instruction in these strategies at this stage is mostly a matter of guiding students before, during, and after reading, calling for

---

✔ Effectively uses strategies to construct meaning: predicting, identifying important information, self-questioning, monitoring, summarizing, and evaluating

✔ Can verbalize process used to construct meaning; that is, is aware of own thinking (metacognition)

the use of the strategies whenever appropriate. If you have some students who are particularly deficient in any strategy, direct reteaching will be appropriate. Remember that students at this stage have had all these strategies taught to them before. However, they may not have been quite ready to learn them at whatever grade they were taught. So reteaching is entirely appropriate. However, helping students make these strategies their own requires monitoring actual reading activities closely to nudge, remind, and elicit strategy use.

Strategies for constructing meaning are not like phonics skills. A reader can master the sound-symbol relationships of letters and know them forever. Constructing meaning is a new challenge each time new and "harder" material is confronted. No one ever "masters" comprehension.

✔ Is learning study strategies such as taking notes

✔ Uses graphic material to construct meaning

Students in the upper elementary grades and in middle school need to use study strategies, especially when reading in the content areas such as social studies or science. You will want to familiarize yourself with the scope and sequence of such skills in your school system to determine if these strategies have been taught prior to the grade you are teaching. Probably this scope will include such skills as outlining, using graphic organizers such as Venn diagrams or webs, notetaking, skimming and scanning, using an index, using library resources, and interpreting charts and tables.

At the beginning of the school year, given a class of mostly Fluent Reading and Writing students, you might informally assess the use of such strategies by setting tasks. For example, assign a piece of reading in a content area and ask students to "take notes" in whatever manner they generally use. Ask students to outline a chapter of an informational book. Distribute text that can be written on, such as a weekly newspaper, and ask students to underline or highlight the information they think is important.

In small groups or one on one, ask students how they approach an assignment to read a chapter in a social studies text on their own. Through such discussion, you will determine whether they preview the text before beginning to read, whether they ask themselves questions based on subtitles, and whether they pre-read summaries and end-of-chapter questions. Ask students whether they look at graphic material before reading, during reading, or not at all. Ask what they are thinking as they look at it.

Don't be surprised if you find students who are not yet adept at using study strategies such as these. Even though the strategies may have been taught previously, students may not have been ready or able to use them independently. Count on having to teach or reteach these strategies.

Instructional Strategies.   Direct teaching followed by immediate and frequent practice and application is probably the best way to ensure that your students learn various study strategies. As an example, we present the following steps for a lesson on notetaking:

1   Present a transparency of informational text.
2   Explain the purpose for notetaking.
3   Model taking notes.
4   Have students collaborate with a partner to take notes on another passage.
5   Debrief with discussion.

6 Have students practice taking notes independently.

7 Debrief students by examining their notes and talking about what they did.

8 Assign notetaking during assigned reading in content areas.

9 Provide for continuing practice in learning centers.

Don't present more than one study strategy at a time. Wait until that strategy seems firm before presenting another one. Make sure the point of learning the strategy isn't lost; that is, students must see the strategy not as an end in itself but as a way to help them do assigned reading more efficiently and with better understanding.

After assigning independent reading, talk with students about strategies they might use to help them grasp and retain the important information. Gradually release students to their own decision making about study strategies. Discussion after reading can help students think about why a strategy was (or was not) helpful and what they might do differently for the next assignment. Your goal, of course, is to have students use strategies independently, without being reminded, and carry that ability into future years of learning.

One final caution: study strategies are somewhat idiosyncratic; that is, your own favorite method of taking notes may not be the choice of all your students. Just because it has stood you in good stead all these years doesn't mean you should force it on your class. For example, you may prefer to take notes in a linear fashion, rather like an outline. Some students may prefer to web ideas. Others may like making tiny checks in the margin next to important ideas (or placing gummed notes on the pages) as they read and then returning to those places to make notes. However, having too many choices is confusing, so you probably should concentrate on teaching thoroughly one or two methods and help students choose the one that works best for them. If some students still are not successful using one of these strategies, you may need to present other methods.

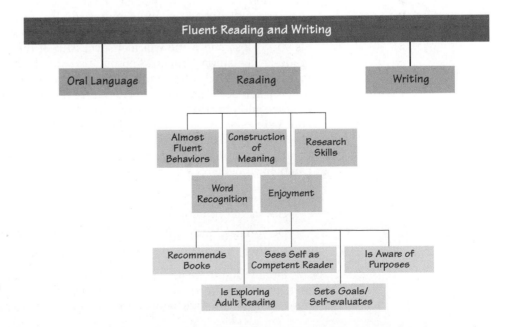

Figure 9.7
Reading: Enjoyment

Test-taking strategies are sometimes considered part of study skills, and these are discussed in Chapter 11.

BENCHMARK

The student enjoys reading (Figure 9.7).

✔ Recommends books to others

✔ Is exploring young adult and adult fiction and nonfiction

✔ Sees self as a competent reader

✔ Sets goals and self-evaluates

✔ Is aware of own purposes for reading

Most students at the Fluent stage probably do enjoy reading. People tend to like doing things they do well. Occasionally, however, someone may read competently but without pleasure. You'll want to look for the following indicators of this benchmark, though there are many more.

People who enjoy reading like to tell others about what they are reading. Such readers also begin to stretch beyond what they have been reading, looking for new challenges and new themes and topics. You'll be able to note which children are exhibiting these behaviors.

Fluent readers are confident. They will tackle unfamiliar text willingly and are not afraid of challenge. They seek wider and wider reading experiences because they know they can deal with them. They know what they want to read and why they have chosen a particular text to read. For example, one student may be reading a biography of John Glenn because she wants to be an astronaut; another could be reading a book by Katherine Paterson because he read one book by that author and liked it; another may be reading a mystery recommended by a friend; and yet another may be reading a book about ancient Greece because he is fascinated by Greek history and mythology.

These students also know whether they have read successfully. That is, they know they understand what they read. They know when something is too challenging and can make another choice without losing self-confidence. You will be able to note which children exhibit these behaviors during the Daily Independent Reading block as well as at other times during the day and by examining records the students keep of independent reading done in school and at home.

Instructional Strategies.   When you note that a student does *not* exhibit the behaviors that indicate enjoyment of reading, try to determine why. For example, if a student is not confident, first identify the student's level of reading for yourself. (See earlier chapters and Chapter 10.) If it turns out that the student is not reading fluently in grade-level materials, adjust your instruction and the materials you use so she or he will feel successful. If the student *can* read fluently in grade-level materials but lacks confidence, your task is related more to psychological and emotional support than to instructional support.

You can do some things to encourage these behaviors, of course. You can encourage and provide time for students to share their reading with each other. You can share what you are reading with your students. You can suggest specific, more challenging books to individual students on the basis of their interests. You can continue to introduce authors and genres through reading aloud to the class. You can help students as they choose what to read by asking questions:

What kind of book are you looking for? A mystery? A scary book?

How could you find such a book in the library?

Do you need more information for a science project? Where might you look?

How will you decide if a book you find will meet your purposes?

Finally, do not neglect reading aloud to your Fluent readers. This is the door to new authors, new genres, new ideas, and new visions. Hearing wonderful books read aloud is still a most potent contributor to pleasure in reading.

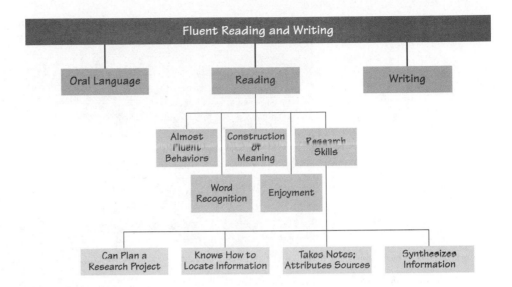

Figure 9.8
Reading: Research Skills

Before students have reached the Fluent Reading and Writing stage, they likely have already been taught some aspects of research. They have "looked things up." They have prepared and presented reports of various kinds. The following indicators will help you assess their progress.

These indicators are quite broad; each could be broken into more discrete aspects of research skills. You may decide early in the school year to assign a small research project and, without instruction of any kind, simply observe closely as students begin to work. You will soon know which students are comfortable with research skills and which need further instruction.

Even if you know there has been considerable prior instruction, summer vacation has intervened, and not all students were necessarily at the literacy stage that allowed them to absorb such instruction. For example, if some students were still struggling with fluency, they might have had a difficult time reading various information sources even though they were competent at locating them.

Students with Internet access at home may be more adept than others at using the computer as a resource. Related but different skills are needed for locating information through a search engine and through an index to a book such as an encyclopedia. Beyond locating information, students need to be taught how to evaluate information for its validity and for its appropriateness for a particular purpose. They need to learn ways to take notes about information they find and how to credit the source of that information. Finally, they need to be able to synthesize information from several sources into one cohesive whole.

You can assess your students' familiarity with and ability to use research skills as you help them prepare for their first project calling for research. Through discussion you can get a general idea of the class's readiness to do research, though there may be wide variation among individuals. On the basis of the initial activi-

Two students collaborate
on a research project using
a computer.
© Michael Newman/PhotoEdit

ties, note which students are able to verbalize how to plan a research project and
which do not participate in a discussion about planning.

Instructional Strategies.   Though some of your students may already be
skilled, chances are you will want to plan very specific lessons for your whole class
in each area of research. These will serve as a refresher for skilled researchers as
well as an introduction for students with no prior instruction.

If you use a published reading or literacy program, it probably has a research
or study skills component. You should examine your program for such lessons
and decide, on the basis of what you are learning about your particular students,
which lessons to teach the whole class, which to teach only to small groups, and
which to omit altogether. You may decide that your students lack prerequisite
skills for some of the lessons in your published program. Your job is to make the
lessons fit the students. We suggest that you spend considerable time presenting
detailed and thorough lessons related to research skills and provide many opportunities for students to apply these skills in authentic assignments related to content areas.

You may also do on-the-spot instruction with individuals. For example, if
Joel is struggling to locate information in an encyclopedia, your best instructional choice may be to give him a quick lesson right then. Model and think
aloud how you would approach the task. Let's say Joel is doing a report about
African animals, and you note that he is reading the entire entry on Africa: political history, geography, crops, and all. You can show him how to scan for pertinent
information and thus narrow his search. If Charmine has found an appropriate
site on the Internet but it offers much more information than she needs, you can
model how to decide what one should take notes on (or print out) and what is ir-

relevant to the project at hand. Perhaps, as Juan is writing a report, you note that he is simply reporting, in sequence, information from each of several sources. You can show him how to go back to his plan and his notes, identify important ideas, then combine information from more than one source to support each main idea.

When you notice several students with similar difficulties, you may decide to plan small-group explicit lessons. You may find that some students who are not quite yet at the Fluent stage can think appropriately about research but lack decoding skills and therefore may struggle with actually reading the information they locate. For them you will provide additional support, including specific instruction in decoding.

Figure 9.9 presents a sample class checklist for all the reading benchmarks at the Fluent Reading and Writing stage. An individual checklist is in the Resource File.

Writing

Most assessment of writing will be done by observing students as they write and by examining various writing products. These observations will guide you in making instructional decisions.

We discuss six major areas of writing at this stage: strengthening and deepening of prior behaviors, writing for a variety of purposes and reasons (Figure 9.10), growing competence in mechanics (Figure 9.11), use of the writing process (Figure 9.12), seeing self as a competent writer (Figure 9.13), and connecting reading and writing (Figure 9.14). A sample class checklist (Figure 9.15) appears near the end of the section, and a checklist for individual students is in the Resource File.

> **BENCHMARK**
> Prior writing behaviors strengthen and deepen.

Your students should be showing evidence of prior writing instruction and experience as the year begins, and you should see their abilities continue to develop.

> **BENCHMARK**
> The student writes for a variety of purposes and reasons (Figure 9.10).
>
> ✔ Is aware of how writing can contribute to self-awareness
> ✔ Uses writing to persuade

The indicators shown in Figure 9.10, if present, can reassure you that a student is writing for a variety of purposes and reasons. There are other purposes, of course, but these should be particularly apparent at the Fluent stage.

Children have probably been doing personal writing ever since kindergarten in the form of personal journals. You'll recall that at first these were probably a recitation of daily events in their lives and perhaps their responses to these events. They have also been writing in response to what they read, responding in a personal way to character and plot. Gradually students become more reflective in their writing, finding that they learn more about themselves as they write. They begin to understand those who say, "I don't know what I think until I write about it." Look for evidence of self-examination and hypothesizing about self. For example, a student may write, "Writing about my reactions to the concert helps me think about why I like certain kinds of music."

Students have been writing to entertain or inform for some time. At this stage, they are also showing their ability to write in order to persuade. They may write about a book they have read, recommending it to others in such a way that others want to read it. They may be writing posters and speeches supporting their opinions about some school issue. They may be expressing their viewpoints through

Reading Checklist:
Fluent Reading and Writing Stage

Teacher_____   Date_____   Grade_____

Student Names

+ = consistently present
- = not present
✓ = somewhat present; recheck;
    insufficient evidence

Benchmark

Behaviors from Almost Fluent Stage

Word Recognition

Construction of Meaning
Grasps genres
Perceives text structure
Appreciates levels of meaning
Varies reading according to purpose
Uses strategies to construct meaning
Is aware of own thinking
Is learning study strategies
Uses graphic material

Enjoyment
Recommends books to others
Is exploring adult reading
Sees self as competent reader
Sets goals/self-evaluates
Is aware of own purposes

Research Skills
Can plan a research project
Knows how to locate information
Takes notes/attributes sources
Synthesizes information

Instructional Plans:

_____
_____
_____

Figure 9.9
Sample Class Checklist for
Fluent Reading and
Writing: Reading
Benchmarks and Behaviors

letters to the editor of a school newspaper or the local newspaper. You can learn whether students understand and use writing for persuasion through discussion about possible courses of action related to an issue of some kind. You might ask, for example, "What can we do to let our elected officials know how we feel?" Students of this age should know they can write letters, either through regular mail or through the Internet.

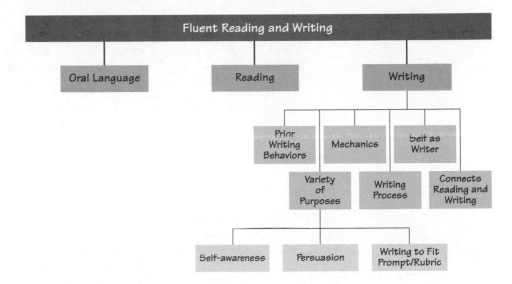

**Figure 9.10
Writing: Variety of
Purposes**

When your students understand that they can use writing for persuasion, they should also realize that powerful writing can be used to persuade them. Discussion of writing that expresses or attempts to sway opinion, including advertisements, will reveal whether students have grasped a little of the power of words.

Instructional Strategies. Even if your students seem to understand the power of persuasive writing, you will want to reinforce what they already are doing and deepen their understanding and abilities. Lessons on persuasive writing may be part of your published reading—language arts program. If so, examine the lessons carefully to determine if they are suitable for your students or if you need to expand them with further examples and exercises.

The skill of critical reading is closely linked to writing persuasively. Students must be helped to recognize persuasive writing, whether its goal is to persuade others to take action, change beliefs, vote for a candidate, or buy a product. One good way to learn to recognize such writing by others is to do such writing oneself.

Lessons and practice are necessary parts of becoming a critical reader and a writer who can use words to persuade. Eventually these abilities must also come into play in authentic contexts in the students' personal lives.

✔ Can write in response to a prompt to fit a given rubric

At school, district, and state levels, writing assessment usually requires students to write in a certain way and in response to a given prompt. Although such assessments are more authentic than answering questions "about" writing, fixing wrong sentences, and identifying parts of speech, they are still a long way from writing one does for one's own purposes. Still, the assessments are a fact of life, and this type of task is realistic in that such writing may be required of students throughout their adult lives. Many jobs, for example, require very specific writing about a given topic.

You may have some information about the previous performance of each student on this kind of task. If so, you'll be glad to have it, but at the same time you must remember that students may have lost some ability over a vacation if they do not make writing part of their everyday lives. On the other hand, those who enjoy writing may have increased in ability during a vacation.

You may want to begin with a discussion about what students remember from prior writing assessments when they were given a topic and knew they would be evaluated on the basis of a rubric. Help them recall the writing process steps, the need for planning, and the need for showing rough drafts. Then mimic the conditions of such an assessment: assign a topic and have them write. You may want to do this twice, once for "creative" writing and once for informational writing.

Collect and read the papers, and sort them roughly into those that seem to show an understanding of the task and ability to carry it out and those that do not. The quality of the writing, of course, is key, and we address that in the next sections. Here we are concerned only with whether students can work in this way.

Instructional Strategies.   If your students are not comfortable with writing to a prompt and meeting the standards of a specific rubric, you'll need to prepare lessons to accustom them to this task. You will need to review with them the many purposes for writing. While much of writing is self-determined, personal, and free, there are times when students will be required to write what they are told to write and in the way they are told to write. They need to learn how to do this. Review or reteach the steps of the writing process, forms such as essay and story, and text structures.

> **BENCHMARK**
> The student is growing in the mechanics of writing (Figure 9.11).

Although writers usually don't address the mechanics of their writing until the final step before publishing, mechanics are apt to be the first thing a reader notices. Ideas are most important, but careless mechanics can interfere with a reader's grasping ideas. By the Fluent stage, your students should understand the importance of mechanics and be on their way to standard use of spelling, grammar, and punctuation.

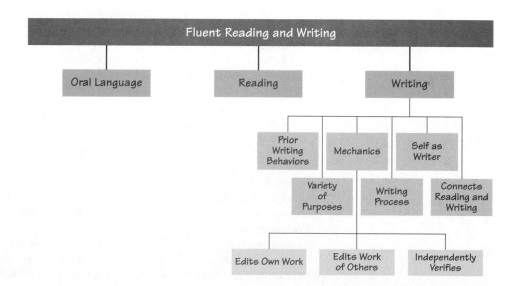

Figure 9.11
Writing: Mechanics

✔ Edits own work

✔ Can edit the work of others

✔ Can independently verify spelling, grammar, and usage

Observe closely as students put the finishing touches on their writing. Note which are editing their own work. All writers need an editor, of course, so understand that it is difficult—perhaps impossible—for a writer to be completely successful in self-editing. Nevertheless, look for behavior showing that the student is going over his or her work after revision to check spelling, punctuation, and usage. Part of self-editing, of course, is recognizing that something may need correcting.

You should also note which students are able to do this editing task for others when asked. Further, which students know how to find answers to their own questions about mechanics, such as by consulting dictionaries, usage references, spell-checking features, or a human authority?

Instructional Strategies.   If students are not editing their own work or are doing it poorly, you'll want to plan specific lessons addressing this important step. You may want to teach your students a system for editing, such as first checking the spelling of each word, then the punctuation, then the grammar. Because it is almost impossible to watch for problems in all these areas in one reading, we suggest you teach students to read for one area at a time.

Spelling is tricky to edit. Successful editing presumes that you will recognize a word that is misspelled and either know how to spell it correctly or know how to locate the correct spelling. Poor spellers may or may not recognize an incorrect spelling when they see one, especially in their own writing. We all tend to see what we expect to see; reading right past an incorrect spelling is common, even for good spellers. Further, relying on a spelling check in a word processing program is risky; if a word is a real word, the computer doesn't care whether it's a homonym of the correct word—hence the many mistaken uses of *their* for *there* or *they're*. Catching these kinds of errors requires an eagle eye.

Assuming your students have detected a spelling error, what next? That is, what if they are pretty sure the word is spelled incorrectly, but they don't know the correct spelling? Here comes the usual objection to dictionaries: if I don't know how to spell it, how can I look it up? Teach your students to hypothesize about probable spelling, a process that can lead them to the correct spelling in the dictionary. Remember what we said in earlier chapters about "invented" spelling? This is what one must do when the correct spelling is unknown: one must invent a probable spelling and use that as a starting point in the dictionary.

Hand-held devices that work somewhat like a computer spell-checking program, such as the Franklin Speller, allow you to input the invented spelling and then watch as various possible choices are presented. Assume you aren't sure how to spell *accommodate*. You enter your guess: *acomodate*. The device will present the correct spelling to you. If your guess might be more than one word (for example, you enter *cach*), the device will present options: *coach, catch, ketch, cache*. Presumably you will recognize which is the correct spelling of the desired word.

For the task of editing another person's writing, you'll need to teach your students how to do so without creating hard feelings or causing the author to become defensive or discouraged. The trick is to stay focused on the work; both students should have the same goal—improving the work. Model ways to point out problems without damaging egos. For example, don't say, "You didn't use quotation marks right." Instead, say, "When I came to this paragraph, I wasn't sure who was speaking. Let's look at the [not "your"] paragraphing and quotation marks to be sure they are clear." Students should use the same system they use on their own work, reading carefully for each area and marking questionable items. You'll need to decide if peer editors should actually make corrections or merely indicate the problems for the author to address. Be sure all students understand that they are looking only for mechanics and perhaps for clarity during this task. They are not criticizing content in any way or suggesting revisions.

You may want to post editing guidelines. In the Resource File, you will find a chart with proofreader's marks and a suggested editing/proofreading checklist for students to use.

Not all writing requires use of the writing process, but fluent writers should be using all the steps of the process when appropriate. Recall those steps from Chapter 3: prewriting, writing the rough draft, revising, editing/proofreading, and publishing the final copy. As you observe your students, you should see evidence of the following behaviors.

Observe closely as students approach a writing task for which the writing process is appropriate. Note which are able to use a prewriting technique to generate ideas and whether the technique chosen seems to produce good thinking. Continue to observe as students proceed through the steps. Note which students are using the steps independently, indicating that they have internalized the process, and which are doing thoughtful revision after producing a rough draft. This seems to us to be one of the last steps students are willing or able to do. Often they want to proceed directly to editing and proofreading or to combine revision with editing.

Instructional Strategies. We believe a writer is never through learning about using the writing process, so even those who seem to use all the steps independently will benefit from continued instruction. However, the type of instruction should vary according to students' present level of skill. Therefore, you may decide to teach to small groups.

> **BENCHMARK**
>
> The student is using the writing process (Figure 9.12).

> ✔ Uses all steps of the writing process independently
> ✔ Varies prewriting techniques according to task
> ✔ Revises own work extensively

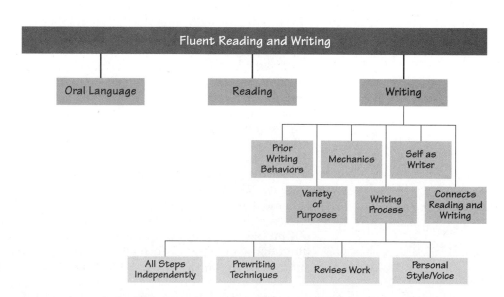

Figure 9.12
Writing: Use of the Writing Process

For example, those students who are using all the steps may need extra guidance in only one area, such as revision. While they may already be revising, you may decide you can teach lessons that will help them increase the effectiveness of their revision.

Other students may need additional instruction related to prewriting techniques. Still others may need reminding of how the writing process can serve them in their efforts to write for their own purposes. Until young writers see the process as an aid to better, more satisfying writing, they may not use it unless requested. You can help them see the process as a means to an end rather than an end in itself.

✔ **Is developing a personal writing style, or voice**

Some students may already be writing in a personal voice, whereas others still write in a lifeless series of declarative sentences such as: "We went to the circus. We had fun. There were lots of animals and clowns." Examine samples of your students' writing frequently to note whether they are developing a personal writing style, remain largely imitative, or still use the stilted language of younger years.

Especially in so-called creative writing (as opposed to informational or report writing), fluent writers will already have a voice, a way of saying things that is uniquely theirs. One student may use fresh metaphors from sports. Another may be developing a gift for moving others with unstructured, free-form poetry. Even in assigned writing that must conform to guidelines, some students will have strong individual styles and others may not.

Instructional Strategies.   Developing a personal style or voice is probably the result of a supportive writing environment and continual encouragement and engagement in writing. Help young writers find their own ways to express ideas and tell stories. This means more than just exercises in avoiding trite similes, although that sort of exercise can help.

When you discuss good literature, help students see beyond plot. Help them note the author's craft. How did the author do what he or she did? How did the author make you feel sad, or happy, or scared? How did this author's way of making you feel sad differ from the approach of that other author who also made you sad? Was it the events? The choice of words? The figurative language? The images?

Ask your students, "Why do you often want to read another book by the same author? Is it because you like the way that author writes? That's the author's voice. Others may try to imitate it, but the best authors have voices so unique that no one can truly imitate them."

BENCHMARK

The student sees self as a competent writer (Figure 9.13).

✔ **Sets goals and evaluates own writing**

Writers at the Fluent Reading and Writing stage feel confidence in their ability to fulfill writing assignments as well as to write for their own purposes. They should be aware that they can still grow a great deal in their ability, but they are not afraid to write; they accept writing tasks willingly, and they are comfortable in doing so.

The one specific indicator we list at this stage is the students' ability to set goals and self-evaluate as they work on various assignments involving writing. For a while, you might devise and post a checklist of some kind to help students monitor their own ability to set goals and evaluate their work. The checklist may be as simple or as elaborate as you choose. Here is a sample:

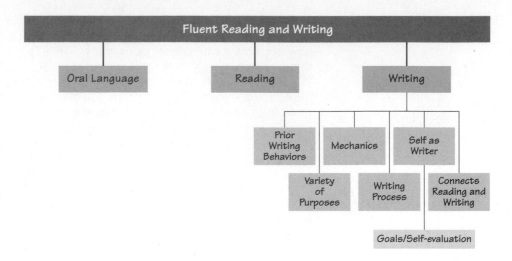

**Figure 9.13
Writing: Seeing Self as a
Competent Writer**

Personal Writing Goals

☐ Can I state my purpose for this piece of writing?

☐ Have I accomplished my purpose?

☐ Did I revise and polish my writing until I am proud of it?

☐ Can I state what needs improvement?

☐ Do I have a plan for becoming a better writer?

Bear in mind, though, that you want your students to set goals and self-evaluate independently—without prompting or checklists.

Instructional Strategies.   Nudging, modeling, and prodding, rather than direct instruction, will move students toward this benchmark. During conferences, and frequently in between, ask the student such questions as these:

What did you want to accomplish with this piece of writing?

Did you accomplish what you wanted to? If not, what will your goal be for the next piece of writing?

What do you want to do better? How can you learn to do it better?

As Calkins (1991), says, "Conferring well is every bit as challenging as writing well" (p. 229). Use your conferences and all your other interactions with students to provide the environment and support they need.

BENCHMARK

The student connects reading and writing (Figure 9.14).

✔ Recognizes author's craft and uses in own writing

Throughout this book we have emphasized the important connection between reading and writing. Mostly we have reinforced that wide reading improves writing, just as writing improves one's ability to read. One constructs meaning when one reads and when one writes. Each process involves similar ways of thinking. At this stage, we highlight only two writing benchmarks that may be new: recognition of the author's craft and experimentation with forms and genres.

Earlier we discussed the importance of helping students become aware of aspects of the author's craft. This serves two purposes: it enhances pleasure in read-

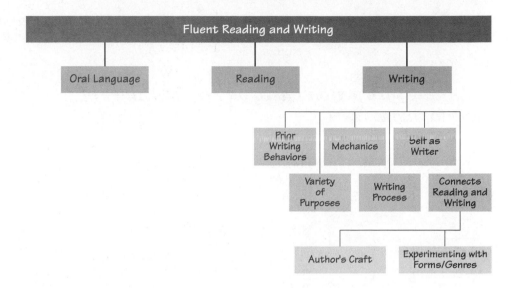

**Figure 9.14
Writing: Connecting
Reading and Writing**

ing, of course, but it also affects the individual's own writing. We believe you should be on the lookout for evidence that students are connecting the craft they are learning to appreciate as they read with their own ability to use such techniques to improve their own writing.

Instructional Strategies.   As you read with students, continue to go beyond discussion of plot, character, setting, and conflict. Address the issue of how authors did what they did and whether the students might attempt similar techniques in their own writing (Atwell, 1987). It may help to comment frequently that such wonderful writing probably did not flow out in the author's first draft but was the result of much thoughtful revision.

You need to help your fluent readers and writers grasp that good writing is not just telling what happened. If it were, we could simply tell this story: A teenage boy and girl fell in love, but their families were enemies. They figured out a way to be together by faking suicide, but it backfired and at the end they both died. Who needs Shakespeare to write *Romeo and Juliet*? Or Leonard Bernstein to write *West Side Story*?

✔ **Is experimenting with writing in many forms and genres**

Observe which students are trying different forms and genres as they write independently. You, of course, will be teaching and assigning many different kinds of writing during the Developmentally Appropriate Writing block. Here you are concerned with students' interest in trying different forms when it is their choice.

Instructional Strategies.   Continue to present many forms and different genres to students so they can at least try them out. With some forms, students definitely need to acquire confidence: letters and reports, for example. Other forms or genres, such as various types of fiction and poetry, may or may not be part of every student's life, but you can nevertheless give students your support as they try different kinds of writing to see which fits them best.

Figure 9.15 presents a sample checklist for all the writing benchmarks and behaviors at the Fluent Reading and Writing stage. An individual checklist is in the Resource File.

Planning Instruction Based on Assessed Stage of Development

Having dealt with the benchmarks for the Fluent Reading and Writing stage, we now address three important questions: what to teach, how to teach, and how to prepare these fluent readers and writers in fifth grade and up for what awaits them in the next stage of their education.

What Do I Teach?

Though this chapter has dealt primarily with the Fluent Reading and Writing stage, you will, of course, have students in your fifth or sixth grade who are not yet at this stage. Your assessment will have made this evident. Instructional decisions are still an important part of your job. Further, you have an increased need to be sure that literacy is a part of the entire curriculum, not just language arts. In addition, you have a responsibility to help your students acquire the study skills they will need to deal with increasingly complex curriculum materials as well as learn to manage and plan their own time to fulfill the requirements imposed by different teachers. In this section, we address the following: meeting the needs of a range of stages, making instructional decisions, literacy across the curriculum, and study skills and strategies.

Meeting the Needs of a Range of Stages

Most likely, the majority of your students in fifth grade and above will be at or almost at the Fluent Reading and Writing stage; in other words, they will be consistently displaying the benchmarks discussed in this chapter and Chapter 8.

It is possible, however, that you will have someone who is still at the Beginning Reading and Writing stage, perhaps a student who has been socially promoted within your school system or transferred from another system. Such students may be given reading instruction in some kind of intervention program. Yet these students may still be with the others during social studies, science, and math. Teachers of these subjects must teach the concepts required by the curriculum even when some students cannot read the material independently. For such students, several instructional strategies and materials discussed in earlier chapters are appropriate: providing content textbooks recorded on audiotape, providing study buddies, varying the questioning to permit all students to participate in a discussion, and providing alternative, simpler materials that cover the same content.

Making Instructional Decisions

At the beginning of the school year, you will need to assess the literacy stage of each of your students, just as you would do for younger students. You can use the

Writing Checklist:
Fluent Reading and Writing Stage

Teacher_____ Date_____ Grade_____

Student Names

+ = consistently present
- = not present
✓ = somewhat present; recheck;
    insufficient evidence

Benchmark

Growth in Prior Writing Behaviors								
Variety of Purposes/Reasons								
Knows writing adds to self-awareness								
Uses writing to persuade								
Can write to fit prompt/rubric								
Mechanics								
Edits own work								
Edits work of others								
Independently verifies								
Writing Process								
Uses all steps independently								
Varies prewriting techniques								
Revises own work								
Develops personal style/voice								
Sees Self as Competent Writer								
Sets goals and evaluates								
Connects Reading and Writing								
Recognizes and uses author's craft								
Experiments with forms/genres								

Instructional Plans:

_____

_____

_____

**Figure 9.15
Sample Class Checklist for
Fluent Reading and
Writing: Writing
Benchmarks and Behaviors**

suggested procedures, tools, and techniques from this and earlier chapters. You may also decide to administer an informal reading inventory to each student during the first two or three weeks of school (see Chapter 10).

Once you have an idea of each student's literacy stage, you will proceed with teaching your curriculum, continuing to use every teaching activity as an opportunity to gather information. When a lesson doesn't turn out the way you planned, evaluate what you did to determine what adjustments you need to make in future lessons to accommodate your students' needs.

An important part of your instructional decision making relates to the range of stages in your class. If you teach fifth grade or above, you may not have expected to have students who are not yet Fluent readers and writers. You may have chosen to teach these upper grades because you prefer dealing with content areas rather than basic skills. Nevertheless, *all* teachers need to be prepared to teach every student in the class, regardless of stage. This may require a great deal of small-group or individual instruction.

Second-Language Learners.   Some students may be fluent in another language but not yet fluent in English, and some may not yet be fluent either in the first language or in English. Such students need programs designed to help them acquire English, and they may need an intervention program as well. It is risky to generalize. An individual plan must be drawn up for each student, and it should be based on whatever combination of needs is present.

Meanwhile, you, as the classroom teacher, will need to make continued adjustments to accommodate students who are not yet fluent in English. Even those who appear to be fluent in English may still wrestle with idiomatic and figurative language. Many teacher manuals now provide suggestions with virtually every lesson for addressing difficult terms and concepts. Students may benefit from having a reading partner to turn to for help, and they may also benefit from literature discussion circles that support their efforts to express ideas.

Give your second-language learners as many opportunities to speak as you can and as they are willing to take, but resist forcing students who may be shy or embarrassed by their accents, their fumbling to find the right word, or their variant cultural background.

Continue to focus on the various cultures represented in your class, whether or not they include other-language speakers. Sometimes you may be able to tie literacy activities to social studies units. Such units may include costumes and foods from various cultures along with study of history and geography. Your job will be to learn what you can of the cultures represented in your particular class, and then use the many ideas found in teacher manuals to make your students feel comfortable and valued as well as enlighten other students about our diverse society. Several sources with many teaching suggestions are listed in For Additional Reading.

Literacy Across the Curriculum

Fluent readers and writers are presumed to be ready to apply their abilities to curriculum areas such as science, social studies, and math. This presumption may be somewhat misplaced; that is, the literacy demands of these content areas may differ somewhat from that of the materials in a reading–language arts program.

Each content area has its own vocabulary, and the organization of each content-area textbook is unique. Information may be incremental; for example, dealing with a chapter in a science book may depend on prior knowledge to a far greater extent than reading a new novel. The type of prior knowledge may also differ: prior knowledge that supports reading fiction is likely personal experience;

prior knowledge that supports content-area reading is often specific to that particular content area. In effect, you must teach your students how to read each particular text along with teaching the content itself.

Study Skills and Strategies

The term *study skills* is sometimes used to refer to a group of abilities, such as dealing with a wide variety of text organization, using learning strategies such as K-W-L, notetaking, summarizing, outlining, using references, test-taking preparation and strategies, managing time, and juggling multiple assignments from several teachers.

Some of these skills have been introduced to students earlier. If you teach fifth to eighth grade, your careful reteaching (and introduction of new skills) may be students' last chance to receive thorough instruction. Teachers in later grades may expect students to know these strategies already and feel no need to provide further instruction.

You need to reinforce what students already know, provide practice, and reteach or introduce skills and strategies students clearly are not yet using competently. While the content of science, social studies, and math is vital to the education of your students, teaching them *how* to learn such things now and for the future is equally valuable.

How Do I Teach What Needs to Be Taught?

In answer to the question of how you will teach, there are three main areas to consider: selecting materials, maintaining a balanced literacy program, and choosing instructional strategies that best support student learning.

Selecting Materials

At every stage of literacy, your job is to provide materials that suit the interests and abilities of your students. Now that students are fluent in reading and writing, you may find you have broader choices, but you must still pay attention to this area.

If you are using a published reading–language arts program, anthologies are probably provided. These contain a wide selection of fiction and nonfiction. They are designed to help students sample many genres, many nonfiction text structures, and a wide range of topics, cultures, and experiences. Such anthologies are wonderful for just this purpose; students can sample a little bit of the infinite published literature available. These tastes will, one hopes, lead students to read widely beyond the prescribed program. You will also want to stay abreast of new books published for readers of this age as well as continuing to read the older, beloved classics. Many of your readers will be sampling young adult and adult literature.

For students who are not yet at the Fluent Reading and Writing stage, you will need books appropriate to their reading level. These may be from the adopted published program or from sets of trade books. The trick is finding interesting books that these students can read successfully.

For all students, you will want to continue to choose books to read aloud. We have never found anyone, including adults, who does not enjoy listening to someone read aloud a good book. Reading aloud stimulates students to read more for themselves. It opens doors to other cultures and times. It expands vocabulary. It provides fodder for intense discussion. It allows you to share the beauty of language.

Maintaining a Balanced Literacy Program

The model of the Balanced Literacy Program 3–8 (introduced in Chapter 4) continues to be vital in your classroom of mostly Fluent readers and writers. All the same pieces are necessary for students to continue to grow: independent reading and writing for power and practice; use of core books for teaching skills and strategies and developmentally appropriate books for application of these skills and strategies; instruction in spelling, grammar, and mechanics and in writing forms and processes, as well as many opportunities designed to apply those skills; and small-group or individual intervention for those students who need it. While all the blocks will still be part of your program, the times allotted for each may be different at this stage.

Daily Independent Reading.   By this stage, students are comfortable with independent reading and able to do so for extended periods. You may decide to allot as much as thirty minutes to this activity, at least on some days. Students may need a refresher and a rehearsal early in the school year to remind them about selecting material and rules of behavior during independent reading.

As with earlier stages, you may choose to read during this time, modeling the value of reading in your life. You may also use the time, if needed, for individual conferences, sampling oral reading, special assessments, checking reading logs, and touching base with students about their interests. Because of time restrictions, it may not be possible to have students write independently during the literacy block every day. Many teachers provide opportunity for this at other times during the day, such as during the period when students are arriving in the morning. Teachers also encourage students to make personal writing a part of their everyday lives outside of school.

Daily Independent Writing.   Students are now more comfortable generating ideas and can write for more extended periods of time. Encourage English-language learners to write in their first language if that is more comfortable; but when they do so, be sure they understand that you may ask them to summarize in English from time to time.

You may use this time for your own writing. You may also use some of it for individual conferences with students—monitoring, coaching, aiding with revisions, and so forth.

Reading: Core Books and Developmentally Appropriate Books.   During the Core Books block, you continue to provide instruction to help students solidify and extend their skills. During the Developmentally Appropriate Books block, you provide the materials and time for students to apply these skills while reading books at their own level.

It may be tempting to think that because your students are at the fluent stage, they no longer need direct instruction. This is a mistake. As we have said repeatedly, none of us is ever as proficient a reader as we might be. Everyone continues to benefit from a wise teacher who helps us interact with text at different levels and for different purposes. Rather than decreased attention to instruction, you may find you want to increase the time you spend interacting with students to teach these finer aspects of literacy.

The scope and sequence of skills in your published reading—language arts series will guide you to teach study skills; story elements; authors's craft; text organization or structure; etymologies; literary techniques such as hyperbole, allusion, irony, and metaphor; and much more. Because Fluent readers are comfortable with decoding and basic comprehension, you can focus on leading them to read critically; for example, they may learn to consider the source, question validity, detect bias, and compare and contrast various viewpoints. You will deal with each and all of these "skills" during the Core Books instructional block and provide material for immediate application during the Developmentally Appropriate block. You want students to become accustomed to applying these skills and ways of thinking even when not directed to do so.

Writing: Teacher-Modeled and Developmentally Appropriate Writing.   As with reading, no one is ever through needing good instruction about writing. You will continue to teach spelling, grammar, and mechanics through direct instruction. In addition, you will continue to model various forms of writing, lead students in collaborative and cooperative writing, teach and reteach the steps of the writing process, and provide a block of time during which students apply what you have taught.

Increasingly, the forms students are writing will connect to various curricular areas. They will be writing informational reports for social studies and science; they will write letters regarding issues and to solicit information; they will compose commentary to post on the Internet; they may correspond with students in other countries. You will also continue to encourage and support personal writing, such as entries in journals, as well as what is often called creative writing–stories and poems.

You will probably spend time during both reading and writing blocks teaching students how to plan and do research for various written reports. This involves not only the critical reading skills that lead to wise identification of sources but also specific instruction about taking notes, carefully recording information about sources, paraphrasing, using direct quotations, synthesizing information from several sources, planning the presentation of information, and revising the plan as new information is learned.

Some students in your classroom may be at the Almost Fluent stage; their needs can probably be addressed in the classroom through careful assessment and small-group and individual instruction. Others may be lagging further in their literacy development and need the additional Intervention block.

Instructional Strategies for Depth and Breadth

Chapter 4 presented an overview of core instructional strategies that support a balanced literacy program. These strategies have all been appropriate in one way or another throughout the developmental literacy stages. You might think these strategies are no longer needed at this stage, but you would be wrong. Many of the basic strategies still serve the needs of students, though you will find your emphasis shifting.

By this stage, you will no longer need the routines for phonics, high-frequency words, or decodable words. You will, however, still teach lessons related to the structure of words as well as etymology. Virtually every routine related to comprehension still belongs in your classroom.

As we said earlier, while one might master the sound-symbol relationship of letters, comprehension is never mastered. As one continues to read more and more challenging material, the demands on the reader increase. Now these demands are seldom related to how to pronounce the words or to answering such questions as "What happened?" and "To whom?" Rather, fluent readers wrestle with such concepts as theme, conflict, allusion, literary techniques, connotation, bias, and layers of meaning. Perhaps an occasional student becomes a deep reader and thinker without any help, but most students need guidance to help them appreciate what reading has to offer.

To that end, here are some comments about routines from Chapter 4 that should still have a place in your classroom at the Fluent Reading and Writing stage.

Minilessons (Instructional Strategy 2). The minilesson is useful no matter what stage you teach, and it will continue to include the five parts described in Chapter 4: (1) introduction, (2) teacher modeling, (3) student modeling and guided practice, (4) summarizing and reflecting, and (5) follow-up. This format is suitable for specific skills, strategies, concepts, or processes, whether in literacy or in any content area.

Explicit Comprehension Routine (Instructional Strategy 4). Recall that this routine involves three main steps: concept, listening, and reading. Thus, if you were preparing a lesson focused on the literary element "conflict," your initial plan might look like the one that follows. Completing the three steps may take several days.

1   *Concept.* Use a familiar story to introduce the concept of conflict. For example, recall the fairy tale *Little Red Riding Hood*. Have students identify the problem and then the source of the problem (another character: the wolf). Have students recall other stories they all know, identify the conflict, and decide whether it is between characters, within a character, between a character and nature, or between a character and society. Here are some examples of the latter types:

   Conflict within a character: In *Ira Sleeps Over* (Waber, 1972), Ira must decide whether to take his favorite teddy bear with him when he goes to spend the night with a friend.
   Conflict between a character and nature: In *Hatchet* (Paulsen, 1987), the main character struggles throughout the book to survive in the wilderness.
   Conflict between a character and society: In *Number the Stars* (Lowry, 1989), the conflict relates to Nazi soldiers marching into the characters' hometown, Copenhagen.

2   *Listening.* Read aloud some short stories and guide students to identify the major problem and what kind of conflict that problem represents. Discuss how the author reveals the conflict.

3 *Reading.* Assign short pieces for students to read for the express purpose of identifying the conflict. Any piece of fiction will be appropriate, since without conflict there is no story.

This model for explicit comprehension routines will suit whatever area of literature you choose to focus on.

Modes of Reading (Instructional Strategy 7).   Recall the modes of reading described in Chapter 4: teacher read-aloud, shared reading, guided reading, cooperative/collaborative reading, and independent reading. Each of these modes still has a place in a classroom of Fluent readers, though they will not look the same in fifth grade and above as they did in first grade.

You should still read aloud to students to share wonderful literature, introduce an author or a book that students will then read independently, read material that may be conceptually difficult so that ideas can be discussed as students listen, and share unfamiliar authors' work.

At the earliest literacy stages, shared reading meant reading to students, then along with students, from big books and classroom sets of little books. At the Fluent stage, you might still read to students as they follow along when studying poetry. Poetry should be read aloud, and you may want to project or provide a blown-up copy of a poem so all eyes are focused on the text as students hear a good reader (you) read it aloud.

Guided reading is often appropriate as students read content-area material such as social studies or science textbooks. You may find that the teacher's manuals that accompany your content textbooks provide detailed ideas for guiding the reading of each chapter. We caution you again that such reading should be silent for the most part. That is, you introduce concepts, present vocabulary, preview the chapter, construct a K-W-L chart, or do whatever is appropriate before students begin to read, but then they should read the first (predetermined by you) chunk of the text silently. After this silent reading, you guide discussion about what they read, going back to the text to clarify thinking if necessary. Then you discuss and set purposes for students' reading of the next chunk—and so on through the day's reading. Some students may be able to read the entire text independent of guidance, but better learning of content will occur (as well as increased skill in reading informational text) if you guide a significant portion of the reading.

Students at this stage will read most self-chosen material independently, and independent reading should continue to play a big part in your day. However, some cooperative/collaborative reading may still be appropriate. Partners may find it helps both of them to read content material together if you are not conducting a whole-class guided reading. Students at this stage also enjoy partnering with younger readers. English-language learners, who may find silent reading difficult, may benefit from reading with another student who speaks the same primary language or with a congenial native English speaker. If ELL students do read alone, their silent reading may involve subvocalization (reading aloud to themselves).

Modes of Writing (Instructional Strategy 10).   You may find you still use all the modes of writing suggested in Chapter 4. Students will continue to need the modeling you provide in a quasi-write-aloud, during which you plan and make a rough draft. They will also continue to benefit from shared whole-class writing, guided writing as they begin to work on a writing project, collaborating with peers, and independent writing.

All writers, even the most prolific and skillful, benefit from the help and guidance of others at some points during the writing process. Like reading, writing is never mastered, and one is never finished learning about it.

Response Activities (Instructional Strategy 8).   As we said in Chapter 4, there are many response ideas in the teacher's manuals that accompany published programs. In addition, other publishers have provided sets of activities to accompany hundreds of books for young fluent readers. We advise you to examine and weigh these response activities and choose carefully those that clearly serve your objectives. Beware of filling your students' days with response activities that consume large amounts of time and have limited value. That time might be better spent reading more books.

We think response to reading is important, but perhaps with Fluent readers the mode of response should be left up to the student. Remember that it isn't necessary to *do* something after every book one reads. Sometimes just keeping a log, perhaps recording a brief response, is sufficient. Another invaluable response is discussion circles, discussed next.

Discussion Circles or Groups (Instructional Strategy 9).   Discussion allows readers to share their thoughts about what they have read. By this stage, students are probably adept at holding and managing discussion groups without much guidance or supervision. At the beginning of the school year, you will assess this ability and step in if needed. Follow whichever steps from Chapter 4 your students need.

At this stage, you may introduce some more sophisticated aspects to literature discussions. For example, you may encourage students to read various books by one author and focus a discussion on the author's themes and craft. You might suggest that students read several books dealing with the same theme or genre. Students may research in the library or on the Internet to find critical commentary about some of the books and authors they are reading and bring that information to the discussion. When a book has a film version, students may enjoy comparing the book with the film, considering the unique challenges of telling a story in each art form.

Reserve some time in your schedule for students to give brief "book chats" about books they have discovered. Great readers have always relied on friends for ideas about what book to read next.

How Do I Prepare Students for What Comes Next?

If you teach students in fifth grade or above, you are probably trying to prepare them for whatever kinds of school experience they might face next. In this section, we address two areas directly related to literacy and to thriving in that new setting: independent learning and change in curriculum and schedule.

Helping Students Become Independent Learners

As your students move into the higher grades, they may find they are being monitored less closely by their teachers. They will be expected to manage their assignments for themselves. They will be expected to know how to read content-area textbooks, how to study for tests on that content, and how to prepare reports and other kinds of projects stemming from various subject areas. Teachers at those higher levels may believe students should already be using the study techniques we discussed earlier; they may not think they should teach such techniques to those who don't already know them.

As the school year progresses, you may want to move your students into situations that are more and more like what lies ahead for them, while at the same time continuing to provide the support they need right now. Such a balance can be tricky, but the payoff is significant.

Some teachers like to suggest ways for students to keep track of assignments in each curricular area, along with blocking out study times so that no area is shortchanged. Even if you teach all subjects, you can help students take charge of this kind of personal time management, just as though they were answerable to several teachers.

For example, let's say your students are doing a long-term project, due on May 1. You can help them learn to lay out a time line of tasks, perhaps working backward from the end date:

> *I need to start writing/inputting the final copy by April 20. So revising and editing must be done between April 15 and April 30. That means I need to have two peers and my teacher read it and suggest revisions before April 15. That may take a week. I need at least two weeks to write the first drafts, so I have to start writing by the last week in March. I need at least two weeks to research my topic; start that by March 8.*

Preparing for Change in Curriculum and Structure

For students who have been in self-contained classrooms, a big change will occur when they have different teachers for each subject and move from one room to the next. Of course, if your elementary school has departmentalized the subjects, students will already be familiar with this procedure, but even so the change will be significant. Teachers at higher grades may not work as closely with each other to be sure that assignments are reasonably distributed among the subjects. These teachers may also not work to link content areas across the curriculum.

Students may or may not be with the same group of peers in all classes. They may or may not be given ample time to ask questions, get individual help during class, and work collaboratively. No matter what your school system does to ease the transition, moving to the next level of schooling isn't easy.

To this end, if you teach the last grade before students move to a different school, gradually change your method of interacting with students as the year progresses. By the end of the school year, your students should be well on their way to managing their own workloads, planning their time, keeping track of assignments, and being responsible for their own learning.

Find out what awaits your English-language learners in terms of bilingual or ESL classes or other special support, and inform the students and their families of the services available to them for the next year. Reassure them that your school system will continue to help them become fluent readers and writers of English.

In the next section, we describe the schedule of a typical sixth grade group of students as they move from classroom to classroom for different subject areas.

A Sixth-Grade Classroom at Work

Once again we use the Balanced Literacy Program 3–8 as a framework for looking at one departmentalized sixth grade (see Table 9.2). If there were students in need of intervention in this class, they would be pulled out on alternate days from the time slot devoted to music, art, physical education, and conferences.

Please bear in mind as you read that this is a hypothetical class. Many variations of scheduling exist across the country. Here we suggest generic ideas related to supporting continued literacy development for fluent readers and writers regardless of scheduling details.

Table 9.2
Daily Schedule for Ms. Lin's Homeroom*

8:00	Ms. Lin's homeroom students report to her classroom. Schoolwide announcements are broadcast on closed-circuit television. Details related to homework, upcoming field trips, library books, and so forth are dealt with.
8:30	Language/literacy block • Independent reading • Direct instruction in mechanics, spelling, grammar • Core Books and Developmentally Appropriate Books • Writing process/report writing • Independent writing
10:00	Ms. Lin's students leave for math class. Another sixth-grade class enters for its block of language/literacy.
11:30	Sixth graders' lunch
12:00	Sixth-grade special classes (music, art, physical education); intervention classes; conferences; study time
1:00	Ms. Lin's third language/literacy block
2:30	Homeroom class back with Ms. Lin; minilesson on scheduling, planning, and homework
2:50	Read-aloud to students
3:15	Dismiss

*Similar schedules exist for the other two sixth-grade teachers: Mr. Martin, who teaches math blocks, and Mr. Santiago, who teaches social studies and science.

FOCUS   **As you read the schedule and plans:**

1. Note how this schedule differs from the samples we presented earlier.
2. Notice which parts of the block are independent of the rest of the curriculum, which are integrated, and how the integration is done.
3. Note the use of whole-class, small-group, and independent activities.
4. Note opportunities for ongoing assessment.
5. Think about how the information presented in this section would be the same (or different) if the sixth grade were self-contained.

Ms. Lin's Language/Literacy Block (28 students in each section)

Each of Ms. Lin's language/literacy blocks is 90 minutes and meets daily. During this time, Ms. Lin makes sure her students spend the appropriate amount of time on each of the Balanced Literacy Program blocks. However, she may not have every student in each block every day.

For example, her week might be arranged as follows:

8:30 9:00	M W F	Independent reading/individual conferences
	Tu–Th	Independent reading/small-group instruction
9:00–9:30		Core Books and Developmentally Appropriate Books (alternate days)
9:30–10:00	M–Tu	Teacher-Modeled and Developmentally Appropriate Writing: instruction in mechanics, spelling, and grammar
	W–Th	Writing process: instruction and application
	F	Independent writing

There is no need to explain each time segment in detail, since they vary only in degree of difficulty from those at the previous stage. Note that reading aloud to students is not part of the literacy block presented here. It occurs instead at the end of each homeroom teacher's schedule.

If the literacy block were longer, Ms. Lin might arrange the time differently. For example, she might have time for students to do independent writing every day. Instead, she encourages independent writing when students first come into their homerooms in the morning. She might also have time for both guided reading and literature circles for every student every day. She might use part of the block to teach literacy skills for specific application to content areas. In the arrangement suggested here, she consults with the content-area teachers and assists them in planning their own literacy lessons in their fields.

Math Block and Science/Social Studies Block

Mr. Martin's math block and Mr. Santiago's alternating science/social studies blocks also meet daily for 90 minutes. Each teacher devotes time during his block to teaching literacy skills and strategies specific to the content area. Ms. Lin has met with both content teachers to help them identify what needs to be taught and help them plan instruction and gather or prepare materials. Lessons are designed to conform to school standards as well as to meet individual and group needs. Some schools may have a staff resource teacher who helps teachers with this sort of planning.

Mr. Martin uses the math text as his guide for math instruction because it matches local standards closely. Within each unit in that book, he has identified literacy skills that are necessary if students are to benefit from math instruction. These include but are not limited to:

- Reading and writing cardinal, ordinal, fraction, and decimal numbers
- Reading and writing specific math terms

- Reading and interpreting charts and tables
- Reading and interpreting picture, circle, line, and bar graphs
- Reading, interpreting, and writing symbols and notations used in math
- Reading, interpreting, and constructing diagrams such as Venn diagrams
- Reading, interpreting, and constructing timelines
- Reading and interpreting narrative problems with relevant and irrelevant information

Mr. Santiago has also examined the curriculum standards for his subject areas, science and social studies, as well as the instructional manuals accompanying his textbooks. There are some generic literacy skills necessary for students to read and write competently in his specific content areas. Some of these connect to math instruction as well as to literacy instruction. These include but are not limited to:

- Reading and writing terminology and concept words specific to each topic
- Reading and writing special notation of various kinds, such as for temperature, elevation, and density
- Reading various kinds of maps, including symbols and legends
- Applying the ability to read and interpret charts, tables, graphs, diagrams, timelines, captions, and any other graphics found in the reading material
- Taking notes and outlining from reading material (both the textbook and multiple other reading sources) as well as listening and viewing material
- Using text structure to aid in understanding text
- Searching through print sources and the Internet for information

Content-area textbooks are changing all the time in terms of format, organization, style, and use of graphic materials. Sharon Walpole (1998–1999) has examined changes in science textbooks; her findings and teaching suggestions appear in the article listed in For Additional Reading.

As you have seen, even when various content areas are taught by different teachers, a great deal of overlap occurs. Literacy skills are needed for most curricular areas. It behooves each content-area teacher to work closely with literacy teachers to be sure students are making the necessary connections.

After Reading the Sixth-Grade Plans

Think about the following questions:

1. How were all parts of the Balanced Literacy Program 3–8 provided for?
2. When would you have done assessment, and what might you have done?
3. Would you like teaching in such a departmentalized school? Why or why not?

Summary

The benchmarks and sample indicators for the Fluent Reading and Writing stage help you identify readers and writers who have moved to a level of competence in literacy that will support continued growth. Fluent readers and writers continue to refine skills, read more widely, explore writing in various forms, and explore literature and subject matter in more depth. Despite students' fluency, teachers still need to promote the development of their students through appropriate assessment and instruction.

In planning instruction based on your assessment of Fluent readers and writers, you will face three major questions: what to teach, how to teach, and how to prepare students for what lies ahead. Decisions related to what to teach involve meeting the needs of the inevitable range of stages and making instructional decisions to serve all your students; in addition, at this stage, you need to think about teaching literacy across the curriculum and teaching study skills and strategies. How to teach what needs to be taught involves selecting appropriate materials, maintaining a balanced literacy program as outlined in the early chapters of this book, and using appropriate instructional strategies. These strategies are the same as those used with earlier stages, though the manner of teaching them and the materials used will change according to students' literacy level.

Students at this stage are likely in upper elementary grades or in middle school and may soon be facing new school experiences. A critical part of teaching Fluent readers is helping them become independent learners who are able to take responsibility for managing their own time. Because significant changes in curriculum and school structure may lie ahead, students must also be informed and prepared for such changes. English-language learners and their families need to know what kinds of services will be available at the next level of schooling.

Though the Fluent Reading and Writing stage is the final stage in literacy development presented in this book, by no means have students finished developing. In fact, no one we know has ever finished developing as a reader or writer. We are all still learning.

FOR ADDITIONAL READING

Cox, C., & Boyd-Batstone, P. (1997). *Crossroads: Literature and language in culturally and linguistically diverse classrooms.* Upper Saddle River, NJ: Prentice-Hall.

Cullinan, B. E., & Galda, L. (1994). *Literature and the child.* Fort Worth, TX: Harcourt Brace.

Harste, J. C., Short, K. G., & Burke, C. (1988). *Creating classrooms for authors.* Portsmouth, NH: Heinemann.

Ioga, C. (1995). *The inner world of the immigrant child.* New York: St. Martin's Press.

Ramirez, R., & Ramirez, J. L. (1994). *Multiethnic children's literature.* Albany, NY: Delmar.

Sloyer, S. (1982). *Readers theatre: Story dramatization in the classroom.* Urbana, IL: National Council of Teachers of English.

Spangenberg-Urbschat, K., & Pritchard, R. (1994). *Kids come in all languages: Reading instruction for ESL students.* Newark, DE: International Reading Association.

Walpole, S. (1998–1999). Changing texts, changing thinking: Comprehension demands of new science textbooks. *The Reading Teacher, 52*(4), 358–369.

FOR EXPLORATION: ELECTRONIC RESOURCES

AskERIC Lesson Plans: Language Arts.
   http://ericir.syr.edu/Virtual/Lessons/ Lang_arts/   A wide variety of lesson plans in literacy and language arts, many of them appropriate for students at the Fluent Reading and Writing stage.

The Children's Literature Web Guide.
   http://www.acs.ucalgary.ca/~dkbrown/ index.html   An omnibus site that aims "to gather together and categorize the growing number of Internet resources related to books for Children and Young Adults."

Paradigm Online Writing Assistant.
   http://www.powa.org/   This "online writing assistant" offers step-by-step guidance for writing informal, thesis/support, argumentative, and exploratory essays. It also includes practice activities and information about documenting sources.

CLASSROOM APPLICATIONS

1. Visit a school that departmentalizes subjects in an upper grade. Record your impressions and draw some conclusions to share with the class.

2. Visit a middle school language arts class (which might be called English or Reading). Record your observations and impressions of instruction and ongoing assessment. How does what you observe match what you have learned in this book? How does it differ?

3. Visit an upper elementary grade during a social studies, science, or math class. Record your observations and impressions related to the following: the literacy demands of the textbook, the competence of the students, adjustments for students who seem to struggle in reading the text, evidence of literacy assessment during instruction, and specific lessons addressing literacy demands of the specific content area.

Using Special Tools for Reading and Writing Assessment

10

Informal and Qualitative Measures for Reading

FOCUS

As you read the Eyewitness section, ask yourself the following questions:

1. What does Ms. Kim need to learn about Bobby's literacy, and how will she find out?

2. How might the procedures Ms. Kim uses differ if this were a first-grade rather than a fourth-grade class?

Eyewitness

A new student, Bobby, is joining Ms. Kim's fourth-grade class today. Records from his previous school haven't yet arrived. Ms. Kim introduces Bobby to the class, finds him a desk, assigns him a buddy, and suggests that he just observe how the class begins the day, joining in whenever he feels comfortable.

Bobby sits quietly, looking around. On the walls and hanging from the ceiling, he sees student projects about global warming. A couple of students quietly straighten shelves crammed with books. Bobby's eyes light up and a smile flickers across his face as he spies the computers. After the morning routines are completed, the other students take out folders and begin writing. Bobby continues to sit, but his left knee begins jiggling up and down. He looks around, apparently unsure of what he should be doing.

Another adult enters the room. Ms. Kim greets him warmly and speaks quietly to him. He hangs up his coat and begins circulating, stopping to chat with various students about their writing. Sometimes he pulls up a chair and talks at greater length with a student.

At a point when Bobby seems about to explode with nervousness, Ms. Kim quietly whispers to him, "Come on back to the workroom with me, Bobby. Let's get to know each other." Looking a bit uneasy, Bobby clutches his jacket and follows Ms. Kim to the back room. There they sit and chat for quite some time. After a while, Ms. Kim points to an array of books on the table. Bobby looks them over, finally selects one, and begins to read aloud to Ms. Kim. She sits back, relaxed and smiling. After he finishes the book, he and Ms. Kim talk some more. When the other students finish writing, Bobby returns to his seat and the class prepares for math.

Later, during the Reading: Core Books block, Bobby is attentive but does not volunteer anything. Ms. Kim watches him, tilting her head and making eye contact occasionally as if to invite him to respond, but she does not call on him. During the Daily Independent Reading block, Bobby chooses some picture books about space and astronauts. He leafs through several and then begins to read one of them, turning the pages thoughtfully. He looks up frequently, but the other students are all engrossed in books, so he returns to his book.

During the Reading: Developmentally Appropriate Books block, Ms. Kim has Bobby join a group that has just completed various biographies. Ms. Kim asks the group members to share with each other the books they have been reading and then discuss what makes an interesting and worthwhile biography. She tells Bobby the group will be happy to help him find a biography to read so he can participate in this group, which will be together for another week or two.

Ms. Kim has been marking various checklists throughout the day during all blocks of literacy instruction.

The next morning, Bobby participates more fully in the morning routines. He has been given a folder for his own independent writing, which he takes out when everyone else takes out a writing folder. He is writing busily when an aide enters the classroom and begins to work with students who are writing. At this point, Bobby and Ms. Kim again go into the workroom. Ms. Kim has several items ready. Bobby begins reading from some lists of words as she marks a paper on a clipboard. After a while, he reads short passages and then answers questions while Ms. Kim continues to write notes as he responds. They seem relaxed but focused. Bobby is cooperative. He is not jiggling his leg.

Later in the day, during the Daily Independent Reading block, Bobby again works one on one with Ms. Kim.

After school, Ms. Kim spreads out all the information she has gathered so far about Bobby's literacy and begins making notes and analyzing results. She then makes notes in her plan book.

The next day, during the Reading: Core Books block, Ms. Kim asks Bobby a direct question calling for an opinion about an event in the story. The question clearly has no right or wrong answer. Bobby ventures an opinion and looks around apprehensively. Ms. Kim nods thoughtfully and invites others to respond to Bobby's idea. Another boy paraphrases Bobby's idea and adds another way of looking at the matter.

During Reading: Developmentally Appropriate Books time, Bobby goes immediately to join the group that has been reading biographies. The group discussion picks up where it left off yesterday, this time without teacher supervision. The others ask Bobby if he has read enough to share his biography with the group. He declines, but tells a bit about the subject of the book and how far he has gotten. Today Bobby asks questions of others freely and asks to read one of the other books as soon as it is available.

Ms. Kim glances over at Bobby's group often. When she sees him entering into the discussion, she smiles to herself.

For most of your ongoing daily instructional decisions, the tools, techniques, strategies, and instruments you have already learned about will be sufficient. However, as our Eyewitness account suggests, there are times when you may want and need more:

- When a new child enters your class and you have no information about the child's reading ability
- At the beginning of the school year
- When a child's reading seems to be dramatically below or above that of the rest of your class
- When a child's reading behavior is puzzling to you for some reason; you have not been able to figure out what's going on using your usual assessments
- When you need more specific information to make a referral for special placement, extra help, or a staffing (a meeting among all people concerned with a child's learning)

• When you need additional information to help you clarify a child's reading performance for the family

In this chapter, we discuss some informal and qualitative measures related to reading. First, we discuss readability, the concept of measuring the difficulty of reading materials. Then we discuss measuring the reader, using an informal reading inventory and other methods. Finally, we examine some issues related to matching readers to reading material in terms of difficulty and ability.

Measuring the Materials

FOCUS As you read about Informal and Qualitative Measures for Reading, ask yourself the following questions:

1. What is readability? How is it figured? What are the precautions you should keep in mind?

2. What is an IRI and how is it used?

3. What does this chapter add to what you already know about assessing students with diverse needs?

4. How is the cloze procedure used to match reader to reading material?

You would probably agree that to teach children effectively, you must use reading material that is neither too hard nor too easy. Not only do you want to provide reading materials the child is interested in, but you want to be confident that the child will be able to recognize or figure out most of the words and be able to grasp the ideas. In other words, you'd like to know both the reading level of the student and the reading level of the materials she or he will read. But how can you know how "hard" a given piece of reading material is? The answer isn't as simple as it might seem.

The term **readability** or **readability level** is often used to refer to the difficulty of a piece of written material. Readability is stated as a grade level. For example, you may hear someone say that a certain book is at third-grade readability. This means the book is just right for a reader with third-grade reading ability; such a reader can both recognize the words and comprehend the ideas. This certainly seems like something you will want to know when you teach.

We believe, however, that readability is a far broader concept than a grade level attached to a piece of text. It encompasses all the factors involved in whether or not a given piece of text is comprehensible to a given reader. Only a small portion of these factors are measurable.

Factors Affecting Readability

We group the factors affecting readability into three general categories: the reader, the text, and the environment. All three are interconnected, as shown in Figure 10.1. We will discuss each of them in turn.

Figure 10.1
Interrelated Factors
Affecting Readability

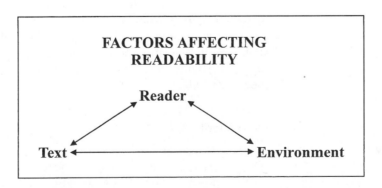

FACTORS AFFECTING
READABILITY

Reader

Text ⟷ Environment

The Reader

Difficulty is, to a certain extent, idiosyncratic; that is, each of us experiences (or does not experience) difficulty with a piece of text depending on our own particular interests, moods, attitudes, abilities, prior knowledge, and so forth. In fact, you probably find that your judgment about how difficult something is to read varies from day to day.

For example, you may find that you can study a certain textbook with good concentration and understanding if you read it when you are rested and well fed, but if you try to read it when you are hungry, or late at night when you are sleepy, you can't make any sense out of it at all. Similarly, you may have found a novel too deep when you were wrestling with some personal problems of your own; then, when you tried again to read it at a more serene time, you were delighted with it.

Your personal growth over time also influences your perception of difficulty. You may have experienced rereading a book you first read at a much younger age and found puzzling. When you read it again, after acquiring more life experience and maturity, you found it satisfying and comprehensible. Furthermore, you have probably found some text that you can't understand (though you know all the words) because you don't comprehend the underlying concepts the author is presuming you know. Then, after an instructor provides the conceptual support, you can read the material successfully.

Finally, there is, of course, the ability of the reader to recognize or figure out the words and put the ideas together. This depends in part on the skills the reader has acquired, either independently or through instruction.

The Text

Some things just seem easier to read than others because of the way they are written. For example:

- A textbook that is arranged logically, supplies graphic aids in the way of charts and tables, explains new terms in context, has pages that are not crammed margin to margin with print, and so forth is easier to read than one without these features.

- Stories that are told in straight sequence from a single point of view seem easier than those that use a great deal of flashback or multiple viewpoints.

- Stories that tap into feelings and experiences you share are easier for you to read than those in which you can't relate to the characters or the problems.

- Beautiful language, while sometimes "difficult," is so rewarding that we stick with it even though it doesn't seem "easy." Similarly, we may enjoy nonsense rhymes just for the pure pleasure of the sounds, not looking for meaning at all.

The Environment

Text can be made less difficult for a reader, or more accessible, through the intervention of the teacher. A teacher can support both the reader and the text by accessing or providing background experiences, discussing concepts, introducing critical terms, encouraging prediction, discussing, questioning, and using the many other instructional strategies that support success.

Other important environmental factors include these:

- A classroom in which reading is treasured and celebrated leads children to read more. A teacher who models his or her own pleasure in reading helps children see that making sense of print is worth doing.

- Children who come from a home that values reading have the additional advantage of support for reading both at school and at home.

Readability Formulas

Given the complexity of the readability factors we just outlined, and the fact that you can't measure most of them or adjust instruction for each child based on individual constellations of factors, it isn't surprising that educators have wanted an easy, quick way to measure the difficulty of text as well as a way to measure the ability of the child.

As early as the 1920s (Klare, 1988), efforts were made to develop a **readability formula** that educators could apply to text to determine how "hard" the text was. Since then, many formulas have been developed. They differ slightly from one another, but all are based on counting certain features of the text and converting the resulting numbers to a grade level.

Recently other ways of leveling text from "easy" to "hard" have been used that do not necessarily use a grade-level designation. We discussed such methods in Chapter 4. Here we want to give you some background on readability formulas so that you will understand them when you encounter them.

Features of Readability Formulas

Readability formulas are based on this assumption: long sentences with hard words are more difficult than short sentences with easy (or short) words. More specifically, the formulas commonly rely on two features: syntax (the sentence structure) and semantics (the words).

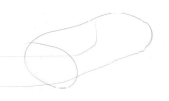

The difficulty of the syntax is usually measured by sentence length; that is, the longer the sentence, the harder it is to read. The difficulty of the semantics is measured in one of two ways. With some formulas, words are checked against a given list of high-frequency words, that is, words that occur so often in print that you would expect a reader at a certain level to recognize them. For other formulas, words are counted as "hard" depending on their length, often as measured by the number of syllables. The presumption is that words with more than one syllable are harder than one-syllable words.

While most educators acknowledge the importance of other factors related to text difficulty, such as those mentioned earlier, as well as factors related to the reader and to the environment, no one has found a consistent, reliable way to measure these abstract factors.

Examples of Readability Formulas

The professional literature contains dozens of formulas and hundreds of references related to readability. One of the first published formulas, and perhaps the easiest to use, is the Fry Readability Formula, first published in 1968 and used widely ever since. It is based on the average sentence length and average syllable count of three 100-word samples from different places in a selection. The averages are plotted on a graph that shows the approximate grade level of the material. (This graph, and step-by-step instructions for using it, appear in the Resource File at the end of the book.) The Fry formula is meant to provide a quick way to judge the approximate grade level of a selection when you have no other information.

Different formulas may yield different results (Klare, 1995). For example, we used three different readability formulas (Fry, 1968; Harris & Jacobson, 1982; Spache, 1953) to check the readability of several books. Notice the variability in the scores (grade-level difficulty) for the following two books:

	Fry	Harris-Jacobson	Spache
The Paper Crane by Molly Bang (1987)	5.0	5.2	3.2
A Bicycle for Rosaura by Daniel Barbot (1990)	4.0	5.4	2.9

This variability doesn't necessarily mean you should not use a readability formula. Rather, it means you should be cautious about relying on the results.

Computer programs are also available for doing readability calculations; two sources for such programs are listed in For Exploration: Electronic Resources at the end of this chapter.

Specially Written and Rewritten Material

Published reading programs sometimes include selections especially written for the beginning reader. These selections are meant to capture children's interest in terms of content and to match the reading development of the beginning reader. Selections may be especially crafted to provide extensive practice with certain words or with certain decoding elements the beginning readers are learning. The rationale for such specially written materials is that readers will more successfully build fluency and confidence when the text challenges they meet are controlled. These materials are frequently called *decodable texts,* a term we have used in earlier chapters.

Trade books that delight young children as read-alouds may present insurmountable difficulties when used as independent reading material for children who are not yet fluent readers. Therefore, publishers may sometimes edit these stories to make the text conform to a certain readability level. That is, they choose a story that seems just right for a certain grade level or age in terms of appeal and content and apply a formula to sample passages. If the selection is found to be "too difficult" for the chosen grade level, long sentences may be broken into shorter sentences, one-syllable words substituted for polysyllabic words, and "hard" words—those not on a given list—replaced with synonyms that are on the list.

In this way, it is possible to adjust a book's readability down to the desired grade level. Yet much may be lost when this is done, not the least being the original language of the author. In addition, breaking up long sentences into shorter ones may reduce the average sentence length but actually result in text that is harder to understand. Consider the following example from *The Wonderful Wizard of Oz* (Baum, 1900/1990):

> Original text: *But it is a long way to the Emerald City, and it will take you many days. The country here is rich and pleasant, but you must go through rough and dangerous places before you reach the end of your journey.*

> Simplified text: *It is a long way to the Emerald City. It will take you many days. The country here is rich and nice. You must go through hard places before you get there.*

As you can see with this short example, breaking long sentences into several shorter ones loses the connecting words that make the relationship between ideas clear to the reader. In this case, because publishers don't like to begin a sentence with the word *but* in material for young children, the contrast between ideas is lost. The passage becomes just a series of short, unconnected declarative sentences. The reader has to make several inferences about how the ideas are related. The result is a loss of clarity as well as a loss of the beauty of the language, which is even further damaged by the substitution of "easier" words. Sadly, the effort to edit a wonderful story to change its readability often results in a story that is no longer worth reading at all.

Joint Statement of the IRA and NCTE

In 1984, the International Reading Association (IRA) and the National Council of Teachers of English (NCTE) issued a joint statement that continues to provide guidance in estimating difficulty. In this statement, the two organizations summarize the factors influencing reading difficulty, many of which we have already addressed, and the problems with reducing the issue of difficulty to a formula. They then suggest the use of three alternative procedures:

1. Teacher judgment of proposed textual material
2. Observation of children using the material
3. Checklists that address such things as student interests, text graphics, new concepts, line length, and so forth.

In essence, the IRA and NCTE urge educators *not* to rely on readability formulas alone for making choices about material. The procedures for leveling books discussed in Chapter 4 reflect the principles of this joint statement.

Some Final Comments on Readability

We believe you should take published readability levels with the proverbial grain of salt, knowing they have been determined through the use of at least one formula and remembering that they are based on limited factors. Keep in mind all the other factors affecting readability that a formula does not take into account.

Short sentences are not necessarily easier than long ones. Consider the often-quoted "To be, or not to be" from Shakespeare's *Hamlet*. This is a short sentence made up of easy words, but what first grader could possibly understand what those words mean? Similarly, long words are not necessarily harder: consider the long names of dinosaurs that very young children learn with delight because they are interested.

The most helpful information about a book is not necessarily a number resulting from a formula. We suggest that you pay attention to the other ways books are being leveled, as described in Chapter 4. Moreover, we think you can learn to rely on your own good sense in judging appropriate books for your students. Use a given readability level if you think you must (or figure the readability yourself), but then use your common sense along with your knowledge about children in general and your children in particular.

Don't sacrifice a wonderful book because a formula says it will be too hard for the child. Instead, if the book is exactly right for the child in all respects except for the difficulty level, make it work by reading it aloud to the child, providing more support before reading, or doing shared or choral reading.

By the same token, a wonderful story is never "too easy" in our view. We acknowledge that for growth to occur there must be challenge, but a book that a child finds easy and interesting provides a pleasurable, successful reading experience and builds fluency as well as adding to the child's confidence, leading to what all teachers have always wanted: children who not only can read but choose to do so.

Measuring the Reader

Imagine it is the beginning of the school year. You are facing a room full of children and wondering how you can possibly meet the needs of each one when you don't know anything about them yet, except possibly scores from standardized tests given to them the previous year. You are aware of the limitations of scores from standardized reading tests (you will learn about these in Chapter 11); you know those figures won't help you make instructional decisions regarding strengths and needs. You might know which books the child (presumably) read the previous year, but not how successfully, or how much was forgotten during the vacation.

You are reluctant to simply put the grade-level book into everyone's hands and assume everyone will be able to read it. Yet how can you know which book to put in the hands of which child? How can you begin to plan lessons? What do you do? It can be an overwhelming feeling even for experienced teachers.

For kindergarten and first grade, we recommend that you simply ask which children can already read. Tell those children to select a book to read to you. Arrange for an aide, a volunteer, or an upper-grade student to be in your classroom for an hour or two each day for the first two weeks of the school year. During that time, hold an individual conference with each child. Be observant, and don't forget that you may have a child who can read quite competently but is reluctant to tell you so for one reason or another. You may also have some who say they can already read but in fact are clearly at the Emergent Literacy stage, just beginning to recognize a few words here and there. However, if a child is already reading fluently, you will want to assess his or her ability further.

From second grade on (or with younger children who are already reading), we recommend that you assess each child using an informal reading inventory. In this section we will discuss the informal reading inventory, as well as some word recognition tests and considerations related to diverse populations.

Instead of using an informal reading inventory to determine a student's reading grade level, some teachers now use an instrument such as the *Developmental Reading Assessment (DRA)* (Beaver, 1997). The DRA uses a series of little books that have been leveled in terms of difficulty on the basis of language and story structure, concepts, vocabulary, pictures, layout, print size, and other factors. Running records and retelling procedures are used for the lower levels; silent reading and retelling are used at higher levels.

The Informal Reading Inventory

An **informal reading inventory (IRI)** is an individually administered instrument designed to sample a child's reading on passages that are graduated in difficulty from very easy to more difficult. Accuracy in word recognition and comprehension are both taken into account. This instrument is designed to give you initial estimates of both placement and diagnostic information.

To do an informal reading inventory, you will need about thirty to forty-five minutes for each child. During this time, the other children can be monitored by another adult or engage in independent work. If you have thirty children and administer an informal reading inventory to three children each day, you will have finished your class in two weeks.

Background and Development of the IRI

In the early 1900s, reading was assessed mostly by judging oral reading accuracy. Later, professionals recognized that comprehension must be measured also. Recognizing that reading comprises both oral fluency and comprehension was a huge step in understanding the many factors that impinge on a reader's success. Professionals wrestled with issues such as standards, what is reasonable to expect at certain ages, how much variation is normal among children of the same age, and what physical behaviors might indicate trouble.

In 1946, Emmett Betts contributed concepts about assessing reading ability that continue to have influence to this day. He believed that standardized tests tend to place students in material that is too difficult for them. According to Betts (1946/1957), readers have three **reading levels:**

Independent: The level at which children are able to read fluently without assistance and with virtually full comprehension

Instructional: The level at which children are able to read capably with good guidance and instruction

Frustration: The level at which children are incapable of either fluent oral reading or good comprehension, regardless of the teacher's skill

Betts used specific percentages of word/recognition accuracy and comprehension as indicators of each of these levels.

At first, teachers made up their own informal reading inventories using passages from classroom reading books. Today there are many published inventories. (Several are listed in For Additional Reading.) Virtually all are based on Betts's original concept, though extensive refinements have been made. For instance, the first published IRIs assessed reading only through grade 6; today some IRIs have passages through grade 12. Each published inventory explains in detail both its debt to Betts's original concept and its own rationale for content, procedures, and percentages.

Recent authors of informal reading inventories take great care in selecting graded passages and devising questions that reflect the changing view of reading. Many adjustments have also occurred regarding the original percentages proposed by Betts. Some IRIs suggest using one form of the graded passages to assess a child's **listening level,** that is, the level of material the child can comprehend when not having to deal with the print. In addition, most inventories now suggest ways to analyze a child's reading in terms of word recognition and comprehension.

Responding to the widespread use of IRIs, most published reading programs now provide some kind of inventory to help place the student in the appropriate level of material. They may also provide diagnostic assessments related to specific aspects of word recognition and comprehension.

Several sources for information about the history and theoretical framework of IRIs, as well as controversies about this widely used assessment technique, are listed in For Additional Reading.

Reading and Listening Levels and Percentages

The following list gives some typical definitions and percentages for the different reading levels, conforming to Betts's original criteria. Published inventories may deviate somewhat from these percentages, but an explanation of the percentages and their rationale will be found in the manual of each published inventory.

- *Independent reading level.* This is the highest level the child can be presumed to read accurately and with good understanding without assistance. This is an appropriate level for homework assignments and for pleasure reading. The typical percentages for defining this level are 99 percent word recognition (no more than 1 significant error in 100 words) and 90 percent comprehension. Also, reading should be smooth, free of signs of anxiety or stress, and fluent. Teacher judgment must be used in some cases about which miscues are significant—that is, which miscues "count." For example, substituting *a* for *the* is not usually considered significant.

- *Instructional reading level.* This is the highest level the child can read with teacher guidance and support. When this level is used for instructional activities, you can expect growth in reading ability. The student is challenged but not frustrated. Difficulties are dealt with through appropriate instruction, and the child feels he or she can read the material with the teacher's help. Word recognition accuracy should be 95 percent (no more than 5 significant miscues in 100 words). Comprehension should be at least 75 percent (fewer than three questions missed out of ten).

- *Frustration reading level.* This is the level of material the student should not be asked to use for anything. When material is at a child's frustration level, he or she is having so much trouble with word recognition or comprehension that learning is not possible. This results in the child's feeling incompetent, which compounds the difficulty. Overt behaviors may include finger pointing, squirming, squinting, word-by-word reading, and lack of expression. The typical percentages are less than 90 percent for word recognition (more than 10 words missed out of 100) and less than 50 percent for comprehension.

- *Listening level.* This is the highest level at which the student can understand material read to him or her. The criterion is at least 75 percent comprehension (70 percent in some inventories). If a child can understand material of a certain level, you can assume she or he has sufficient vocabulary and background experience to handle the material. If, therefore, the child is unable to *read* material at that level, there should be a potential for reading growth with appropriate instruction.

Later in this chapter, we discuss how to deal with scores that do not fall neatly into the given percentages, such as 99 percent word recognition but only 60 percent comprehension.

Variations in IRI Percentages

The upper portion of Table 10.1 sums up the typical IRI percentages based on Betts's criteria. It has been suggested, though, that at the lower grade levels, a lower word recognition percentage should be tolerated because these children are just beginning to read (Clay, 1985). The lower portion of Table 10.1, based on the

Table 10.1
Informal Reading Inventory Criteria

	Word Recognition		Comprehension
Original criteria (Betts)			
Independent	99%+	*and*	90%+
Instructional	95%+	*and*	75%+
Frustration	Less than 90%	*or*	Less than 50%
Revised criteria (Burns & Roe, 1999)			
Independent	99% or higher	*and*	90% or higher
Instructional			
Grades 1–2	85% or higher	*and*	75% or higher
Grades 3–12	95% or higher	*and*	75% or higher
Frustration			
Grades 1–2	Below 85%	*or*	Below 50%
Grades 3–12	Below 90%	*or*	Below 50%

IRI published by Burns and Roe (1999), reflects such an adjustment. In the Burns and Roe version, the word recognition expectation is lower for grades 1 and 2 at the instructional level.

If you use a published IRI, the percentages you encounter will be dictated by the particular publication chosen. When making your choice, it is wise to read the introductory material and the author's rationale for the percentages.

Generally, despite the variations, we are comfortable using the Betts criteria coupled with common sense. Remember, the suggested percentages are just guidelines to help you estimate a child's reading levels. Rigid application of the numbers is never wise. As you will see later, percentages are only part of the picture an IRI yields.

Components of the IRI

All IRIs are made up of the same basic components:

- *Graded word lists.* These are sample lists of words at each grade level, beginning with preprimer and going up to the highest-graded passage covered by the particular IRI. Some teachers use these lists to judge which passage to have the child read first. Some teachers analyze errors from these lists to see which parts of words the child seems to miss most often.

- *Graded passages.* These are passages of text beginning with the preprimer level and proceeding up. Some go to grade 6; some continue to much higher grades. Comprehension questions and sometimes a retelling guide are provided for each passage. Most published inventories provide at least two equivalent sets of passages, and often more. Some include one set of narrative passages and one set of expository material. Some include a set of longer passages for alternate use. These multiple sets of passages allow a number of options:

  One set (or form) can be used to assess oral reading (word recognition in context) and comprehension, while another set is used for silent reading comprehension.
  One set can be used at one time and another at a later time to assess growth.
  One set can be used to estimate a child's listening level.

- *Summaries and analyses.* These include various ways to record and analyze a child's performance after administration of the inventory. These may include:

  A summary form to pull all information together.
  A method for analyzing a child's miscues or errors.
  A method for analyzing the types of comprehension questions missed, comparing comprehension on oral passages with comprehension of passages read silently and considering reading performance in light of listening level.

The following sections discuss these IRI components in more detail and offer illustrations of each. The sample forms we will use are from Johns's *Basic Reading Inventory* (1997), listed in For Additional Reading at the end of the chapter.

IRI Procedures

Each published informal reading inventory provides extensive, detailed steps for administering, scoring, and analyzing performance. Although there are many differences, the basic steps are similar:

1 *Decide what level of passage to have the child read first.*

- We recommend starting one year below the child's grade placement for children in grades 1 and 2 and two years below for children in grade 3 and up.
- Alternatively, to estimate which passage the child should read first, you can administer the graded word lists. The graded word lists usually have twenty words each. The lists are duplicated for you to mark on and can be photocopied for such purposes without permission. Figure 10.2 shows a sample graded word list. The procedures for using word lists may vary from one IRI to another, but the following sequence is typical:

    Have the child read the words on the list quickly.
    Mark + or ✓ if read correctly. If a word is incorrect, write what the child said.
    Have the child return to the missed words and try to figure them out.
    Credit all words read correctly plus all those the child reads correctly when given time to analyze the word.
    Have the child begin reading the passages at the highest grade level on which he or she read nineteen or twenty words fluently on the graded word list.

2 *Present the first graded passage from one form. (Usually the first form to be used is called Form A.)*

- You may be told to introduce the passage in some way, perhaps by asking the child to predict on the basis of the title. This procedure helps to check for prior knowledge.
- The child is told to read aloud. The child reads from a page with only the passage on it. You have a copy with the passage, the comprehension questions, and other information.
- You mark every deviation from the exact text, using the marking system presented in the IRI or one you already know, such as the one we presented in Chapter 3 (Figure 3.1, page 63). The passages and accompanying questions are available for you to photocopy for your marking purposes. Figure 10.3 shows a sample of a marked form.
- A variation of this procedure calls for having children above grade 3 first read the passage silently and then read it aloud as you mark miscues. This reduces the amount of time needed for administration to about twenty to thirty minutes per child (since you do not use separate oral and silent reading forms). This procedure is more like classroom reading tasks, in which silent reading typically precedes oral reading with older children. Though we recommend this variation, you should feel free to use the procedure of oral reading at sight for older children who exhibit many word recognition

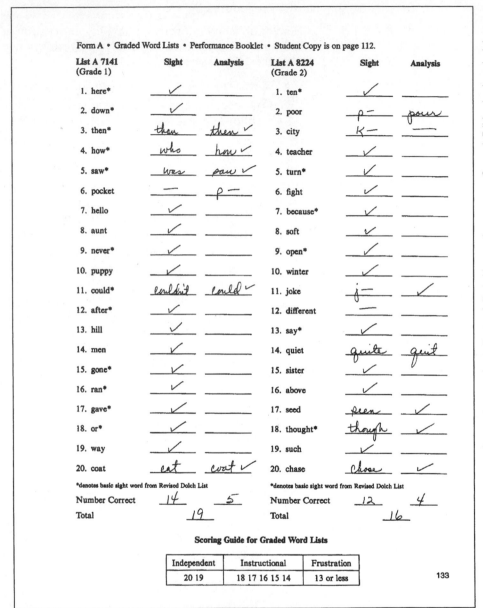

**Figure 10.2
Sample Graded Word List
(Johns, 1997).
(Note: The "Scoring Guide
for Graded Word Lists"
shown at the bottom is not
an indication of actual reading level.)**

problems. This may provide more useful insights into the word recognition processes the child uses with unfamiliar material.

• As you are listening to the child read and marking miscues, you also record observations of the child's behavior, such as fidgeting, word-by-word reading, long pauses, nervousness, frequent requests to be told the word, and other indications of attitude and mood. Some teachers return to passages

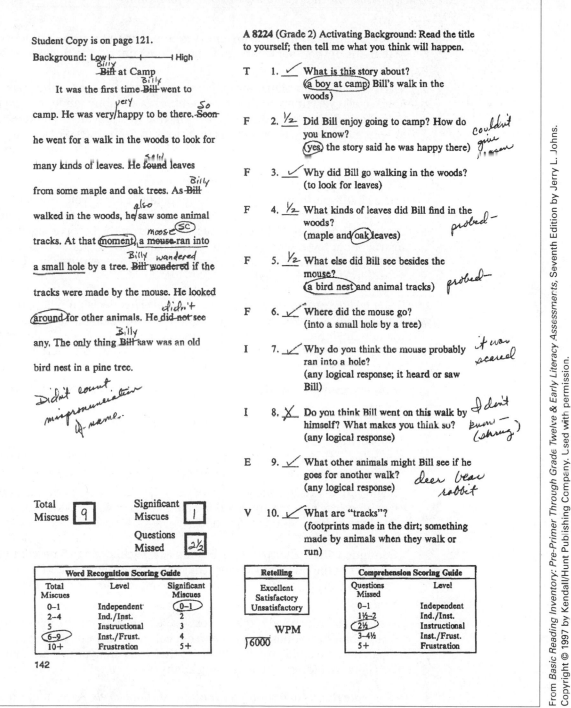

Student Copy is on page 121.

Background: Low |———|———| High

Billy
~~Bill~~ at Camp

Billy
It was the first time ~~Bill~~ went to

very
camp. He was very/happy to be there. *So* ~~Soon~~

he went for a walk in the woods to look for

smell
many kinds of leaves. He ~~found~~ leaves

Billy
from some maple and oak trees. As ~~Bill~~

also
walked in the woods, he/saw some animal

moose (SC)
tracks. At that ⟨moment⟩ a ~~mouse~~ ran into

Billy *wandered*
a small hole by a tree. ~~Bill~~ ~~wondered~~ if the

tracks were made by the mouse. He looked

didn't
⟨around⟩ for other animals. He ~~did not~~ see

Billy
any. The only thing ~~Bill~~ saw was an old

bird nest in a pine tree.

*Didn't count
mispronunciation
of name.*

Total Miscues: 9

Significant Miscues: 1

Questions Missed: 2½

Word Recognition Scoring Guide

Total Miscues	Level	Significant Miscues
0–1	Independent	⟨0–1⟩
2–4	Ind./Inst.	2
5	Instructional	3
⟨6–9⟩	Inst./Frust.	4
10+	Frustration	5+

142

A 8224 (Grade 2) Activating Background: Read the title to yourself; then tell me what you think will happen.

T 1. ✓ What is this story about?
⟨a boy at camp⟩ Bill's walk in the woods)

F 2. ½ Did Bill enjoy going to camp? How do you know?
⟨yes⟩ the story said he was happy there) *couldn't give reason*

F 3. ✓ Why did Bill go walking in the woods?
(to look for leaves)

F 4. ½ What kinds of leaves did Bill find in the woods?
(maple and ⟨oak⟩ leaves) *probed*

F 5. ½ What else did Bill see besides the mouse?
⟨a bird nest⟩ and animal tracks) *probed*

F 6. ✓ Where did the mouse go?
(into a small hole by a tree)

I 7. ✓ Why do you think the mouse probably ran into a hole?
(any logical response; it heard or saw Bill) *it was scared*

I 8. ✗ Do you think Bill went on this walk by himself? What makes you think so?
(any logical response) *I don't know — (shrug)*

E 9. ✓ What other animals might Bill see if he goes for another walk?
(any logical response) *deer bear rabbit*

V 10. ✓ What are "tracks"?
(footprints made in the dirt; something made by animals when they walk or run)

Retelling

Excellent
Satisfactory
Unsatisfactory

WPM

6000‾

Comprehension Scoring Guide

Questions Missed	Level
0–1	Independent
1½–2	Ind./Inst.
⟨2½⟩	Instructional
3–4½	Inst./Frust.
5+	Frustration

Figure 10.3
Sample Marked IRI Passage (Johns, 1997)

when administration of the inventory is complete to probe for students' explanations of their behaviors. You may or may not decide this is worth the time it takes.

- After the child completes the passage, you remove it and either have the child retell everything he or she remembers (a retelling guide may be provided) or ask the questions (usually ten) that are provided. The questions are often labeled by type, such as questions on topic, fact, vocabulary, and so forth. Note the child's responses and the examiner's notes shown in Figure 10.3; the examiner has circled or recorded what the child said and has given half-credit for three questions.

- If the child's performance is at the independent level, you proceed to the next higher grade level and continue until the child's performance falls to the frustration level. If the child's performance on the first passage is at the instructional level, you go back to passages for lower grades to determine the child's independent reading level; then you proceed upward until the frustration level is reached.

3 *Decide whether to administer any other form.* This decision will depend on what you feel you need to know. We do not recommend spending any more time administering an IRI than is necessary for you to begin to plan appropriate instruction. However, you may occasionally make one of the following choices:

- Administer another form to measure comprehension when the child reads silently.

- Administer a form with expository material rather than narrative (if available).

- Administer one form as a listening-level assessment. For this, the procedures may vary from one inventory to another, but they are basically as follows:

  Begin with a passage one year lower than the child's instructional level.
  Introduce the passage and ask the child to predict about the content.
  Read the passage aloud to the child.
  Ask the questions.
  Continue with higher passages as long as the child gets 75 percent (or 70 percent) of the questions correct (misses three or fewer out of ten). When the score falls below this level (the child misses four or more questions), stop.

The child's listening level is the highest grade level at which he or she missed no more than three questions (70 percent comprehension). This level is then compared to the child's reading levels so that you can hypothesize about the child's potential for growth in reading ability.

4 *Transfer the results to a summary sheet to estimate levels.* A sample summary sheet is shown in Figure 10.4 in the next section.

5 *Analyze the results, using factors such as types of miscues and categories of comprehension questions.* Later in this chapter, we will discuss procedures for this kind of analysis.

Estimating Levels

When you transfer results to a summary sheet, you have data from each marked passage the child has read. You record the number of miscues or questions missed, along with the associated levels for word recognition and for comprehension of orally read passages. You also include comprehension results from silently read passages if you have them. Most summary sheets also provide a place for various other information related to performance, such as listening level, most prevalent type of word recognition error, and rate (if you timed the readings).

Then you look at the total picture of reading performance and estimate the child's three reading levels. If scores fall neatly into the given percentage ranges, your job is easy. Usually, however, the outcome isn't neat, and you have to make a decision. Look, for example, at Figure 10.4, which shows a summary sheet for Gordon, a fourth-grade student. How would you determine his reading levels?

From the first day of school, Gordon's teacher was concerned about his reading. Hence she did not follow her usual procedure of having the student read the same passage twice, first silently and then orally. Instead, she followed the procedure for a younger child, using separate passages for oral reading and silent reading, as indicated by the separate columns on the summary sheet. She suspected that Gordon's needs justified the additional time required.

To estimate this student's reading levels, we will use not only the summary of miscues and comprehension questions missed but also the additional information related to attitude and behavior recorded in the box labeled "General Observations." This information comes from notes the teacher made during the administration of the inventory. Notice, too, these other features of the summary page in Figure 10.4:

- The grade levels, from preprimer (PP) to grade 12, are listed down the left side of the form.

- This particular sheet records the number of miscues and the number of questions missed, not the percentages. In the following discussion, though, we will refer to the percentages as well.

- Although the teacher will have marked all miscues for later analysis, only significant miscues are counted for the purpose of figuring reading levels. **Significant miscues** are miscues that were not self-corrected and that affect syntax or semantics, resulting in a loss or change of meaning.

- When a score falls between two levels, this fact is indicated with a slash mark; for example, "Ind/Inst" means the child's score fell between the independent and the instructional level.

We estimate Gordon's reading levels to be as follows:

> Independent   grade 1
> Instructional   grades 2–3
> Frustration   grade 4

The following sections explain these choices.

Independent Reading Level. Gordon's independent level is not immediately clear. While his word recognition was at the independent level through grade 1,

Seventh Edition

BASIC READING INVENTORY PERFORMANCE BOOKLET

A Oral Reading

Jerry L. Johns
Northern Illinois University

Student GORDON Grade 4 Sex (M) F Date of Test ____

School ____ Examiner ____ Date of Birth ____

Address ____ Current Book/Level ____ Age 9

SUMMARY OF STUDENT'S READING PERFORMANCE

Grade	Word Recognition: Isolation (Word Lists) Sight	Analysis	Total	Level	Context (Passages) Miscues	Level	Comprehension: Oral Reading Form A Questions Missed	Level	Silent Reading Form B Questions Missed	Level
PP									1	Ind
P					0	Ind	1	Ind	2½	Inst
1					0	Ind	3	Inst/FR	4	Inst/FR
2					2	Ind/Inst	2	Ind/Inst	1	Ind
3					4	Ind/Inst	0	Ind	5	FR
4					5	Inst	4	Inst/FR		
5					15	FR	6	FR		
6										
7										
8										
9										
10										
11										
12										

SIGNIFICANT

ESTIMATE OF READING LEVELS

Independent 1 Instructional 2-3 Frustration 4

LISTENING LEVEL

Form ____

Grade	Questions Missed	Level
PP		
P		
1		
2	0	
3	3	
4	2	
5	3 ←	
6	5	
7		
8		

ESTIMATED LEVEL: 5

GENERAL OBSERVATIONS

Oral—
Reading is flat-monotone
Made a "yuck" face at Gr 1—said story was babyish
GR 3- volunteered info about bears
GR 4- liked story
GR 5- tired—wanted to stop

Silent—
Squirmy during GR. 1—asked for break right after
GR 2—100% but said "Can we quit now?"
GR 3- seemed almost determined not to answer questions.
Despite behavior—attitude positive. He wants to be a better reader.

INFORMAL MISCUE ANALYSIS SUMMARY

Types of Miscues	Frequency of Occurrence: Seldom	Sometimes	Frequently	General Impact of Miscues on Meaning: No Change	Little Change	Much Change
Substitutions						
Insertions						
Omissions						
Reversals						
Repetitions						

Figure 10.4
Sample Results from an Informal Reading Inventory of a Fourth Grader (Johns, 1997)

his comprehension at grade 1 was only 70 percent ("Inst/Fr") for the oral passage and 60 percent (again "Inst/Fr") for the silent passage. However, his comprehension scores on higher-level passages were higher: his oral passage comprehension was 100 percent at grade 3 (zero questions missed), and his silent passage comprehension was 90 percent (only one question missed) at grade 2.

Several things could account for this inconsistency:

- Gordon may have thought the grade 1 oral story was "babyish."
- The syntax of the preprimer and primer passages is so unlike natural speech that it may have inhibited his comprehension.
- He may have been unused to silent reading.
- He asked for a bathroom break right after the grade 1 silent passage (as noted in the General Observations) and probably was uncomfortable as he read it.

Considering that Gordon is in fourth grade, that his word recognition is independent at grade 1, and that his comprehension is independent at the third-grade level for oral passages and at the second-grade level for silent passages, we think you could assign him grade 1 material for independent reading to begin with. You might very well find that he can handle higher-level material when he is focused, interested, and not being assessed.

At the same time, you would plan to provide instruction in silent reading strategies and metacognition. Remember that this is just an estimate—a way to begin. As you actually begin work, you might find that you under- or overestimated Gordon's independent reading level. Then you would adjust up or down as needed.

Frustration Reading Level.   Having estimated at what level a child can work independently, we next like to determine the frustration level—the level at which you never want to put the student. For Gordon, we would say grade 4. Why? Although his word recognition was still at the instructional level at grade 4, his comprehension was not so strong: on the oral passages his comprehension bordered on the frustration level at grade 4, and on the silent reading passages he was at the frustration level at grade 3.

Consulting our notes on the grade 3 silent reading passage (not shown in the figure), we recall that Gordon simply shrugged when asked the three questions that called for inference or judgment. This, coupled with his forgetting a detail (where the first steam engine was built) and his inability to articulate a definition of *steam,* added up to five questions missed out of ten—clearly the frustration level. However, it may turn out that he is reluctant to venture a response unless he is absolutely sure of being right. This could account for his shrugging and not responding to the questions that had no clear right-or-wrong answers. With encouragement, he may comprehend better than the numbers indicate.

Most work in the fourth grade, Gordon's current grade, requires strong comprehension and silent reading. A frustration level of grade 4 means that Gordon cannot be expected to learn well from grade-level material. For subjects such as science and social studies, Gordon needs easier materials on the same topics, both for instruction and for independent work. If such materials are not available, he will need extraordinary support to learn from the grade-level materials. For example, he may need to listen to the material read aloud, or he made need elaborate study guides or the help of a study buddy. He will need additional prereading instruction to build concepts and teach new vocabulary, as well as more guidance during silent reading, with the text broken into small, meaningful chunks.

During the Core Books block, as we discussed in Chapters 7 through 9, the teacher will provide additional support and vary the participation elicited from students depending on their ability. With this help, Gordon will be able to participate in a discussion even if the material is a bit too challenging for him.

Instructional Reading Level.   Developmentally appropriate books for Gordon will be those at his instructional level, which falls between the independent and frustration levels. Often the instructional level involves a range, as it does for Gordon. Since his independent level is grade 1 and his frustration level grade 4, his instructional level is grades 2 to 3.

Instruction should begin with second-grade material. At that grade level, Gordon's word recognition is strong (just 1 percent below the independent criterion), and his comprehension is also strong on both oral and silent passages. With grade 2 materials, Gordon will not need to struggle with word recognition or comprehension and will probably quickly build fluency, stronger comprehension, and self-confidence. He will probably soon move on to grade 3 materials.

Taking into account Gordon's positive attitude (see the last comment in the General Observations) and his listening level of grade 5, which shows his ability to deal with higher-level concepts and language, there is every reason to believe he will make rapid growth when instructed with materials at the appropriate level.

Remember, the reason for giving an IRI is to permit a quick estimate of a child's reading ability in order to begin appropriate instruction. As you begin to teach, you may find you need to make an adjustment almost immediately. From then on, you will use the kinds of observational informal assessments discussed in earlier chapters.

Analyzing Miscues and Comprehension

Using information from the IRI, you may want to do a detailed analysis of the student's miscues and comprehension. Often published informal reading inventories provide a method for summarizing and analyzing miscues and responses to various kinds of questions as well as information to help you interpret your analysis and use it to inform instruction.

Keep in mind as you read about such analyses that you must be cautious about drawing conclusions based on scanty evidence. You use IRI information, which you acquire early in your work with a child, to draw tentative conclusions on which to base instructional plans. As new evidence occurs during instruction, you will continually revise your conclusions.

Miscues.   As you know, a miscue is any oral response to print that differs from the actual print—saying something else instead of exactly what is on the page. Everyone miscues occasionally, even you! If your miscue doesn't upset your ability to construct meaning, you probably read right on without being aware of having miscued. To return to the example mentioned earlier, if you substitute *a* for *the,*

the meaning is not affected significantly and you read on. If you substitute *want* for *went,* the meaning is lost and you probably catch yourself and self-correct. If you substitute *emerge* for *immerge,* you may or may not know that you've miscued, depending on whether you know the difference between the two words.

Educators used to talk about mistakes or errors. But the concept of "miscue" is a better one. It suggests that when a reader's oral response isn't a perfect match for the print, it is because the reader has not paid attention to all the cues in the print: the meaning of the passage, the parts of the word, the graphic symbols and their associated sounds, the punctuation, and so forth. Looking closely at a reader's miscues may give us a hint about the mysterious, unobservable processes one uses to make sense of print.

Although the principles for analyzing miscues are fairly standard, there is some variation in procedures from one IRI to another, and you will want to follow the instructions in the manual that comes with your chosen IRI. Some manuals direct you to analyze only the miscues that occur during the reading of the passages (not the word lists) and only those that occur in passages at the independent or instructional level for word recognition. Not everyone agrees on the latter point; some IRIs have you analyze miscues from all passages attempted.

Reading specialists who limit analysis to the independent and instructional levels suggest that when a reader struggles with material at the frustration level, the miscues may not be typical. For example, the reader may begin to guess wildly, miscall words that were read accurately on an earlier passage, or ignore word recognition strategies that he or she would usually use. All this is often accompanied by physical indications of frustration such as sweating, fidgeting, finger pointing, word-by-word reading, losing one's place, and so forth. In other words, little may be learned by analyzing miscues that occur when a reader is frustrated.

Procedures for Analyzing Miscues. Recall that when we counted miscues for the purposes of figuring percentages and estimating reading levels, we focused only on significant miscues, those that resulted in loss of meaning. For purposes of analysis, however, we use *all* miscues, including those that were self-corrected and those that were not counted as significant (such as *house* for *home*).

The first step is to look at each oral reading passage and transfer the miscues and the corresponding text to the summary sheet. Figure 10.5 shows an example of a child's miscues recorded on the appropriate form for the *Basic Reading Inventory* (Johns, 1997). Detailed instructions are given in the manual; our discussion here is meant only to give you an idea of how such an analysis is done.

Next, you examine each miscue in terms of each of several qualities. For example, the "Graphic Similarity" columns ask you to compare the miscue (what the child said) with the text (what is on the page) in terms of letters at the beginning, middle, and end of the word. The "Context" columns ask that you judge whether a miscue was "acceptable in context," which requires that you refer to the passage in which the miscue occurred. There is also a place to record which "unacceptable in context" miscues were self-corrected by the child. The coding in Figure 10.5 uses a check mark if the category applies to a particular miscue, a dash if it does not, and an X if the child did not attempt to say the word. The check marks in each column are then added to produce the totals at the bottom of the form. We have

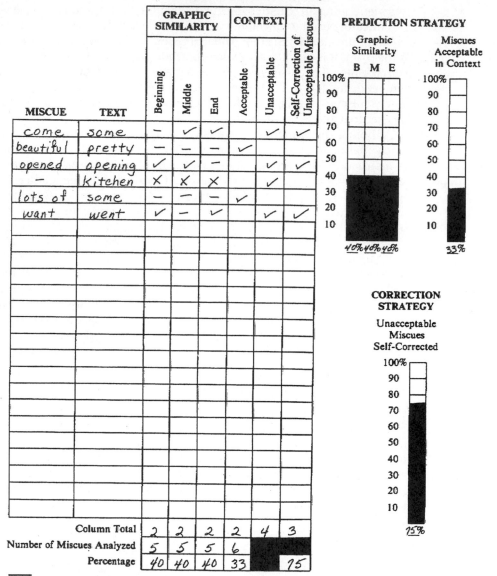

Qualitative Summary of Miscues on the Basic Reading Inventory

Jerry L. Johns
Northern Illinois University

MISCUE	TEXT	GRAPHIC SIMILARITY			CONTEXT		Self-Correction of Unacceptable Miscues
		Beginning	Middle	End	Acceptable	Unacceptable	
come	some	—	✓	✓		✓	✓
beautiful	pretty	—	—	—	✓		
opened	opening	✓	✓	—		✓	✓
—	kitchen	✗	✗	✗		✓	
lots of	some	—	—	—	✓		
want	went	✓	—	✓		✓	✓
Column Total		2	2	2	2	4	3
Number of Miscues Analyzed		5	5	5	6		3
Percentage		40	40	40	33		15

PREDICTION STRATEGY

Graphic Similarity
B M E

40% 40% 40%

Miscues Acceptable in Context

33%

CORRECTION STRATEGY

Unacceptable Miscues Self-Corrected

15%

Figure 10.5
Sample Miscue Summary, Basic Reading Inventory (Johns, 1997)

done the arithmetic, the procedures for which are provided in the manual. The column totals are then transferred to the graphs at the right of the form.

The Prediction Strategy, shown at the right of Figure 10.5, has two parts. The "Graphic Similarity" graphs show whether the child relied more heavily on one part of the word than another and to what extent. The "Miscues Acceptable in Context" graph shows instantly what percentage of miscues analyzed did not result in loss of meaning. A comparison of these two graphs may (we realize we may be overgeneralizing) show something helpful in terms of planning instruction. For example, high graphic similarity and low acceptability in context might mean that a child relies on phonics to the exclusion of what makes sense. The "Correction Strategy" graph at the lower right of Figure 10.5 helps you see at a glance whether a child frequently recognizes when meaning is lost and self-corrects.

Interpretation of Miscues. How might you interpret the information in Figure 10.5? The pattern of this child's miscues reveals several bits of information that could help you make instructional plans:

- The percentages of graphic similarity were low for all parts of the words, indicating that the child pays little attention to the letters on the page.
- A third of the miscues did not result in a loss of meaning; in those cases, the child's substitutions fit the story. This child often seems to say the word he expects in terms of meaning, and if it works, he reads on.
- Of the miscues that did result in loss of meaning, 75 percent were self-corrected. Meaning is clearly of highest priority for this child. The only miscue not self-corrected was "kitchen," a word he refused to attempt.
- Despite the strengths of self-correction and acceptable miscues, this child needs to pay closer attention to the words on the page. This will be increasingly important as he reads more factual material in social studies and science texts.

For this child, a good instructional strategy would be to let him practice reading into a tape recorder and then assess himself. This would help him become more aware of accuracy. You would not want to make him so self-conscious, however, that he lost his very real strength in constructing meaning.

Table 10.2 shows examples of what might have been learned about other children through the analysis of miscues and what initial instructional plans might be appropriate.

Comments

Analysis of miscues from the child's independent and instructional reading levels may be misleading. Often so few miscues occur that it is risky to draw conclusions about typical strategies the child might be using. However, we believe the analysis is worth doing for the initial insights you get. For most children, we believe the IRI miscues can provide enough information to get you started with instruction that is on target.

Also, doing such analysis helps you begin to think appropriately about what can be learned from miscues whenever a child is reading, not just during an assessment. It will help you resist the temptation to jump to conclusions or to judge a child harshly for not recognizing a word you think he or she "should" know. For a discussion of the history and evolution of miscue analysis, see Murphy (1998), listed in For Additional Reading at the end of the chapter.

Your analysis of miscues after an IRI may be sufficient for one child but not for another. If you think you do not have enough miscues from an IRI to provide a useful analysis and fear you are not providing appropriate instruction for a given child, you can take a running or fluency record, as described in Chapters 3 and 7, to generate more miscues to analyze. Other, more elaborate types of miscue analysis also exist, each with written procedures for administering, coding, and interpreting data. (See Goodman, Watson, and Burke, 1987; Rhodes and Shanklin, 1990; and Rhodes, 1993). A reading spe-

Table 10.2
Summary, Interpretation, and Instructional Plans Based on Miscues of Three Children

Name	Summary of Miscues	Interpretation	Instruction
Jorge	Most miscues were semantically and syntactically acceptable, but little attention was paid to graphic clues. Examples: *pony* for *horse, kids* for *children.* Self-corrected most miscues that resulted in loss of meaning.	Obviously understood the text, but needs to learn that such substitutions may not always work and that accuracy is important.	Have him audiotape himself and then check his own tape to raise his awareness of how often he substitutes his own words for those of the author.
Heather	Miscues were graphically similar in most cases: *when* for *where, ever* for *every, house* for *horse.* Meaning was seldom maintained. Syntax sometimes was appropriate. Few miscues were self-corrected.	Seems so intent on figuring out the sound of the word that she neglects to think about meaning.	Provide many books at her independent reading level to relieve the need to decode every word and allow focus on meaning. Build prior knowledge and encourage prediction. Chunk guided silent reading to help her monitor meaning. Model monitoring: "Does it make sense? Does it sound the way the language is supposed to sound? If it doesn't, I need to reread to see if I miscued."
Wesley	Few miscues and efficient use of strategies when reading narrative material, but not when reading expository text, for which he seemed to use only phonics.	May not have sufficient background information for content material.	Teach strategies for reading content material such as science texts: previewing, predicting, reflecting and retelling to self, summarizing, and reviewing. Deal carefully with new vocabulary and concepts before reading.

cialist or clinician might choose one of the elaborate varieties, but you would want to weigh the time involved against the potential for improved ability to meet the child's needs.

Comprehension.   When you have completed the IRI, you have the reader's responses to many kinds of questions. Many IRIs label each question as to type, such as main idea or topic, vocabulary, literal or factual, inferential, evaluative, and so forth. Using information only from passages at the child's independent and instructional levels, you may want to look at which kinds of questions the child consistently answers acceptably and which kinds consistently give trouble.

Figure 10.6 shows one summary of a student's comprehension performance on an IRI. Such an analysis makes it easier to look at the total picture of a reader's responses to certain kinds of questions. The manual for this IRI gives detailed directions for filling out the summary, doing the arithmetic, and drawing conclusions. For both oral and silent reading forms, you record how many of each kind of question a child missed out of how many possible for each passage read. You then use these numbers to derive percentages.

Interpretation of Comprehension Scores.   You may first look to see if there are gross differences between the student's performance on oral and silent forms. The child whose performance is summarized in Figure 10.6 had slightly more difficulty with fact questions when reading silently. You may then compare the student's response to literal (fact) questions with all the other (higher-level) questions. The child shown had a slightly higher percentage of higher-level questions missed. In addition, you can look at the percentage missed of each different kind of question.

Initial instructional planning may flow directly from such an analysis. If the child has more difficulty with higher-level questions, your instruction will focus on comprehension at inferential and evaluative levels. If the child missed many factual questions, you may focus on the strategy of identifying important details. If the performance is fairly even in all areas (as it is here), you should continue to emphasize all areas of comprehension.

Comments

Once again, you will not have very large numbers, so drawing conclusions is risky. Say a child scored 67 percent on "topic" questions. That sounds dreadful—but would the score be meaningful? If the child read only three passages at the independent and instructional levels, there were only three "topic" questions altogether, and the child missed only one. It isn't reasonable to expect to make a sound judgment based on only three responses and a single error.

However, if you find on analysis that a child has answered every literal question correctly and missed almost all the inferential questions, you have useful information for planning instruction. The key is consistency in the child's performance.

Summary of Student's Comprehension Performance on the Basic Reading Inventory
Jerry L. Johns
Northern Illinois University

ANALYSIS BY TYPE OF QUESTION

Grade	Fact Oral	Fact Silent	Topic Oral	Topic Silent	Evaluation Oral	Evaluation Silent	Inference Oral	Inference Silent	Vocabulary Oral	Vocabulary Silent
P	/5	/5	/1	/1	/1	/1	/2	/2	/1	/1
1	/5	/5	/1	/1	/1	/1	/2	/2	/1	/1
2	0/5	0/5	0/1	0/1	0/1	0/1	0/2	0/2	0/1	0/1
3	1/5	0/5	0/1	0/1	0/1	0/1	1/2	0/2	0/1	0/1
4	0/5	1/5	0/1	0/1	0/1	0/1	0/2	0/2	0/1	0/1
5	1/5	2/5	0/1	0/1	0/1	0/1	2/2	2/2	1/1	0/1
6	/5	/5	/1	/1	/1	/1	/2	/2	/1	/1
7	/5	/5	/1	/1	/1	/1	/2	/2	/1	/1
8	/5	/5	/1	/1	/1	/1	/2	/2	/1	/1
9	/5	/5	/1	/1	/1	/1	/2	/2	/1	/1
10	/5	/5	/1	/1	/1	/1	/2	/2	/1	/1
11	/5	/5	/1	/1	/1	/1	/2	/2	/1	/1
12	/5	/5	/1	/1	/1	/1	/2	/2	/1	/1
Ratio Missed	2/20	3/20	0/4	0/4	0/4	0/4	3/8	2/8	1/4	0/4
Percent Missed	10 %	15 %	0 %	0 %	0 %	0 %	37½%	25 %	25 %	0 %
Total Ratio Missed	5/40		0/8		0/8		5/16		1/8	
Total Percent Missed	12½ %		0 %		0 %		31 %		12½ %	

ANALYSIS BY LEVEL OF COMPREHENSION

	Lower-Level Comprehension (Fact Questions Only) Oral	Lower-Level Comprehension (Fact Questions Only) Silent	Higher-Level Comprehension (All Other Questions) Oral	Higher-Level Comprehension (All Other Questions) Silent
Ratio Missed	2/20	3/20	4/20	2/20
Total Ratio Missed	5/40		6/40	
Total Percent Missed	12½ %		15 %	

From Jerry L. Johns, *Basic Reading Inventory* (7th ed.). Copyright © 1997 by Kendall/Hunt Publishing Company (1-800-228-0810). May be reproduced for noncommerical educational purposes.

362

Figure 10.6
Sample Page for Summarizing and Analyzing Comprehension from an Informal Reading Inventory (Johns, 1997)

Interpretation of All Data

When you interpret the information gathered from an informal reading inventory, you look at the total picture of the reader's performance. We have shown you several pieces to look at first separately and then together: the percentages of word recognition and comprehension accuracy, the listening level, the analysis of miscues, and the summary of comprehension. Along with these, you must also consider behavior, attitude, interest, and other information you may have gleaned from conversations with the child.

Remember that this instrument is designed to give you an *estimate* of the child's reading levels and an *estimate* of specific needs in word recognition strategies and comprehension, along with information about what the child is doing competently. On the basis of all these bits and pieces, you begin to work. If the estimates turn out not to be appropriate—for example, you find the child isn't working well at the instructional level you estimated—you make an adjustment. As we have repeatedly said, nothing about literacy can be measured with the accuracy of a ruler.

Using Results to Plan and Adjust Instruction

Because the IRI gives you a quick estimate of reading levels as well as strengths and needs, you can place a child into a developmentally appropriate book immediately. You also will know the probable extent to which the child can participate during the Core Books block, in which you are likely to use grade-level books. Further, you are ready to help the child find books to read during independent reading time. While this may not be a complete picture of a child's reading, it is a beginning.

With an IRI you know something about what the reader is already doing competently, so you can capitalize on that strength. At the same time, you learn what the child seems not to do, or ignores, or does poorly. These two types of information guide you to prepare minilessons to help the child acquire and build new strengths. For example, if the child's miscues showed a high percentage of graphic similarity but mostly resulted in a loss of meaning, you know you do *not* need to urge the child to use phonics more often. Rather, you need to encourage the child to use his or her sense of language and meaning.

As another example, if the child was unable to respond acceptably to evaluative questions but answered virtually all fact questions accurately, you do not need to urge the child to pay attention to detail. Rather, you will emphasize personal response to text, reading critically, and building confidence in voicing opinions.

Suppose the child has read haltingly, unwilling to try unfamiliar words, reading right through punctuation marks, and apparently focused on "attacking" one word at a time. You might decide to work on building fluency at the child's independent reading level, using a tape recorder, a reading buddy, or a volunteer. You might defer more challenging reading temporarily until the child has built confidence and pleasure in reading at this lower, more comfortable level.

Precautions

The informal reading inventory has been a useful tool for several decades and will continue to play a role in assessing reading. However, you need to bear in mind a number of concerns:

- Informal reading inventories are based on an assumption that it is possible to accurately determine the reading level of a piece of text, that is, that one can judge a piece of writing to be of second-grade difficulty, sixth-grade difficulty, or whatever. Earlier in this chapter, we discussed some of the complexities involved in this concept of readability.

- Estimates of the child's reading levels are based on a limited sample of performance. While not as inauthentic as a standardized paper-and-pencil test, the IRI is still not completely authentic. The child has not chosen this material to read. It is a contrived situation, calling for a child to read under conditions that may create a certain amount of stress.

- Passage content may be a poor match for the child's oral vocabulary, background experiences, and interests. That is, given two passages of equal (according to a formula) reading difficulty, a child may read more competently when material matches his or her interests and background than when it doesn't.

- Many factors may impinge on a child's performance on an IRI on any given day: health, weather, noise, mood, hunger, and so forth. Of course, you will note as many of these as you can and take them into consideration. Too often, however, only the numbers and levels are used for decision making or reported to parents. The lengthy notes that might explain those numbers and levels are set aside.

- Estimates based on an IRI presume it is possible to establish clear reading levels for a given child. In fact, though, all of us read with more accuracy and deeper comprehension on some days than on others, and we read some types of material better than other types.

Some Final Comments on IRIs

We believe informal reading inventories have a place in virtually every classroom. You will want to "practice" administering an IRI to several children to build confidence in your ability to administer the inventory and to analyze, draw conclusions, interpret, and plan instruction based on the reader's performance.

Plan to spend a considerable amount of time preparing before you do your first IRI. Read the manual from cover to cover. Make reminder charts for yourself; flag the pages you need to use during the administration of the inventory. Do whatever will help you get through the procedure in the prescribed manner while putting the child at ease.

When you become adept and are using informal inventories regularly, don't fall prey to the "tail wagging the dog" syndrome. Having so much data may fool you into thinking you have concrete information. Don't let the information govern all your decision making, only your initial planning. From then on, let your daily interaction with the child guide you. Learn to trust your own instincts more than the numbers.

Word Recognition Tests

In this section, we briefly discuss three kinds of specific tests of word recognition. *Sight word tests* assess a child's instant recognition of a given body of words.

Phonics tests purport to isolate which phonic elements a child knows and uses to figure out the probable pronunciation of unfamiliar words. *Structural analysis tests* assess a child's knowledge of and ability to use the structure of words, such as prefixes, suffixes, inflectional endings, and sometimes syllabication. Recall that we have discussed nontest assessment of these aspects of word recognition throughout this book.

Sight Words

In Chapter 6 we discussed the concept of sight words, including the fact that the term has more than one meaning. Briefly, a **sight word** can be defined in any of the following ways:

- A word recognized instantly ("at sight"), without analysis or decoding
- A word taught as a whole, without attention to its parts
- A word from a published list of words that occur with high frequency in all written material and therefore need to be recognized by any reader

We will discuss each of these definitions and then focus on procedures for administering and interpreting sight word tests.

Recognition of a Word "At Sight" Without the Need to Analyze or Decode It. When a child can read a word instantly, without hesitation, you say that word is a sight word for that child. Instant recognition of words on the lists provided with an IRI indicates that those words are sight words for the child in question. Yet such lists are made up of a sampling of words taken from passages at each grade level. Therefore, performance on them cannot be taken as an indication of a child's general sight word knowledge, which usually refers to a specific body of high-frequency words that have been determined necessary for all reading.

Words Taught as a Whole. Some educators also use the term *sight words* to refer to any words that are taught or must be learned by sight rather than through analysis of the parts. Sometimes such words do not follow phonic or structural generalizations and therefore do not lend themselves to analysis or decoding. At other times, the child has not yet learned the necessary skills for analysis.

For example, analysis of the word *Titanic* will result in a close approximation of the pronunciation. However, six-year-olds have not yet been taught the skills for such analysis. If you wanted to teach the word to them, you'd probably present it as a whole word, perhaps noting only the beginning sounds.

Words Determined to Be Necessary for All Reading Because of Their High Frequency. A broader and more common meaning for the term *sight words* is "a group of words that children 'should' recognize at sight by a certain grade." Lists of such words have been made by examining children's reading material, counting how often each word occurs, and identifying the "high-frequency" words—the ones that occur so frequently that fluent reading cannot take place without instant recognition of them.

The *Dolch Basic Sight Word Test* (Dolch, 1942) consists of 220 high-frequency words divided into lists from preprimer to third grade. Many teachers use this list to assess children's familiarity with basic sight words. Johnson (1971) reexamined the list and found that it continued to have value. Other lists are also available (Fry, 1980; Fry, Kress, Fountoukidis, & Polk, 1993), and the Resource File provides samples.

Procedures for Sight Word Tests.   There are two simple ways to administer a basic sight word list to a child: with flash cards or with a printed list. In either case, words should be exposed for about one second. This is easily done if the words are printed on flash cards. If the child is reading from a list of words, you may need to use an index card to cover and then briefly reveal each word. While the child reads, you mark responses on another copy of the list. After the child has gone through a list, you may want to present the missed words again to see if they are recognized on second look or whether the child can analyze them.

As with any kind of test, reassurance is important; tell the child you just want to find out which words he or she already knows and which you both still need to work on. You may decide to change your procedure if a child begins to miss one word after another. In that case, some teachers like to ask the child to silently look at the list and find words he or she knows.

Figure 10.7 shows a partial marked list. A + indicates the word was said correctly. When the child misread a word, the teacher attempted to record what the child said instead. The "Flashed Word" column indicates the child's first try; the "Second Look" column records the child's efforts when the missed words were presented again. Notice that the teacher also made some behavior notes during the test administration.

Analysis and Summary.   If you record the child's exact responses as shown in Figure 10.7, you can analyze the nature of the words not known or miscalled. You might look at such things as the following:

Very soft voice
Rising inflection on each word—unsure

Sight Word List

		Flashed Word	Second Look
1.	the	+	
2.	of	+	
3.	and	+	
4.	to	+	
5.	a	+	
6.	in	*t*	*i+*
7.	that	*what*	*then*
8.	is	+	
9.	was	*saw*	+
10.	he	*she*	+

Figure 10.7
Partial Sample of a Marked Test of Sight Words

- Were words often skipped? If so, did the child usually not attempt the word on the second try either?
- Did errors increase with each list or occur evenly on all lists?
- Were substitutions mostly at the beginnings of words? Middles? Ends?
- Was there any other pattern of errors?
- How did behavior change as the task increased in difficulty?

These analyses are not precise; rather, they give you a general picture of a child's miscues that might not have been apparent had you relied solely on classroom reading experiences. Simply recording results is of little use unless you follow up with an analysis and a summary that can lead to improved instruction.

The following list is a possible summary and analysis of third-grader Brian's performance on a sight word test. He was given a second look at words he missed the first time. For these purposes, it is not necessary to know the specific words Brian read or missed. Notice how each summary statement is followed by an instructional statement.

1 Brian read instantly all the words on the preprimer, primer, and first-grade lists.

Instructional note: Concentrate only on second- and third-grade words. All earlier words are known and will continue to be practiced in any daily reading.

2 Brian missed fewer words at the second-grade level (12) than at the third grade level (20).

Instructional note: Show Brian how he is gradually mastering the lists and is close to "knowing" all the words.

3 His attitude is positive: he thinks he will know all the words "before fourth grade."

Instructional note: Support his positive attitude.

4 Brian attempted to pronounce (sound out) all unknown words when given a second chance. He was persistent and did not want to give up. He kept apologizing, saying, "I should know that word."

Instructional note: Get "should" out of the issue. Focus on the strength of his persistence.

5 Most errors occurred at the middle or end of a word. That is, Brian always began his attempts to decode the words by associating an appropriate sound with the letters at the beginning of the word.

Instructional note: Devise practice activities that call for distinguishing words by middles and ends. Further assess his knowledge of medial and final sounds if necessary.

6 Once Brian assigned a sound to a vowel, he seemed unable to try an alternative sound when the first one did not produce a recognizable word. For example, he pronounced the word *great* as /greet/. He asked if he was right, and I said, "Not quite, try again," but he could not think of an alternative sound.

Instructional note: Plan specific lessons on vowel digraphs as well as strategy lessons about trying alternative pronunciations when the first attempt fails to result in a real or correct word.

7 Several miscalled words may have been read correctly in context. Lack of context seems to inhibit Brian. He kept saying, "I'd know that word if it was in a sentence."

Instructional note: Keep a list of miscalled words handy, and try to notice whether they are known during normal classroom reading activities.

8 Sometimes Brian strung together close approximations of each syllable of a word without ever having the "Aha!" experience of recognizing what he had just said. Example: *un-i-ted.* He kept saying these syllables over and over, pronouncing *un* with a short *u* sound and using a short *i* in the middle. He didn't want to give up; he kept saying, "I can get it. Just a minute." Finally, when we were all finished and I pronounced the word for him, he grinned and said, "Oh, yeah, like the United States of America. Right! I just didn't know it without a capital *U*."

Instructional note: Build on Brian's persistence and expectation that print should make sense.

9 We discussed his performance. Brian thought he did "pretty good." I agreed. He said he could learn the rest of the words: "Easy—piece of cake." I asked him what he thought would help him learn the words. He said he thought he would write them while he said them. Then he would ask a friend to test him. I told him I thought that was a good plan, and we made a date to retest in two weeks.

Instructional note: Use Brian's ideas and check frequently to be sure he and his friend are working well together. Retest in two weeks.

Interpretation and Planning.   Instructional plans should be based on the kind of summaries and instructional notes just illustrated. For Brian, such plans might be as follows:

- Use his idea of saying and writing words. Help him choose a friend to test him.
- Encourage fluency by helping him locate books at his independent reading level to tape record.
- Plan minilessons based on vowel digraphs and alternative sounds of vowels. Teach him steps to think through if his first try isn't a word he recognizes. For example: "If a word ends in *e,* try the long sound for the other vowel first. If that isn't a word I know, try the short sound. If that isn't a word I know, make a schwa sound and reread the sentence for clues."

As with most assessments, results on the day of testing merely sample a child's reading behavior and are useful only for beginning planning. From then on, daily observation and possibly the use of checklists may be sufficient to monitor progress, though it would be easy to readminister a sight word test to track progress in this area.

A Caution.   We do not recommend paper-and-pencil, group-administered tests of sight words. Such tests call for a child to look at a row of several words, listen to a word the teacher says, and mark that word. This procedure tests only whether the child can find the word the teacher says. It does not test whether the child can read the word.

Phonics Tests

Unquestionably, children need to use phonics as they read. We addressed this issue earlier in the book, and we reiterate here the importance of phonics in learning to read. We believe phonics needs to be taught early and taught well. Therefore, it is important for you, the teacher, to keep close track of which children are "getting it" and which are not. Furthermore, at grades beyond first grade, you need to know which children may need reteaching because they did not "get it" when it was first taught or because they were not taught phonics at all, perhaps due to pedagogical ideas that prevailed when they were in an earlier grade.

We believe the best way to assess a child's knowledge of and ability to use phonics is through careful observation during classroom reading experiences, both while reading text and during instruction focused on word recognition strategies. As you saw earlier in this chapter, analyzing miscues on an IRI can also provide insights into a child's use of phonics.

What about specific tests of isolated phonics elements? In our view, the information from these tests may not be very reliable. A child may do well on a test of isolated phonics skills but fail to apply this ability while reading. The true test of phonics ability occurs as the child is actually reading. Nevertheless, you may have occasion to use some phonics tests in your classroom.

If you are using a published reading program or a stand-alone phonics program, frequent assessment will be built into the program. Your school system may have devised its own assessment or have selected a certain published test to use. Such tests may assess other aspects of reading along with word recognition elements. Some published tests are listed in For Additional Reading at the end of this chapter.

Most phonics assessments attempt to isolate which phonics skills a child is able to use successfully. Some do this using nonsense words or syllables, since the use of real words may be misleading: there is no way to predict which children may already recognize a word at sight. Sometimes one part of the word is held steady while another is manipulated.

For example, assume the child either knows the word (rime) -*in* or is taught it. Then various initial consonants (onsets) are added to that syllable—*hin, jin, lin, vin*—and the child attempts to pronounce the resulting words aloud. (Consonants that would result in a real word, such as *bin, din,* and *fin,* are not used. Those beginning sounds would be assessed with a different rime.) This kind of assessment requires one-on-one administration. Some children find it difficult to deal with the notion of nonsense words and continue to try to force a real word out of every combination of letters. Keep in mind that such an assessment is devoid of context.

Less helpful are assessments that are entirely paper and pencil. These might require children, for example, to listen to the sound at the beginning of a word the teacher says and circle a word (or picture) from a list that starts with the same sound. Unless the child is actually applying phonics to the oral pronunciations, this kind of test will not reveal his or her ability with phonics.

As we said, we believe phonics ability is best assessed as children deal with meaningful text. If you do assess phonics in isolation, the published tests that accompany your reading or phonics program probably are as good as any other. Remember, though, what we have said before: phonics is one tool for helping a reader predict the probable pronunciation of an unknown word (or helping a writer predict the probable spelling). It has no end other than that.

Interpretation and Planning.   Whatever your source of information regarding a child's needs in terms of phonics skills, you must use this to plan for instruction or it is of no real value to the child. First, match the skill against your own school system's scope and sequence of skills or its standards to see which particular phonic elements your students are expected to have mastered at this point. Then you can begin to make plans.

There is little value in having children who already use a skill practice isolated drills. Rather, they will best grow by using the skill in actual reading of connected text.

For children who are not yet using the skill effectively, you must plan specific lessons. In many cases, careful reteaching will be all that is required. As you begin to teach or reteach skills, pay attention to whether or not the child is able to hear the phonic element you are targeting. If a student beyond the Emergent Literacy stage does not seem to hear the sound, or cannot make the association of sound with symbol and use that to figure out unfamiliar words, you may want to consider a conference with a special reading teacher or a referral for additional diagnosis from an exceptional education specialist.

Structural Analysis Tests

Most published reading programs include tests of structural analysis ability. Diagnostic and standardized tests often include aspects of structural analysis as well. The abilities tested include recognition and application of affixes such as prefixes, suffixes, and inflectional endings. They also include the use of patterns of vowels and consonants, such as CVC (a vowel between two consonants) and CVVC (a pair of vowels between two consonants), to predict vowel sounds and accents.

As with phonics, we believe you will be able to note which children are successfully using structural analysis in the course of everyday reading activities. For example, as you review a morning message with second graders, you might talk about how you could figure out the pronunciation of *September* by applying the CVC pattern and breaking the word into syllables, then pronouncing each syllable to get close to the exact pronunciation. Then you would encourage children to consider the context in confirming that *September* is a likely pronunciation.

While any good teacher supports, encourages, and reminds children throughout the day to use their growing abilities, it is difficult to remember which children are struggling and which are not. You may therefore decide to construct a checklist of some kind or keep anecdotal records. For many of your children, you may just note that they seem to be applying their growing knowledge of phonics and word structure as they wrestle with unfamiliar words. For some children, though, you may observe that they do not seem to apply phonics or structural analysis to unfamiliar words. Your notes would include some examples and, during subsequent group reading activities, you might specifically address clues and prompts to these children. If some of the children still did not respond, you may want to assess further using a published test or one you have devised.

Interpretation and Planning.   For each structural analysis element found lacking, plan a lesson for those children who need it. For example, if several children are having trouble with words beginning with the prefix *un-*, plan a lesson about this. Present the concept of prefixes, the specific prefix and its meaning, examples (*unhappy*), and nonexamples (*under*); then provide guided practice with isolated words, followed by practice in reading words in context. Also, remember to call attention to (or ask the children themselves to note) examples of words in their day-to-day reading that have the prefix or could have the prefix. Guide them to think about how the meaning of each base word is affected by the prefix.

Diverse Populations

In addition to IRIs and word recognition tests, your process of measuring the reader should include attention to the diverse populations represented in your school and your classroom. Here we will give you some ideas for assessing children with special needs as well as those from diverse language and cultural backgrounds.

Children with Special Needs

Within any classroom, you will likely have some children who are or will be classified as part of a special population of one kind or another. These may include students with learning disabilities as well as those with various emotional, mental, or physical challenges. Most terms for such students eventually come to be seen as pejorative, and they change over time. However, the existence of children with special needs will remain.

We have recommended that when you think you have such a child who has not yet been identified, you consult your school policies about the proper procedures to follow. Usually these will include keeping careful anecdotal records based on observation, completing certain checklists, consulting with specialists, and trying one or more interventions within your classroom.

At some point, the special education teacher may begin additional testing with instruments not used routinely for all children. These are special diagnostic tests used to further define a child's needs and help prescribe a suitable instructional plan. While you will not be expected to administer or interpret these assessments, you may want to inform yourself about them since you will participate in staffings and parent conferences. For further information on assessment in exceptional education, see For Additional Reading.

Language and Cultural Diversity

Cultural and language diversity will influence your interpretation of children's miscues, their retelling, and their responses to comprehension questions. Keep in mind that your goal is to draw conclusions that will help you help the child grow in literacy. Rigid adherence to counting the number of correct items and assigning the child to a level based on percentages is not helpful. You need to give weight to the child's culture and first-language patterns as you decide how to interpret test results.

Miscue or Language Difference?   Two basic kinds of language differences may affect a child's oral reading: pronunciation and syntax. A child whose first language assigns a different sound to a letter or combination of letters may retain that sound while pronouncing English words. For example, if a child gives a /th/ sound to the letter *c*, this may not be a miscue; it may reflect a pronunciation difference arising from the child's first language. If you are uncertain whether or not a miscue is the result of a simple pronunciation error, ask the child for clarification to see if she understood the word she said (Garcia, 1994).

Similarly, if a child reverses the order of words in a sentence, it is not likely that he saw the words in mixed-up order. Rather, the child may be changing the syntax to match his first language. In some languages, for example, the adjective follows the noun rather than preceding it, as in "the sweater yellow" rather than "the yellow sweater."

Comprehension Difficulty or Cultural Difference?   As a child is asked to retell what he or she has read or to answer a series of questions, you need to consider why the child might give a certain response. What you want to know, of course, is whether the child is able to read the words and grasp the ideas sufficiently to construct meaning from the passage. Your procedure is predicated on the assumption that readers will have a somewhat shared background of experience and frame of reference through which to consider the content. Yet a child who has grown up in a different culture from that reflected in your classroom and community likely has quite different experiences and, therefore, a different frame of reference. This could affect recollection of facts in a passage as well as the kinds of conclusions the child might draw.

Here is a very simple example of what we mean: a passage might tell about a child's getting lost and finally being found by his mother. If you were to ask a reader what the mother will do when she finds the lost child, answers might reflect the reader's culture. These are some possible answers:

The mother cries tears of happiness.

She spanks the child for wandering off.

Someone snatched the child and his mother never finds him.

He's probably trying to get away because he's scared to go home.

He would never get lost—he's too little—his momma should be holding his hand.

The point is, we all respond to text out of our own cultures, backgrounds, and personal life experiences. Your job is to try to decide whether a deviation from the expected response is based on failure to construct meaning or on cultural differences.

Comments

Some children in your class may be speaking English as a second language and not yet have acquired literacy in either their first or second language. Others may already have been literate in their first language before they began to acquire English. If students can read in their first language, you should assess them in that language if possible. Obviously, those who are already literate in some language have a grasp of how language systems work, even if theirs is quite different from English. Conceptual knowledge about print as well as the ability to draw on one's own experiences is generalizable across languages. (See Farr and Trumbull [1997], p. 138ff., listed in For Additional Reading.)

Far more is involved in communication than a simple sharing of the phonological and syntactical aspects of language. Just think of how many misunderstandings arise between two people who speak the same language and share the same household. This text is not, of course, the place for an extensive discussion of the subtleties of diversity and literacy. We can, however, keep nudging you to reserve judgment, keep an open mind, continue to study, and welcome diversity rather than shunning it.

Matching the Reader and the Material

So far in this chapter, we have discussed measuring both materials and readers. We want to remind you of the limitations in the procedures we have discussed. When a readability formula is applied to a piece of written text, the result is given as a grade level, but such formulas do not take into account many of the factors related to what makes material easy or difficult for a given reader. Similarly, when an inventory (or, indeed, any test) is given to a child, it measures the child's reading levels only on that day, with that material, and in an "inauthentic" situation.

Probably the most common reason for measuring materials and for measuring children is to try to put the right materials in the hands of each child. Yet, given the limitations of these measures, we hope you now accept that they offer only estimates. They merely give you a starting point when no other information is available.

In this section, we further discuss these concepts as well as the published interest levels often provided for books. We also present an alternative strategy (the cloze procedure) that can help you match a child to reading material without knowing either the difficulty level of the material or the reading level of the child.

We don't want to seem to be against the concept of measuring the difficulty levels of materials or the ability levels of readers. On the contrary, we think it is important to try to ascertain both and to use what you learn as you try to match children and books. But we want you to use these concepts with your eyes wide open, aware of the limitations. And we want you to expand your thinking to include the broader aspects of putting children together with the right books. In other words, pay attention to readability level (or other kinds of levels) and to children's reading levels, but don't be a slave to the numbers.

Reading Levels

It would be nice if you could simply determine the readability of the books you have available, assess the reading levels of your children, and then match one to

A biography about a well-known dancer captures this reader's interest.

© Elizabeth Crews

the other. You have already seen, however, some of the complications involved, and in this section we address that matter further.

Using the Published "Reading Levels" of Written Material

For many children's trade books, the publisher defines the readability by means of a "reading level," sometimes abbreviated RL. When a book is given a certain reading level—for example, 2.5—it means that a formula of some kind has been used. The 2.5 means second grade, fifth month—in other words, just right for children who read at the second-grade, fifth-month reading level.

Some publishers of trade books indicate the reading level on the books themselves. For example, *Piano Lessons Can Be Murder* (Stine, 1993) has "RL4" on the back cover, which means fourth-grade reading level. *Anastasia Krupnik* (Lowry, 1979) says "RL: 6.0," meaning a reading level of sixth grade, zero months. *Amelia Bedelia* (Parish, 1963/1981) has a note on the copyright page stating that a third-grade reading level was determined using the Fry Readability Formula, thus telling the purchaser not only the presumed difficulty level but the means by which it was determined.

As you deal with such reported reading levels of books, here are some ideas you'll want to keep in mind:

- The notion that there is a significant difference in text difficulty and in a child's reading ability from one month to the next—that is, that 2.4 is significantly different from 2.5—is misleading because it suggests a "three bears" view of matching a book with a child: too hard, too easy, and just right. Is it meaningful to say that a child reads at second grade, fourth month, but not at second grade, fifth month? Does such a child even exist?

- Even if ability does change significantly from one month to the next, the notion that we can know a child's reading level with such precision is questionable. A child who has a reading level of 2.5 usually acquired that "score" through an averaging of his or her performance on several discrete parts of a standardized test—a process that many consider to yield a child's *frustration* level. (Standardized tests are discussed in Chapter 11.)

- The readability level reported is the result of taking several samples from a book and averaging them. This is misleading as well as mathematically unsound. For example, if a sample from the beginning of a book is found to be at the sixth-grade difficulty level, a sample from the middle at the second-grade level, and a sample from the end at the fourth-grade level, it just doesn't make sense to average them and call the whole book fourth-grade level. The fact is, for a child who reads at the fourth-grade level, some of it will be difficult, some quite easy, and some about right.

- Readability levels on published books cannot, of course, take into account an individual reader's interest in or prior knowledge of the content.

Using the Assessed Reading Levels of the Child

We have presented the concept of finding a child's three reading levels: independent, instructional, and frustration. These are reported in terms of a grade level. For example, Suzy is independent with materials written at the second-grade level, instructional with third- and fourth-grade materials, and frustrated with fifth-grade material. This information may well be more useful to you than being told that a child achieved a single reading level of 2.5 on a standardized test. Nevertheless, you should keep the following ideas in mind:

- The passages used to determine the child's independent, instructional, and frustration reading levels were presumably graded for difficulty using one of the several available formulas (this information is given in the manual of the IRI). So you must be willing to accept that a passage can indeed be graded for difficulty.

- Then you must accept that a child's performance on said passages can reflect his or her true reading ability for other material that has been similarly graded for difficulty using the same or another formula.

Comments

> Despite the pitfalls of using readability levels for written material and reading levels for children, we still think the effort is worthwhile. Paying attention to both can save time and narrow your choices, giving you a better shot at a good match between materials and reader. Little harm is done as long as you accept the need to make adjustments continually in light of new information.

Interest Levels

When publishers provide information related to interest, they usually report it as **interest level,** or IL. Sometimes this is specified by grade level(s) and sometimes by an age range.

When you see an IL, you know that someone—one hopes someone who knows children, child development, and children's literature—has judged the age of a child who might be interested in a given book regardless of how "difficult" it might be. This information can be helpful, because you can read a book to children who are interested in the subject even when they cannot yet read it to themselves. This, in fact, is true of many picture books, which are intended to be read aloud. The language, subject, story line, and art are all perfectly suited to a child who is not yet reading independently. It is assumed that an adult or other reader will read the book aloud.

This same information is also provided for many chapter books that are meant to be read by children. For example, *Where the Red Fern Grows* (Rawls, 1961/1974) bears the designation "RL 6, IL age 10 and up." This book has been determined to be at sixth-grade difficulty level, but children from about fifth grade on may be interested in the story. As the classroom teacher, you would be comfortable reading this chapter book aloud to your fifth-grade class. Even those who might read it on their own will enjoy hearing it. All will benefit from sharing the ideas and the beauty of the language.

You are the final expert on the interests of your students. If you pick up a book and think it would interest your children, share it with them no matter what interest level is given. Remember that if a book is judged to be of interest to a certain age of reader, that doesn't imply that all children of that age will be interested in that particular book. You will soon know if you have misjudged your students' interest.

Another Way to Match Material and Reader: The Cloze Procedure

Imagine that you are a fourth-grade teacher and you want to know whether your students will be able to read the social studies book you plan to use. No readability level is given for the book, and you have not yet determined your children's reading levels. What can you do?

A simply constructed and simply administered procedure can give you a quick estimate of how well the material will match the children. This procedure, called the **cloze procedure,** is used with the particular text from which your children are expected to read. The information you gain does not generalize to other material.

Using the Cloze Procedure

The following procedures and percentages for the cloze procedure are based on the work of Bormuth (1968):

1 Choose a passage from the text of about 250 words in length. Be sure the passage makes sense from beginning to end; that is, it would not be necessary to have read the previous section to understand it.

2 Reproduce the passage in this way: Leave the first and last sentences intact. For all sentences in between, delete every nth word (usually every fifth word) and substitute blanks. Make all the blanks of equal length so that the length of the blank does not provide a clue as to what word belongs there. There should be fifty blanks in all. See Figure 10.8 for an example.

3 Tell your students the purpose for this exercise: to help you know what reading materials will suit them. Reassure them that you are not testing them. Tell them to try to think like the author and replace the missing words, but that you know they may not know what all the words should be, and that's fine.

4 Have students read the text and write in the missing words. There is no time limit.

5 Score the papers, counting as correct only words that are the exact words you deleted. Synonyms are not acceptable. (See Bormuth [1968] for the rationale.)

6 The following percentages are used to judge the fit of the text to the reader:
   Above 57 percent: independent reading level
   44 to 57 percent: instructional reading level
   Below 44 percent: frustration reading level

This procedure is meant to yield only a "ballpark" estimate of the match between a particular text and the children in your class. You should not use it as an estimate of an individual child's overall reading level. That is, if you happen to use a selection whose readability level has already been determined, don't assume a child with a score of, say, 50 percent is at the instructional reading level for that level of material.

After you have scored the papers and sorted them into three groups based on the percentages just given, you can presume the following:

- Scores above 57 percent: This text will be quite easy for these children. They will be able to read it on their own and do additional reading on the subject.

- Scores from 44 to 57 percent: Most children will probably have scores that put them in this, the instructional, range for this text; they will do fine with guidance, good instruction, practice, and other sound instructional procedures.

- Scores below 44 percent: This text will probably be too difficult for these children, even with your good instruction. They can still deal with the themes, topics, and subjects of the curriculum, but they will need extraordinary support, other material, or the opportunity to listen to the text read aloud by you, a volunteer, or an aide.

Annie Oakley, who became known as the world's greatest female sharpshooter, was born Phoebe Ann Moses in 1860. The family was very ____, and Annie began shooting ____ a very young age ____ order to help feed ____ family. She brought home ___ the grouse and quail ____ family could eat. Word ____ her amazing accuracy with ____ rifle spread. More and ____ people heard about her ____ talked about her skill.

____ sharpshooter with a circus, ____ Frank Butler, was scheduled ____ play in Columbus, Ohio ____ April 1881. Frank always bragged ____ how good a shot ____ was and that he ____ shoot better than anyone. ____ bet Frank that there ____ someone who could shoot ____. Frank accepted the challenge, ____ Annie Moses met Frank ____ in a contest near ____ little town of Greenville, Ohio.

That contest made show ____ history. Annie won the contest ____ well as Frank's heart. ____ began to perform together, ____ in love, and were ____. After a while, Frank ____ performing, but he continued ____ serve as Annie's manager. ____ were a huge success. ____ traveled all over this ____ and to Europe and ____. Everywhere she went, Annie ____ people. She could shoot ____ from the side of ____ horse. She could shoot ____ looking at the target ____ a mirror. One of ____ most famous tricks was ___ slice a playing card ____ two as it was ____ in her husband's fingers. ____ trick resulted in a ____ slang term. An "Annie ____ " was a term used ___ a pass, or complimentary ____, which was punched to ____ it was a free ____.

Frank and Annie remained a devoted couple until they died within days of each other in 1926.

Annie Oakley, who became known as the world's greatest female sharpshooter, was born Phoebe Ann Moses in 1860. The family was very poor, and Annie began shooting at a very young age in order to help feed her family. She brought home all the grouse and quail the family could eat. Word of her amazing accuracy with her rifle spread. More and more people heard about her and talked about her skill.

A sharpshooter with a circus, named Frank Butler, was scheduled to play in Columbus, Ohio in April 1881. Frank always bragged about how good a shot he was and that he could shoot better than anyone. Someone bet Frank that there was someone who could shoot better. Frank accepted the challenge, and Annie Moses met Frank Butler in a contest near the little town of Greenville, Ohio.

That contest made show business history. Annie won the contest as well as Frank's heart. They began to perform together, fell in love, and were married. After a while, Frank stopped performing, but he continued to serve as Annie's manager. They were a huge success. They traveled all over this country and to Europe and England. Everywhere she went, Annie amazed people. She could shoot hanging from the side of a horse. She could shoot by looking at the target in a mirror. One of her most famous tricks was to slice a playing card in two as it was held in her husband's fingers. This trick resulted in a new slang term. An "Annie Oakley" was a term used for a pass, or complimentary ticket, which was punched to show it was a free ticket.

Frank and Annie remained a devoted couple until they died within days of each other in 1926.

Figure 10.8
Sample Cloze Passage and Completed Passage

Comments and Cautions

You may already be familiar with the term *cloze,* but with different meanings. The word itself relates to closure: making something complete by filling in the missing parts. The procedure we have described is just one use of cloze passages. Other uses also have to do with filling in missing words, but have other purposes and procedures.

Sometimes you may be compelled to put the same book in the hands of all children, including those who clearly cannot read the text. We have seen some teachers try to accommodate the frustrated children by using the social studies (or other) text as round-robin oral reading. Their rationale is that some children cannot read the text on their own; this way they at least hear it read aloud. We do not agree with this practice, for two principal reasons. First, if those who cannot read it are expected to benefit from listening, the text must be read extremely well, by someone who has previously read it and already knows the content. Second, there is little reason to make the entire class sit through the oral reading of a text in social studies or a similar content area. Sadly, this practice of round-robin oral reading often consumes the entire period. Such teachers may be "covering" the text, but they are not teaching.

If you are locked into using the same text with all students, we suggest you find other ways to accommodate the children for whom the text is at the frustration level. For example, have the text recorded by a volunteer or use a study-buddy system. You can also expand your prereading activities: building or accessing background, presenting new concepts, using prereading overview and study guides, and presenting new vocabulary.

Discussion following silent reading should include summarizing, drawing conclusions, and further predicting. Following the summarization by a competent reader, the child who was unable to read the text should be able to participate in the higher-level activities of drawing conclusions and predicting. In this way, even children who were frustrated by the text can learn the important information.

During the discussion, focus questions to the struggling readers on those they can answer successfully. For example, assume there is only one date in a certain paragraph and you know Johnny knows how to read dates. After the class has read the paragraph silently, you can say, "Johnny, find and read for us the date when ____ ____ happened." The point is to find a way to ask specific questions that a specific child can answer from the text. This allows the child to participate at a level that almost guarantees success.

Summary

In this chapter we have presented some tools, techniques, and ideas that go beyond the ordinary daily assessments you will use with all students in your classroom. We have looked at ways to measure the difficulty of reading materials, measure a child's reading ability, and create a good match between reader and material.

Measuring the materials typically involves the concept of readability. Actual readability depends on the interaction of reader, text, and environment, including factors that are not measurable. Readability formulas, however, concentrate on the text itself, analyzing certain features and converting the resulting numbers to a grade level. These formulas are convenient, but a number of risks are associated with depending on them. As a result, the joint statement from the International Reading Association and the National Council of Teachers of English urges educators to use methods other than formulas to estimate the difficulty level of text.

Measuring the reader often involves use of an informal reading inventory (IRI), which can provide valuable information about a student's three reading levels—independent, instructional, and frustration—as well as the student's listening level. Besides estimating these levels, you can use the IRI results to analyze miscues and comprehension performance to get an overall picture of a child's reading performance and decide how to plan appropriate instruction. Similarly, you can gain information from tests that focus on word recognition strategies: sight word tests, phonics tests, and structural analysis tests. All of these measures, however, have limitations and pitfalls.

You'll need to be particularly careful when assessing diverse populations in your classroom. For example, language differences may cause apparent miscues, and cultural differences may make you think a child is having comprehension difficulties.

As you attempt to match the right material to the right reader, you will note the reading levels and interest levels that publishers often supply for their books. These may be useful as a quick guide, but you are in a better position than the publisher to judge a book's suitability for your students. The cloze procedure is one way to determine how well a particular textbook might fit your students.

However you make use of these various tools and techniques, it is important to regard them merely as a starting point. As you work with your students to develop their literacy, you will need to make continual adjustments in light of new information.

FOR ADDITIONAL READING

General Sources

Murphy, S., with Shannon, P., Johnston, P., & Hansen, J. (1998). *Fragile evidence.* Mahwah, NJ: Lawrence Erlbaum. See especially Chapter 8, "Toward Reform: Lessons from Miscue Analysis."

Salvia, J., & Ysseldyke, J. E. (1998). *Assessment* (7th ed.), Chapter 21. Boston: Houghton Mifflin.

Informal Reading Inventories: Background

Caldwell, J. (1985). A new look at the old informal reading inventory. *The Reading Teacher, 39,* 168–173.

Flippo, R. F. (1997). *Reading assessment and instruction,* pp. 54–64. Ft. Worth, TX: Harcourt.

Johns, J. L. (1993). *Informal reading inventories: An annotated reference guide.* Dekalb, IL: Communitech International, Inc.

Johnson, M. S., Kress, R. A., & Pikulski, J. J. (1987). *Informal reading inventories.* Newark, DE: International Reading Association.

Pikulski, J. J. (1990). Informal reading inventories. *The Reading Teacher, 43*(7), 514–516.

Informal Reading Inventories: Partial List of Published Inventories

Burns, P. C., & Roe, B. D. (1999). *Burns/Roe informal reading inventory* (Preprimer to twelfth grade) (5th ed., rev. by B. D. Roe). Boston: Houghton Mifflin.

Johns, J. L. (1997). *Basic reading inventory* (Preprimer through grade 12 and early literacy assessments) (7th ed.). Dubuque, IA: Kendall/Hunt.

Leslie, L., & Caldwell, J. (1995). *Qualitative reading inventory–II* (Preprimer through junior high). New York: HarperCollins.

Silvaroli, N. J. (1990). *Classroom reading inventory* (6th ed). Dubuque, IA: William C. Brown.

Swearingen, R., & Allen, D. (2000). *Classroom assessment of reading processes* (Grades 1 through 6) (2nd ed.). Boston: Houghton Mifflin.

Tests of Specific Word Recognition

Prescott, B. A., Balow, I. H., Hogan, T. P., & Farr, R. (1987). *Metropolitan achievement tests: Reading diagnostic tests.* New York: Psychological Corporation.

Richardson, E., & DiBenedetto, B. (1985). *Decoding skills test.* Parkton, MD: York Press.

Woodcock, R. W. (1997). *Woodcock diagnostic reading battery.* Chicago: Riverside Publishing Company.

——— (1998). *Woodcock reading mastery tests—revised.* Circle Pines, MN: American Guidance Service.

Exceptional Education

Lerner, J. (2000). *Learning disabilities: Theories, diagnosis, and teaching strategies* (8th ed.). Boston: Houghton Mifflin.

Lerner, J., Lenthal, B., & Lerner, S. (1995). *Attention deficit disorders: Assessment and teaching.* Pacific Grove, CA: Brooks/Cole.

Rhodes, L. K., & Dudley-Marling, C. (1996). *Readers and writers with a difference.* Portsmouth, NH: Heinemann.

Children with Diverse Cultural or Language Backgrounds

Farr, B. P., & Trumbull, E. (1997). *Assessment alternatives for diverse classrooms.* Norwood, MA: Christopher-Gordon.

Garcia, G. E. (1994). Assessing the literacy development of second-language students: A focus on authentic assessment. In K. Spangenberg-Urbschat & R. Pritchard (Eds.), *Kids come in all languages: Reading instruction for ESL students* (pp. 180–205). Newark, DE: International Reading Association.

FOR EXPLORATION: ELECTRONIC RESOURCES

Reading Assessment Tools

High-Frequency Word Assessment.
> **http://www.elm.maine.edu/assessments/ 100word/index.stm**   A reading assessment, developed by an elementary school teacher in Maine, designed to measure the number of high-frequency words a student can recognize.

Informal Reading Inventory.
> **http://lrs.ed.uiuc.edu/students/srutledg/iri.html**   A tutorial to assist teachers in developing an informal reading inventory.

Software for Readability Formulas

Readability Calculations.

Software for Macintosh or Windows. Figures readability using eight formulas. Available from Micro Power & Light Co., 8814 Sanshire Ave., Dallas, TX 75231, 1–214–553–0105. http://www.micropowerandlight.com/

Readability Master 2000.

Software for PC or Macintosh. Calculates readability using the New Dale-Chall Readability Formula plus Spache and Fry. Available from Brookline Books, P.O. Box 381047, Cambridge, MA 02238, 1–800–666-BOOK.

CLASSROOM APPLICATIONS

1. Administer any published informal reading inventory, following the procedures outlined in its manual. Summarize and analyze the data, and write a conclusion and initial instructional plan.

2. Choose some print material that does not report a readability level. Try both narrative and expository material. Read the material and use your understanding of children to estimate the interest level of the material and the reading difficulty level. Then figure the readability using the Fry Readability Formula (see the Resource File). Draw some conclusions.

3. Make up an interview guide to help you talk with several children about how they decide which books they will read—that is, how they determine which books will interest them and which will be about right in terms of readability.

4. Observe in an ESOL class. Listen to the children, and try to detect which mispronunciations are apt to result from language differences and which from failure to recognize words. Note how the teacher handles such mispronunciations. Share your conclusions with the class.

5. Prepare a cloze passage using a text designed for fourth grade or higher. Administer it to a class or group. Score and sort the papers, and draw conclusions about the suitability of that text for that class. Plan how you would meet the needs of all the children, including those for whom the text is at the frustration level.

Formal and Standardized Assessments

FOCUS   As you read the
Eyewitness section,
ask yourself the following
questions:

1. How can Mr. Singh use results from the testing that is
going on in his classroom to
improve his instruction?

2. What is Mr. Singh learning
about his children while
observing them? How might
this information affect next
year's plans for test preparation?

Eyewitness

A sign hangs on the door of Mr. Singh's fourth-grade classroom: TESTING—DO NOT ENTER. Inside, the children sit quietly with booklets and pencils on the tables in front of them. Mr. Singh speaks to the children from the front of the room. He holds a copy of the test booklet and points to various places, demonstrating what the children are to do. Some children fidget, roll their eyes, and twirl their hair around their fingers. Others are alert, their eyes sharply focused on Mr. Singh's face. It is achievement test day.

For several weeks, part of each day has been devoted to getting ready for the state test. The children have taken one practice test after another. They have been told it is important to do one's best on the test, while at the same time they have been told not to get anxious about it. No matter what anyone says, the children know the test matters. This knowledge will lead some children to, in fact, do their best. It will drive others to give up and not try at all because they feel defeated before the test even starts.

Now Mr. Singh has set his timer, written the start and stop times on the chalkboard, and signaled the children to begin work. Almost immediately, several hands shoot up. Mr. Singh tiptoes around, whispering to the children individually, reassuring them, pointing to where they should be, reminding them that, unlike his usual practice, he cannot tell them any words, answer any questions about things they don't understand, or help them figure out answers. They must do the work on their own.

Let's imagine we can actually see inside each child's mind during the testing. The following are only a few examples of how children (and adults) might approach the standardized test. As you will see, responses vary.

Sam usually likes to sprawl on the floor with his nose in a good book. He isn't sprawling today, though. Instead, he sits up straight, both feet on the floor, takes a deep breath, and reads the directions on the first page. He appears to be totally focused, looking neither right nor left. After reading the directions, he turns to the first test item and begins. The passage has several paragraphs, followed by a series of multiple-choice questions. Sam reads the questions first. After reading two or three, he begins reading the passage. He stops reading after a short while with a kind of "Got it!" smile on his face and marks the answer to the second question. Then he returns to the passage until he finds the answer to the first question and the third. He continues reading two or three questions, then the passage, moving back and forth between passage and questions until the first passage is completed. He quickly checks each answer and makes sure he has recorded it in the right place. He smiles and gives a little shake as though to say, "There, that's done." Then he moves to the next item. He doesn't look up. He doesn't fidget. He works straight through the test.

Sally is an average reader, but she is fearful of any kind of test and anxious about disappointing her parents and teacher. She skips the directions and begins reading the first passage, bending down with her nose close to the page. She uses her finger to keep her place. Finally, she finishes the first passage and looks at the first question. She marks her answer without referring to the passage. She continues to choose answers to the questions without once looking back at the passage. She leaves two or three questions unanswered and moves on to the next passage. She seems tense: brow furrowed, feet twined around the chair legs, making noises in her throat as though trying not to read aloud to herself.

Stuart is the picture of cool. He lounges back, tipping his chair on two legs and draping one arm over the back. Stuart doesn't read much in class beyond what he has to. He seldom reads for pleasure. He likes to talk, though; he'll participate in discussions even when he hasn't read the story. He boasts of not caring about grades or test scores and says his parents don't care anyhow. When Mr. Singh signals they can begin, Stuart looks around to see what everyone else is doing. He jiggles one leg and drum-beats his pencil against his desk. He skips the directions and glances at the passage. Then he skips that also and goes directly to the questions. After filling in the bubble for the first answer, he doesn't look at the test booklet again. In fact, he continues filling in bubbles on the answer sheet without even referring to the questions. He seems to be making a pattern of filled-in bubbles on the page.

Shirley gets about halfway through the passage and stops. Her lips move as she apparently tries to sound out an unfamiliar word. She raises her hand, but of course Mr. Singh can't help her during the test. She goes back to the word and continues to try to figure it out. She is fighting tears and hiding her eyes. She raises her hand again and begs to be excused to go to the bathroom. She says she feels sick to her stomach. Mr. Singh clearly aches for her, but there isn't much he can do beyond murmur words of support and encouragement.

Later we see Mr. Singh making notes with pencil and paper. If we asked, he would tell us that he observed his children very closely today as they went through the often stressful period of standardized testing. He took many notes about behaviors and has vowed to find a way to better prepare students to do their best without increasing their anxiety. He also has promised himself to become better acquainted with the test formats his children will be required to use and with the procedures he will be required to follow so that he can maintain "standardization" of administration yet give as much support to his students as possible. Further, he thinks he can do a better job of helping children think like test makers, which will help them be more successful test takers.

All over the country, children like those in Mr. Singh's class are taking similar kinds of tests every year. Some take several such tests in a single year. These are standardized tests designed to measure how well children have achieved in various areas of learning and to compare one group of children to the rest of the school system, county, state, or country.

Such tests consume precious instructional time. The results may or may not seem to be used in any productive way. The published results may cause consternation or gloating, depending on the scores. Low performance sometimes causes schools and even whole states to scrap everything they've been doing and completely revamp their teaching. Sometimes entire curricula seem to be written to match the achievement tests; in other words, the test publishers are, in effect, determining curriculum.

Sometimes it may seem that both educators and the public think standardized tests are close to useless at best and damaging at worst—but every year schools continue to administer them. Why? The answer actually may be simple, understandable, and defensible: taxes support schools. Taxpayers deserve to know that their money is indeed educating children. They want tests given to prove that children are learning what they should be learning: reading, writing, and arithmetic, as well as history, geography, and science. What's the easiest way for educators to demonstrate that children are learning? By giving tests that purport to measure what children are supposed to have learned at various points in their education and by making sure those tests allow one school to be compared to another. Thus, we know (or think we know) that children in Arkansas and children in New Hampshire, children in Oregon and children in Tennessee—in fact, all the children in the country—are meeting the same standards of achievement.

This chapter introduces some basic concepts concerning the standardized testing of reading. We will discuss the purposes of standardized testing and the limitations. We will give you some historical perspective, define some terms, explain how results are reported, and offer advice on interpreting such reports. We will discuss the state of the profession in standardized testing and the classroom teacher's role in preparing children to take standardized tests. We will also describe several standardized tests and provide sources for you to explore for further information.

FOCUS **As you read about Formal Assessment, ask yourself the following questions:**

1. How does formal assessment differ from informal assessment?

2. What are norm-referenced and criterion-referenced tests, and how do they differ in terms of reflecting and reporting student learning?

3. What are the commonly reported derived scores, and what do they mean?

4. What are the big issues nationally (and locally) concerning formal testing?

5. What are some issues related to standardized testing of diverse learners?

Basics of Formal and Standardized Measurement

Considering the amount of money allocated to providing an education for every child in the nation, it is no surprise that voters as well as educators have a strong need to know whether or not goals are being met. Are educators indeed teaching children? Are children learning? What are they learning? Are they learning the right stuff? Is it what they need now and in the future? Will our children grow up to be adults who are capable of holding their own in a global economy? Before we can figure out if anything needs to be changed in our instruction, don't we have to try to determine the results of our present methods?

Clearly, what is assessed must be closely linked to what is taught. That is, schools must establish educational objectives: what children should know and be able to do. Then educators can plan curriculum: what, when, and how to teach in order for children to meet the established objectives. Logically, then, educators need some way to find out if children are reaching the objectives that have been established. This might be easier if every single school system in the country had established exactly the same objectives. But they have not—and we're certainly not suggesting that they should. Still, there seems to be some agreement that schools should assess all children using the same or like instruments to compare them. Some states have developed their own tests, or their own norms (norms will be discussed later in this chapter), but even in those states the individual school districts may not have identical educational objectives. The whole subject is fraught with pitfalls. Every time one aspect of standardized testing seems clear, another becomes muddied.

Some would say that the whole notion of standardized testing began with the work of Binet and Simon, the authors of an intelligence test for draftees for the armed forces in 1905 (Glazer, 1998). These tests were not meant to measure achievement; rather, they were designed to separate those who were mentally capable from those who were not.

Eventually various tests were devised to test what were thought to be elements of the reading process, such as word identification, comprehension, study skills, and fluency. Today we have many published tests that purport to measure every aspect of literacy. Such tests state that their purpose is to show achievement. The test items cover what each child *should be doing* at each grade level in each area of literacy. To allow for children who are performing considerably below or above that grade level, some test items are much easier and others are much harder.

Every classroom teacher needs to know some basics about standardized tests. They are a fact of life in every school system to one degree or another. This book is not a forum for debate about the issue of standardized testing. Instead, we hope to provide enough information for you to begin thinking independently about the issue.

Standardized Tests: What Are They? Why Use Them?

Up to now in this text, we have discussed mostly informal assessment. Such assessment is based on observation and sampling of a child's performance as well as looking at products such as written work. Informal assessment also includes many tests that accompany published curriculum materials in subjects such as reading, math, science, and social studies, as well as teacher-made "tests" covering something that has been taught and studied.

Each classroom teacher may carry out informal assessment and testing somewhat differently. Teachers are careful when they give such tests in order to be fair and get as true a picture of each child as possible, but there is variation from one teacher to the next. The classroom climate, the testing conditions, the support the teacher offers, and even the score deemed "passing" may differ from school to school, from classroom to classroom, and from teacher to teacher.

Standardized tests, in contrast, are administered under identical (as nearly as possible) conditions every time, no matter where or by whom. This means the same time limits, the same directions, and the same testing circumstances. Since standardized tests are designed to allow comparison between one child or group of children and another, everything about the conditions of the test must be kept identical except for the child's performance.

If you think about it for a minute, you'll realize that ensuring this standardization of conditions is virtually impossible because there are simply too many variables to be controlled. Still, the attempt to impose standard conditions is important if results are to have any meaning at all. Therefore, test publishers dictate many things, including what to say to the children as you give directions.

A fifth grader is taking a standardized test.
© Elizabeth Crews

The following sections define and describe three major types of standardized tests: norm-referenced, criterion-referenced, and diagnostic.

Norm-Referenced Tests

A **norm-referenced test** compares the performance of an individual to that of the group on which the test was standardized. When the scores of such a group are displayed, those scores distribute in a **bell curve**. A bell curve shows a very few scores at the upper end, a very few at the lower end, and most in the middle. If you plot all the scores on a graph and draw a line connecting them, the shape resembles a bell—hence the name of the curve.

Figure 11.1 illustrates a bell curve. The horizontal axis indicates the range of scores, from the lowest scores on the left to the highest scores on the right. The vertical axis, labeled "Frequency," shows how often each score occurs in the population. Scores distributed in this way are said to follow a **normal distribution,** and the regularity of the curve allows us to calculate the percentages shown on the graph: for instance, 68 percent of the scores will fall in the center portion of the graph, only 2 percent will be at the extreme right side (very high scores), and 2 percent will fall at the extreme left (very low scores).

How do test makers determine which **raw score** (the number correct) on a test corresponds to which position on the curve? They try out the tests on a **norming population,** often consisting of children from various socioeconomic backgrounds; in cities, suburbs, small towns, and rural communities; and from every part of the country. Test publishers then determine the average score of children

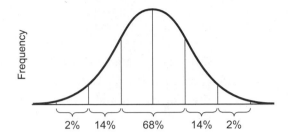

**Figure 11.1
Normal Distribution of
Scores Shown on a Bell
Curve**

at various points in their schooling (which grade and sometimes even which time of year), and the resulting scores become the reference for various derived scores (to be discussed later in this chapter). Occasionally a school district will develop **local norms** based on its own children rather than comparing scores to the broader population that includes children from many parts of the country.

You may have heard Garrison Keillor on public radio describe the mythical town of Lake Wobegon, where "all the children are above average." While it is possible that the children of one school (or some other defined group) might all be above average, *all* children cannot be above average. It is statistically impossible. But, you may be thinking, what if all children achieve at higher and higher levels? Wouldn't that mean they could all be above average? No, it would not. The test scores would still distribute in a curve, though the middle or average might then be a higher raw score. In other words, given large numbers of test takers, there will *always* be a normal distribution. Average isn't what "should be"; average is what "is."

To illustrate the concept of average, Figure 11.2 shows a normal distribution of IQ scores, with which you are probably familiar. You can see that an IQ of 100 is right in the middle, at the peak of the bell curve; therefore, an IQ of 100 is "average."

Much more is involved in understanding normal distribution than what we say here, but the main points you must understand are these:

- Test scores distribute themselves as shown in Figures 11.1 and 11.2, reflecting the wide variance of performance within any group.
- Most scores cluster near the middle.
- Only a very few scores occur at the extreme low or extreme high end.

Norm-referenced reading and literacy tests are apt to be broad measures of achievement, yielding little in terms of particular areas of strength or weakness. Remember that each norm-referenced test is designed to show the entire possible

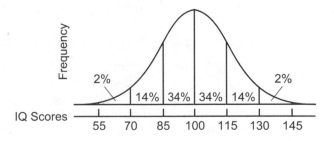

**Figure 11.2
Normal Distribution of IQ
Scores**

range of performance, so there will likely be items that almost no child in your classroom can know.

Criterion-Referenced Tests

Unlike norm-referenced tests, which measure performance in relation to the entire norming population, **criterion-referenced tests** measure performance in terms of an absolute mastery of particular skills that the child is expected to have learned. Achievement on a criterion-referenced test depends on the stated objective. Although the child who has completely mastered the skills would get every item correct, 80 percent correct is usually considered to be acceptable evidence of mastery. The test will not tell you if a child can perform beyond the scope of the test, since the test items are restricted to skills that have been taught, usually ones that are grade-level appropriate.

Published criterion-referenced tests may have a number of subsections, each intended to measure a subskill of reading or literacy. Levels of performance corresponding to mastery are indicated by the publishers. If a child does not achieve mastery, that indicates that review or reteaching is needed. After reteaching, the same test (or an alternate form) may be readministered to see if the child has now reached mastery.

To the degree that a criterion-referenced test matches your own objectives for your children, it may be considered diagnostic if it helps you pinpoint trouble spots for children and leads you to plan appropriate instruction.

Diagnostic Tests

Diagnostic tests are designed to lead you directly to specific instructional plans for a child. Such tests are standardized in that you, the test giver, are told exactly how to administer them. Unless you use the standard procedures, the results are not considered valid. These tests sample many components of an area of achievement, and the resulting scores show which areas need instruction for the individual child. The publishers of these tests may suggest particular teaching strategies and techniques to improve each area found deficient.

As you no doubt have realized, all of the informal assessment we have discussed earlier in this text is diagnostic; that is, all of it leads to instructional planning. Here, however, we are considering published tests with parameters determined by the publishers, not by you. While such tests may be helpful in screening and in planning educational experiences for some special populations, they may not be necessary for the grade-level classroom teacher. Later in this chapter, we will give you the names of some specific diagnostic tests.

Concepts and Terminology of Testing

You may already be familiar with the terminology related to standardized norm-referenced tests. Even so, the following discussion will remind you of concepts that you must understand in order to use standardized tests, interpret their results, and discuss the implications with colleagues, parents, and members of your community. We will also define and explain some of the several ways scores are reported.

Statistical Concepts

In addition to the standardization and norming procedures discussed earlier, the following common concepts are important: validity, reliability, and standard error of measurement.

Validity. A test has **validity** if it measures what it says it measures. Three types of interrelated validity are content validity, criterion validity, and construct validity. The publisher's technical manual will explain how validity was determined for any particular test.

Content Validity. **Content validity** is the degree to which a test's content reflects the content it is intended to measure. In terms of your classroom, it means that the content of the test is related to what your students have had a chance to learn, and the items are directly related to what you want to measure.

Criterion Validity. **Criterion validity** refers to how well a particular test compares with other measures. The comparison is reported as a statistical correlation ranging from +1.0, which is perfect correlation, to –1.0, which indicates no correlation.

Construct Validity. **Construct validity** is more complicated; suffice it to say that it relates to (1) the likelihood that the score on the test actually reflects what you wanted to test and, conversely, (2) the likelihood that inability to score well on the test cannot be accounted for by any other factor than inability to do that particular task. In other words, the test must have been conceived with a clear notion of what it aimed to test; then it should test that and only that.

Reliability. **Reliability** has to do with consistency. It helps you answer the question: Would Johnny get the same score if he took this test another day? A high degree of reliability indicates a high degree of likelihood that the person tested would receive the same score if the test were repeated. The degree of reliability is reported as a score: 1.0 is perfect reliability; .80 is usually considered an acceptable degree of reliability, though some programs require .90. The publisher's technical manual will report how reliability was determined for any particular test.

Two common kinds of reliability are test-retest and internal. To determine *test-retest reliability,* test developers give the same tests to the same group two times; they then correlate the two sets of scores to see whether individuals perform close to the same on both testings. To determine *internal reliability,* test developers correlate items within a test; one way of doing this is to correlate performance on one-half of the test items (say, even-numbered items) with performance on the other half (odd-numbered items).

Standard Error of Measurement. Since no test is absolutely perfect, the **standard error of measurement,** sometimes written *SEM,* allows you to say that a score can be trusted, give or take a certain number of points. Based on the normal distribution, the SEM allows you to say that 68 percent of the time the "true" score will fall within the range of plus or minus 1 SEM of the actual score.

For example, let's say a child scores 83 on a test with an SEM of 6. Most likely, the child's "true" score is 83 plus or minus 6, or somewhere between 77 and 89.

However, since this fluctuation holds true only 68 percent of the time, 32 percent of the time the "true" score might be even further from the actual score of 83. If you wanted to be even more confident that you were being truthful about results, you could expand your interpretation to include plus or minus 2 SEM; this would give you a 95 percent degree of confidence. In our example with the score of 83 and SEM of 6, you could be 95 percent certain that the true score would be 83 plus or minus 12—that is, somewhere between 71 and 95.

The important point about SEM is the concept that no test can be said to be completely accurate. The best it can do is yield a score for the day the student took the test; you must think of that score as the middle of a range of possible scores the child might receive. The publisher's manual will provide the SEM for each particular test.

Test Scores

As mentioned earlier, the actual number of items correct on a test is called the raw score. Let's say Susie gets 88 items correct on a standardized test; from that raw score, we have no idea whether to cheer or moan. This number is useless because too many things are unknown: How does her score compare to those on whom the test was normed? Did this test cover what has been taught in Susie's class? What's average for someone her age or in her grade? How reliable is that score? Even figuring a percentage for the 88 isn't helpful. We need a score that allows us to make inferences and draw conclusions.

To that end, test publishers provide what are called *derived scores* for each possible raw score. These derived scores allow you to look at an individual or at your class in terms of larger groups, from your school to your state to the whole country. Derived scores also allow you to compare one year's scores to those from prior years.

The most common derived scores are percentile rank, standard scores such as stanine and normal curve equivalent, and grade- and age-equivalent scores. Figure 11.3 will help you compare some of these derived scores as we discuss them.

Percentile Rank. The test publisher converts each raw score to a **percentile rank** that indicates a student's performance on that test in relation to the compa-

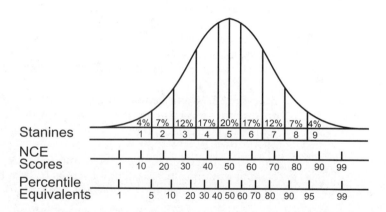

**Figure 11.3
Comparisons of Three
Types of Derived Scores**

rable group (same age or grade/month) on which the test was normed. The percentile score tells how an individual score compares in terms of the percentage of students in the norming group who scored above or below that individual score. On the bell curve shown in Figure 11.3, note that the 50th percentile is precisely in the middle: exactly average.

Let's say that Susie's raw score of 88 has a percentile rank of 70 on the particular test involved; this means that 70 percent of the students in the reference group (the group on which the test was normed) had a raw score of 88 or lower. Another way to look at it is this: Susie's score was the same as or higher than the scores of 70 percent of the norming group.

Cautions. Do not confuse percentile with percentage. A percentile rank of 70 does *not* mean that Susie had 70 percent of the items correct; a percentile rank of 70 could be associated with many different raw scores, depending on the group with which Susie's score was being compared. Percentile rank also does *not* compare Susie with the other children in her class; that is, it does not mean she scored higher than 70 percent of her classmates. It compares her *only* with the norming group; it would be possible that every child in her particular classroom was at the 70th percentile or higher.

A limitation of the percentile rank score is that the units are not equal. This can be important when cutoff scores are established for eligibility for special programs. Because percentile equivalents are clustered around the middle of the bell curve and lie far apart at the extreme upper and lower ends (see Figure 11.3), a difference of only one or two raw-score points in the middle might mean the difference between being at the 45th percentile and being at the 55th percentile. At the ends of the curve, in contrast, a difference of several raw-score points might not alter the percentile score.

Therefore, if your school has a special program that admits children with percentile scores, say, "at or below the 40th percentile," it is important to consider how many raw-score points put a child on one side or the other of that magic number. Let's assume a child's raw score converts to the 41st percentile, making the child ineligible for a special program according to the 40th-percentile cutoff. If the SEM (standard error of measurement) were taken into account, perhaps the child might be eligible after all.

Comments

We don't mean to suggest that percentile ranks are not valid or valuable ways to consider scores; they are very good when you want to look at large numbers of children or at trends. We do want you to learn what you can about what such numbers mean (or don't mean) in terms of looking at individual children. But we don't want you to risk making a judgment about an individual child based on a percentile rank without taking into account the limitations of percentile numbers.

Standard Scores. Standard scores differ from percentile scores in that the difference between one score and the next represents the same raw-score interval at the extremes that it does in the middle, expressed in terms of standard units of measurement. Two commonly used standard scores are the stanine and the normal curve equivalent. Publishers provide tables that allow you to convert any raw score into these standard scores.

Stanine Scores.   The **stanine score** places pupils in one of nine bands from the lowest stanine of 1 to the highest of 9. Stanine scores are assigned to represent a normal distribution, so most students will be in the 4th, 5th, or 6th stanines (around the middle), while only a few will be at the extremes. You can see in Figure 11.3 which percentiles compare with each stanine.

Normal Curve Equivalent Scores.   **Normal curve equivalent (NCE) scores** range from 1 to 99 and are equal units; the difference between the 40th and the 45th NCE is the same number of raw-score points as the difference between the 90th and the 95th. While the numbers 1 to 99 might suggest that the NCE is the same as the percentile, the equal (standard) units show that it is not.

Comments

Stanines are widely used and may be more understandable than percentile rank among laypeople. Each stanine encompasses a range of raw scores, and a child whose performance falls in stanines 4 through 6 is usually considered to be doing average work.

The nature of stanines is such that significant improvement (or decreased performance) is reflected by a change in either direction of two or more stanines. For example, if Joe was in the 5th stanine last year and this year his score falls in the 4th stanine, those scores are not sufficiently different to be cause for alarm. If Joe's score this year falls in the 3rd stanine, however, it would be considered a problem that needs exploring.

Grade- and Age-Equivalent Scores.   **Grade-equivalent scores** have often been reported to the community and to parents. Most people think they can understand such scores, though these scores are perhaps the most commonly misunderstood of all.

Grade-equivalent scores are derived from the performance of students in the norming group on a particular test. Let's say the test is designed for fifth graders at the beginning of the school year. The tests are given to a large number of students and scored. The average raw score obtained by the fifth graders at the beginning of the school year is then given a grade-equivalent score of 5.0 (fifth grade, zero months). Tests are often normed at various points in a school year so that the publishers can establish grade-equivalent scores for other months as well: for instance, the norming might indicate raw scores equivalent to a grade-equivalent score of 5.4 (fifth grade, fourth month) or 5.7 (fifth grade, seventh month). Sometimes the fifth-grade test is also "normed" on fourth graders and on sixth graders. As long as the grade-equivalent scores are roughly at the child's grade level, little misunderstanding probably occurs.

Age-equivalent scores are derived similarly. The difference lies in the way the score is reported. Rather than by grade and month, the score is reported in terms of an age and a month. Grade-equivalent scores conform to a school year in that they run from 0 months (5.0) to 9 months (5.9). Age-equivalent scores conform to calendar years, running from 0 months to 11 months.

Cautions. Grade-equivalent scores have several problems that must not be overlooked. In fact, the problems are so considerable that some publishers no longer publish grade-equivalent scores. These problems have to do both with how the scores are derived and with how they are misunderstood.

Publishers use average student scores at the intended grade level to estimate equivalent performance at higher and lower grades. That is, grade-equivalent scores are mathematically extrapolated both down to lower grades and up to higher grades. Thus, publishers can provide tables showing that a given raw score might correspond to a grade equivalent much lower or higher than the actual grade for which the test was intended, even though the test wasn't actually administered to students in those grades.

Let's say George, a fifth grader, has a raw score of 34 with a grade equivalent of 5.2 on a reading test. This is supposed to mean his score is the same as that of the average fifth grader in the second month of the norming group.

Now let's look at Jimmy, another fifth grader. Jimmy's raw score has a grade equivalent of 8.5. One can probably safely say that Jimmy is a competent reader who reads above grade level. However, you *cannot* say that Jimmy reads at the eighth-grade level; he wasn't reading eighth-grade material. All you can say is that *on this fifth grade test,* Jimmy performed the same as the average student in the eighth grade would probably have done *on this fifth-grade test* if the test had actually been given to eighth graders.

By the same token, if fifth-grade classmate Sheri receives a lower raw score with a grade equivalent of 3.5, it does not necessarily mean that she is a third-grade reader or that she should be put in third-grade material. The test wasn't made up of third-grade reading material, and it probably wasn't normed on third graders. The only thing one can honestly say about her score is that Sheri performed on this fifth-grade test the way the average child in the third grade, fifth month, would probably perform. It will be obvious to the teacher (and family) that she is struggling and not doing "average" work, but that's all the score means.

An additional problem occurs because grade-equivalent scores are not standard. That is, growth from one grade equivalent to the next might not mean the same thing from one year to the next or from one test to the next.

Moreover, reading scores on formal measurements may not be consistent with a child's actual reading performance in the classroom. You will remember that in our discussion of informal reading inventories in Chapter 10, we explained that it is important to determine a child's instructional reading level—the level at which the child will grow with good instruction. The score an individual child obtains on a standardized norm-referenced assessment probably does *not* reflect his or her instructional level (Betts, 1949) and is not a reliable guide to placement in reading material. If anything, the score may be closer to the child's frustration level. This is what the child did on a day when trying his or her hardest, perhaps—and made a few lucky guesses.

Practicing What You Have Learned. As we have said, derived scores corresponding to each possible raw score are presented in tables in the manuals accompanying tests. Usually, however, schools return tests to the publisher for scoring; the publisher then sends a report with the raw scores and the requested derived scores.

The following list presents derived scores for three children. Read each derived score and try stating what you know and what you don't know from the given information. Then read our discussion of each student and compare your thinking with ours.

- *BILLY: third grade; percentile rank 66.* Percentile rank compares an individual's score to the curve of the norming population. Billy read as well as or better than 66 percent of the students on whom this test was normed, which puts him slightly above the middle. The percentile rank does not compare him to his classmates, however, nor do we know how it compares to his previous performances. We must keep in mind, too, that a percentile difference of 5 or even 10 in the middle of the curve represents a much smaller difference in test performance than the same difference at the extreme high or low ends.

- *JILL: fourth grade; stanine 4; last year's stanine 6.* Stanines are nine bands of scores, with 4, 5, and 6 representing average performance. Jill's score this year is within the average range for students in her grade in the norming group, but it is two stanines lower than last year's score. We will look more closely at Jill's daily classroom behavior and performance to see if this score seems reasonable. We will also do informal diagnostic assessment to try to determine if there is a problem we can do something about.

- *CARLA: second grade; grade equivalent 5.8.* The grade-equivalent score compares an individual score to the average score of children in the norming population at different grade levels; it is expressed in terms of years and months. This test was normed on second- and third-grade students. A mathematical formula was used to project how children at higher or lower grade levels might perform on this test. Carla's grade-equivalent score of 5.8 reflects such a projection. We know that Carla reads well above grade level, but this does not mean she should be reading fifth-grade material. Rather, we can say that she performed on this second-grade test the way a student in the fifth grade, eighth month might have performed on this second-grade test.

Using Formal Measurements

Whatever the problems, formal assessment with standardized norm-referenced tests will undoubtedly continue to occur in most, if not all, school systems. In the following sections, we will summarize some of the concerns associated with such testing and describe current thinking in the profession regarding formal assessment. We will also show you some ways to accommodate such assessment in your classroom without undue stress and suggest some ways you can help your children perform to the best of their abilities.

Concerns About Formal Testing

Many educators have reservations about the value and perhaps even the need for the widespread norm-referenced testing that is still part of almost every school system. Actually, decisions about such testing are often not in the hands of educators but in the hands of politicians and school boards. And the content of the tests is largely in the hands of publishers.

Each school system must decide its purpose for testing and how best to report the results to the public or to whatever regulatory authority is involved in funding programs. As our discussion thus far has revealed, risks of misinterpretation and lack of understanding on the part of the public exist with the reporting of any of the standardized test scores.

A related problem arises when schools allow curriculum to be driven by performance on national assessments. Much of what is done in each classroom, then, is directed toward nudging students to score better and better on the test. Local standards and benchmarks may even be rewritten to conform to whatever test is chosen. This, in effect, hands curriculum over to test publishers.

You, the individual classroom teacher, may have little to say about which tests are given to your children. However the choices about testing are made by educators and communities, you can vow right now to be involved in such decision making. Choosing a formal assessment that is a good match with your local notions about what should be taught, learned, and tested makes sense. Therefore, informed people must examine tests carefully and make informed decisions about which tests to use.

Further, once a test is chosen, careful decisions must be made about how to report the results honestly and in a way that is clear to the community. Are all derived scores for each school reported in the newspaper? If so, are the scores accompanied by an explanation of what they mean? Will it be clear that 40th percentile is average and what being average actually means? Are scores of some children not included, and, if so, which children's scores are omitted and why? Are the scores of special education students left out of the report? Those of bilingual students? What kinds of decisions are being made as a result of a single child's score, an individual teacher's class scores, a school's scores, or a county's scores?

The State of the Profession: Local and State Assessments

Some movements are afoot across the country to change the way children (and, by extension, educators) are tested (Tierney, 1998). Some states have established criterion-referenced or curriculum-referenced assessment that ties directly to established performance standards. In such assessments, the link between curriculum and assessment is strong. Some systems may use a published test but establish their own norms, a procedure that allows comparison with similar programs that share the same goals and objectives. No doubt you will see additional movements to change assessment in such a way as to match learning more closely. Most such changes occur only when people with strong beliefs become informed and involved. You must decide whether you will be one of those people.

At the time this text is being written, state mandates for assessment are still in a state of flux. Practices vary from one state to the next and from one year to the next. At this point, several states mandate that a particular assessment be used for all students in certain grades in every school. Florida, for example, requires the administration of the Florida Comprehensive Assessment Test (FCAT) in reading to grades 4, 8, and 10.

The Southwest Educational Developmental Laboratory (1999) reports a number of states in that region that have implemented legislation requiring early assessment of reading in grades K–2. The assessments, often individually administered, are to be ongoing. Some states stipulate which areas are to be assessed but allow individual districts to select the assessments. Other states specify the instrument to be used. For example, Louisiana requires that the Developmental Reading Assessment (Beaver, 1997) be used to assess the reading level of every first-grade student at the end of the year. Second- and third-grade students are to be assessed at the beginning and end of each year. If students perform below grade level, they are given further assessment.

Texas has mandated a battery of tests called the *Texas Primary Reading Inventory (TPRI)* (Texas Education Agency, n.d.) for all kindergarten, first-, and second-grade children. The TPRI is an early reading instrument designed to be individually administered by the classroom teacher. (For more details, see the section "Individually Administered Tests" later in this chapter.)

New Mexico and Oklahoma have no recommendations about specific early reading assessments. In New Mexico, each district is to test reading and report the data to the state annually, though specific assessments recommended at the state level may be forthcoming in the future. Oklahoma stipulates testing all children in grades K–3 on phoneme awareness, phonics, spelling, reading fluency, and comprehension; the means of assessing these areas is left to the district.

As results of widespread testing are reported in a community, you will notice a groundswell of reaction. If the scores are not as good as previously, have fallen, or have failed to improve significantly, a scapegoat is sought. We as a profession (and as members of the taxpaying community) may want to find something or someone to blame when children are not learning what we think they should be learning. Remember that events are seldom caused by a single other event or condition; and remember that two events that may exist together, or correlate (such as single-parent homes and low reading scores), do not necessarily indicate cause and effect. Correlation is not the same as causation. There are many, many ways to look at data and infinite ways to interpret that data. For an excellent discussion of the politics of testing, see pages 137–182 in Calkins, Montgomery, and Santman (1998), listed in For Additional Reading at the end of the chapter.

There are many reasons you will want to keep reading and learning about standardized testing in your school system as well as in the nation. You need to look at standardized test results of high school students also; these students are products of your elementary and middle school programs. Significant decisions based on the results of such testing include, but are not limited to, the following matters: special funding from the state; which program to use; how children are assigned to special classes; changes in mandated materials; and, as in Florida recently, whether or not students in a given school will be eligible for a voucher that can be used to attend another public school or a private school.

At the very least, you will want to inform yourself about the assessment policies of your local school system. Then learn about your state's policies. Read professional journals. Visit web sites (these change frequently, but are easily found with any search engine; we list some sites at the end of this chapter). Ask questions. Be a part of change that grows out of the concerns of educators rather than one who passively allows decisions to be handed down from the top. Learn about the existing state of assessment in your community; then either support it if you agree with it or work for change if you do not.

The Role of the Classroom Teacher

In an ideal world, there would be a perfect fit between what you teach and what is tested. The standardized test would exactly cover what you were teaching in your class. In other words, in this ideal world, we would teach what we test and test what we teach. This is not a perfect world, of course; therefore, you must help your students demonstrate what they have learned on whatever assessment you are required to use.

Mandated standardized tests may be quite unlike your students' regular daily activities. The tests are paper and pencil. They may require filling in bubbles on a separate answer sheet. They may require reading a short, decontextualized paragraph and answering a series of questions. They may require connecting items or circling items. They may emphasize recall and details.

Not only are the tasks required of the students apt to be different; your behavior during such testing will differ from your daily behavior. You will be required to use the publisher's language to explain what your children are to do. During the test, you will not be allowed to answer questions, nudge children toward using their skills to figure things out, or ask stimulating questions that will lead to understanding. Time limitations will be rigidly imposed.

As in Mr. Singh's class described at the beginning of this chapter, your children will display a range of behaviors in response to the demands of testing, despite what you do or do not say to them:

- Some children are extremely anxious; no matter how much you reassure them, they will feel they should be perfect.

- Young children cannot really understand why the test publisher would put items on the test that are clearly too hard for most of them.

- Some children may be quite cavalier about the whole experience; they decide this test has little to do with their real lives, so they scarcely look at the test items. Rather, they just make interesting designs as they fill in bubbles on the answer sheet or pick C for every multiple-choice item.

- Some capable, hard-working, agreeable children work slowly and methodically; they are thrown into a near panic when time limits are imposed.

- Others rush through everything they do and see no reason to work differently on a test.

- There may be a scattering of physical symptoms of stress: stomachache, headache, coughing, crying, or excessive thirst. Your heart will ache especially for these children.

Many teachers spend some time each year teaching their children how to take the tests. Such preparation in addition to the actual testing can take quite a bite out of instructional time. Glazer (1998) reports studies showing that each child in the United States faces, on average, two thousand test items a year. In addition to the test time, teachers spend an average of 14 hours a year preparing children to take tests. Special education students spend even more time being tested.

Let's begin with the assumption that your students will be spending some time each year being tested on standardized, norm-referenced tests. Given that, we think you might as well accept it (for now, at least) and help your children perform as well as they can. Therefore, we suggest that you spend some time teaching your children about the formats, layouts, constrictions, language, and so forth of such tests. This is not cheating; you are not using actual test items. Rather, you are helping children learn how to respond to the way material is presented in the test. You are teaching them to think like test makers so that they can become good test takers.

Helping Your Students Prepare

Your children may be used to demonstrating their understanding of what they have read in a number of interesting and personal ways, such as through discussion, writing in a response journal, giving an oral report, drawing a picture, recasting a story as theater, debating issues, or comparing themes among novels. There is no choice about one's response on a standardized test, nor is there room for divergent opinions. A common format requires the student to answer a series of questions by choosing from several options: the familiar (to you) multiple-choice item. Students are expected to give or identify "the" correct answer—the one the test makers had in mind. This is only one way a test may vary widely from the way your children are used to thinking.

Simply leading children through practice tests is not true preparation; such practice does not help them learn how to think as they take the test. Following are some simple ways you might plan instruction and teach your children what they will find helpful as they take standardized tests:

- Examine past tests to discover which formats are commonly used. Examples might be cloze passages, multiple choice, and matching.

- Take the test yourself, and think about the strategies you used to determine the "correct" answers. Compare your strategies with those of colleagues.

- Observe your children as they take tests, and make notes of various strategies you see them using.

- Talk with your children about strategies they use.

- Prepare specific sample test items. Model how you would read and respond to each item, but tell children there are several ways to approach any task, and help them find their own best way.

- Invite children to share ways to read and respond to an item.

- With your children, examine each possible response to each item, clarifying why it is or is not the best choice.

- Make evident what children do as they take tests. Discuss their behaviors. Ask questions, examine incorrect answers, and ask children to explain why they chose the answer they did. Then redouble your efforts to teach them to think like a test maker during standardized testing.

- Replicate the testing conditions and let children get used to working silently and independently, without asking questions, within time limits.

- Share things you and others do that help you, and urge children to try these strategies, reassuring them that they may or may not choose to adopt them. For example, you may prefer reading the questions before you read a test passage so you can look for answers as you read. This may seem the most sensible approach in the world to you, but it may not be the best for everyone. Some test takers prefer to read the passage first while holding in their minds the thought "What are they [the test makers] looking for?" There is no one right way to perform successfully on every test. Each person must find his or her own best way.

- Give children assistance on using answer sheets. Begin with how to fill in the personal information. Then show them exactly how the page is set up: how each row of choices matches items in the test; whether one should move across or down; what to do if there are five possible bubbles but some test items have only four options; how to keep their place as they move back and forth from the test booklet to the answer sheet.

- Stress to your children that the goal in responding on a test is to get right answers, not to be creative or personal, even though this may be quite different from what you emphasize in everyday responses to reading.

You will undoubtedly enlarge your scope of helping your children become competent, confident test takers as you learn more about the tests they will be taking and more about your individual children's responses to testing.

Teacher, family and student share pleasure in the student's work.

Talking to Families

Another important job for you is helping families understand what the scores mean. Your school may have a particular way of reporting scores and of interpreting performance to parents. You, however, may find you want to do more than the standard communication. Remember that your understanding of what various scores represent and how to interpret them came only after a considerable period of study. The families of your students may not have had that advantage. They may appreciate a letter informing them of upcoming testing as well as a later letter containing your careful explanation, with examples, of exactly what Susie's score means in terms of her performance in this school in this grade on this particular measure.

Figure 11.4 shows a sample of a letter you might send home to explain upcoming standardized testing. Figure 11.5 is a sample letter you might send explaining an individual child's score on a standardized test, putting the derived score into words that a layperson can understand.

You may want to create a template on your computer that will minimize the amount of time it takes to write individual letters but will allow individual pieces of information to be inserted. Working from the template, you can fill in data and add a personal statement for each student. Figure 11.5 shows the individual information for Jeremy in **boldface** to illustrate what is standard and what is individualized. (In the actual letter, of course, you would not use boldface.)

The tone of the letter should always be positive. For those children whose performance is worrisome, try to find a way to reassure the parents. For example, tell parents that you see evidence of growth in the child's daily activity that is not reflected on the test. Of course, you must be truthful; don't hide your concerns if you have them.

Even if you have communicated with families via letters, at certain times you will probably want to talk face to face. In a conference following the reporting of test results, you should try to do all of the following:

1. Give family members a chance to say how they feel about the child's learning at this point.

2. Share work such as writing, reports, projects, checklists—the kinds of informal assessment we have been suggesting throughout this book.

3. Give a report and review of the child's performance on the standardized test and an interpretation of what the score means. Explain what is meant by a percentile rank, grade equivalent, or stanine. Explain where the child falls. Compare the child's score to his or her previous scores (not to the rest of the class).

4. Encourage questions and welcome concerns.

5. Describe your reaction to the child's performance and how it matches (or fails to match) the child's daily performance in the real world of the classroom.

6. Together with the family, draw up a plan to support continued growth.

Chapter 12 contains additional suggestions related to working with families.

Dear Family,

Standardized testing will take place next week on [insert dates and times]. This letter explains why we give these tests and how you can help your child handle them with as little stress as possible.

Why? Standardized tests help us know how our students are doing in comparison to [insert whatever norming population is used in your system: national (the rest of the country), state (other schools in the state), local (other schools in this district)]. Results of this testing also help us plan future instruction in our school.

After the tests have been scored, which will take several weeks, we will report school-wide results to the public. Your child's scores will be reported to you by letter [and conference, if appropriate].

What can you do? We need a clear picture of how our students are doing, which means each child must be able to do his or her best on test days. Children need to take the tests seriously but also not panic about them. This is a tough balance to achieve, and you can help in the following ways.

Tell your child you know about the tests and are sure the child will do his or her best work. Talk about the purpose of the tests: to help teachers help kids. Fooling around on the answer sheet or guessing wildly spoils the results.

Explain that there may be some things your child won't know on the test. Point out that "they make the test hard enough for the smartest kid in the whole world."

Tell your child not to be "creative." For example: When asked to "pick the best title," your child should simply pick the answer that tells what the passage or story is about, even though real titles often don't tell what a story is about. Unlike some of our class work, on standardized tests, children need to try to find "right answers."

Be sure your child is well rested and well fed. Sleepy, hungry children can't think well.

Telling a child "don't worry" or "don't be nervous" doesn't help much. Testing IS stressful . . . it's best to acknowledge it.

Reassure your child that you are proud of him or her . . . no matter what.

Thank you for all of your support.

Sincerely,

Figure 11.4
Sample Letter About
Standardized Tests

Dear family of **Jeremy**,

Here is **Jeremy's** score from the standardized test he took in **February** and an explanation of what that score means. I've also made some comments about how these scores fit with what I'm seeing in the classroom every day.

At our next conference we'll talk about these scores, **Jeremy's** daily work, and any concerns you or I have.

Jeremy's percentile rank on the reading test was **45**. This means that he did as well as or better than **45** percent of the students on whom this text was developed. It DOES NOT compare him to the rest of this class. His percentile rank of **45** shows him to be **an average reader. Jeremy's** percentile rank this year is **slightly higher than** it was last year.

Jeremy has worked very hard this year. This test may not have given him a chance to show everything that he can do. For example, there is a time limit on the test and Jeremy likes to work slowly and carefully. He might have had a higher score if he could have worked longer.

One thing that always delights me about Jeremy is his imagination. When he reads, his mind leaps from one interesting idea to another. We certainly don't want him to curb his imagination, but on a standardized test it may have kept him from concentrating on the "right answers" such tests demand.

I look forward to our conference. Please call 555-5555 and leave a message. I'll call you back to schedule a time for us to meet.

Sincerely,

Figure 11.5
Sample Letter Reporting an Individual Child's Test Results (Boldface Indicates Individualized Additions to the Basic Template)

Formal Tests for Measuring Literacy

This section briefly describes several tests. The publishers' addresses are listed in For Additional Reading at the end of the chapter. We have organized the tests into three types: group tests, individual tests, and tests for special populations. We describe some achievement tests, designed to measure how well students are able to do whatever the test publisher deemed appropriate for that population. We also describe some diagnostic tests, designed to measure specific subskills of literacy to support a prescription for teaching.

    Some reading tests are part of an achievement test (sometimes called a *survey* test) that covers other aspects of literacy such as spelling or language (grammar). Some are part of a battery of tests that also includes math. Some include specific skills involved in reading such as phonics or structural analysis. Some are standardized but not normed.

This is not a comprehensive list; we are simply naming and briefly describing some tests to give you an idea about what is published. Inclusion of a test here does not imply recommendation.

Group-Administered Tests

Group survey or achievement tests are the most common tests used in schools. These are chosen by the administration and are used for one or more of the following purposes: to assess progress in reading (and perhaps other subjects), to target children who may have problems, or to provide evidence regarding the success (or failure) of a particular program. These tests are norm-referenced, so each individual score, class average score, or school average score can be compared to a large norming sample. (Sometimes local norms are developed as well.) A survey test usually has several levels so that it can be used with students in every grade. Sometimes one level is designed to be used with more than one grade. Often there are alternative, equivalent forms for the same level to allow pre- and post-testing.

Don't forget: the tasks required on the achievement test may be quite different from the kind of reading your children do on a daily basis. In addition, the test situation itself often inhibits children and keeps them from doing what they might normally do easily.

Remember, too, that group survey tests may be unsatisfactory when used with children who are having reading problems; the test that is appropriate for the child's grade may be much too difficult for the child to read. Let's say you teach fifth grade, and you know Johnny will be unable to read most of the fifth-grade test. In many cases, you can't give Johnny a lower-level form such as the second-grade test (which he might be able to read) because no norms are provided for fifth-grade children on the second-grade test, and therefore the score Johnny obtained would have no meaning. Some publishers do, however, provide norms for students on either side of the grade level for which the test was written. This allows a certain amount of "out-of-level" testing. In such a case, you might be able to make better sense of Johnny's performance.

The following are some widely used group-administered tests:

- *California Achievement Tests, 5th edition (1992)*

  CTB/Macmillan/McGraw-Hill

  Grades K–12

  Series of tests includes the area of reading/language arts. Allows testing based on performance level rather than grade level. Yields usual derived scores and curriculum-referenced score.

- *Iowa Tests of Basic Skill (ITBS)(1996)*

  Riverside Publishing Company

  Grades K–8

  Series of tests includes measures of literacy areas. Yields usual derived scores. Both norm- and criterion-referenced.

- *Metropolitan Achievement Tests (MAT), 7th edition (1993)*

  Psychological Corporation

  Grades K–12

  Series of tests covers several disciplines, including reading. Criterion-referenced scores available as well as practice and locator tests (to allow testing out of grade level).

- *Stanford Diagnostic Reading Test, 4th edition (1995)*

  Psychological Corporation

  Grades 1.5–12; several levels from grades 1.5 through 12.8

  Assesses various components of reading from auditory discrimination through scanning and skimming. Provides all usual derived scores. Norm- and criterion-referenced.

- *TerraNova Reading (1996)*

  CTB/McGraw-Hill

  Grades K, 1, 2, 3 and higher

  Group or individual; Spanish version available

  Tests comprehension, vocabulary, reference skills, and word analysis (which includes decoding and reading high-frequency words). Part of a series of assessment tools.

- *Gates-MacGinitie Reading Test, 3rd edition (1989)*

  Riverside Publishing Company

  Grades K–12; several levels

  Subtests include various aspects of reading from concepts and oral language at the lower level to vocabulary and comprehension. Provides usual derived scores.

Individually Administered Tests

Individually administered tests are often designed to yield diagnostic information. Though some group tests claim to provide diagnostic information, we believe such information is better learned through individually administered tests such as those described here and, of course, through the many informal assessments described throughout this text.

Norm-Referenced Tests

- *Woodcock Reading Mastery Test—Revised (1998)*

  American Guidance Service, Inc.

  Ages 5–75

  Forms include readiness tests and achievement tests in reading (and other curricular areas). Provides usual derived scores.

- *Wide Range Achievement Test, 3rd edition (WRAT–3) (1993)*
  Wide Range Inc.
  Ages 5–75 (group or individual)
  Includes reading and spelling. Provides raw and derived scores.

- *Test of Early Reading Ability, Revised (TERA–2)*
  PRO-ED, Inc.
  Ages 3–9
  Norm-referenced. Administration takes about 30 minutes. Tests construction of meaning, including logo and environment reading, alphabet knowledge, reading words and comprehension, and conventions of written language. Raw scores can be converted to various derived scores.

- *Comprehensive Test of Phonological Processing (CTOPP) (1999)*
  PRO-ED, Inc.
  Grades K, 1, 2, 3 and higher
  Requires approximately 30 minutes per student for administration. Norm-referenced on a nationwide sample.

- *Test of Phonological Awareness (TOPA) (1994)*
  PRO-ED, Inc.
  Grades K, 1, and 2
  May be individual or group administered. Normed on a large sample in thirty-eight states.

- *The Phonological Awareness Test (1997)*
  LinguiSystems
  Grades K, 1, 2, and 3
  Requires 20 to 30 minutes per student for administration. Covers the major skills of phonological awareness. Raw scores can be converted to age-equivalent scores, percentile scores, and standard scores.

Criterion-Referenced Tests

- *BRIGANCE Comprehensive Inventory of Basic Skills (1999)*
  Curriculum Associates
  Birth through adult
  Several inventories assessing early development, basic skills, essential skills. A Spanish-language assessment is also available. The inventories are criterion-referenced and helpful in writing IEPs (individual education plans) for exceptional education students. Software for IBM and Macintosh is available.

- *Texas Primary Reading Inventory (TPRI) (n.d.)*
  Texas Education Agency

Grades K, 1, and 2

Provides a screening section and an inventory section at each level covering appropriate graphophonemic knowledge, phonemic awareness, book and print concepts, listening comprehension, reading accuracy, word reading, and reading comprehension. An Intervention Activities Guide provides helpful suggestions for the teacher.

Related Formal Assessments

The publishers of the tests just cited also publish other individually administered assessments in related literacy areas. These include language development, oral language, spelling, writing, intelligence, cognitive functioning, school readiness, and more. As a classroom teacher you will be unlikely to administer them, though you may need to understand reported scores for children who have been given such tests. To that end, you will want to acquaint yourself with the assessments used in your school system.

Testing to Accommodate Special Populations

Have you ever done poorly on a test of some kind and said to yourself, "But the test wasn't fair!"? Perhaps in a physical education class you were supposed to clear a hurdle, but you were much shorter than the others. Maybe you thought the height of the hurdle should have been proportionate to the height of the child. Everyone has had the experience of feeling judged unfairly because of being held to a standard of performance that did not take into account individual differences. Accommodating differences does not mean making excuses; it does mean trying to adjust for an uneven playing field.

Here's a question to consider: how can educators use the same instrument to test every child when our children are so diverse? We believe this is an important question for you to think about.

For some years, education policy has focused on equity. Farr and Trumbull (1997) report some principles on equity and educational testing and assessment that should guide the development of standards and assessments in the future. These stress the importance of establishing standards that reflect a diverse population and assessments that have been field tested on a diverse population. Farr and Trumbull also include the "Guidelines for Equitable Assessment" from FairTest in Cambridge, Massachusetts. This document emphasizes the need for significant changes in assessment practices that until now, the authors say, have been harmful to various groups of students, among them language minorities.

Students in Exceptional or Special Education

Testing plays a critical part in special education programs: tests help educators decide what a program for students with disabilities should look like, how the program might be carried out, and whether or not it is successful. Every program planned for a special population must address several questions:

- Who needs the help?
- How will we identify those children?

- What do we need to teach them?
- How will we teach them?
- How will we know if we have been successful?
- What will we do if we have not been successful?

Moreover, as with any other program funded by tax dollars, there must be accountability for the use of the funds. This becomes even more important when funds are limited and schools must compete for them by showing greater need or by demonstrating greater success.

As a classroom teacher, you may not need to choose or administer any formal tests other than those required by your school for all children. School-wide standardized tests may, however, be the first signal that a child should be tested further to determine whether she or he needs special services of some kind. Further tests will probably be administered by special school personnel. If such a need is determined to exist, an individual education plan will be written, and your job will be to provide instruction in your classroom that supports what the special teachers are providing.

You will probably want to keep informed about the assessment of special populations even though you don't administer the tests yourself. This is part of your development as a professional, a subject we consider in detail in Chapter 12. Reports of investigations and research are often summarized in professional publications, and we recommend that you consult such publications regularly.

For example, *Reading Today* (International Reading Association, 1999a) summarized the report "Performance Trends and Use of Accommodations on a Statewide Assessment," issued by the National Center on Educational Outcomes at the University of Minnesota. This report examines the use of accommodations for students with disabilities in Kentucky. (An example of an accommodation is using sign-language interpreters during testing so that deaf students can have the same conditions during testing that they have during instruction.) The report suggests that though performance of students with disabilities remains below that of the general student population, the gap may be closing. In fact, such students may be showing gains that exceed those of the general population.

For information about this and other pertinent reports, you can visit the National Center on Educational Outcomes web site, cited in the For Exploration section at the end of this chapter. Simply scanning the topics there will yield worthwhile information. For example, under "Issues and Considerations in Alternate Assessments," you will find discussion of many issues that arise when some portion of a school population cannot be assessed through typical testing procedures.

Another web site that may yield up-to-date information about assessment of special populations (as well as about other current issues) is the one maintained by *Education Week* (see the listing in For Exploration). For example, the following information (from Hoff, 1999) was available at the online site:

Education Dept. Examining Rise in Students Excluded from NAEP

Federal statisticians are reviewing scores from a 1998 national reading assessment to see if some states improved their standing because they excluded higher proportions of students with disabilities and limited English skills than they did in earlier tests.

> *States that registered some of the largest gains on the 4th grade test also increased the rate at which they removed students from the testing sample because of their disabilities or their inability to understand English.*

Keep your purpose in mind as you read such information in print and on the Internet. Use your critical thinking skills, considering where the information appears, who wrote the report, and whether it seems valid to you.

Title I Students

Another group of students who can be considered a special population are those who participate in a Title I program. As reported in *Reading Today* (International Reading Association, 1999b), this program, which was established in 1965 to help poor children achieve at the same levels as their better-off peers, has failed to reach its goal. The Elementary and Secondary Education Act, of which Title I is a part, is currently approaching its time for reauthorization. This means decisions will need to be made. The International Reading Association (IRA) has taken a position (reported on page 8 of the same issue of *Reading Today*) on all aspects of the program and its revision. Regarding assessment, the IRA states, "Assessment needs to be ongoing and linked directly to instruction."

The IRA also addresses the issue of accountability, the importance of making public the goals of a Title I program, and the need to work with a community when results are not satisfactory. Remember that when such a report talks about "results," it is likely referring to results as measured by a standardized test of some kind. The issue of assessment underlies many of the discussions of educational reform in this field, as in most other fields.

Second-Language Learners

A major concern, of course, is using assessment to make wise decisions about the education of every student, no matter what element of our diverse population the student represents. A child who is not yet proficient in English cannot demonstrate what he or she knows when the test is written in English. A child from a minority culture may not understand test items reflecting only mainstream culture.

Many of the published tests mentioned here (and many others as well) are available in a Spanish version. Consult publishers' catalogs or web sites to find out which provide tests in another language. When you have the opportunity, you will want to assess literacy without limiting that assessment to English. It is important to learn which children are already literate in another language and to what extent they are using literacy skills in that language.

Although students may develop conversational proficiency in English fairly rapidly, it takes much longer to develop academic literacy skills. According to Collier (1992), it takes five to nine years for English-language learners to reach grade level on many standardized tests.

Conclusions

Accountability, a term that comes up repeatedly in discussions of assessing diverse populations, is not a bad word; it means that educators need to continue to find ways to demonstrate what children are learning, support what is being taught, monitor whether what is assessed matches what is taught, and show that schools are doing the job they are supposed to be doing. When students are living with differences that inhibit the use of the usual assessment instruments and procedures, educators must find ways to accommodate those differences without contaminating the results. Educators must be especially vigilant when considering evidence that can lead to potentially life-altering decisions about a child.

Summary

In this chapter, we have introduced some basic information about formal and standardized assessments. Standardized tests, designed to be administered under the identical conditions every time, are often used to measure how well schools are teaching as well as how well children are achieving.

A norm-referenced test compares performance of an individual to that of the norming population, the group on which the test was standardized. Plotted on a graph, the scores on such tests take the shape of a bell curve, with the largest portion of scores concentrated near the middle (the "average") and very few at either the high end or the low end.

Criterion-referenced tests differ in that they measure performance in terms of an absolute mastery of particular skills the child is expected to have learned; that is, they are tied directly to specific areas of curriculum. Diagnostic tests, another major type, are designed to lead directly to instructional decisions.

Critical for all these tests are validity (the extent to which a test measures what it is supposed to measure) and reliability (the consistency of results). Another important statistical concept is the standard error of measurement, which tells us how confident we can be that a particular score is a child's "true" score.

In addition to a student's raw score on a test, publishers usually provide one or more derived scores. Common derived scores include the percentile rank, standard scores such as the stanine and the normal curve equivalent, and grade- and age-equivalent scores. All of these have benefits as well as disadvantages. Teachers need to be careful not to misinterpret derived scores or to foster confusion among students and their families.

Besides the risks of misinterpretation, concerns about standardized testing include the degree to which tests may drive the curriculum. Partly because of such concerns, many changes are occurring in standardized testing across the United States—changes about which you will want to keep informed, especially as they affect your own district. Your role as a teacher will also include helping students prepare for standardized tests and conveying the results to families in a positive, helpful way.

For measuring literacy, hundreds of formal tests are available. They include group and individual tests, norm- and criterion-referenced. The chapter has listed some specific tests, though this is in no way a comprehensive catalog.

A major concern in all standardized testing is the degree to which it may be unfair for special populations. Accommodations may be needed for students in special education programs, Title I students, and students for whom English is a second language. At the very least, educators should be aware of the pitfalls in using a single test for a diverse population.

The information in this chapter is intended simply to introduce some very basic terms and concepts for an area of testing with which all classroom teachers must deal. Ideas about such testing are being challenged daily, and decisions about how best to assess all students fairly are always evolving.

FOR ADDITIONAL READING

General Sources

Barrentine, S. (Ed.) (1999). *Reading assessment: Principles and practices for elementary teachers.* (A collection of articles from *The Reading Teacher*). Newark, DE: International Reading Association.

Calkins, L., Montgomery, K., & Santman, D. (1998). *A teacher's guide to standardized reading tests.* Portsmouth, NH: Heinemann.

Farr, B., & Trumbull, E. (1997). *Assessment alternatives for diverse classrooms.* Norwood, MA: Christopher-Gordon.

Salvia, J., & Ysseldyke, J. E. (1998). *Assessment* (7th ed.). Boston: Houghton Mifflin.

Publishers of Tests and Other Formal Assessment Tools

American Guidance Service, Inc., 4201 Woodland Rd., Circle Pines, MN 55014. Phone: 1–800–328–2560; web site: **http://www.agsnet.com/**

CTB/McGraw-Hill, 20 Ryan Ranch Rd., Monterey, CA 93940. Phone: 1–800–538–9547; web site: **http://www.ctb.com/**

Curriculum Associates, Inc., P.O. Box 2001, North Billerica, MA 01862–0901. Phone: 1–800–225–0248; web site: **http://www.curriculumassociates.com/**

LinguiSystems, 3100 4th Ave., East Moline, IL 61244–9700. Phone: 1–800–776–4332; web site: **http://www.linguisystems.com/products.asp**

PRO-ED Inc., 8700 Shoal Creek Blvd., Austin, TX 78757–6897. Phone: 1–800–897–3202; web site: **http://www.proedinc.com/**

Psychological Corporation, 555 Academic Court, San Antonio, TX 78204–2498. Phone: 1–800–228–0752, 1–800–211–8378; web site: **http:// www.hbtpc.com/**

Riverside Publishing Company, 8420 Bryn Mawr Ave., Chicago, IL 60631. Phone: 1–800–823–9540; web site: **http://www.riverpub.com/products/**

Texas Education Agency, 1701 N. Congress Ave., Austin, TX 78701–1494. Phone: 521–463–9734

Wide Range Inc., 15 Ashley Place, Suite 1-A, Wilmington, DE 19804–1314. Phone: 1–800–221–9728

FOR EXPLORATION: ELECTRONIC RESOURCES

Education Week on the Web.
   http://www.edweek.org/   Reports on various topics related to education.

ERIC Clearinghouse on Reading, English, and Communication.
http://www.indiana.edu/~eric_rec/   Offers many links to assessment sites.

FairTest Fact Sheets.
http://www.fairtest.org/facts/main.htm   Links to a number of different assessment-related "fact sheets" produced by FairTest: The National Center for Fair and Open Testing. These documents include information about different types of tests as well as pointed discussions of the problems with standardized testing.

Links to State Education Agencies.
http://www.ccsso.org/seamenu.html   This site contains a map of the United States. Click on any state and you will be routed to the web site of the state's education agency, where you can usually find information about the state's assessment programs.

National Center for Education Statistics.
http://nces.ed.gov/   The primary federal entity for collecting and analyzing data related to education in the United States and other nations. The site includes many links to other sites: for example, to the National Assessment of Educational Progress site, known as "The Nation's Report Card," and to information about the National Reading Conference.

National Center on Educational Outcomes.
http://www.coled.umn.edu/nceo/   Part of the College of Education and Human Development at the University of Minnesota, the NCEO focuses on educational outcomes for students with disabilities.

Southwest Educational Development Laboratory.
http://www.sedl.org/   Presents information about forty-five reading assessments used in grades K–2 in the southwestern states and information about state-mandated tests in the Southwest.

CLASSROOM APPLICATIONS

1. Volunteer as a proctor during "test" days at a local school. As soon after each stint of proctoring as possible, record everything you observed about the situation. Then draw some conclusions about how what you observed might affect your instruction if this were your classroom.

2. Examine the test manuals (and tests, if available) for the standardized, norm-referenced reading test given at one grade level in your school system. Then examine the standards or benchmarks and the curriculum for that grade. In writing, compare the test to the school standards. Draw conclusions about whether there seems to be a good match between what is taught and what is being tested.

3. Talk to special teachers about the formal assessments they use. Ask to examine some of the tests and their manuals. Compare different assessments of the (stated) same area. Be prepared to defend your choice of one assessment over another.

4. Do an Internet search for reports related to standardized assessment of literacy issues. Summarize the sites you find, and indicate whether you recommend them for others to examine and why.

Beyond the Classroom

Part IV

Collaborating with Families, Peers, and Other Professionals

FOCUS As you read the Eyewitness section, ask yourself the following questions:

1. What other responsibilities do teachers have besides teaching their classes?
2. Who participates in the family conference that Mr. Bingham arranges?
3. What can you learn from this scenario about conducting a good family conference?
4. What does the scenario tell you about teachers' committee work?

Eyewitness

Today we are following Mr. Bingham, a second-grade teacher, on the afternoon of a released day at his school. The released day is for home/family conferences and professional committee meetings. First, we see a part of Mr. Bingham's last family conference; then we see him attend the school's Professional Development Committee meeting.

As we catch up with Mr. Bingham, he is meeting with his student Fred and Fred's grandmother, Mrs. Higgenbottom. He begins by telling Mrs. Higgenbottom that he feels Fred has made a great deal of progress in figuring out words and reading more smoothly, which were the two goals set for Fred at their last conference.

Mr. Bingham then asks Fred to show his grandmother the two best pieces of reading work he has done during the past two months. Fred shows her two pictures: each is of a different bird, and each has three sentences written below the picture. Fred says these are pictures of the birds that he liked best in a book he finished a few weeks ago. His grandmother asks Fred to read aloud what is written under each picture. Fred reads what he has written smoothly and accurately. You can tell that Fred is proud of his drawings and his reading—and so is his grandmother.

Next, Mr. Bingham asks about Fred's reading at home. Mrs. Higgenbottom says that Fred reads a little each night to her or to his grandfather. She notes that Fred reads the words but can't always remember what he reads when she asks him questions.

At this point, Mr. Bingham takes out the benchmark checklist for Fred (the one for the Beginning Reading and Writing stage). He tells Mrs. Higgenbottom that he and Fred look at this checklist every two weeks. He says that Fred is doing fine with figuring out the words, but he is still struggling with getting the meaning of what he reads. (The checklist shows that Fred has pluses or checks in most word recognition categories, but has only a few checks and several minuses in the constructing meaning categories.) "What Fred does with you when he reads at home," Mr. Bingham says, "is the same thing he does at school."

After some discussion about understanding what you read, Mr. Bingham, Fred, and Mrs. Higgenbottom decide that the goal for Fred should be reading for understanding. Mr. Bingham suggests that Fred do all his home reading silently and then practice retelling what he has read. He suggests that Mrs. Higgenbottom and Fred take turns retelling sections of the story to each other. In this way, Mrs. Higgenbottom will serve as a model for Fred. At first, Mr. Bingham says, Fred should retell while looking at the book. After he is comfortable with this, he should try to retell from memory. Mr. Bingham further points out that when Fred retells, he should give only the most important or "big" ideas; he does not need to give all the details. The conference concludes with everyone agreeing that Fred's goal should be to improve his understanding of what he reads by doing silent reading and some retelling at home.

After completing this family conference, Mr. Bingham goes to the Media Center to meet with the four other teachers on the Professional Development Committee: Ms. Liong, who teaches special education for grades 3–6; Mr. Anders, a fifth-grade teacher; Ms. Washburn, who teaches first grade; and Ms. Fishbein, the assistant principal. The committee is finalizing plans for two **inservice** *meetings—meetings of practicing teachers that will form part of the school's* **staff development** *program, its ongoing training for teachers and other professionals in the school.*

The two upcoming meetings will be about ongoing assessment and inclusion for students in grades 1–6. Ms. Washburn has contacted Dr. Garcia, a professor at the local college who specializes in managing inclusion programs in elementary schools. She has a list of suggested workshop topics, ideas, and available dates from Dr. Garcia. The committee must now decide on the specific topics for the meetings. After some discussion, all the members agree that Dr. Garcia's suggestions should be followed.

Ms. Liong, however, expresses her concern, as she has before, about how teachers will accept these new ideas about inclusion. She suggests that the committee meet with Dr. Garcia prior to the inservice to discuss how the teachers in the school think about assessment.

Think back to the Focus questions. Consider some of the things that took place in our Eyewitness:

The Family Conference

- The teacher, student, and grandparent participated in the conference.
- Mr. Bingham operated from a positive point of view.
- Mr. Bingham focused on goals set at the last conference and tried to build on and connect to what Mrs. Higgenbottom said.
- Mr. Bingham was careful to use terminology that Fred's grandmother understood rather than educational jargon that might be unfamiliar to her. For example, he talked about Fred's "getting the meaning of what he reads" rather than about "constructing meaning."

The Committee Meeting

- Teachers were collaborating, working together to plan and implement the school's programs.
- The staff development and inservice planning involved topics of critical importance to the classroom.
- Teachers assumed part of the responsibility for seeing that staff development was implemented properly.

As you can see from this Eyewitness, teachers must work together to support an ongoing, assessment-based literacy program. No one should simply close the

FOCUS **As you read about collaboration with families and other professionals, ask yourself the following questions:**

1. Why is it important to involve families in the literacy assessment process?
2. What are some good ways to involve families?
3. Why is collaboration with colleagues essential to the successful literacy program?
4. What are some types of collaboration that should take place in your school?
5. What are some ways to continue your professional growth and development?

classroom door and work alone. To rephrase a common saying, "It takes a whole school" to create literate students.

In this chapter, we focus on the importance of collaboration in maintaining a well-balanced literacy program. We examine three main issues related to collaboration:

1 Involving families in the ongoing literacy assessment process.

2 Working together with colleagues, other classroom teachers, administrators, and specialists throughout the instructional process.

3 Maintaining one's own professional development through study and collaboration with colleagues.

Involving Family Members in Assessment

Research over many years clearly shows that when parents and other family members are involved in their children's education, the benefits for improving learning are great (National PTA, 1998). When family and school work together, some of the research-proven benefits are as follows:

- Children achieve more, regardless of their socioeconomic level.
- Students get better grades and have higher test scores.
- Students have more positive attitudes about school and learning.

One aspect of family involvement is to have parents and other family members participate in the ongoing assessment process. There are many ways to do this effectively. We will examine five such ways: conferences, reporting systems, portfolios, self-evaluation, and newsletters. First, however, you must begin by getting to know your community.

Getting to Know Your Community

Your process of collaborating with families should begin at the community level, which includes the entire spectrum of local diversity. The more diverse our classrooms, the greater the opportunities to provide better instruction for all students.

You can contact various organizations and groups representing different cultures within your community. You can find out about special programs, festivals, and materials they might have to help you bring particular cultures into your classroom. You can also invite family members of students in your room or your school to give talks and share their customs and traditions. They might talk about their food, dress, language, celebrations, and so on. These visits will help lay the groundwork for good instruction and for involving family members in the assessment process for individual children in your class.

Conferences

As you saw in our Eyewitness, family conferences are an important part of the ongoing assessment process. Nearly all schools require that teachers have a certain number of such conferences each year. Some schools provide released days when students go home early so that teachers can hold conferences. At other schools, conferences are held in the late afternoon or evening.

Usually the school's requirement is one conference per semester or one per grading period. In fact, if family members are to be truly involved in assessment, it is best that you have a conference for every grading period or at least for every other grading period. The exact number of family conferences you have will be directly influenced by the size of your class as well as by your school's policies.

We see ten steps to having an effective conference. Study each of these steps and think about how you can use them in your classroom.

1   *Schedule an appropriate time.* Many family members work outside the home. Sometimes everyone in the household has a job. Therefore, it is important to schedule your conference at a time that is convenient for the family members attending. This may be before school, during the day, after school, in the early evening, or even on a Saturday. Some schools allow teachers to go to the student's home for a conference. You must adhere to school policies on this matter.

Notify the family about the conference in enough time to allow for needed adjustments. This notification may be done over the telephone, by mail, or by a note taken home by the student. Figure 12.1 presents a sample notification form. Notice that it provides family members with a way to give alternative times and make suggestions for things they might want to discuss. Also, notice that the form indicates that the student is to attend. When children come from a second-language background and their parents don't speak or read English, send the notice in the family's native language, if possible.

2   *Prepare for the conference.* Advance preparation is critical for a successful conference. Figure 12.2 presents a sample form that many teachers use both to prepare for the conference and to consult during the conference. Even though our focus in this text is on assessment, conference time will also be devoted to other issues. You should think about the topics you want to discuss and the materials you need to illustrate any points you want to make. Recall that Mr. Bingham had Fred share some samples of his work. It is always important to have work samples, checklists, and so forth to illustrate points you want to make.

There may be times when you want to involve the principal or other building-level specialists in the conference. Plan ahead for this, but don't let so many people get involved that the conference becomes overwhelming to the student or the family.

When working with second-language families, be sure to check in advance to see if family members speak English. If they do not, try to arrange for a translator to be present during the conference. The translator might be an older student or one who is more proficient in English. It is also important to try to learn something about the attitudes toward school and teachers of the culturally diverse family.

3   *Involve the student in the conference.* When students are involved in the critical learning and assessment process, they know that everyone is working together for their benefit. Ask the student in advance of the conference to identify some work samples in particular areas to share during the conference. If

FAMILY CONFERENCE NOTIFICATION

Your family conference for _____ has
been scheduled as follows: (Child's Name)

        Date: _____

        Day.   _____

        Time: _____

        Location: _____

Please return the bottom of this form by _____.

You should plan for _____ to be present for the conference.
               (Child's Name)

_____
            (Teacher)

_____
      (School Telephone)

- -

Family Conference Agreement

_____   The scheduled time is good for me.

_____   I am unable to attend at the scheduled time. Better dates/times for me
         would be:

_____

Here are some things I would like to discuss in the conference:

_____

_____

_____
        (Signature)

_____
        (Telephone)

**Figure 12.1
Conference Notification
Form (Have copies available in other languages as
needed.)**

there are things you and the family member want to discuss without the student, you can simply ask the student to go to another area during this time. Have some books, magazines, or computer activities available for students during this period.

4   *Arrange a comfortable, pleasant, professional environment for the conference.* You are a professional. When you have conferences with family members and students, you are sharing your best professional image. Therefore, hold your

CONFERENCE FORM

Student's Name _____

Date of Conference _____ Time _____

Persons Attending _____

_____

Topics to Discuss: _____

_____

_____

Materials: _____

_____

_____

Conference Notes: _____

_____

_____

_____

_____

Goals: _____

_____

Next Conference: _____

_____

**Figure 12.2
Sample Conference Form**

conference in an area that is neat, clean, attractive, and organized. Usually conferences are held in the classroom, so make sure your room is organized, neat, and attractive. Such a room helps families have confidence in you.

Have comfortable seating available, preferably at a round table. If you do not have a round table, arrange comfortable chairs in a circle. Avoid arrangements with yourself on one side of the table and the family member(s) and student lined up on the other side, which can be seen as threatening or authoritarian.

5 *Begin your conference on a positive note.* Students and family members should not perceive conferences as a time when the teacher tells what is wrong with the student. Begin your conference with positive points, focusing on the good things the student has been doing. Show good, representative work chosen by you or by the student. If this is a follow-up conference, begin by discussing progress toward goals established at the previous conference.

6 *Build your conference from goals.* Involve the student in setting some goals before the conference. For example, one student said he had two goals for the conference: "Show my mom my good writing, and let her hear my oral reading to show her I can read." Having goals for the conference keeps it focused and on target.

7 *Listen.* Resist the temptation to talk too much. Listen to what family members and students are saying; you can gain some valuable insights. In a conference that one of the authors once held, a parent kept comparing her son (the student) to his older sister. It was easy to see why the child, who was an excellent student, always felt he was not doing a good job. Even when shown his good work, the mother always brought up something that the sister did better. During the year, we worked to help this parent see her son's strengths and understand the danger of comparing one child to the other.

8 *Use nontechnical language.* Recall that Mr. Bingham used language that Mrs. Higgenbottom could easily understand. Family members may not always understand educational terminology. Therefore, use clear, simple explanations without too much "jargon." Just put yourself in the family member's place. If you've ever taken your car to a mechanic who explains the problem using terminology you don't understand, you'll understand how some teachers make family members feel. Avoid this situation. Using educational "lingo" thoughtlessly creates a wall between you and the family.

9 *Give specific suggestions.* Parents and other family members really do want to help their children. Give them suggestions that they can readily follow. Recall that in our Eyewitness, Mr. Bingham suggested that Fred's grandmother have him read silently and retell what he read. He gave her specific ideas for doing this. Avoid vague suggestions like "Teach your child these words" or "Study spelling with your child." These are not helpful.

10 *End your conference with goals.* Just as you started your conference with goals, end it with goals. Conclude with one or two learning goals that the family can focus on at home and that you will work on at school. Keep the goals simple and doable. Recall how Mr. Bingham did this.

Reporting Systems

Another way to involve families in the literacy assessment process is through some type of reporting system. The most commonly known reporting system is the report card, with which everyone is familiar. Ever since we began our careers in education, report cards have been an issue. We remember no school situation in which the report card seemed exactly right. There was always a committee working on a new type of report card.

LOGAN SCHOOL
SIX-WEEK REPORT

Name _____Sara James_____   Grade ___4___

Teacher _____Mr. Watters_____   Date __10-15-99__   Report __#1__

Language Arts

Sara is making good progress with her reading, writing, and spelling. She is at the Almost Fluent Reading and Writing stage. She has improved in her comprehension and spelling. She needs to focus more on her writing, especially noun/verb agreement.

Math

Beginning geometry is Sara's favorite area in math. She is grasping the concepts and enjoying what she is learning. She needs to improve in the addition of fractions and in long division.

Social Studies

We have been studying a geography theme. Sara has good understanding of the concepts of continent, country, state, and province. She is beginning to understand the use of a map legend.

Figure 12.3
Sample Narrative Report

You probably remember the traditional report card. You were given letter grades in specific subjects: Reading, Math, English, Social Studies, and so forth. The traditional letter grade system was used: A, B, C, D, and E or F.

Over the years, educators came to realize that these letter-grade reporting systems had little meaning and were not helpful to families, students, or teachers. Schools began to try other alternatives. For example, sometimes a narrative was written giving information about the student's growth. Figure 12.3 provides an example. Often narratives are used only in the primary grades, though some schools have used them in the upper grades as well. Some schools combine some type of grading-scale system with a narrative, as shown in Figure 12.4. While narrative re-

TEACHER COMMENTS

First Report

Second Report

Third Report

Fourth Report

Growth in School Studies

		First Report			Second Report			Third Report			Fourth Report		
		Progressing Slowly	Progressing Satisfactorily	Progressing Very Well	Progressing Slowly	Progressing Satisfactorily	Progressing Very Well	Progressing Slowly	Progressing Satisfactorily	Progressing Very Well	Progressing Slowly	Progressing Satisfactorily	Progressing Very Well	

This section reports your child's achievement in studies listed. Items not checked were not evaluated at this time.

INTEGRATED LANGUAGE ARTS

1.	Displays comprehension skills and strategies													
2.	Self selects a variety of reading material													
3.	Reads independently													
4.	Reads with fluency													
5.	Reads with expression													
6.	Expands vocabulary													
7.	Identifies elements of a story													
8.	Identifies elements of fiction and nonfiction													
9.	Writes in response to reading													
10.	Uses the writing process													
11.	Writes for a variety of purposes													
12.	Expresses ideas in writing													
13.	Uses capitalization correctly													
14.	Uses puctuation correctly													
15.	Uses grammar correctly in speaking and writing													
16.	Spells assigned words correctly													
17.	Spells correctly in written work													
18.	Forms letters and numerals correctly													
19.	Writes neatly and legibly													
20.														
21.														
	EFFORT													

Figure 12.4
Sample Report Card Using a Grading Scale and Narrative (Used by permission of the Marion Community Schools, Marion, Indiana)

ports are very helpful, they are also very time consuming for teachers and have been abandoned by many schools.

The reporting system used in your school is an important part of the ongoing literacy assessment process and is one important way to involve families in this process. We believe you should consider the following guidelines to help you use your school's reporting system effectively:

- Find out about the reporting system in your school early. Look at previous reports sent home for your students, if they are available.

- Talk with other teachers who are familiar with the system to learn about any issues or problems.

- If a letter grading system is being used, talk with your principal and, if possible, other grade-level teachers about what each letter grade means and how to determine the criteria.

- At the beginning of the year, find out exactly when reports are to be sent home so that you can make sure you have the information you need to complete them.

- Study the reporting system carefully to make sure you know how to complete each report.

Portfolios

We introduced the concept of the portfolio in Chapter 3. Portfolios are a good way to involve family members in the ongoing assessment process (Farr & Tone, 1994). They can be used in family conferences as a way to show a student's progress. Family members can see the type of work a child has done at school and has selected to show in the portfolio. It is also helpful for family members to read the reflections of both the child and the teacher on work the child has done.

For further reading on this topic, see Tierney, Carter, and Desai (1991) and Pierce and O'Malley (1992), both listed in For Additional Reading at the end of the chapter.

Family Evaluations

Another effective way to involve the family in the assessment process is through evaluations of various aspects of a child's literacy activities at home. Figure 12.5 presents a sample home evaluation form.

A form of this type can be sent home at the beginning of the year and as often as you need. You will want to customize the form to suit your own special needs. By using such a form, you will learn about how family members perceive what their child is doing at home. Many times this information will help to explain why a child does or does not do certain things at school.

Newsletters

Newsletters are another good way to involve family members in the literacy learning and assessment process. These can be sent home periodically to keep families abreast of what's taking place in school. Students themselves can contribute to

---

HOME EVALUATION

Student's Name _____ Grade _____

Teacher _____ Date _____

Dear Family Member,

Please complete this form and return to school within five days. Think about your child in relation to each item.

1. This student reads a lot at home. ___ Yes ___ No

   Estimate the amount of time spent in daily reading: _____

2. List the types of things you see your child reading at home:

   _____

   _____

3. Circle the words that best describe the quality of your child's reading at home:

   Excellent - Good - Fair - Poor - Does Not Read

4. How often do you read to your child?

   Every Day - Once in a While - Whenever I Have Time

5. This student often likes to write stories, letters, and other things at home. ___ Yes ___ No

6. Circle the word(s) that best describe(s) the quality of your child's writing at home:

   Excellent - Good - Fair - Poor - Does Not Write

7. Make any comments that would help me work with your child in reading and writing.

   _____

   _____

   _____

   _____

Figure 12.5
Home Evaluation of
Literacy Activities

the newsletters. For example, one teacher with whom we work features two or three children in each newsletter. All children are included throughout the year.

If you are using a published reading—language arts series, you may find that newsletters are available as a part of the instructional program. See the example in Figure 12.6. Sometimes these letters are available in other languages as well, such as Spanish, as shown in Figure 12.7.

NEWSLETTER

Dear Family,

For the next few weeks, we'll be studying the theme "It's Cool. It's School." Your child will be reading about how real and imaginary fourth-grade students cope with the challenges and rewards of life at school.

Theme-related Activities to Do Together

When I Was in School...

Compare memories of your own school experiences with those of your child. Talk about classrooms, playground activities, teachers, friends, favorite subjects and not-so-favorite subjects, funny moments, and sad ones.

Is School Cool on TV?

As you watch TV together, pay attention to school-related stories and settings. Talk about whether they seem realistic. What are characters' attitudes toward school? How is the "TV school" like and unlike our school?

The Ideal School

Share ideas about your ideal school. Where would it be? What would it look like? What would the schedule be? What would you study?

Theme-related Books to Enjoy Together

Anna, the One and Only by Barbara Joosse. HarperCollins 1988 (144p) No matter how hard she tries to be good, high-spirited Anna seems to end up in trouble.

The Cat That Could Spell Mississippi by Laura Hawkins. Houghton 1992 (160p) Linda, the new girl in class, learns the hard way how to make friends.

Mrs. Cole on an Onion Roll and Other School Poems by Kalli Dakos. Simon 1995 (40p) A collection of humorous school poems.

Serious Science: An Adam Joshua Story by Janice Lee Smith. Harper 1993 (80p) When his little sister destroys his science fair project, Adam Joshua comes up with a new invention to save the world.

★ ***Thank You, Dr. Martin Luther King, Jr.*** by Eleanora E. Tate. Putnam 1992 (98p) Mary Elouise learns to appreciate her heritage after an African American story-teller visits her school.

Wayside School Gets a Little Stranger by Louis Sachar. Morrow 1995 (176p) The kids at the famous thirty-story school have a series of substitute teachers.

★ = Multicultural

➡ **Read with your child every day.**

Parenting Tip

Your child will have a more positive attitude and an improved ability to learn if the day gets off to a good start. Try to begin each school day with

- a healthy breakfast.
- a calm atmosphere.
- reliable transportation arrangements.
- a smile and a hug as a sendoff.

Figure 12.6
Sample Newsletter in English (Houghton Mifflin Company, *Invitations to Literacy*, Grade 4. Used by permission.)

BOLETÍN

Queridos familiares:

Durante las próximas semanas vamos a estudiar el tema "¡Vuela, vuela! ¡A la escuela!". Su hijo/a leerá relatos sobre niños de cuarto grado (reales o imaginarios) que se enfrentan a los desafíos de la vida escolar y disfrutan de sus satisfacciones.

Actividades para hacer con su niño/a

Cuando yo iba a la escuela...

Compare su experiencia como estudiante con la de su hijo/a. Platiquen acerca de los salones de clase, las actividades del recreo, los maestros, los amigos, las materias preferidas y materias "odiadas", los momentos felices y los tristes.

¿Cómo es la escuela en televisión?

Cuando vean televisión juntos, presten atención a los programas relacionados con la escuela. Observen si se parecen o no a la realidad. ¿Qué actitudes tienen los personajes con respecto a la escuela? ¿En qué se parecen la escuela de la televisión y nuestra escuela? ¿En qué se diferencian?

La escuela ideal

Expongan sus ideas sobre cómo debería ser la escuela ideal. ¿Dónde estaría? ¿Qué aspecto tendría el edificio? ¿Cuál sería el horario? ¿Qué estudiarían?

Libros con que su niño/a puede disfrutar

Anna, the One and Only por Barbara Joosse. HarperCollins 1988 (144p) Por mucho que intenta ser buena, Anna siempre termina en problemas.

The Cat That Could Spell Mississippi por Laura Hawkins. Houghton 1992 (160p) Linda, la niña recién llegada a la clase, aprende cómo hacer amigos.

Mrs. Cole on an Onion Roll and Other School Poems por Kalli Dakos. Simon 1995 (40p) Una colección de graciosos poemas escolares.

Serious Science: An Adam Joshua Story por Janice Lee Smith. Harper 1993 (80p) Cuando su hermanita le destroza el proyecto para la feria de ciencias, Adam Joshua crea un invento para salvar al mundo.

★ ***Thank You, Dr. Martin Luther King, Jr.*** por Eleanora E. Tate. Putnam 1992 (98p) Mary Elouise aprende a apreciar su origen después de que un narrador de cuentos afroamericano visita su escuela.

Wayside School Gets a Little Stranger por Louis Sachar. Morrow 1995 (176p) Los niños de la famosa escuela de treinta pisos tienen una serie de maestros sustitutos.

★ = Multicultural

➡ Lea con su niño/a cada día.

Consejo para los padres

Su hijo/a tendrá una actitud más positiva y una mejor predisposición para aprender si empieza bien el día. Trate de que los días de clase comiencen con

- un desayuno nutritivo
- una atmósfera tranquila
- un medio de transporte seguro
- ¡y una sonrisa y un abrazo de despedida!

Figure 12.7
Sample Newsletter in Spanish (Houghton Mifflin Company, *Invitations to Literacy*, Grade 4. Used by permission.)

Regardless of how you approach the collaborative process with families, you must involve family members in the literacy learning and assessment process. Use some of the ideas presented here. Seek out others from other sources. For Additional Reading lists some books that provide further ideas.

Collaborating with Colleagues

Throughout this text, we have stressed the importance of all teachers building their classroom programs around the stages of literacy development and a balanced literacy program. To make the school one that truly prevents failure and promotes success, all staff members must be seen as a team collaborating and working together (Hiebert, Pearson, Taylor, Richardson, & Paris, 1998). In this section, we examine the second important part of collaboration: working with colleagues.

To collaborate means to work together in a joint effort. Here we are talking about working together with colleagues in one's school in a joint effort to help all children become successful literacy learners. We address four aspects of collaborating with colleagues: planning with other teachers, working with building-level specialists, inclusion, and coaching. Even though these overlap, we address each separately.

Planning with Other Teachers

A significant part of collaboration within your school involves long-term planning with other teachers at your grade level or related grade levels. This planning focuses on examining the various stages of literacy development within each teacher's class and talking about what each is teaching and how students' learning is progressing.

We suggest that you meet at least once a month with teachers at your grade level or with teachers at related grade levels if you are in a multi-age teaching situation. During these meetings, you should cover such things as the following:

- Talk about the stages of development represented in your class. Review students' progress.

- Discuss instructional procedures that have worked particularly well and those that have not.

- Review individual students who have particular problems. Brainstorm alternative teaching ideas.

- Review assessment data for individual students or for the school as a whole; discuss areas of literacy that seem strong or weak.

Working with Building-Level Specialists

In most buildings, you will find a variety of specialists who operate as part of the educational team. These may include such individuals as a reading teacher or specialist, a special education or resource room teacher, a language specialist, an intervention teacher, a technology specialist, a music teacher, an art teacher, and so forth. You may work more directly with some of these teachers than with others. Some specialists may come into your classroom to work (see the next section on inclusion), and others may pull students from your classroom for special classes and programs. Whatever the arrangement, a number of things will make working with special teachers easier:

- Meet with special teachers periodically to let them know where your students are in their literacy development and what the students are studying. This type of information helps the special teacher coordinate his or her instruction with yours. If students are pulled from your room for any type of literacy instruction, you should meet with the special teacher at least once every two weeks to ensure close coordination. For example, discuss how a given student performs in your class and how he or she performs for the special teacher.

- If students are pulled from your room individually or in small groups, make sure they leave your room early enough to get to the special teacher on time. Special teachers work on a tight schedule and have a limited time with each individual or group.

- Include special teachers in family conferences when appropriate or needed. Often what a student does in special classes can provide important information for the family about the student's overall literacy learning.

- Consult with special teachers when completing home reports of any type. Information obtained from the special class may be very helpful in formulating your evaluation.

- If any of the special teachers do demonstration lessons, invite them to come into your class to provide a demonstration in an area where you need particular help with one or more students.

- If possible, visit the special classes from time to time to see how your students are performing. Insights gained by observing students' literacy behavior with a different teacher, in a different setting, and with different materials will help you to better understand each student's literacy development.

Building-level specialists are a part of your educational team. Working with them helps to make your instructional program stronger.

Inclusion

As a classroom teacher, you will definitely face the policy known as inclusion. *Inclusion* refers to the policy and procedures used in placing students with various disabilities in the regular classroom program for instruction (Lerner, 2000). **Full inclusion,** a policy followed in many districts, is the placement of *all* children with any and all special needs within the general education program for *all* instruction.

When you have students with special needs or disabilities within your class, remember they are to be held accountable for basically the same benchmarks as other students. Your task is to modify instruction as necessary to enable these students to achieve the benchmarks.

Depending on a student's disability, you may often have a paraprofessional or resource teacher to assist you with the instruction. This means that you and any person working in the room with you must plan together using the concepts, ideas, and suggestions presented in this text. Your ability to work with such a colleague will be vital to the student's success in your classroom.

The policy of inclusion and, especially, full inclusion are both highly debated topics among general educators and special educators. For a full discussion of this topic, see Lerner (2000), listed in For Additional Reading. Recent analyses of existing research do not clearly support any one type of program for *all* students with disabilities. In fact, current data appear to support the idea that pullout programs may be best for some students with disabilities (Swanson, Hoskyn, & Lee, 1999).

Coaching Other Teachers

An important aspect of collaborating with your colleagues is coaching. **Coaching,** as the term is used here, is the process of helping a teacher internalize a set of instructional strategies through observation and feedback. Research over many years (Showers, Joyce, & Bennett, 1987) has shown the importance of this process. As a new teacher, or even as a veteran teacher who is learning some new instructional strategies, it is important that you have a coach to help you internalize what you learn.

If your school does not have a plan for coaching, we suggest that you locate another teacher with whom you can establish a partnership in which you coach each other. A full discussion of coaching is beyond the scope of this text. However, we suggest the following steps to develop a collaborative coaching model between yourself and your colleague:

1   *Identify areas for growth.* Together, you and your colleague should identify two or three teaching areas you would like to strengthen. For example, you might need help in working with a particular student or in using a particular strategy.

2   *Schedule a time for observation or make a video.* If possible, schedule a time to observe each other teaching or make a videotape (or an audiotape if video is not available) of a lesson. If an observation is being made, the observer should make notes about what was observed during the lesson.

3   *Meet to discuss observations or to review videos.* During this time, talk about the things that were taking place during the lesson. Offer each other feedback and suggestions for continued growth. Identify one area on which each of you should focus.

4   *Schedule another observation or make another video.* Continue this process until you believe you have developed strength in the particular area of concern. Then move on to another area.

Collaboration with colleagues through coaching is an important part of building teaching strength within your school. It is also an important part of continuing your own professional development, a subject which we will now address.

Continuing Professional Development

As you have just seen, collaboration through coaching supports your professional development. Yet in terms of professional development you will want to do much more than that, because you realize that a good teacher is never finished with

Teachers learn some new ideas during an inservice meeting.
© Elizabeth Crews

learning about children and about teaching. In this section, we discuss four ideas for continuing your professional development. You should select the ones that best suit your needs.

Attending Workshops and Taking Classes

Teachers can maintain a high level of knowledge in their fields and continue to update that knowledge through workshops and classes. Watch school bulletin boards for notices from local colleges and universities. Many school districts also have a full range of workshop and class opportunities to help teachers continue learning and keep up to date on the newest ideas.

In addition, there are private groups that offer full-day workshops for teachers on a variety of literacy-related topics affecting instruction and assessment. Following are some groups that present workshops throughout the country:

- Staff Development Resources (SDR)
  2535 West 237th Street, Suite 126
  Torrance, CA 90505
  1–800–678–8908

- Bureau of Education & Research (BER)
  P.O. Box 96068
  Bellevue, WA 98009–9668
  1–800–735–3503
  http://www.ber.org/
  email: info@ber.org

- Charlesbridge Seminars
  85 Main Street
  Watertown, MA 02472–4411
  1–800–225–3214

Contact these organizations to get on their mailing lists and find out what offerings they have in your area.

You will also want to attend professional meetings designed for teachers of second-language learners. You can find out about such meetings by contacting the following:

- The National Association of Bilingual Education
  1200 L Street NW, Suite 605
  Washington, DC 20005–4018
  202–898–1829

- Teachers of English to Speakers of Other Languages (TESOL)
  700 S. Washington Street, Suite 200
  Alexandria, VA 22314
  703–836–0774

Collect materials about working with bilingual students and their families. Use the above addresses plus the following:

- National Clearinghouse for Bilingual Education
  1118 22nd Street, NW
  Washington, DC 20037
  http://www.ncbe.gwu.edu/library/

Joining Professional Organizations

Becoming a member of some professional organizations is an important part of your professional growth. You will learn about local and state organizations from colleagues in your area. These organizations will help you keep up with the latest research, adopt good ideas from other teachers, and share ideas of your own.

You will also want to join a national organization related to literacy. The two largest national literacy organizations are:

- International Reading Association
  800 Barksdale Road
  Newark, DE 19714–8139
  302–731–1600
  http://www.reading.org/

- National Council of Teachers of English
  1111 W. Kenyon Road
  Urbana, IL 61801–1096
  1–800–369–6283
  http://www.ncte.org/
  email: public_info@ncte.org

When you join one of these organizations you receive many benefits, such as professional journals, special workshops, and information on political issues related to education.

Maintaining Professional Reading

Reading professional journals and magazines for teachers is also an important part of your continuing professional development. The two professional organizations mentioned in the preceding section offer a number of professional journals. You get one journal with your membership and can subscribe to other journals for an additional fee:

International Reading Association

- *Lectura y vida:* Spanish-language journal for all teaching levels
- *The Reading Teacher:* for preschool, primary, and elementary teachers
- *Journal of Adolescent and Adult Literacy:* for teachers of middle school, high school, and adult learners
- *Reading Research Quarterly:* a journal of reading research

National Council of Teachers of English

- *Language Arts:* for elementary teachers and teacher educators
- *Primary Voices K–6:* a journal written by different teams of elementary educators
- *School Talk:* a newsletter for classroom teachers
- *Voices from the Middle:* for middle school teachers

The following are some other widely read magazines published for teachers:

- *Instructor*
  Scholastic Inc.
  555 Broadway
  New York, NY 10012
  1–800–544–2913
  http://teacher.scholastic.com/products/instructor.htm
- *Early Childhood Today*
  Scholastic Inc.
  555 Broadway
  New York, NY 10012
  1–800–544–2913
  http://teacher.scholastic.com/products/ect.htm
- *The Mailbox*
  Education Center Inc.
  3515 West Market Street
  Box 9753
  Greensboro, NC 27403
  1–800–334–0298
  http://www.theeducationcenter.com/

- *Teaching K–8*
  40 Richards Avenue
  Norwalk, CT 06854
  1–800–249–9363
  http://www.teachingK–8.com/
- *Copycat Magazine*
  Copycat Press, Inc.
  P.O. Box 081546
  Racine, WI 53408–1546
  414–634–0146
  http://www.copycatpress.com/navcm.htm
- *Creative Classroom*
  Children's Television Workshop
  One Lincoln Plaza
  New York, NY 10023
  1–800–759–6383
  http://www.creativeclassroom.org/

Networking

Networking is the process of getting to know other individuals who do the same or a similar type of work that you do. Networking gives teachers the opportunity to discuss and share issues and problems with others who have similar concerns. Networking within one's own building is invaluable; in part, this is what we have been discussing in terms of collaboration and planning with other teachers and specialists.

In today's world, however, networking goes far beyond the building where one teaches. Attending conferences at which you can meet and talk with other teachers is also a powerful part of networking. You are able to find out how teachers in another school, district, state, or country handle various aspects of education.

Networking has been greatly enhanced by advances in technology. By using email and the Internet, it is possible to find out what other schools are doing; in fact, with email you can maintain an ongoing dialogue. Many schools and educational programs have their own web pages on the Internet. It is possible to find schools and classrooms similar to yours. Not only can you have a dialogue with the teachers, but your students can communicate with each other.

Following are some web sites that may be helpful to you:

- *Pathways to Literacy*

  http://www.tiill.com/

  Provides teacher resources, links to professional organizations, a live chat line, and a news forum.

- *Illinois Literacy Resource Development Center*

  http://www.ilrdc.org/

  Gives information on fourteen sites with programs in family literacy, work force education, and adult literacy.

- *California Early Literacy Learning*

  http://www.cell-exll.com/

  This is a professional development program to help elementary teachers strengthen their teaching of reading and writing.

- *Co-nect*

  http://www.co-nect.net/

  Provides information on how to become a Co-nect school, focusing on re-structuring and planning, using existing resources, and the wise use of technology.

- *The Learning Space* (Washington State)

  http://www.learningspace.org/

  Gives information about literacy programs, funding sources, classroom web pages, and so forth. Online tutorial training modules are provided.

Conclusion

You have devoted a great deal of your personal time to reading and studying the principles of this text. Your focus has been on becoming a strong teacher of literacy.

Being an assessment-based literacy teacher requires knowledge about literacy and instruction. It also requires that you work together with everyone involved in each child's learning process. This is why collaboration with families, colleagues, and other professionals is so critical to your continued professional growth as a teacher.

For all of us who teach, collaboration helps us carry out the job that we have chosen as our career: to help all children and young adults achieve success in literacy.

Summary

Collaboration is extremely important to successful literacy programs. This collaboration must involve families, peers, and other professionals.

Involving students' family members in the assessment process is important to effective literacy instruction. You need to begin by getting to know your community in terms of its cultural makeup. Then you can promote family involvement through conferences involving family members and students, the use of family-sensitive reporting systems, student portfolios, family evaluations, and newsletters.

Collaborating with peers and colleagues entails planning with other teachers and with building-level specialists to develop consistency within your program. Where inclusion is involved, planning and collaborating with others becomes especially important. Another important aspect of collaboration is the coaching that teachers can provide to each other. Every school needs some type of program in which teachers are coached by peers and other professionals.

Ongoing professional development can support and deepen what you gain through direct collaboration. Opportunities for professional development include attending workshops and classes, joining professional organizations, maintaining your professional reading by keeping up with journals in your field, and networking with other teachers and education professionals.

FOR ADDITIONAL READING

Baghban, M. (1989). *You can help your young child with writing.* Newark, DE: International Reading Association.

Grinnell, P. C. (1984). *How can I prepare my young child for reading?* Newark, DE: International Reading Association.

Lerner, J. (2000). *Learning disabilities: Theories, diagnosis, and teaching strategies* (8th ed.). Boston: Houghton Mifflin.

Pierce, L., & O'Malley, M. J. (1992). *Performance and portfolio assessment for language minority students.* Washington, DC: National Clearinghouse for Bilingual Education.

Rich, D. (1994). *Helping your child succeed in school with activities for children aged 5 through 11.* Washington, DC: U.S. Department of Education.

Thomas, A., Fazio, L., & Stiefelmeyer, B. L. (1999a). *Families at school: A guide for educators.* Newark, DE: International Reading Association.

———— (1999b). *Families at school: A guide for parents.* Newark, DE: International Reading Association.

Tierney, R. J., Carter, M. A., & Desai, L. E. (1991). *Portfolio assessment in the reading-writing classroom.* Norwood, MA: Christopher-Gordon Publishers, Inc.

FOR EXPLORATION: ELECTRONIC RESOURCES

In addition to the web sites mentioned in the chapter text, the following may be useful:

ABC's of Inclusion.
http://ink.sped.ukans.edu/ksbe/abc.html   This site contains a manual, sponsored by the Kansas State Board of Education, on collaborative teaming in inclusive classrooms.

The National Coalition for Parent Involvement in Education (NCPIE).
http://www.ncpie.org/   NCPIE is committed to developing effective family-school partnerships throughout the United States. The web site provides guidelines for developing partnerships and information about NCPIE organizations, special activities, and resources.

Teachers.Net.
http://www.teachers.net/   This web site provides access to a number of different online chat rooms covering topics relevant to teachers. Teachers can use these chat rooms to ask for advice, post lesson plans, and share their experiences.

Working Hand in Hand to Educate Children: Tips for Parents, Families and Teachers.
http://www.handinhand.org/tips.html   Emphasizing the importance of good relationships between teachers and families, this site provides specific advice useful for both teachers and parents.

CLASSROOM APPLICATIONS

1. Interview several teachers to find out how they handle family conferences. If the school approves, sit in on one or more conferences. Summarize your observations and compare them with the suggestions given in this chapter.

2. Talk with the teachers in a school about how they work with the building-level specialists. Interview at least one specialist to get his or her perspective on how this process works.

3. Observe a classroom that has an inclusion program. Talk with the educators involved to discover their feelings about how this process works.

4. Attend a professional meeting of a local, state, or national literacy organization. Go to some of the sessions, seek opportunities to talk to other teachers, and see what types of exhibits are available.

Resource File

This part of the book contains resource materials that classroom teachers should find useful throughout the elementary and middle school grades. The first section lists all the benchmarks for literacy development introduced in Chapter 1 and discussed in detail in Chapters 5 through 9. The following sections, grouped by the chapter to which they most directly pertain, include a wide variety of assessment forms and other materials useful in a balanced literacy program. As you teach, you will want to adapt these materials to the needs of your own individual students. Remember that the stages of literacy development are not rigid, and tools useful at one stage may still be appropriate at later stages.

The following listing will help you locate individual items in this Resource File.

BENCHMARKS

Introduction

The term *benchmark* was first used by surveyors. It referred to something that has a permanent position, such as a rock, that can be used as a reference point for making other determinations. It has come to be used as a term for any standard of merit or achievement.

In education, we use the term *benchmarks* when we suggest behaviors that typify certain stages of achievement or development. The following sections list benchmarks for various stages of literacy development. Although these benchmarks are widely acknowledged to be true (see the rationale and evidence for the benchmarks in Chapter 1), they come with a cautionary note: a child does not develop smoothly from one stage to the next, nor does a child develop equally in all areas. Therefore, while these benchmarks generally hold true for all children, an individual child will seldom fit neatly into just one slot.

Along with the benchmarks, we present behaviors that indicate whether a child has achieved them. See Chapters 5 through 9 for suggestions for assessing and recording these behaviors and planning instruction based on what this knowledge tells you.

Another caveat is that separating the language systems—oral language (listening and speaking), reading, and writing—is almost impossible. They work together and, in part, develop together. For example, the child who listens to and can retell a favorite story (a reading benchmark) is also, obviously, showing development in both listening and speaking. Nevertheless, for the purposes of this book, we describe the categories separately. As you examine the benchmarks, note the overlap between one category and another.

These benchmarks should be used to guide instruction for all students. However, English-language learners may not exhibit some of the behaviors at the same time native speakers do because they have not had enough exposure to English. Often, because of the "silent period" in language production (see Chapter 3), their oral performance may not reflect their underlying competence. Getting at true competence may require use of the students' first language and alternative means of expression, such as gestures, pointing, or drawing.

THE EARLY EMERGENT LITERACY STAGE

Oral Language

The child shows through both receptive (listening) and productive (speaking) behaviors that language development is occurring.

✔ The child shows pleasure in stories, poems, and informational texts.

✔ Attends to read-alouds

✔ Attends to programs on television and will predict future events during commercials

✔ Can retell stories in sequence or tell what a story or expository text is "about"

✔ Uses book language when retelling story (example: "Once upon a time . . .") and informational text

✔ Likes to make up stories

✔ Tells a story or gives information to go with a picture

The child shows growing facility with the functions (uses) of language.

✔ Retains oral directions to do more than one thing; usually can tell the directions back

✔ Makes verbal requests or gives verbal orders that are understood by others

✔ Asks questions for information and for permission

✔ Converses with peers and adults

✔ Reports orally on events in his or her life

The child enjoys word play.

✔ Likes to play word games

✔ Pretends or role-plays using appropriate language

✔ Repeats and uses (sometimes inappropriately) new words

The child shows increasing knowledge of grammar and other language conventions.

✔ Tells you a sentence doesn't make sense or sound right if incorrect syntax or incorrect facts are presented

✔ Is generalizing about such language oddities as irregular plurals and verb forms

✔ May be able to identify what is or is not a complete sentence, though cannot tell why

Reading and Book Knowledge

The child has acquired many concepts about print.

✔ Has concepts about books and print

✔ Knows that labels name products or tell about something

✔ Asks questions about print and about own writing, scribbling, or drawing

✔ Knows the purpose of some print

✔ Likes playing with movable and/or magnetic letters, arranging them into "words" and "reading" them or asking an adult, "What word did I make?"

The child is familiar with various genres.

✔ Knows several/many nursery rhymes

✔ Knows several/many traditional stories such as fairy tales

The child begins to construct meaning.

✔ Predicts what will happen next or what word or phrase comes next during read-aloud

✔ Makes up stories to go with pictures

✔ Can retell a story he or she has heard

✔ Can play games such as "What if . . . "

The child enjoys literature and language.

✔ Enjoys listening to stories read aloud

✔ Wants favorite stories read over and over

✔ Looks at books independently

✔ Pretends to read

✔ Enjoys playing with sounds and words

Writing and Uses of Writing

The child knows the purpose of writing.

✔ Understands that the marks on a paper mean something

✔ Wants to write messages, letters, greeting cards, and shopping lists

The child tries to communicate in writing.

✔ Uses paper and pencil (marker, crayon, chalk, typewriter, computer) to attempt to write

✔ Arranges movable letters, writes string of letter-like shapes, or hits random string of letters on a keyboard, then asks, "What did I say?"

The child connects reading and writing.

✔ Wants to label own pictures

✔ Understands that stories are made up by a person who thought of the story and then wrote it down—and that he or she can do this also

✔ Can spin out a story to go with attempts at writing and with drawings

THE EMERGENT LITERACY STAGE

Oral Language

The student exhibits behaviors of the Early Emergent Literacy stage to a greater degree.

The student uses standard sentence construction and grammar.

✔ Is recognizing use of nonstandard language in self and others

✔ Is developing a sense of school/book language being perhaps different from home or neighborhood language

The student's facility with oral language is growing.

✔ Makes self understood by peers and adults

✔ Follows "rules" for conversation and discussion

✔ Retains oral directions

✔ Can ask questions for clarification

✔ Can paraphrase what others have said

✔ Participates in sharing

The student's oral language reflects literature to which the child is exposed.

✔ Uses new words from stories

✔ Uses "book language" when appropriate; that is, storytelling narrative is clearly different from conversation or simply relating an event

✔ Enjoys "making a play" of a favorite story

The student shows pleasure in language.

✔ Enjoys jokes related to words, such as puns

✔ Enjoys tongue twisters

✔ Enjoys hearing humorous books related to idioms

✔ Is proud of learning new words

✔ Tries out new words and asks what words mean

Reading

The student exhibits behaviors of the Early Emergent Literacy stage to a greater degree.

The student has acquired most or all of the concepts about print.

✔ Handles book in correct position; knows where to begin reading and what direction to read

✔ Can point to a word, two words, a letter, two letters

✔ Knows that print should match the voice of the reader

✔ Knows about such book parts as title, author, and so forth

The student is using print in everyday life.

✔ Can locate a specific book, record, tape, and so forth

✔ Recognizes some environmental print such as brand names and fast-food restaurant signs

The student is acquiring word-recognition skills.

✔ Recognizes and can name most letters

✔ Can match many upper- and lower-case letters

✔ Recognizes and can name some words

✔ Recognizes own name in print and perhaps other names

✔ Shows evidence of phonemic awareness

✔ Has a sense of letters "making sounds"

✔ Is beginning to use phonics; knows many letter-sound associations, including both consonants and vowels

✔ Is beginning to use other decoding strategies such as sight words, context, graphics, and word structure

The student is constructing meaning.

✔ Can retell a story page by page

✔ Can summarize

✔ Participates in small group and whole-class discussions about books and stories

✔ Talks about books with others

✔ Responds to books in writing

✔ Begins to see self as a reader

Writing

The student exhibits continued growth in many of the Early Emergent Literacy behaviors.

The student is using spelling and other writing conventions.

✔ Can write own name (perhaps first name only), with all or most of the letters present, though not necessarily formed correctly

✔ Can name most letters in random presentation

✔ Forms letter-like shapes and some correct letters

✔ Uses some punctuation

✔ Shows phonemic awareness and beginning association of letters and sounds in attempts to spell

✔ Can give letter sound or say a word that begins with the letter sound

The student is using writing for own purposes.

✔ Can keep a journal that may combine drawing and writing

✔ Attempts to read others' writing

✔ Shares writing with others

✔ Shows interest in practicing writing, often through copying favorite stories from books

The student is becoming familiar with the writing process.

✔ Uses the steps of the process appropriately with guidance

✔ Understands that the author of what is read has also gone through a process of some kind

The student is constructing meaning in writing.

✔ Responds to reading

✔ Composes both narrative and expository pieces

✔ Expresses and reports on personal events and feelings

THE BEGINNING READING AND WRITING STAGE

Oral Language

The student exhibits behaviors from the Emergent Literacy stage to a greater degree.

The student's use of standard English continues to develop.

✔ If speaker of nonstandard English, is learning to switch between two languages

✔ Self-corrects while speaking

The student's facility with language is growing.

✔ Listens to classmates and can paraphrase what others have said

✔ Oral language reflects increasing vocabulary

✔ Will ask for meaning of unknown words used in class

✔ Is interested in collaborative work with classmates

✔ Can participate in a discussion

✔ Can plan and ask oral questions

✔ Will plan and present an oral report

The student continues to show pleasure in words.

✔ Makes jokes related to plays on words

✔ Shows interest in the history of words

✔ Enjoys nonsense and silly poems such as those by Shel Silverstein and Jack Prelutsky

✔ Enjoys making own dictionary

Reading

The student continues to show growth in many of the behaviors from the Emergent Literacy stage.

The student is acquiring additional word-recognition skills and strategies.

✔ Recognizes and can name all letters in random order

✔ Recognizes and can name many words at sight

✔ Uses phonics and structural elements to determine the pronunciation of words

✔ Chooses appropriate strategies and skills to sound out words

✔ Uses context to determine word meaning

The student constructs meaning from print.

✔ Can read and retell familiar stories

✔ Reads own writing

✔ Is beginning to use critical strategies such as predicting, identifying important information, self-questioning, monitoring, summarizing, and evaluating

✔ Attempts to read and retell unfamiliar texts (narrative and expository)

✔ Self-corrects when reading

✔ Is confident and willing to take risks

✔ Chooses to read during free time

✔ Sees self as a reader

✔ Likes to read to others

✔ Begins to explore using research tools and skills such as glossary, table of contents, dictionary or picture dictionary, beginning encyclopedias, and reference sources on CD-ROM and in library

Writing

The student exhibits continued growth in many of the Emergent Literacy behaviors.

The student exhibits a variety of general writing behaviors.

✔ Enjoys writing

✔ Is confident about own writing

✔ Communicates with others spontaneously

✔ Attempts to read others' writing

✔ Shows interest in writing

✔ Writes in a variety of formats for different purposes, such as journals, learning logs, notes, lists, stories, poems, reports, and labels

The student is growing in the use of mechanics and conventions of writing.

✔ Forms letters conventionally for the most part

✔ Shows increased phonemic awareness along with increased visual memory and spelling sense

✔ Invents spelling when conventional spelling is not yet known and edits/proofreads later if writing is to be published

✔ Is beginning to learn spelling patterns that reflect phonics knowledge

✔ Recognizes nonstandard usage and grammar in own writing and edits/proofreads

✔ Uses word processing

The student uses the writing process.

✔ Participates in and understands the purpose of all steps of the writing process

✔ Uses the writing process collaboratively and independently

✔ Listens to or reads the writing of others and makes appropriate positive comments related to story parts or text structure

THE ALMOST FLUENT READING AND WRITING STAGE

Oral Language

The student exhibits continued growth in many of the behaviors from the Beginning Reading and Writing stage.

The student's use of standard English continues to develop.

✔ Is aware of own problem areas

✔ Accepts diverse usage or varieties of English from others without criticism

The student's facility with language is growing.

✔ Uses new vocabulary

✔ Collaborates with classmates in speaking and listening situations

✔ Participates in discussion without adult supervision

✔ Can listen to and then question or respond to (use an idea expressed by) a speaker

✔ Speaks in front of a group using written notes but no script

The student continues to take pleasure in the use of language.

✔ Appreciates symbolic language such as metaphor

✔ Enjoys listening to and telling riddles and jokes

✔ Begins to appreciate shades of meaning, connotation, precise word choice, the evocative power of certain words

✔ Recognizes and begins to use persuasive techniques

Reading

The student exhibits continued growth in behaviors from the Beginning Reading and Writing stage.

The student regularly uses all word-recognition strategies.

✔ Uses structure, phonics, and syntax (language structure) to determine word pronunciation

✔ Uses context

✔ Selects appropriate skills and strategies to sound out unknown words

✔ Reads orally with 90 percent accuracy in grade-level materials

✔ Self-corrects

✔ Takes risks

✔ Uses a dictionary both for pronunciation and for meaning

The student's ability to construct meaning is growing.

✔ Enjoys listening to selections that may be beyond reading ability

✔ Reads independently

✔ Enjoys reading a variety of genres

✔ Reads outside of school even without reward

✔ Prefers to read silently

✔ Continues to grow in the use of strategies for constructing meaning: predicting, identifying important information, self-questioning, monitoring, summarizing, and evaluating

The student reads for a variety of purposes.

✔ Appreciates levels of meaning in stories

✔ Has a growing interest in authors, illustrators, and genres

✔ Is aware of own purpose(s) for reading

✔ Is beginning to understand text structure in expository text

✔ Uses variety of print sources for information

✔ Is learning to synthesize information from more than one source

The student is learning research skills.

✔ Uses card catalog or the computer equivalent

✔ Operates the computer

✔ Is learning to narrow search, whether for print or Internet sources

✔ Is learning to read graphic materials such as graphs, charts, tables, time-lines, and maps

✔ Uses dictionary, thesaurus, encyclopedia, and other references, either in book form or on CD-ROM

Writing

The student exhibits continued growth in behaviors from the Beginning Reading and Writing stage.

The student writes for a variety of purposes.

✔ Is aware of the power of the written word

✔ Can identify a topic and theme and develop a paper to fit a given rubric

✔ Can plan and put together a report

✔ Writes stories with all the literary elements present

The student shows growth in the mechanics and conventions of writing.

✔ Uses spelling patterns to attempt to spell words

✔ Uses increasingly conventional spelling, demonstrating increased visual memory and spelling sense

✔ Uses increasingly more appropriate grammar and punctuation in writing

✔ Uses word processing tools to check spelling, to format, to revise, and to edit

The student shows pleasure in writing.

✔ Sees self as a writer

✔ Offers constructive comments to peers about their writing

✔ Seeks suggestions for revision during peer and teacher conferences

✔ Chooses to write in free time and at home

✔ Enjoys sharing writing with peers either by reading aloud or by publishing in print

✔ Enjoys and supports the writing of classmates

The student connects reading and writing.

✔ Uses what is learned about narrative writing, such as form, theme, literary techniques, style, idioms, and colorful language, in own writing

✔ Uses what is learned about text structure in expository writing and attempts to use a variety of structures in own informational writing

✔ Appreciates poetry forms and attempts to write them

THE FLUENT READING AND WRITING STAGE

Oral Language

The student exhibits continued growth in behaviors from previous stages.

The student's facility with language is growing.

✔ Oral language reflects increasing vocabulary

✔ Shifts from formal to informal usage to suit occasion

✔ Listens to oral presentations with understanding

The student uses oral language for a variety of purposes.

✔ Discusses literature with pleasure and understanding

✔ Enjoys role-playing and Readers' Theater

✔ May enjoy debate or speech competition

The student continues to enjoy language.

✔ Is sensitive to body language and tone of others and self

✔ Can appreciate the importance of speech in interpreting the written word; for example, news reporters, actors, comedians

Reading

The student continues to display many of the behaviors from the Almost Fluent Reading and Writing stage.

The student seldom seeks or needs assistance with word recognition.

The student uses a wide variety of strategies to construct meaning.

✔ Grasps differences in genres

✔ Perceives text structure

✔ Appreciates levels of meaning in a story

✔ Varies reading according to purpose for reading

✔ Is effectively using strategies to construct meaning: predicting, self-questioning, monitoring, summarizing, and evaluating

✔ Can verbalize process used to construct meaning; that is, is aware of own thinking (metacognition)

✔ Is learning study strategies such as taking notes

✔ Uses graphic material to construct meaning

The student enjoys reading.

✔ Recommends books to others

✔ Is exploring young adult and adult fiction and nonfiction

✔ Sees self as a competent reader

✔ Sets goals and self-evaluates

✔ Is aware of own purposes for reading

The student is refining research skills begun at the previous stage.

✔ Can plan a research project

✔ Knows how to locate information

✔ Takes notes in a variety of ways; attributes sources

✔ Synthesizes information into a final product

Writing

Prior writing behaviors strengthen and deepen.

The student writes for a variety of purposes and reasons.

✔ Is aware of how writing can contribute to self-awareness

✔ Is using writing to persuade

✔ Can write in response to a prompt to fit a given rubric

The student is growing in the mechanics of writing.

✔ Edits own work

✔ Can edit the work of others

✔ Can independently verify spelling, grammar, and usage

The student is using the writing process.

✔ Uses all steps of the writing process independently

✔ Varies prewriting techniques according to task

✔ Revises own work extensively

✔ Is developing a personal writing style, or voice

The student sees self as a competent writer.

✔ Sets goals and evaluates own writing

The student connects reading and writing.

✔ Recognizes author's craft and uses in own writing

✔ Is experimenting with writing in many forms and genres

K-W-L Chart (Chapter 2)

K-W-L Study Guide

Name _____ Date _____

Topic (be specific) or reading assignment _____

K What I **Know**	W What I **Want** to Know	L What I **Learned**

New questions after completing chart: _____

_____

_____

My plan for what to do next: _____

_____

_____

_____

_____

_____

Interest Inventory

Read-Aloud Items

Directions: Distribute Response Forms to children. Discuss each of the "faces," explaining what each might represent. Tell children there is no right or wrong answer. They are to be completely honest. Tell them you will read each statement twice. They are to put an **X** on the face that shows how they feel about each.

Practice Item:

1. I like to roller skate.

Repeat the statement. Say: Find number 1. Look at each face. Put an **X** on the face that shows how you feel about roller skating. *Circulate to be sure each student has followed directions. Continue with the remaining items. (Omit or add items if you choose.)*

2. I like to read at home.
3. I like to read about animals.
4. I like to read fairy tales.
5. I like scary stories.
6. I am interested in stories about space.
7. I like to use computers.
8. I like to watch television.
9. I would rather watch television than read a book.
10. I like to play outside with my friends.
11. I would rather play outside than read.
12. I like to do sports.
13. I like arithmetic.
14. I like reading books as much as television and playing outside.
15. I like to listen to someone read a story out loud.
16. I like to draw pictures about stories.
17. I wish I owned more books.
18. I think I am good at school.
19. I read in bed before I go to sleep.
20. I like to make up stories.

Interest Inventory

Response Form

Name _____ Date _____

1. 😊 😊 😐 😟 😞   11. 😊 😊 😐 😟 😞

2. 😊 😊 😐 😟 😞   12. 😊 😊 😐 😟 😞

3. 😊 😊 😐 😟 😞   13. 😊 😊 😐 😟 😞

4. 😊 😊 😐 😟 😞   14. 😊 😊 😐 😟 😞

5. 😊 😊 😐 😟 😞   15. 😊 😊 😐 😟 😞

6. 😊 😊 😐 😟 😞   16. 😊 😊 😐 😟 😞

7. 😊 😊 😐 😟 😞   17. 😊 😊 😐 😟 😞

8. 😊 😊 😐 😟 😞   18. 😊 😊 😐 😟 😞

9. 😊 😊 😐 😟 😞   19. 😊 😊 😐 😟 😞

10. 😊 😊 😐 😟 😞   20. 😊 😊 😐 😟 😞

Interest Inventory for Older Children (Chapter 2)

Interest Inventory

Name _____ Grade _____ Date _____

1. Name your favorite book and tell why you like it. _____

   _____

2. How many books do YOU own? What kind? _____

   _____

3. Tell about any members of your family who like to read. _____

   _____

4. About how many books did you read last month? What were they? _____

   _____

5. What kinds of things do you read outside of school? (Which magazines? Which parts of

   newspapers? Which kinds of books?) _____

   _____

6. Who are your favorite authors? Why? _____

   _____

7. What topic interests you most? (For example: space, animals, adventure, other parts of the

   world, how things work, stars, etc.) _____

8. What kinds of stories do you like best? (For example: horror, realistic, historical, ghost,

   mystery, legend, myth, biography) _____

9. Do you enjoy listening to someone read aloud to you? Why or why not? _____

   _____

10. How important is reading in your life? Think about how you would feel if you could never
    read a book again . . . if you had to choose between books and television or movies . . .

    _____

    _____

Literacy Attitude Survey for Young Children (Chapter 2)

Literacy Attitude Survey
(Items to be read aloud by teacher)

Name _____ Date _____

(Do * sample before numbered items.)

*   I like animal shows on television.

1. I am a good writer.

2. I make up good stories.

3. I am good at helping others read.

4. I like to read at school.

5. I like to read at home.

6. I like to write at school.

7. I like to write at home.

8. I like to read my stories to my friends.

9. I am a good reader.

10. Reading is important at my house.

Literacy Attitude Survey for Older Children (Chapter 2)

Literacy Attitude Survey

Name _____ Date _____

1. When I go to the library, I _____

   _____

2. At Drop Everything And Read time, I _____

   _____

3. When we work in groups, I _____

   _____

4. I wish I could read _____

   _____

5. In school, I am very good at _____

   _____

6. My favorite class is _____ because _____

   _____

7. I learned to read (tell when and how) _____

   _____

8. I think _____ is the best reader I know because _____

   _____

9. The hardest thing for me about reading is _____

   _____

10. Tell about your reading and writing in the future: _____

    _____

Homework Cover Sheet (Chapter 2)

Homework Packet

PLEASE KEEP YOUR CHILD'S WORK AND RETURN THE EMPTY PACKET WITH THE COVER PAGE ATTACHED AND YOUR COMMENTS. THANK YOU.

_____
(teacher's name)

- -

Child's Name _____ Date _____

(Numbers 1–5 to be completed by the teacher)

1. Homework returned   Mon   Tues   Wed   Thurs   Fri

2. Books returned   On Time   Late   Not at All

3. What we are studying next week: _____

4. Papers/work/test(s) in this packet: a. _____

                            b. _____

                            c. _____

                            d. _____

                            e. _____

5. Comments: _____

_____

_____

_____

- -

6. Family comments or concerns: _____

_____

_____

_____

Self-Reflection — Literature Circle

Name _____ Date _____

Title of Book _____

Author _____

Illustrator _____

Use the scale for each of the following:

(Scale: 5 = Wonderful, 4 = Pretty good, 3 = Okay, 2 = Not so Good, 1 = Ooops)

How I felt about the book _____

How well I read the book _____

My part in discussion circles _____

My journal response during the reading of the book _____

Write about your literature discussion circle. What is the best part? What is the worst? How would you change it? How would you change the way you participate?

_____

_____

_____

_____

_____

_____

_____

Self-Reflection Form for Independent Reading (Chapter 2)

Self-Reflection — Independent Reading

Name_____ Date_____

Title and Author_____

Mark the scales:

1. How I felt about the book:

> Loved it   Okay   Didn't like it

> Explain your marking _____

> _____

> _____

2. I understood the ideas:

> Mostly   Some   Not much

> Explain your marking _____

> _____

> _____

What else would you like to say about reading this book?

_____

_____

_____

_____

_____

_____

_____

THINKING ABOUT MY READING

Name _____ **Date** _____

Title and Author of Book _____

_____

	All the time	Sometimes	Hardly ever
Before reading, did I			
* Preview the book			
* Predict			
During reading, did I			
* Stop and think			
* Change predictions			
After reading, did I			
* Retell to myself			
* Respond			

What do I need to do better? _____

_____

_____

_____

_____

_____

Levels of Language Production: Informal Checklist for Classroom Teacher (Chapter 3)

Levels of Language Production

Name _____ Date _____ Grade _____

Check behavior that is most typical. Add comments.

	Check	Comments
Preproduction		
Mostly silent		
Points to pictures of some words		
Draws pictures if asked		
Answers with yes/no card		
Early Production		
Listens attentively		
Speaks/one–two words		
Uses key words only		
Speech Emergence		
Uses phrases/short sentences		
Sometimes fluent		
Uses some articles, verb endings, adjectives and adverbs		
Intermediate Fluency		
Oral language similar to classmates		
Other Behaviors to Note		
Participates in class discussion		
Participates in small-group discussion		
Talks with classmates on playground		
Talks with other adults		
Family members speak English		

Form for Fluency Record or Running Record (Chapter 3)

FLUENCY RECORD

Name _____

Date _____ Time: from _____ to _____

Source of reading [give name of book or other reading material as well as page(s)]:

_____

p.___ _____
p.___ _____
p.___ _____
p.___ _____
p ___ _____
p.___ _____
p.___ _____
p.___ _____
p.___ _____
p.___ _____
p.___ _____
p.___ _____
p.___ _____
p.___ _____
p.___ _____
p.___ _____
p.___ _____
p.___ _____
p.___ _____
p.___ _____
p.___ _____
p.___ _____

—— x 100 = _____%

Notes:

RETELLING: NARRATIVE

Name _____ Date _____

Title of Story and Source _____

✓ = indicates whether student told about element unaided or after prompting by teacher
- = indicates student could not tell even with prompting

Elements Included	Unaided	Prompted
1. Setting (time, place, weather)		
2. Character		
Major(s)		
Others		
3. Problem		
4. Story Events		
Includes all major events		
Tells mostly in sequence		
5. Solution		
Tells how the problem was solved		
Tells how the story ended		

Comments/Analysis: _____

_____

_____

Future support needed: _____

_____

_____

_____

Retelling (Summarizing) Record for Expository Text (Chapter 3)

RETELLING: EXPOSITORY TEXT

Student Name ____________________ **Date** ____________

Selection/Author ______________________________

____

Parts Included	Unaided	Prompted
Topic		
Main idea(s)		
Supporting details		
Explanation/relating ideas/conclusion		

Comments/Analysis: ______________________________

____

____

____

____

Future support needed: ______________________________

____

____

____

____

Discussion Observation Grid (Chapter 3)

Discussion Check

Book/Story _____

Date _____

+ = often
S = sometimes
- = hardly ever
N/O = not observed

Poster to Encourage Good Discussion Behaviors (Chapter 3)

HOW TO HAVE A GOOD DISCUSSION

- Don't interrupt.

- Stick to the topic.

- Talk loud enough.

- Call people by name.

- Listen to other ideas.

- Don't argue.

- Don't hurt anyone's feelings.

- If one or two people haven't said anything, ask them what they think.

Oral Language Checklist for Individual Student (Chapter 5)

**ORAL LANGUAGE CHECKLIST:
EARLY EMERGENT LITERACY STAGE**

Name_____ Grade_____ Age _____

Key: Y = behavior present consistently
S = behavior sometimes present
N = behavior not yet present

Benchmark	Date						Comments
Pleasure in Stories, Poems, Information							
Attends to read-alouds							
Predicts							
Retells:							
story/sequence							
information/main ideas							
Uses book language when retelling							
Makes up stories							
Tells story to go with picture							
Functions of Language							
Retains oral directions							
Makes verbal requests/gives orders							
Asks questions							
Converses							
Reports							
Word Play							
Likes word games							
Role-plays							
Uses new words							
Grammar							
Knows when sentence doesn't sound right							
Generalizes irregular plurals and verb forms							
Identifies complete sentence							

Instructional Needs: (over)

Reading and Book Knowledge Checklist for Individual Student (Chapter 5)

READING AND BOOK KNOWLEDGE CHECKLIST: EARLY EMERGENT LITERACY STAGE

Name _____ Date _____ Grade/Year in School _____

Key: P = behavior present
S = some knowledge
L = little knowledge
N = behavior not present

Benchmark	Date							Comments
Concepts About Print								
Has concepts about books and print*								
Recognizes labels								
Questions about print								
Purpose of print								
Plays with letters								
Familiarity with Genres								
Nursery rhymes								
Traditional stories								
Construction of Meaning								
Predicts								
Makes up stories								
Retells								
Plays "What if . . ."								
Enjoyment								
Enjoys listening								
Has favorite stories								
Looks at books independently								
Pretends to read								
Plays with sounds/words								

Instructional Needs: (over)

* See also separate checklist in Chapter 5, Figure 5.8

Writing and Uses of Writing Checklist for Individual Student (Chapter 5)

Writing and Uses of Writing Checklist:
Early Emergent Literacy Stage

Name _____   Date _____   Grade/Year in School _____

Key: P = behavior present
     S = some knowledge
     L = little knowledge
     N = behavior not present

Benchmark	Date						Comments
Purpose							
Marks mean something							
Wants to write							
Communicates							
Uses tools							
Manipulates letters							
Connects to Reading							
Wants to label own pictures							
Understands stories are made up and he or she can do this also							
Can make up stories							

Instructional Needs

Oral Language Checklist for Individual Student (Chapter 6)

Oral Language Checklist:
Emergent Literacy Stage

Name _____ Age _____ Grade _____

+ = behavior present
- = behavior absent
✓ = somewhat present

Benchmark	Date	Comments
Early Emergent Literacy Behaviors		
Standard Usage and Grammar		
Recognition of nonstandard usage		
Sense of school/book language		
Facility with Oral Language		
Makes self understood by peers and adults		
Follows "rules" for conversation and discussion		
Retains oral directions		
Can ask questions for clarification		
Can paraphrase what others have said		
Participates in sharing		
Reflecting Literature		
Uses new words from stories		
Uses "book language" when appropriate		
Enjoys "making a play" of a favorite story		
Pleasure in Language		
Enjoys jokes related to words		
Enjoys tongue twisters		
Enjoys hearing humorous books		
Is proud of learning new words		
Tries out new words		

Comments:

Reading Checklist for Individual Student (Chapter 6)

Reading Checklist:
Emergent Literacy Stage

Name _____ Age _____ Grade _____

Dates

+ = consistently present
- = not present
✓ = somewhat present; recheck

Benchmark

Early Emergent Literacy Behaviors							

Concepts About Print

Handles book correctly							
Points: word, two words; letter, two letters							
Knows print matches voice							
Knows book parts							

Using Print in Everyday Life

Locates specific book							
Recognizes some environmental print							

Word Recognition Skills

Names most letters							
Matches upper- and lower-case letters							
Recognizes some words							
Recognizes own name							
Phonemic awareness							
Alphabetic principle							
Phonics							
Other strategies:							
sight words							
context							
graphics							
word structure							

Constructs Meaning

Retells stories							
Summarizes							
Discusses							
Talks about books							
Responds in writing							
Begins to see self as reader							

Comments:

Writing Checklist for Individual Student (Chapter 6)

Writing Checklist:
Emergent Literacy Stage

Name _____ Age _____ Grade_____

Dates

+ = consistently present
- = not present
✓ = sometimes present/needs instruction

Benchmark

Early Emergent Literacy Behaviors

Spelling and Other Conventions
Writes own name
Names most letters
Forms letterlike shapes/letters
Uses some punctuation
Shows phonemic awareness
Gives letter-sound or says word with sound

Purposes of Writing
Keeps a journal
Attempts to read others' writing
Shares writing with others
Practices writing

Writing Process
Uses steps
Knows all authors have used a process

Construction of Meaning
Responds to reading
Composes narrative and exposition
Expresses/reports personal events and feelings

Comments:

Test of Phonemic Awareness (Chapter 6)

Yopp-Singer Test of Phoneme Segmentation

Student's name _____ Date _____

Score (number correct) _____

Directions: Today we're going to play a word game. I'm going to say a word and I want you to break the word apart. You are going to tell me each sound in the word in order. For example, if I say "old," you should say "/o/-/l/-/d/." (*Administrator: Be sure to say the sounds, not the letters, in the word.*) Let's try a few together.

Practice Items: (*Assist the child in segmenting these items as necessary.*)   ride, go, man

Test items: (*Circle those items that the student correctly segments; incorrect responses may be recorded on the blank line following the item.*)

1. dog	_____		12. lay	_____
2. keep	_____		13. race	_____
3. fine	_____		14. zoo	_____
4. no	_____		15. three	_____
5. she	_____		16. job	_____
6. wave	_____		17. in	_____
7. grew	_____		18. ice	_____
8. that	_____		19. at	_____
9. red	_____		20. top	_____
10. me	_____		21. by	_____
11. sat	_____		22. do	_____

From: Yopp, H. K. (1995). A test for assessing phonemic awareness in young children. *The Reading Teacher, 49,* pp. 20–29.

Oral Language Checklist:
Beginning Reading and Writing Stage

Name _____ Grade _____ Age _____

+ = behavior present
- = behavior absent
✓ = somewhat present

Benchmark	Date						Comments:
Emergent Literacy Behaviors							
Use of Standard English							
Switches between standard and nonstandard English							
Self-corrects							
Facility with Language							
Listens and paraphrases							
Increasing vocabulary							
Asks for meanings of words							
Works collaboratively							
Participates in discussion							
Plans and asks oral questions							
Plans and presents oral report							
Pleasure in Words							
Makes jokes related to plays on words							
Shows interest in word history							
Enjoys nonsense and silly poems							
Makes own dictionary							

Comments:

Letter-Name Knowledge Record Sheet (Chapter 7)

Letter-Name Knowledge

Name_____   _____   Date_____

Upper Case   **Match**   **Lower Case**

Upper Case	Lower Case
___ A	___ a
___ B	___ b
___ C	___ c
___ D	___ d
___ E	___ e
___ F	___ f
___ G	___ g
___ H	___ h
___ I	___ i
___ J	___ j
___ K	___ k
___ L	___ l
___ M	___ m
___ N	___ n
___ O	___ o
___ P	___ p
___ Q	___ q
___ R	___ r
___ S	___ s
___ T	___ t
___ U	___ u
___ V	___ v
___ W	___ w
___ X	___ x
___ Y	___ y
___ Z	___ z

Observations:

___ Says all upper- and lower-case letters by name

___ Matches all upper- and lower-case letters

___ Needs help with:

_____

_____

_____

Reading Checklist for Individual Student (Chapter 7)

Reading Checklist:
Beginning Reading and Writing Stage

Name _____ Grade _____ Age _____

+ = consistently present
- = not present
✓ = somewhat present; recheck

Benchmark	Date					Comments
Emergent Literacy Behaviors						
Word Recognition Skills/Strategies						
Names letters in random order						
Recognizes many sight words						
Uses phonics and structural analysis						
Chooses strategies for sounding words						
Uses context to determine meaning						
Construction of Meaning						
Reads and retells familiar stories						
Reads own writing						
Begins to use:						
- predicting						
- identifying important information						
- self-questioning						
- monitoring						
- summarizing						
- evaluating						
Reads and retells unfamiliar texts (narrative/expository)						
Self-corrects						
Takes risks						
Reads in free time						
Sees self as reader						
Reads to others						
Begins to use research tools and skills (list:)						
_____						
_____						
_____						

Comments:

Writing Checklist for Individual Student (Chapter 7)

Writing Checklist:
Beginning Reading and Writing Stage

Name _____ Grade _____ Age _____

+ = consistently present
- = not present
✓ = sometimes present/needs instruction

	Date					Comments
Benchmark						
Emergent Literacy Behaviors						
General Writing Behaviors						
Enjoys writing						
Is confident about writing						
Communicates spontaneously						
Reads others' writing						
Shows interest in writing						
Writes in a variety of formats						
Mechanics and Conventions of Writing						
Forms letters conventionally						
Shows increased phonemic awareness						
Uses invented spelling and edits						
Learning spelling patterns						
Recognizes nonstandard usage and edits own writing						
Uses word processing						
Writing Process						
Participates in writing process						
Writes collaboratively and independently						
Reacts to others' writing						

Comments:

Teacher Observation Sheet for Independent Reading and Writing (Chapter 7)

Independent Reading and Writing Log Sheet

Name	Reading	Writing

Student's Learning Center Record (Chapter 7)

Name _____

My Center Record

Center Number	Name	Date Completed

Oral Language Checklist:
Almost Fluent Reading and Writing Stage

Name _____ Grade _____ Age _____

+ = behavior present
- = behavior absent
✓ = somewhat present

Benchmark	Date						Comments
Beginning Reading and Writing Behaviors							
Use of Standard English							
Is aware of own problems							
Accepts diverse usage							
Growing Facility with Language							
Uses new vocabulary							
Collaborates in speaking and listening							
Participates in discussion without adult							
Listens to and questions speakers							
Speaks with notes							
Pleasure in Use							
Appreciates symbolic language							
Listens to and tells jokes/riddles							
Appreciates shades of meaning							
Recognizes and uses persuasive techniques							

Comments:

Reading Checklist for Individual Student (Chapter 8)

Reading Checklist:
Almost Fluent Reading and Writing Stage

Name_____ Grade_____ Age_____

+ = consistently present
- = not present
✓ = somewhat present; recheck

	Date					Comments
Benchmark						
Beginning Reading and Writing Behaviors						
Word Recognition Strategies						
Uses structure						
Uses phonics						
Uses syntax						
Uses context						
Selects appropriate strategies						
Reads orally at 90% accuracy						
Self-corrects						
Takes risks						
Uses dictionary						
Construction of Meaning						
Enjoys listening						
Reads independently						
Enjoys reading a variety of genres						
Reads outside of school						
Reads silently						
Continues to grow in use of:						
- predicting						
- identifying important information						
- self-questioning						
- monitoring						
- summarizing						
- evaluating						
Variety of Purposes						
Appreciates levels of meaning						
Has growing interest in authors, illustrators, genres						
Is aware of own purpose						
Begins to understand expository text structure						
Uses variety of sources						
Synthesizes information						
Research Skills						
Uses card catalog/computer						
Operates computer						
Narrows search						
Reads:						
- graphs						
- charts						
- tables						
- timelines						
- maps						
Uses:						
- dictionary						
- thesaurus						
- encyclopedia						
- CD-ROMs						
- internet						

Comments:

Writing Checklist for Individual Student (Chapter 8)

Writing Checklist:
Almost Fluent Reading and Writing Stage

Name _____ Grade _____ Age _____

+ = consistently present
- = not present
✓ = sometimes present/needs instruction

Benchmark	Date						Comments
Beginning Reading and Writing Behaviors							
Variety of Purposes for Writing							
Is aware of power of writing							
Writes paper to topic/theme/rubric							
Writes reports							
Writes stories							
Mechanics and Conventions of Writing							
Uses spelling patterns							
Uses increasingly conventional spelling							
Uses increasingly appropriate grammar							
Uses increasingly appropriate punctuation							
Uses word processing tools							
Pleasure in Writing							
Sees self as writer							
Offers constructive comments to peers							
Seeks suggestions for revision							
Writes in free time							
Enjoys sharing							
Supports classmates							
Connects Reading and Writing							
Uses learning about narrative writing							
Uses learning about expository writing							
Appreciates and writes poetry							

Comments:

Oral Language Checklist for Individual Student (Chapter 9)

Oral Language Checklist:
Fluent Reading and Writing Stage

Name _____ Grade _____ Age _____

+ = consistently present
- = not present
✓ = somewhat present; recheck;
    insufficient evidence

Benchmark	Date						Comments
Continued Growth in Previous Behaviors							
Facility							
Shows increasing vocabulary							
Shifts from formal to informal language							
Listens to presentations with understanding							
Variety of Purposes							
Discusses literature							
Enjoys role-playing/Readers Theater							
Enjoys debate/speech competition							
Enjoyment							
Is sensitive to body language and tone							
Appreciates speech interpretation							

Instructional Plans:

_____

_____

_____

_____

_____

_____

Reading Checklist for Individual Student (Chapter 9)

Reading Checklist:
Fluent Reading and Writing Stage

Name _____ Grade _____ Age _____

+ = consistently present
- = not present
✓ = somewhat present; recheck;
    insufficient evidence

	Date					Comments
Benchmark						
Behaviors from Almost Fluent Stage						
Word Recognition						
Construction of Meaning						
Grasps genres						
Perceives text structure						
Appreciates levels of meaning						
Varies reading according to purpose						
Uses strategies to construct meaning						
Is aware of own thinking						
Is learning study strategies						
Uses graphic material						
Enjoyment						
Recommends books to others						
Is exploring adult reading						
Sees self as competent reader						
Sets goals/self-evaluates						
Is aware of own purposes						
Research Skills						
Can plan a research project						
Knows how to locate information						
Takes notes/attributes sources						
Synthesizes information						

Instructional Plans:

_____

_____

_____

Writing Benchmark Checklist:
Fluent Reading and Writing

Name _____ Grade _____ Age _____

Key. T = behavior present consistently
S = behavior sometimes present
N = behavior not yet present

	Date						Comments

Benchmark

Growth in Prior Writing Behaviors

Variety of Purpose/Reasons
Knows Writing Adds to Self-awareness
Uses Writing to Persuade
Can Write Prompt/Rubric

Mechanics
Edits Own Work
Edits Work of Others
Independently Verifies Mechanics

Writing Process
Uses All Steps
Revises Own Work
Developing Personal Style/Voice
Varies Prewriting Techniques

Sees Self as Competent
Sets Goals and Evaluates

Connects Reading and Writing
Recognizes and Uses Author's Craft
Experiments with Forms/Genres

Instructional Plans:

_____

_____

_____

_____

_____

_____

Editing/Proofreading Checklist

	Peer Editor	Author
1. Paragraphs as needed	☐	☐
2. Complete sentences/no sentence fragments	☐	☐
3. Capitals		
Beginnings of sentences	☐	☐
Proper names	☐	☐
4. Incorrect capitals changed to lower case	☐	☐
5. Punctuation		
Ends of sentences/questions	☐	☐
Commas	☐	☐
Apostrophes	☐	☐
Other	☐	☐
6. Insertions clearly marked	☐	☐
7. Deletions clearly marked	☐	☐
8. Possible misspellings		
Corrected	☐	☐
Circled for checking	☐	☐

Signed:

Peer editor _____ Date _____

Author _____ Date _____

Proofreading/Editing Marks

Command	Mark	Example
Capitalize	≡	My brother's name is sam.
Lower case	/	My Brother's name is Sam.
Add period	⊙	My brother plays football He also plays basketball.
Add comma	⋏	My brother plays football and basketball but he doesn't like baseball.
Add apostrophe	⌄	My brothers name is Sam.
Insert	∧	My brother is very tall. *thin and*
Delete	ℓ	My brother is very tall and skinny.
Make new paragraph	¶	...doesn't like baseball. My sister, on the other hand, loves baseball.

Fry Readability Formula (Chapter 10)

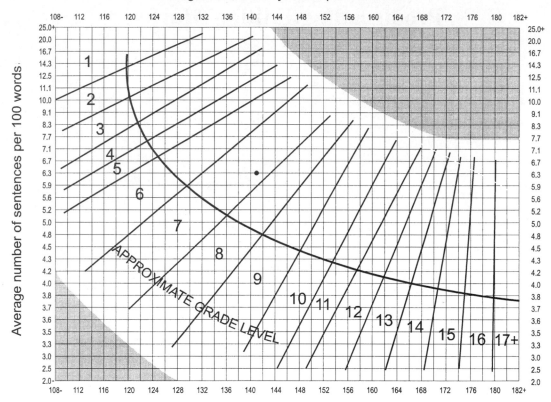

Average number of syllables per 100 words

Instructions:

1. Select three 100-word selections from the beginning, middle, and end of the text. Don't count proper nouns.
2. Count the number of sentences in each selection. Estimate to the nearest tenth of a sentence.
3. Average the sentence count.
4. Count the number of syllables in each selection.
5. Average the syllable count.
6. Plot the two scores on the graph to get the grade level.

From "A Readability Formula That Saves Time" by Edward Fry (1968), *Journal of Reading, 11*, pp. 513-516, 578. International Reading Association. Reprinted by permission.

The Fry Instant Word List: 300 High-Frequency Words (Chapter 10)

The Fry Instant Word List

The Instant Words: First Hundred

First 25 Group 1a	Second 25 Group 1b	Third 25 Group 1c	Fourth 25 Group 1d
the	or	will	number
of	one	up	no
and	had	other	way
a	by	about	could
to	word	out	people
in	but	many	my
is	not	then	than
you	what	them	first
that	all	these	water
it	were	so	been
he	we	some	call
was	when	her	who
for	your	would	oil
on	can	make	now
are	said	like	find
as	there	him	long
with	use	into	down
his	an	time	day
they	each	has	did
I	which	look	get
at	she	two	come
be	do	more	made
this	how	write	may
have	their	go	part
from	if	see	over

Common suffixes: *s, ing, ed*

The Instant Words: Second Hundred

First 25 Group 2a	Second 25 Group 2b	Third 25 Group 2c	Fourth 25 Group 2d
new	great	put	kind
sound	where	end	hand
take	help	does	picture
only	through	another	again
little	much	well	change
work	before	large	off
know	line	must	play
place	right	big	spell
year	too	even	air
live	mean	such	away
me	old	because	animal
back	any	turn	house
give	same	here	point
most	tell	why	page
very	boy	ask	letter
after	follow	went	mother
thing	came	men	answer
our	want	read	found
just	show	need	study
name	also	land	still
good	around	different	learn
sentence	form	home	should
man	three	us	America
think	small	move	world
say	set	try	high

Common suffixes: *s, ing, ed, er, ly, est*

The Instant Words: Third Hundred

First 25 Group 3a	Second 25 Group 3b	Third 25 Group 3c	Fourth 25 Group 3d
every	left	unit	idea
near	don't	children	enough
add	few	side	eat
food	while	feet	face
between	along	car	watch
own	might	mile	far
below	close	night	Indian
country	something	walk	real
plant	seem	white	almost
last	next	sea	let
school	hard	began	above
father	open	grow	girl
keep	example	took	sometimes
tree	begin	river	mountain
never	life	four	cut
start	always	carry	young
city	those	state	talk
earth	both	once	soon
eye	paper	book	list
light	together	hear	song
thought	got	stop	leave
head	group	without	family
under	often	second	body
story	run	late	music
saw	important	miss	color

Common suffixes: *s, ing, ed, er, ly, est*

The instant word list, pp. 286–87 from "The New Instant Word List," by Edward Fry, *The Reading Teacher*, December 1980. Reprinted with permission of Edward Fry and the International Reading Association.

227 Core Words Derrived from 400 Storybooks for beginning Readers (Chapter 10)

The numeral to the right of each word indicates the number of times it occurred in the storybooks surveyed.

the	1334	good	90	think	47	next	28
and	985	this	90	new	46	only	28
a	831	don't	89	know	46	am	27
I	757	little	89	help	46	began	27
to	746	if	87	grand	46	head	27
said	688	just	87	boy	46	keep	27
you	638	baby	86	take	45	teacher	27
he	488	way	85	eat	44	sure	27
it	345	there	83	body	43	says	27
in	311	every	83	school	43	ride	27
was	294	went	82	house	42	pet	27
she	250	father	80	morning	42	hurry	26
for	235	had	79	yes	41	hand	26
that	232	see	79	after	41	hard	26
is	230	dog	78	never	41	push	26
his	226	home	77	or	40	our	26
but	224	down	76	self	40	their	26
they	218	got	73	try	40	watch	26
my	214	would	73	has	38	because	25
of	204	time	71	always	38	door	25
on	192	love	70	over	38	us	25
me	187	walk	70	again	37	should	25
all	179	came	69	side	37	room	25
be	176	were	68	thank	37	pull	25
go	171	ask	67	why	37	great	24
can	162	back	67	who	36	gave	24
with	158	now	66	saw	36	does	24
one	157	friend	65	mom	35	car	24
her	156	cry	64	kid	35	ball	24
what	152	oh	64	give	35	sat	24
we	151	Mr.	63	around	34	stay	24
him	144	bed	63	by	34	each	23
no	143	an	62	Mrs.	34	ever	23
so	141	very	62	off	33	until	23
out	140	where	60	sister	33	shout	23
up	137	play	59	find	32	mama	22
are	133	let	59	fun	32	use	22
will	127	long	58	more	32	turn	22
look	126	here	58	while	32	thought	22
some	123	how	57	tell	32	papa	22
day	123	make	57	sleep	32	lot	21
at	122	big	56	made	31	blue	21
have	121	from	55	first	31	bath	21
your	121	put	55	say	31	mean	21
mother	119	read	55	took	31	sit	21
come	118	them	55	dad	30	together	21
not	115	as	54	found	30	best	20
like	112	Miss	53	lady	30	brother	20
then	108	any	52	soon	30	feel	20
get	103	right	52	ran	30	floor	20
when	101	nice	50	dear	29	wait	20
thing	100	other	50	man	29	tomorrow	20
do	99	well	48	better	29	surprise	20
too	91	old	48	through	29	shop	20
want	91	night	48	stop	29	run	20
did	91	may	48	still	29	own	20
could	90	about	47	fast	28		

From "Bookwords: Using a Beginning Word List of High Frequency Words from Children's Literature K–3" by M. Eeds, *The Reading Teacher*, January 1985, p. 420. International Reading Association. Reprinted by permission.

Dolch Basic Sight Vocabulary (Chapter 10)

a	don't	if	over	they
about	down	in	own	think
after	draw	into	pick	this
again	drink	is	play	those
all	eat	it	please	three
always	eight	its	pretty	to
am	every	jump	pull	today
an	fall	just	put	together
and	far	keep	ran	too
any	fast	kind	read	try
are	find	know	red	two
around	first	laugh	ride	under
as	five	let	right	up
ask	fly	light	round	upon
at	for	like	run	us
ate	found	little	said	use
away	four	live	saw	very
be	from	long	say	walk
because	full	look	see	want
been	funny	made	seven	warm
before	gave	make	shall	was
best	get	many	she	wash
better	give	may	show	we
big	go	me	sing	well
black	goes	much	sit	went
blue	going	must	six	were
both	good	my	sleep	what
bring	got	myself	small	when
brown	green	never	so	where
but	grow	new	some	which
buy	had	no	soon	white
call	has	not	start	who
came	have	now	stop	why
can	he	of	take	will
carry	help	off	tell	wish
clean	her	old	ten	with
cold	here	on	thank	work
come	him	once	that	would
could	his	one	the	write
cut	hold	only	their	yellow
did	hot	open	them	yes
do	how	or	then	you
does	hurt	our	there	your
done	I	out	these	

Glossary

aesthetic listening   Listening for pleasure. The term *aesthetic* in this sense can also apply to reading.

age-equivalent score   A score based on the average age of the people in the standardization population who earned that score; also called *age norm*.

Almost Fluent Reading and Writing (stage)   The fourth stage of literacy development, during which the student becomes more sophisticated in all aspects of literacy.

alphabetic principle   The assumption that each speech sound has a corresponding graphic representation.

anchor papers   Samples of writing that illustrate the levels of acceptability in terms of a given rubric.

anecdote   A brief note you make about something you have observed in a particular child; part of the observing process. Sometimes called *anecdotal records*.

apply (application)   To use a skill, strategy, or process in an authentic literacy situation.

assessment   The process of collecting data about a student's performance.

assessment-based literacy classroom   A classroom in which instructional decisions about literacy are based on each student's performance in relation to stages of literacy development.

attention-deficit disorder (ADD)   A developmental disorder involving one or more of the basic cognitive processes relating to orienting, focusing, or maintaining attention (Harris & Hodges, 1995).

attention-deficit—hyperactivity disorder (ADHD)   Difficulty in concentrating and staying on a task, accompanied by hyperactivity (Lerner, 2000).

attitude/self-concept check   An instrument designed to reveal students' attitudes toward themselves as learners and toward school and learning.

authentic assessment   Using actual literacy tasks for the purpose of determining student performance, as opposed to relying solely on typical kinds of tests.

Author's Chair   A special chair in which students sit while reading aloud their writing to others.

balanced literacy program   A plan for literacy instruction that incorporates essential blocks for effective learning.

Beginning Reading and Writing (stage)   The third stage of literacy development, during which the student actually starts to read and write.

bell curve   A bell-shaped graph that represents the probability of distribution of large numbers of scores or results on a given measure; also called *normal curve* or *normal frequency curve*.

benchmarks   Behaviors exhibited by students at a certain stage of development.

checklist   An instrument that allows a teacher to check whether behaviors or abilities are present, sometimes present, or not present in an individual child or a group or class. May be teacher-made to meet a particular purpose.

cloze procedure   A method of assessing comprehension of a passage by asking the reader to replace missing words.

coaching   In teaching, the process of helping teachers internalize a set of instructional strategies through observation and feedback.

conference   Usually a meeting between a teacher and a student to discuss some aspect of the student's work. Conferences can also be held between two students or between the teacher and a student's family members.

connected text   Two or more words that convey meaning. Can be narrative or expository.

construct validity   The degree to which a test assesses the theoretical characteristic it is said to measure.

content validity   The degree to which the content of a test reflects the content it is intended to measure; sometimes also called *curriculum* or *instructional validity*.

context   The words surrounding a given word; they may constitute a phrase, a sentence, a paragraph, or the entire text. Attention to context sometimes aids a reader to figure out an unfamiliar word.

conventional stage   The last stage of spelling development, in which a child spells most words correctly, is aware of when a word is spelled incorrectly, and knows how to locate words not known.

core book   A common book experienced by all students in a class; students do different activities in accordance with their abilities and needs.

criterion-referenced test   A test that measures what a person is able to do in terms of what the test maker decides should be tested; compare *norm-referenced test.*

criterion validity The degree to which a given test predicts future performance; or the degree to which the test correlates with a different test that is supposed to measure the same factors.

critical listening   Listening in order to make judgments. The term *critical* also applies in the same sense to reading.

decodable text   A text that has been identified or created as one that allows application of previously taught phonic skills.

decoding   The process of translating written language into verbal speech. Decoding is one part of reading.

developmentally appropriate books   Books that are at the students' instructional reading level.

developmentally appropriate writing   Writing in which the teacher assigns a type or mode of writing appropriate to students' abilities, but individual students are allowed to select their own topics; a block in the balanced literacy programs described in this book.

diagnostic test   A test designed to reveal the strengths as well as weaknesses of an individual; such tests often include suggestions for analyzing strengths and weaknesses in order to plan appropriate instruction.

directionality   The understanding that print goes from left to right and top to bottom on the page; one of the key concepts about print.

discussion circle (or **discussion group**)   A small group of students (usually three to five) who get to-gether to talk about a piece of text they have read; for instructional purposes, the teacher may give them some prompts.

domains of writing   Particular types of writing; usually discussed as sensory/descriptive, imaginative/narrative, practical/informative, and analytical/expository.

Early Emergent Literacy (stage)   The very beginnings of literacy development, in which the foundations are laid for future learning.

efferent listening   Listening in order to learn, as from informational text. The term *efferent* can also apply to reading.

Emergent Literacy (stage) The second stage of literacy development, during which children become more interested in literacy.

encoding   Changing spoken language into written symbols. Encoding is the process associated with spelling.

English-language learners   Students acquiring English as a second language; often abbreviated as *ELL students* or *ELLs.*

evaluation   Judging assessment data about a student on the basis of a set of criteria or guidelines.

explicit teaching   Teacher modeling of a specific skill, strategy, or process.

expository text   Text written to inform or explain something; often called *informational writing* in K–8 programs.

extended-day program   A program in which instruction beyond the core program is made available to a small group before or after school hours.

fluency   In reading, the ability to read words of connected text aloud smoothly and without significant word recognition problems. A fluency record is taken by keeping track of words read correctly and those not read correctly. (See also *running record.*)

Fluent Reading and Writing (stage)   The fifth stage of literacy development, during which the student uses all aspects of literacy. This stage continues to develop throughout one's life.

formative   Pertaining to ongoing assessment for the purpose of judging progress toward a goal; often used in the phrase *formative assessment* or *formative evaluation.* Compare *summative.*

frustration reading level   The level of material that is too difficult for a reader, even with good instructional support.

full inclusion   The policy of placing and instructing all children, including all categories of disability and levels of severity, in their neighborhood schools and in the general education classroom (Lerner, 2000).

functions of language   Term used by Halliday (1975) to describe seven ways one uses oral and written language: instrumental, regulatory, interactional, personal, imaginative, heuristic, and informative.

gifted and talented   Demonstrating sufficient talents or abilities to warrant special programs. *Gifted* often refers to students with high intellectual or cognitive ability; *talented* to outstanding ability in a particular area, such as one of the arts.

grade-equivalent score   Score on a standardized test typical of the norming group at a certain grade. The score is given as year and month: for instance, 3.5 means third grade, fifth month.

grade level   Can refer to the student's position in the educational program, the student's achievement, the level of educational materials, or the level of performance on a test.

graphic organizer   A visual way to show how a text is organized; see also *story map*.

graphics   Nonprint information and special arrangement or presentation of print material. Includes illustrations, photographs, charts, tables, maps, sidebars, special typefaces, different type sizes, arrows, colors, and more.

graphophonic cues   Cues that arise from the relationship between the orthology (written symbol) and the phonology (sound) of letters.

guided reading   A process in which the teacher guides students through the reading of a text. Guided reading may be *observational* (teacher observes students' use of strategies and skills in reading a complete text) or *interactive* (teacher guides students in reading a text in meaningful chunks).

holistic scoring   In writing, assigning one score based on a combination of several factors, including both content and mechanics; may use anchor papers for samples of levels of performance.

inclusion   The practice of placing students with special needs or disabilities in the regular classroom program for instruction.

independent reading   A time when students self-select materials they want to read. The models for a balanced literacy program described in this book feature a block of Daily Independent Reading.

independent reading level   The level of material that a reader can read, with few word-recognition problems and good comprehension, without instructional support.

independent writing   A time when students select what they want to write. The models for a balanced literacy program described in this book feature a block of Daily Independent Writing.

informal reading inventory (IRI)   A series of graded passages designed to measure a reader's overall ability, as well as strengths and needs in word recognition and comprehension.

inservice   Occurring during a teacher's employment; often used to describe staff development programs (see *staff development*).

instructional reading level   The level of material that a reader can read with instructional support.

instructional routine   A pattern of teaching that always includes specified steps; a pattern used over and over.

interactive writing   A process in which students help the teacher write a piece by taking the pen, chalk, or marker and trying to spell specific words.

interest level   Information sometimes provided by a publisher to suggest the grade or age level(s) of readers who would find a particular book or story of interest.

interest inventory   An instrument designed to reveal a student's interests in school subjects, topics, outside activities, and so forth. Such inventories can be paper-and-pencil or oral.

inter-rater reliability   A scoring system's ability to produce the same score for a given piece of work no matter who does the scoring.

intervention   In a balanced literacy program, an additional support block provided for students who are experiencing difficulty in learning to read or who have special learning needs; see also *reading intervention program*.

K-W-L   A strategy for guiding the reading of nonfiction. The letters stand for What I **K**now, What I **W**ant to Learn, and What I **L**earned.

language experience   A method of teaching that involves recording (writing down) a child's language and using that text as reading material for the child.

language-rich environment   A setting, at school or at home, in which oral and written language is pervasive, allowing a child's language and literacy to flourish.

learning center   A specific space (table, desk, or cubicle) within a classroom where individual students go to perform a particular task related to learning.

learning disabilities   Difficulties in the acquisition and use of speaking, listening, reading, writing, or mathematics.

learning log   A student's record of learning activities and understanding of concepts.

listening level   The highest grade level of material that can be understood when the material is read aloud to the student.

literacy development   Learning to speak, listen, read, write, and view. Thinking is an integral part of all of these processes.

local norms   The range of test scores of a restricted or defined population, used to compare scores to that population rather than to the national population on which many tests are normed.

metacognition   Knowledge and control of one's own thinking and learning. In reading, metacognition relates to the reader's being aware of when reading makes sense and adjusting his or her reading when comprehension fails.

minilesson   A short, teacher-directed, planned lesson focused specifically on a skill, strategy, or process.

miscue   A mismatch between the word on the page and the word a reader says (Goodman, 1965). The term implies that a reader's misreading may result from paying attention to inappropriate cues.

modeling   The process of demonstrating or showing students how to use a strategy, skill, or process. Think-alouds are often involved.

modes of reading   Different ways in which a text may be read, moving from teacher directed to independent.

morning message   A written activity many teachers use to begin the day. The message may be written by the teacher or by students. It may be collaborative. It can serve to remind students of a schedule, inform them about events, or share news. It is sometimes also used to reinforce reading and writing skills.

morphology   The study of the meaningful parts of words such as bases, roots, compounds, inflections, and affixes.

narrative   In K–8 education, usually refers to a story, whether true or fictional (as contrasted with expository text).

networking   Connecting and communicating with other professionals in your field.

nonstandard English   Usage that deviates from standard English in some way.

normal curve equivalent (NCE) score   A score based on a normal curve and ranging from 0 to 99, with the points on the scale defined so that there is an equal number of raw-score points between each pair of scores.

normal distribution   The probable way (graphically represented by a bell curve) in which a very large number of values (such as scores on a test) will distribute from lowest to highest, with most falling in the middle; also called *normal frequency distribution.*

norming population   The group of individuals used to establish the norms for a particular test; often composed of many subgroups.

norm-referenced test   A test that allows comparison of individual scores to those of the group (the norming population) on which the test was standardized.

observing   An assessment tool that involves close watching of student behavior—while the student is engaged in a particular activity or task—to make inferences about the student's literacy.

onset   The consonant sound that precedes the vowel in a syllable. For example, in the word *cat,* /c/ is the onset.

parallel talking   Activity in which children (usually very young children) take turns talking but do not actually have a conversation that involves an exchange of ideas.

percentile rank A score that allows comparison of an individual performance to that of the norming population.

performance assessment Assessment of learning based on the student's performance of certain tasks. These may be either regular activities or tasks specially assigned for the express purpose of assessment.

phonemes The smallest units of sound in speech, for example, the word *cat* has three phonemes.

phonemic awareness Awareness of sounds (phonemes) that make up words.

phonetic Pertaining to speech sounds; in spelling development, the stage when children develop phonemic awareness (also called the *phonemic stage*).

phonics Using one's knowledge of the relationship between the letters and the sounds the letters represent to aid in figuring out the pronunciation of a word.

picture walk Talking through a story or book by looking at and talking about the pictures; see also *text walk*.

portfolio A collection of an individual student's work designed to show evidence of performance and growth.

practice To try out, in a directed situation, a skill, strategy, or process that has been taught.

precommunicative stage In spelling development, the stage when children do writing that is not meaningful to anyone else; they may use letters or marks that resemble letters.

predictable text A text with some type of repeated pattern that allows the reader to anticipate what is likely to follow on subsequent pages.

print-rich environment An environment, at home or school, in which print is evident in books, magazines, signs, and labels; such an environment stimulates and supports literacy.

productive language Language an individual generates by speaking or writing.

pullout program A program in which students who need special assistance leave their regular classroom to receive instruction beyond the core program.

raw score The number of items correct on a given test.

readability (or **readability level**) Ease or difficulty of a piece of text; may be based on a formula or on a combination of variables within the reader, the text, and the environment.

readability formula A numeric formula for estimating text difficulty.

read-aloud Session during which someone reads aloud to children.

reading expectation level An estimate of the reading level a student should be able to reach given certain factors such as age, grade, IQ, or listening comprehension, or based on a formula that uses these or other factors.

reading intervention program Instruction designed to prevent or stop reading failure given *in addition to* the core classroom program.

reading levels The three levels—independent, instructional, and frustration—identified using an informal reading inventory; the term is also used to indicate the grade levels appropriate for written material.

receptive language Language an individual receives through listening or reading.

reciprocal teaching An instructional strategy in which teacher and students take turns modeling four strategies—predict, question, clarify, and summarize—after silent reading of a chunk of text.

reliability The degree to which a test's results are consistent from one time to another and one set of conditions to another.

retelling Restating in one's own words the essential parts of a story or expository text; can be used as a measure of comprehension and of knowledge of story elements.

rime The vowel and any following consonants in a syllable. For example, in the word *school,* /ool/ is the rime, while /sk/ is the onset.

risk taking Students' willingness to make an effort, try new things, and express opinions. A classroom in which students feel free to behave in this way may be referred to as a "risk-free environment."

rubric A standard by which to measure a piece of work. In education, a rubric generally includes specific guidelines and criteria for assessing students' performance.

running record A record of the accuracy of a child's oral reading. As used by Clay (1985), it involves a particular way of listening and coding.

scaffolding   The process of providing strong teacher support at the beginning of new learnings and gradually taking it away to allow the student to achieve independence.

scope and sequence   A listing of strategies and skills that are developed in programs and/or ones that individuals are expected to learn. These are most often organized by grade level.

second-language learner   One who is learning a language other than his or her native language.

self-correction   Recognizing a miscue and spontaneously correcting it.

self-reflection   Thinking about oneself in terms of learning. The term is sometimes used interchangeably with *self-assessment* and *self-evaluation,* which refer to making a judgment about one's own work and drawing conclusions about one's ability.

semantic   Pertaining to the meanings of words, phrases, sentences, or longer texts.

semiphonetic stage   In spelling development, the stage when children have grasped the alphabetic principle but may not yet represent every sound with a letter or letters.

sight words   Words recognized instantly without the need to apply word recognition strategies. *Basic sight words* are those considered to be of such high frequency that every reader must learn them.

significant miscues   Miscallings or misreadings of words that significantly change the meaning; in calculating fluency, often only significant miscues are counted as wrong. See also *miscue.*

SQ3R   A study strategy composed of several steps: **S**urvey (look over the entire assignment), **Q**uestion (ask yourself questions about what you might learn), **R**ead (read to answer the questions), **R**ecite (say orally or in writing what you have learned), and **R**eview (the material).

staff development   Educational and training programs offered by a school district for its teachers and other professional staff members.

standard   A degree or level of performance that is expected for students at a certain time.

standard error of measurement   A measure of how much one can trust an individual score; for example, a standard error of measurement of 6 means that an earned score of XX probably really is XX, give or take 6.

standardized tests   Tests whose value depends on their being given in specific ways, following specific procedures; tests that have been normed.

stanine score   A standard score, ranging from 1 to 9, based on the norming population; a stanine of 5 represents average performance.

story map   A graphic organizer visually showing the elements of a story.

summarizing   Retelling the story elements in narrative text or the main points in expository text.

summative   Pertaining to a final assessment used to assign a grade. The term generally appears in the phrase *summary assessment* or *summative evaluation.*

syntactic   Pertaining to the grammatical construction of language.

syntax   The grammatical construction of language; the rules by which words and other elements are combined to form sentences.

teacher-modeled writing   A procedure in which the teacher shows students how to do a particular type of writing and shares his or her thinking about the process; this is a block in the Balanced Literacy Program 3–8.

text walk   Talking students through a segment of text before they read it so they will know what is coming in the text. Sometimes called a *picture walk* at the primary levels and a *guided preview* at the intermediate levels.

think-aloud   The process of verbalizing to model or demonstrate one's thinking process.

transitional stage   In spelling development, the stage when children spell all the sounds in a word, are beginning to learn spelling generalizations, and are applying knowledge of morphology.

validity   The degree to which a test measures what it says it measures; see also *construct validity, content validity,* and *criterion validity.*

voice-to-print match   The ability to look at print as someone reads aloud and point to a word as it is heard.

word structure   The way words are formed. Understanding word structure means knowing the parts of a word that carry meaning—including prefixes, suffixes, inflected endings, base words, and roots—as well as compound words and contractions.

word wall   A space, usually on the wall of a classroom, where words are posted in alphabetical categories as they are taught to students. Word walls may focus on high-frequency words, phonic or structural elements, or new vocabulary by categories.

work sample   Evidence of a child's actual classroom work. Can be a paper, report, project, model, or any product that shows what kind of work a child has done.

Literature

Ackerman, K. (1988). *Song and dance man.* New York: Scholastic.

Bang, M. (1987). *The paper crane.* New York: Mulberry Books.

Barbot, D. (1990). *A bicycle for Rosaura.* Brooklyn: Kane/Miller Book Publishers.

Baum, L. F. (1900/1990). *The wonderful wizard of Oz.* Chicago/New York: Geo. M. Hill Company.

Blume, J. (1974). *Blubber.* New York: Bradbury.

Cox, J. A. (1980). *Put your foot in your mouth and other silly sayings.* New York: Random House.

Galarza, E. (1971). *Barrio boy.* Notre Dame, IN: University of Notre Dame Press.

Galdone, P. (1972). *The three bears.* New York: Clarion.

Gibbons, G. (1994). *Emergency.* New York: Holiday House.

Greenfield, E. (1992). *Koya Delaney and the good girl blues.* New York: Scholastic.

Leedy, L., & Street, P. (2001). *There's a frog in my throat.* New York: Winslow Press.

Lewis, C. S. (1950/1994). *The lion, the witch and the wardrobe.* New York: HarperCollins.

Lowell, S. (1992). *The three little javelinas.* New York: Scholastic.

Lowry, L. (1979). *Anastasia Krupnik.* Boston: Houghton Mifflin.

——— (1989). *Number the stars.* Boston: Houghton Mifflin.

Marshall, J. (1989). *The three little pigs.* New York: Dial Books for Young Readers.

Martin, B., Jr. (1967). *Brown Bear, Brown Bear.* New York: Henry Holt and Company.

Munsch, R. (1986). *Love you forever.* Willowdale, Ontario, Canada: Firefly Books Ltd.

Nevin, A., & Nevin, D. (1977). *From the horse's mouth.* Englewood Cliffs, NJ: Prentice-Hall.

Numeroff, L. F. (1985, 1989). *If you give a mouse a cookie.* New York: Scholastic Big Books.

Parish, P. (1963/1981). *Amelia Bedelia.* New York: Harper & Row/Avon Camelot.

Patent, D. H. (1992). *Pelicans.* New York: Clarion Books.

Paulsen, G. (1987). *Hatchet.* New York: Macmillan, Bradbury.

Rawls, W. (1961/1974). *Where the red fern grows.* New York: Scholastic.

Say, A. (1988). *A river dream.* Boston: Houghton Mifflin.

Sendak, M. (1963). *Where the wild things are.* New York: HarperCollins.

Seuss, D. (1938). *The 500 hats of Bartholomew Cubbins.* New York: Vanguard.

Stine, R. L. (1993). *Piano lessons can be murder.* New York: Scholastic.

Taylor, M. (1976). *Roll of thunder, hear my cry.* New York: Dial.

Terban, M. (1983). *In a pickle and other funny idioms.* New York: Clarion Books.

Vogt, G. (1989). *Predicting earthquakes.* New York: Watts.

Waber, B. (1972). *Ira sleeps over.* Boston: Houghton Mifflin.

Westcott, N. B. (1988). *The lady with the alligator purse.* Boston: Little, Brown and Company.

White, E. B. (1952). *Charlotte's web.* New York: HarperCollins.

Yee, W. H. (1992). *Eek! There's a mouse in the house.* Boston: Houghton Mifflin.

References

Adams, M. J. (1990). *Beginning to read: Thinking and learning about print.* Cambridge, MA: MIT Press.

Allen, R. V. (1976). *Language experiences in communication.* Boston: Houghton Mifflin.

Allington, R. L., & Walmsley, S. A. (Eds.). (1995). *No quick fix: Rethinking literacy programs in America's elementary schools.* New York: Teachers College Press.

Anderson, R. C., Hiebert, E. H., Scott, J. A., & Wilkinson, I. A. G. (1985). *Becoming a nation of readers: The report of the Commission on Reading.* Washington, DC: National Institute of Education.

Atwell, N. (1987). *In the middle: Writing, reading, and learning with adolescents.* Portsmouth, NH: Boynton/Cook, Heinemann.

Au, K. H. (1979). Using the Experience-Text-Relationship method with minority children. *The Reading Teacher, 32,* 677–679.

Au, K. H., Carroll, J. H., & Scheu, J. A. (1997). *Balanced literacy instruction: A teacher's resource book.* Norword, MA: Christopher-Gordon.

Beaver, J. (1997). *Developmental reading assessment.* Parsipanny, NJ: Celebration Press, an Imprint of Pearson Learning.

Betts, E. A. (1946/1957). *Foundations of reading instruction.* New York: American Book Company.

Betts, E. A. (1949). Adjusting instruction to individual needs. In N. B. Henry (Ed.), *Reading in the elementary school (Forty-eighth Yearbook of the National Society for the Study of Education,* Part II, pp. 266–280). Chicago: University of Chicago Press.

Bormuth, J. R. (1968). Cloze test readability: Criterion scores. *Journal of Educational Measurement, 5,* 189–196.

Brown, A. L. (1980). Metacognitive development and reading. In R. J. Spiro, B. C. Bruce, & W. F. Brewer (Eds.), *Theoretical issues in reading comprehension* (pp. 453–481). Hillsdale, NJ: Lawrence Erlbaum Associates.

Burns, P. C., & Roe, B. D. (1999). *Burns/Roe informal reading inventory* (Preprimer to twelfth grade) (5th ed., revised by B. D. Roe). Boston: Houghton Mifflin.

Calkins, L. M. (1986). *The art of teaching writing.* Portsmouth, NH: Heinemann.

Calkins, L. M. (with Harwayne, S.). (1991). *Living between the lines.* Portsmouth, NH: Heinemann.

Calkins, L. M. (1994). *The art of teaching writing* (rev. ed.). Portsmouth, NH: Heinemann.

Chall, J. S. (1967). *Learning to read: The great debate.* New York: McGraw-Hill.

Chamot, A. U., & O'Malley, J. M. (1994). Instructional approaches and teaching procedures. In K. Spangenberg-Urbschat & R. Pritchard (Eds.), *Kids come in all languages: Reading instruction for ESL students.* Newark, DE: International Reading Association.

Chard, D. J., & Osborne, J. (1999). Phonics and word recognition instruction in early reading programs: Guidelines for accessibility. *Learning Disabilities Research and Practice, 14*(2), 107–117.

Clay, M. M. (1985). *The early detection of reading difficulties* (3rd ed.). Auckland, New Zealand: Heinemann Education.

————. *Becoming literate: The construction of inner control.* Portsmouth, NH: Heinemann.

Collier, V. (1992). A synthesis of studies examining long-term language minority student data on academic achievement. *Bilingual Research Journal, 16*(1&2), 187–212.

Cooper, J. D. (1986). *Improving reading comprehension.* Boston: Houghton Mifflin.

———— (2000). *Literacy: Helping children construct meaning* (4th ed.). Boston: Houghton Mifflin.

Cooper, J. D., Boschken, I., McWilliams, J., & Pistochini, L. (1998). *Soar to Success: The Intermediate Intervention Program,* Levels 3–6. Boston: Houghton Mifflin.

————*A study of the effectiveness of an intervention program designed to accelerate reading for strug-*

gling readers in the upper grades Final report. Boston: Houghton Mifflin.

Cooper, J. D., Warncke, E., Shipman, D., & Ramstad, P. A. (1979). *The what and how of reading instruction.* Columbus, OH: Charles E. Merrill Publishing Company.

Cummins, J. (1996). *Negotiating identities: Education for empowerment in a diverse society.* Ontario, CA: California Association of Bilingual Education.

Cunningham, P. M., & Allington, R. (1994). *Classrooms that work: They can all read and write.* New York: HarperCollins.

Cunningham, P. A., Hall, D. P., & Defee, M. (1998). Nonability grouped, multilevel instruction: Eight years later. *The Reading Teacher, 51*(8), 652–664.

Delpit, L. D. (1986). Skills and other dilemmas of a progressive Black educator. *Harvard Educational Review, 56*(4), 379–385.

Dolch, E. W. (1942). *Basic sight word test.* Champaign, IL: Garrard.

Durkin, D. (1966). *Children who read early.* New York: Teachers College Press.

Ehri, L. S., & Sweet, J. (1991). Fingerpoint-reading of memorized text: What enables beginners to process the print. *Reading Research Quarterly, 24,* 442–462.

Eldredge, J. L. (1995). *Teaching decoding in holistic classrooms.* Englewood Cliffs, NJ: Merrill: An Imprint of Prentice Hall.

Farr, R., & Tone, B. (1994). *Portfolio and performance assessment: Helping students evaluate their progress as readers and writers.* Orlando: Harcourt Brace College Publishers.

Farr, B., & Trumbull, E. (1997). *Assessment alternatives for diverse classrooms.* Norwood, MA: Christopher-Gordon.

Flood, J., Jensen, J. M., Lapp, D., & Squire, J. R. (Eds.). (1991). *Handbook of research on teaching the English language arts.* New York: Macmillan.

Fountas, I. C., & Pinnell, G. S. (1996). *Guided reading: Good first teaching for all children.* Portsmouth, NH: Heinemann.

Freeman, D., & Freeman, Y. (1999). The California reading initiative: A formula for failure for bilingual students? *Language Arts, 76*(3), 241–248.

Freeman, Y. S., & Freeman, D. (1997). *Teaching read-*

ing and writing in Spanish in the bilingual classroom. Portsmouth, NH: Heinemann.

Freppon, P., & Dahl, K. L. (1998). Theory and research into practice: Balanced instruction: Insights and considerations. *Reading Research Quarterly, 33*(2), 240–251.

Fry, E. B. (1968). A readability formula that saves time. *Journal of Reading, 11,* 513–516.

——— (1980). The new instant word list. *The Reading Teacher, 34,* 284–289.

Fry, E. B., Kress, J. E., Fountoukidis, D. L., & Polk, J. K. (1993). *The reading teacher's book of lists* (3rd ed.). Englewood Cliffs, NJ: Prentice Hall.

Garcia, G. E. (1994). Assessing the literacy development of second-language students: A focus on authentic assessment. In K. Spangenberg-Urbschat & R. Pritchard (Eds.), *Kids come in all languages: Reading instruction for SL students* (pp. 180–205). Newark, DE: International Reading Association.

Gentry, J. R., & Gillett, J. W. (1993). *Teaching kids to spell.* Portsmouth, NH: Heinemann.

Gibbons, P. E. (1993). *Learning to learn in a second language.* Portsmouth, NH: Heinemann.

Glazer, S. M. (1998). *Assessment is instruction: Reading, writing, spelling, and phonics for all learners.* Norwood, MA: Christopher-Gordon.

Goodman, K. S. (1965). A linguistic study of cues and miscues in reading. *Elementary English, 42,* 639–643.

Goodman, Y. D., & Watson, C. B. (1987). *Reading miscue inventory.* Katonah, NY: Richard C. Owen.

Goodman, Y. M. (1986). Children coming to know literacy. In W. H. Teal & E. Sulzby (Eds.), *Emergent literacy: Reading and writing* (pp. 1–14). Norwood, NJ: Ablex.

Goodman, Y. M., Watson, D. J., & Burke, C. (1987). *Reading miscue inventory: Alternative procedures.* Katonah, NY: Richard C. Owen.

Graves, D. H. (1983). *Writing: Teachers and children at work.* Exeter, NJ: Heinemann.

——— (1991). *Build a literate classroom.* Portsmouth, NH: Heinemann.

——— (1994). *A fresh look at writing.* Portsmouth, NH: Heinemann.

Hall, D. P., Prevatte, C., & Cunningham, P. M. (1992). *Eliminating ability grouping and failure in the pri-*

mary grades. Paper presented at the National Reading Conference, San Antonio, TX.

Halliday, M. (1975). *Learning how to hear.* London: Edward Arnold.

Hancock, J. (Ed.). (1999). *The explicit teaching of reading.* Newark, DE: International Reading Association.

Harris, A. J., & Jacobson, M. D. (1982). *Basic reading vocabularies.* New York: Macmillan.

Harris, A. J., & Sipay, E. R. (1985). *How to increase reading ability* (8th ed.). New York: Longman.

Harris, T. L., & Hodges, R. E. (Eds.) (1995). *The literacy dictionary.* Newark, DE: International Reading Association.

Hasbrouck, J. E., & Tindal, G. (1992). Curriculum-based oral reading fluency norms for students in grades 2 through 5. *Teaching Exceptional Children,* pp. 41–44, Spring.

Henderson, E. (1990). *Teaching spelling* (2nd ed.). Boston: Houghton Mifflin.

Hiebert, E. H., Colt, J. M., Catto, S. L., & Gury, E. C. (1992). Reading and writing of first-grade students in a restructured Chapter 1 program. *American Educational Research Journal, 29*(3), 545–572.

Hiebert, E. H., Pearson, P. D., Taylor, B. M., Richardson, V., & Paris, S. G. (1998). *Every child a reader.* Ann Arbor, MI: Center for the Improvement of Early Reading Achievement (CIERA).

Hiebert, E., & Taylor, B. (Eds.). (1994). *Getting reading right from the start: Effective early literacy interventions.* Needham Heights, MA: Allyn & Bacon.

Hillerich, R. L. (1977). Let's teach spelling—Not phonetic misspelling. *Language Arts, 54,* pp. 301–307.

Hoff, D. J. (1999). Education Dept. examining rise in students excluded from NAEP. *Education Week, 18*(28), p. 5.

Holdaway, D. (1979). *The foundations of literacy.* Sydney: Ashton Scholastic, distributed by Heinemann, Portsmouth, NH.

International Reading Association. (1999a). Report shows performance of students with disabilities improving in schools. *Reading Today, 16*(4), 26.

———— (1999b). Title I and the 21st century. *Reading Today, 16*(4), 1.

Johns, J. L. (1997). *Basic reading inventory* (7th ed.). Dubuque, IA: Kendall/Hunt.

Johnson, D. D. (1971). The Dolch list reexamined. *The Reading Teacher, 24,* 455–456.

Jones, C. (1997, Sept. 24). Educators challenged by diversity's demands. *USA Today,* pp. 1–2.

Juel, C. (1988). Learning to read and write: Longitudinal study of 54 children from first through fourth grades. *Journal of Educational Psychology, 80,* pp. 437–447.

———— (1991). Beginning reading. In R. Barr, M. L. Kamil, P. Mosenthal, & P. D. Pearson (Eds.), *Handbook of reading research* (Vol. 2, pp. 759–788). New York: Longman.

Klare, G. R. (1988). The formative years. In B. L. Zakaluk & S. J. Samuels (Eds.), *Readability: Its past, present, and future* (pp. 14–34). Newark, DE: International Reading Association.

———— (1995). Readability. In T. L. Harris & R. E. Hodges (Eds.), *The literacy dictionary* (p. 204). Newark, DE: International Reading Association.

Krashen, S. (1982). *Principles and practice in second language acquisition.* New York: Pergamon Press.

———— (1993). *The power of reading.* Englewood, CO: Libraries Unlimited.

Krashen, S., & Terrell, T. (1983). *The natural approach: Language acquisition in the classroom.* Hayward, CA: Alemany Press.

Lerner, J. (2000). *Learning disabilities: Theories, diagnosis, and teaching strategies* (8th ed.). Boston: Houghton Mifflin.

Learning First Alliance. (1998, June). *Every child reading: An action plan of the Learning First Alliance.* Washington, DC.

Lipson, M. Y., & Wixson, K. K. (1997). *Assessment and instruction of reading and writing disability: An interactive approach* (2nd ed.). New York: Longman.

Martinez-Roldan, C. M., & Lopez-Robertson, J. M. (1999/2000). Initiating literature circles in a first-grade bilingual classroom. *The Reading Teacher, 53*(4), 270–281.

Menyuk, P. (1988). *Language development: Knowledge and use.* Boston: Scott, Foresman.

Moll, L. C. (1988). Some key issues in teaching Latino students. *Language Arts, 65*(5), 465–472.

Morrow, L. M. (1989). Using story retelling to develop comprehension. In K. D. Muth (Ed.), *Children's comprehension of text: Research into practice* (pp. 37–58). Newark, DE: International Reading Association.

Moustafa, M. (1997). *Beyond traditional phonics: Research discoveries and reading instruction.* Portsmouth, NH: Heinemann.

Mulligan, J. (1974). Using language experience with potential high school dropouts. *Journal of Reading, 18,* pp. 206–211.

Mullis, I. V. S., Campbell, J. R., & Farstrup, A. (1993, September). *NAEP, 1992: Reading report card for the nation and states.* Washington, DC: U.S. Department of Education.

NAEP. (1995). *NAEP 1994 Reading: A first look—Findings from the National Assessment of Educational Progress* (Rev. ed.). Washington, DC: U.S. Government Printing Office.

National Assessment of Educational Progress. (1987, June). *Reading objectives, 1986 and 1988 assessments.* Princeton, NJ: National Assessment of Educational Progress, Educational Testing Service.

National Council of Teachers of English (NCTE) & International Reading Association (IRA). (1996). *Standards for the English language arts.* Urbana, IL/Newark, DE: NCTE/IRA.

National PTA. (1998). *National standards for parent/family involvement programs.* Chicago: Author.

Norton, D. E. (1997). *The effective teaching of language arts* (5th ed.). Upper Saddle River, NJ: Prentice-Hall.

Ogle, D. M. (1989). The know, want to know, learn strategy. In K. D. Muth (Ed.), *Children's comprehension of text* (pp. 215–223). Newark, DE: International Reading Association.

Palincsar, A. S., & Brown, A. L. (1984). Reciprocal teaching of comprehension-fostering and comprehension-monitoring activities. *Cognition and Instruction, 1*(2), 117–175.

——— (1986). Interactive teaching to promote independent learning from text. *The Reading Teacher, 39*(8), 771–777.

Pearson, P. D. (1985). Changing the face of reading comprehension instruction. *The Reading Teacher, 38,* 724–738.

Pearson, P. D., Roehler, L. R., Dole, J. S., & Duffy, G. G. (1992). Developing expertise in reading comprehension. In S. J. Samuel & A. E. Farstrup (Eds.), *What research has to say about reading instruction* (pp. 145–199). Newark, DE: International Reading Association.

Pehrsson, R. S., & Robinson, H. A. (1985). *The semantic organizer approach to writing and reading instruction.* Rockville, MD: Aspen Systems Corporation.

Peterson, B. (1991). Selecting books for beginning readers. In D. E. DeFord, C. A. Lyons, & G. S. Pinnell (Eds.), *Bridges to literacy* (pp. 119–147). Portsmouth, NH: Heinemann.

Pikulski, J. J. (1994). Preventing reading failure: A review of five effective programs. *The Reading Teacher, 48*(1), 30–39.

Pinnell, G. S., Fried, M. D., & Estice, R. M. (1990). Reading Recovery: Learning how to make a difference. *The Reading Teacher, 43,* 282–295.

Pressley, M. (1998). *Reading instruction that works: The case for balanced teaching.* New York: The Guilford Press.

——— (1999). Self-regulated comprehension processing and its development through instruction. In L. Gambrel, L. M. Morrow, S. B. Neuman, & M. Pressley (Eds.), *Best practices in literacy instruction* (pp. 90–97). New York: The Guilford Press.

Rhodes, L. K. (Ed.). (1993). *Literacy assessment: A handbook of instruments.* Portsmouth, NH: Heinemann.

Rhodes, L. K., & Shanklin, N. (1990). Miscue analysis in the classroom. *The Reading Teacher, 44,* 252–254.

Rosenshine, B. V. (1980). Skill hierarchies in reading comprehension. In R. J. Spiro et al. (Eds.), *Theoretical issues in reading comprehension* (pp. 535–554). Hillsdale, NJ: Lawrence Erlbaum Associates.

Rosenshine, B. V., & Meister, C. (1994). Reciprocal teaching: A review of research. *Review of Educational Research, 64*(4), 479–530.

Rupley, W. H., Wilson, V. L., & Nichols, W. D. (1998). Exploration of the developmental components contributing to elementary school children's reading comprehension. *Scientific Studies in Reading, 2*(2), 143–158.

Salvia, J., & Ysseldyke, J. (1998). *Assessment* (7th ed.). Boston: Houghton Mifflin.

Shanahan, T. (1990). Reading and writing together: What does it really mean? In T. Shanahan (Ed.), *Reading and writing together* (pp. 1–18). Norwood, MA: Christopher-Gordon Publishers, Inc.

Sharp, S. J. (1990). Using content subject matter with LEA in middle school. *Journal of Reading 33*, pp. 108–112.

Showers, B., Joyce, B., & Bennett, B. (1987). Synthesis of research on staff development: A framework for future study and a state-of-the-art analysis. *Educational Leadership, 45*(3), 77–87.

Slavin, R. E., Madden, N. A., Dolan, L. J., Wasik, B. A., Ross, S., Smith, L., & Dianda, M. (1996). Success for All: A summary of research. *Journal of Education for Students Placed at Risk, 1*(1), 41–76.

Smith, N. B. (1965). *American reading instruction.* Newark, DE: International Reading Association.

Snow, C. E., Burns, M. S., & Griffin, P. (Eds.) (1998). *Preventing reading difficulties in young children.* Washington, DC: National Academy Press.

Southwest Educational Development Laboratory. (1999). Southwest region statewide K–2 reading assessments. Austin, TX. Online: http://www.sedl.org/pitl/rci/rad/states.html.

Spache, G. (1953). A new readability formula for primary-grade reading materials. *Elementary School Journal, 53*, 410–413.

Stahl, S. A., Duffy-Hester, A. M., & Stahl, K. A. D. (1998). Everything you wanted to know about phonics (but were afraid to ask). *Reading Research Quarterly, 33*(3), 338–355.

Stauffer, R. G. (1969). *Teaching reading as a thinking process.* New York: Harper & Row.

Strickland, D. S. (1994). Reinventing our literacy programs: Books, basics, and balance. *The Reading Teacher, 48*(4), 294–306.

Strickland, D. S., & Taylor, D. (1989). Family storybook reading: Implications for children, families, and curriculum. In D. S. Strickland & L. M. Morrow (Eds.), *Emerging literacy: Young children learn to read and write* (pp. 27–34). Newark, DE: International Reading Association.

Swanson, H. L., with Hoskyn, M., & Lee, C. (1999). *Interventions for students with learning disabilities: A meta-analysis of treatment outcomes.* New York: The Guilford Press.

Swartz, S. L., & Klein, A. F. (Eds.). (1997). *Research in Reading Recovery.* Portsmouth, NH: Heinemann.

Taylor, B. M., Frye, B. J., Short, R., & Shearer, B. (1992). Classroom teachers prevent reading failure among low-achieving first-grade students. *Reading Teacher, 45*, 592–597.

Teale, W. H., & Sulzby, E. (1986). *Emergent literacy: Writing and reading.* Norwood, NJ: Ablex.

Templeton, S., & Bear, D. (Eds.). (1992). *Development of orthographic knowledge and the foundation of literacy: A memorial festschrift for Edmund H. Henderson.* Hillsdale, NJ: Lawrence Erlbaum Associates.

Texas Education Agency. (n.d.) *Texas primary reading inventory* (TPRI). Austin, TX: Author.

Tierney, R. J. (1998). Literacy assessment reform: Shifting beliefs, principled possibilities and emerging practices. *The Reading Teacher, 51*, pp. 374–390.

Vygotsky, L. S. (1978). *Mind in society.* Cambridge, MA: Harvard University Press.

Walp, T. P., & Walmsley, S. A. (1989). Instructional and philosophical congruence: Neglected aspects of coordination. *The Reading Teacher, 42*, 364–368.

Weaver, C. A., & Kintsch, W. (1991). Expository text. In R. Barr, M. L. Kamil, P. Mosenthal, & P. D. Pearson (Eds.), *Handbook of reading research,* Vol. II (pp. 230–245). New York: Longman.

Wilson, R. M., & Cleland, C. J. (1989). *Diagnostic and remedial reading for classroom and clinic.* Columbus, OH: Charles E. Merrill.

Yopp, H. K. (1995). A test for assessing phonemic awareness in young children. *The Reading Teacher, 49*, pp. 20–22.

Acknowledgments

Chapter 4: p. 118, 122, 123: unnumbered art taken from Cooper, *Literacy*, 4/e. Copyright © 2000 by Houghton Mifflin Company. Used by Permission.; p. 139: Table 4.9, "Sources of Predictability in Groups of Levels" reprinted by permission of Barbara Peterson. In *Bridges to Literacy: Learning From Reading Recovery* edited by Diane P. Deford, Carol A. Lyons, and Gay Su Pinnell: (Heinemann, A division of Reed Elsevier Inc., Portsmouth, NH, 1991); p. 140: Table 4.10, from Houghton Mifflin School Division report by J.D. Cooper, I. Boschken, J. McWilliams, & L. Pistochini. *A study of the effectiveness of an intervention program designed to accelerate readings for struggling readers in the upper grades—Final report.* Copyright © 1999. Reprinted by permission of J. David Cooper.

Chapter 7: p. 278: Figure 7.10, from Cooper, *Literacy*, 4/e. Copyright © 2000 by Houghton Mifflin Company. Used by permission.

Chapter 8: p. 341: Figure 8.19, from IT'S COOL. IT'S SCHOOL. Teacher's Book: A Resource for Planning and Teaching in HOUGHTON MIFFLIN READING: INVITATIONS TO LITERACY by Cooper, et al. Copyright © 1996 by Houghton Mifflin Company. Reprinted by permission of Houghton Mifflin Company. All rights reserved.; p. 341: Figure 8.20, from AMERICAN SNAPSHOTS Teacher's Book: A Resource for Planning and Teaching in HOUGHTON MIFFLIN READING: INVITATIONS TO LITERACY by Cooper et al. Copyright © 1996 by Houghton Mifflin Company. Reprinted by permission of Houghton Mifflin Company. All Rights reserved.

Chapter 12: p. 497: Figure 12.4, used by permission of Marion Community Schools.; pp. 500–501: Figures 12.6 and 12.7, from HOUGHTON MIFFLIN READING: INVITATIONS TO LITERACY Home/Community Connections. Level 4 by Cooper et al. Copyright © 1997 by Houghton Mifflin Company. Reprinted by permission of Houghton Mifflin Company. All rights reserved.

Author Source Index

Subject Index

Quickly find handy material including benchmarks, sample checklists, and many useful forms for classroom use in the tabbed pages of the Resource File at the back of this book.

Reading Checklist for Individual Student (Chapter 7)

Reading Checklist:
Beginning Reading and Writing Stage

Name _____ Grade _____ Age _____

+ = consistently present
- = not present
✓ = somewhat present; recheck

	Date	Comments

Benchmark

Emergent Literacy Behaviors

Word Recognition Skills/Strategies
Names letters in random order
Recognizes many sight words
Uses phonics and structural analysis
Chooses strategies for sounding words
Uses context to determine meaning

Construction of Meaning
Reads and retells familiar stories
Reads own writing
Begins to use:
- predicting
- identifying important information
- self-questioning
- monitoring
- summarizing
- evaluating
Reads and retells unfamiliar texts
(narrative/expository)
Self-corrects
Takes risks
Reads in free time
Sees self as reader
Reads to others
Begins to use research tools and skills (list:)

_____

_____

_____

Comments:

Retelling Record for Narrative Text (Chapter 3)

RETELLING: NARRATIVE

Name _____ Date _____

Title of Story and Source _____

✓ = indicates whether student told about element unaided or after prompting by teacher
- = indicates student could not tell even with prompting

Elements Included	Unaided	Prompted
1. Setting (time, place, weather)		
2. Character		
Major(s)		
Others		
3. Problem		
4. Story Events		
Includes all major events		
Tells mostly in sequence		
5. Solution		
Tells how the problem was solved		
Tells how the story ended		

Comments/Analysis: _____

_____

_____

Future support needed: _____

_____

_____

_____